NONGOVERNMENTAL POLITICS

NONGOVERNMENTAL POLITICS

edited by Michel Feher
with Gaëlle Krikorian and Yates McKee

ZONE BOOKS · NEW YORK · 2007

© 2007 Urzone Inc.
Zone Books
1226 Prospect Avenue
Brooklyn, NY 11218

Printed in Canada

Distributed by The MIT Press,
Cambridge, Massachusetts, and London, England

Some of these essays originally appeared in French in *Politique
non gouvernementale*, edited by Michel Feher and Gaëlle Krikorian
in *Vacarme* 34 (Winter 2006).

Library of Congress Cataloging-in-Publication Data

Nongovernmental politics / edited by Michel Feher.
p.   cm.
Includes bibliographical references.
ISBN-13: 978-1-890951-75-7
ISBN-10: 1-890951-75-7
ISBN-13: 978-1-890951-74-0 (gatefold)
ISBN-10: 1-890951-74-9 (gatefold)
1. Non-governmental organizations—Political aspects.
2. Non-governmental organizations—International cooperation.
3. International relief. 4. Human rights. I. Feher, Michel.
JZ4841.N64   2007
361.7—dc22

2006052825

STAKEHOLDER CLAIMS

STAKEHOLDER ACTIVISM:

WAYS

SITES

DESIGNS

The Governed in Politics

Michel Feher

NEITHER APOLITICAL NOR GOVERNMENTAL. To be involved in politics without aspiring to govern, be governed by the best leaders, or abolish the institutions of government: such are the constraints that delineate the condition common to all practitioners of nongovernmental politics. What these activists seek to accomplish ranges considerably: providing humanitarian aid, protecting the environment, monitoring human-rights and civil-liberties violations, adding new entitlements to the list of fundamental rights and liberties, defending the interests of corporations' stakeholders — workers, suppliers, consumers — and expanding public access to knowledge are only the most frequent among their pursuits. The ideological leanings of nongovernmental activists are hardly less widespread than their areas of involvement. For instance, it is fair to say that the liberal promoters of "velvet" revolutions in the former Soviet bloc do not share the political priorities of the critics of neoliberal globalization who gather in the World Social Forums. But at the same time, both groups are equally at odds with the evangelical charities that George W. Bush has called "the armies of compassion" and, with their Islamic counterparts, branded as terrorists by the U.S. State Department. Yet heterogeneous concerns and conflicting sensibilities notwithstanding, what nongovernmental activists of every stripe recognize is that both the legitimacy and efficacy of their initiatives demand that they refrain from occupying the realm of governing agencies — whether with the purpose of taking them over, filling them with worthy stewards, or doing away with them. (That the same people can successively work for NGOs, national governments, international institutions, or private corporations does not blur the distinction between governmental and nongovernmental politics: it only shows that the border between the two domains can be crossed — in both directions.)

Does forsaking the ambitions that pertain to the art of governing amount to withdrawing from politics altogether? It is certainly true that many nongovernmental activists are prone to downplay, if not deny, the political character of their endeavors. Eager to avoid the accusations of cynicism and dogmatism that are so often leveled at professional politicians, they tend either to focus on the moral and sometimes religious nature of their concerns or to stress the scientific and technical competence that underlies their activities. However, no matter how beneficial activists find it either to drape themselves in the purity of ethics or to rest on the authority of science, neither their alleged philanthropy nor their claims to expertise enable them to eschew the conflicts and transcend the power relations that make up the social fabric in which they intervene. To put it simply, nongovernmental politics is no more apolitical than governmental — neither more impervious to the ways in which governmental agencies operate nor endowed with the legal or institutional authority to which these agencies lay claim. Nongovernmental politics can thus be envisioned as encompassing the political involvements of the governed, or better still, as the politics in which the governed as such are involved.

Should we infer from this definition that what characterizes nongovernmental activism is essentially a combination of humble ways and modest objectives? There again, nongovernmental activists are inclined to claim these attributes as their distinctive features. Selfless devotion to a noble cause and steadfast preoccupation with limited, but concrete progress are indeed qualities that, in the eyes of the public, contrast favorably with the self-interested strategizing, unrealistic promises, and vapid slogans that are customarily imputed to candidates for governmental offices. In practice, however, the distinction between governmental and nongovernmental politics proves more complicated than an opposition between top-down arrogance and bottom-up earnestness — or, for that matter, between cold-blooded efficiency and well-meaning irrelevance.

These complications are a function of the appeal that each of the two realms has for the actors who operate in the other. On the one hand, there are instances where nongovernmental agencies get involved in tasks that fall under the purview of government. This is the case when the United Nations High Commissioner for Refugees (UNHCR) delegates the actual management of refugee camps to humanitarian NGOs or when human-rights advocates negotiate with representatives of the military in order to establish regulations for the use of violence.[1] On the other hand, the fact that nongovernmental activists tend to be associated with higher moral standards than government officials incites the latter to impress upon their constituents that they, too, are moved by the concerns that inspire the activism of the most popular exponents of civil society. To make such a point, some heads of governments appoint either a secretary of humanitarian affairs or a minister of the environment — or both — while a number of elected officials eagerly display their civic involvement in grassroots campaigns advocating debt relief for developing countries or warning against the nefarious consequences of climate change.

As these examples indicate, adjectives such as "sincere," "local," and "powerless" are not very helpful when it comes to specifying the character of nongovernmental politics. Rather than good intentions, limited ambitions, or insufficient means, what distinguishes the various political involvements of the governed as such is that they are all predicated on an intolerance of the effects of a particular set of governmental practices—regardless of whether the governing agency responsible for these practices is a state, an international organization, a public institution, or a private corporation. Because the domain of nongovernmental politics comprises a wide range of topical involvements and ideological orientations, both the measures that nongovernmental activists do not tolerate and the reasons for finding them intolerable are bound to vary greatly. Yet what these activists all have in common is that they are driven by a shared determination not to be governed *thusly*.[2] In other words, what specifically concerns nongovernmental activists is not *who* governs—who is in charge, for whose benefit, and to what alleged end—but *how* government is exercised. One can therefore speak of a dual relationship between nongovernmental politics and government according to what the latter term designates. Insofar as it refers to the empowering mechanisms upon which governing agencies rely, government is indeed that from which nongovernmental politics is severed. However, when it is understood as the normative procedures to which the governed are subjected, government is the very object of nongovernmental politics.

Can the various refusals to be governed thusly that demarcate the field of nongovernmental politics all be traced back to a common urge? For instance, should we presume that behind their intolerance for a particular mode of government, what really drives nongovernmental activists is the desire not to be governed at all? Conversely, are we to believe that the underlying motive of nongovernmental activism is a quest for "good governance," namely, for the norms that, once properly enforced, would make it tolerable—and even comfortable—to be governed?

Once again, in light of the topical and ideological diversity of nongovernmental endeavors, it would seem improbable that the specific intolerances upon which nongovernmental activism is predicated would all be subsumed under one and the same affect—be it an irremediable aversion to being governed or a longing for the kind of government that would render nongovernmental politics unnecessary. But more importantly, what is problematic about these two hypotheses is that they subordinate the question of how government is exercised to that of who exercises it, thereby denying the autonomy of nongovernmental politics. Indeed, to suggest that the governed are either allergic to their condition or seeking the proper kind of government is to convey that they themselves see their involvement in politics as inherently transient and anomalous. In other words, both suggestions amount to claiming that, were it not for the dysfunctions in the governmental realm, the governed as such would not be involved in politics—either because the institutions of government would have been abolished or because the political role of the governed would merely be that of citizens delegating their sovereignty to their elected representatives. Yet in spite of the fact that nongovernmental activism is largely fueled by outrage, there is no reason to believe that what unites nongovernmental activists is a shared ambition to bring about the conditions under which they could retire from politics.

UNIVERSAL PRINCIPLES, PARTICULAR EXPERIENCES. Recognizing that the governed as such are at home in politics still leaves us with the question of how they actually make it their home. In that respect, the first issue that needs to be addressed regards the ways in which nongovernmental activists seek to legitimize their own initiatives. According to their critics, especially those who work in government, nongovernmental agencies do not have what is required of a political actor to be legitimate, namely, a mandate conferred by a constituency. And there is no denying that this allegation has some merit: nongovernmental activists are indeed deprived of the authority bestowed on elected officials, which makes them vulnerable to the accusation of being neither representative nor accountable.

In order to compensate for their lack of democratic credentials, some practitioners of nongovernmental politics are prone to display the good governance that distinguishes the organization to which they belong — that is, the democratic procedures within their organization and the transparency of its financial operations — while others tend either to boast of their grassroots origins or emphasize their solidarity with the beneficiaries of their activism. Yet no matter how hard they try to don the trappings of representative institutions, to exhibit the features of exemplary citizens, or to identify with the people they seek to help, the fact remains that nongovernmental activists operate outside the realm of sovereignty. What this means is both that they do not represent anyone but themselves and also that governmental representatives are no more accountable to them than to their other constituents. Accordingly, the most coherent exponents of nongovernmental politics are those who simply renounce any claim to representation and turn instead to two other sources of legitimacy.

The first of these two sources consists of principles and preoccupations that are largely deemed universal, such as the rights included in the United Nations Universal Declaration of Human Rights (UNDHR), the humanitarian duties to which the Geneva Conventions subject warring parties, and the environmental responsibilities that the UN Kyoto Protocol and other international treaties assign to both states and private corporations. Because governing agencies are not only legally bound by these principles and preoccupations, but also are keen to proclaim their allegiance to them, nongovernmental activists are able to seize upon such proclamations and hold those who make them accountable for the discrepancies between the values which they espouse and their actual policies. In short, what the practitioners of nongovernmental politics are able to draw from universally recognized entitlements and obligations is the legitimacy of monitors. Mindful of the fact that those who govern are bound to predicate their own legitimacy on their commitments to be respectful of human rights, responsive to humanitarian emergencies, and attentive to environmental concerns, nongovernmental activists, for their part, can legitimately assert that for the governed to grant their willingness to be governed, they must see to it that these commitments are effectively honored.

The second source from which nongovernmental activists derive their legitimacy does not involve universal precepts. Instead, it consists of particular experiences that are judged intolerable by the people who are subjected to them and for which the actions of governing agencies can be held responsible. Though these two sources of nongovernmental legitimacy may be perceived as polar opposites, both of them are correlated to the ways in which governing bodies seek to legitimize themselves. Indeed, the authority of those who exercise a form of government does not rest merely on the respect they pledge to the set of fundamental rights and duties that constrain their power. It also depends on their ability to argue persuasively that they contribute to the welfare of the governed.

For instance, state officials are prone to justify their sway over other people's conduct by pointing to the public services they provide, while corporate executives are given to claiming that their management optimizes the prosperity of their stakeholders. These justifications, which attest to the "pastoral" origin of modern governmental power, prove useful for nongovernmental activists.[3] The latter are able to draw on what their governmental counterparts claim — that only a "caretaker" is legitimately entitled to govern — in order to hold them accountable for the effects of the measures they take. Thus, in this instance, what authorizes the governed to challenge the way they are governed is their experience of governmental measures — the suffering these measures inflict, the uncertainties they create, the opportunities they suppress — regardless of whether the procedures under which these measures are taken and the motives invoked for taking them are respectively legal and principled.

MONITORING COMMITMENTS, QUESTIONING NORMS. Obviously, these two ways of legitimizing nongovernmental activism are not mutually exclusive — despite the fact that, in the first case, policies are faulted for not meeting standards, regardless of their effect, while in the second case, policies are taken to task for what they effectively do, regardless of the standards underwriting them. In most of their endeavors, nongovernmental activists avail themselves of both to formulate their grievances and empower their initiatives.[4] (After all, when governments fail to abide by the principles to which they are allegedly committed, there is a good chance that shattered lives will result from it; and when intolerable experiences are caused by governmental measures, it is often the case that the agencies responsible for these measures have violated the fundamental rights of their victims.) Yet distinguishing between the two sources of nongovernmental legitimacy still has considerable heuristic value: even as nongovernmental advocates draw from both sources, the alternative ways in which they articulate universal precepts with unique experiences make for two very different types of advocacy.

In the first instance, nongovernmental activists cite intolerable experiences as material evidence against institutions accused of violating the rights and shunning the obligations to which they are explicitly pledged. The status of these experiences is thus that of a symptom of the divergence between what governing agencies profess and what they actually do. (Watchdogs relying on the texts where the liberties and protections of the governed are enshrined — the Bill of Rights, UNDHR, and the Geneva

Conventions, among others — are typical examples of this first type of activism.) In the second instance, however, the political purpose of citing specific intolerable experiences caused by a mode of government is not to expose the discrepancy between governmental professions and governmental deeds, but to question the social norms that enable governing bodies to call upon unimpeachable principles in order to justify objectionable policies. (Exemplary of this mode of intervention are those activists who endeavor to challenge the norms defining intellectual property, because such norms are what enable national governments and private corporations to call upon the widely recognized rights of creators — rights to control the use and to reap the benefits of their creations — in order to prevent AIDS patients from gaining access to generic drugs. In a similar vein, other nongovernmental advocates question the norms pertaining to the understanding of national sovereignty, because these norms make it seem "normal" when state officials lay claim to the rule of law to justify sequestering undocumented immigrants in detention camps.) According to this second way of combining the two sources of nongovernmental legitimacy, what subjects governing agencies to the political activism of the governed is not that they flout the formal conditions of their authority, but that they exploit the formality of these conditions in order to conceal, or worse, to encourage, unjust and harmful practices.

ENGAGING INSTITUTIONS, FOSTERING SOCIAL PRACTICES. Along with discerning what authorizes nongovernmental activists to challenge governing agencies, another condition for understanding how the governed establish their place in politics involves the strategic options available to them. Just as nongovernmental legitimacy is drawn from two different sources, nongovernmental strategies can also be divided according to two main orientations — largely along the lines of what Albert O. Hirschman calls "voice" and "exit."[5] The first one comprises the various forms of nongovernmental activism that truly deserve to be called advocacy. Regardless of the cause they defend, all advocates basically mobilize either to change the laws and regulations enabling the persistence of intolerable modes of government or to protect the rights and liberties threatened by the establishment of new modes of government. As for the second strategic orientation, it does not consist of advocating for or against institutional change, but of warding off institutional scrutiny and pressure. Rather than calling for an authoritative suspension of the legal measures and regulatory norms to which they attribute intolerable effects, activists who follow the second path look for ways to eschew the prescriptions to which they object and, by doing so, secure a social space where the targets of these prescriptions can develop alternative ways of governing themselves and of relating to each other.

The proponents of these two strategic orientations are generally perceived as being at odds with each other. And it is true that both groups are inclined to claim that there is no valid alternative to their strategy. On the one hand, advocates who mobilize public opinion and petition governing bodies — whether to promote or challenge legislation, expose discriminating institutions, or protect vested interests — often see their work as the only responsible way of engaging in nongovernmental politics. On the other hand, activists involved in developing informal sociabilities — as well as in saving them from being either institutionalized or scrutinized by the law — are prone to claim that social creativity, for some, and cultural authenticity, for others, are entirely on their side. Accordingly, the former dismiss the latter's strategy alternatively as sectarian, apolitical, and ineffective, while the latter argue that, to earn their seat at the institutional table, the former must consent to mitigating their demands, accommodating their interlocutors, and thus, ultimately betraying their own cause. Yet despite the familiar ring and persistent appeal of such disputes, in practice, nongovernmental agencies are not necessarily faced with the necessity of choosing once and for all between the two strategic options available to them.

First, it is hardly uncommon for an activist to shift from one approach to the other according to circumstances: hackers and members of more or less clandestine networks can become civil-liberties advocates and vice versa, squatters may decide to take part in public debates about housing laws and regulations, and so on. Second, some sections of the nongovernmental domain cannot function without combining the two strategies. This is especially true for the various strands of activism that are concerned with "access": whether their purpose is making knowledge and technology more widely accessible or gaining access to a population in need of humanitarian rescue, nongovernmental activists preoccupied with accessibility tend to alternate between claiming — or advocating for the recognition of — "access rights" and working around the constraints that international legislation and national authorities impose upon their endeavors. Third, there are certain types of nongovernmental tactics, such as civil disobedience and boycotts, that can be claimed by the proponents of both strategic orientations. Civil disobedience, while belonging to the repertoire of public advocacy, is also a practice that initiates an alternative sociability. Similarly, boycotting a brand, a specific technology, or all the imported products coming from a particular country is an act that is simultaneously about putting pressure on the governing agencies that the boycott is meant to affect and about promoting new trading and consuming patterns, at least among the boycotters themselves.

Fourth and finally, what further complicates the relationship between the two strategic options that are ostensibly polarizing the field of nongovernmental politics is their propensity to affect each other's aim. On the one hand, there are instances where an advocacy, whether aimed at securing rights, bolstering opportunities, or making an institution more inclusive, turns out also to be conducive to new social practices. (Queer advocates of gay marriage, especially in Western Europe, are keen to emphasize this underestimated outcome of institutional change. In their view, the main merit of opening the institution of marriage to same-sex couples is not that it will "normalize" gays and lesbians in the eyes of the straight majority but, on the contrary, that it will foster new and more inventive ways of approaching and appropriating marital relationships — for straight as well as for gay spouses.)[6] But on the other hand, it may also occur that an alternative sociability, though originally developed outside any institutional framework, becomes not only eligible for legal protection, but also formative of new rights and entitlements. (In the United States, queer activists who are critical of gay marriage — or at least of the prominence of this issue in the gay and lesbian agenda — are a good illustration of this second twist in the relationship between nongovernmental strategies. As these activists see it, the real order of the day is neither to make marriage more inclusive nor to celebrate the marginality of queer culture, but to demand legal recognition and protection for the alternative forms of unions and kinship that have been developed within gay and lesbian communities over the last four decades.)[7]

Some activists go back and forth between engaging and dodging institutions; some tactics simultaneously pertain to both options; and the proponents of one strategy can sometimes forward the aim of the other. For all these reasons, the polarization of the nongovernmental domain should not be overstated. While the two strategic orientations available to them often pit nongovernmental activists against one another, the complexities of their actual relationship also provide the practitioners of nongovernmental activism with the opportunity to question overly facile oppositions — whether between responsible and irresponsible or, conversely, authentic and compromised politics.

MORE ACCOUNTABLE, LESS DEPENDABLE. To improve further our understanding of how the governed establish themselves in politics, we need to look at the realm of nongovernmental politics from yet another perspective. Rather than the ways in which nongovernmental activists establish their legitimacy and develop their strategy, what this new perspective brings to light is the nature of their dissatisfaction with a governing agenda. And just as there are two sources of nongovernmental legitimacy and two main orientations in nongovernmental strategy, it appears that governing agencies face two opposite kinds of reproaches from their nongovernmental counterparts. They can either be accused of abusing their power and privileges or be blamed for relinquishing their duties and responsibilities. In the first case, nongovernmental activists seek to counter the intrusiveness of governing agents. They thus take them to task for governing too much. Conversely, in the second case, what is deemed intolerable is the carelessness of those who govern. The latter, in other words, are indicted for not governing enough, or at least for not exercising their license to govern in the proper areas and with the appropriate zeal.

Looking at the governed's involvement in politics from the point of view of their grievances against governing agendas does more than provide us with a better sense of the boundaries of nongovernmental politics. What this perspective reveals — that governing bodies are alternatively blamed for being meddlesome and for being negligent — also proves especially enlightening with respect to the recent development of nongovernmental activism. The latter can certainly claim deep and venerable roots — such as in the abolitionist movement, trade unionism, and Victorian and Progressive era charities.

Yet, it is undeniable that in the course of the last three decades, the field of nongovernmental politics has expanded dramatically, both in terms of the number of people it involves and the diversity of issues it addresses.

That nongovernmental activism has been able both to attract more candidates and to cover new ground can be traced to two major trends in governmental politics. The first consists of an increasing public demand for governmental accountability. Starting in the early 1970s and until the beginning of the new millennium, executive privilege has indeed been the object of an unprecedented defiance. Prompted by the wearing down of Cold War disciplines whereby militants — committed to the "defense of the free world" or, alternatively, to the "construction of socialism" — were required to subordinate their critical inquiries to their ideological allegiance, this multifaceted onslaught has been successively inspired by post-1968 radicals involved in the critique of authoritarian institutions, antitotalitarian liberals arguing for the autonomy of civil society, and largely neoliberal advocates of "good governance" calling for public scrutiny of governmental practices. The ensuing intolerance faced by unaccountable governing bodies has proved damaging for the standing of the various principles — such as national sovereignty and institutional authority — that are designed to curtail the autonomy of the governed and thus to dissuade them from entering politics in their own name.

As for the second trend in governmental politics to which nongovernmental activism owes its current prominence, it originates in the monetarist policies implemented by Margaret Thatcher and Ronald Reagan at the turn of the 1980s and consists of the steady decrease of public funding that national governments and international institutions have henceforth devoted to social programs and economic development. Pervasive and enduring, this assault on the welfare state has been successively facilitated by the decrepitude of the various models of state socialism, the wider crisis of revolutionary politics, and the erosion of the social compact provided by the so-called "Fordist" regime of capital accumulation based on regulated markets and collective bargaining between labor and business. The ensuing consensus among ruling elites has not only left capitalism's foes in a state of temporary disarray, but also has proved damaging to the standing of those institutions — such as labor unions and class-based political parties — that are designed to fend for the interests of their affiliates and thus encourage the governed to center their political activity on the acts of choosing and supporting delegates.

CHECKING INTRUSIVENESS, CONFRONTING NEGLIGENCE. As these two trends coalesced, in the years immediately following the demise of the Soviet empire, governing agencies found themselves in a situation where, compared with what was expected of them in the first half of the Cold War, they both had a harder time warding off public scrutiny and an easier time renouncing their social obligations. For their part, nongovernmental activists saw this twofold evolution of governmental politics as propitious to the development of their own operations, regardless of whether they found it to their political liking. Faced with governments that were becoming simultaneously more accountable and less dependable, the governed had indeed two good reasons for either entering politics or claiming new political ground. First, the growing intolerance of opaque institutions and unanswerable officials provided nongovernmental activists with enhanced opportunities both to monitor the conduct of their governing counterparts and to hold them to their commitments. Second, the increasing negligence of governing bodies, especially in the domain of social services, enticed nongovernmental agencies to devise innovative ways of either countering or compensating for governmental divestments. Consequently, the 1990s were arguably the golden years — or at least the boom decade — of nongovernmental politics.

At the same time, however, the two kinds of impetus that can be credited for the soaring number of the governed entering politics during the last decade of the twentieth century have also been responsible for producing newfound tensions among nongovernmental activists. Though these tensions often seem like a post–Cold War tribute to Cold War ideological disputes, what best accounts for them is the already-mentioned fact that the governed's involvement in politics can be fueled by two opposite types of grievances, namely, governmental intrusiveness and governmental negligence. Hence the potential rifts between activists intent on exploiting the public's impatience with unaccountable authorities and activists mobilized against the propensity of public officials to unburden themselves of their social obligations. While the former are in the business of preventing governing agencies from governing too much, the latter's purposes consist of exposing and mending the damage caused by governing agencies that don't govern enough.

Accordingly, supporters of governmental accountability and critics of governmental negligence tend to be suspicious of each other. On the one hand, civil-society advocates concerned with curbing executive prerogative — by means of challenging the precedence of state sovereignty over human rights, public order over civil liberties, and national unity over the rule of law — are often accused of contributing, more or less unwittingly, to the legitimacy of neoliberal conceits such as that of "lean and clean" government. On the other hand, detractors of hegemonic neoliberalism — who challenge the precedence of private interests over public services, of free over fair trade, and of shareholders' dividends over stakeholders' claims — are just as often suspected of either longing, more or less consciously, for the return of bureaucratic socialism or at least wasting militant energies by channeling them toward the restoration of an obsolete welfare state.

Though sometimes justified, these mutual accusations have also served to enhance the vigilance and bolster the inventiveness of both groups. For their part, activists who purport to stave off governmental overreach by championing human rights, civil liberties, or humanitarian care have become acutely aware that, while governing agencies are still prone to renege on their obligations in these matters, they are also increasingly inclined to appropriate them for their own purposes. For instance, Western governments have proved keen to cite humanitarian motives either to justify their determination to remain neutral with respect to a bloody conflict or, conversely, to support their decision to mount a military operation against the authorities of a sovereign state. (The genocide of the Rwandan Tutsis in 1994 and NATO's intervention in Kosovo in 1999 respectively exemplify the two opposite roles played by humanitarianism in these governments' rhetoric.) In a similar fashion, putting an end to human-rights violations has been used as an argument for waging war — most recently in Afghanistan and Iraq — whereas unfettering civil society has figured as a frequent excuse for removing social safety nets. Confronted with this other form of governmental intrusiveness — the abusive appropriation of their own discourse — the more sophisticated among the nongovernmental foes of unaccountable governments have thus striven to improve their own analytical skills and rhetorical techniques in such a way as to forward their agenda while at the same time avoid its co-optation by governing agencies. These efforts entail either narrowing down the definition of their activism to protect it from being instrumentalized or expanding its purview, for instance to reframe social protections as human rights.

As for critics of governmental neglectfulness, their predicament involves remaining intransigently critical of the neoliberal global order while, at the same time, discarding the presumption that what they aspire to is simply to rehabilitate the strictures of a state-managed economy. Meeting these two requirements thus amounts to performing a balancing act whereby a radical critique of privatization and market hegemony does not lead to calls for the nationalization of the means of production and the reinstatement of industrial and commercial protectionism. The most creative outcomes of this balancing act include the development of areas where "free access" or common usage prevails over the usual conditions of private appropriation, the promotion of competition not for profit but against profit-driven corporations — as in the case of manufacturers of generic drugs competing with pharmaceutical companies — and the infusion of noncommercial components into the value of a product or a company. This last type of intervention can take two opposite forms. The first one consists of negative campaigns aiming at the devaluation of a brand because the company associated with the brand is known for its unsavory financial practices, the unsafe and exploitative conditions under which its employees are made to work, the danger that its products present for the health of consumers, and so on. Conversely, the second way of acting on the value of a brand involves marketing devices such as "fair trade" or "organic" labels that are purported to enhance the value of certain products, as well as the conduct of those consumers who choose these products over regular commodities.

Acrimonious as it may be, the mutual suspicion harbored by liberal champions of governmental accountability and antineoliberal detractors of governmental remissness has thus proved beneficial to the inventiveness of both groups. However, liberal advocates of civil society and radical critics of neoliberal globalization are no longer the only contenders in the world of nongovernmental politics. In the last decade, these two "secular" wings of nongovernmental activism have been increasingly exposed to the competition of ambitious and often wealthy religious organizations. Whether they are evangelical Christians concerned with hastening the return of the Savior or fundamentalist Muslims seeking to reinstate the social order prescribed by the Prophet, the activists who belong to these organizations have managed to occupy a sizable portion of the nongovernmental field, especially as purveyors of humanitarian care and protectors of rights and liberties. Their growing prominence can be explained by the same two trends in governmental politics that are also responsible for the expansion of the rest of the nongovernmental realm, namely the tendencies among governing agencies to be at the same time more accountable and less dependable. For religious NGOs, especially the most powerful among them, both trends have proved beneficial: the latter because the neglectfulness of national governments enables them to substitute their own services for those of the ailing welfare state, and the former because the corroding effect of democratic accountability on the authority of secular institutions makes religious organizations appear to be the only agencies that are still capable of satisfying a popular demand for authoritarian norms.

What the preceding paragraphs seek to portray are the stakes faced by nongovernmental politics at the turn of the twenty-first century. However, it must be added that, in the aftermath of September 2001, there has been a new inflection in the evolution of governmental politics and that this inflection has at least temporarily modified the conditions under which nongovernmental activism is exercised. While the post-9/11 world has proceeded apace with the dismantling of social-welfare programs, at the same time, both the threat widely attributed to global terrorism and the ever-growing fears that immigration inspires in the richest parts of the globe have managed to provide a new lease on life to the hitherto compromised standing of governmental privilege and unaccountability. Though it is too early to tell whether this blow to the "Whiggish" hopes of civil-liberties and human-rights advocates will prove enduring, there is hardly any doubt that it will affect — and indeed, it is already affecting — the ways in which nongovernmental activists endeavor to establish their legitimacy, devise their strategies, and prioritize their grievances. Addressing these impending and to an extent ongoing developments is one of the main ambitions of the critical essays, profiles of NGOs, and interviews with activists that make up the present volume.

Nongovernmental Politics is divided into four sections. The first one, entitled MOTIVES, examines the founding principles, guiding rules, but also the structural predicaments pertaining to three major areas of nongovernmental activism: those concerned with protecting human rights, providing humanitarian care, and forwarding stakeholders' claims. Each of these three instances revolves around a particular problem that is simultaneously responsible for subjecting activists to frustrating constraints and for triggering both their doctrinal and practical inventiveness.

In the case of human-rights advocacy, this defining problem regards the issue of enforcement. Because the governing agencies that are endowed with the legitimacy to stop and prevent human-rights violations are often not the ones that have either the means or the will to do so, human-rights activists are frequently exposed to the difficult task of warding off two opposite — and potentially crippling — pitfalls: that of letting their work be reduced to a testimony "for the record," and that of providing a pretext and a justification for an agenda other than human rights.

For their part, humanitarian workers encounter a different dilemma, albeit one that is just as daunting — and just as stimulating — as the predicament facing human-rights advocates. In their case, the problem centers on the issue of witnessing. Because the emergency operations in which humanitarians are involved can often be traced to either neglectful or abusive conducts on the part of governing agencies, nongovernmental rescuers find themselves torn between two equally problematic attitudes. They can decide that the care of those they seek to rescue requires them to keep a low profile — but only at the risk of appearing to be silently complicit with the neglectful or abusive agencies that they fail to denounce. Conversely, they can also consider it their moral duty to express their outrage — but only at the double risk of compromising the humanitarian aspect of their mission and thus of appearing to abuse or neglect their own vocation for the purpose of posturing as the voice of justice.

Finally, the nagging, yet productive difficulty that informs the various strands of stakeholder activism relates to the question of ownership. The traditional socialist perspective on social struggles — whether it proceeds from a revolutionary or social-democratic strategy — presents the social classes involved in these struggles as vying for the possession of what Marxist parlance calls the means of production. Stakeholders, that is, the motley crew of suppliers, workers, consumers, patients, and even neighbors who happen to have a stake in a corporation's activities, can hardly be defined as was the proletariat of yore — the people who do not own the means of production, but who should. Rather, what differentiates them from their counterparts, the shareholders, is the fact that their claims over the process of production are not predicated on ownership. Hence the predicament of stakeholder activists who, on the one hand, are loath to proclaim that were corporations to meet their financial, social, and environmental duties, shareholders and stakeholders would live in good capitalist harmony, but who, on the other hand, are unlikely to call for a sweeping transfer of property rights from the former to the latter.

The second section of *Nongovernmental Politics,* entitled WAYS, inquires about the various ways of practicing nongovernmental activism. The first part of this inquiry addresses the aesthetic or performative dimension of nongovernmental politics. This dimension entails both the modes of self-presentation through which nongovernmental agencies establish their credibility and the modes of expression through which they publicize their causes. The former involve the organizational and managerial technologies that enable some nongovernmental entities to display the kind of accountability and professionalism expected of exemplary institutions, thereby satisfying their grantors and earning the respect of governing agencies. Yet nongovernmental self-fashioning also includes the techniques that are deployed for the sake of producing the opposite effect, that of conveying intransigence or authenticity by means of staving off any sign of institutionalization. As for the modes of expressing nongovernmental agendas, they include the rhetorical and media resources of which activists avail themselves — whether to "mobilize shame" or to stimulate pride, to maximize the public exposure of their cause or to diffuse it through discrete networks, to unpack deceptions or to complicate deceptively simple depictions.

The second perspective on the ways of the governed in politics focuses on the registers of nongovernmental activism. Its purposes are first to take stock of the diversity of these registers, but also to examine how they interact and translate into one another. On the one hand, the spectrum of what qualifies as nongovernmental activism is remarkably wide. It ranges from emphatically modest "lifestyle" decisions, such as boycotting certain commodities produced in sweatshops or opting for environmentally friendly technologies, all the way to ostensibly grandiose initiatives such as drafting a proposition for an international treaty.[8] On the other hand, activists either combine different registers — for instance, when humanitarian organizations report on the medical consequences of denying civil rights to asylum seekers — or translate one type of advocacy into the language of another. In this last respect, questions such as whether and how certain kinds of activism previously formulated in terms of class interest, national solidarity, or resistance to governmental scrutiny should be reframed in terms of human rights have proved both contentious and prominent among nongovernmental circles.

Entitled SITES, the third section of *Nongovernmental Politics* delves into two types of terrain — borders and disaster areas — that have a particular significance for the political activism of the governed. Both are sites to which nongovernmental agencies commit a great deal of their resources and energy, because each of them is a template for one of the two main forms of misconduct imputed to governing agencies. Borders, especially on the dividing line between the global North and global South, prove especially challenging for nongovernmental activists concerned with executive prerogative. Immigration is indeed an issue where national authorities exercise their governmental power in the most unaccountable way — but also an instance where their unaccountability is condoned by a large portion of their constituents. On the other hand, disaster zones, whether they consist of neighborhoods afflicted by an industrial disaster, countries torn by war, forests and seashores ravaged by profit-driven development, or the planet itself, threatened by the accumulation of such debacles, are privileged working sites for activists mobilized by governmental neglectfulness. For whatever the scale and specific nature of these catastrophes, the plight of the people affected by them can usually be associated with defective governance — in the form of decrepit public infrastructures, remiss or corrupt civil servants, callous and cynical corporate executives, or international organizations mired in paralyzing bureaucracy.

The fourth and last section of *Nongovernmental Politics,* entitled DESIGNS, investigates two major, and competing, designs presiding over the political activism of the governed. The first, which revolves around the contentious notion of civil society, consists of optimizing the ability of the governed to govern themselves. The nature and consistency of what constitutes this optimum are the issues that account for the contentiousness among the promoters of the governed's self-government. For some, the guiding purpose of nongovernmental activism is to maximize the autonomy of civil society and thus to minimize state encroachment on its agencies. For others, however, lionizing civil society at the expense of public social services and utilities merely serves to subject the governed to corporate governance. For others still, if the governed are to optimize their ability to govern themselves, they must strive to associate the autonomy of civil society with the development of a "third sector," one that is neither publicly managed nor driven by profit.

The second major design to which nongovernmental activists subscribe is the one inspiring the various strands of religious activism that have recently risen to prominence in the nongovernmental realm. These religious activists are encouraged to awaken the governed to the urgency and desirability of complying with God's wishes. Neither of these designs, it should be noted, transgresses the boundaries of nongovernmental politics: religious activists do not aspire to govern in the name of God, while their secular counterparts do not claim to act as the representatives of the governed. Though they both apply themselves to checking what they see as the intrusiveness and the neglectfulness of governing agencies, substituting for these agencies is not the objective of either group. Tensions among them notwithstanding, the champions of civil society merely purport to enhance the ability of the governed to govern themselves, whereas the facilitators of God's designs endeavor to open the governed's hearts and minds to the call of a superior form of government.

Nongovernmental politics is neither the site of the good nor the domain of the powerless. It is not a substitute for governmental politics, yet its growing appeal in no way signifies that the citizenry is increasingly disengaged from "real" political issues. The strategic and ideological rifts among nongovernmental activists are just as wide as the divisions among parties and factions vying for governmental power and just as unlikely to be mended. Consequently, a focus on nongovernmental politics provides us less with an alternative to traditional forms of politics than with a perspective that complicates our understanding of politics in at least two related ways.

First, it shows that politics extends beyond the realm of representation. In other words, representing the people or, alternatively, choosing and supporting worthy representatives are not the only options available for those who want to engage in politics. Second, taking nongovernmental politics seriously not only expands the realm of what counts as politics, but also emphasizes the open-endedness of the political process. If it is indeed true that an improved system of representation is not meant to solve the tensions between governing and nongovernmental agencies — meaning that the latter does not see the advent of "good" representatives as a valid reason to retire from politics — then looking at the political field from the perspective of its nongovernmental dimension arguably undermines the notion that there should ever be an end to politics.

1   See Michel Agier, "Le camp des vulnérables; Les réfugiés face à leur citoyenneté niée," *Les Temps Modernes* 59, no. 627 (2004), and David Kennedy, *The Dark Side of Virtue: Reassessing International Humanitarianism* (Princeton: Princeton University Press, 2003).

2   Refusing to "be governed thusly" (d'*être gouverné comme cela*) is the definition given by Michel Foucault to the notion of critique as it developed alongside and in relation to the arts and techniques of government from the sixteenth century on. See Michel Foucault, "Qu'est-ce que la critique?" *Bulletin de la société française de philosophie* 84, no. 2 (1990), pp. 35–63. For an enlightening meditation on Foucault's conception of critique, see Judith Butler, "What is Critique? An Essay on Foucault's Virtue," in David Ingram (ed.), *The Political,* Blackwell Readings in Continental Philosophy (Oxford: Blackwell, 2002), pp. 212–28.

3   The relationship between modern governmental power and the pastoral authority of the "shepherd " — first in its Jewish then in its Christian versions — is key to Michel Foucault's genealogy of what he calls "governmentality." See, in particular, Michel Foucault, *Sécurité, territoire, population: Cours au Collège de France, 1977–1978* (Paris: Seuil/Gallimard, 2006), pp. 167–260.

4   Thomas Keenan stresses this point eloquently — on the subject of human-rights claims — in "'Where Are Human Rights...?': Reading a Communiqué from Iraq," included in this volume, pp. 57–71.

5   See Albert O. Hirschman, *Exit, Voice, and Loyalty: Responses to Decline in Firms, Organizations, and States* (Cambridge, MA: Harvard University Press, 1970) and *Essays in Trespassing: Economics to Politics and Beyond* (Cambridge: Cambridge University Press, 1981).

6   For a subtle and lucid perspective on debates surrounding gay marriage, both in the United States and in Europe, see Eric Fassin, "Same Sex, Different Politics: Comparing and Contrasting 'Gay Marriage Debates in France and in the United States,'" in *Public Culture* 13, no. 2 (Spring 2001), pp. 215–32 , and "Lieux d'invention: L'amitié, le mariage et la famille," in *L'inversion de la question homosexuelle* (Paris: Éditions Amsterdam, 2005), pp. 93–102.

7   See "Beyond Same-Sex Marriage: A New Strategic Vision for all Our Families & Relationships," available online at beyond-marriage.org, and Fassin, "Same Sex, Different Politics."

8   See "Nongovernmental Generation of International Treaties," an interview with James Love, included in this volume, pp. 359–67.

MOTIVES

HUMAN RIGHTS

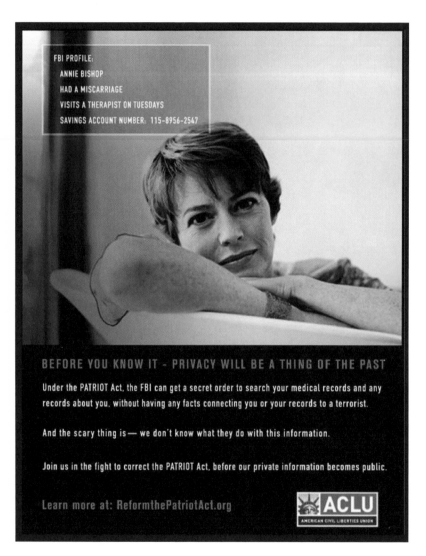

In July 2006, as the House and Senate voted to extend and expand the USA Patriot Act, the ACLU ran a nationwide campaign to alert the public about the dangers that such a vote presented to the constitutional rights of American citizens (www.aclu-nj.org).

Radically Civil

Anthony D. Romero interviewed by Michel Feher,
Thomas Keenan, and Gaëlle Krikorian

Anthony D. Romero is the executive director of the American Civil Liberties Union (ACLU),
the nation's premier defender of civil liberties and civil rights. He took the helm of the ACLU
in September 2001, a week before the attacks on the World Trade Center and the Pentagon,
and has presided over the most successful membership growth in the ACLU's eighty-six-year
history. Born in New York City to parents who hailed from Puerto Rico, Romero is a gradu-
ate of Stanford University Law School and Princeton University's Woodrow Wilson School of
Public Policy and International Affairs.

PART ONE: OCTOBER 25, 2005

Can you tell us about the history of the ACLU?

I'm only the sixth executive director in eighty-five years, and I'm the first to come from
outside the organization in almost forty years. Most of my predecessors came up through
the ranks. I had always known the ACLU, but when I accepted this position in 2001, I looked
into its history and discovered some pretty remarkable things, especially in light of 9/11 and
how one thinks of the ACLU after 9/11.

But to start at the beginning, in 1917, Roger Baldwin, a patrician Boston Brahmin who
had opposed the First World War, got together with some of the leading suffragists—
for example, Crystal Eastman and Jane Addams—to create the National Civil Liberties
Bureau (NCLB). The founders of our predecessor organization, which was renamed the
American Civil Liberties Union just three years later, were very concerned, even after the
successful conclusion of the First World War, about whether the way that war was fought
was right or wrong.

The NCLB emerged in the context of a burgeoning immigrant population that was
mostly Eastern European and often Jewish, a newly aggressive, at times even violent labor
movement, and the Bolshevik Revolution of 1917, in which an allegedly nefarious power,
that is, one that challenged American values and principles, came into being. In 1919, a
series of bombs went off across this country and prompted a great storm and fury from the

federal government. One bomb went off on the doorstep of the attorney general at the time, A. Mitchell Palmer, threatening the life of his daughter. In 1920, a bomb exploded at the New York Stock Exchange, closing it down for a while. Palmer, in response, unleashed the full force of the Justice Department, which summarily arrested and deported more than five thousand immigrants, mostly Eastern Europeans, many of them union organizers, conscientious objectors, and other dissidents. Reading all this in the early papers of the ACLU, I found it sounded eerily reminiscent of the current context, with the rise of al-Qaeda, a hostile force of global terrorism that challenges American values and principles.

The early papers make it clear: the NCLB was based on the idea that we needed some kind of effective mechanism to stand up to governmental power. It was not until the 1930s, when the ACLU and other organizations, such as the National Association for the Advancement of Colored People and the Anti-Defamation League, began to assert Americans' First Amendment rights, that the Supreme Court realized that these rights weren't just going to be guaranteed by edict: they had to be enforced. Until you had someone really take them seriously, give teeth to them, these rights would just remain paper aspirations.

So the NCLB began not as a nonprofit organization, but as a political movement.

It was a membership organization. Baldwin, who remained the director for more than three decades, spent the first part of his tenure traveling to local civil-liberties unions. He had this idea that you couldn't just be in New York and Washington; you had to be closest to the ground, where people directly confronted challenges to their civil liberties and civil rights. These citizen brigades, if you will, are really where we came from. Some of our local chapters are almost as old as the ACLU itself. We have fifty-three state offices — one in almost every state, as well as Puerto Rico and Washington, D.C., and three in California.

What makes the ACLU different from many similar organizations is that the membership, the *unions*, is where we came from. We added a legal arm *later*, a nonprofit and charitable arm *later*, a lobbying arm *later*. Our early focus remains true even now. We have five hundred and fifty thousand members today, and we only count those who, in a fifteen-month period, give $20 or more for their membership card. It's a crazy thing in the American political landscape, but there actually is an ACLU membership card. It got a little bit of notoriety when the first President Bush accused his opponent Michael Dukakis of being a *"card-carrying* member of the ACLU." Today, people get mad at us if we don't send them their cards!

Are there other defining moments in the ACLU's early history?

In 1941, we opposed the internment of Japanese Americans in the middle of the Second World War, a very popular war. The government arrested and detained one hundred and twenty thousand people of Japanese descent in the American West, denying them due process, information, and volition. It was the ACLU, especially our California offices, that challenged internment and eventually brought the case to the Supreme Court. We lost the case in 1944, but it shows what the organization is able to do, even in circumstances when its actions are very unpopular.

The issue of the internment camps almost divided the organization. When you read the minutes from that period, familiar issues appear. Do we need to change our conceptions of liberty and freedom during wartime? Should we make compromises on rights, imagining that what is temporarily given up will later be returned? It was a time when even good-willed civil libertarians argued that we needed to be much more cognizant of the Japanese threat, that we were fighting a war for our lives and our values. Some people asked, "Don't you understand that this is not the same world order that we once inherited?" But others replied, "Let's retain our values; let's preserve what's best about who we are." And the latter prevailed.

Today, it's a point of pride for us to look back and say, "Look, we were right in 1944, even though the Supreme Court ruled against us." These days we're fighting George Bush and the political right, but then it was liberals we were up against: it was President Franklin Roosevelt who signed the executive order for internment; Hugo Black, the Supreme Court justice, argued that the internment was appropriate; and Earl Warren, who was then the California state attorney general, carried it out. These were three of the greatest names in American liberalism, all saying that the internment was an unfortunate, but necessary compromise of freedom for security. It shows that our battles and challenges remain, regardless of which party is in power.

Today the ACLU is probably best known for its activism and expertise in court. Was this juridical focus in the original design of the organization, or did it grow out of other activities?

The original design of the ACLU was very much volunteer-based, and it has only slowly professionalized. In the United States, most injustices, most social issues, most issues related to rights sooner or later end up being formulated as questions before the courts. Even things that are political in nature are almost always encapsulated in some important legal case.

One of the earliest cases for the ACLU was the Scopes trial, in which a teacher in Tennessee was put on trial for teaching Darwin's theory of evolution in the classroom. It is remarkable that today, this very week, we have fourteen lawyers, not in Tennessee, but in Pennsylvania, arguing about whether or not they should teach "intelligent design" there. It's inevitable that we're going to keep coming back to some of these questions, which are at the heart of the American experience and democracy. We're always going to have to deal with the secular and the sectarian in a country that is as ambivalent as ours — tolerant of different denominations and religions, but at the same time very religiously motivated. But to go back to the Scopes trial, Roger Baldwin raised money from New York liberals, went to Tennessee, and placed an ad in a Tennessee newspaper saying, "If any teacher wants to step forward and challenge this ban on teaching evolution, we will be glad to provide the legal assistance." And then he found a lawyer to work with us in defending the rights of that teacher.

Over time, this capacity has grown, and we have brought it in-house, to the point that we are now probably the world's largest public-interest law firm, with 150 full-time lawyers who litigate cases before courts at the state and national levels, including, of course, the Supreme Court. Our lawyers develop areas of expertise. The issues we take up are complicated and not easily farmed to outside counsel. The more the jurisprudence has evolved, the more we have expanded that aspect of the organization.

We have, in total, over seven hundred staff members nationwide. There are about three hundred people in the national office, which is based primarily in New York and Washington, D.C. We have a national voting-rights project, based in Atlanta. We are one of the few national organizations that advocate for the legalization of all drugs. We argue that they should be regulated just as we regulate tobacco or arms, but individuals should have the right to determine what and how and whether they wish to put things in their body. That effort is based in California. And then we have local offices in all the states, varying in size from five or six people to about one hundred twenty people in California.

So despite the prominence of the courts in the United States, not every ACLU program is geared toward judiciary action.

We have three major programs, three major strategies, if you will, for enforcing rights. One revolves around litigation: because many of the issues we address are unpopular, the law and the possibility of litigating are what allow you to create political will. It's the big stick that you can hold over the heads of elected politicians, who are often too afraid to do the right thing. Then, second, you have legislative work in Congress and in all the state capitals to try and promote good laws and prevent bad ones from passing. We've had some success in different places at different times, even with this Congress.

What was your most recent success?

Our effort to reenfranchise felons. In America, the states determine when felons regain the right to vote; in places like Nebraska and Rhode Island, we've begun to change legislative rules around.

Finally, the third program is a communications and public-education program, because you can win in Congress or in state legislatures, and you can win in the courts, but unless you change the hearts and minds of people, you can win the battles and lose the war. That's what I think, frankly, has happened with much of the human-rights movement in the United States. As we've become more professionalized, we've become less able to communicate with ordinary people about why things matter. The more civil rights becomes the realm of professional litigators and lobbies and communications experts, the more we lose the people like my mother and my sister and my cousin. Part of what we're trying to do at the ACLU, especially within the last year or so, is to do a much better job of explaining why we do something.

For example, we've just started an experiment, producing a monthly half-hour television show. It doesn't read like an infomercial. It doesn't read like a talking head. It tells a story. It takes our clients, and tells what happens to them and why. The first show is on the Patriot Act. We tracked a number of people who were being affected by the law and told their stories. Children crying about fathers being deported, women talking about their husbands being deported without access to lawyers. Not the abstractions of Fourth and Fifth Amendment protections, not the abstractions of "due process" or "surveillance," but stories about what happens when a country goes to war with its own people and who gets clipped in that war, namely, immigrants and minorities.

We picked this subject because it's one we are currently working on. The Patriot Act is before Congress, which is now debating whether to extend or rescind or shrink it.[1] We wanted a show that could be used as an organizing tool for the American people to say, "Holy shit, this is really happening in people's lives, this is why it matters." You see the significance of the larger policy issues by telling stories about people who encounter injustice.

The second show, which we just produced, is on the Supreme Court. It features one client — a high-school girl in Oklahoma — who refused to submit to a urine-sample drug test to sing in the choir. We followed her case all the way up to the Supreme Court. We want to show that the Supreme Court is more than just some marble box on Maryland Avenue in Washington, D.C. We want to show why the Court matters to ordinary people, why it matters to this girl to be able to bring her case before it. The story is told in a very compelling way: she's a kind of Everygirl, a very typical American, very cute, very emotional, and very high-strung. Her parents talk about how it was important to support her and her efforts to challenge the policy. We show the different justices and their different judicial temperaments and philosophies. We talk about what you should look for in a justice. We want to tell you why you should care who the next nominee is.

We took a leap of faith — we'd never done a TV show before. We negotiated to get it distributed on a satellite television outlet called Link TV, but now we've also signed a contract with a major cable outlet, Court TV, which will get out to about eighty-five million people. They liked the first two shows so much that they want to run all of our shows. We have spent $2 million on the project thus far. We had a hunch that if you build it they will come. If we can make emotionally engaging, well-done, edgy content, put it out there with help from people we know in the entertainment world, it will reach people. That was our hypothesis, which now seems to be paying off.

You need to litigate well, and you need to lobby well, of course. But in the last four years, we've pushed the ACLU out of its comfort zone. We should always be trying new approaches — in both our programs and our tactics. For instance, regarding the latter, we hired Bob Barr, a former congressman from Georgia, a far-right-winger, the one who was trying to impeach Clinton, the writer of the Defense of Marriage Act — great civil libertarian credentials. But on some of the issues, he agreed with us, especially on surveillance under the Patriot Act. So we put him on retainer, hired him as a consultant. You should have seen the firestorm within the ACLU. People were saying, "What is Romero doing? We actually hired *this* guy to work with *us*?" I believe that in a political climate so difficult, unless we find a way to work with conservatives and Republicans, we'll become irrelevant.

I have always thought that the most important thing is to hold on to your principles, but be tactically relevant. We didn't change our position on gay marriage. We didn't change our position on abortion. Yet we don't have a litmus test for whom we work with.

Tactical alliances are hard for a lot of groups to set up, but it's one of the places where we've had some payoffs. We've had the U.S. Chamber of Commerce and other business-sector groups — who all oppose parts of the Patriot Act — with us because we've built topical contacts across the political aisle. If we had only stayed with the Quakers, the pacifists, and the librarians, we would not have the political muscle that we now have.

So you're working on three levels: jurisprudence, legislation (lobbying Congress), and what we might call norms. This third level — addressing what is and is not considered normal — is the focus of your education program. This issue of norms is an essential part of your work, especially given that there is a culture war going on. As you implied earlier, if you want to change the jurisprudence and the law, you have to change the culture.

Yes, and gay rights would be a perfect example of such cultural change. *Lawrence v. Texas,* which in 2003 overturned the criminality of sodomy, said less about where the Supreme Court was than where the country was. In 1986, there was a very similar case out of Georgia, an ACLU case, *Bowers v. Hardwick,* that had the same set of facts and circumstances: two gay men are in the privacy of their own home, consensually making love, and a cop walks in and arrests them under the sodomy statute of the state of Georgia. The case goes all the way to the Supreme Court — Laurence Tribe is fighting for us — and we lose. The opinion is a travesty. They quote Leviticus, for instance, and the result is this crazy doctrine and dogma that's more about religious life than about civil rights or human rights. Then you fast-forward to *Lawrence v. Texas,* and the Court does a complete reversal. What's changed is not the Court, but the fact that it's no longer tenable in this country to have that level of explicit discrimination sanctioned by the state. By that point, norms had changed considerably: you had TV shows with gay characters, you had gay families with kids, you had a lot more people out. You had much more recognition that this is a fact of life, whether you like it or not. In a lot of ways, the Court played catch-up on that issue. So you're right: there's jurisprudence, and there are norms.

Would you talk about the lawsuits the ACLU has filed against the Bush administration regarding acts of torture committed at the Abu Ghraib prison, in Guantánamo Bay, and at the Baghram air base?

We were very concerned, when the U.S. went off to war in Afghanistan and then to Iraq, about how the war was being prosecuted — about the mechanics of the war. The ACLU was on this in October 2003, even before the Abu Ghraib incident came to light. One day at a staff lawyers meeting, one of our younger lawyers asked, "Why don't we fire off some Freedom of Information Act requests and ask for all the information the government has on torture and abuse in Guantánamo, Iraq, and Afghanistan?" One of my top lawyers said, "I'll give you a dollar for every page you get of any relevance." Then the Abu Ghraib photos came out, and our judge in New York — where we had filed our request — began to get a little bit of fire under his feet and mandated that the government start turning over these documents. So far, we have received seventy thousand pages of U.S. government documents, all of which somehow relate to torture and abuse in Afghanistan and Iraq and Guantánamo. In total, there are one hundred and fifty thousand pages of documents, but they haven't all been released yet. Regardless of the content, you have to ask, "What the hell is going on here—the U.S. government has one hundred and fifty thousand pages relevant to torture and abuse overseas?" What has happened to the moral authority of the rules of war, the Geneva Conventions?

Once you pull the string, the whole thing begins to unravel. You begin to piece together this picture, and it is incredible what you see. You see hundreds of cases of deaths that are not investigated. You see tons of cases of young men who die under suspicious circumstances—blunt force, hypothermia, internal bleeding—that are never investigated. You read, for instance, about a father being forced to watch a mock execution of his fourteen-year-old son. You read stories about men's hands being bathed in alcohol and then lit on fire. You read stories of lit cigarettes being placed in detainees' ears. You read of men being shackled to the floor for twenty-four hours, unable to relieve themselves in a bathroom, forced to defecate and urinate on themselves. What's incredible when you read these documents—what makes them so poignant—is that they don't put the word *torture* in quotation marks. The FBI doesn't say *so-called* torture techniques, or *alleged* ones—they just talk about torture techniques.

Why is there a paper trail on that?

Because complaints have been raised within the system. For instance, one document reveals that the FBI instructed its agents not to participate if in any instance they thought interrogations were going beyond what was allowable under the Geneva Conventions. You look at this document and see that they're fighting with each other. Some say, "This is wrong." Others reply, "This is effective." Others still protest, "This goes too far." This argument is going on within this monolith called the Bush administration. Here the bureaucracy, the government, works to our advantage. It gets more interesting when you understand the internal battles between different parts of the government involved. For instance, the first documents we got were from the FBI, because the FBI was pissed off at the Department of Defense and the State Department, whose employees were dressing up as FBI officials when they interrogated detainees in Guantánamo and elsewhere so that they would not be left "holding the bag." In response to this deception, someone in the FBI wanted us to see these documents and released them as a part of the court mandate.

Now we're in court on the issue of photographs. We've been arguing that the definition of the word "document" applies not only to memos and legal opinions, but also to digital documents, whether video, audio, or photographs. We have a great judge in New York on this case who ruled that the government had to turn over seventy-seven photos and three videos from Abu Ghraib. What's interesting here is that the government pulled out the big guns on this issue. We submitted our papers and an affidavit from a former army lieutenant as to why these documents should be released. The government filed its papers, and

In September 2003, the ACLU launched an advertising campaign featuring renowned actors, authors, musicians, and directors speaking out in their own words in support of fundamental civil liberties and the ACLU's role in defending those liberties (courtesy of ACLU).

its affidavit came from General Richard B. Myers, the chairman of the Joint Chiefs of Staff. Here you have a federal district court litigation — it's high, but it's not huge — and the government is so concerned that it has pulled out *the* top general to tell the court why we should not be given these photographs. They obviously understand that the public outcry that hasn't yet been ignited by all these memos and legal papers could be ignited once people *see* what is going on. Many of these facilities have built-in cameras, built-in surveillance, so we can get a much fuller picture of the breakdown of the law. We are interested in these images not because we have some prurient interest in seeing people humiliated or tortured or killed, of course, but because they offer the best chance of holding these individuals accountable.

Images resonate with people; they help paint the human face of what happened to our clients. In fact, to that end, two of our plaintiffs will come to New York next week, to visit the Bellevue/NYU Program for Survivors of Torture and to help prepare for our case, and then we're going to bring them around to meet members of Congress, including Senator John McCain, and some members of the press.

Were the plaintiffs detained?

They've all been released. Our clients were once detained and tortured by the United States and ultimately released by the United States. So freeing detainees is not our task per se. What we're trying to do is insist that responsibility goes to the highest levels of our government. Donald Rumsfeld is still the secretary of defense. That is remarkable by itself. You have this great scandal rocking the American military, and you still have the same secretary of defense. Alberto Gonzales, who as White House counsel was responsible for calling the Geneva Conventions "quaint" and "obsolete," was promoted to attorney general. Lieutenant General Ricardo Sanchez, who was identified in the Fay report as being responsible for Abu Ghraib, is rumored to be up for a fourth-star promotion.[2] Major General Geoffrey Miller, who was specifically identified in the Schmidt and Furlow report as having been responsible for the abuse in Guantánamo, was *not* held accountable, even though the army's own reports said he should be charged.[3] The government decided to override the recommendations from the army inspector general's report. This is ludicrous!

We sued Rumsfeld because we think you should go all the way to the top, but you have to connect the top of the chain of command all the way to the bottom. Another organization didn't want to sue the military officers below him, because it felt that it might be a mistake — given the fact that America is at war — to look antimilitary. We thought otherwise — I thought otherwise — so on our own, we also sued Brigadier General Janis Karpinski, Colonel Thomas Pappas, and Sanchez, three uniformed military officers we think are essential.

What about General Miller?

We are still looking for a way to connect him, too. The difficulty with Miller is a lack of clients. We had a much more difficult time getting access in Guantánamo than in Iraq and Afghanistan — tracking down clients who have been released from there has been much harder. We'll see.

Why are there only seventy thousand out of one hundred and fifty thousand documents available and only seventy-seven photos and three videos? Is that all that you know about specifically, or is that all there is?

That's all that we know about specifically, all that the government says exists in the context of Abu Ghraib. The government has yet not released the full index of the hundred and fifty-thousand documents that it initially said were relevant. When it completes the production, it usually gives us an index of the documents, both released and unreleased. We march through the list and fight document by document about which should or should not be released. So we've already identified the seventy-seven images and three videos from Abu Ghraib. Obviously, the fact that the judge ruled that these particular images and videos should be released means that next we'll ask what videos they have about Guantánamo, about Baghram. What videos do they have on these naval carriers where they're holding ghost detainees? The fact that we've established a precedent to have access to these videos is probably why General Myers went in on this case — because they realized it would open the floodgates. I don't know what we're going to find, but it can't just be Abu Ghraib photos. They wouldn't have gone to such lengths to fight us for, essentially, duplicate pictures of whatever *60 Minutes* already has.

I also think there's something more there, because the judge has suggested that it's not just a matter of a few rogue soldiers, but that the evidence raises questions about command responsibility. Most of the photos we saw of Charles Graner and Lynndie England humiliating detainees don't necessarily implicate the commanders. But perhaps there are other images that do. This is purely speculation, which is what you do when you have a government that's a black hole — you try to figure it out. There may be photographs of the so-called initial reaction forces (IRF) used to quell prison riots, where the guards dress in full riot gear, with shields and masks and plastic on their arms, and they march in, almost like ancient Greek soldiers, and plow down the recalcitrant detainees. If we can get videos of how an IRF operation plays out, with someone getting trampled and hurt, that implicates the chain of command much more aggressively.

We are also looking at the use of dogs for intimidation in interrogations. General Sanchez authorized the use of dogs. We think he perjured himself in Congress, because he said, under oath, that he had never approved the use of dogs, but we have a memo he signed — one the government turned over — that lists environmental manipulation, sleep "adjustment," and *the use of dogs*. If we can show how the guards urged the dogs to attack the prisoners — in pictures — then we can really begin to connect the dots between what happened, what the policy is, and what senior commanders like Sanchez authorized.

Five years ago, did you think you would be suing the U.S. government about torture?

No! It was unthinkable. I'm sorry if this sounds naive, but I thought those questions were fully resolved for the American people. In my own myopia, in my own ethnocentrism, if you had asked me, "Would you have to deal with an American government that arrests and detains American citizens and does not grant them access to a lawyer?" I would have thought, "That will not happen here." I mean, I thought, "We have other problems in America, but you can't just suspend the Bill of Rights that way." And yet we have the case of Jose Padilla, an American citizen, arrested in the United States, who has never been charged with a crime. He has just been labeled by the American president as a "bad guy" and not given access to his lawyer for *two years*. I would have thought this to be absolutely unthinkable; that's the type of stuff you'd imagine seeing in the developing world, but not in America.

In October 2003, when we started this case, we were just being healthily skeptical. At that point, we were still being told how humanely the prisoners were being treated and that Guantánamo was the best prison camp in the world. I remember going to Guantánamo in August 2003 with the whole press corps, and they thought I was being overly aggressive. I was asking questions about detention, the facilities, and the treatment. I remember asking one of the doctors about the use of medicine as a tool for interrogation. A reporter from one of the major media outlets said, "Oh, Anthony, come on, they're not going to do that. Don't be preposterous." I said, "You know, it's not beyond the military to use 'truth serums' and other drugs to alter prisoners' minds and their physical states, in order to break them down." And that was exactly what they were doing.

In December 2004, the ACLU created a new section called the Human Rights Working Group. This would seem to mark a shift from understanding civil-rights problems as something we have in the U.S., while human-rights problems are what "they" have in the developing world. You are bringing human rights home at just the moment when the administration is violating human rights in the name of promoting civil rights abroad.

There's always been this idea that we export human rights and we consume civil rights and civil liberties. There's certainly some irony in the situation now, as the administration says we're exporting human rights while simultaneously contradicting those rights in the way it fights the war.

The ACLU is the largest-staffed human-rights organization on the globe. We fight for human rights in the U.S. context, with the U.S. government, but we can benefit from putting our work in a global context. What the ACLU does and how the Americans prosecute the wars in Afghanistan and Iraq will have an enormous impact in other countries. As advocates here, we have to see our work in the context of other advocates working on comparable issues in Europe, in South America, and elsewhere. We are going global; the economy did it before us, law enforcement as well. The human-rights community is just beginning to ask others elsewhere what they did and how they can learn and how we can help one another. Using the same framework, the same language, and dealing with American arrogance — this idea that we're different — is important. Thinking we should use a different language for the same type of work is hubris, another idea of American exceptionalism.

In our human-rights project, we try to apply international human-rights norms and standards domestically, which has now led us to focus on Mississippi, specifically on the conditions of confinement for juveniles there. Some of what we've uncovered in our human-rights research — we're working there just as any human-rights organization would, collecting and organizing data and facts — is really remarkable. We are shocked about what we allow ourselves to do overseas, but you should see what we do in juvenile detention centers in Mississippi. Kids in lockdown for eighteen to twenty-four hours. Young girls and young boys with full, hooded restraints on their heads, almost reminiscent of the Abu Ghraib photographs. Corporal punishment, not like what you see in Abu Ghraib, but still extreme — there are skulls being fractured. And these local juvenile officials get away with it with impunity.

Remember where the guards in Abu Ghraib came from.

Yes, they were prison guards. Some of them had been defendants in ACLU cases. So we can't think about Abu Ghraib and Guantánamo as separate from what happens in Mississippi.

The ACLU has recently experienced exceptional growth in staff and in membership.

The staff at the national office has grown about 73 percent, and our membership has almost doubled since 2001. We have been aggressive and strategic in our efforts to reach the American people. The big factor is the climate. This time around, Americans have begun to realize how this affects their lives and civil liberties. Our membership is not huge for America. The National Rifle Association — what does it have, three million members? But our growth shows that there is at least recognition of what needs to change.

Do you work differently since you've expanded?

Right now we're at a turning point. Up until this point, I have felt that the organization should focus on a couple of things really aggressively and push them forward as far as we can. I'd say the Patriot Act, torture, and the values debate around issues such as gay rights and abortion are where we've put the most staff, resources, publications, and programs. Today, in our staff meeting, we discussed our opportunity to take advantage of the weakened presidency, to go completely full throttle. The administration does not have its former control over the Republican Party, so we have an opportunity to open up a much fuller debate.

Do you have any specific fronts in mind?

For instance, the whole public reaction to the Terri Schiavo case remains unexploited. George Bush tried to insert himself into this decision about the end of this woman's life, tried to override the courts and the wishes she had expressed to her husband, tried to exert influence on the side of religion and the parents who wanted to keep her alive. The backlash was huge: 83 percent of Americans thought that was wrong. But the Democrats, being incapable of playing the opposition party they need to be, didn't exploit it. Now, I still think there is a public understanding of the Schiavo case that could be brilliantly exploited. We were discussing it just this morning: let's think about dropping a bill in the House that deals with the Schiavo facts, demanding that Congress never allows that to happen again. Let's ignite a petition campaign. Let's bring back public action. Let's have these local resolutions on Schiavo — just as we did on the Patriot Act, where thousands of towns across the country said the Patriot Act went too far.

The religious right has done this kind of thing brilliantly. They take one of our issues, expose its underbelly, and make us fight defensively. Now we need to go on the offensive. With this weakened presidency, there's a chance to create much more havoc in a way that we activists need to be thinking about. If we can get the videos of abuse, then we'll go to religious leaders, especially the Christian evangelicals, and get them to say, "Is this what America stands for?" Religious congregations, whom we don't usually work with, can say how immoral this is. Scientists could address the stem-cell issue this way. They could portray the Republicans and the right wing as Neanderthals turning their backs on science. That's not something we would do, but pursuing the Schiavo case, or at least what it brought up, could be a lot of fun. You have local resolutions, local legislation, local bills, you drop it into the state legislatures, and you have a bill in Congress. And then you have a multipronged campaign. When 83 percent of the public agrees with the ACLU on something, God, we should be jumping all over it!

Is there a way to promote cultural change to protect abortion? Poll after poll shows that the majority of Americans are pro-choice, yet you have Senator Hillary Clinton trying to stake out a middle-ground position between the evangelicals and her own constituency.

The evangelicals have been able to do precisely what we are hoping to do: define something about the larger issue in such a narrow way that it becomes impossible to gain traction on it. So the debate about abortion in America has recently become the partial-birth-abortion ban. Now they're redefining "fetal pain" as the abortion issue. It's a way to insinuate life into the discussion by asking about whether or not the fetus feels pain. It's exactly what they've been so good at. We, too, have to learn how to capture the public narrative. We still have work to do.

PART TWO: MARCH 28, 2006

In the last few months, the exposure of the National Security Agency's (NSA) spying program and the CIA's "extraordinary rendition" program have certainly bolstered your case against the Bush administration's propensity to abuse executive power. However, it is far from clear that these revelations about shrinking civil liberties at home and human-rights violations abroad play a major role in the declining popularity of the president. More importantly, you now have to deal with a Roberts Supreme Court that is even more hostile to your causes than the Rehnquist Court. How do you assess these recent developments?

First, regarding the Supreme Court, you know that today — March 28, 2006 — there was a hearing in the case of Salim Ahmed Hamdan. Hamdan was Osama bin Laden's driver in Afghanistan and is now a Guantánamo detainee challenging the legality of the military commissions established by George W. Bush in November 2001. During the argument, Paul Clement, the solicitor general, tried to convince the Court that it should dismiss the case. His twofold argument was that the president, as commander-in-chief, had the authority to create such military commissions and that the Detainee Treatment Act — although it was adopted by Congress after Hamdan's appeal had been granted — retroactively prevents the Court from reviewing their legality. Well, at least regarding the jurisdictional issue, the Court seemed unconvinced by the administration's argument. We obviously don't know if the votes will end up reflecting the tone and content of today's questions at the argument.[4] But if they do, it will mean that, in spite of the clearly conservative views now held by a majority of justices, most of them still remain very protective of their own role in the system of checks and balances that are purported to safeguard our constitutional democracy. In other words, it will mean that even a body as conservative as the Roberts Court is disturbed by the abuse of executive power that is one of the distinctive features of the Bush presidency.

Now what this means for us is that we need to be more relentless than ever in going after these abuses and that we should be on the offensive on all fronts. We need to keep reminding legislators, Republicans as well as Democrats, that the Bush administration is both violating the principles they claim to hold dear and trampling on their constitutional prerogatives. We need to keep taking the administration to the courts each time it transgresses the constitutional limits of its authority. And we need to make headway in the court of public opinion by showing how the current pattern of abuse of executive power is a menace to the rights and liberties of any American citizen.

Let's start with the courts.

Shortly after the *New York Times* exposed the NSA spying program, in December 2005, we filed a lawsuit in Detroit challenging the program. We are charging that a program allowing the NSA to monitor and collect e-mails and phone calls from American citizens without a warrant or any other form of judicial oversight violates all Americans' rights to free speech and privacy under both the First and the Fourth Amendment of the Constitution. We are filing this suit on behalf of a group of eight plaintiffs.

What we want to demonstrate is not only that this program is illegal, but also that it is causing "concrete harm" to a wide range of individuals and organizations — journalists, lawyers, scholars, advocacy groups — regardless of their position on the political spectrum. Therefore, it was important for us to find plaintiffs whose work is disrupted by the NSA wiretapping — if only because they now have to travel overseas in order to communicate freely with their clients or sources — but who cannot be identified as notorious critics of the administration's foreign policy. So while some of our clients' profiles fit what you would expect — the National Association of Criminal Defense Lawyers, the Council on American-Islamic Relations, Greenpeace, and the ACLU itself — others don't. For instance, we are representing Christopher Hitchens, an author and journalist who, as you know, was a prominent supporter of the military interventions in Afghanistan and Iraq. Our plaintiffs also include Larry Diamond, who is a senior fellow at the Hoover Institution and a former member of the Council on Foreign Relations' Independent Task Force on United States Policy Toward Arab Reform, and Barnett Rubin, who is an expert on Afghanistan currently collaborating with the Afghan government.

The fact that these people are joining us in challenging the NSA spying program is a remarkable sign. It shows that the administration's disregard for our basic rights and liberties is not merely an object of concern for those who oppose the war in Iraq and every other aspect of George W. Bush's agenda. We want to send this message to the president's allies in Congress, who are actively preparing to cover up his illegal program. More importantly, maybe, we want to send it to those other members of Congress who still believe that it is in their political interest to stand on the sidelines of issues like this — for fear of having their patriotism questioned.[5]

What about the CIA's "extraordinary rendition" program?

We are representing Khaled el-Masri, a German citizen who was abducted by the CIA while he was vacationing in Macedonia. He was beaten, drugged, and flown to a secret CIA prison in Afghanistan, where he was subjected to unlawful detention and interrogation for five months. Even when CIA agents realized that he was innocent, they still held him for two more months. Then, without explanation, they flew him again and deposited him, at night, on a hill in Albania. In December 2005, we filed a lawsuit against George Tenet, who was the head of the CIA at the time of el-Masri's abduction, and also against the airline companies that facilitated his kidnapping. We charge that the extraordinary rendition program — which seems to have been applied to about 150 foreign nationals in the past few years — violates both international law, such as the United Nations Convention Against Torture and Other Cruel, Inhuman or Degrading Treatment or Punishment, and the Fifth and Eighth Amendments of the U.S. Constitution.

We may not be in the best position to win this case, because it involves a foreign national whose rights were violated outside U.S. territory. And I'm sure the government will invoke a state-secrets defense.[6] But it is still very important that we pursue it, if only to encourage and help international institutions, especially the Council of Europe and the European Parliament, with their own investigations of the CIA's practice of extraordinary rendition and of the complicity of European governments in this matter. Domestically, it is also crucial that we keep this issue in the public eye, that we don't let the administration bury it. In that respect, I am especially pleased by the effect we managed to produce with the press conference we held last December. It took place while Secretary of State Condoleezza Rice was in Europe and about to meet with the newly elected German chancellor, Angela Merkel. We organized this press conference to announce that we were filing a lawsuit on behalf of Khaled el-Masri. We wanted our client to be present, but he was not allowed to enter the country. So we had him anyway, via satellite feed, on a giant screen, and this turned out to be even more spectacular, so much so that Rice was forced to address the issue and defend the administration's policy on German soil. We got her knickers in a twist, while Merkel was pressured into expressing concern and welcoming European investigations of the extraordinary-rendition programs. Both the press conference itself and its outcome certainly were a lot of fun.

Indicting as they may be, these pending cases still don't seem to raise that much outrage in Congress: Senator Russell Feingold's motion to censure the president, for instance, is not likely to be very successful. Tell us about your lobbying strategy in Congress.

Let's start with the Republican side of the aisle. I am convinced — indeed, I know — that many Republican members of Congress are increasingly uncomfortable with the constant executive overreach of the Bush administration. They feel that, in the long run, being identified with such a pattern of abuse is bad for them and bad for their party. However, with midterm elections looming, they are paralyzed. On the one hand, they don't want to pay the price for the growing unpopularity of the president, but on the other hand, they

At a news conference in Washington on December 6, 2005, ACLU executive director Anthony Romero discusses a lawsuit filed against former U.S. Central Intelligence Agency director George Tenet on behalf of Khaled el-Masri. El-Masri, a German citizen kidnapped by the CIA, was detained, interrogated, and beaten at a prison in Afghanistan (Jonathan Ernst/Reuters).

fear that breaking ranks now will, in the short term, worsen the crisis of the Republican Party and jeopardize their own election or reelection. So there again, we have to be both relentless and patient. Basically, we keep telling the Republican members of Congress two things. First, we remind them that they are supposed to be the champions of small government, that nothing is more at odds with Republican philosophy than an administration that tramples on the prerogatives of the legislative and judicial branches of government and, even more importantly, on the business of private citizens. Second, we warn them that if they don't oppose the current abuses of executive power, they have to face the possibility that the next Democratic administration will take advantage of Bush's impunity and immunity to act in the exact same way. I believe that more and more Republican legislators hear what we say and privately agree with our arguments. Yet it may take time — and a lot of nagging on our part — before they publicly criticize the Bush administration for its way of waging the so-called war on terror.

On the other side of the aisle, we are still dealing the Democrats' usual fear of being called either unpatriotic or soft on national-security issues. So as the lack of support for the Feingold censure motion demonstrates, they remain very reluctant to take on the administration when it comes to abuses of power allegedly committed in the name of "keeping America safe." But it may be that the problem is even deeper than that. For a long time now, Democrats have been in this process of defining their own agenda. They constantly reframe and refrain: reframe what it means to be progressive and refrain from tackling contentious issues. They believe that skirting their own values is a winning strategy because their liberal constituents have nowhere else to go, while moderately conservative voters will recognize their positions as that of some "sensible center" and join them on that basis. We need to challenge this strategy. We need either to convince Democrats that playing it safe is not the road to success or, if they remain unconvinced, simply force them to take a stand on risky matters. We have no other option than that of playing the part of the obnoxious dinner guests who constantly embarrass their hosts. And we have to play that part unsparingly, with Democrats—who expect to be spared by us—as well as with Republicans.

Your determination and relentlessness notwithstanding, both the makeup of the Roberts Supreme Court and the persistent timidity of what is supposed to be the opposition in Congress clearly limit your ability to advance your causes through the rulings of either the judiciary or the legislative branch of government. Thus, I imagine that making inroads with what you call the court of public opinion is an even more pressing concern than it was a few months ago.

Yes. More than ever, we are aware that fighting for our issues in the courts and lobbying Congress are only part of what we must do. More than ever, our task today is to convince everyone in America that violations of human rights and shrinking civil liberties are issues that concern all of us, if only because they can harm any of us. Now, to fulfill such a task, we still have to learn how to tell better stories, stories that bring home the concreteness of the harm and the fact that anyone can be targeted. And it is true that the administration is providing us with amazing scenarios that should help us tell good stories. For instance, when you have homeland security officials spying on and wrongly arresting vegans who were peacefully protesting outside a Honey-Baked Ham store, as they did in Georgia in 2003, or when you have the FBI using counterterrorism resources to infiltrate animal-rights groups, which they call "ecoterrorists," you are clearly given good material for compelling stories about random and widespread abuse that could affect just about anyone. On our Web site, you can already see an impressive list of ordinary people who were targeted by the FBI, the NSA, or the Department of Homeland Security and who tell their stories. But we still need to find better ways to communicate the danger that such practices of widespread and unchecked surveillance, arbitrary arrest, and brutal interrogation represent, both for the fabric of our political system and for virtually any citizen.

Speaking of strategic reassessments based on the recent changes in the Supreme Court, the abortion ban passed by the South Dakota legislature and signed by the governor of that state on March 6, 2006, clearly conveys the newfound confidence of the religious right in the Roberts Court's readiness to overturn *Roe v. Wade*—since the promoters of the ban know that its constitutionality will be challenged and thus eventually reviewed by the Court. What do you plan to do on that front?

As we discussed before, I believe that it is crucial for us to venture beyond our comfort zone, especially when we are faced with exceptional challenges. And the abortion ban in

South Dakota certainly is a major challenge, both because it is extraordinarily far-reaching — virtually all abortions are banned — and because some Southern states are about to follow suit. So while we are obviously not a political party, which means that we can't substitute for the lack of nerve of the Democratic opposition, I believe that the situation calls for trying something that we have never done before, namely, sponsoring — or at least cosponsoring — a ballot initiative. We, that is, the ACLU of the Dakotas, joined a coalition called the South Dakota Campaign for Healthy Families, which is calling upon South Dakotans to sign a petition that would place a repeal of the abortion ban on the November 2006 ballot.[7] This is clearly unexplored and risky terrain for us, but I think that it is consistent with the notion that we can no longer rely simply on the protection of the courts and on our ability to lobby legislatures.

For decades now, the common wisdom has been that social conservatives were reflecting public sentiment, while we were just hanging on to legal protections. I think that we need to start challenging our adversaries on what is supposedly their turf. We need to do that in part because of recent judicial nominations, but also because we can't expect to do our job of protecting human rights and civil liberties if we take it for granted that ballot initiatives and, more generally, any motion seeking popular support are out of our reach. In that respect, nothing is more encouraging than the recent mobilization and marches — of students and others — against the proposed legislation on immigration by the House of Representatives. The fact that these marches gather so many people in the absence of any central organizer really shows us that bringing our cases to the court of public opinion is a challenge that we have to meet.

CODA: OCTOBER 12, 2006

The ACLU celebrated the end of the 2005 Supreme Court term as the country moved one step closer to stopping the Bush administration's relentless abuse of power. In a 5-3 decision in *Hamdan v. Rumsfeld*, the Court ruled unconstitutional the system of military commissions established by the President to try detainees at Guantánamo Bay. It was a victory for the ACLU and the other human rights groups that filed briefs in the case. Most importantly, it was a victory for the rule of law in the United States.

The celebrations didn't last long. Less than four months after the announcement of the *Hamdan* decision, the President signed into law the Military Commissions Act of 2006, an alarmingly unconstitutional end run around the will of the Court. The law essentially gives the President free reign to allow torture and ignore the Geneva Conventions. It gives retroactive immunity to government officials who authorized or ordered illegal acts of torture and abuse. It weakens the judiciary — yet another blow to the separation of powers. It eliminates *habeas corpus* for nearly all detainees and permits convictions based on evidence that was literally beaten out of witnesses. In other words, what the Court did to protect the rule of law, the Congress and the President undid. And then some.

Needless to say, we may be going to court again soon.

1 The Patriot Act was renewed on March 2, 2006 by the U.S. Senate and on March 7 by the House of Representatives. The renewal was signed into law by President Bush on March 9, 2006.

2 Major General George Fay chaired the army panel that looked into the torture and abuses at the Abu Ghraib detention center at Guantánamo Bay, Cuba. Fay told reporters that "there were some instances where torture was being used." The army report cited twenty-seven people who are accused of being associated with abuses at Abu Ghraib, including criticism of Lieutenant General Ricardo Sanchez, who was the commander of U.S. forces at the time of the abuses. The U.S. Senate refused to approve Sanchez's promotion, and he retired from the U.S. Army in November 2006.

3 Lieutenant General Randall Schmidt of the U.S. Air Force and Brigadier General John T. Furlow's report was one of several to report on detainee treatment at the Guantánamo Bay detention center. Their report recommended that Major General Geoffrey Miller should receive official reprimand for his failure to monitor the interrogation of a detainee, who experienced abusive treatment. Miller retired from the army on July 31, 2006.

4 The U.S. Supreme Court ruled on June 29, 2006 in the case of *Hamdan v. Rumsfeld* that President Bush did not have the authority to set up military commissions at Guantánamo Bay, Cuba. The ruling stated that such commissions were in violation of the Uniform Code of Military Justice (UCMJ) and the Geneva Conventions.

5 On August 17, 2006, in the case of *American Civil Liberties Union v. National Security Agency,* U.S. District Court Judge Anna Diggs Taylor held that the NSA's Terrorist Surveillance Program is unconstitutional on the grounds that it violates the Administrative Procedures Act, the Separation of Powers Doctrine, the First and Fourth Amendments of the U.S. Constitution, the Foreign Intelligence Surveillance Act (FISA), and Title III of the Omnibus Crime Control and Safe Streets Act (Title III). On September 20, 2006, the House Judiciary Committee and the House Permanent Select Committee on Intelligence approved H.R. 5825, the "Electronic Surveillance Modernization Act." The bill, authored by Representative Heather Wilson (R-NM), relaxes warrant requirements for electronic surveillance of certain domestic communications. Among its many provisions, the legislation would permit wiretaps on U.S. citizens for up to ninety days following a terrorist attack and would retroactively shield people and companies from liability for complying with surveillance requests from government intelligence programs.

6 On May 18, 2006, Khaled el-Masri's suit was dismissed on account of the CIA's claim that further court proceedings would disclose "state secrets." On July 25, 2006, the ACLU filed an appeal on this ruling on behalf of el-Masri.

7 South Dakota repealed the strict law limiting abortions in the November 7, 2006, referendum.

Missing Persons

a project by Trevor Paglen

Since the mid-1990s, the CIA has spearheaded a covert program to kidnap suspected terrorists from all over the world. Since late 2001, these disappeared people have been brought to a network of secret CIA-operated prisons, called "black sites," where torture is commonplace. The CIA calls this the "extraordinary rendition" program.

The locations of these black sites, which are only known by code names such as "Salt Pit" and "Bright Light," are some of the CIA's deepest secrets. The people who are taken to these black sites are effectively "disappeared." No public records of these prisoners are kept. Their identities are secret. Among CIA operatives, they are called "ghost detainees."

To capture and subsequently transport these ghost detainees, the CIA uses a fleet of unmarked airplanes. These airplanes are owned by intricate networks of front companies.

Missing Persons is a study of the front companies that own these aircraft. This collection of documents is culled from — and inspired by — corporate and aviation documents associated with the unmarked CIA aircraft used in the program.

The names, addresses, and phone numbers of companies such as "Premier Executive Transport Services, Inc." and "Stevens Express Leasing, Inc." are those of "paper companies" serving as CIA proxies.

The names of these companies' officers, such as "Colleen A. Bornt," and "Tyler E. Tate," are what the CIA calls "sterile identities." These people have no credit histories, fixed addresses, employment histories, or telephone records — none of the records that one would expect real people to leave behind.

Stevens Express Leasing, Inc.
92 Timber Creek Dr., Suite 101
Cordova, TN 38018
(901) 680-0888

Corporation Annual Report
Tennessee Secretary of State Document
March 28, 2002

James J. Kershaw
James J. Kershaw, President

Premier Executive Transport Services, Inc.
339 Washington Street, Suite 202
Dedham, MA 02026
(617) 326-8848

Aircraft Bill of Sale (N313P)
Federal Aviation Administration Document
November 10, 2004

James J. Kershaw
James J. Kershaw, Secretary/Treasurer

Keeler and Tate Management Group, LLC.
245 E. Liberty Street, Suite 510
Reno, NV 89501-2256
(702) 322-0673

Initial List of Manager or Members
Nevada Secretary of State Document
October 14, 2003

Tyler E. Tate
Tyler Edward Tate, Member

Keeler and Tate Management Group, LLC.
245 E. Liberty Street, Suite 510
Reno, NV 89501-2256
(702) 322-0673

Assignment of Special Registration Numbers (4476S)
Federal Aviation Administration Document
December 1, 2004

Tyler E. Tate
Tyler Edward Tate, Member

Premier Executive Transport Services, Inc.
339 Washington Street, Suite 202
Dedham, MA 02026
(617) 326-8848

Aircraft Registration Application (N313P)
Federal Aviation Administration Document
May 1, 2002

Bryan P. Dyess

Bryan P. Dyess, President

Devon Holding & Leasing, Inc.
129 West Center Street
Lexington, NC 27292
(336) 243-2730

Business Corporation Annual Report
North Carolina Secretary of State Document
April 29, 2003

Bryan P. Dyess

Bryan P. Dyess, President

Premier Executive Transport Services, Inc.
339 Washington Street, Suite 202
Dedham, MA 02026
(617) 326-8848

Aircraft Registration Request (N379P)
Letter to Federal Aviation Administration
September 13, 1999

Colleen A. Bornt

Colleen A. Bornt, Vice President

Premier Executive Transport Services, Inc.
339 Washington Street, Suite 202
Dedham, MA 02026
(617) 326-8848

Expedited Aircraft Registration Request (N313P)
Letter to Federal Aviation Administration
November 30, 2001

Colleen A. Bornt

Colleen A. Bornt, Vice President

بسم الله الرحمن الرحيم

الحمد لله رب العالمين والصلاة والسلام على أشرف المرسلين نبينا محمد وعلى اله وصحبه وبعد:

قال تعالى: (يَا أَيُّهَا الَّذِينَ آمَنُوا مَنْ يَرْتَدَّ مِنْكُمْ عَنْ دِينِهِ فَسَوْفَ يَأْتِي اللَّهُ بِقَوْمٍ يُحِبُّهُمْ وَيُحِبُّونَهُ أَذِلَّةٍ عَلَى الْمُؤْمِنِينَ أَعِزَّةٍ عَلَى الْكَافِرِينَ يُجَاهِدُونَ فِي سَبِيلِ اللَّهِ وَلَا يَخَافُونَ لَوْمَةَ لَائِمٍ ذَلِكَ فَضْلُ اللَّهِ يُؤْتِيهِ مَنْ يَشَاءُ وَاللَّهُ وَاسِعٌ عَلِيمٌ) الْمَائِدَة 54

في اول بشارة يوصّلها لنا إخوانُنا في كتيبة الفرقان في شهر رمضان المُبارك هذا الشهر الذي شهد انتصارات المسلمين على مر التاريخ، تمكن إخوانكم يوم أمس من نصب كمين محكم للعميلة المرتدة (نافعة نافع عزيز) العضوة في الاتحاد الوطني الكردستاني وعضوة مجلس محافظة نينوى ورئيسة ما يسمى بلجنة حقوق الأنسان في نينوى إضافة الى عملها داخل القواعد الأمريكية في الموصل (والمبينة في وثائقها أدناه)، حيث اعترضها المجاهدون في حي البريد في الساحل اليسر بمدينة الموصل وانقضوا عليها بوابل من أسلحتهم الرشاشة مما أدى الى مقتلها في الحال بالإضافة إلى قتل حارسها الشخصي الذي كان يقود سيارتها.

أين حقوق الإنسان حين يقبعون في سجونكم ولمدة أشهر أكثر من 200 مسلماً في غرفة (4*5م) لا يجد أحدهم مكان لجلوسه، بل أين حقوق الإنسان وفي كل يوم يعذب هؤلاء على أيدي الوثنين السكارى، بل أين حقوق الأنسان حين يقتل المسلمين من جراء تعذيب جلاديكم فترمى جثثهم في العراء ... قال تعالى (وَلَوْ تَرَى إِذْ وُقِفُوا عَلَى رَبِّهِمْ قَالَ أَلَيْسَ هَذَا بِالْحَقِّ قَالُوا بَلَى وَرَبِّنَا قَالَ فَذُوقُوا الْعَذَابَ بِمَا كُنْتُمْ تَكْفُرُونَ) الأنعام الآية 30

والله اكبر... ولله العزة ولرسوله وللمؤمنين

وصلى الله على نبينا محمد وعلى اله وصحبه اجمعين
الهيئة العسكرية لجيش أنصار السنة
الثلاثاء 1/رمضان/1426
4/ تشرين الأول/2005

بشير السنة
(جيش أنصار السنة)

لتحميل نسخة من المرفقات إختر احد الروابط التالية :
http://www.twa9ef.com/uploads/b7673d0c6d.jpg
http://9q9q.com/get.php?filename=1128448227.jpg
http://roohalkaleej.net/up/Up/Nafeah.JPG

Screen shot of the October 4, 2005 communiqué by the military wing
of Jaish Ansar al-Sunna claiming responsibility for the assassination
of Nafi'a Nafeh 'Aziz.

"Where are Human Rights...?":
Reading a Communiqué from Iraq

Thomas Keenan

Where are human rights when more than two hundred Muslims are rotting for months in your prisons in a 4x5 meter room, without any of them finding a place even to sit down? Where are human rights when every day prisoners are tortured at the hands of drunken pagans? Where are human rights when Muslims are killed as a result of the torture of your executioners, and their bodies are thrown out in the open?

— Jaish Ansar al-Sunna

This is not a statement from a human-rights group, although it might sound like one (with the exception of the phrase about the "drunken pagans"). It is a communiqué from the military wing of Jaish Ansar al-Sunna (the Army of the Protectors of the Tradition) in Iraq that was distributed on October 4, 2005, on a number of Arabic-language Islamist Internet forums, including Ansar-Jehad and the now-defunct al-Firdaws. It was widely recirculated in similar forums elsewhere, including the French Al-Mourabitoune, where I first read it.[1]

Jaish Ansar al-Sunna is one of the Sunni jihadist militant groups fighting a guerrilla war, against not just the United States and coalition military forces in Iraq, but also against those said to be in league with them — primarily the Iraqi National Guard and the New Iraqi Army, the police, the Shi'ite and Kurdish militias and their offshoots, government officials at all levels, would-be employees of the government, and, frequently, civilians from the wrong sect or neighborhood.[2]

The full communiqué, dated the first day of Ramadan, claimed responsibility for and celebrated the assassination of Nafi'a Nafeh 'Aziz, who was identified as not only an "apostate" and a collaborator with the occupation authorities, but also as "a member of the Pagan Union of Kurdistan, member of the Nineveh provincial council, and president of the human rights committee in Nineveh."[3] She was killed, the communiqué said, by the "brothers" of the al-Furqan Brigade, along with her bodyguard, in an ambush in Mosul. As evidence, links to an image of her U.S. military identification cards were

Image of one of Nafi'a Nafeh 'Aziz's identity cards, as attached to the communiqué announcing her killing.

posted in various Internet forums, along with the communiqué from which I am quoting. On the French forum where I read it, the photograph was erased from each of the three cards.

Nafi'a 'Aziz was a forty-nine-year-old female Kurdish local government official in Mosul and a respected women's and human-rights activist. Her death was briefly noted in wire-service dispatches, but not widely covered in the Western press.[4] It was also reported on the Iraqi television network al-Sharqiya that evening and by the two most important Arabic-language satellite television stations, al-Jazeera in Qatar and al-Arabiya in Dubai, the following day.[5] Al-Jazeera's report apparently included footage of 'Aziz and her son dead inside their car.

Some days later, the public affairs staff of the Multinational Force Northwest marked her killing in its bulletin, *This Week in Iraq,* with an article titled "Respected Council Member Loses Life, Legacy Lives On."

> Nafiaa Aziz, one of the most active members of the Ninevah Provincial Council, was killed in a drive-by shooting, along with her son, in Mosul on Monday.... She was an advocate for human rights, ensuring humane treatment. She visited many detention facilities and was the first council member to visit the division jail in Mosul. Considered one of the most vocal council members, Aziz participated in radio call-in shows and televised events, and spoke often during weekly council meetings.[6]

Her death also registered in the blogosphere, inspiring one military wife, who called herself Angoraknitter, to start a blog called Dear Home Front. Angoraknitter's husband appears to be a senior U.S. officer stationed in Mosul, and her first entry — "Tragic Lose [*sic*] for Progress" — quotes him: "Very bad day today. The top woman on the Provincial council, Nafia Aziz, was assassinated this morning in a drive by shooting.... She was the chairman of the Human Rights committee and she worked very hard to improve the conditions of the jails and ensure that the families of detainees were informed about their whereabouts and stuff like that."[7]

Two weeks after 'Aziz's killing, Louise Roug of the *Los Angeles Times* profiled her. She wrote:

> Aziz counted Brig. Gen. Kevin Bergner, the deputy commander of the 20,000-member multinational force here, among her friends. She called him her "brother." The two visited prisoners together, going as far as Abu Ghraib near Baghdad.
>
> To prisoners, she was a comforting, maternal presence.
>
> "She would walk into a jail and at once be in charge and compassionate," he said early this week. Though they did not always agree, he said, he admired her.[8]

A month later, I wrote to an Iraqi blogger in Mosul and asked about Nafi'a 'Aziz. My correspondent wrote back in broken, but precise English: "Her death was a great loss to all the citizens of Mosul particularly the poor and the detainees. My own idea, is her murder are planned to frighten the honest people like her from involved in the political process; it is a terroristic act but not a ressistant [*sic*] act. We usually differentiate between the two acts (one against the people, the other against the occupation)."[9]

None of the bloggers or reporters seemed to know who had killed 'Aziz. Roug quotes an American intelligence officer investigating the killing: "There are many people in this city who had a motive to kill her."[10]

But the brothers of the al-Furqan Brigade knew whom they were killing, or claiming to have killed, needless to say. And it was in reaction to 'Aziz's status precisely *as* a militant for women's and human rights, with a special interest in detention, that their sardonic set of questions about the location of human rights — or, perhaps, their implicit protest against their absence — is posed.

Setting aside its context, the statement is a powerful, even typical appeal against human-rights violations and particularly against a pattern of prisoner abuse that has been widely documented and criticized by partisan and independent observers worldwide. Unlike many such communiqués from Iraq, which typically mix dreary celebrations of slaughter with exaggerated claims of enemy casualties, this one seeks to justify a killing in terms that go beyond the sectarian or political affiliation of the victim and to exploit the gap between the discourse of democratization and the practice of the occupation. Rather than rely only on the absolute authority of the Prophet and the certainty of religious conviction (although those authorities are invoked elsewhere in the communiqué), this statement also seeks to present the act in other, more secular terms.

In that sense, the communiqué belongs to the kind of strategy apparently advocated by al-Qaeda's senior thinker Ayman al-Zawahiri, who wrote — in his now-celebrated intercepted letter of summer 2005, which was released later by the U.S. Office of the Director of National Intelligence — on the *political* character of the jihadist struggle, which is to say, on the necessity not just of sowing terror, but also of persuading, and negotiating with, public opinion: "The strongest weapon which the mujahedeen enjoy — after the help and granting of success by God — is popular support from the Muslim masses in Iraq, and the surrounding Muslim countries."[11] Hence, he wrote, there is an urgent need to

> spare the people from the effect of questions about the usefulness of our actions in the hearts and minds of the general opinion that is essentially sympathetic to us.... I say to you: that we are in a battle, and that more than half of this battle is taking place in the battlefield of the media. And that we are in a media battle in a race for the hearts and minds of our Umma. And that however far our capabilities reach, they will never be equal to one thousandth of the capabilities of the kingdom of Satan that is waging war on us.[12]

This may seem trivially obvious; isn't terrorism always in a codependent relationship with the media; doesn't it thrive on the oxygen of publicity; doesn't it — unlike, precisely, a simple military confrontation between two conventional forces — essentially work through public opinion, hearts and minds, and persuasion?

It would take too long to consider this fully, and this is not the place to do so. I would suggest only the following. The answer is yes (terrorism needs and attracts the media), but these clichés are nevertheless not so obvious in this case. Zawahiri needed to write this. And the fact that he did so indicates one of the most interesting and fundamental tensions of the contemporary jihadist movement. On the one hand, terrorism is characterized by a rhetoric and a practice of absolute demands, a walled-up insularity, even a monolingualism, of unequivocal doctrinal conviction. It is one that requires no countersignature, no approval, no negotiation, and even no outside — other than the enemy. The slogan of this would be the famous phrase of Shaykh Abdullah Yusuf Azzam, who created Maktab al-Khadamat (the Afrghan Services Bureau, which later morphed into al-Qaeda) in Peshawar: "Jihad and the rifle alone: no negotiations, no conferences and no dialogues."[13]

On the other hand, there *are* press releases, communiqués, statements, spokesmen, Web sites, the Jihad Information Brigade, the Global Islamic Media Front, and all the rest — in short, there is a struggle for public opinion. This implies the relative demands characteristic of a political contest, the need to take the other into account, to listen and pay attention, to compromise or at least appear to do so, to trade and to share, to anticipate and to compensate for the fact that the line between "us" and "them" is not clearly given in advance. Zawahiri was worried about losing support among the Muslim masses, so he insisted on "the need to direct the political action equally with the military action."[14] Military action generates publicity, but not all publicity is good publicity.

The battle for public support requires, he said, not "neglect[ing] the realities on the ground."[15] Among those realities are not just territory and ground, but something more amorphous, a state of mind, what "the Muslim populace…will…find palatable."[16] Politics passes by way of opinion, mass opinion, which is formed in the media, especially the visual media. Zawahiri was worried, among other things, about the public-relations effect in Iraq of al-Qaeda's videotaped and widely distributed beheadings of its hostages. He wrote directly and critically about these "scenes of slaughter": "Among the things which the feelings of the Muslim populace who love and support you will never find palatable — also — are the scenes of slaughtering the hostages." He imagined an answer: "And your response, while true, might be: Why shouldn't we sow terror in the hearts of the Crusaders and their helpers?" And he advised, from a distance: "We can kill the captives by bullet. That would achieve that which is sought after without exposing ourselves to the questions and answering to doubts. We don't need this."[17]

We are on the edge of an enormously complex question here, a question about the relation between politics and violence.

Carl von Clausewitz argued famously in *On War* that "war is a true political instrument," a means and nothing more, "merely the continuation of policy by other means," and went on to ask: "Do political relations between peoples and between their government stop when diplomatic notes are no longer exchanged? Is not war just another expression of their thoughts, another form of speech or writing? Its grammar, indeed, may be its own, but not its logic."[18]

On the other hand, there is another, equally commonsensical notion that, in fact, war marks the breakdown of politics, its failure. The latest exemplar of this might be the phrase attributed to Colin Powell in David Hare's play *Stuff Happens*:

> *Powell* Maybe because my whole life has been in the army I'm less impressed by the use
> of force. I see it for what it is.
>
> *Bush* What is it?
>
> *Powell* Failure.[19]

Politics hovers between the principles of ethics and the irreversibility of violence, between two kinds of absolutes. It should not be reduced to either one. But it always is. We are — politics is — forever losing sight of these boundaries, turning (in)to fundamentalism and war, without any possibility of mastering those limits once and for all.

Sometimes — perhaps this is the case with Ansar al-Sunna and al-Zawahiri — political action is a mere instrument in the service of absolute control. There are risks, though. Sometimes, absolutism turns (in)to politics. The language of politics is just that, a language, and not merely a tool. However necessary it may seem, it puts something at stake — and the game is not a fully predictable or reliable one.

The status of "human rights" in the announcement of 'Aziz's assassination provides a case in point. Why did her killers feel the need to take this rhetorical path? They did not, it should be noted, provide a videotape of her death — they did not capture her, or hold her hostage, or execute her before a camera (by sword or by gun), as they have done with so many others. They simply ambushed her car, keeping only her identification cards as evidence of the operation, and then wrapped them in a communiqué for public distribution. Here, again, are their questions:

> Where are human rights when more than two hundred Muslims are rotting for months in
> your prisons in a 4x5 meter room, without any of them finding a place even to sit down?
> Where are human rights when every day prisoners are tortured at the hands of drunken
> pagans? Where are human rights when Muslims are killed as a result of the torture of
> your executioners, and their bodies are thrown out in the open?

It's a communiqué about, more than anything else, human rights. That alone should be reason for surprise, given the authors. But what does it say when it asks "Where are human rights?"

They ought to be someplace, and they are not. They are said to characterize the very space and time of human existence, and yet there is no sign of them. They are missing, evidently. People — or, more precisely, Muslims — are there, in terrible places, and rights are lacking. Perhaps the question is: Do Muslims have human rights?

But that is a difficult question. Are 'Aziz's assailants *invoking* the "rights of man"? In deploring their absence, are they appealing to them, calling for their realization, seeking to find them? Is the answer: "Yes, we ought to have human rights, just like everyone

(TOP) Screen shot of Jaish Ansar al-Sunna logo, from a videotape of an attack on a U.S. military vehicle in Mosul, June 2006.

(BOTTOM) Screen shot from Jaish Ansar al-Sunna videotape of fighting in Ramadi, June 2006.

else, but they are being denied to us—and by precisely those who propose to export them to the entire world"? In exposing this hypocrisy, the communiqué would be making a profound claim for rights, the most powerful possible claim, from the position of utter deprivation. Through us, the prisoners, stripped of everything, imprisoned and tortured and executed, without a place (even a place to sit down), demand what ought to be theirs already. Utterly exposed, they seek protection.[20] Treated like disposable material, they protest against this radical exclusion and claim for everyone—starting with themselves, here—these rights.

There is no necessary reason to suspect that these sentences say anything other than this. Many eloquent versions of this appeal have been written using just the same strategy.

Or is the cascade of rhetorical questions designed, on the contrary, to illustrate the bankruptcy of the discourse? The questions, read this way, would be another way of saying: "There are no human rights," or even, "There are no humans." The vocabulary of human rights would be exposed as hollow, fraudulent, false, misleading, chimerical. Obviously, in conditions such as these, human rights are a lie, and a dangerous one, at that—and those who pretend to advocate or to defend them are not only in league with the Americans, but illegitimately hiding their particular interests in universal clothing.

Human rights are absent. But is the absence of these rights temporary or permanent, accidental or essential? Is this powerful statement a cry for rights or an exposé of their essential nature as a lie?

It is extraordinary that the same sentences could suggest two such diametrically opposed interpretations. I am not sure what the correct answer is here. My instinct is that this ambiguity (between invocation and dismissal) is in fact the most interesting political gesture of the statement. It may even be intentional.

Without simply belonging to it, the statement certainly points to a critical feature of contemporary human-rights discourse.

Consider the divided status of many speech acts enunciated today in terms of rights. On the one hand, the speaker demonstrates, expresses, or makes manifest a singularity, an identity, status, or behavior, often a wounded one. We suffer, we are a target, there is something unique about us that exposes us to violence, harm, or wrong. Utterances of this sort come from the victims of genocidal attacks; from the targets of persecution based on race, gender, or nationality; from those who happen to live in the wrong city at the wrong time; from people infected with HIV, or exposed to toxic chemicals, or displaced and ruined by a flood or an earthquake. (Or from those who speak on their behalf.) It frequently has a plaintive structure, but not always: sometimes it is the valiant assertion of a marginalized existence, the entry into visibility of something otherwise hidden. "We're here, we're queer, get used to it." In either case, my singularity is the place from which I speak.

On the other hand, rarely do the speakers in question speak simply in the name of that local, isolated suffering or that experience. Rather, phrases structured like that of Bernard Kouchner — "man was not made to suffer" — follow immediately or even precede the expression of an experience.[21] More often than not, we make a claim to redress or to visibility based not merely on ourselves, but also on our membership in something larger, the largest something of all, something that all are entitled to — because we are human, because we speak, because we are part of humanity, just like everybody else to whom we are speaking.

Human-rights discourse is thus, structurally, the opposite of special pleading: it is *general* pleading; it is a plea on behalf of everyone, passing through someone in particular. I have a claim to make on others only insofar as it is not simply mine, only if my condition — not my suffering, but the possibility of my suffering — can be extended to all humanity.

This is a structural feature: it would be meaningless to speak of a *right* that belonged only to me. A property, yes, but not a right. And yet the claim to a right, to something by definition shared with others, extendable to an unlimited (in principle) set of subjects, is never abstract — it comes from a particular place, experience, existence (whether primary or secondary), to respond to a particular wound. One does not enunciate rights claims abstractly. This is the paradox of rights talk: the claim is meaningless if it is not universalizable, but it is effective only if it is rooted concretely.

Today we more or less take this paradox for granted, but how does this acceptance happen? The answer is not obvious. How does this universalization of particulars become plausible, audible, practical?

Jacques Rancière offers an answer to this, in *La mésentente* (Disagreement) and elsewhere, by retelling the story of the secession of the Roman plebeians on Aventine Hill, based on Pierre-Simon Ballanche's rewriting of Livy. Here is the most essential form of his question: "How do you recognize that the person who is mouthing a voice in front of you is discussing matters of justice rather than expressing private pain?"[22] He summarizes the scene:

> The patricians at Aventine do not understand what the plebeians say; they do not understand the noises that come out of the plebeians' mouths, so that, in order to be audibly understood and visibly recognized as legitimate speaking subjects, the plebeians must not only argue their position but must also construct the scene of argumentation in such a manner that the patricians might recognize it as a world in common.[23]

To be clear: the burden on those who would be heard is a double one — not simply to speak, exchange, communicate, but, first of all, to be understood as speaking at all. The event is their entry into a political space that by definition excludes them. Moaning, lowing, crying — expressing one's private suffering — makes no claims on others, remains outside of discourse, humanity, the political sphere. For this to become a matter of justice, of sharing and division, of politics, it is first of all necessary to transform the boundaries and definition of the political or public space; that is, to change the definition of who speaks and what counts as speaking within it. Thus Rancière can claim nothing less than this: "In order to enter into political exchange, it becomes necessary to invent the scene upon which spoken words may be audible, in which objects may be visible, and individuals themselves may be recognized."[24]

This is his fundamental insight: that we cannot take for granted the possibility of communication, let alone the common human status that would seem to underpin it, but that communication nevertheless does happen…and that making it possible is the political act par excellence.

How is this "common" scene constructed?

> They do not set up a fortified camp in the manner of the Scythian slaves. They do what would have been unthinkable for the latter: they establish another order, another partition of the sensible, by constituting themselves *not as warriors* equal to other warriors but as speaking beings sharing the same properties as those who deny them these. They thereby execute a series of speech acts that *mimic* those of the patricians.[25]

I have tried elsewhere to understand this inaugural act of repetition, quotation, mimicry, and the conditions that enable the transformation of the conditions of understanding.[26] Here is what is essential: sometimes a speech act, dependent on its context to be understood, can change that context or those conditions themselves…by changing the definition of who counts as a speaker and what counts as speaking. The language changes when the plebeians, copying, speak it.

Rancière calls this the "capacity for polemical particularization of their universality" and associates it with human rights (not, he underlines, humanitarianism).[27] Precisely because universality cannot be taken for granted, this claim has a militant dimension.

As Slavoj Žižek has insisted, commenting on Rancière, universality is hence not merely the outcome of a struggle or multicultural compromise of particular versus particular, identity versus identity. Rather, it belongs to the rhetoric of the counterintuitive claim. For Žižek, Rancière suggests that "democracy began when we said: 'We, the ones who are excluded, we are the all, we are the people, we stand for universality.'"[28]

Is this what the leading human-rights organizations — and thinkers — of our day mean when they calmly proclaim the universality of human rights? Kofi Annan celebrated the fiftieth anniversary of the adoption of the Universal Declaration of Human Rights with this claim: "Human rights are foreign to no culture and intrinsic to all nations. They belong not to a chosen few, but to all people. It is this universality that endows human rights with the power to cross any border and defy any force."[29] When he wrote this, was he agreeing or disagreeing with Rancière and Žižek?

What sort of activity is "human-rights activism"? Although the discourse of human rights got its modern start with the revolutions that overthrew the French monarchy and British rule in the American colonies, today an assault on the state in the interest of seizing power is far from the norm for political action undertaken in the name of human rights.

Rather, the ethos is much closer to that expressed by Michel Foucault in the short text he read at a press conference in Geneva in June 1981 inaugurating the Comité International Contre la Piraterie, an initiative for nongovernmental intervention in the defense of Vietnamese boat people being attacked in the Gulf of Thailand by pirates. Later published under the title "Face aux gouvernements, les droits de l'homme," it sketched the conceptual outline of a properly nongovernmental politics.[30]

Proposing, together with a number of nongovernmental organizations and celebrities, to launch a ship to protect those drifting refugees, Foucault asked the obvious question about the status of the initiative — "Who has commissioned us?" — to which he replied, "No one." He proposed simply that there was "an international citizenry, which has its rights, has its duties, and promises to rise up against every abuse of power, no matter who the author or the victims. After all, we are all governed and, to that extent, in solidarity." He traced the creation of this right to such nongovernmental projects as Amnesty International, Terre des Hommes, and Médecins du Monde, and concluded his brief speech with something like a motto for this sort of action: "The will of individuals has to inscribe itself in a reality over which governments have wanted to reserve a monopoly for themselves — a monopoly that we have to uproot little by little every day."

"We are all governed" — and without seeking to become governors, we intervene, address those who govern, hold them accountable, act where they refuse. The politics of human rights is, in this sense, largely a "politics of the governed" — not a project that aims to govern, precisely not that.[31]

"If governments make human rights the framework and even the frame of their political action, that's great," Foucault said the following year in an interview about Poland. "But human rights are above all what we oppose to governments. They are the limits that we pose to all possible governments."[32]

There is little danger, I suppose, that this opposition or difference between governmentality and the nongovernmental will ever *fully* collapse. Rights will always be violated — by governments and would-be governors, among others — and rights claims will be made in response. But things are certainly getting complicated. Human-rights discourse depends and even thrives on the basically enigmatic or indeterminate character of its two key terms (if we knew, once and for all, who counted as human and what their rights were, there would be a lot less confusion and a lot less work to do). The structural complications of this situation are now asserting themselves with considerable force.

Who doesn't support human rights today? In the aftermath of the Cold War, as David Rieff and Alex de Waal, among others, have pointed out, the major European and American human-rights organizations have found themselves suddenly and surprisingly close to the very state powers they had been campaigning against for so long. "Kosovo" became a metaphor for this new situation, and "Iraq" its terrible hyperbole.[33] "Human rights" can easily become another form of political administration, of governmentality, and sometimes even an excuse for worse.[34]

Where are human rights? Everywhere? Nowhere? What are the limits, the borders, of this discourse, and where is it elastic? What kind of word is "human," and what does it have to do with the particularity of those who are suffering in Iraq's prisons and detention centers, of those who imprison and torture them, of those who advocate on their behalf, and of those who kill the advocates? Jaish Ansar al-Sunna understands the complexity of its question at some level. Its members are not human-rights activists, I repeat: they killed this particular human-rights activist. But the killing and the communiqué somehow also implicitly confess that there is something else attractive for them, like it or not, in the discourse of human rights. Rancière says, "They do not set up a fortified camp" — they constitute themselves not as "warriors equal to other warriors, but as speaking beings."[35] Nafi'a 'Aziz's killers took the armed path, with terrible results. And they did something else....

Perhaps the American occupation is the more typical case of the paradigm of "concrete universality" — "we are the universal" — that Žižek finds in Rancière. But, even taking all the disjunctions into account, there is something like it at work as well in Jaish Ansar al-Sunna's deeply ambivalent communiqué. It pushes the question of the relation between politics and violence to its difficult extreme. What happens when those who set up a fortified camp, who constitute themselves as warriors equal to other warriors — and who aim to defeat those other warriors unconditionally, without mercy — also speak the language of human rights? Not only speak, but ask "Where are human rights?" I do not have an answer to either question (and I'm not sure anyone does), but I think that lingering with the questions will be worth our while.

1   "Jaish al-Ansar al-Sunnah/Awwal bisharah fi Ramadan yazaf-
fuha Mujahidin Katibat al-Furqan fi 'l-Mawsil," Shabakah
"Ana 'l-Muslim" (muslm.net discussion forum), October 4,
2005, 11:44 p.m., www.muslm.net/vb/archive/index.php/t-
119518-p-3.html; also posted at al-Firdaws discussion forum,
October 4, 2005, 11:48 p.m., www.alfirdaws.org/forums/
showpost.php?p=16156&postcount=1, and Ansar-Jehad,
mirrored at http://clearinghouse.infovlad.net/showpost.
php?p=1336&postcount=7; Abou-Zoubayr, "Communiqués
des Moujahidines des deux fleuves (mardi)," al-Mourabitoune discussion forum, October 4, 2005, www.ribaat.org/
services/forum/showpost.php?p=267912&postcount=5. I
am extremely grateful to Samera Esmeir, who translated the
text of this communiqué into English for me and went over
it word by word, many times, helping me think about what
it says and what it does. I also owe a great debt of thanks to
Andras Riedlmayer, who has translated forum postings and
video stills for me too many times to count and has helped
me understand much more about what I've been seeing and
reading. Here is the full text of the Jaish Ansar al-Sunna
statement as rendered in English by Laura Mansfield, a blogger and translator experienced with such documents:

In the Name of Allah, the Beneficent, the Merciful.

Praise be to Allah the Lord of the Worlds; and
prayers and greetings to the most honest of messen-
gers, our prophet Mohamed, and to his family and his
companions.

Allah above said O ye who believe! if any from
among you turn back from his Faith, soon will Allah
produce a people whom He will love as they will
love Him, lowly with the believers, mighty against
the rejecters, fighting in the way of Allah, and never
afraid of the reproaches of such as find fault. That is
the grace of Allah, which He will bestow on whom
He pleaseth. And Allah encompasseth all, and He
knoweth all things. Surah: The Table, Ayat 54.

First, we bring glad tidings to our brothers in
the Al Furqan Brigades in the Holy month of Ramadan, which has witnessed the victories of Muslims
throughout history.

Your brothers among them yesterday sprung a
well-planned ambush on the apostate Nafi'a Nafeh
Aziz, a member of the Kurdish Pagan Union, and a
council member in the Ninevah governorate, and
president of the Human Rights Committee in Ninevah, and who worked inside the American bases in
Mosul (as made clear in the documents). The muja-

hideen blocked her cat [sic] in the City of Mosul and
attacked it, spraying it with gunfire, leading to her
immediate killing and the death of the bodyguard
driving the car.

Where are the human rights when they hide you
in their prisons and where for months more than two
hundred Muslims are held in a room with no place to
even sit down? Where are the humans rights when
they torture and kill the Muslims, who are tortured
by executioners, and their bodies thrown outdoors.

Allah above said: If thou couldst but see when
they are confronted with their Lord! He will say: "Is
not this the truth?" They will say: "Yea, by our Lord!"
He will say: "Taste ye then the penalty, because ye
rejected Faith." Surah: The Cattle, Verse 30.

Allah Akbar! Honor be to Allah and to his mes-
senger and to the believers.

May the peace of Allah be upon our prophet
Mohamed, and upon his family and his friends.

Military Wing

The Ansar al Sunnah Army

Tuesday 1 Ramadan 1426

4 October 2005

Laura Mansfield, "Ansar al Sunnah Army Claims Execution of
Female Member of Ninevah Governing Council in Iraq," Lau-
raMansfield.com: Arabic Translations and Terrorism Analysis,
October 6, 2005, www.lauramansfield.com/j/showarticle.
asp?id=27. Although the communiqué appeared in October 2005 on a variety of Arabic-language jihadist Internet
forums, including al-Firdaws and Ansar-Jehad (cited above),
as of May 2006, I could find only one copy, in the forum
called Shabakah "Ana 'l-Muslim" (The "I Am the Muslim"
Network), or muslm.net.

Ansar al-Sunna also took responsibility for 'Aziz's killing in a videotape distributed online by the Global Islamic
Media Front, in the third edition of a simulated news broadcast called Sout al-Khalifa (Voice of the Caliphate) the following week. At six minutes and fifty-five seconds into the
twenty-seven-minute program, during a section devoted
to operations by Ansar al-Sunna, the masked anchorman
announced the shooting and 'Aziz's identification cards were
shown in the small window over his left shoulder. Global
Islamic Media Front, "Sout al-Khalifa" (Voice of the Caliphate) 3, October 11, 2005, www.clandestineradio.com/audio/
meast_aq_caliphate_051010.wmv; Global Islamic Media Front
Releases "Third News Program," *Foreign Broadcast Information Service,* October 12, 2005.

2   The organization dates from September 2003; its formation was announced with a statement declaring that "a number of scattered jihad factions and groups…[had] formed a big army under one emir." Quoted in Michael Rubin, "Ansar al-Sunna: Iraq's New Terrorist Threat," *Middle East Intelligence Bulletin,* May 1, 2004; available online at www.aei.org/news20691. In the group's first videotape, *Banners of Truth,* a spokesman declares: "A group of resistance fighters who have experience in the struggle against the infidels from north of Iraq to its south organized themselves on the basis of the shari'ah in the Koran and the Sunnah and we called it the Ansar al-Sunnah Army. We call on everyone to join it so as to raise the Word of Allah and obliterate the word of the crusader and Jewish infidels. We assert that the agents, hypocrites, and renegades will not stand before us and that the battle will be between the soldiers of the Merciful One and the soldiers of Satan. He who fights Allah is defeated." Quoted in Ahmad al-Masri, "'Ansar al-Sunnah Army' Views in Videotape for the First Time Its Operations against Occupation Forces in Iraq," *al-Quds al-Arabi,* February 21, 2004, p. 4; translated as "Ansar al-Sunnah Army's First Video," *DARPA Tides Project,* February 21, 2004; available online at www.why-war.com/files/2004/06/ansar_alsunnah_army.html. The Iraq insurgency has many components — nationalist, Ba'athist, and Sunni jihadist, as well as some Shi'ite anti-occupation fighters — and (to be clear) they do not all share the ideology or the tactics of Ansar al-Sunna.

3   Laura Mansfield, "Ansar al Sunnah Army Claims Execution." The communiqué writer indulges here in a little play on words: 'Aziz was a member of the Patriotic Union of Kurdistan, but the communiqué says "pagan [*wathani*]," not "patriotic [*watani*]."

4   "Security Incidents in Iraq, October 3," Reuters, October 3, 2005; Mohammed Barakat, "U.S. Helicopters Fire on West Iraq Town," Associated Press, October 3, 2005; "Au moins 12 insurgés tués dans l'opération américaine dans l'ouest de l'Irak," Agence France Presse, October 3, 2005; "Two Policemen, Local Official and Son Killed in Northern Iraq," BBC Monitoring Middle East — Political, October 5, 2005. Nafi'a 'Aziz's death is incident k1997 at www.iraqbodycount.org, based on reports from Reuters and the Associated Press of October 3, 2005. For more information on the setting in which she worked, see the testimony about the women's rights activists of Mosul in U.S. Congress, House Subcommittee on the Middle East and Central Asia, Committee on International Relations, *Human Rights Violations Under Saddam Hussein: Victims Speak Out,* 108th Congress, 1st session, 2004; available online at www.house.gov/international_relations/108/91184.pdf.

5   For al-Arabiya: "Al-Arabiya TV Updates Security Developments In Iraq," BBC Monitoring International Reports, October 4, 2005; for al-Sharqiya: "Iraqi Suicide Bomber Attacks US Convoy in Mosul; Gunmen Kill Local Official — TV," BBC Monitoring Middle East — Political, October 3, 2005.

6   Multinational Force — Northwest Public Affairs, "Respected Council Member Loses Life, Legacy Lives On," *This Week in Iraq,* October 5, 2005, p. 7, available online at www.mnf-iraq.com/Publications/TWII/05Oct.pdf.

7   Angoraknitter, "Tragic Lose [*sic*] for Progress," Dear Home Front, October 3, 2005, http://dearhomefront.blogspot.com/2005/10/tragic-lose-for-progress.html. See also "The Sons of Nafia," Dear Home Front, October 4, 2005, http://dearhomefront.blogspot.com/2005/10/sons-of-nafia.html, and "More on Nafia Aziz," Dear Home Front, October 20, 2005, http://dearhomefront.blogspot.com/2005/10/more-on-nafia-aziz.html.

8   Louise Roug, "A Dynamic Advocate Is Now a Statistic," *Los Angeles Times,* October 19, 2005.

9   Truth Teller, e-mail to the author on November 5, 2005. Truth Teller's blog is available at http://moslawi.blogspot.com/.

10 Roug, "Dynamic Advocate."

11 "Letter from al-Zawahiri to al-Zarqawi," Office of the Director of National Intelligence, News Release No. 2–05, October 11, 2005, www.dni.gov/press_releases/20051011_release.htm, p. 4.

12 *Ibid.,* p. 10.

13 Quoted in Jonathan Fighel, "Sheikh Abdullah Azzam: Bin Laden's Spiritual Mentor," *Institute for Counter-Terrorism,* September 27, 2001, www.ict.org.il/articles/articledet.cfm?articleid=388.

14 "Letter from al-Zawahiri to al-Zarqawi," p. 14.

15 *Ibid.,* p. 7.

16 *Ibid.,* p. 10.

17 *Ibid.*

18 Carl von Clausewitz, *On War,* ed. and trans. Michael Howard and Peter Paret (New York: Knopf, 1993), pp. 99 and 731.

19 David Hare, *Stuff Happens* (London: Faber and Faber, 2004), p. 49.

20 Samera Esmeir underlined to me that the Arabic al-'ra' suggests, more precisely, "outdoors" or "in the open" — where there is no shelter, nothing to cover you, no protection, a space of total abandonment.

21 Bernard Kouchner, *Ce que je crois* (Paris: Grasset, 1995).

22 Jacques Rancière, "The Politics of Aesthetics," Kein Theater, August 9, 2004, http://theater.kein.org/node/99.

23 Jacques Rancière and Davide Panagia, "Dissenting Words: A Conversation," *Diacritics* 30, no. 2 (2000), p. 116.

24 *Ibid.*

25 Jacques Rancière, *Disagreement: Politics and Philosophy*, trans. Julie Rose (Minneapolis: University of Minnesota Press, 1999), p. 24, emphasis added.

26 Thomas Keenan, "Drift: Politics and the Simulation of Real Life," *Grey Room* 21 (2005), pp. 94–111.

27 Rancière, *Disagreement*, pp. 125–26.

28 Slavoj Žižek, "Human Rights and Its Discontents," Lecture, Human Rights Project at Bard College, November 16, 1999, available online at www.bard.edu/hrp/resource_pdfs/ keenan.zizek.discontents.pdf. Compare Žižek's proposition to Jacques Rancière's notion, articulated in "Dissenting Words": "In a very real sense, it all began with the May '68 assertion that 'we are all German Jews' — an entirely ideological statement, the validity of which, if analyzed at the level of its content, one finds to rest entirely on the capacity to overturn the political relationship between the order of designations and that of events by emphasizing the gap that separates subject and predicate. From there, an entire field of understanding speech acts as political gestures opened up: a field that reconfigured the division between words and things while rearranging the distinction between legitimate and illegitimate speakers (i.e., claimants)." "Human Rights and Its Discontents," p. 114.

29 Kofi A. Annan, foreword to Yael Danieli, Elsa Stamatopoulou, and Clarence J. Dias (eds.), *The Universal Declaration of Human Rights: Fifty Years and Beyond* (Amityville, NY: Baywood, 1999), p. v.

30 Michel Foucault, "Face aux gouvernements, les droits de l'homme," *Dits et écrits: 1954–1988; IV: 1980–1988* (Paris: Gallimard, 1994), pp. 707–708. I wrote about this text long ago, in Thomas Keenan, *Fables of Responsibility: Aberrations and Predicaments in Ethics and Politics* (Stanford, CA: Stanford University Press, 1997), pp. 155–61, and it still surprises me.

31 On "the politics of the governed," see especially the second section of Michel Feher, "Les divisions de la gauche mouvementée," *Vacarme* 20 (2002), pp. 36–44; Partha Chatterjee, *The Politics of the Governed: Reflections on Popular Politics in Most of the World* (New York: Columbia University Press, 2004), ch. 3, is also valuable in this regard.

32 Michel Foucault, "L'expérience morale et sociale des Polonais ne peut plus être effacée," *Dits et écrits IV*, p. 349.

33 See David Rieff, "The Precarious Triumph of Human Rights," *New York Times Magazine,* August 8, 1999; *A Bed for the Night: Humanitarianism in Crisis* (New York: Simon and Schuster, 2002); and *At the Point of a Gun: Democratic Dreams and Armed Intervention* (New York: Simon and Schuster, 2005); and Alex de Waal, "Human Rights Organisations and the Political Imagination: How the West and Africa Have Diverged," *Justice Africa*, October 2002, www.justiceafrica.org/new_variant_famine.htm.

34 David Chandler, notably, has underlined this again and again, for better and for worse: "Introduction: Global Civil Society and the Future of World Politics," in David Chandler and Gideon Baker (eds.), *Global Civil Society: Contested Futures* (London: Routledge, 2005), pp. 1–14. I learned a great deal about the potential for "human rights" to act as a form of governmentality, in the Foucauldian sense, at a workshop on government and humanity organized by Miriam Ticktin and Ilana Feldman at New York University in April 2005, where Samera Esmeir was particularly insistent and helpful on this point.

35 Rancière, *Disagreement*, p. 24.

Speaking Plainly about Chechnya: On the Limits of the Juridical Model of Human-Rights Advocacy

Bridget Conley-Zilkic

In November 1999, the military of the Russian Federation invaded the breakaway republic Chechnya, pounding it into submission. Chechnya's capital, Grozny, fell to Russian forces in February 2000 after being largely reduced to rubble. In an op-ed piece published a few weeks later, Peter Bouckaert, an investigator with the New York–based international human-rights organization Human Rights Watch (HRW), allowed his personal frustration to break through the usual distance that characterizes human-rights reporting. Bouckaert wrote: "I am tired of going to funerals and expressing my condolences for senseless murders, acts of sheer brutality. There is little I can promise: There is no indication that the abuses will end or that the perpetrators of these crimes will be punished.... The silence of the international community on Chechnya is deafening. To date, the international community has given the Russian government no reason to fear any repercussions for its actions."[1]

Four years later, in January 2004, Bouckaert's colleague Rachel Denber authored a comparably remarkable document, *"Glad to Be Deceived": The International Community and Chechnya*. Labeled a "commentary" on Chechnya, it was a more frank assessment of the international response to Chechnya than any document HRW had produced since Bouckaert's. Its central argument was simple: "The international community's response to it [armed conflict in Chechnya] has been shameful and shortsighted." The international community, the commentary continued, had "chosen the path of self-deception, choosing to believe Russia's claims that the situation in Chechnya is stabilizing, and so be spared of making tough decisions about what actions are necessary to stop flagrant abuses and secure the well-being of the people of the region."[2]

Denber reviews the history of human-rights abuses in Chechnya — which she describes as "the most serious human rights crisis of the new decade in Europe" — alongside the major milestones in the international response to Chechnya, noting moments where it looked as if some progress was being made.[3] This progress, when and where it

A Chechen woman carries her child past a Russian solder sitting on an armored personnel carrier near a polling station opened for the presidential elections in the village of Kurchaloi in Chechnya, October 5, 2003 (Yuri Kabodnov/AFP/Getty Images).

appeared, was ultimately subsumed by the acceptance of Vladimir Putin and all that came with him as the symbol of a new Russia with which Western governments could work. Denber writes:

> By mid-2000, Western leaders understood that Putin, until then a political unknown, had consolidated power and would lead Russia for at least four more years. They generally ceased to press Russia for concessions on Chechnya. This meant that the international community's most important multilateral achievements in Chechnya—resolutions at the United Nations Human Rights Commission, resolutions by the PACE [Parliamentary Assembly of the Council of Europe], and the like—received no reinforcement at the bilateral level, and so went unheeded.[4]

Mid-2000, it should be noted, marks a very early point in the history of the current conflict in Chechnya.

Between the appearances of these two unique documents, Human Rights Watch issued several reports, letters to relevant parties, and statements about abuses in Chechnya. The reporting was excellent throughout, but the recommendations, dependent as they are on a legal model that places all its hope in "accountability," played a role in aiding the willing deception that Denber describes. How can this be? How can such an organization—and Human Rights Watch stands out for the consistency and quality of its reports on Chechnya—contribute to states' self-deception as they consider their responses to a conflict?

Although HRW's reports often depend largely on the work of Chechen and Russian colleagues on the ground who are associated with the Russian human-rights organization Memorial, they have provided front-line information to an international audience about where, against whom, and by whom abuses are committed. At issue here is not this aspect of HRW's reporting, but its recommendations to the governments of Russia and other countries, which create the paradoxical situation whereby recommendations for "accountability" obfuscate responsibility for the very abuses that demand "accounting."

CHECHNYA: SPRING 2002

The events of spring 2002 offer ample evidence of this paradox: HRW published two reports on abuses and sent other communications to world leaders about the situation; the Russian government issued a new regulation to its armed forces in an attempt to forestall criticism at the meeting of the UN Commission on Human Rights; and violence continued in Chechnya.

The second Chechen war had begun on September 30, 1999, when a Russian force of one hundred thousand men entered Chechnya to reclaim control of the breakaway republic. When Grozny fell in February 2000, Russia declared the war won. With Grozny in Russian hands and the bulk of Chechen fighters regrouping in the mountains, the Russians installed a pro-Moscow Chechen government and declared that all that was left to do was a little more work—"pacification."

The characteristic "pacification" operation was the *zachistka*. A *zachistka* was ostensibly a checking of civilians' papers: Russian forces would seal off a town and search for Chechen fighters house by house. In practice, though, *zachistka* were often free-for-alls for the Russian soldiers.[5] Looting was among the most common crimes that took place. Vandalism, wanton destruction of Chechen property, and indiscriminate shooting regularly occurred. Beating and torture, on the spot or after taking people (usually men) to a holding area near headquarters, were also common. Many detained men reported that they had been tortured with electric-shock treatment, often on their genitals, which harmed their ability to have children. Rapes also occurred. And people were killed or "disappeared."

Sometimes detained Chechens could be bought back from the Russians, depending on their families' resources. A thousand dollars, weapons (easily bought in the markets), a golden necklace: Chechens exchanged their meager possessions for a loved one's life. Or a loved one's body; the trade also included the dead.

Throughout this period, Russian forces were the largest threat to Chechen civilians, but civilians were also targeted by Chechen forces. For example, Shamil Basayev claimed responsibility for several suicide attacks, some in Chechnya and others, larger and more dramatic, in Russia proper. Although the larger assaults on Russian targets have garnered more press coverage, many Chechens have been killed by suicide attacks within the republic.

Responding to these patterns of abuse, on February 2, 2002, HRW released a report, *Swept Under: Torture, Forced Disappearances, and Extrajudicial Killings during Sweep Operations in Chechnya*, about six Chechen villages that had faced "exceptionally harsh" sweep operations (*zachistka*) during June and July of the previous year.[6] One of these occurred in Alkhan-Kala, a town to which we will return shortly. During these operations, Russian forces extrajudicially executed people (that is, murdered them), illegally detained people, "disappeared" and tortured detainees, and looted and vandalized Chechen property. Of the dead, some were so disfigured that they had to be identified by their clothing.

After providing eyewitness testimony about what had occurred during these *zachistka*, HRW offered recommendations that centered on a series of investigations that the organization thought should take place, each of which should result in "accountability." Investigations were to be undertaken by the Russian government, a national commission, various UN special rapporteurs, the international community, and the Organization for Security and Cooperation in Europe (OSCE). Further, HRW recommended that the investigations undertaken by the Russian government be scrutinized by the Council of Europe and OSCE, indicating HRW's lack of faith in the Russian government's ability to carry out the very investigations it had recommended. Russian military units, the report also stated, should be taught the standards laid out in all relevant international agreements, particularly those relating to the treatment of detainees. Citing an article of the European Convention on Human Rights, HRW suggested informing the Russian military that detainees should be arrested only if there was "reasonable suspicion" that they had committed an offense, that their names should be documented on a publicly available list, that they should not be tortured, that Russian law demands that the procuracy be informed of a detention within twenty-four hours of an arrest, and so forth. It might be asked whether legal instruction could counter abuses that were as intentional and brutal as those the Russian soldiers inflicted on the townspeople of Alkhan-Kala, where one of the *zachistka* that *Swept Under* documented took place. For instance, one woman spent days after the *zachistka* searching for her detained son. His body was later found in a shallow grave:

> Her son had been shot through the head, just above the right eye, and two more times on the left side of the chest. His right arm, which was unnaturally positioned behind the back, had been dislocated or possibly broken. Khasaeva also said his legs and chest were severely bruised. Khasaeva said that people from the village told her the two other men found in the makeshift grave were brothers from Urus-Martan named Rustam and Rakhman. She did not know their last names. She believed their bodies had already been in the grave for a while, as they had started to decompose. She said both bodies were headless and had been wrapped in canvas.[7]

A resolution critical of Russian actions in Chechnya was tabled at the 2002 meeting of the UN Commission on Human Rights. The commission had been successful in passing resolutions condemning Russia's actions in Chechnya in other years since the war had begun, but this time it proved more difficult. At the same time, the Russian government issued an order to its military, ostensibly designed to counter abuses during searches. Order 80, introduced on March 27, 2002, issued new guidelines for Russian behavior during searches for rebels, responding directly to many of the recommendations human-rights organizations had made: soldiers were forbidden to wear masks; soldiers were required to introduce themselves and give the reason for the search; they were not to cover the license plates on their vehicles and armored personnel carriers; a prosecutor and head of village was to be present at every search; witnesses had to sign a statement that no abuses had occurred; and the names of people killed or detained, as well as where they were being taken and what they were accused of, were all to be released to village authorities.

This order intervened at the level of discourse alone. It was composed in terms comparable to those HRW had used in its recommendations. Thus, Order 80 was able to capitalize on the distance between these recommendations and the actual abuses. The order responded to a human-rights discourse that itself was one step removed from the situations in which abuses happened.

On March 28, 2002, HRW sent a letter to the Parliamentary Assembly of the Council of Europe's joint working group and to the Russian Duma, asking them to "end impunity for crimes committed by federal forces in the region, including crimes committed against women."[8] Given the very information that HRW brought to international attention — that is, the lack of accountability and the need for investigations and investigations of those investigations — the "respectful request" that the government "abide by international humanitarian and human rights law; investigate and, if the evidence warrants, prosecute soldiers and officers found to have committed atrocities; provide training on international humanitarian law for all soldiers and forces serving in Chechnya; and provide victim and witness protection to those women and other civilians who agree to testify against their perpetrators" seems misplaced. What reason is there to believe that any of this would occur?

In Chechnya, Order 80 was greeted by some as a positive development: "I was very hopeful about Order 80," Malika Umazheva, head of the administration in the Chechen town of Alkhan-Kala, explained, "but my hopes were short-lived."[9] Her hopes survived only until the events of April 11–15, 2002, when Alkhan-Kala was subjected to yet another violent *zachistka*. None of the promised provisions were followed. When Umazheva demanded that she be allowed to carry out her duties under Order 80, she was prevented from doing so. What she was not allowed to witness, although she later compiled evidence of it from villagers, was a series of violent acts: indiscriminate violence, torture, and beating of men taken into custody, as well as looting. In addition to stealing from private homes, a recently renovated plywood shop, and a poultry factory, the soldiers looted the local hospital and administration buildings. A woman whose belongings had been stolen later tried to issue a complaint, along with Umazheva. They were asked, "What did you think? We are here to take everything that we need."[10]

When Umazheva asked Prosecutor Ferlevsky to intervene and help stop these abuses, he replied that he had no authority over the troops. At the end of day on April 12, Umazheva, Ferlevsky, and General Igor Bronitsky (whose forces carried out the operation) met. "The prosecutor then asked me to sign a document that the *zachistka* was conducted in an orderly manner without any violations of human rights," Umazheva later told a reporter. She stood up to Bronitsky and Ferlevsky, refusing to sign the document, "because human rights were violated." They pushed her, saying that the operation was finished, and they would leave once she had signed. After speaking with fellow villagers, Umazheva decided it was worth signing the paper to end the suffering the *zachistka* had caused. In the end, the actual document she signed was blank.[11]

Even as that *zachistka* was under way, HRW released a report, *Last Seen... : Continued 'Disappearances' in Chechnya*. The report documented eighty-seven disappearances between September 2000 and January 2002, noting that the actual number of disappearances was believed to be much higher. The report argued, "Despite its international legal obligations, Russia is failing to prevent 'disappearances' by its security forces, and failing properly to investigate and prosecute such cases after they occur. The response of the civilian and military procuracies—the agencies charged with the investigation and prosecution of 'disappearances'—remains inadequate, allowing abusive security personnel to act with impunity." The report cited some "cosmetic" improvements, such as Order 80, but commented that a previous regulation, Order 46, "appears to have had little impact." Its recommendations were not very different from those given in *Swept Under*.[12]

In Alkhan-Kala, Order 80 was again mocked. Umazheva's calculation that it was worth signing the document attesting that the *zachistka* had been conducted properly to protect the people from further abuses was proven grossly wrong: "I believed them, but they deceived me. They got the document from me, but the next day they murdered people."[13] The soldiers returned for another two days and executed more men. Several days later, Russia's human-rights representative for Chechnya, Viktor Kalamanov, made a public statement that Order 80 was being followed and that there were no complaints or abuses. The same day, the UN Commission on Human Rights voted down a motion to censure Russia for violations in Chechnya. As a result, the commission no longer hears regular reports on conditions in Chechnya.

In May, HRW sent two more letters, one to President George W. Bush and one to heads of state and other prominent figures in the European Union. Both letters suggested that the recipients "speak plainly" to President Putin and the Russian people about the problems that stand in the way of democracy in Russia, including abuses against the Chechen people. Both letters noted the deterioration of the human-rights situation in Chechnya and again asked that Russia be "pressed" to release a list of detainees in the hope that transparency would someday lead to accountability. Then, in January 2003, almost a year to the day after the release of *Swept Under*, HRW released *Into Harm's Way: Forced Return of Displaced People to Chechnya,* which repeated the pattern of not speaking plainly about what could be expected from the Russian government.[14] HRW again asked the Russian government to guarantee the safe return of displaced persons, to investigate atrocities, to allow UN special rapporteurs to conduct their own investigations, and to maintain transparency of detainment.

Is the failure of international organizations and governments to confront fully the scale of abuses and the disingenuousness of the Russian government's commitment to democratic principles any surprise when even human-rights organizations refuse to *speak plainly* about what could be expected from the Russian government?

ON THE PURSUIT OF HUMAN RIGHTS

The problem in the relationship between how abuses occur, how they are documented, and the recommendations that human-rights organizations then give is not by any means limited to Chechnya. For example, in an article on international human rights and Liberia, Kenneth Cain describes the absurdity of human-rights organizations' recommendations to the Liberian government headed by Charles Taylor, all of which are comparable to those made for Chechnya. He writes: "These organizations tended to advocate that abstract, ideal standards be met and to articulate aspirational human rights goals that had no hope of actually being implemented in the real world.... It is difficult to ascertain precisely how victims of human rights abuses are actually served by fanciful references to international covenants and whimsical human rights cheerleading."[15]

The problem of relying on states to implement human-rights reforms is consistent throughout the field of international human-rights advocacy; as David Kennedy says, "by structuring emancipation as a relationship between an individual rights holders and the state, human rights places the state at the center of the emancipatory promise."[16]

International human-rights advocacy as currently practiced by professional human-rights organizations offers a conservative model of engagement. The profession places its hopes in institutional and statist models of change, focusing on altering perpetrator behavior, rather than on empowering or declaring solidarity with victims. The goal of such organizations is to hold up international legal standards in the hope that perpetrator governments (the most common target of such organizations) will conform to them. Conformity is measured by a state's willingness to prosecute legally those who carry out their policies, rather than by any real change in the policies themselves. This is the role "accountability" plays in the discourse of contemporary human-rights advocacy.

When accountability is the paramount end of human rights, rather than "speaking plainly" about a situation, then the rights of those whose states refuse to acknowledge their status as rights bearers become nonexistent. At this point, there are two options left: either continue speaking as if juridical rights were achievable despite conditions that suggest otherwise, or forge a way out of rights discourse altogether.

International human-rights organizations generally choose the first option. The second has become a matter of theoretical debate. If the point at which an individual no longer has a state to guarantee his or her rights marks the moment when rights language is no longer relevant, then one could agree with Giorgio Agamben that the rights of man (as opposed to those of the citizen) constitute rights only to "bare life," that is, apolitical rights. Agamben argues: "Rights…are attributable to man only in the degree to which he is the immediately vanishing presupposition (indeed, he must never appear simply as man) of the citizen." Rights, as such, are declared and declarable only in relation to the juridical position of the subject. Agamben ultimately suggests that the way out of this is to escape politics and rights discourse altogether: "Until a new politics — that is a politics no longer founded on the exception of bare life — is at hand, every theory and every praxis will remain imprisoned and immobile."[17]

However, if one were to begin from a different understanding of rights, the limitations of the juridical model would no longer announce the end of rights talk, but would suggest a different way of thinking and speaking about rights claims. What if the fundamental question of rights began not with reliance on and then disappointment in the state as the guarantor of rights, but with a question of the politics of rights? Such a politics would be situated at the border between those who have rights they can claim (citizens within a political system that acknowledges that citizenship) and the promise of the rights of man (human existence regardless of the state's guarantees). What if the subject of rights were conceived, as Jacques Rancière has suggested, as "the subject, or more accurately the process of subjectivization, that bridges the interval between two forms of the existence of those rights"?[18] In this sense, rights do not belong to a subject, but are asserted in the disjunction between the rights of the citizen (one who claims rights in a state) and those of the human (one who asserts political existence where it is not recognized). Rancière refers to this as a process of dissensus, "putting two worlds in one and the same world. A political subject…is a capacity for staging such scenes of dissensus."[19]

Lest we forget the stakes of this discussion, let's return briefly to Chechnya in 2002. Malika Umazheva, the head of the administration in Alkhan-Kala who tried to activate the terms of Order 80 for the protection of her town, was dismissed from her job for her efforts and for her refusal to remain silent. She spoke to human-rights advocates, to audiences at conferences in the region, and to the media. She also refused simply to give up her position, protested her dismissal, and was reinstated. On the day before she was due to return to her duties, she was murdered — shot in the back three times by Russian forces.[20]

Asking how to engage human rights is not a luxury; it is, at least for some, a life-threatening endeavor. How can a politics of rights, moving away from the current jurid-ical monopoly, respond to abuses as they occur in life-threatening situations? By way of a conclusion, I offer below suggestions — recommendations — to human-rights orga-nizations as a starting point.

First, change the terms of human-rights reporting to include the agency of those who are brutalized by abuses. Acknowledge what people are doing to help protect themselves and to assert their rights. The juridical monopoly reduces such people to "victims" of abuses, a preassigned role that gives them meaning in the current modes of documenting human rights. This is grossly reductive. How would human-rights report-ing produce a different understanding of abuses if every report included something about what people are doing to help themselves? What if, in addition to making recom-mendations to governments and international and multilateral organizations, reports also directly addressed those who are suffering from and responding to abuses?

Second, change the terms of analysis so that abuses and facts are not solely discern-ible through the lens of international legal categories. It might be surprising what would emerge as issues if the entity considered wronged and abused was not the law, but rather the individuals and groups at risk. (See the above recommendation.)

Third, at a minimum, speak plainly. In the field of humanitarian action, the organi-zation Médecins Sans Frontières (MSF) operates under the assumption that the basic principles that make humanitarian action meaningful — impartiality and neutrality — are not givens in moments of conflict, but must be vigorously defended. A similar grappling with the fundamental conditions that make human-rights recommendations achievable — this is even within the dominant juridical mode — has not occurred within the professional human-rights community. International human-rights organizations are particularly bad about openly acknowledging when the goal of standing with "vic-tims" comes into conflict with the goal of accountability. To change this, such organiza-tions need to be willing to err a little more on the side of honesty than on the side of the law. This would mean making difficult decisions about recommendations, but there is no reason human-rights advocacy should be premised on ease.

The views expressed in this essay are those of the author alone and do not necessarily reflect those of the United States Holocaust Memorial Museum or its council.

1   Peter Bouckaert, "The Real War Begins," *Washington Post,* February 25, 2000. Available online at www.washingtonpost. com/ac2/wp-dyn?pagename=article&contentId=A31468- 2000Feb24&notFound=true.

2   Rachel Denber, *"Glad to Be Deceived": The International Community and Chechnya* (New York: Human Rights Watch, 2004). Available online at http://hrw.org/wr2k4/7.htm#_ Toc58744956.

3   *Ibid.* Denber notes that there were some minor developments in terms of accountability. A few Russian soldiers were brought to trial for their crimes in Chechnya, but the number was, and remains, outrageously small compared with the number of abuses. The case of Colonel Budanov, who was accused of raping and killing a young Chechen woman, illustrates the limitations of Russian accountability: the trial dragged on, with his defense at first winning an argument that he was mentally unfit at the time of the crime, then under pressure from human-rights organizations found competent to stand trial. He was ultimately found guilty of murder and kidnapping. On the international front, criticism of Russia was rarely on the agenda of any forum not specifically reserved for addressing human-rights concerns.

4   *Ibid.*

5   For example, in Aldi, on February 5, 2000, Russian soldiers killed approximately forty-six civilians; in Alkhan-Yurt, between December 1 and 18, 2000, sixteen people were killed; in the Grozny district of Staropromyslovsky, between December 22 and January 21, thirty-eight civilians were killed. In 2001, a mass grave was found just outside the main Russian base at Khankala. Human-rights organizations found fifty-one corpses, only a few of which could be identified.

6   Human Rights Watch, *Swept Under: Torture, Forced Disappearances, and Extrajudicial Killings during Sweep Operations in Chechnya* (New York: HRW, 2002). Available online at www.hrw.org/reports/2002/russchech/.

7   *Ibid.* Nine days after releasing this report, HRW also wrote President Putin an open letter focusing on the rights of refugees, because the presence of Chechens in Georgia's Pankisi Gorge had become a matter of international debate. The letter cites both the Russian government's "record of pressuring internally displaced persons within its juridiction to return to unsafe conditions in Chechnya" and a hope that "the security and well-being of refugees will be an incontestable priority" in Putin's talks with Georgian authorities about forcibly returning Chechens from Georgia's Pankisi Gorge to Chechnya.

8   Elizabeth Andersen and LaShawn R. Jefferson, "End Impunity for Crimes in Chechnya: HRW Letter to Members of the Russian Duma," March 28, 2002. Available online at www. hrw.org/press/2002/04/Duma0328.htm.

9   Maura Reynolds, "Chechens Report Abuses Despite Safeguards," *Los Angeles Times,* April 23, 2002.

10 Human Rights Center, "Memorial" and "'Mopping-Up' in the Village Alkhan-Kala 11–15th April, 2002," April 19, 2002. Available online at www.memo.ru/eng/memhrc/texts/ alkhan-kala.shtml.

11 "I consulted with the elders," Umazheva explained. "People were suffering. Children couldn't go to school. Sick people couldn't go to the hospital. People couldn't take their cattle and sheep into the fields. So it was decided that I should sign this document to make the soldiers leave the village." Reynolds, "Chechens Report Abuses."

12 Human Rights Watch, *Last Seen…: Continued 'Disappearances' in Chechnya* (New York: HRW, 2002). Available online at http://hrw.org/reports/2002/russchech02/.

13 Reynolds, "Chechens Report Abuses."

14 Human Rights Watch, *Into Harm's Way: Forced Return of Displaced People to Chechnya* (New York: HRW, 2003). Available online at http://hrw.org/reports/2003/russia0103/.

15 Kenneth Cain, "The Rape of Dinah: Human Rights, Civil War in Liberia and Evil Triumphant," *Human Rights Quarterly* 21, no. 2 (1999), pp. 296–97.

16 David Kennedy, "The International Human Rights Movement: Part of the Problem?" *Harvard Human Rights Journal* 15 (2002), p. 113.

17 Giorgio Agamben, *Homo Sacer: Sovereign Power and Bare Life,* trans. Daniel Heller-Roazen (Stanford, CA: Stanford University Press, 1998), p. 113.

18 Jacques Rancière, "Who Is the Subject of the Rights of Man?" *South Atlantic Quarterly* 103, no. 2/3 (2004), p. 302.

19 *Ibid.,* p. 304.

20 For more on Malika Umazheva, see Bridget Conley, "For the Women of Chechnya, Hope Dies Last," *Journal of Human Rights* 3, no. 3 (2004), pp. 331–42.

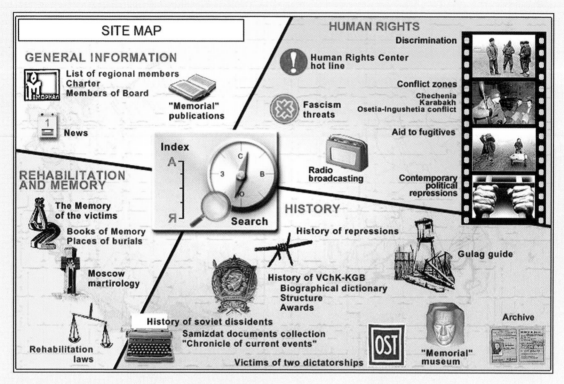

Site map from Memorial's Web site (www.memo.ru/eng/map1.htm).

Continuities

a profile of Memorial by Philippe Mangeot

For anyone who has heard of Memorial only through its reports on human-rights violations in the Russian Federation, the name of the organization may be somewhat surprising. Indeed, from today's perspective, Memorial seems more preoccupied with current emergencies than with the demands of memory. However, when Memorial was founded — in January 1989, amid the political effervescence of the last years of perestroika — its name accurately described its purpose. At the time, the focus of the group's founders was the past: Memorial's first tasks consisted of seeking justice for the victims of political persecution in the USSR by providing a tombstone, however symbolic, for the dead, and thereby writing an alternative history of the Soviet empire.

Yet this emphasis on the past soon gave rise to a triple gamble on the future. First, Memorial staked its hopes on the hypothesis that unearthing the history of Soviet repressive policies and practices would foster the emergence of an autonomous civil society in the territories of the former Soviet empire. Second, Memorial's founders gambled on the idea that commemorating the lives and deeds of yesterday's victims would both increase the prestige of the principles and mandate the implementation of the rights for which these victims had fought. Finally, Memorial's third bet was that its research and methodology regarding the establishment of historical truth would also prove a useful tool for monitoring the human-rights record of post-Soviet states.

Taking stock of the past in order to pave the way for a less tragic future was thus Memorial's initial preoccupation. Its founding members began by setting up research groups whose missions involved collecting archives of political persecution and, more generally, gathering and processing incomplete and scattered information about Stalin's regime and its immediate successors. This research constituted Memorial as a memory "entrepreneur," to draw on Howard S. Becker's terminology, insofar as the organization aimed, against official history, at both prompting and framing the resurgence of a collective memory that had all but entirely disappeared. To perform these tasks, a number of Memorial centers were established in all the regions of Russia, but also in former Soviet republics such as the Ukraine, Kazakhstan, and Georgia, among others. Acting as a memory entrepreneur also entailed unearthing stifled family memories and other hitherto untold stories. For that purpose, Memorial organized an annual competition for the best familial story called "Man in the History of Twentieth-Century Russia," which is still being run today.

As its memorial and historical work got under way, Memorial also sought to give it spatial, temporal, and legal traces. First, the organization was instrumental in the establishment of monuments, steles, and commemorative plates in all the places of the former Soviet Union where massacres had been committed. Second, Memorial also endeavored to impose commemorative rituals in post-Communist Russia. Thanks to its efforts in 1991, October 30 was declared a day in memory of the victims of political repression in homage to the prisoners of the camp in Mordovia who, seventeen years earlier, had started a hunger strike to protest their conditions of detention. Third, Memorial's advocacy also contributed to a law rehabilitating victims of political repression, which returned civil rights to thousands of surviving Russian citizens.

While accomplishing their work on memory, Memorial activists soon developed another pole of activity, one that specifically focused on human-rights advocacy in the present. The organization thus became a watchdog against ethnic discrimination and political persecution in the countries of the Commonwealth of Independent States (CIS), comprising the former Soviet Republics of Armenia, Azerbaijan, Belarus, Georgia, Kazakhstan, Kyrgyzstan, Moldova, Russia, Tajikistan, Ukraine, Uzbekistan, and, until 2005, Turkmenistan — in particular, their "hot spots": the armed-conflict zones in Nagorno-Karabakh, South Ossetia, Tajikistan, and, of course, Chechnya. The group also formed an alternative and independent media center whose primary mission was to account for violations of international law in the conflicts taking place on the territory of the CIS and for infringements on minority rights in Russian regions.

To guarantee the credibility of its inquiries, Memorial submitted them to a particularly rigorous methodology, which remains its trademark. Indeed, from the beginning, all of Memorial's reports have been based on the solicitation and confrontation of testimonies and sources from opposing parties. Meant as a counterweight to the states' official versions, these inquiries are distributed both within and beyond the Russian Federation. Memorial is therefore one of the rare voices in Russia that not only has protested against the Chechen conflict, but also has alerted the international community to the massacres committed against the civilian population in Grozny. Memorial has also been responsible for filing the first complaints that have been deemed admissible by the European Court of Human Rights regarding the exactions of Russian forces in Chechnya.

The conjunction between two exigencies, that of reclaiming the past and that of monitoring the present, distinguishes Memorial from all other Russian human-rights groups. This distinctive feature is no doubt as much the result of Memorial's unique expertise — its ability to make use of the tools of historical research and analysis in contemporary conflict zones — as it is the consequence of an ethical demand; for human-rights activists can hardly limit their investigations to the history of the Gulag when national and ethnic minorities are being killed and persecuted in their own country. But the members of Memorial are also convinced that there is a continuity between the practices of Soviet totalitarianism and current violations of human rights in post-Soviet states in terms of structures, practices, and even personnel. Indeed, among the members of Memorial, the belief that current human-rights violations are directly linked to those of the past is an essential article of faith. To be part of Memorial is thus to profess that a commitment to history and an involvement in the present are inseparable and that exposing the links and connections between past and present abuses is at the core of the organization's mandate.

Whether they endeavor to undo the official history of yore or to counter its contemporary avatars, Memorial activists always predicate their work on the claim that the state should respect the autonomy of civil society and that there is no rule of law unless the independence of public space is preserved. Acting on that claim translates into two types of practices for Memorial: confrontations with governmental agencies, on the one hand, and self-organization, on the other. For instance, under President Boris Yeltsin, the group used the knowledge it had acquired and information it had collected about the history of totalitarianism to pressure the state into providing material compensations for the surviving victims of Soviet brutality. Yet at the same time, Memorial was independently acting as a care provider for these survivors, organizing services such as housework and the distribution of free medicines. Similarly, Memorial's inquiries and counterinvestigations have enabled the group to expose the discrepancies between the principles that governmental authorities claim to abide by and their actual practices, thereby pressuring them into bringing the latter into conformity with the former. But at the same time, and parallel to its monitoring activities, Memorial has also been busy promoting civic initiatives, whether by sponsoring educational programs on legal scholarship and culture, creating "human-rights schools," or proposing specific classes on civic education for schools. All of these practices are described by Memorial as "legal literacy campaigns" that are indispensable for the effective democratization of the country.

This twofold approach relates to the fact that, from the outset, Memorial saw itself as the avant-garde of a civil society yet to come, but one already grounded in the experience of dissidence during the last decades of the Soviet regime. And indeed, the initial members of Memorial included some of the most prestigious dissidents: the physicist Andrei Sakharov, 1975 Nobel Peace Prize laureate and Memorial's first president; Serguei Kovalev; the writer Anatoli Rybakov; and the historian Roy Medvedev; among others. Many members' children also became involved, for example, Aleksandr Daniel, whose mother, Larisa Bogoraz, was condemned to four years of exile in 1968 for protesting in Red Square against the Soviet intervention in Czechoslovakia. Memorial's constant preoccupation with its own independence from the state, but also its determination to subject governmental agencies to its intransigent scrutiny, can thus be perceived as a legacy of the founding and formative experience of Soviet dissidence. Accordingly, the organization systematically refuses all forms of state funding. Instead, it relies on various modes of self-financing, such as the concert tours with student performers from the St. Petersburg Conservatory — organized by Vladimir Schnittke, nephew of the composer Alfred Schnittke — and on foreign aid, which comes from the main promoters of civil society in the former Soviet bloc, the MacArthur, Soros, and/or Ford Foundations, the National Endowment for Democracy, the International Federation of Human Rights (FIDH), and the European Union.

In an increasingly nationalistic Russia, Memorial's dependence on foreign funds has become a potential liability. In the last trimester of 2005, the Douma, the Russian parliament, considered passing a law on NGOs that would have simply prevented Russian organizations from receiving any form of foreign assistance. While the law that was finally adopted proved somewhat less stringent, it still stipulates that the government is entitled to oversee the ways in which foreign donations are used and, even more significantly, that the activity of any NGO can be suspended if it is deemed a threat to "the sovereignty, independence, territorial integrity, national unity, cultural heritage or national interests of Russia." Under this law, which is clearly meant to prevent the possibility of an Ukrainian-style "Orange Revolution" in Russia during the 2007 and 2008 elections, Memorial's systematic denunciation of the Russian army's crimes in Chechnya is likely to fall under the category of "anti-Russian propaganda." Along with other NGOs critical of Vladimir Putin's regime — in particular, the Helsinki Committee for Human Rights and the Organization of Soldiers' Mothers — Memorial has vehemently objected to this new law, but in vain. Either subservient or increasingly controlled, the media did very little to publicize the protests of the NGOs and to foster any debate about the law. Thus, the law was easily adopted and did not provoke any reaction from public opinion.

This episode is revealing in terms of Memorial's situation in contemporary Russia. Seventeen years after its creation, the NGO is a venerable, but also an aging operation. The people who experienced Memorial's glorious beginnings are the first to concede that, in Russia proper, the enthusiasm that had greeted the group, particularly around its work on memory, has largely faded. Over the years, Memorial has certainly garnered quite a lot of international respect and notoriety. Today, its members are still the main interlocutors for foreign NGOs concerned with human rights, but also for foreign journalists whose ability to conduct inquiries in Russia has considerably diminished over the last several years. At the same time, however, Memorial activists are fewer than before. Though the group still boasts around fifteen thousand members in Moscow and several dozen full-time researchers, and though it can lay claim to a hundred local affiliated organizations, all observers agree on the relative exhaustion of an organization that is no longer able to mobilize widely in protest against official lies and the restriction of liberties.

In short, its power both to intervene in the public sphere and to affect the political climate has dramatically decreased. Moreover, because most newspapers, TV and radio stations have pledged allegiance to Putin and his authoritarian regime, Memorial's investigations and press releases are barely taken up by the Russian media.

In the profoundly unstructured Russian society of the early 2000s, Memorial seems to have escaped from another world: as if the avant-garde of a civil society yet to come had turned out to be the last of the Mohicans.

Translated by William Bishop.

The Trouble with Evenhandedness: On the Politics of Human Rights and Peace Advocacy in Sri Lanka

Alan Keenan

Since the fall of the Soviet empire and the apparent global triumph of liberal capitalism, much hope has been placed in civil society and nongovernmental organizations (NGOs) as engines of liberalization and democratization throughout the world.[1] Despite the existence of many persuasive critiques of the transformative power of civil society, especially in postcolonial (which are often also neocolonial) contexts, "civil society building" remains a popular goal and practice for international donors from the wealthy nations of the global north.[2] This has been particularly true in situations of protracted civil conflict, especially during internationally sponsored peace processes or in the period of postconflict reconstruction. Foreign states and international organizations seeking to encourage political stability and integration into the global economic system are in need of organizations and institutions that can contribute to the range of activities that have come to be known as "peace building." While civil society and NGOs have been asked to play important roles in numerous transitions out of violent conflict, the jury is still out on just how effective they can be as agents of lasting and democratic change.

   This essay hopes to contribute to debates over this question. It is part of a larger study that examines the roles that NGOs and civil-society networks have played during the Sri Lankan peace process of 2002–2006. The larger study seeks to understand what forms of political action and critique are open to various kinds of organizations within civil society and what approaches hold out the most promise for effecting sustainable and democratic change in situations of protracted identity-based conflict, especially during peace processes supported by foreign governments and international organizations. Of special importance to the pages that follow here is the question of what, if any, democratic political potential lies in the discourse of human rights. Claims that human rights have been violated obviously have great power as partisan political weapons, especially in situations of violent group conflict. It is less clear, however, that the discourse of human rights as a whole actually contains the potential for advancing positive democratic political change, especially in deeply divided societies.[3] Is it possible for human-rights advocacy by NGOs and networks of activists to promote democratic practices in such a context? What would be required for such groups to be able to help

Sri Lankan women shout slogans during a protest demanding peace talks between the government and Tamil Tiger rebels in Colombo, December 10, 2004. The demonstrators, marking the International Human Rights Day, staged the protest demanding that stalled peace talks be revived to find a permanent solution to Sri Lanka's drawn-out ethnic conflict (Sena Vidanagama/AFP/Getty Images).

transform the dynamics of violent conflict in sustainable and democratic ways?

Over the past decade, and especially over the past five years of intense international involvement to help resolve Sri Lanka's twenty-year-old civil war, the political activities and interventions of liberal and democratic civil-society groups and activists in Sri Lanka have increasingly been shaped by the ideas and practices of conflict resolution. With the sponsorship and encouragement of international donors, the discourse of conflict resolution has brought with it a particular model of political transformation and conflict reduction. This model has been adopted by NGOs and other civil-society organizations with important effects on how they imagine their own political roles and possibilities and how others in society see them. As part of a larger professionalization, even bureaucratization, of civil-society political activity, Sri Lankan NGOs and activists have been encouraged to take up practices of "peacebuilding" and "conflict transformation" that are generally quite technical, even apolitical. However, they have rarely been encouraged to engage directly with the power structures and ideological formations that sustain Sri Lanka's various violent conflicts.[4]

As part of the increasingly hegemonic discourse of conflict resolution, the principle of remaining evenhanded with respect to the two main negotiating parties — the government of Sri Lanka and the Tamil Tigers — emerged as a powerful influence on political discourse and on the interventions undertaken by many different actors in the Sri Lankan peace process, including foreign governments, multilateral organizations, international NGOs, and various Sri Lankan NGOs. Despite its obvious attractions in a situation of violent conflict, I argue that the ideal of evenhandedness has played a destructive role in Sri Lanka's peace process. More specifically, I contend that the concern with being evenhanded with respect to the positions of the Sri Lankan government and the Tamil Tigers has contributed to a neglect of crucial human-rights protections. The neglect of rights has, in turn, undermined trust and security between different ethnic and political groups. Furthermore, the imperative to be evenhanded has weakened the democratic and transformative potential of Sri Lankan NGOs, civil-society organizations, and activists. Promising a nonpolitical — because nonpartisan — means of transforming violent conflict into peaceful relations, the ideal of evenhandedness has in fact involved such groups in interventions that are highly political, even if this political aspect is disavowed.

After examining the various factors that have made evenhandedness so counterproductive — both those factors specific to Sri Lanka's peace process and those basic to the ideal of evenhandedness as such — I describe an alternative, more explicitly political model of engagement and critique that can be seen in the work of a small number of Sri Lankan human-rights activists. This approach, which I call "the politics of neither/nor," allows allegiance to basic democratic rights and principles to guide nongovernmental political interventions, rather than the ideal of balance or evenhandedness. By actively defending human rights, these activists attempt to reclaim the fundamental right of average, unarmed citizens to speak freely and engage in independent political activities, against the deliberate destruction of political space by the violence and arbitrary rule of both the state and counterstate agents. A neither/nor approach, I argue, ultimately holds out the promise of better integrating human rights and conflict resolution efforts. For this promise to have a chance of being fulfilled, however, the neither/nor approach must be incorporated into a broader, democratized social movement of NGOs and other political forces within civil society.

SRI LANKA'S ETHNIC CONFLICTS AND THE CRISIS OF THE STATE

The violent struggle by the Tamil Tigers (officially known as the Liberation Tigers of Tamil Eelam, or LTTE) to establish a separate state in the name of the Tamil people of Sri Lanka began in the mid-1970s. It had its origins in the failure of Sri Lanka's postindependence political leadership to agree on a political system that would grant citizens of all ethnicities equal access to the resources and protections of the state. By the mid-1950s, Sinhalese politicians had discovered the power of a discourse that pledged to use the state to rectify what many average Sinhalese and Buddhists (roughly 75 percent of the population) saw as the humiliations and disadvantages they had suffered under British colonial rule. Their grievances centered on the loss of prestige accorded to Buddhism, the dominance of English as the language of the elite and of economic opportunity, and the disproportionate number of Tamils holding civil-service jobs and gaining entrance to universities. Exploiting popular conceptions of democracy as unrestrained majority rule and popular myths about the essentially Buddhist character of the island, Sinhalese politicians passed a series of laws — with regard to language, education, religion, and land use — that effectively defined the state as Sinhalese and Buddhist. From 1956 onward, nonviolent Tamil protests against their second-class citizenship were met with increasingly violent repression by government forces. Thus, original demands by Tamils for limited forms of political autonomy for the Northern and Eastern Provinces, where Tamil speakers (mostly Hindu, but also Christian and Muslim) combine to form a majority, eventually became demands for a separate state. Small-scale antistate violence by various groups of Tamil youth in the north exploded into full-scale war in 1983 after a Tamil Tiger ambush of an army truck triggered massive state-sanctioned anti-Tamil violence throughout the island.

The separatist war has since led to the deaths of an estimated seventy thousand people and displaced upwards of one million others, out of a population of less than twenty million. Atrocities have been committed by both the government and the LTTE, including LTTE violence against other Tamils. Even as the Tigers have fought the Sinhalese-dominated state, they have also been responsible for the deaths of thousands of Tamils aligned with rival political and militant movements. The Tigers' claim to be the sole representative of the Tamil people has been enforced through violence and fear, including the assassinations of the most prominent Tamil politicians of the past three decades. Tens of thousands of Sinhalese were also killed in the course of two separate insurrections, in 1971 and 1987–1990, by militants of the left-wing nationalist People's Liberation Front, or Janatha Vimukthi Peramuna (JVP). The violence by both the state and the JVP was merciless in the extreme. Sri Lanka's small Muslim population has also suffered violence at the hands of the Sri Lankan state, and, to a much larger degree, from the Tamil Tigers, who in 1990 forcibly expelled some ninety thousand Muslims from the northern Jaffna peninsula then under their control. The violent and unaccountable power of the Sri Lankan state, in other words, ultimately bred ruthless and totalizing forms of counterstate resistance, in the form of the LTTE and the JVP, both of which have gone on to sow further destruction and hatred along lines of ethnicity, religion, and class.

The past several decades have witnessed a series of attempts to find a negotiated settlement of political demands made in the name of the Tamil people. Various proposals for constitutional reforms that would grant some degree of self-rule to the Northern and Eastern Provinces have come and gone with no success, because they offered either too much autonomy to gain consensus among Sinhalese or too little to win acceptance from the LTTE. The Norwegian-brokered cease-fire of February 2002 is the longest-running cease-fire to date, though at the time of this writing, in mid-2006, it survives in name only. Despite close involvement by governments of the European Union, the United States, and Japan, and promises of billions of dollars of aid for postwar reconstruction should a negotiated settlement be reached, talks between the Tigers and the government have failed to resume after the LTTE's withdrawal in April 2003.[5]

Thanks in part to the stresses of the peace process itself, including the many violations of basic human rights that have accompanied it, political divisions between Sinhalese parties and within the LTTE have effectively paralyzed attempts to restart negotiations. Tiger proposals for an LTTE-run interim administration in the north and east have to date not been discussed. Soon after its unveiling in November 2003, the fragile interparty cohabitation of the Sri Lankan government collapsed, which ultimately led to elections in 2004 that brought to power a new coalition of parties—now including the resurrected JVP—which took a much harder line on negotiating with the Tigers. Almost simultaneously, the LTTE suffered the defection of its Eastern Province military commander, Colonel Karuna. His initial defeat by the main body of the LTTE has been followed by guerilla resistance of increasing intensity, as the remnants of Karuna's forces have benefited from increasingly strong assistance from the Sri Lankan military. Since the election in November 2005 of a new Sri Lankan president, who ran on a platform opposing any changes to the "unitary" character of the Sri Lankan state and any concessions to the Tigers, violence between the LTTE and the Sri Lankan military has escalated to dangerous levels, with civilians of all ethnicities being targeted from all sides.

EVENHANDEDNESS AND BALANCE ON THE SRI LANKAN ROAD TO PEACE

By the spring of 2006, with the Sri Lankan peace process on the verge of collapse into full-scale war, accusations of bias and a lack of evenhandedness—directed both at the so-called international community as well as at domestic political actors — had become central to Sri Lankan political discussions.[6] This was especially true just before and immediately after the European Union's decision — in reaction to repeated cease-fire violations and political assassinations attributed to the LTTE — to add the Tamil Tigers to its list of banned "terrorist organizations," which prevents the Tigers from conducting any activities in EU countries. Even prior to this, however, the concern with being evenhanded and with revealing and criticizing "bias" and "partiality" on the part of others had been present on all sides of Sri Lanka's complicated political conflicts.

The intuitive attractiveness of evenhandedness, especially in an environment riven by explosive human-rights charges, is not hard to understand. It is especially appealing for those who take up the role of mediators or for any outside party that wants to assist others to escape a destructive cycle of conflict. It would seem almost in the nature of their role to resist taking sides and instead to try to treat the various parties equally and impartially, without adding to the sense of disadvantage or insecurity generally felt by those in conflict.[7] Indeed, the desire by outsiders to remain evenhanded is likely to be encouraged and intensified by the natural resistance of groups within a conflict to account for the activities that they deem unfair or biased, especially when such accounts take the form of human-rights criticisms that can be used as potent political weapons against them. The desire for evenhandedness would seem to flow directly from the obvious appeal — even to would-be peacemakers within the society in conflict — of a model of conflict resolution or transformation that seeks to get outside of the conflict and see (the truth of) all sides, none of which, so the thinking goes, is either entirely blameless or entirely to blame, since there are always two sides (or more) to every story.

In Sri Lanka, however, the desire to be evenhanded has in fact contributed to the slow, but steady collapse of the cease-fire. As I will argue below, the ideal of evenhandedness is a risky guide for political work in any situation of protracted violent conflict. In the case of Sri Lanka, however, the quest for evenhandedness became especially destructive because it accentuated certain underlying assumptions of the official Norwegian-facilitated peace process — assumptions that ultimately proved not only incorrect, but counterproductive.[8] If one thinks of conflict-resolution initiatives as generally aiming to transform a zero-sum or either/or conflict between identity-based groups into a win/win, or both/and, process, the problems plaguing the Sri Lankan peace process had much to do with whom the both/and approach aimed to bring together and on what terms.

The basic design flaw in the peace process was its highly exclusive nature. That is, it brought together and aimed to satisfy the interests of *both* the Tamil Tigers *and* the government, each of which was presumed to adequately represent their "own" people: the Tamil minority concentrated in the north and east of the island and the Sinhalese majority concentrated in the south, center, and west. Left out of this limited and binary structure, and thus from any ideal of evenhandedness that followed its parameters, were other important constituencies whose acceptance of the process would be a crucial factor in the sustainability of any agreements between the warring parties. Those denied any meaningful role in the process included the Muslim minority, concentrated in the volatile Eastern Province, Tamil parties and activists that rejected the Tigers' claim to be the "sole representative of the Tamil people" (including the renegade faction of the LTTE led by the Eastern Province military commander Karuna, who broke away two years into the process), and, finally, more strongly Sinhalese nationalist parties and others who didn't feel themselves adequately represented by the Sinhalese-dominated government.[9]

The second major problem with the peace process was that engagement in it involved no serious commitment on anyone's part — not from the government, the Tigers, the Norwegians, or from other international supporters of the process — to transform the antidemocratic activities of the two major antagonists.[10] Whether with respect to the fundamental issues of constitutional reform at stake in the conflict or with respect to the ways in which each party governed its "own" populations, questions of justice — directed toward the past, the present, or the future — were off the table. Instead, the peace process was structured as a purely pragmatic deal meant to empower each entity in its current incarnation while preserving the balance of power between them. In effect, the two parties agreed that they would not challenge each other's power and position for the time being, but made no promises about — or showed much interest in — a principled process that would transform either their long-term relationship or how they treated those under their political control.[11] Instead of a process designed to move toward a just settlement based on meaningful democratic power sharing and accountable governance, there was a simple exchange: the government was to get the peace and quiet necessary for economic development based on international investment, while the Tigers were to get international recognition and investment, together with the consolidation and expansion of their military and political control over the Tamil-speaking areas they claim as their homeland.[12]

Equally damaging was the fact that the peace process included no mechanisms designed to enable *others* to pressure the two major parties to change their modes of governance, to act as checks on their behavior, or to develop independent initiatives for reconciliation or accountability that might ultimately transform the larger political environment. Thus, the cease-fire monitoring mission, staffed by representatives of Nordic countries, was given no powers of enforcement or remedy in the event of cease-fire violations. Nor did the monitors or the Norwegian government show any interest in interpreting their mandate to include the prevention of human-rights violations against the civilian population. The Norwegian government and other foreign states involved in the process actively resisted calls to establish an independent human-rights monitoring mission that would have been less involved with maintaining the confidence of the two parties involved in the cease-fire agreement. Nor was there any international support offered to those in Sri Lankan nongovernmental organizations who attempted to develop their own independent monitoring procedures.

Finally, and perhaps most importantly, the entire structure of evenhandedness between the two parties was built on top of a cease-fire agreement that in various ways allowed the Tigers to expand and deepen their coercive control over the north and east of the island, as well as over Tamils living in other regions. The cease-fire agreement required non-LTTE Tamil political parties to disarm, even as it allowed the Tigers to establish "political" offices for work in government-held territories. Yet it granted no reciprocal right for government forces or for cease-fire monitors to enter areas controlled by the Tigers. The result was the expansion and further entrenchment of Tiger control throughout the north and east, aided by a range of coercive methods: the assassination of hundreds of members of rival Tamil parties, the murder and harassment of Muslims who rejected LTTE control of the north and east, the forcible recruitment of thousands of underage fighters, widespread extortion from the civilian population, the manipulation of elections in 2004 and 2005, and the near-complete destruction of all independent political spaces in the north and east of the island.

In this context — in which the Tamil Tigers violated the cease-fire at will and exploited many opportunities available for the expansion of their rule through coercion and intimidation — the ideal of evenhandedness and the principle of balance between the two parties that underlay the whole process had devastating effects. Particularly damaging was the interpretation of evenhandedness that informed many people's responses to cease-fire and human-rights violations. According to this view, one was only allowed to criticize the violations of one of the two parties (generally the Tigers) so long as the other party (generally the government) had committed equivalent violations. Given that each side was violating different rights to varying degrees — the vast majority, and certainly the most egregious, cease-fire and human-rights violations being committed by the Tigers — focusing on the violations of the Tigers was seen by many, both within Sri Lankan civil society and within the world of international organizations and the diplomatic community, to be "unbalanced" and therefore both unfair and destabilizing. (Many were afraid that highlighting Tiger violations would run the risk of scaring them away from the peace process.) As a result, for the first three and one-half years of the peace process, until the Tigers' assassination of the Sri Lankan foreign minister in August 2005, only a handful of local and international groups were willing to speak out publicly against such violations.

The years of widespread Tiger violence and intransigence,[13] especially in the context of a noninclusive process, ultimately provoked Sinhalese, Muslim, and even Tamil "spoilers" who felt disrespected, disempowered, and in many cases, physically endangered by the direction that the peace process had taken.[14] Their growing resistance, both violent and nonviolent, to the terms on which "peace" was being offered has ratified the long-standing resistance of the Sri Lankan state to real reforms. That the Tigers were allowed to get away with murder not only weakened support for a peaceful and just settlement among Sinhalese and Muslims; it also fueled a desire for righteous payback in similar currency by violent Sinhalese supremacists and their supporters in the Sri Lankan government — a government that has continued its long tradition of using violence to quell dissent and maintain ethnic and class hierarchies.

In other words, the closures and counterproductive forms of evenhandedness that characterized the Norwegian-led peace process, both with respect to the "balanced" structure of the formal process and with respect to how cease-fire and human-rights violations were downplayed, have merely ratified and legitimated impunity on all sides, with destructive effects in all directions. They have also undermined the legitimacy of the Norwegian facilitators among many Sri Lankans, who view their reluctance to criticize Tiger "terrorism" either as a sign of weakness or as evidence of their pro-Tiger bias and bad faith. Since democratic and liberal elements in Sri Lankan civil society have been discouraged from raising human-rights issues, both by the ideal of evenhandedness and by the direct instructions of their international donors, the job of denouncing such violations has increasingly been taken up by Sinhalese hardliners who have no interest in reforming the Sri Lankan state. Their highly partisan use of human-rights language has had the effect of delegitimating such claims in the eyes of many. In the end, then, the lack of effective human-rights protections has meant that all constituencies — Tamil, Muslim, and Sinhalese civilians; government soldiers and police; LTTE fighters and anti-LTTE militants — have been made to feel less secure over the past four years. It is thus no surprise that violence of all kinds and from all sides has now escalated to the point that the cease-fire is effectively dead, even if it has not, as of this writing, been explicitly abrogated.

THE LIMITS OF EVENHANDEDNESS AS AN IDEAL

The inadequacy of evenhandedness as an ideal for intervening in violent identity-based conflicts or for judging such interventions goes beyond the specific design flaws and mistakes in mediation that have undermined the Sri Lankan peace process. As I will show with reference to current Sri Lankan controversies, the danger of using evenhandedness as a guide to intervening in such conflicts, whether these are carried out by international or local actors, goes much deeper. Attempts to respect evenhandedness as a guiding ideal inevitably depoliticize fundamental aspects of a conflict, even as they necessarily depend on — and help naturalize — particular and contestable political interpretations of what the conflict is really about.

The idea that it is important *not* to be biased or partial as a mediator in a conflict would seem, on the face of it, to make sense. Avoiding bias or partiality presumably includes not ignoring the legitimate interests of one or more group or party to the conflict and not having the interests of only one party at heart. But given that one can never fully satisfy all the interests, needs, and concerns of all the parties involved in a conflict, respecting this principle requires one to make choices about which interests, needs, or positions to attend to, to determine whose claims seem important and whose not, which are legitimate and which excessive or mistaken. Making such choices, however, amounts to making judgments that are fundamentally political and go to the heart of the conflict(s) in need of resolution. In short, while trying not to be biased or partial makes sense, it can have value only as a negative injunction, as a reminder of the ease with which one's interventions can be interpreted as favoring one side over another. When one attempts to give it positive content in the form of evenhandedness or impartiality, however, one is immediately forced to take a political stance on the conflict, a stance that is almost certain to appear less than evenhanded to one or more significant stakeholders or constituencies.

To put this point another way, the ideal of evenhandedness relies on a conception of balance. But imposing a balanced framework on a conflict that is certain to be unbalanced in multiple and incommensurable ways threatens to impose a particular vision of what the conflict is about and what its settlement should look like, precisely those issues that should be open for debate and discussion by all parties. Conflict resolution is certainly facilitated by recognizing that all parties and communities have suffered, that representatives of all communities have done terrible things in their names, and that the entirety of this suffering and violence, from all sides, needs to be recognized and taken into account. One can do one's best to respect this form of impartiality, however, without in any way holding that responsibility for past or present injustices lies in equal measure or in any kind of measure that one can ultimately hold evenly in one's metaphorical hands. Once again, then, the danger is that in the guise of a balanced, evenhanded, impartial intervention, a particular and contestable political vision is smuggled into conflict-resolution initiatives without public acknowledgment.

ASYMMETRIES IN VIOLATIONS

A more specific form of this problem rests in the fact that the ideal of evenhandedness offers no resources for negotiating the basic asymmetries that exist between the parties, whether they be the different forms of rights violations that each party commits or their distinct modes of power and domination. Ultimately, the ideal of evenhandedness founders on the absence of a common standard for judging the urgency or importance of rights violations, injustices, and antidemocratic forms of power.

As mentioned above, the cease-fire violations that received the most publicity over the course of the Sri Lankan peace process, especially during its first three and one-half years, were those committed by the Tigers, which included political assassinations, the recruitment of underage fighters, extortion, attacks on rival political parties, election fraud and enforced election boycotts, and the forcible control over civil society. These are all violations of civil and political rights considered fundamental, such as the right to life, freedom of movement and property, and the right to vote, speak freely, and organize politically.

Although Tiger violations were publicly criticized to a limited extent, many Tamil nationalists and supporters of the LTTE responded by strongly arguing that other violations needed to be discussed alongside, and in some cases, instead of, Tiger violations.

These LTTE supporters cited a host of other rights that they felt were of equal or greater importance and that were being violated by the government and ignored by many human-rights advocates and critics of the Tigers. Violations they cited included the continued existence of the Sri Lankan military's so-called High Security Zones, which have displaced Tamils from their land and thus violate the property rights of tens of thousands of families; the right of internally displaced and war-affected people to humanitarian assistance and to longer-term rehabilitation and reconstruction efforts; the denial of socioeconomic rights, including the right to health care, education, sanitation, and housing, suffered disproportionately by Tamils in the Northern and Eastern Provinces; the continued denial of the language rights of Tamil speakers; and, most important of all, the denial of the right to self-determination that belongs to the Tamil nation, the demand for which is at the heart of the Tigers' liberation struggle.[15]

Unfortunately, the ideal of evenhandedness cannot help us work our way through these disputes. Even if one agrees that all of these violations — whether of property rights, language rights, the right to life, or the right to organize politically — are of equal importance, which many would dispute, they simply cannot all be addressed in the same way, or at the same speed, or starting at the same time. The violation of most civil and political rights, for instance, can in principle be ended immediately, as long as the violating party has the will to change its behavior.[16] But the same is not true of other kinds of violations. For example, returning the property of those with houses in army-controlled High Security Zones would require reciprocal and negotiated demilitarization by both sides or risk destabilizing the balance of military forces on which the cease-fire rests.[17] While many of the rights to humanitarian assistance at issue should, in principle, be amenable to relatively quick practical interventions, the actual experience of the peace process revealed that serious progress on these issues can be achieved only through sustained cooperation between the Tigers and the Sri Lankan government and the through establishment of new administrative mechanisms.[18] With respect to violations of internationally recognized socioeconomic rights, this is a problem that plagues the whole of Sri Lanka, and it requires major institutional and economic changes in order to be overcome. Even in the (unlikely) best-case scenario, such reforms will take years, though they could certainly *begin* quite quickly, in part through attempts to address the especially high levels of poverty and lack of economic opportunities in the north and east. Finally, even if the right to self-determination of the Tamil people were accepted by all major parties as a legitimate claim — which is far from being the case — this right to self-determination would, by definition, require being elaborated and defined in institutional terms over the course of a long and complicated negotiating process. It is certainly not something that can be granted in any meaningful sense at the beginning of a peace process.

Trying to apply an evenhanded approach to disputes over the existence, value, and priority of the various rights said to be violated over the course of a given conflict is, then, ultimately destined only to provoke frustration and endless, unproductive debates.

Debates over the priority of different kinds of rights violations are particularly difficult to resolve, in part because they are generally informed by essentially political judgments about which entity, given its specific forms of power and domination, is the greater threat to justice and to peace — in the case of Sri Lanka, the Tamil Tigers or the Sri Lankan state.

On the one hand, the Sri Lankan state is formally democratic and preserves certain democratic features, such as regular competitive elections that produce changes in the ruling parties; freedom to organize politically, up to a certain point; media that are relatively free, though deeply — even ferociously — divided along ethnic and partisan lines; and a formally independent judiciary. The formal legitimacy of the Sri Lankan state thus garners it some degree of sympathy, along with material benefits, from fellow members of the international community of states.

Nonetheless, the Sri Lankan state has for the past fifty years effectively been an ethnocracy. Utilizing a definition of democracy as pure majoritarianism and dispensing with safeguards for minorities whose concerns are consistently outvoted, government policies have systematically favored the majority Sinhalese in both symbolic and material ways.[19] Moreover, the Sri Lankan state has proven itself capable of the most terrible forms of extralegal political violence in defense of both the ethnic and class hierarchies on which it is based. Maintained by an increasingly politicized and violent police force and a judiciary largely unwilling to challenge either elected authorities or powerful interests, the Sri Lankan state has proven itself able to resist all calls for legal accountability. In terms of its basic features, the Sri Lankan state and political system are effectively immune to political challenge and reform.[20]

The political closures of the state, however, are matched, if not exceeded, by those of the Tamil Tigers, who are more ruthlessly and fully antidemocratic and are easily labeled as "terrorists" by foreign states and by local critics.[21] More important than their use of standard terrorist forms of violence such as attacks on civilian targets is the terror produced by their desire for total control over the "Tamil nation." This desire for control is evidenced by the human-rights violations committed over the course of the peace process, including the murder and exile of dissenting voices, the elimination of rival political groups, the forcible recruitment of child soldiers, and the effective control over the activities and statements of organizations ostensibly part of civil society. The University Teachers for Human Rights, Sri Lanka's longest-lived and best-known human-rights group, which is composed of a small number of Tamil academics, describes LTTE violence in the following terms:

> The terror [felt by members of Tamil political parties forced to align with the Tigers] is an object lesson in the LTTE's methods of terror. Its terror has a dimension beyond being simply vindictive and irrational. One cannot play safe with the LTTE. The TULF MPs killed by the LTTE thought themselves to be playing safe. They all but acknowledged its totalitarian claims, never criticised it publicly and remained obligingly silent when their own

colleagues were picked off by LTTE killers, one by one. People are thus driven to be cautious to the point of not risking doing anything that may be taken amiss by the LTTE. *It is a degree of terror that a state cannot match.*[22]

And yet, many Tamils still see the LTTE as their best defender and their only source of political respect and leverage, especially since the Sri Lankan state continues to brutalize Tamil civilians with impunity.[23] Many also argue that, if given the proper support from the international community, the LTTE could slowly evolve into a more legitimate and statelike entity, able either to rule "Tamil Eelam" independently or to share power with a democratized Sri Lankan state. Indeed, many Tamil activists are reluctant to criticize the Tigers publicly for fear of undermining their struggle against the Sri Lankan state, which is considered to be the greater threat to their freedom and dignity.

Judgments about the different modes of power of the warring parties and the dangers they pose, in other words, are inevitably influenced by the forms and strength of a given critic's ethnic identification and by his or her particular ideological beliefs. With no procedure available for bracketing out such beliefs and forms of identification, it simply makes no sense to speak of an *evenhanded* accounting of the respective crimes and the level of danger posed by the different entities.

However much one might want to be evenhanded, the choices one makes about these issues, whether as an international or a local actor, will inevitably have *uneven* effects. One's interventions, that is, can never be neutral, because they will inevitably affect the balance of power, whether symbolic or material, between the parties in conflict. Nor would there be any way of knowing in advance what it would mean to be evenhanded in the sense of applying equal pressure to all sides.[24]

In the absence of a coherent and workable practice of evenhandedness, then, advocates of human rights, democracy, and peace are left with the task of challenging and attempting to transform the different modes of power of the parties on the basis of complex, contextual, and fully political judgments. Such judgments will be concerned with how the different forms of undemocratic and arbitrary power characteristic of the Tigers, the state, and other armed groups can best be engaged, in what contexts, and at what speeds.[25] More specifically, one must judge how to tackle different forms of rights violations, determining which ones are more urgent, how to sequence them, which are more open to redress, and so on. Far from heightening our awareness to these questions, much less helping us develop better ways of addressing them, the ideal of evenhandedness ignores or downplays the tactical, contextual, contestable, and risky nature of all forms of pressure and political intervention in conflict situations.

THE COSTS OF EVENHANDEDNESS TO DEMOCRATIC CIVIL SOCIETY

The dangers of attempting to follow an evenhanded or balanced approach are particularly acute for civil-society organizations — whether NGOs, popular movements, or small networks of activists — that seek the democratic and/or liberal transformation of society. The ideal of evenhandedness can easily undermine the ability of both local groups and their international allies to take an independent stand in pursuit of their own critical political agendas. Under the spell of the ideal of evenhandedness, liberal and democratic civil-society activists and organizations are easily tempted and at times actively encouraged by their donors to play the role of the mediator. In doing so, their central concern becomes balancing the interests and maintaining the confidence of the various negotiating parties, rather than holding them to account and trying to transform their methods.

Such has certainly been the case in Sri Lanka. Thanks to the influx of relatively large amounts of international funding, the Sri Lankan peace process saw the proliferation of peace and conflict-resolution initiatives. New organizations emerged, and established organizations expanded and/or redirected their work in support of "peace" and "conflict transformation." From small-scale grassroots community organizations holding peace rallies and undertaking interethnic community-service projects to Colombo-based elite research and advocacy groups sponsoring workshops on various aspects of the peace process, activities in support of "peace" proliferated. The goal for international donors in encouraging and funding this work was to tap into the peace-building power of Sri Lankan civil society. The job assigned to Sri Lankan organizations was to build peace by supporting the Track One process, which advocated a top-level both/and approach to the conflict. Thus, in the initial years of the Sri Lankan peace process, most civil-society activities in support of peace and conflict transformation primarily took the form of advocacy in support of the peace efforts of the Tigers and the Sri Lankan government, who were assumed to be the only important players and whose efforts needed to be communicated and sold to the general public.[26] The goal of these organizations was decidedly not to criticize either of these parties and their international sponsors or to articulate an independent political agenda of their own.

Unfortunately, these developments had a devastating effect on the work of human-rights activists and organizations. Most of the established organizations whose work had centered on the defense and promotion of human rights lost large amounts of their funding, as international financial support for civil-society initiatives was channeled almost exclusively to groups doing "peace-building" or "reconciliation" work of various sorts. Indeed, human-rights criticisms were particularly frowned upon by international donors and by many of the most prominent Sri Lankan civil society supporters of peace. Given that it was impossible to present a fully balanced list of charges against all parties in the conflict, the popularity of the ideals of evenhandedness and balance paralyzed critiques of human-rights abuses by making them seem unfair and/or destabilizing.[27]

Had the two main warring parties shown real interest in changing their ways, one might argue that public advocacy and engagement with them in support of Track One negotiations — rather than active criticism and resistance — would have made political sense. Unfortunately, many donor-funded civil-society organizations were so wedded to a model of conflict resolution that gave pride of place to evenhandedness and to supporting the negotiating parties that they failed to shift tack even as these parties actively continued to destroy the space for independent political activity while defending their ability to violate rights with impunity. This was most obviously the case with the LTTE, whose use of violence was blatant and relentless. But it was also true of the Sri Lankan state, which failed to criticize or try to prevent the LTTE's violence during the initial years of the process, and actively worked to preserve its own impunity for its past and ongoing rights violations.[28]

The lack of response to human-rights violations by those supporting the peace process, including civil-society groups, international organizations, and foreign states, had the effect of ratifying, in the name of peace, the underlying patterns of impunity the Tigers and the Sri Lankan government had exploited to maintain their domination for decades. Failure to address their systems of unaccountable power not only seemed to endorse a very violent form of "peace," it also helped undermine security and trust on all sides of Sri Lanka's multiple conflicts. Moreover, this lack of attention to abuses of power had the unintended effect of leaving the role of speaking in defense of basic human rights to Sinhalese supremacist groups. While they were legitimately outraged at the Tigers' repeated cease-fire and human-rights violations, these groups nonetheless had little interest in a just settlement of Tamil grievances. Their increasing prominence in debates over human-rights issues has reduced the discourse of human rights to an arsenal of rhetorical weapons used by partisans who refuse to apply the same human-rights principles to each side.

The failures of the Sri Lankan peace process reveal, among other things, that human-rights protections are a necessary aspect of effective and sustainable conflict-transformation initiatives. The ideal of evenhandedness undermines the ability of civil-society activists to articulate human-rights concerns. By doing so, it can also cripple effective *peace* work, which requires weaning people from their identifications with the warring parties, or at least from their acceptance of militarist nationalism and anti-democratic violence. Ultimately, for it to be effective, peace advocacy needs to argue against militarism and exclusive forms of nationalism and in support of democracy and human rights.[29]

FROM BOTH/AND TO NEITHER/NOR: TOWARD A MORE FULLY POLITICAL PRACTICE OF HUMAN-RIGHTS AND PEACE ADVOCACY

From among a small, but increasingly influential number of Sri Lankan political activists, there has emerged a different, more critical style of political intervention, one that appeals to human-rights principles to support the development of deeper, more sustainable forms of peace. Articulated through overlapping networks of supporters inside and outside the island, rather than through established donor-funded organizations, a shared style of political critique can be found in reports by the long-established network of activists known as the University Teachers for Human Rights, the work of the recently established and increasingly influential Sri Lanka Democracy Forum, and

A Sri Lankan journalist carrying a puppet depicting the country's police chief participates in a demonstration to mark International Human Rights Day in front of the police headquarters in Colombo, December 10, 1999 (Anuruddha Lokuhapuarachchi/Reuters).

the interventions by more ad hoc initiatives such as the Collective for Batticaloa, the Multi-Ethnic Coalition for Child Security, and the Coalition of Muslims and Tamils for Peace and Coexistence.[30] Their shared approach abandons the ideal of evenhanded-ness in favor of more confrontational and more fully political forms of critique, adopt-ing what might be called a neither/nor approach.[31] As we have seen, the both/and approach of the Norwegians and other international supporters of the Sri Lankan peace process allowed the Tamil Tigers and the Sri Lankan state to define the two (and only two) "sides" that were in conflict and that needed to be brought together. In contrast, the neither/nor approach uses the language and principles of human rights to *challenge* the militarism and exclusive nationalism of *both* the Sri Lankan state and the Tigers. This approach also challenges other groups that are party to the conflict to the extent that they share these militaristic characteristics, such as the breakaway faction from the LTTE commanded by Karuna and the Sinhalese-supremacist JVP, which has a long history of brutal, terror-filled insurrections and continued militarist and antidemocratic practices.

Seeking to defend and expand the space "in between" the various warring parties and in solidarity with all those who are literally caught in the middle of the violence from different sides, the politics of neither/nor invokes basic principles of human rights so as to say "no" to all forms of arbitrary, unaccountable, and antidemocratic power.[32] This politics demands instead that the people themselves be allowed to reenter and re-create the political space itself, enabling them to share power in nonviolent ways.[33]

The central principle of the neither/nor approach is that in their distinctive ways, both the Sri Lankan state and the Tigers have violently usurped the constitutive power of the people to govern themselves and to determine their shared fate and common policies. The underlying claim is that the people themselves — of all ethnicities — have political priority over both the state and those fighting to create a new state of their own. Thus, proponents of the neither/nor approach have explicitly rejected the idea that either the LTTE or the government represents those for whom they claim to speak — "the Tamil nation" and "the Sri Lankan people," respectively — and have rejected their right to monopolize the limited political space opened up in the name of "peace."

The neither/nor approach is thus clearly not evenhanded with respect to the major protagonists or their particular acts of violence and injustice, since it explicitly aims to weaken and undermine their power according to whatever political means are available. It does, however, consciously aim to challenge *all* human-rights violations, regardless of the agent, particularly those that destroy the fragile political space through violence, fear, and the deliberate targeting of dissenting voices. It aims to expand and democratize the tenuous space "in between" partisans, making it more inclusive, more equal, and more open to question. Nonetheless, it recognizes how fraught, uncomfortable, and unstable this middle position is: it's not the middle of evenhandedness or balance, but of being "caught in the middle" — as in "between the devil and the deep blue sea."

The neither/nor approach, then, in its ideal form, would be a quintessentially democratic mode of nongovernmental politics to the extent that it would be an independent project aimed at defending the democratic rights of all citizens against arbitrary, abusive, and illegitimate power, whether that of the state or of counterstate entities, and at resisting the closure of political space. While such a political practice would not claim to be the sole legitimate approach in situations of violent, identity-based conflicts, its proponents argue that it is the specific task of at least some significant portion of civil society to challenge and ultimately delegitimate the warring parties by naming their modes of power as one of the primary sources of the collective crisis that must be addressed.

Such an approach is political in another sense, too. While it is grounded in respect for basic rights for all and in principles of political openness and plurality, its universalism is a minimalist one and doesn't claim to offer neutral principles to resolve the dilemmas of democratization and peacebuilding. Instead, it consciously accepts the need to make strategic choices about which set of rights to defend and to emphasize at any given moment, recognizing that these choices will have political consequences that inevitably affect the course of the macrolevel conflicts, even as these consequences will be largely incalculable in advance.

THE PROMISE OF A NEITHER/NOR APPROACH

The argument here, then, is not that the neither/nor approach, through its attachment to basic democratic principles and to the fundamental rights to the political space, can overcome the problems and dilemmas that plague the ideal of evenhandedness. Indeed, the neither/nor approach is a more fully political practice precisely because it accepts and publicizes the inevitability of these dilemmas and the risks that come with having to negotiate them. The wager of this approach, however, is that such acceptance makes it possible to handle the dilemmas somewhat more effectively and thus offers an important resource for conflict transformation of a different, hopefully more democratic, sort.

How is this the case? First, a neither/nor approach helps define a minimal common ground of basic (democratic) rights that Sri Lankans from all ethnicities should, at least in principle, be able to agree on, given their shared vulnerability to arbitrary and violent forms of political power. In the case of Sri Lanka, as in so many other parts of the world, members of all religious and ethnic communities have suffered from — or are presently threatened by — abusive power from unaccountable political groups, both from their own and from other communities.

Second, a neither/nor approach aims to strengthen this sense of common rights by tapping into the power of political opposition that defines an "us" — Sri Lankan citizens and agents of democratic change — and a "them" — antidemocratic militarists, violent nationalists, and rights violators — that allows Sri Lankans to identify along new, political, differently ethnicized lines. The claim here is that any movement for political change requires a negative, critical edge that allows it to be against something, in part so as to help people clarify the deeper sources of their political suffering and in part to draw together otherwise divided constituencies. Citizens and agents of democratic change cannot re-create the political space destroyed through violence and fear without their own symbolic forms of negativity and exclusion. It is crucial to their political engagement to have an opponent that they want to defeat.[34]

Third, a neither/nor approach offers a position from which to criticize, challenge, and perhaps transform the antidemocratic nature of governance in Sri Lanka, which is at the heart of Sri Lanka's multiple conflicts, maintaining and aggravating polarized, violent group relations thanks to the universal impunity for gross violations of human rights. A neither/nor approach clarifies the nature of the political phenomena that need to be addressed for there to be a sustainable and just peace. By directly naming and challenging the violent and unaccountable modes of power characteristic of both the Sri Lankan state and its counterstate challengers — today, the LTTE — a neither/nor approach allows one to see more clearly the extent to which Sri Lanka's ethnicized violence was originally a manifestation of state crisis and still is to a large degree. The ethnopolitical divisions and violence that dominate political discussions are the product of that crisis, at least as much as its cause. This is true even as the two strands have, in practice, become inseparable as polarized and exclusive communal identifications take on a power of their own in reaction to violence and social exclusion done in the name of one group or the other. In order to address effectively the specific role played by the dynamics of antidemocratic power and governance, a neither/nor approach offers resources that the both/and ideal of evenhandedness cannot.

Fourth, where evenhandedness depoliticizes the nature of conflict transformation and operates on the terrain of good or bad faith, a neither/nor approach is more fully political and strategic; debates about how to pursue such an approach can follow accordingly. A neither/nor approach is rooted in a strong democratic project of reestablishing a political space freely and equally open to all and in a set of principles that are laid out as clearly and as persuasively as possible. Hence, a neither/nor political practice of human-rights advocacy makes considerations of how best to challenge and change undemocratic power the central criteria for doing its work and judging others' interventions, rather than the balance, bias, or good faith of the intervener.[35]

Finally, there are advantages that come from acknowledging that all political interventions, especially those in the name of basic rights, will have diverse consequences that can't be predicted in advance — consequences that might, in some cases, benefit those whom one wishes to weaken. For example, when human-rights critiques of the Tigers embolden the Sri Lankan state and Sinhalese supremacist parties to continue denying the role each plays in perpetuating the systematic injustices suffered by Tamils. By acknowledging the open-ended, unpredictable, and risky character of political interventions, a neither/nor approach opens up the possibility of more honest and productive debates about the politics of human-rights and peace advocacy, debates that will likely be focused on the costs and benefits of different styles of human-rights interventions and of particular rights claims and critiques.

REFRAMING THE USES AND LIMITATIONS OF EVENHANDEDNESS

A neither/nor approach thus ultimately aims to use human-rights principles to achieve a distinct form of both/and politics in which Tamils, Sinhalese, and Muslims can struggle together to create and control their own inclusive, nonviolent, and democratic forms of politics in the space "in between" and in opposition to the various warring parties. Developing this form of political struggle, however, is necessarily a long-term and exceedingly complex process. In particular, it is only through the slow and careful working through of conflict dynamics within and between different organizations and political groupings within civil society that one can have any hope of successfully generating common political identifications in opposition to unaccountable, antidemocratic, and illiberal power. Building a shared sense of being equal members of the same political community united by a shared set of rights requires acknowledging and reconfiguring, to some degree at least, existing — at times competing — ethnic and ideological identifications.

By articulating a larger ideological and strategic framework within which LTTE and government violations of rights can be battled together and where this shared struggle is accepted as necessary to making progress with *either* group, an effective neither/nor politics both requires and enables a sharper attunement to conflict dynamics than has sometimes been the case among human-rights advocates over the course of the Sri Lankan peace process. Just as proponents of peace need to recognize that defending basic human rights is indispensable for the achievement of their own central goal, so, too, human-rights advocates and proponents of a politics of neither/nor need to learn from conflict-resolution practitioners. Despite its challenge to the dominant modes of conflict resolution work in Sri Lanka, then, a neither/nor approach can be successful only to the extent that its proponents — and human-rights advocates in general — are better attuned to the play of ethnopolitical identifications and conflict dynamics when making their critical interventions. As part of this, something that resembles a practice of evenhandedness and balance is indispensable.

For example, during the first three and one-half years of the Sri Lankan peace process, many Tamil political activists were inhibited from joining the small number of human-rights advocates who were speaking out publicly against LTTE violations. This was not only because of fear of LTTE reprisals or simply because of ideological allegiance to the LTTE, but also because many Tamil activists saw the dominant approach of human-rights advocates as overly fixated on the crimes of the Tigers and insufficiently critical of the Sri Lankan government and military and their deep ties to Sinhalese supremacist conceptions of the Sri Lankan state. From this perspective, many Tamils remained silent in the face of Tiger killings and child recruitment out of a desire not to provide further ammunition for the propaganda work of Sinhalese nationalists.

Irrespective of the accuracy or inaccuracy of the criticism that most human-rights advocacy was "unbalanced" in its criticisms, the widespread nature of that impression among many Tamils suggests that human-rights advocates would have done well to frame their criticisms of the LTTE more clearly in terms of a global, neither/nor critique of all forms of violent, exclusive, antidemocratic power, which would also have put the structural and specific injustices of the Sri Lankan government front and center. Making clearer and more forceful criticisms of the government and/or the state, even in a context where the Tigers were the more frequent and bloody violators, would have provided greater cover for Tamils who might have been tempted to add their voices to such criticisms. It would have done so in part by undercutting the ability of Sinhalese supremacists to interpret the violations of the Tigers as evidence of a "terrorist" threat so urgent that it obscures the necessity of reforming the state and addressing Tamil grievances.

A neither/nor approach to peace and human rights, then, doesn't rule out all concern with evenhandedness or balance. Yet the evenhandedness at work here is different in important ways from the evenhandedness of the official peace process that was forced onto or adopted by so much of Sri Lankan civil society. Rather than aiming to respect the interests of the negotiating/warring parties, it aims to address the concerns of nongovernmental political activists across different ethnic and ideological identifications. This form of evenhandedness works to facilitate, rather than to shut down, criticisms of human-rights violations without any pretense of producing equivalent effects on the different parties. What appears as balance in this context is perhaps better understood as an attempt to expand the space in between the warring parties. By making clear the full range of those actions, institutions, and parties open to criticism in the name of democratic and human rights, a neither/nor approach better illuminates the historical and structural context for understanding specific violations. It aims, in short, to make it more possible for everyone, regardless of their present ethnopolitical identifications, to criticize *all* closures of political space.

In another sense, too, evenhandedness should not simply be ruled out from serving as a useful tactic. However clear the advantages of the neither/nor approach, the argument here is not that it could or should be the sole mode of intervention in situations of protracted identity-based conflict. Indeed, were one truly to accept the risky, contextual, and tactical nature of all interventions in the name of peace or human rights, one would have to recognize that in some cases the risks of adopting the ideal of evenhandedness might themselves be worth taking. In other words, the theoretical critique of evenhandedness sketched out above doesn't require the rejection of evenhandedness as a political tactic. For some organizations or political actors, invoking the ideal of evenhandedness might bring important enough benefits for its risks to be worth taking. This would most clearly be true for those organizations that place importance on maintaining access to the various parties in conflict, for example, representatives of foreign states that might usefully maintain channels of communication necessary for negotiations between warring parties, humanitarian NGOs and development organizations that work on both sides of a cease-fire line, or even local NGOs or activists who take on the role of maintaining contact across conflict lines in particularly tense times or locations. For this sort of political work, it is generally necessary to adopt a nonconfrontational posture and to convince the relevant parties in conflict that one's interventions aren't going to weaken them vis-à-vis other parties and that one recognizes their basic interests and has no interest in challenging or undermining their power. In such cases, the language and tactics of evenhandedness are clearly very useful.

For such interventions not to be counterproductive, however, it is important that evenhandedness be recognized as a particular tactic for intervention, rather than a goal that can actually be achieved. The idea and language of evenhandedness, that is, needs to be understood as a sometimes useful fiction, but a fiction that can be dangerous for all the reasons argued above. Its risks need therefore to be clearly understood by those who choose to adopt it for tactical reasons, and measures need to be taken to reduce those risks to a minimum. Equally important, evenhandedness must not be allowed to monopolize the political space and to present itself as the only legitimate mode of intervention (as happened with such disastrous effects in Sri Lanka). More confrontational and critical approaches must not be silenced.

Indeed, the argument here is that the risks of tactical evenhandedness are in fact manageable only to the extent that such interventions are placed in a larger, more political, and more critical framework. According to this framework, the overall aim of all those working for peaceful and democratic transformation of a given conflict — whether foreign states and multilateral organizations, international NGOs, local NGOs, or small-scale networks of activists — should be to defend and expand the space for democratic, nonmilitarist forms of politics that can challenge the hold of warring ethnonationalisms and the unaccountable power of their various representatives. The neither/nor approach is a crucial means to attain this goal, but not the only one: attempts at tactical evenhandedness or at "constructive engagement" designed to work in a balanced way with the warring parties can at times assist in this quest. But such attempts at evenhandedness need to be carried out with the overall goal of expanding the possibilities for democratic politics clearly in mind and only to the extent that one's best judgment actually holds that such engagement is necessary to and consistent with this goal.

FULFILLING THE PROMISE: DEMOCRATIZING THE INSTITUTIONAL CONDITIONS FOR HUMAN-RIGHTS AND PEACE ADVOCACY

Since the Sri Lankan cease-fire collapsed further into de facto war in late 2005 and early 2006 and the "peace process" became more of a misnomer, there have occurred a variety of international and local human-rights interventions that follow the general contours of the neither/nor approach sketched out above. These have included various reports and interventions by local human-rights groups that challenge Tiger, government, and other armed groups' killings and disappearances, as well as a long and detailed report by the United Nations Special Rapporteur on extrajudicial executions. The latter report clearly states that the purpose of political killings over the course of the cease-fire "has been to repress and divide the population for political gain. Today many people — most notably, Tamil and Muslim civilians — face a credible threat of death for exercising freedoms of expression, movement, association, and participation in public affairs. The role of political killings in suppressing a range of human rights explains why members of civil society raised this more than any other issue."[36]

While the increase in human-rights interventions is encouraging, they continue to have very limited effects. The force of the neither/nor approach remains primarily at the level of critique, so far without tangible effects, either on the warring parties or in terms of increased public protest or expanded opportunities to express oppositional views in public or to act in ways that defy the warring parties.[37] Interventions that follow neither/nor principles remain the work of a very small network of activists, largely without official support or endorsement from established local NGOs or prominent members of civil society.

For the democratic promise of the neither/nor approach to be fulfilled, it will have to move beyond this small band of activists and ad hoc networks and begin to shape the discourse and practices of the larger world of professionalized civil society concerned with political reforms along liberal-democratic lines.[38] But for the neither/nor approach to be taken up by this wider range of organizations and for the transformation of their political discourse and political strategy, in turn, to have meaningful democratic effects on Sri Lankan society, professionalized liberal-democratic civil society must itself first be significantly democratized.[39] Without more inclusive, representative, egalitarian, and contestable institutions and practices, Sri Lankan NGOs, intellectuals, and activists who invoke the principles of peace, justice, and human rights while pushing for liberal and/or democratic political reforms will remain cut off from the broader popular support base needed to give them their democratic energies and credentials. It is only by being in close physical, intellectual, and political contact with those actually caught in the space in between the warring factions that Sri Lanka's liberal-democratic civil-society organizations can come to understand and identify with their concerns in such a way as to speak for and defend them effectively.

In its present form, the world of established liberal-democratic reform-minded civil-society organizations suffers from severe democratic deficits. Primarily staffed and controlled by Sri Lanka's small, cosmopolitan, internationally connected, and English-speaking middle-class (read elite), this community of activists and organizations is neither socially nor politically representative of or very in touch with the experiences of the larger Sri Lankan public. Elite civil-society NGOs are also generally quite disconnected from the lower-profile, less professionalized, and more grassroots NGOs and popular movements that work on human-rights, justice, and governance issues outside of Colombo, as well as from the larger public with whom they work.

In part because of this lack of sustained social and institutional connections to non-elite Sri Lankans, politically reform-minded NGOs and activists find their primary sources of financial and ideological support in foreign states, multilateral organizations, and international NGOs, rather than in their own fellow citizens. This nondemocratic relationship at the heart of reform-minded civil society — a relationship of mutual but unequal dependence between more and less powerful elites —helps undermine the democratic potential of Sri Lankan civil society in a number of interconnected ways.[40]

Most obviously, it does so by giving international donors the power to set the overall political agenda of professional liberal-democratic civil society. Despite the rhetoric of and, in some cases, genuine belief in civil society as an independent source for transparency, accountability, and other democratic values, the financial leverage of donors means that much of the time, Sri Lankan NGOs function as the implementing agencies for policies devised elsewhere, without the knowledge or input of Sri Lankans. This instrumentalization of local civil-society organizations can take different forms. It can, at times, be fairly direct, as when NGOs are funded to perform specific tasks that they would not independently choose to pursue, or, as we have seen, when they are effectively restrained from being anything other than loyal agents of the donor ideology of evenhandedness and related models of peacebuilding.

The transformation of putatively independent NGOs and activists into instruments of nondemocratic donor agendas also takes place through the very form of the internationally financed projects they are funded to carry out. According to the implicit logic of such work, political change is imagined to come from discrete, short-term interventions carried out by Colombo-based elite organizations and shaped by the bureaucratic norms of proposal writing, budgeting requirements, monitoring and evaluation reports, consultant reviews, and so on. But rather than aiming at or facilitating the long-term political organization and empowerment of marginalized communities or those who have suffered injustice, such projects generally seek to train or to produce knowledge about non-elite populations (refugees, farmers, child soldiers, etc.) so that their needs and actual or potential crises can be better managed by others (the Sri Lankan state, INGOs, or other international organizations).[41] With their work shaped to a large degree by the imperative to produce and disseminate this sort of knowledge, and with the bureaucratic management and control it makes possible, local NGOs and activists have little room to develop or pursue their own democratic agendas. Instead, they find themselves incorporated into the larger apparatus of global governmentality.

Finally, the dependence of professionalized liberal-democratic NGOs on foreign support over the course of the violence-filled peace process has provoked an anti-NGO backlash among many Sri Lankans, most strongly from Sinhalese, but including those from all ethnicities and religions. Among many Sinhalese, there are grave and growing suspicions that NGOs are the covert agents of international forces designed to destroy Sri Lanka's territorial integrity (by dividing the island along ethnic lines), to weaken its sovereignty (through forms of neocolonial economic exploitation), and to undermine its cultural traditions (through increased Christian conversions of Buddhists and Hindus). Unfortunately, the anti-NGO and anti-Western backlash from Sinhalese (and to a lesser extent Tamil) nationalists — born of colonial humiliation and half a century of majoritarian hegemony and now exacerbated by fears of loss of sovereignty due to economic globalization — has been misread and underplayed by international donors and their elite brokers in professional liberal-democratic civil society. This is in part due to an insufficient appreciation of the roles that Sri Lanka's colonial legacy and resentment at class inequalities continue to play in Sri Lanka's conflicts and in part due to the lack of social contact between elite Colombo NGO leaders and the proponents — and non-elite recipients — of anti-NGO ideology. This social and ideological gulf severely limits the ability of established liberal-democratic NGOs to reach out beyond Colombo to a larger audience of potential supporters.[42]

For all these reasons, then, if they wish to do more than preach to the small world of the already converted, Sri Lanka's elite, liberal-democratic, reform-minded NGOs must begin to open up space — inside their organizations, between different organizations, and between the world of elite NGOs and the rest of Sri Lanka — in which their institutional forms and political priorities are open to question and to change. They must begin to address directly the widespread suspicions about their foreign connections and elite status; they must diversify their staffs and actively seek greater contact with and support from non-elite NGOs and the wider public, in part through adopting different modes of political organizing and different forms of rhetoric and dissemination of information; and they must devise ways to challenge their donors to take seriously their own liberal-democratic ideals of transparency, autonomy, and accountability so that the specific political agendas of international donors, as well as the bureaucratic and governmentalized organizational forms they insist upon, are open to criticism and change.

It is only when these democratic deficits begin to be addressed that a politics of neither/nor and human-rights interventions more generally will have any chance of gaining the political traction necessary to pose a real challenge to established modes of power. As it now stands, especially with violence and fear reaching ever greater levels, the most one can hope for is for the small community of activists already attached to a neither/nor approach to continue to plant its seeds of critique and challenge and to continue to make use of what remains of free political space, democratic energies, and habits to see their ideas and practices further accepted and institutionalized. The hope must be that someday, sooner rather than later, the political and organizational context will shift in ways that could allow for the growth of something resembling a democratic neither/nor movement for social and political change, one that could increase the chances that Sri Lanka's next "peace process" will be both peaceful and sustainable.

1   For one statement of this hope, see Mary H. Kaldor, *Global Civil Society: An Answer to War* (London: Polity Press, 2003). See also Kaldor, *New and Old Wars: Organized Violence in a Global Era* (Stanford: Stanford University Press, 1999), where (particularist) "new wars" are said to deliberately target (universalist) "civil society" for destruction. Finally, see Helmut K. Anheier, Marlies Glasius, and Mary H. Kaldor, "Introducing Global Civil Society," in *Global Civil Society Yearbook 2004/5* (London: SAGE, 2004) pp. 3–17. Also available online at the Centre for the Study of Global Governance, London School of Economics, www.lse.ac.uk/Depts/global/yearbook04chapters.htm#introduction.

2   The term "civil society" is a complex and contested one. It is often used in academic writings to refer to the social realm that is not the state, the family, or the market, or else, in a closely related understanding, to the range of groups, formal and informal, that attempt to effect social and political change without entering the formal political process of elections and party politics. Civil-society groups, in these definitions, would include trade unions, religious groups, small-scale community groups, and established nongovernmental organizations (NGOs). In either case, the ideological content of the political activity undertaken "within" civil society or by "civil-society organizations" is understood to be diverse. In the pages that follow, it is this meaning of civil society that is intended. In the discourse of international donors, however, "civil society" is often discussed as if "it" were a unified political agent acting on the basis of shared liberal and democratic values. Its existence — and growth — is thus generally taken to be by its very nature politically beneficial and something that donors should support. Operating on the basis of this homogenized vision of civil society, however,

has the effect of ignoring the antidemocratic and illiberal forces within civil society or else of defining them as outside the bounds of acceptable politics, an exclusion that often only further strengthens such forces. The idealized vision of civil society as necessarily liberal and democratic also has the effect of downplaying the democratic and liberal deficits within the actual operations of existing donor-supported organizations. For three distinct, and powerful critiques of the hopes placed in the idea of civil society as an agent of liberal democratization, see Neera Chandhoke, *The Conceits of Civil Society* (New Delhi: Oxford University Press, 2003), esp. chs. 1 and 2; David Rieff, "Civil Society and the Future of the Nation-State: The False Dawn of Civil Society," *The Nation*, February 22, 1999, pp. 10–16; and Partha Chatterjee, *The Politics of the Governed: Reflections on Popular Politics in Most of the World* (New York: Columbia University Press, 2004), esp. chs. 2 and 3.

3   For two criticisms of the emancipatory power of human rights, see Wendy Brown, "'The Most We Can Hope For...': Human Rights and the Politics of Fatalism," *The South Atlantic Quarterly* 103, no. 2/3 (2004), pp. 451–63; and David Kennedy, "The International Human Rights Movement: Part of the Problem?," *European Human Rights Law Review* 3 (2001), pp. 245–67. The latter essay is reprinted in David Kennedy, *The Dark Sides of Virtue: Reassessing International Humanitarianism* (Princeton: Princeton University Press, 2004).

4   For an analysis of one significant donor-sponsored civil-society peacebuilding initiative, see Alan Keenan, with Sunila Abeysekera, Dunja Brede, Wijaya Jayatilika, and Devanesan Nesiah, "Final Report of the Review Mission for FLICT (Facilitating Local Initiatives for Conflict Transformation), Colombo, Sri Lanka, June 2005. Available online at http://humanrightsandpeace.blogspot.com/2006/09/final-report-of-review-mission-for.html. The preference in internationally funded conflict transformation projects for relatively technical approaches that avoid engagement with the local power structures that fuel violence is part of the larger tendency of internationally sponsored civil-society initiatives to privilege technical activities — for instance, project proposals, seminars, training workshops, report writing — over political consciousness raising, organizing, and agitation.

5   The government and the LTTE met in Geneva in February 2006 to discuss strengthening implementation of the cease-fire agreement after a dramatic rise in cease-fire violations had occurred during the previous months. Despite official reaffirmations of their commitment to respect the cease-fire agreement fully, both sides again engaged in violence within a few weeks of the Geneva meetings, and a follow-up meet-

ing originally scheduled for April was ultimately canceled.

6   For an example, see the January 2006 exchange between the U.S. ambassador to Sri Lanka, Jeffrey Lunstead, and representatives of U.S.-based Tamil diaspora organizations at www.tamilnation.org/intframe/050110ugly.htm.

7   This is not meant to deny that there can be advantages to having a state with greater ties to and sympathy for one of the parties in conflict play the mediator. Thus, in the case of the role of the United States in brokering the Palestinian-Israeli peace process in the 1990s, the fact that Israel was so economically and militarily dependent on the United States gave the U.S. government significant leverage to push for concessions while also offering the Palestinian leadership domestic cover by allowing them to blame this "bias" for any failure to strike a stronger bargain. Of course, the advantages of such a model depend on the mediator's willingness to use its leverage.

8   The most consistent and prescient critics of the cease-fire agreement and the Norwegian approach to peace have been the University Teachers for Human Rights. Since before the formal start of the peace process, their reports (available at www.uthr.org) have warned of an unprincipled peace ultimately leading to an even more destructive round of warfare. For a review of the peace process written in late 2005, which analyzes in great depth its various limitations , see Jonathan Goodhand and Bart Klem, *Aid, Conflict, and Peacebuilding in Sri Lanka,* vol. 1 of *Sri Lanka Strategic Conflict Assessment 2005* (Colombo, Sri Lanka: The Asia Foundation, 2005). For an earlier critique of the excessively pragmatic nature of the Sri Lankan peace process, see Tyrol Ferdinands, Kumar Rupesinghe, Paikiasothy Saravanamuttu, Jayadeva Uyangoda, and Norbert Ropers, "The Sri Lankan Peace Process at a Crossroads: Lessons, Opportunities, and Ideas for Principled Negotiations and Conflict Transformation" (Colombo, Sri Lanka: Berghof Foundation, 2004), available online at www.cpalanka.org/research_papers.html. Finally, for an excellent early analysis of the need for the peace process to be "widened" (made more inclusive) and "deepened" (made to address the underlying political issues in dispute), see Sumanasiri Liyanage, "What Went Wrong?," *Polity* 1, no.3 (July–August 2003).

9   For a valuable theoretical and historical argument that Sri Lanka's conflicts can be understood and resolved only by taking into account the existence of multiple conflicts *within* the different ethnic groups, see Kenneth Bush, *The Intragroup Dimensions of Ethnic Conflict in Sri Lanka: Learning to Read between the Lines* (New York: Palgrave Macmillan, 2003).

10 The sole exception to this rule were the regular pronouncements by the U.S. government demanding that the Tigers "renounce violence in word and deed" and enter the democratic mainstream. See for example, Ambassador Jeffrey Lunstead's address to the American Chamber of Commerce in Sri Lanka, January 9, 2006. Unfortunately, the exclusively antiterrorist framework in which such demands were made obscured the role that the violence and injustice of the Sri Lankan state played in producing Tiger "terrorism."

11 This was the central argument made in Ferdinands, et al., "The Sri Lankan Peace Process." For a critical analysis of this reading of the peace process, see Alan Keenan, "Critical Engagement or Constructive Engagement?: Sri Lankan Civil Society at the Crossroads of Politics and Principle," *Lines Magazine,* May 2004, www.lines-magazine.org/Art_May04/alan.htm.

12 See Liyanage, "What Went Wrong?"

13 For example, the LTTE repeatedly raised its flag during public events in government-controlled territory, despite rulings by the Sri Lanka Monitoring Mission that this violated the cease-fire.

14 For a useful essay on the nature of "spoilers" in peace processes, see Marie-Joëlle Zahar, "Reframing the Spoiler Debate in Peace Processes," in John Darby and Roger Mac-Ginty (eds.), *Contemporary Peacemaking: Conflict, Violence, and Peace Processes* (New York: Palgrave MacMillan, 2004), pp. 114–24.

15 It is only more recently, with increased violence from Sri Lankan government forces from late 2005 onward, that LTTE supporters have raised complaints concerning murder, disappearances, and destruction of property carried out or condoned by army, police, and armed groups working with their assistance.

16 Most political and civil rights would be classed as "negative" rights, which require only forbearance on the part of political authorities in order to be respected. Some, however, such as the right to vote, do require significant human and financial resources in order to be realized in practice and made available to citizens.

17 For many analysts, the publicity given to this issue by the LTTE was rooted less in concerns for the well-being of those displaced than in the strategic advantage that would accrue to them from a reduction of the Sri Lankan military presence in the Jaffna peninsula. Evidence in support of this suspicion is the fact that the LTTE rejected the "Report on the Aspect of High Security Zones" written by former Indian Army Chief of Staff, Lieutenant General Satish Nambiar. Commissioned by the Sri Lankan government, the report called for a

process of reciprocal confidence-building measures between the Sri Lankan military and the LTTE in which the high-security zones would be progressively dismantled as the LTTE withdrew its long-range artillery and other offensive capabilities in the Jaffna peninsula. See www.hinduonnet.com/fline/fl20011/stories/20030606007713000.html.

18 The limited cooperation that was achieved, in the form of the joint LTTE-GOSL (government of Sri Lanka) Subcommittee for Immediate Humanitarian and Rehabilitation Needs (SIHRN), broke down within six months of its establishment, when the LTTE abandoned talks in April 2003.

19 The ways in which majority electoral systems, under certain conditions, can transform votes into ethnic censuses, with a high potential for political marginalization and ultimately violent resistance by minorities, has been noted by many political scientists and conflict analysts. For two particularly useful examples, see Donald Horowitz, *Ethnic Groups in Conflict* (Berkeley: University of California Press, 1985), pp. 83–89, and Jack Snyder, *From Voting to Violence: Democratization and Nationalist Conflict* (New York: Norton, 2000), esp. ch. 6, for related arguments about the destabilizing power of formally democratic elections in newly decolonized multiethnic societies.

20 Jayadeva Uyangoda's analysis of the obstacles to reforming the Sri Lankan state continues to be applicable today. See Jayadeva Uyangoda, "A State of Desire: Some Reflections on the Unreformability of the Sri Lanka's Post-Colonial Polity," in S.T. Hettige and Markus Mayer (eds.), *Sri Lanka at Crossroads: Dilemmas and Prospects After 50 Years of Independence* (New Delhi: Macmillan, 2000), pp. 92–118.

21 The decision by the European Commission in May 2006 to include the LTTE on its list of banned "terrorist" groups was a turning point in the Sri Lankan peace process and a delayed response to the Tigers' consistent and serious violations of the cease-fire agreement, as well as a result of intensive lobbying by the Sri Lankan government. The decision's ultimate effects on the conduct of the Tigers and on the prospects for a negotiated settlement remain to be seen.

22 University Teachers for Human Rights, "In the Name of 'Peace,' Terror Stalks the North-East," *Information Bulletin,* no. 28 (February 1, 2002). Also available online at www.uthr.org/Bulletin.htm.

23 Within the first few months after the November 2005 presidential election of Mahinda Rajapakse, there were a series of killings, disappearances, and mob attacks against Tamil civilians throughout the north and east and Sri Lanka, resulting in the deaths of more than one hundred Tamil civilians. See Matthew Rosenberg, "Sri Lankan Government Using Civilians

as Targets, Critics Say," Associated Press, June 19, 2006, www. signonsandiego.com/uniontrib/20060619/news_1n19sri.html, and D.B.S. Jeyaraj, "Again, in Trincomalee," *Himal Southasian,* May–June 2006, www.himalmag.com/2006/may/analysis_1.html. See also the reports from this period by the University Teachers for Human Rights (available at www.uthr. org), as well as reports by various ad hoc coalitions of representatives from a variety of NGOs, including INFORM, the Centre for Policy Alternatives, the Law and Society Trust, the Movement for the Defence of Democratic Rights, and the Free Media Movement, some of which are available at www. cpalanka.org.

24 Indeed, attempting to determine what "equal" pressure would mean raises a host of difficult conceptual and political issues. For instance, would equal pressure mean pressure that is equally damaging symbolically? Or pressure that pushes each party an equal distance toward democratization and/or liberalization? Or perhaps pressure that angers each party's supporters to an equal degree? Asking such questions reveals the impossibility of devising a calculus for gauging equality of pressure.

25 Part of the challenge here involves different asymmetries of support for and vulnerability to critique faced by the LTTE and the Sri Lankan state. On the one hand, there is the clear pro-state bias of the international community (composed primarily of states and multilateral organizations), whose essentialist discourse and policies of "antiterrorism" rule out the possibility of state terror. On the other hand, the Sri Lankan state is potentially more vulnerable to international pressure precisely because of its greater links to and dependence on outside forces. It is also subject to higher expectations — and thus potentially to greater demands — of democratic behavior, given its claims to legitimacy.

26 This is a point made nicely by Sumanasiri Liyanage's "Civil Society and the Peace Process," in Kumar Rupesinghe (ed.), *Negotiating Peace in Sri Lanka: Efforts, Failures, and Lessons,* 2 vols., 2nd ed. (Colombo: Foundation for Co-existence, 2006).

27 The logic of evenhandedness not only threatens to displace or devalue the importance of critical interventions in the name of human rights, it can also have the effect of colonizing and distorting such work. Thus, in the case of Sri Lanka, when activists and human-rights organizations have publicly challenged human-rights violations, their interventions have at times been shaped and constrained by the model of evenhandedness as balance. For example, such a notion of balance is relied upon in a press release titled "Sri Lanka: Act Now to Prevent Escalation of Violence and Abuse," issued on

December 5, 2005 by Amnesty International, available online at http://web.amnesty.org/library/Index/ENGASA3700420 05?open&of=ENG-LKA):

> The Government and the Liberation Tigers of Tamil Eelam must act urgently to stop the downward spiral of violence and human rights abuses in the north and east of the country, said Irene Khan, Secretary General of Amnesty International as she concluded her four-day visit to Sri Lanka. "Both sides use Human Rights as a political weapon — each accusing the other of abuses but doing little to stop the spate of killings, abductions, and harassment over the past year.... In this climate of fear, the voices of civil society and ordinary people are being stifled." The Amnesty International delegation listened to reports of rising tensions between communities. Muslim groups expressed concerns about murder, marginalisation, and discrimination. As one man put it to Amnesty International's research team: *"The Sinhalese are afraid of the LTTE, the Tamils are afraid of the government, and the Muslims are afraid of both." People of all communities are deeply fearful of what lies ahead.* [My emphasis.]

Explicitly intending to counter the use of human rights as a "political weapon," Amnesty's "balanced" approach nonetheless obscures the nature of the different forms of power and violence characteristic of each protagonist. In this case, it leaves out entirely LTTE violence against dissident Tamils. Until a few months prior to Amnesty's visit to Sri Lanka, most human-rights and cease-fire violations committed by the LTTE during the previous three and one-half years were directed at dissident Tamils. The Amnesty formula for balance also leaves out the crucial role played by anti-LTTE violence that came from Tamil fighters who broke off from the Tigers — the so-called Karuna faction — as well as the violence perpetrated by the Sri Lankan state against Sinhalese, which has historically been widespread and brutal and linked in important ways to the ethnic conflict between the state and Tamil militants.

28 The most important recent case of impunity and failure of the Sri Lankan judicial system to punish state-sanctioned ethnic violence is the May 2005 Supreme Court acquittals of those convicted in the October 2000 massacre of twenty-seven Tamil detainees in a government rehabilitation center in the Sinhalese village of Bindunuwewa. For an analysis of the case and a critique of the legal grounds for the acquittal, see Alan Keenan, "Making Sense of Bindunuwewa: From Massacre to Acquittals," *Law and Society Trust Review* 15, no. 212 (June 2005). Available at http://humanrightsandpeace.

blogspot.com/2006/03/bindunuwewa-massacre-justice-undone.html.

29 What this suggests, in turn, is that it is important to over-come the sharp distinction between civil-society organiza-tions that work on "peace" and those that work on "human rights." While "peace groups" might legitimately conduct a specific set of activities, such as interethnic dialogue work-shops, seminars on experiences of peace processes in other countries, workshops on power-sharing models, and so on, their work ultimately needs to be directed toward the same goal as that of human-rights advocacy. This goal includes the establishment of new, more inclusive, less violent, and more accountable political relationships, not only between the (formerly) warring parties or between civilians from dif-ferent "communities," but, crucially, between governing par-ties — whether state or counterstate — and those they claim to represent. Similarly, human-rights advocates need to think carefully about how their interventions can best sup-port moves toward peaceful coexistence, rather than adding to partisan and ethnic polarization. This is a point I elaborate below. For a useful discussion of the shared principles and practical tensions between human-rights and conflict-reso-lution advocates, see Ellen Lutz, Eileen Babbitt, and Hurst Hannum, "Human Rights and Conflict Resolution from the Practitioners' Perspectives," *Fletcher Forum of World Affairs* 27, no. 1 (Winter/Spring 2003), pp. 173–93.

30 Reports by the University Teachers for Human Rights are available at www.uthr.org. Statements and reports by the Sri Lanka Democracy Forum are available at www.lankademoc-racy.org. The report from the Collective for Batticaloa is avail-able at www.lankademocracy.org/documents/batticollective.html, while the recent report from the Coalition of Muslims and Tamils for Peace and Coexistence, "New Year in Trinco-malee: What is Wrong with the Geneva Talks and the Peace Process?," can be found at http://humanrightsandpeace.blogspot.com/2006/05/new-year-in-trincomalee-what-is-wrong.html. Some of the individuals involved in the ad hoc networks work in larger, more established organizations. It is important to note here that there are no established human-rights groups in Sri Lanka that address conflict-related abuses by the government *and* the LTTE. There do exist organiza-tions, mostly law-oriented, that take on cases against the government. These groups are generally staffed entirely by Tamils or entirely by Sinhalese. Finally, there exist multieth-nic research, lobbying, and policy reform NGOs, but these organizations do not generally pursue human-rights issues or cases and never take a clear neither/nor position.

31 My analysis of what I am calling the "neither/nor approach" builds on work by Sri Lankan writers and activists. It attempts to conceptualize the commonalities underlying various recent interventions, including those mentioned in the previous note. Notable recent essays informing this work include Sunil Bastian, "No War, No Peace?," *Polity* 3, no. 3 (April/May 2006), Liyanage's "Civil Society and the Peace Process," and various writings in *Lines Magazine* (www.lines-magazine.org).

32 A representative example of this "no" can be found in the report "Also in Our Name," published in July 2004 by the Collective for Batticaloa at www.lankademocracy.org/docu-ments/batticollective.html, which states that "unless peace makers attend to the imperatives of peace and not of war they will be greatly failing in their mission. Peace mak-ing should involve resistance to the operations of the war machinery." For another example, see Ahilan Kadirgmar, "Anti-War," *Lines Magazine* 4, no. 3/4 (November 2005/Feb-ruary 2006), www.linesmagazine.org/Art_Nov05_Feb06/Ak_EditorialNov2005.htm.

33 While the neither-nor approach has used the language of human rights to challenge LTTE and government forms of power, it could equally stress the importance and speak the language of interethnic reconciliation and apology (and perhaps even forgiveness). The discursive frames of recon-ciliation and apology can be powerful forms of neither/nor politics as long as the interventions done in their name are clearly oriented toward challenging and rejecting the spe-cific modes of power responsible for violence and injustice, for example, by generating acknowledgment that those who claim to speak in the names of one's own community have in fact committed crimes worthy of repudiation and/or apol-ogy. My point here is similar to that made with respect to postconflict truth commissions by Michel Feher, "Terms of Reconciliation," in Carla Hesse and Robert Post (eds.), *Human Rights and Political Transitions: Gettysburg to Bosnia* (New York: Zone Books, 1999), pp. 325–38.

34 For an argument to this same effect, see Liyanage, "Civil Society and the Peace Process." Liyanage's argument, how-ever, would be stronger if it acknowledged the difficulties that this oppositional approach to peacemaking and human-rights activism faces from the ethnic divisions that exist across civil society and between NGOs. Hence, I argue that the neither/nor approach needs to learn from the techniques of conflict resolution in order for human-rights and peace advocates to negotiate their way through and ultimately beyond divisive ethnic identifications.

35 Such a practice is political not only in distinction from the depoliticizing approach of evenhandedness, but also in contrast to the tendency of much human-rights advocacy, on either legalistic or moralistic grounds, to denounce violations as wrong in themselves.

36 United Nations Commission on Human Rights, Report of the Special Rapporteur on Extrajudicial, Summary, or Arbitrary Executions, Philip Alston, "Mission to Sri Lanka (28 November to 6 December 2005)," E/CN.4/2006/53/Add.5, March27, 2006. Available online at www.ohchr.org/english/bodies/ chr/docs/62chr/E_CN4_2006_53_Add5.doc.

37 Of course, it is during a period of rising violence and de facto war that we would least expect democratic activism and risk taking to be on the increase. This highlights a basic paradox of human-rights activism in situations of violent civil conflict: generally speaking, the more urgently the interventions are needed, the more difficult they are to generate, and when conditions shift and space opens up for more challenging forms of political interventions, the sense of urgency wanes, and other concerns — such as those of "maintaining the cease-fire" and "remaining evenhanded" — take precedence for many activists and international donors.

38 These groups, which I will refer to here as "professionalized liberal-democratic civil society," might also be termed "self-conscious" civil society. While they don't exhaust the realm of civil society, they often monopolize the discourse of civil society, especially among foreign donors and those intent on "civil-society building." Of these groups, only a fraction are concerned directly with human-rights issues. And of this fraction, only some approach human-rights issues in a political way, that is, challenging those in power. And of these, only a small part is political in a neither/nor way, consciously addressing the collapse of democratic and liberal governance, clarifying its links to the war and political violence, and struggling to challenge all warring parties and carriers of antidemocratic ideology.

39 This is a point I make at greater length in the closing sections of Alan Keenan, "Building a Democratic Middle-Ground: Professional Civil Society and the Politics of Human Rights in Sri Lanka's Peace Process," in Jeff Helsing and Julie Mertus (eds.), *Human Rights and Conflict: Exploring the Links between Rights, Law, and Peacebuilding* (Washington, D.C.: United States Institute of Peace, 2006). For similar arguments, see Jude Howell, "Making Civil Society from the Outside — Challenges for Donors," *European Journal of Development Research* 12, no. 1 (2000), pp. 3–22; and Peter Uvin, *Human Rights and Development* (Bloomfield, CT: Kumarian Press, 2004), ch. 5, esp. pp. 98–109. By "democratization," I

have in mind processes that would lead to elite civil-society organizations becoming more inclusive in the voices and positions and identities involved in the organizations' work; developing less hierarchical institutions; advocating positions that are more representative of the concerns, needs, and interests of non-elite Sri Lankans; cooperating more closely with non-elite organizations and non-NGO forms of civil society, such as trade unions; allowing their agendas and institutional ideology to be more actively questioned and revised by staff and supporters; and claiming the right to develop their agendas and institutional ideology more autonomously, with less control from donors.

40 The dependence is two-way, since NGO leaders are the local brokers for international donors, receiving financial support and status in exchange for providing information about, access to, and implementation in the rest of Sri Lanka. What they don't receive is encouragement to set an independent political agenda.

41 The anthropologist Steven Sampson offers a similar, but more lengthy and more devastating analysis of what he calls "project life," or the bureaucratic and governmentalizing practices of donor-built NGOs and civil society "capacity building," in "'Trouble Spots': Projects, Bandits, and State Fragmentation," in Jonathan Friedman (ed.), *Globalization, the State, and Violence* (Lanham, MD: AltaMira Press, 2003).

42 It is worth noting that there are other barriers to robust democratic and civil-society politics within Sri Lanka and other poor countries trapped in postcolonial conflicts. Partha Chatterjee, for instance, makes a fascinating case that to discover the full range of democratic energies in postcolonial contexts, one needs to recognize the limited applicability of the Western idea of civil society as the realm of the liberal, individual citizen. In a context such as India's, he argues, it is only a small and unrepresentative middle-class civil society that presses an explicit agenda of human rights and democratic pluralism. But there exist other hybrid forms of democratic politics at work in other social domains, including what Chatterjee calls "political society," in which average people, without the de facto status of full citizenship on the liberal model, nonetheless negotiate their interests with and through state and local forms of "governmental" power. In the case of Sri Lanka, analogous forms of political action remain largely unstudied. Were they better understood, there might be the chance to form more effective alliances between activists from non-elite "political society" and "official" or "standard," Western-style civil-society advocates. See Chatterjee, *The Politics of the Governed,* esp. chs. 2 and 3.

Principled Pragmatism

Gareth Evans interviewed by Michel Feher

Since January 2000, Gareth Evans has been president of the Brussels-based International Crisis Group, an independent global NGO with one hundred and twenty full-time staff members on five continents working to prevent and resolve deadly conflict. He came to the Crisis Group after twenty-one years in Australian politics, thirteen of them as a cabinet minister. As foreign minister (1988–1996), he was best known internationally for his role in developing the UN peace plan for Cambodia, helping conclude the Chemical Weapons Convention, and helping initiate new Asia-Pacific regional economic and security architecture. He has written or edited eight books, including Cooperating for Peace, *launched at the UN in 1993, and has published over ninety journal articles and chapters on foreign relations, human rights, and legal and constitutional reform. He was cochair of the International Commission on Intervention and State Sovereignty, which published its report,* The Responsibility to Protect, *in December 2001. He was also a member of the UN Secretary General's High-Level Panel on Threats, Challenges, and Change, which reported in December 2004, and the Blix Commission on Weapons of Mass Destruction, which reported in June 2006. He is currently a member of the Zedillo International Task Force on Global Public Goods and the UN Secretary General's Advisory Committee on Genocide Prevention.*

I'd like to start by discussing the origins, history, and purposes of the International Crisis Group.

The International Crisis Group (ICG) was formed in 1995 by a group of key international figures who were outraged at and disgusted with the international community's failure to anticipate and to respond effectively — in policy terms — to the series of disasters in the early 1990s that we all remember: Somalia, Rwanda, Bosnia, and Srebrenica, in particular. The feeling was that there had to be some new kind of international organization, with which many familiar and forceful international names would be associated, to send a real wake-up call to policy makers and force them to think about things they don't want to think about and do things they don't want to do.

UN peacekeepers and Sarajevo citizens take cover from gunfire on
the city's infamous "Sniper Alley" during Bosnia's 1992–1995 war
(Hidajet Delic/AP Photo).

The idea was born in 1993 on a plane coming out of Sarajevo with an interesting cast of characters on board: Morton Abramowitz, the U.S. diplomat; Mark Malloch Brown, then working with the United Nations and now with the UN Development Program; and Fred Cuny, a larger-than-life Texan humanitarian who was an engineer by trade and an energizer by disposition. Cuny almost single-handedly helped save Sarajevo during the siege by developing a water-supply system and generally cutting through bureaucracy and getting things done. The feeling was that his kind of experience on the ground could be translated into an organization that would be a stimulator, provoker, and shamer of governments, aimed at turning these situations around in the future. It was a very large ambition.

Yet the organization itself started small, with a series of preparatory meetings. There was a large group of supporters, but the initial implementation was low-key: two people operating out of a small back-room office in London, with the initial focus on the Balkans in general and Bosnia in particular. The organization came into its own in 1999, while campaigning to mobilize a response on Kosovo, where yet another human-rights catastrophe seemed imminent and the West was again dragging its feet. Right from the start, the Crisis Group became known as a nonwimpy NGO in that it was willing to advocate strongly for interventionist — namely, military — action if circumstances called for it.

So that's the birth of the organization, a successful birth with high aspirations in those first three to four years in the Balkans. But the subsequent development of the organization turned out to be more problematic: it faced a number of internal problems before consolidating into the kind of organization you see today.

By internal problems, do you mean technical or political?

The first executive director of the organization, Nicholas Hinton, who had been general director of Save the Children, died of a heart attack during a field visit to Bosnia in 1997; his succession was not a particularly happy event for the organization.

And Fred Cuny had already died in Chechnya.

Right, before he could play any substantial role in the Crisis Group, he was murdered in Chechnya. Also, in the first few years, the organization didn't quite know whether it wanted to be a supercoordinator of humanitarian relief organizations or a sort of super think tank, energizing the responses to problems without engaging in on-the-ground operations. This ambiguity is evident in the documentation of early debates about the organization. But once these various birth pains were resolved and the organization regained stable organizational footing, which seems to have coincided with my arrival in early 2000, we made a decision that we have stuck to ever since: we decided not to pretend that we're an operational organization capable of coordinating either governments or intergovernmental organizations such as the UN or its agencies, let alone bilateral donors and humanitarian relief organizations and NGOs on the ground such as Médecins Sans Frontières (MSF), Oxfam, CARE, or World Vision. These organizations, which all have very clear ideas of what they're doing, purport to intervene in situations of conflict as providers of humanitarian aid. Instead, we're focusing on being an interesting — and, I think, unique — combination of think tank, campaign advocacy organization, and group of policy analysts.

Our mission, in short, is conflict prevention in all its dimensions: preventing the outbreak of conflict, preventing its escalation and/or continuation, and preventing its recurrence. We have a role in all stages of the conflict cycle. Our methodology is also three-legged: the first leg is field-based analysis; the second is making policy recommendations designed not to be just abstract pronouncements, but very user-friendly to policy makers; and the third is high-level advocacy designed to influence opinion makers directly, rather than addressing the community at large. Though we are involved in grassroots campaigning from time to time, for example in Darfur, more often, we immerse ourselves in very complex problems that demand multidimensional solutions. Traditional mass campaign techniques — seven-second sound bites, relatively simple messages, and mobilizing broad community responses in the hope that they will translate into decision-maker sensitivity — are not what we do. That gives us a less visible profile, but it also means that we're playing a distinct role, one that complements the efforts of grassroots campaigners and human-rights monitors.

If there is any single characteristic that distinguishes Crisis Group, it is an intense focus on achieving a level of professionalism that will be recognized as such by foreign-affairs departments, presidential offices, and the higher reaches of the UN and EU systems. I don't say this to cast a negative aspersion on those who do things in a different way. It's just that we have our particular niche, our particular effectiveness, in being able to talk with policy makers in a language they understand. And of course, with our board being actively involved in advocacy and the organization employing so many former government people — starting with me as a former foreign minister, which is rather unusual for NGOs — we see our role as complementary to other organizations, not competitive with them.

It is true that expertise and professionalism play a very important role in the way that the Crisis Group seeks and manages to establish the legitimacy of its interventions. Yet, as you explained earlier, the sense of outrage that led to the creation of the organization did not arise from the lack of expertise and professionalism of the so-called international community, but from its failure to live up to the promises of 1989, namely, that of fostering the advent of a world where the Universal Declaration of Human Rights would become a binding text and where the democratic rule of law would become the norm, rather than the exception. Inciting policy makers to make good on these promises was thus an essential part of your original agenda, and I imagine that it still is. But do you now deliberately keep this aspect of your mission implicit?

The ethical foundations of the organization are based on a very simple proposition: that violent conflict and the horror, misery, loss of life, damage to property, and loss of expectations that go along with it is an acute human-rights violation. We are not a human-rights organization as such. We are a conflict prevention and resolution organization. I make that distinction because there are temptations for us to involve ourselves in situations all over the world that cry out for intervention, but don't have a particular conflict dimension to them. Very often, of course, we do plunge into human-rights situations in the broadest, socioeconomic sense, but only because they generate and sustain conflict.

To the extent that we stick to the prism of conflict prevention and resolution, we can legitimately claim that our action transcends left and right, that it is genuinely nonpartisan and genuinely nonideological. Whatever our personal orientations, all of us in the organization are driven by a single-minded focus on preventing conflict and the human misery it causes. Our ideology is essentially pragmatic — if pragmatism is an ideology in its own right. My touchstone in these matters is Deng Xiaoping, who said, "It doesn't matter whether the cat is black or white, as long as it catches the mouse." What matters is what works, whatever the ideological sensitivities we might trade on. Global policy decision makers share this perspective, so we speak the same language.

In my time as president, I've focused on getting the foundations right, on having a quality product that will withstand the utmost factual scrutiny. I am particularly obsessed with not exaggerating the evidence to make a campaign point. For instance, I've argued with my team about mortality figures in Darfur and the Congo, always insisting that we articulate figures we are confident about, and not merely present those we think will make a bigger impact. Whenever we make a mistake on any matter of factual analysis, I insist on immediate corrections, at least on the Web site. This can be embarrassing, but I think getting the facts right is a very important part of building a reputation. When it comes to policy recommendations, we try to be level-headed, clear, and well grounded. We want to push people to the edge of their comfort zones, but always have our own feet firmly planted on planet Earth. There is an important distinction here, I think, between us and other NGOs that seek to energize, sensitize, and mobilize constituencies, but don't necessarily come up with sharply focused, practical solutions, or at least with the compromises that are inevitably part of getting things right in the real world.

Let's go back to the notion of "what works." Human-rights organizations claim that they monitor and denounce human-rights violations regardless of context. It is both their mandate and their mandatory rhetoric to be perceived as giving precedence to their principles over the pragmatic compromises that policy makers consent to in the name of getting things done. In practice, however, these human-rights organizations are concerned with figuring out "what works" for their purposes, and they shape their strategies accordingly. It seems to me that you are in a symmetrical situation, in that you have to persuade policy makers that your proposals offer workable solutions, rather than strictly principled ones. In other words, you have to "sell" your efficiency and your pragmatism, even though there are clearly some political confines and ethical conditions that determine "what works" for you.

I don't mean "what works" in terms of what makes the trains run on time. I mean "what works" in terms of preventing violent conflict, which does mean that from time to time we will embrace pragmatic solutions that are perceived as offensive to some human-rights norms. A good example would be Charles Taylor in West Africa. The deal with Nigeria gave him amnesty on a conditional basis in order to stop the final stages, at least, of a very, very ugly war that would certainly have resulted in tens of thousands of more deaths if not for that tactic.

Were you instrumentally involved in Taylor's extraction?

No, we weren't, but we supported it. There'd been a lot of policy debate on whether Nigeria should just give up Taylor, as it eventually did, or whether amnesty should be perpetually observed so that future amnesty negotiations can be made with confidence. We favored a fairly firm position whereby only if the conditions of the amnesty were breached should Taylor be handed over, and that ended up being more or less the intellectual basis on which the Nigerians agreed to change course.

The Taylor case is a classic example of the kind of dilemmas we face. Another one we've confronted is the role of the International Criminal Court and the impunity issue. In the case of the northern Uganda Lord's Revolutionary Army, we squared the circle by saying to the ICC and to governments that influence the ICC: "Don't move too quickly in issuing arrest warrants and indictments against these characters; give the diplomatic route another chance. Listen to what civil society is saying in the region. Give the process time. It may well be disastrous to go to the court, because once you create that specter, you will never get these guys to accommodate." But when it became clear that time was not delivering results, we very firmly and publicly supported Luis Moreno-Ocampo [the ICC's chief prosecutor] and the court in their indictments, even though a number of NGOs still argue that it was counterproductive.

There is a constant tension; there are no absolutes here. On the issue of democratization, for example, and the rush to hold elections to produce a legitimizing government, we very often say, "Let's be cautious about an early validation process." If the conditions are not there to change the underlying dynamics of the country, and if the election is simply reinforcing what produced the country's problems in the first place, it may not be a good idea to move so quickly. That's the very unpopular position we took in Bosnia back in 1996; we said that the first priority is not elections, but consolidating civil society's structures to create a way out of the ethnic boxes in which everybody was firmly located.

This view has in fact become almost conventional wisdom over the last decade. Organizations such as the International Institute for Democracy and Electoral Assistance (IDEA), for example, have very clearly taken this position. There is much more of a focus on getting the "rule of law" and civil society structures right so that alternative political actors can find their footing, rather than engaging in reflex enthusiasm for democratic trappings as such.

Faced with a tension between different ideals, we always respond by prioritizing one ideal over another. Cambodia, for instance, is a classic example of a country that resolved its violent conflict, but sure as hell has not solved its civil-rights or democracy problems. I, personally, have had a long and close involvement in the Cambodian situation, and even though I have fought passionately about the human-rights situation there and would want to be involved in ongoing reform efforts, we have decided that this is not a role for the Crisis Group because it is not about conflict, but about other points on the human-rights spectrum. I think there is a logic and a consistency about our position throughout, but I can't pretend there aren't tensions from time to time. Our pragmatism is never at the expense of a very core, basic, highly emotional commitment to resolving and preventing conflict.

How do you "square the circle," to pick up that expression, in forcing your main addressees — for instance, Western governments acting as the leading members of the international community — out of their comfort zones when they are also your board members or close affiliates?

I would resist the suggestion that our addressees are narrowly defined. Our recommendations are targeted toward anybody who has leverage or decision-making capacity — direct or indirect — in a given situation. For example, we're publishing a report on Afghanistan as we speak. Target recommendations are made first to the Afghan National Assembly, then to the executive government of Afghanistan, who would contribute to the process of making the representative assembly more effective. The international community players are third, last in line because the particular issue here is developing a legitimate conflict-resolving internal structure that can be delivered by local players.

An awful lot of our recommendations on the Aceh situation were directed to internal Indonesian players, rather than to external ones. In other situations, the big guys and the UN will have the most leverage, either because there is no government, as in Somalia, or a totally ineffectual government, or in cases where local governments are so much beyond the pale, as in Uzbekistan or Turkmenistan, that there's no way to communicate effectively with them. In these cases, it's a matter of finding the leverage point that actually works.

The EU and the United States and the other big guys are very often the primary leverage appliers. Does that mean, in terms of the composition of our board, that we can't be as robust in making unpalatable recommendations? In my experience, that has not been a problem. Over and over again, we have come up with recommendations that are at odds with the prevailing wisdom both in Washington, D.C., and in London — and in Brussels, insofar as there is a Brussels. For instance, regarding the Israel-Palestine conflict, we have been very unhappy with the quartet approach to the peace process — or the "quartet minus three," as it has been more accurately described — in light of the minimal influence exercised by the EU, the UN, and Russia, compared with the United States.

In the context of Iran right now, too, we are advocating an approach that departs from that of the United States and the European Three, but we hold the board together because the underlying analysis has been unimpeachable — nobody can claim we are distorting the evidentiary foundations to make a particular case. The board understands our policy recommendations as thoughtful, well-intentioned, and nonideological — practical by nature. While the board itself is all over the place in terms of its ideological orientation, we still have a predominance — to my mind, an unhealthy predominance — of North American and

Western European board members. Achieving the right balance is still a work in progress. But even with that predominance, there are so many internal divisions. If you look at Zbigniew Brzezinski's position on Iran in comparison with that of Kenneth Adelman or William Shawcross, for example, you immediately see their ideological diversity.

Does this ever create barriers to your working together?

There was only one time in our history that an internal division almost caused a meltdown in the organization: in the run-up to the Iraq war. I wanted to publish a report saying that the case for military intervention had simply not been made. A majority of my executive committee at that stage took a very different view. Some have since moderated their position as history has caught up with them. But then, I faced a problem — an interesting one for many in my sort of position — in that, technically, I am bound in policy matters by the approval of the board and executive committee. In practice, however, I am given an enormous amount of freedom; with these fast-moving reports, you couldn't possibly seek formal endorsement for everything. But the process, as always with chief executives, is to use your own judgment about what will be going too far, what will bring down the wrath of the board upon you and make you lose your job.

In this case, I had to decide whether to accept the majority position of the executive committee, which happened to be meeting at the time, or appeal to the full board to contradict them. Had I gone to the full board, I probably would have had a 70-30 vote against the paper I wanted to put out, so I made a political judgment not to publish it. I knew that the whole world was intensely divided on this issue, and it was likewise a hugely divisive event in this organization. It would have constituted grounds for resigning for a whole bunch of people, which would have torn the organization apart and split us along left/right lines. And so I decided that, all things considered, we were more useful to the universe as a united organization. We compromised and produced a report that didn't take a position, but meticulously examined the pros and cons of each side of the argument. In the end, I suspect that the balanced report we published proved more influential — and more efficient as an indictment of the war — than one that passionately concluded that the war was misconceived.

What is the atmosphere like in your board meetings?

The board meetings are extremely interesting. They are spread over two days, with three of the sessions devoted to policy discussion and one to housekeeping. We articulate the issues and give guidance, without drawing conclusions, which has been extremely valuable in supporting debate. The discussions are of higher quality than at any university conference I've ever been to and certainly than at any other governmental meeting. People get engaged, have great ideas, and very clear thinking emerges. On an issue such as the Middle East, which one might think would be incredibly divisive, we've managed to sustain a broad consensus on the two-state solution through all the ups and downs of the last ten years. I don't really recognize the universe you might be imagining, of strongly held positions and conflicts between superpower representatives. It's a much more fluid foreign-policy-making and -recommending environment.

Structurally, how is the "we" constructed? "We" advocate, "we" decide how. . . .

Technically, deciding which projects we take up starts with me and the staff, who determine which issues we can add value to. For example, for a long time, we decided to stay out of the Sri Lanka situation because we thought it was moving toward a resolution. We also thought the Norwegians were doing as much as anyone could as mediators, and there were plenty of other NGOs on the ground. But over time, it has become apparent that this is an intractable conflict with the prospect of full-scale war breaking out again. So we've reconsidered.

Then there's the formal business of board endorsement. Financial considerations are important, because our projects are quite expensive. We don't like just sitting behind computers in capital cities such as Washington, D.C., or Brussels, and we don't like having consultancies with people flying in and flying out, if we can avoid it. We like to establish an organization on the ground and really immerse ourselves in the problem, and that's from $250,000 to $300,000 a year minimum, per project.

When it comes to our written analysis, I write the reports based on recommendations from the program directors, who in turn consult with people on the ground and with our people in Washington and New York who listen to the UN agenda and consider the issues coming up on the horizon. A good report takes at least three or four months of solid fieldwork to produce. It's not just a matter of getting something from the field and putting staples in it and a cover around it — it's an iterative process. We try to stay ahead of the curve but, of course, our predictions are constantly overturned by the real world. Things — events — happen.

Finally, there's input from New York, Washington, and Brussels, the Europeans especially, and the UN. The report goes in draft form to our board, which is divided up into regional working groups. At the penultimate stage of a paper, twelve to fifteen board members see a copy and have a few days to respond to it, to provide a reality check and to offer new ideas. Then, ultimately, it comes back to me to sign off on, or not, as the case may be. I have two or three reports in my bag at the moment that have been going back and forth by e-mail for weeks now among our team. The final product is an institutional product that bears all of our imprints. The personal touch of people on the ground and program directors comes in via the op-eds and interviews they do under their own names, but we never allow anyone to define himself or herself as the primary author of a particular Crisis Group product. It's a house product with a house style.

We focus on consistency. If we're talking about Islamism as a phenomenon in North Africa, we want to apply the same terminology and conceptual framework to a Southeast Asia report. To the extent that there are differences, we adjust, but we have a principled conceptual framework. And when we change our mind or direction, we articulate that change: you'll find footnotes saying, "In the last report we had a different take on this and here's why our position has changed." I think policy makers appreciate this continuity, because in their institutional frameworks, they can't really flit about like butterflies or mosquitoes from one thing to another. We recognize that the engines grind that way.

I'd like to end by asking about two recent developments. The first is your new appointment to the UN Genocide Committee. I'm wondering how you are going to negotiate between that role and leading the Crisis Group. And second, it seems that the Crisis Group is involved in new ways in the grassroots movement gathering around the Darfur conflict and in giving its seal of approval, or at least its name, to the new MTV/George Clooney digital activism project. Joining in these kinds of civil-society campaigns seems to be a departure for an NGO like yours that usually insists on speaking the same language as the policy makers.

The UN appointment is just to an advisory panel and will not be very time consuming. It's an opportunity to bring a Crisis Group perspective to the UN and to work much more closely with Juan Mendez [the UN's Special Advisor on the Prevention of Genocide] and the small group of people around him. It also provides us better insight into crafting appropriate policy responses for him to recommend to the Security Council. We've maneuvered ourselves into a position of having a relevant voice on policy-making issues in this area, so this appointment is an opportunity.

As for Darfur, as I said, we are not usually a message-bearing campaign organization. We don't need to be one financially and, in fact, we choose not to be, because it might compromise our effectiveness with policy makers. Nonetheless, there are times when the magnitude of a particular situation requires mobilizing a grassroots constituency in order to get governments into action mode — as distinct from analysis mode — and this leads us to participate in campaigns. Darfur is such an exception, where I think we belong with Human Rights Watch and Amnesty and a whole bunch of others. We've been particularly effective on U.S. college campuses. John Prendergast, one of our senior advisors, is a force of nature in these grassroots methods, speaking to campuses all over the country. He succeeded in mobilizing the Los Angeles Star Brigade to get involved in Darfur and Uganda. My constant refrain to him has been, "Hey, you do it, but the message that you are getting out there must be a Crisis Group message." While there are these occasional exceptions — all quite complementary to our basic mission — we've made a very deliberate decision not to turn ourselves into a generic campaign organization, because that would be counterproductive to our basic mission. We do best by sticking to our particular niche.

MOTIVES

HUMANITARIAN CARE

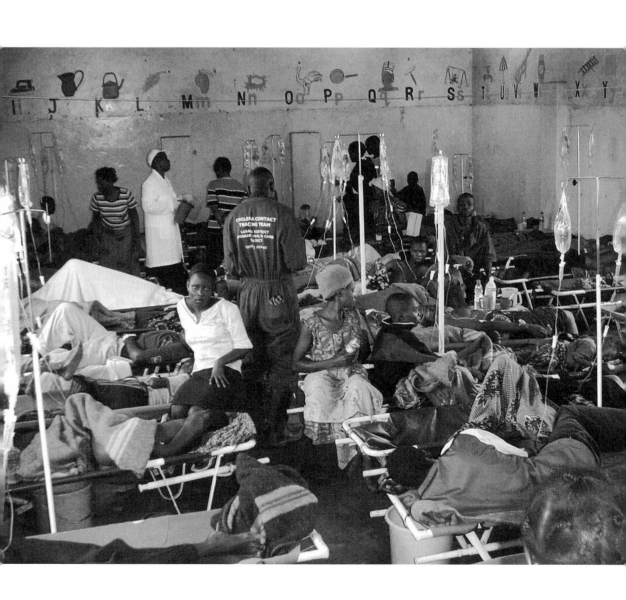

Learning from Dilemmas

Rony Brauman interviewed by Michel Feher and Philippe Mangeot

Rony Brauman was the president of the French humanitarian organization Médecins Sans
Frontières from 1982 to 1994 and founder of Liberté Sans Frontières. He is the coauthor,
together with Eyal Sivan, of the documentary film The Specialist *on the Eichmann trial.*
His publications include Devant le mal — Rwanda: Un génocide en direct *(1994);* L'Action
humanitaire *(1995);* Les Médias et l'humanitaire *(1996); an interview with Philippe Petit,*
Humanitaire: Le dilemme *(2002); and an interview with Catherine Portevin,* Penser dans
l'urgence: Parcours critique d'un humanitaire *(2006). Brauman is a researcher at the Méde-*
cins Sans Frontières Foundation and teaches at the Institut d'études politiques in Paris.

Let's start with two recent public positions taken by Médecins Sans Frontières (MSF)
on the war in Iraq and the situation in Darfur. In the case of Iraq, from the outset of
the U.S.-led campaign, you have refused to take a stand either for or against the war.
On the one hand, MSF has been very critical of those NGOs that have accepted being
embedded in U.S. military units. But, on the other hand, you did not sign the statement
released by another group of humanitarian NGOs that called the war unjustifiable.[1]
Concerning Darfur, MSF has not only challenged the claims of genocide in Darfur but
has also questioned the value of the so-called "humanitarian interventions" that such
claims are meant to bring about.[2] How do these two stances fit with previous public
positions taken by MSF — in particular, vis-à-vis the Bosnian war between 1992 and 1995
and the Rwandan genocide in 1994, when MSF famously proclaimed that "doctors can't
stop a genocide"? Would you say that your outlook has changed over the last decade?

There was nothing particularly special about our position on Iraq. What *was* special was
the context in which we took it, the web of discourses of the campaign launch. After all,
humanitarian organizations very rarely take it upon themselves to declare that a war or a
resistance movement is or is not justified. Whether you look at Mozambique, Afghanistan,
Colombia, the Israeli-Palestinian conflict, or the civil war in Algeria, in all those cases, no

A school building converted by MSF into a cholera treatment center
during an epidemic in Chawama, Mozambique (Keni Soler/MSF).

one called for intervention or made statements of support for this or that side. From the standpoint of humanitarian action, there is indeed no reason to distinguish either between this and that conflict or between any of the parties involved in a conflict — even when some of the parties are international organizations such as the MONUC (United Nations Organization Mission in the Democratic Republic of the Congo) in the Congo or the ISAF (International Security Assistance Force) in Afghanistan. I myself can have opinions on these matters, but a humanitarian organization as such cannot. An NGO such as MSF must seek to establish a purely pragmatic relationship with the warring parties on the ground; we must fashion our interactions with them according to the goals of our humanitarian mission — regardless of whether these parties are there to keep peace, maintain war, fight terrorism, or accomplish any sort of project, laudable or otherwise. The fact is, we are a party with a specific involvement in the conflict, and we demand to be treated as such. Thus, from our standpoint as a humanitarian agency, the American intervention in Iraq was not a special case. Of course, it generated substantial opposition, but the political rifts created by the war were not relevant to our perspective; this is why we refused to take sides.

The same goes for our position on the Sudan: we treat the different factions involved in the Darfur crisis (militias, insurgents, inter-African forces, government forces, and soon, perhaps, UN peacekeepers) as parties with whom we maintain close and more or less tense relations — based on whether they respect our position and our work — but among whom we don't consider it our place to take sides.

There is still something unique and novel about your approach to Darfur. MSF has not only rejected the notion that the terror campaign led by the Sudanese government constitutes genocide. You have also questioned the wisdom of the military intervention that the qualification of genocide is meant to prompt. That seems to go beyond your professed neutrality about whether military interventions are justified. Moreover, there have been moments in MSF's history when the organization's preoccupation with impartiality could be seen as compatible with actual calls for such military interventions.

To understand our position, it is important to ponder the very unusual semantic and political context in which the term "genocide" is currently situated. Today, "genocide" is given two very different meanings. One of them is overwhelmingly and inevitably tied to the Holocaust, the Shoah (I don't usually use that term, but it is unavoidable here). Yet there is another usage of the word "genocide," just as frequent, albeit less explicitly recognized, that entails applying it to any major massacre. And this is not merely a "popular" usage of the term. The United Nations International Law Commission has given genocide a broad definition that now informs jurisprudence whereby any massacre of a certain magnitude that occurs in a limited time and space may be called "genocide." Why? First, because such a massacre is necessarily the result of logistical planning. Among other things, it involves preparing the terrain and procuring material assets (for example, the requisition of public-works equipment to dig holes and bury bodies, as occurred in Srebrenica). Then, from the evidence of planning, the UN texts deduce the existence of an intention to commit the massacre, linked to the targeting of a specific population. They thus conjure up the two main characteristics of genocide. This extensive legal definition of genocide coexists more or less harmoniously with the first meaning of the word — whereby genocide refers to events of the magnitude of the Holocaust. The conflation of the two definitions means that a massacre called "genocide" is considered a more serious evil than all other crimes and thus one that requires military intervention either to prevent it or, at least, to stop it. In other words, once you call something a "genocide," it necessarily affects the prioritization of the response. In that respect, bringing food and medicines to people who are about to be massacred is bound to be a low priority. It could even be considered a somewhat shocking proposition, almost an insult to the future victims. This is the famous paradigm of the Red Cross at Auschwitz: to call a massacre "genocide" is to suggest that emergency aid is secondary and that the only important thing to do is to incite a public outcry capable of generating pressure for an international military intervention. This frames the question in all-or-nothing terms.

Thus, the purpose of the position we took on Darfur was to escape this deceptive framework. If we follow UN jurisprudence, it is perfectly correct to speak of "genocide" in Darfur — we are indeed witnessing a planned and targeted massacre. However, the only thing that this reveals is the malleability of the term and the inability of the UN legal texts to describe a political situation accurately. What is happening in Darfur? At the outset of the crisis, insurgents took up arms in order to demand a fairer distribution of power and resources. And their demand was met by a strictly violent — that is military, rather than political — response on the part of the Sudanese government and its allies in the region. What ensued was a brutal and extremely deadly counterinsurgent campaign similar to those the Sudan had experienced at other times. In Darfur, as previously in southern Sudan, the Sudanese regime is marginalizing certain regions and populations to benefit those who constitute its main base. What we are witnessing is the violent construction of a national space where the demands being expressed by the marginalized groups are political. However, the political dimension of the situation is overshadowed by the metaphysical representation of the situation entailed by the notion of genocide.

Consequently, we have relied on the work of people such as Roland Marchal and Marc Lavergne, just to name two of the most subtle French thinkers on the topic of Darfur. Their work has allowed us to recognize the value of the political aspect of the conflict and thereby to reopen the question of humanitarian aid and stress its urgency. Our position was that providing humanitarian aid was indeed urgent for the people of Darfur if "death by attrition" was to be avoided ("death by attrition" in the sense that one speaks of "genocide by attrition" for the American Indians or for the Armenians). Such a death would result from either the exhaustion or the explosion of the diseases that would inevitably occur when two million people have been displaced. For us, producing an intelligible political description of the situation was thus a way of reintroducing the need for humanitarian aid and the conditions necessary for providing it as a vital priority — something that was simply foreclosed when the situation was analyzed in terms of genocide.

So, to answer your question: no, I don't believe we changed our position. On the contrary, it seems to me that both reflect MSF's ethos: MSF is an organization that insists on remaining outside the political arena, yet seeks to understand the political context in which it intervenes in order to demarcate better the humanitarian field and to safeguard the conditions necessary for humanitarian work.

At the risk of delighting the Khartoum regime — which could hardly have expected that a Nobel Peace Prize recipient would lend support to its claim that there was no genocide taking place in Darfur?

Khartoum, of course, assumed our position and used it as an argument against the accusation of genocide. The appropriation of our discourse certainly created tensions within MSF. But we quickly got over that — what's important for us is to know that we can stand behind what we are saying; we are not concerned with how our positions are used in public debates and for political purposes. To worry about that would mean condemning ourselves to silence. Our role is not — and I want to emphasize this — to take part in the debate over legal definitions: it is not our place to argue about when a massacre should be called a "crime against humanity," a "war crime," or a "genocide." Our role is to describe a situation with tools that are relevant to *us*, focusing on the consequences that the description has for an aid organization that refuses to discriminate between the populations it assists. Thus, for our purposes, it is crucial to stay clear of notions that obfuscate the situation. Avoiding these notions is a necessary condition if one is to speak with any precision about the destruction of villages, harvests, and livestock, terror strategies, and killings that are taking place in Darfur — all these counterinsurgency techniques, dating back to colonial times, that are meant to impose order on the outlying areas of the Sudan. In short, our goal is to describe war processes, the techniques of violence employed by the parties involved, and the consequences of these practices so that we can identify the kind of responses that are available to us as a humanitarian agency.

This effort to repoliticize situations is at the heart of MSF's ethics. During the first half of the 1990s, you criticized the concept of "humanitarian crisis," which was then frequently used to describe violent regional and local conflicts, because you saw it as a way of "depoliticizing" the situation it sought to describe. Today, you criticize the frequent use of the word "genocide" because you see it as a way of giving a "metapolitical" meaning to local and regional conflicts. And yet, despite this undeniable consistency on the part of MSF, there is still a difference between your position on Darfur today and the one you held in the early 1990s regarding the wars in the former Yugoslavia. Such a contrast is all the more striking because there are some remarkable similarities between Omar Hassan Al-Bashir's strategy in Darfur and Slobodan Milosevic's project. In both cases, the same relationship exists between a central power with nationalist ambitions (in Belgrade yesterday, in Khartoum today) and its local clients who exploit the situation to carry out their own agendas (the Bosnian Serb militias of Mladic and Karadzic in Bosnia a decade ago, the Janjaweed militias today in Darfur); there is also the same

Recognizing that many parents are unable to bring their children to the vaccination points, MSF deploys a mobile vaccination team to fight measles in Darfur (Kris Torgeson/MSF).

type of ethnic instrumentalization, and so on. Despite these structural similarities, MSF declared that delivering sandwiches to a population facing an impending massacre was improper back in the early 1990s. Moreover, you emphasized the remissness of the international community — which, at the time, claimed to be essentially concerned with delivering humanitarian aid to the besieged population of the Bosnian cities — in the face of a program of ethnic and nationalistic cleansing. Should we not then speak about a shift in the way MSF has decided to treat a similar type of conflict?

One can even name it a contradiction. I think with Bosnia, we went too far in our criticism of the "humanitarian alibi." At the time, I was president of MSF-France, and my public positions determined the orientation of the organization. I was obsessed with the idea that we would become like the Red Cross delegation during the Second World War, handing out packages to people who would be exterminated shortly thereafter. I have managed to move beyond this misplaced fear, if only by informing myself, thanks to Jean-Claude Favez's pioneering work on what the ICRC [International Committee of the Red Cross] did — and did not do — during the Second World War.[3] The work that I did with Eyal Sivan for our film on Eichmann also helped to change my mind.[4] But I also think that my positions on Bosnia could be looked at as expressions of *inertia* — in the physical sense of the word. To a large extent, I still inhabited the perspective developed within MSF during the 1980s. At the time, with people such as Claude Malhuret, we were clearly stating that MSF's mission was to defend a liberal conception of human rights. In the context of the Cold War, we believed that liberal democracies were the natural base for humanitarian organizations because of their undeniable superiority over totalitarianism. We were very explicitly influenced by Hannah Arendt, and, in our own way, we adopted Raymond Aron's schema of the conflict between *human rights* — civil and political rights derived from a categorical imperative — and *collective rights* — which belong to the realm of desirable social projects.

During the Bosnian war, I was at a crossroads. On the one hand, I continued to pursue positions inherited from the Cold War; on the other, I was trying to get my bearings in the new world we were suddenly living in after the Berlin Wall came down. I saw Bosnia as the final resurgence of the beast. For me, the traditional confrontation between liberal democracy and totalitarianism had reemerged on the Bosnian front, and I responded in the traditional liberal way, by raising the flag of human rights. Regarding Bosnia, our position was thus determined, on the one hand, by our determination not to repeat the conduct of the Red Cross at Auschwitz, which can be seen as the founding concern of French humanitarianism and, on the other hand, by our commitment to the liberal ethos we had developed during the 1980s.

Would you then say that you now regret denouncing the international community for the way it dealt with the wars in the former Yugoslavia — namely, for having treated ethnic cleansing as if it were a natural disaster and for having been resigned, from the outset, to the victory of Serbian nationalism?

When I say that we went too far, I'm not thinking of that type of criticism, which anyway dovetailed to a large extent with the protests of the entire humanitarian community. Europe, we said to ourselves, needed to stop the reemergence of fascism, but instead of doing that, it was using humanitarian action as a kind of alibi for inaction. We felt that the United Nations had deployed a peacekeeping "protection force" that in fact protected no one besides itself — and then only with the greatest difficulty. Misleading and propagandistic uses of humanitarianism affected our own legitimacy, and we were right both to expose them and to confront those responsible for this abusive co-optation of humanitarianism. Not only do I not regret having taken such positions but I think that, for the most part, the entire NGO community responded to the situation pretty well.

It is only afterward that we tumbled into error — for example, when MSF went public with a report on crimes against humanity just after the discovery of the detention camps in Bosnia. We had conducted an inquiry with Bosnian refugees. We had set out to show that murder, torture, and deportation had, in fact, been carried out and that they constituted crimes against humanity. The facts were established but, even then, the psychological effects of their definition as crimes against humanity limited our capacity for reflection.

I remember saying to the press that humanitarian action made no sense under such conditions. That's the position that I find untenable today: the idea that delivering humanitarian aid would have somehow involved us in the crimes perpetrated by the Serbian militias, that it would have made us passively complicit with the murderers. There was something metaphysical — or metapolitical, to use your expression — in a posture that put forward the thesis of crimes against humanity to discredit humanitarian aid. It is now clear to me that calling something a "crime against humanity" — an epithet that applies to a whole range of crimes — doesn't tell us a whole lot, either about the concrete conditions under which humanitarian work can be exercised, or about the ways in which humanitarianism can be abusively appropriated for other agendas. And this is crucial to me, because humanitarianism is both about delineating the space in which humanitarian agencies can operate and about articulating the conditions under which they are able to work. It is not about building moral and legal cases against governmental agencies.

Looking back at the history of MSF, it seems as if you have moved back and forth between two postures. On the one hand, you have turned to politicians and governments either to denounce their intolerable practices or to demand that they assume their political responsibilities. On the other hand, you have turned inward, so to speak, in order to reflect both on the conditions that make your own activity possible and on the effects that your actions might produce. Is it the case that that the latter posture has gradually taken precedence over the former? Or is it that you have found a stable equilibrium between those two postures?

Indeed, one can say that during its history, MSF has assumed two emblematic roles. We began by seeking what I would call a witnessing role, a role of authoritative eyewitnesses with a mission to alert the public, since we were doctors operating in the field. For me, this stance now seems questionable, to say the least. First, it is at the root of certain mistakes the organization made — for instance, at the end of the 1960s, the future founders of MSF felt they had to denounce a genocide, which wasn't actually one, in Biafra. Second, the very notion of an "eyewitness" is problematic — eyewitness of *what*? What does it mean to be a "witness" to genocide? Who are the witnesses? As Raoul Hilberg has said concerning the extermination of the Jews by the Nazis, the witnesses were the criminals themselves. It's Eichmann who was the witness, rather than the insurgents in the Warsaw Ghetto or the "Muslims" of Auschwitz.

Hindsight skepticism notwithstanding, this emphasis on witnessing remained a distinctive feature of MSF for a long time. It still exists, in a way, at least in the way the public sometimes thinks about our organization, as became evident when we received the Nobel Peace Prize. In France, the association between MSF and the witness posture was pervasive in the supposedly well-informed press — I mean *Le Monde, Libération,* and *Le Nouvel Observateur* — which chose to dwell on the legend of the organization's founding. What is certain is that this rhetoric of witnessing and accusation, culminated in 1980 when MSF, in collaboration with the International Rescue Committee (IRC), organized a march on the border between Thailand and Cambodia in order to protest the confiscation of humanitarian aid by the pro-Vietnamese authorities in Phnom Penh. At that time, we were convinced that there was a major famine in Cambodia, which turned out to be false.

However, the substance of MSF's public statements has changed considerably since then. The famine in Ethiopia in 1985 is the moment when we articulated an entirely different conception of our role. It took some effort to understand that the Ethiopian regime had actually used the entirety of resources contributed by international solidarity — financial, logistical, and political — to buttress its Stalinist approach to modernization — including transferring populations, dismantling the rural economy and culture, eliminating the "kulak," and so on. We did not want merely to denounce these policies. The main issue for us was that, as members of the humanitarian community, we found ourselves contributing to the destruction of a people we had come to help. (Indeed, what the Ethiopian government wanted us to do was to get people back on their feet so that they could be deported.) Therefore, instead of focusing on the crimes committed by a Stalinist regime, we entered a new stage in our critical thinking: we began to reflect more seriously upon our own role, upon the potentially negative consequences of our activity — upon the fact that we could inadvertently play into the hands of agencies whose objectives had nothing to do with humanitarianism.

The coexistence of these two postures — bearing witness to the misdeeds of others and reflecting upon our own course of action — was clear in our approach to Bosnia: the press conference on crimes against humanity belonged to our old witnessing/denunciation mode; yet at the same time, we were also involved in a process of self-examination regarding our specific responsibilities in a given context. In this latter respect, even though I still think that our presence in Srebrenica was helpful, I must admit that a number of questions remain unanswered. In particular, it is entirely possible that our presence and work contributed to the illusion of security among the people of Srebrenica — when in fact very real threats hung over them. For my part, I went there twice, and it did not occur to me to say to people: "Watch out, make sure you are not being trapped!" There was a Canadian and then a Dutch battalion there, the ICRC was visiting from time to time, and we had convinced ourselves that we could rely on the guarantee of protection from the international community — we all saw in 1995 what that amounted to.

In hindsight, that experience created a feeling of malaise and guilt that is still felt by many of us who were involved in Bosnia. This feeling might explain the tenacity with which MSF sought to involve itself in the investigation and the collection of evidence regarding the Srebrenica massacre — although this kind of involvement is ordinarily foreign to our mode of operation.

In terms of our ongoing reflection upon our role as humanitarians and the consequences of our actions, another defining moment was that of the war in the Congo in 1996–1997, following the attacks on the refugee camps in Kivu and the march on Kinshasa by Laurent Désiré Kabila's troops. In my opinion, humanitarian NGOs should probably substitute this war for the Red Cross at Auschwitz as their main negative paradigm — as the template of what should be avoided at all costs. Indeed, we have to recognize that in the instance of the 1996–1997 Congo war, the humanitarian agencies that were on the ground — the UNHCR (United Nations High Commissioner for Refugees), the ICRC, and MSF — all became directly implicated in the killing of the refugees that were fleeing the camps. In order to search for these fleeing refugees, we were required to have liaison officers in our vehicles. Whenever we found refugees, these officers immediately informed Kabila's ADFL (Alliance of Democratic Forces for the Liberation of Congo-Zaire), which at the time was allied with the RPA (Rwandan Patriotic Army), about our position. Consequently, because of the humanitarian organization's assistance, all the RPA troops had to do was to arrive immediately and, acting as killing squads, begin executing groups of two hundred, five hundred, even a thousand people. In short, we humanitarians were nothing but hunting dogs for the killers of the RPA.

For humanitarian agencies, this was arguably the worst situation ever. As for myself, at the time, I tried to remember the lesson we had learned during our Ethiopian experience in 1984: to put it in Arendt's terms in *Eichmann in Jerusalem,* if you can't prevent a crime, you should at least avoid taking part in it. Along with others, I harshly criticized the UNHCR for enabling the AFDL and the RPA to carry out massacres and, although such a response tore MSF apart, I strongly advocated that we just leave the scene. In a situation so tragically predetermined, I could not — and still cannot— see how it was possible to do otherwise than suspend our activity immediately and protest vehemently, even though I knew that it was already too late.

The reason I am dwelling on this episode is that I want to emphasize once more how necessary it is for humanitarian organizations to examine systematically the consequences of our actions. I will add that this kind of self-reflection is all the more necessary because of the considerable symbolic weight that humanitarian positions and rhetoric have acquired since the beginning of the 1990s.

In short, it is true that in the history of MSF there has been a tension between a witnessing function and an analytic function. However, since the Ethiopian crisis, this tension has gradually diminished as the analytic function has become more prominent.

You present your position on Bosnia as though it is still largely defined by your old witnessing posture. But can't it also be perceived as an expression of the self-reflective posture to which you give precedence today? At the time, people said that there was a "humanitarian crisis" in Bosnia. In responding the way you did — that is, in questioning the wisdom of delivering humanitarian aid in the context of the Bosnian war — weren't you simply wondering about the political meaning and the political consequences of your actions? In other words, weren't you already raising the same questions that you would be compelled to address in the Congo in 1996? And aren't these questions the ones that must be raised again today regarding the situation in Darfur? After all, you mentioned just a little while ago how General Al-Bashir was able to use your analysis of the situation in western Sudan for his own purposes. Isn't this a case where you should ponder the political consequences, if not of your actions, then at least of your statements?

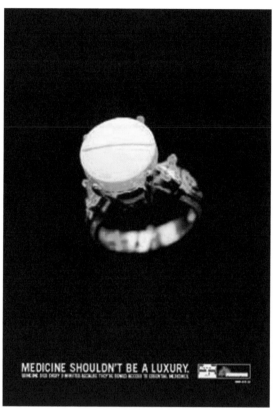

Two posters from MSF's Access to Essential Medicines campaign.

Indeed, there is probably a limit beyond which everything can backfire, a kind of threshold beyond which the meaning of any position is turned on its head. But I think that we can overcome this contradiction, at least in part, by upholding a vision of humanitarianism in general as the policy of the lesser evil — or as the policy of the "least worst," to borrow an expression from Philippe Mesnard. For a long time, I was very critical of this kind of idea. Today, I consider it to be an acceptable policy and, in some cases, even a desirable one. So accepting the notion of a policy of the lesser evil, or at least declining to deny its legitimacy, seems to me to be one way to live with the contradiction that you refer to without completely becoming a victim of it.

Besides, in a situation such as the war in Darfur, we want to describe it, to create a narrative that fits our purposes — not to qualify the situation in either moral or legal terms. I don't agree that our position amounts to acquitting a criminal power — that avoiding the notion of genocide amounts to exonerating the Khartoum regime of its crimes. On the contrary, what this position made possible was, as I said before, a concrete description of the crime: it allowed us to recall that the Darfur region was the site of a brutal counterinsurgency campaign and of asymmetrical violence orchestrated by the Sudanese authorities, that there were and still are two million people displaced in a region of six million, that it was and still is an extremely serious situation. Once again, what we wanted to escape was the terrible alternative between genocide — a situation calling for a public outcry in favor of immediate military intervention — and nothing, meaning a situation that would not call for any kind of emergency because it did not amount to genocide.

What is it that I am really defending? Perhaps the rather modest idea that politics, history, and the future are written by and with the living — and that if you are on the side of the living, the minimal policy consists in *caring for bodies*. I would have rejected such a formula with the utmost vehemence in the 1980s in the name of the very idealistic conception of humanism I had at the time. Today I am advocating it as a minimal — and thus not imperial — policy. Caring for bodies means taking meaningful action to help those who otherwise would have tremendous difficulty surviving; helping them get through a difficult period — whether it is a period of six months or six years. In southern Sudan, such a period lasted for twenty years, and we were there the whole time. So, that's it — I understand your question, but I don't know how to go any further than that.

As long as the witnessing posture prevailed, MSF's ethic was articulated around the following proposition: "We can make the politicians face their responsibilities because we are nonpolitical actors caught in a political situation." In other words, you insisted on claiming humanitarianism as your domain, defining it as a nonpolitical domain in order to prevent governments from appropriating the cause of humanitarianism and, by that token, evading their specifically political responsibilities. However, once you substitute the analytical posture elaborated in Ethiopia for that of the witness, you are no longer able to present yourselves as nonpolitical observers of a political situation. Instead, you must embrace the status of a particular political agency operating among other political agencies and pursuing a political agenda that consists of fulfilling your humanitarian mission at the lowest political cost. It is as if MSF's determination to give politics its due has come full circle.

When we are at the forefront of the Campaign for Access to Essential Medicines, when we accuse international institutions, pharmaceutical companies, and governments of not taking sufficient responsibility in this matter — of merely paying lip service to it — we are indeed adopting the position that you describe. So I agree with you, with the caveat that the words "politics" and "policy" can mean a lot of different things. It seems to me that the "nongovernmental politics" we try to pursue goes against the grain of what traditionally has been thought of as fundamental to politics. Today, MSF operates in a vast arena that is also occupied by other groups such as Act Up and the various participants in world social forums. Along with these groups, we are inventing new forms of political involvement insofar as each of our interventions focuses on one specific social objective, one dimension of life. It is not about changing or preserving life "in general," but, on the contrary, about addressing life in its details. This is something important, but difficult to assess, precisely because it does not correspond to any institutionalized form or tradition — and even I cannot see where such efforts will lead. Our state-centered or, more generally, institution-centered vision of politics tends to cloud our perspective and keeps us from comprehending and fully appreciating the originality and dynamics of these new movements. Not that I situate MSF among the social movements and NGOs mobilized against neoliberal globalization. I did not support "Third World socialism" in the 1980s, and I still do not. Moreover, I think it is important to maintain boundaries between different types of agencies and mobilizations. However, it seems to me that MSF and these critics of neoliberal globalization are taking part in a larger dynamic that, in a few years, with the distance that I now lack, historians and sociologists will be able to properly assess.

Let's go back one last time to the shift from witnessing to self-reflection, from MSF as a nonpolitical witness of political situations to MSF as a particular political agent. To what extent do you think this is an endogenous evolution and to what extent is it a function of the evolution of governmental politics? In the early 1990s, when the governments, acting as the leading members of the international community, were describing regional conflicts in humanitarian terms in order to evade their political responsibilities, it made perfect sense for MSF to insist on the separation between the realms of humanitarianism and politics. However, depoliticization is hardly the problem today. One can indeed accuse the Bush administration of many things, but fleeing from politics is not one of them. Accordingly, one may wonder whether MSF's repositioning of itself as a political agency operating alongside other political agencies is not dictated, at least in part, by the changing strategies of governments — especially the most powerful among them.

Obviously, our ongoing reflection on humanitarianism does not take place in a vacuum. It happens in the context of changing political configurations that necessarily implicate organizations such as ours. Thus, I don't see how one can distinguish between what is endogenous and what is reactive in our evolution. The same would be true if I were to analyze the evolution of humanitarianism at the end of the Cold War era. The issue, it seems to me, is less about figuring out whether we can or should stay clear of politics than about defining the kind of politics we are involved in. We don't know any better than the politicians what the "highest good" might be, or even if it exists. However, we should be able to say why we are doing one thing rather than another, whether it is in the context of the wars in Iraq or the Sudan, the 2005 tsunami, the famine in Niger, or the battle against AIDS. If that's what you call being a political actor, then yes, it's absolutely essential to be a political actor in that way — and only in that way.

Let's move now to internal politics. How does the decision-making process work at MSF international?

The various national sections are independent. They are subject to the national laws of the countries where they are based, and each of them is totally autonomous. Accordingly, there are no official positions of MSF international unless all the national groups have come to agree on one. For instance, all the national sections of MSF agreed to suspend aid collections for the emergency in Asia one month after the tsunami. (We all agreed that we had already received more funds than we could make use of and that it would be dishonest on our part to reallocate the surplus to other projects without the explicit consent of the donors.)

For especially thorny situations, we have an arbitration body located in Geneva — the world capital of humanitarian neutrality. This is a permanent office with a president, a secretary, and a few executives.

Can you map out the tensions that run through a unique political organization such as MSF? For instance, what were the tensions surrounding the Campaign for Access to Essential Medicines that you launched in 1999?

That campaign was run by some sections of MSF international and was criticized by others, principally MSF-Netherlands, which felt that it was outside the scope of what MSF is legitimately entitled to do. The conflict was limited, and MSF-Netherlands simply remained on the sidelines of that particular campaign. The campaign has led to the creation of an R&D institution for the development of new drugs. A few months from now, we plan to come out with a new drug therapy to fight malaria — it involves a combination of two existing products and has been approved by the two laboratories concerned. We are working on similar projects specifically for tropical diseases. Because there remains some disagreement over these projects, funding will be handled only by the national sections that support them.

How is the scope of legitimate action determined?

We have a certain tradition and the precedents of past positions. If you will, it is a kind of common law, a global jurisprudence. For instance, if MSF had to deal with a major financial crisis, we would have to abandon projects such as the Campaign for Access to Essential Medicines in order to continue our activities in Darfur, Liberia, and all the areas that are experiencing major political crises. We all know what is at the core of MSF's project and what belongs on the periphery. So it's only when there is a relative abundance of financial resources that we are able to think about expanding the scope of our actions.

To continue the subject of internal tensions, was there a debate within MSF regarding the position you took on the war in Iraq?

No. The decision not to take a stance on the conflict did not raise any problem. There was some discussion about what we needed to do specifically — but the debates occurred in every section; they did not pit one section against another.

Before the invasion, we debated the idea of setting up a facility to take in refugees. It was a well-intentioned, but misguided idea. In fact, such a project has often proved misguided. On the eve of war, we tend to imagine that there will be a massive influx of refugees who will pour into the site we have prepared — only to realize that they don't come, they go elsewhere, or that, in fact, there are not very many displaced persons or that they leave the camps soon after arriving. All forms of planning in these circumstances end up trapping those who make them, because reality ends up trumping predictions.

The second phase came with the declaration of war. We decided that we had to be on the scene, so we went, along with MSF-Belgium, but the conditions were bad. Our team was arrested and imprisoned by Saddam Hussein's forces.

Then there was the third phase, after the actual invasion. For some, myself included, there was no longer anything for us to do in Iraq. The Ba'athist regime had certain strengths that Stalinist regimes tend to have, such as a public infrastructure — a managerial class, lots of doctors and hospitals — that, while definitely deficient, still existed. The only thing these doctors had to do was to go to work — which made our presence unnecessary. The other argument in favor of leaving was that the occupier was the most powerful nation in the world. As an occupying force, it had specific conventional obligations to fulfill. Its agents certainly had the means to fulfill them, and we had no special reason to help them out. However, others within MSF saw things differently: the Iraqi people were still very much in trouble — they were emerging from a long history of dictatorship, and the invasion had caused considerable destruction. There were needs, and some of us felt that we needed to be there.

The debates within MSF were pretty intense. Each section confronted the same tensions, the same divergence of opinions. Those who opposed an Iraq mission finally won out. For a few months, MSF-Belgium attempted to carry out a very interesting operation: they quietly set up in Sadr City, the huge Shiite slum in Baghdad, used their connections with the political-religious leadership, and did public-health work, medicine, and surgery. But they had to stop because of the unacceptable security situation for their personnel. In a way, I saw it as a confirmation of my position: We were not able to operate there for the same reasons that also prevented Iraqi doctors from working in that area; we were thus in exactly the same situation as local health providers — which only proved that our presence was unnecessary. Though undeniably courageous and well intentioned, the intervention of MSF-Belgium in Sadr City was predicated on the old self-aggrandizing fantasy that is rather common among people who are working under the banner of humanitarianism. We say to ourselves: Well, if others are not succeeding, that's because they are incompetent — we never say that aloud, but that is what we think and act upon. Of course, it's not true. We don't succeed for the same reasons that others don't succeed.

Still under the rubric of tensions within MSF, there seems to be some disagreement over the issue of abortion in certain countries.

The disagreement is not over principles — no one among us questions the medical act as such. Rather, the discussion concerns the degree of liberty we should allow ourselves with respect to national legislation. How far do we go in challenging a law — in this case, a law that criminalizes abortion — when we know that challenging it may endanger both our activities in the country concerned and the local personnel who would be implicated in the procedure, especially when they are not aware of the legal consequences accompanying certain medical gestures. Today, we are facing this problem in the Sudan and the Congo in particular, and more generally in all the regions where mass rapes are being committed. There is a clear demand made on us by the victims, but we don't have clear guidelines for responding to it.

Are there other instances of this type of problem?

It's the same with treatment protocols. In almost all of the countries where we work, the treatment protocols, which are imposed by the ministries of health, are the result of negotiations between the local authorities and multinational pharmaceutical companies — under extremely uneven conditions, as one can easily imagine.

Over the last decade, we have witnessed a dramatic and deadly resurgence of malaria due to the displacement of populations, wars, and climatic changes. So it's a fundamental public-health issue. For the most part, the treatments we're using to fight these epidemics are outdated. In certain cases, the rate of resistance to the drugs being used is close to 80 percent — one might as well pass out sugar. This simulation of medical assistance is ethically untenable. The problem for us, then, is posed in these terms: can we impose our views on what the therapeutic approach should be — insofar as we can demonstrate the validity of our perspective — and thus override the instructions of a national government and break the habits to which it conferred legitimacy? It is a delicate situation that stages a conflict between two forms of authority — scientific legitimacy versus political legitimacy; humanitarian legitimacy — if I dare say so — against governmental legitimacy.

So far, by adopting a rather confrontational strategy, we've made some progress, at least in places such as Burundi, Sierra Leone, and Liberia. Our toughest confrontation involved the Ethiopian government. For the second time in our existence, we were almost expelled from the country. But it was an interesting sign of the times that the situation was resolved in our favor. Following a publicized shouting match between us and the Ethiopian Ministry of Health, the latter publicly recognized its scientific errors and agreed to implement a new protocol.

Yet these battles have also caused disputes between different national sections of MSF. Some have wondered whether such policies should have been pursued at all, considering that the outcome was uncertain and that our obstinacy carried the risk of destabilizing local teams by having them accused of neocolonial arrogance. These divergences, I want to stress, are largely tactical; they are about practical approaches. For example, we often have debates about whether we should try to mobilize the local press and opt for open confrontation or, on the other hand, pursue discreet talks.

What exactly is the range of tactical options that are available to you — aside from either resigning yourself to passing out sugar pills, crossing all the red lines, or leaving the country altogether ?

There is a fourth option, which consists of establishing power relations between ourselves and governments. We now have the ability to do this; ten years ago we did not. Our Nobel Peace Prize helps, but more broadly, the recent years have endowed NGOs with unprecedented political leverage. Today, the Ethiopian situation of 1985 would be very unfavorable to the Ethiopian government.

Exploring power relations is perhaps the signature motif of MSF-France — our happy conscience. This may be what distinguishes us from the other national sections. In a certain number of situations, it just seems obvious to us that establishing a power struggle — with no predetermined outcome — is the way to go. I would even say that all our actions are undertaken with the assumption that there will be tensions between us and the state authorities of the countries where we intervene. However, for other sections of MSF, as well as for other NGOs, such an attitude is not a given, if only because they have traditions of cooperation with state governments that situate them as subcontractors with respect to state agencies. When you're there to implement a policy, you don't question it and are not prone to create a conflict with the authorities.

What interests me particularly about MSF is our capacity to establish and assume power relations on the ground. Nothing guarantees that this will always be the case. We may very well become an agency of institutions subcontracted by states and in charge of the private implementation of public-health policies. Given the disastrous state of public health in Africa, we might end up building nonprofit hospitals financed by the World Bank or the European Union and so fall back into a secularized and social version of the missionary tradition. That would most likely be productive, but I'll admit that it is not the type of action that inspires me.

Translated by Michel Feher and Blake Ferris.

1   Statement released on March 3, 2003, and signed by Action
    contre la Faim (ACF), Médecins du Monde (MDM), Handicap
    International, Première Urgence, Solidarités, and Enfants du
    Monde.

2   See, in particular, the op-ed piece written by Jean-Hervé
    Bradol, the current president of MSF-France, entitled "D'un
    génocide à l'autre" and published in the French daily *Le
    Monde*, September 14, 2004. Available online at www.msf.
    fr/site/bibli.nsf/documents/trib140904bradol.

3   Jean-Claude Favez, with Geneviève Billeter, *Une mission
    impossible?: Le CICR, les déportations et les camps de concen-
    tration nazis* (Lausanne: Payot, 1988).

4   *Un spécialiste: Portrait d'un criminel moderne*, DVD, by Rony
    Brauman and Eyal Sivan (Paris: Montparnasse, 2000).

Aid supplies gathered by MSF are unloaded from the Greek navy vessel
Ierapetra at the seaport of Beirut, Lebanon, July 25, 2006. The ship
brought eighty tons of tents, blankets, and cooking and hygiene sets
after Israel loosened its thirteen-day blockade of Lebanon's ports to
allow aid ships into Beirut (Mahmoud Tawil/AP Photo).

Humanitarianism: A Nongovernmental Government

Didier Fassin

On August 23 and 24, 2005, during his trip to Niger to survey the effects of the famine afflicting the country, Kofi Annan began by visiting a feeding center in Zinder run by Médecins Sans Frontières (MSF). He praised the health workers at the site for their "very valuable work," but when journalists asked him about the recent criticism the humanitarian group had lodged against the United Nations, he diplomatically refused to comment. His only statement was that he "was very impressed by what MSF was trying to do in Niger."[1] This comment came as a surprise to no one. The anecdote is a familiar part of the political landscape. Nor was it surprising that the representative of the world assembly of states would make an obligatory stop at the local office of a nongovernmental organization and be called to comment on public attacks against his agency: humanitarian workers have now become legitimate actors on the international stage.

These self-proclaimed spokespersons of the planet's poor and suffering have staked out a territory in global public space as privileged interlocutors with the powers that be. MSF's moral authority — solidified by a Nobel Peace Prize — lends their representatives a power that the secretary-general of the United Nations cannot not take into account in his politics, whether it be through handling with kid gloves those humanitarians whose word has come to be if not truly representative, at least extremely legitimate, or, on the contrary, using them as a conduit for expressing an idea his institutional position does not permit him to articulate. This is no different for heads of state who, even in wartime, cannot afford to avoid negotiating with nongovernmental organizations, which invoke their right to assist victims of conflict and to express themselves in the name of an emerging global civil society.

This is, one might think, nothing new. The International Committee of the Red Cross (ICRC) has, after all, been intervening in battlefields for over a century by inserting itself into relationships between states, sometimes even replacing these states by virtue of the "protecting powers" that the 1949 Geneva Conventions gave it. Nevertheless, beyond maintaining a privileged relationship with the public powers in every country with a Red Cross branch, the ICRC also benefits from the rights and prerogatives attributed to it by these states in the context of its charters. It even benefits from a "humanitarian mandate" that gives the group the power to protect civilians, wounded soldiers, and prisoners of war. Although nongovernmental, the Red Cross is closely and officially tied to states that, in their own name, have assigned it this higher mission.

This is not the case for organizations dating from what might be called the "second humanitarian era." This era began in 1971 with the creation of MSF whose core founders, in a reaction to the constitutive political ambiguity of the Red Cross, volunteered their services. During the Biafran war, the founders of this new group had volunteered with the Red Cross to aid endangered populations. However, in order to distance themselves from the Red Cross, they abandoned neutrality and grouped themselves together so as to be able to testify freely about what they saw. The "Sans Frontières" movement, as some have come to call it, understood itself to be emancipated from the tutelage of any state. Even more, it constructed itself "against the state" via rhetoric that affirmed its independence by denouncing established powers.[2] When Jean-Hervé Bradol, the president of MSF, contrasted his organization's "humanitarian spirit" with the violence of "the cannibalistic regime," he intended to reference states, and their governments and armies, who, in his eyes, incarnate this regime with the complicity of various sections of the United Nations — such as the High Commissioner for Refugees in the case of victims of persecution, the World Health Organization, in the case of malaria and AIDS, and the World Food Programme, in the case of Niger.[3] In other words, what MSF has come to denounce does not only include the warring or occupying powers that were its initial targets, but also the states and international organizations that were complicit and silent.

In this essay, I reexamine the supposedly self-evident distinction between states and humanitarians, between what is governmental and what is nongovernmental. Given that this dualism is so self-evident, I begin with what might appear to be an oxymoron: the existence of a humanitarian government. I aim to expand the political dimension of humanitarian action beyond the purview of groups claiming to act under its prerogative and to consider how its politics is one of the moral resources for public action in contemporary society. My analysis, therefore, focuses on the many forms of interference and interpenetration between state institutions and social organizations. In particular, concentrating on the ways people and projects move in and out of two worlds often understood as being strictly delineated, I will reveal just how porous the border between them has in fact become and how, in the end, the state has been humanitarianized. I then proceed to show how, particularly in the realm of international conflicts, this evolution has crystallized around the multiplication of militaro-humanistic structures that wed armies of intervention to mechanisms of aid. Deploring this confusion, nongovernmental organizations strive to differentiate themselves from belligerent states without really being able to erase the ties that structurally link the organizations to those states. Ultimately, another landscape for humanitarianism exists, one characterized less by the presence of new actors than by new configurations of agency and new forms of action.

Humanitarian government can be defined as the administration of human collectivities in the name of a higher moral principle that sees the preservation of life and the alleviation of suffering as the highest value of action.[4] This definition does not imply any particular state or nonstate form as the foundation of this government.

In the scholarly literature, there are usually two ways of thinking about humanitarian government. On the one hand, for international relations and international law scholars, "humanitarian government" stands for both a new mode of action available to national governments and a new mode of regulation of global society.[5] Concretely, what these scholars seek to understand are the motives and justifications advanced by state and suprastate organizations for their interventions in recent conflicts—for example, in Somalia, Bosnia, and East Timor. One of their typical foci is the shift from the classical problem of just war to that of so-called humanitarian interventions. In this perspective, nongovernmental organizations are not considered per se but only insofar as they participate in the transformation of international politics. On the other hand, for specialists in social movements and political activism, humanitarian government corresponds to the emergence of a new set of actors onto national and international stages.[6] Their primary concern is to analyze the motives and modalities of NGOs—MSF and Médecins du Monde (MDM) being the most frequently studied. What matters here is the emergence of those transnational structures of mediation that play a crucial role in the reconfiguration of the international order. In this second perspective, NGOs are foregrounded while states recede into the background.

As such, humanitarian government can be understood as being grounded in two almost opposite political figures, one governmental and the other nongovernmental. If that is the case, it means that the notion of humanitarian government pertains to a broader political and moral logic at work both within and outside state forms. This logic can be called humanitarian reason. Although in this article I will refer to nongovernmental politics, that is, to modes of governmentality that escape the state's grip, it is necessary to interrogate the fact that this logic is so powerful that everyone considers it the greatest good in international power relations, so efficient that it underwrites both governmental and nongovernmental politics and tends to abolish the boundaries between the two, and so desirable that it creates competition between them as governmental policymakers more and more frequently contest nongovernmental organizations' claim to a monopoly on the concept. Humanitarian government, then, is grounded in this form of reason, which, precisely, blurs the boundary between what is governmental and what is nongovernmental.

In order to show the extent of humanitarian reason and its power over contemporary moral economies, two very different cases where it was recently used officially and literally in France can be cited. First, as France's immigration policies have become more restrictive, leading to an increasing number of undocumented foreigners, one category proved particularly problematic: seriously ill patients—for example, those suffering from AIDS and cancer—who would not be adequately treated in their home countries. A procedure was put in place to regularize these patients' situations. At first, it applied only to exceptional cases left to the authority of city governments, but later it was generalized and made official through law. This procedure was referred to as "humanitarian reason," which made it possible to give a foreigner the provisional right to live in France. In the second case, after a scandal exposed the poor conditions of French prisons, a question emerged about prisoners in the terminal phases of an illness or whose course of treatment could not be administered while they were being detained. In order to justify the liberation of these prisoners, "humanitarian reason" was once again invoked to designate an argument based on compassion. Certain prisoners' sentences were thus suspended.[7] In both cases, the same formula described magnanimous gestures of public power, and the initiatives went beyond the realm over which humanitarian organizations strove to maintain a moral monopoly. The state showed that it, too, could act and speak in this way.

THE HUMANITARIAN STATE

Over the last twenty-five years, nongovernmental politics grounded in humanitarian reason has grown exponentially—allowing for the creation of numerous national and transnational groups increasingly active on the global public stage. Up until the 1970s, the Red Cross claimed a quasi monopoly on humanitarianism, even as the neighboring fields of human rights, medical aid, and development were already comprised of a plurality of organizations. Thereafter, however, "humanitarianism" not only became a key word for justifying intervention but also, and perhaps more importantly, in the communication campaigns surrounding interventions. This is true to such an extent that today, many organizations in human rights and other neighboring fields act in the name of humanitarianism, even though they previously criticized the tendency of humanitarian organizations to emphasize emergency operations. At the present time, most of the largest nongovernmental organizations have branches in several countries: for example, MSF has around twenty sections of variable size that have grouped into an "international movement." Remarkably, almost all these branches, whose autonomy varies according to the central apparatus, are based in Western societies whose global territory they practically define: of the twenty branches of MSF, fourteen are European, two North American, one Australian, one Japanese, one is based in Hong Kong, and finally one branch is based in the United Arab Emirates.[8] Nonetheless, the wide usage of the term "humanitarian" to describe the interventions of actors from Northern countries in Southern ones is not limited to nongovernmental organizations. States and supranational institutions have each in turn taken up the symbolic mantle of humanitarian reason in order to justify and legitimate their actions, including military ones.

One could say that the state has been humanitarianized: in other words, it has developed a humanitarian rhetoric and politics to describe its own governmental practices. This might seem surprising since, as we have already seen, humanitarianism emerged

(TOP) At a October 31, 2001, House International Relations subcommittee hearing on Afghanistan and the Taliban, representative Cynthia McKinney (D-Georgia) made the point that an unexploded U.S. cluster bomb packet (LEFT) looks very similar in size and color to a U.S. food ration (RIGHT). Both were dropped from planes onto Afghanistan (Kenneth Lambert/AP Photo).

(BOTTOM) To avoid confusion between food parcels wrapped in yellow and unexploded yellow cluster bombs in Afghanistan, the Pentagon announced on November 1, 2001, that it would change the color of air-dropped humanitarian packages to blue. (LEFT) U.S. Army major Tim Blair holding a sample of the "Humanitarian Daily Ration" packages of food that the U.S. Defense Department said were dropped over Afghanistan, October 7, 2001. (RIGHT) A part of what police claimed was a cluster bomb dropped by NATO during their bombing campaign over the Kosovo village of Vrbovac, April 4, 1999 (Reuters).

with the Red Cross, which claimed an autonomous space on battlefields at the margins of the barbaric bloodshed perpetrated by nation-states and their armies. Furthermore, the second birth of humanitarian activism in the form of MSF and then MDM, among other organizations, was not merely predicated on humanitarianism's independence from state violence, but on its opposition to this violence. The state, by appropriating humanitarian rhetoric in order to give meaning to its own public actions, endeavored to undermine this social division of moral labor. The state's refusal to let NGOs be the sole bearers of humanitarian care can be explained by reasons both anthropological — compassion and its companion emotions are increasingly valued in the contemporary world — and tactical — having to do with the increasing symbolic value of humanitarianism in the public sphere.[9] Yet there is also a more trivial reason for the appropriation of humanitarianism by the state, namely, that of intricate connections and forms of transition between the governmental and nongovernmental spheres — despite protestations by humanitarian organizations to the contrary.

Movements that involve actors themselves are much more frequent than humanitarian organizations generally want to admit, especially in France. Bernard Kouchner, who cofounded MSF and MDM, was appointed to the governments of several French prime ministers — Michel Rocard, Edith Cresson, Pierre Bérégovoy, and Lionel Jospin — before becoming the special representative for the United Nations in Kosovo. Claude Malhuret started as president of MSF, then was appointed state secretary for humanitarian action under Jacques Chirac, and later elected mayor of Vichy for the Liberal Democratic party. Xavier Emmanuelli, another cofounder of MSF, was state secretary for humanitarian action under Alain Juppé. Jacques Lebas, a former president of MDM, was named head of several committees on poverty issues. Gilles Brücker, also a former president of MDM, was named director of France's Institute for Health Surveillance. In the opposite direction, more recently, Jean-François Mattéi was the minister of health and subsequently became the president of the French Red Cross. The presence of humanitarian actors within state mechanisms and ministries — and now of politicians in humanitarian organizations — demonstrates their eclectic political affiliations, since they may be linked to right-conservative or liberal parties as well as center-left or left parties. This tendency is not, however, limited to these well-known and emblematic figures.

The history of policies concerning childhood lead poisoning in France, for example, can only be understood in the context of the intimate interactions between governmental and nongovernmental humanitarianism.[10] For many years, doctors had believed that lead poisoning occurred very rarely. Once its frequency and seriousness was revealed, elected officials tried to sidestep the issue. Humanitarian organizations, along with public-health officials and social workers, were the ones who actually discovered the problem, which is now deemed a top priority. In the late 1980s, MSF proceeded to organize and finance a medical study in the United States with the mandate of obtaining the expertise necessary for testing and thus preventing an illness whose epidemiological reality had, at the time, been denied by the Direction Générale de Santé (General Health Directorate). In the early 1990s, MDM protected tenants' groups, allowing them to mobilize and to decry publicly the government's inefficiency in rehabilitating decrepit living spaces and the forced relocation of families exposed to lead poisoning. It was also a former member of MSF—a graduate of the École Nationale d'Administration—who became the director of the agency at the Ministry of Health that was responsible for at-risk populations and who convinced two of her former colleagues in the humanitarian world—first the secretary of humanitarian affairs, Xavier Emmanuelli, and then the next government's minister of health, Bernard Kouchner—to include provisions against lead poisoning in the 1998 Prevention of Social Exclusion Act.

The examples of how the governmental and nongovernmental realm interfere with one another could be multiplied indefinitely. In 1999, for example, the Couverture Maladie Universelle (Universal Health Coverage) law granting individuals without health coverage, including undocumented immigrants, the right to medical treatment was in the process of being drafted. The then labor minister, Martine Aubry, collaborated closely with a group of social organizations, including MDM, while her cabinet negotiated off the record with MSF representatives about the way to provide free health insurance to the poorest among this population. In 2005, when the Aide Médicale de l'État (State Medical Aid) program, which provided undocumented immigrants free medical treatment, was threatened by pressure from both ministers and parliamentary representatives, the administration of the health minister, Xavier Bertrand, relied on support from a group of social organizations, including MDM, to prepare new governmental directives concerning this right. Each of these changes in policy relied much more on an invisible work of conviction, negotiation, and collaborative construction than on a frontal attack.

This porous border between the governmental and nongovernmental spheres thus moves according to multiple logics rarely seen for what they are. On the international scene, this porousness has been most evident in the domain of war, as states have, little by little, appropriated the language humanitarian organizations believed to be their own.

THE MILITARO-HUMANITARIAN MOMENT

It is difficult to know exactly when the history of this appropriation began, since it is possible, after the fact, to interpret many military interventions carried out in the name of a threatened population in humanitarian terms. In fact, most political analysts do just that when they introduce criteria purported to establish which kinds of international actions pertain to humanitarianism, even when the term "humanitarian" was not originally predicated to them.[11] Instead of this after the fact and allegedly objective perspective, which endows the observer with the authority to determine what actions qualify as humanitarian, it may be preferable to adopt an inside or subjective perspective, which conversely endeavors to discover when the notion of humanitarianism explicitly emerges in the rhetoric justifying interventions. Instead of implementing the criteria for allegedly just wars, this second perspective focuses on the lexicon

NEGLECTED DISEASES: HAVE OUR GOVERNMENTS GOT SLEEPING SICKNESS?

SIGN UP TO URGE YOUR GOVERNMENT TO SUPPORT RESEARCH IN DISEASES OF THE POOR.
DND*i*
Drugs for Neglected Diseases Initiative

www.dndi.org

Poster for the Drugs for Neglected Diseases Initiative.

elaborated by the actors themselves. This perspective has the advantage of identifying when a new political vocabulary emerges, when new international norms form, and when the moralization of action is publicly articulated.

According to this subjectivist approach, the beginning of the 1990s marks the moment when military interventions were first qualified as humanitarian. The deployment of military forces by the United States and the United Nations in Somalia in 1992 was no doubt the turning point since, for the first time, not only was the situation presented as a "humanitarian crisis," but the international resolution also relied on the notion of the impossibility of "distributing humanitarian aid." It is also at this moment that the confusion between the military and the humanitarian, and between the governmental and the nongovernmental became most visible.[12] Kouchner, who was then the health minister, but whose legitimacy was largely predicated on his former positions as president of MSF and MDM, became an emblematic figure for this mix of registers when he dressed in a khaki outfit and, surrounded by American troops, distributed sacks of rice.

Yet it is perhaps even more pointedly the 1994 genocide in Rwanda that further legitimized the notion of a humanitarian war: while the systematic extermination of the Tutsi was sheepishly defined by the United Nations as a "humanitarian crisis," what the humanitarian NGOs denounced was the lack, or at least the delay, of military intervention. MSF, in particular, evacuated one of its offices after some of its personnel was massacred. The question was no longer whether a war could be carried out for humanitarian reasons, but whether the refusal to intervene was not a criminal offense under humanitarian law.[13] Thereafter, states, whether by themselves or as members of the United Nations, became the primary agents of the humanitarian international. Each of the West's subsequent military interventions, from East Timor to Kosovo to Iraq, has been justified thusly.

Over the last several years, however, nongovernmental organizations have relentlessly denounced the abusive appropriation of humanitarianism in order to give a moral justification to war as well as the persistent blurring of boundaries on the ground between the military and humanitarian workers. Furthermore, they have publicly expressed concern about the inherent risks at stake: not only to their members' security, but also regarding the mediatization of their interventions. Yet, it may be that humanitarians have failed to take stock of their own role in the confusion between the two registers: for example, when they heard Václav Havel and Tony Blair speak of "humanitarian war" to describe the NATO intervention in Kosovo, they were indignant. At the very same moment, however, MSF issued a report on the crimes and acts of violence perpetrated by Serbs against Albanian Kosovars—a document that the armed allied forces duly seized on to attest to the soundness and urgency of their intervention. Humanitarian organizations also condemned the simultaneous dropping of food and cluster bombs in 2002 which was meant to both alleviate the famine afflicting the Afghan population and force the Taliban to flee. But from the beginning of the Soviet invasion, MDM and other NGOs had aided the Afghan resistance in its war against the Russian invaders, first medically and then politically. Always defending causes that strike them as just and denouncing situations they find intolerable, these organizations, despite themselves, end up playing an active role in such conflicts.

More generally, humanitarian organizations complain about the military's instrumentalization of them. In doing this, they underestimate the ambiguous relationship they themselves have cultivated with the armies, whose protection these organizations expect in the form of humanitarian corridors and sanctuaries, even as they demand their autonomy be maintained. Moreover, they demand that the military refrain from appropriating humanitarian rhetoric, while at the same time calling upon them to intervene in order to prevent massacres and genocides. This proves just how precarious the line drawn by humanitarian organizations is and just how high the tensions are both between and within them over how to confront this treacherous position.

On the ground, humanitarian agents tend to shift between ideological posturing and pragmatic negotiations. On the one hand, they accuse heads of states of confusing registers when they ask humanitarian organizations to collaborate with missions of war described as humanitarian and they also resent military chiefs of staff who submit humanitarian work to their own procedures. But, on the other hand, humanitarians are also involved in a complex web of relations that extends from negotiating corridors and secure spaces—for example, during the second Iraq war—all the way to participating in intelligence operations, something that has been verified in the case of at least one Canadian organization in Kosovo.

Yet even beyond these objective and sometimes inevitable alliances, the very temporality and form of humanitarian interventions tend to be based on those of military actions: the foreboding sense of urgency, especially in cases of massive landing and brutal retreat; the setting up of structures and mechanisms meant to make humanitarian work more efficient, but end up isolating humanitarians from local populations. Under these conditions, it should probably come as no surprise that many aid recipients can hardly tell the difference between military personnel accomplishing humanitarian acts and humanitarian workers who arrive with the military—regardless of whether they actually welcome their presence or resent their intervention. One can certainly understand why humanitarian organizations deplore this state of affairs and insist on independence. But one can just as easily understand why the difference between them and the military is not always clear to local populations—a situation that warring parties can easily exploit.

Ostensibly constructed against the state, humanitarian intervention thus actually proves to be taken up in a complex web of relations with the state's agents and institutions. This observation is true at local, national, and even global levels but does not necessarily entail unacknowledged complicities or hidden interests. It should, however, make us think about politics in a different way and, in particular, strive to understand what a nongovernmental government actually looks like. Humanitarian organizations have today become political actors engaged in power relations, plays of alliance, and systems of negotiations with states and international institutions, which, in turn, rely on the legitimacy of humanitarian reason and those who promote it.

The expression "humanitarian nongovernmental government" therefore indicates forms of action available to nongovernmental organizations in the management of world affairs. These forms lie on a spectrum that goes from frontal opposition to states as a way of denouncing violations of humanitarian law to often invisible collaborations in global health-policy reform. The independent inquiries carried out by MDM in Chechnya are an excellent illustration of the first instance. A remarkable example of the second is the Drugs for Neglected Diseases Initiative, which brought together MSF, the World Health Organization, public research institutes, and private pharmaceutical laboratories to encourage the development of medicines considered unprofitable, but necessary for the treatment of infectious diseases in poor countries. In both cases, humanitarianism is an inspiration for ways of inventing new modes of what is called governing, both beside the state and along with it.

Translated by William Bishop.

1   Dalatou Mamane, "Annan: U.N. to Help End Hunger in Niger," Associated Press Online, August 25, 2005.

2   Just as Pierre Clastres considered the society of "savages" an alternative paradigm to a state regime, humanitarian agents almost invariably consider the international society of states a cannibalistic regime, dismissing it as "savage." In both cases, of course, this is an ideological construction. Pierre Clastres, *Society Against the State,* trans. Robert Hurley with Abe Stein (New York: Zone Books, 1989).

3   See Jean-Hervé Bradol, "The Sacrificial International Order and Humanitarian Action," in Fabrice Weissman (ed. and trans.), *In the Shadow of "Just Wars": Violence, Politics, and Humanitarian Action* (Ithaca, NY: Cornell University Press, 2004), pp. 1–24.

4   In "Le camp des vulnérables: Les réfugiés face à leur citoyenneté niée," *Les temps modernes* no. 627 (2004), p. 132, Michel Agier uses the expression "humanitarian government" to refer to the ways refugee camps are controlled by "aid organizations and the United Nations." I will be using the expression, without quotation marks, in a somewhat different, more general sense, beyond the frame of organizations referred to as humanitarian, in a manner inspired by the work of Michel Foucault, who speaks, for example, of "the government of men." On this, see Didier Fassin, "L'espace moral de l'action humanitaire: À propos de quelques épreuves récentes," paper presented at *Autour de l'intervention: Protagonistes, logiques, effets,* Université de Montréal–McGill University, 2003.

5   See, for instance, "The Dilemmas of Humanitarian Intervention," special issue, *International Political Science Review* 18, no. 1 (1997).

6   See, especially, Pascal Dauvin and Johanna Siméant, *Le travail humanitaire; Les acteurs des ONG du siège au terrain* (Paris: Presses de Sciences Po, 2002).

7   In France, the most famous prisoner to benefit from this measure was Maurice Papon, an official of the Vichy government who collaborated with Nazi Germany in the Second World War, a past that he hid after the war, when he went on to have a career in politics until revelations about his past resulted in his trial and conviction for crimes against humanity in 1997–1998. Given the accusations against him, this shows the strength of the principle that won his liberation. In this real moral dilemma, compassion won out over the sense of justice. It is worth noting that the regulations that allowed for humanitarian reason to be used in these circumstances were established by one of the founders of MSF, Bernard Kouchner, who was then minister of health. On these questions, see Didier Fassin, "Quand le corps fait loi: La raison humanitaire dans les procédures de régularisation des étrangers," *Sciences sociales et santé* 19, no. 4 (2001), pp. 5–34, and "Compassion and Repression: The Moral Economy of Immigration Policies in France," *Cultural Anthropology* 20, no. 3 (2005), pp. 362–87.

8   A certain de-Westernization of the international humanitarian movement might nonetheless be under way, at least according to a study of Muslim charities carried out by the founder of the branch of MSF in the United Arab Emirates. However, one can still wonder whether this is really humanitarian work or if it is rather a question of traditional religious organizations working in the no less traditional field of helping the poor. We find no moral values (the exaltation of bare life) or ethical principles (a universalizing approach to victims) or action (an appeal to urgency) here. See Abdel-Rahman Ghandour, *Jihad humanitaire: Enquête sur les ONG islamiques* (Paris: Flammarion, 2002).

9   It is well known that Hannah Arendt theorized the emergence of compassion in public action in "The Social Question," *On Revolution* (New York: Penguin, 1965), pp. 59–114. As for the tactical reasons, Luc Boltanski and Eve Chiapello have shown that capitalism absorbs the criticisms levied against it: *The New Spirit of Capitalism,* trans. Gregory Elliott (London: Verso, 2005).

10 On this history, see Didier Fassin, *Faire de la santé publique* (Rennes: Editions de l'Ecole Nationale de Santé Publique, 2005), and Didier Fassin and Anne-Jeanne Naudé, "Plumbism Reinvented: Childhood Lead Poisoning in France, 1985–1990," *American Journal of Public Health* 94, no. 11 (2004), pp. 1854–63.

11 This is the case for Nicholas J. Wheeler in *Saving Strangers: Humanitarian Intervention in International Society* (Oxford: Oxford University Press, 2000). Wheeler admits that the four criteria he uses are hardly any different from the ones used to qualify a war as just. For him, both India's interventions in Pakistan to stop the massacre of the Bengali population in what would become Bangladesh and Vietnam's intervention against Pol Pot's regime to end the mass crimes against Cambodians belong to the register of humanitarian intervention, even if he also discusses their strategic motivations.

12 For a critical analysis of the ambiguities surrounding the militaro-humanitarian intervention in Somalia, see Sherene H. Razack, *Dark Threats and White Knights: The Somalia Affair, Peacekeeping, and the New Imperialism* (Toronto: University of Toronto Press, 2004).

13 The genocide of the Tutsi left a profound trace in the humanitarian organizations that were on-site, as is clear in the three volumes of "public testimony" edited by Laurence Binet for MSF: *Génocide des Rwandais tutsis 1994; Camps de réfugiés rwandais Zaïre-Tanzanie 1994–1995; Violences du nouveau régime rwandais 1994–1995.*

Rescue workers remove a dead body from a collapsed building next to the U.S. embassy in Nairobi, August 8, 1998. One day earlier, terrorist bombs exploded minutes apart outside the U.S. embassies in both Kenya and Tanzania, killing at least 107 people, injuring over 2,200, and turning buildings into mountains of shattered concrete (Khalil Senosi/AP Photo).

The Sovereign, the Humanitarian, and the Terrorist

Adi Ophir

If sovereignty is the power granted by a juridical order proclaiming an exception to this order, as Carl Schmitt said, and if the state of exception proclaimed by a sovereign is a moment at which life is abandoned by the law, forsaken, and exposed to violence that the law does not punish, as Giorgio Agamben explains, then large-scale disasters challenge the very principle of sovereignty.[1] An emergency and a state of exception are created without being proclaimed by the sovereign, life is forsaken, and violent forces — natural as well as social — roam about, footloose, paying no heed to the sovereign's claim to have sole authority over life and death.

Contemporary humanitarianism is a more or less distinct formation of power and knowledge that specializes in lifesaving and relief technologies, which I would like to call "technologies of disaster" (henceforth TDs). The moral discourse and globalized practices embedded in these technologies present a different relationship to the exception and, hence, a different challenge to the political sovereign. In this paper, I propose an analysis of this challenge and some of its consequences. The agents of global humanitarianism are moral entrepreneurs whose discourse and practices propose — sometimes implicitly — a new model of relations between politics, law, and morality in which a certain form of biopolitics turns into a mode of resistance to state power.

MORAL TECHNOLOGIES

For centuries, the main task of political authorities in the West in times of calamity was to contain the disaster, to keep it from spreading into the safer areas, where the court and members of the elite took shelter. In the wake of a disaster, the forces of law and order would return to the scene, trying to restore their rule and sometimes taking advantage of new opportunities created by the disaster, enhancing their domination or transforming their power. This pattern existed in the West from the Middle Ages until at least the beginning of the eighteenth century. Then, gradually, with the expansion of the state, the emergence of the concepts of risk and probability, and the growth of new kinds of knowledge and the techniques associated with them, political authorities came to assume more and more active responsibilities for the direct management of large-scale disasters (natural as well as man-made). States developed and adopted new practices of preparation for expected disasters and new practices of control and relief when disasters did occur. Instead of containment, the task of political authorities and state apparatuses evolved into the efficient management of social space and the physical environment, the reduction of damage and injuries, and the political control and manipulation of the distribution of risks and losses. Disaster may still have been conceived as a natural event, and the state of emergency may have been imposed from the outside, but the sovereign insisted on controlling the exceptions created by the disaster and on making political use of its consequences. The modern state cannot tolerate no-man's-lands and hence mobilizes all its resources to prevent or eliminate them.

It was only around the turn of the twentieth century that modern states in the West assumed full responsibility for the way their societies cope with large-scale disasters, prepared for them before they happened, tried to limit the damage when they did happen, cared for the survivors, and rebuilt disaster zones. But as early as the end of the fourteenth century, in the wake of the Black Death, when the first technologies of spatial segregation appeared in Europe (the lazaretto, the quarantine, and the closure of houses, cities, and entire regions), political authorities recognized the importance of the TDs related to the plague, investing in and trying to gain control over them.[2] When both territoriality and the political problematization of life became essential components of the modern form of state power, TDs became political technologies, and their control and operation were at stake in political struggles. Plague regulations, issued and enforced by both local and central authorities, were widespread by the seventeenth century and served as one of the first and most important spheres for the development of the mechanism of biopower. Earthquakes called for building regulations and provided ample opportunity for rescue and restoration, as Sebastião de Carvalho, the marquess of Pombal, the virtual dictator of Portugal, demonstrated in an exemplary way in the aftermath of the 1755 earthquake in Lisbon.[3] By the second half of the nineteenth century, after the Crimean War (1853–1856), the Battle of Solferino (1859), the American Civil War (1861–1865), and the establishment of the International Committee for the Relief of the Wounded, now the International Committee of the Red Cross (1863), Western states gradually recognized war as a disaster of sorts and adopted new technologies to save the lives and ease the suffering of its survivors.

However, alongside the political and governmental aspect of TDs, and sometime through it, TDs have always also been moral technologies. This is so for the same reason they are the business of the sovereign — because they involve life-and-death decisions. In another sense, these technologies were moral even before they became political, because they involved the care of the living before such care became the daily business of political authorities; they remain moral, even after being completely dissociated from any institutionalized religion, because they involve the concrete, technical, and mate-

First aid on the front line during the First World War in Champagne, France (Photothèque CICR[DR]).

rial embodiment of compassion, mercy, pity, and sacrifice for the sake of others. Indeed, the care of the living and the special attention given to suffering and its reduction are common to TDs and to some of the disciplinary technologies, insurance mechanisms, and welfare institutions of the modern state. Like other mechanisms of biopower and governmentality, of which they are certainly a part, TDs are at one and the same time concerned with — and capable of dealing with — entire populations and specific individuals. The logic of their improvement and specialization means a growing capacity to integrate individuals into specific populations that endow them with essential characteristics while differentiating individuals according to characteristics that make them singular. But there is a real difference that distinguishes TDs from other mechanisms of biopower and governmentality. It is this difference that I would like to present now.

I am using the term *technology* in a wide sense, to designate a more or less structured assemblage of power and knowledge that includes more or less coordinated physical instruments, spatial arrangements, means of communication, means of data collecting and processing, organizational procedures, and discursive practices. The entire instrumental apparatus is embedded in and activated through distinct discursive regimes that direct the operation of instruments, determine these instruments' goals and set standards for their evaluation, educate skilled technicians, and maintain different kinds of interfaces with other technical and discursive environments.

This technological assemblage has multiple origins, and its genealogy contains contingent circumstances, conflicting motivations, and unintended consequences. But to the extent that this assemblage has a certain structure, it already has a logic of its own that cannot be reduced to its multiple genealogies.[4] This is the logic of the care for more or less anonymous others who are subject to severe hardship or threatened by imminent death. This type of care is made possible by the modern technological apparatus and is articulated through it; however, it is the care for others in distress that provides the technological apparatus with its direction, goals, and standards of operation. Care for others in distress is embedded in modern TDs and makes them a distinct part of the apparatuses of biopower. This distinction is most vividly realized today in nongovernmental humanitarian organizations, which are based in a globalized civil society and are relatively independent of both the state and its political interests and the global market and its economic interests.

This may seem like a naive presentation of contemporary humanitarianism, but I would like to insist on the following: notwithstanding everything we know about the more or less tacit ways humanitarian organizations are manipulated by political powers and serve their interests despite the humanitarians' best intentions — despite their clear ideological role and the role they play in legitimating and stabilizing a new, immoral global economic and social order — the humanitarian organizations that operate TDs follow a clearly moral imperative: to save lives and to reduce suffering wherever possible.

Moreover, the moral interest has assumed here a distinct form — it is no longer an interest in the good or the just, or in moral law or duty, or even a more general interest in what ought to be done, but a specific interest in the misery of others — alongside a complex technological apparatus for pursuing this interest. Other interests and motivations — political, economic, libidinal, and so on — certainly play crucial roles in the ways humanitarian mechanisms are put to work. But in times of disaster, and the closer one gets to the disaster zone itself, the more all these "heteronomous" interests, as Kant would have called them, come to be articulated in the language of the ruling moral interest: interest in the misery of others. Everything must be justified in terms of the moral imperative — reduce suffering wherever possible — and whatever cannot be thus justified is open to criticism and sanction. As in the realms of science, art, and law, the question is not the purity of a seemingly autonomous judgment but the material existence of mechanisms — discursive, institutional, and technical — that serve to expose, separate, and exclude elements foreign to the judgment at stake. Such mechanisms have become an integral part of the contemporary apparatus of TDs due to the process of their specialization, which includes the education of experts, the emergence of a culture of expertise, and the institutionalization of a differentiated field (in Bourdieu's sense) of symbolic capital where these experts take positions.[5]

Contemporary TDs are moral before they are political and economic, and they may assume amoral meanings and be used toward political and economic goals only because and only insofar as they are directed by the logic of the care for life in distress. A recent, cynical example occurred during the U.S. wars in Afghanistan and Iraq, when some U.S.

planes dropped humanitarian aid while others were dropping bombs. The American war machine mobilized TDs, just as it mobilized technologies of communication or computation, to prove to the Afghan and Iraqi people, and to the rest of the world, that the war was not directed against the people. Many critics were quick to note that the American aid operation was too little, too late and cynically used as American propaganda in order to justify reckless, futile wars. But in order to do precisely what the critics said they were doing, the Americans had at least to simulate actions driven by care for people in distress. In this they had to demonstrate neither moral sentiment nor moral virtue, but the measurable efficiency of their lifesaving operations. Had it been impossible to simulate rescue and relief, TDs would have been useless as a means of propaganda; had it been impossible to separate (if only in principle) proper from improper use of TDs, the critique of military humanitarianism would have been invalid to begin with.[6]

The management of disaster is a skillful, sophisticated operation of a variety of techniques of rescue, relief, spatial control, and distribution of aid and risk, good and evil. In any large-scale disaster, TDs are inevitably interwoven with the mechanisms, institutions, and rules of the state and the market. For this reason, the management of disaster provides a special opportunity for the "moralization" of the state apparatus and civil society and for the politicization of the morally motivated civil society. Facing a more or less imminent disaster, coping with one as it unfolds, or working in the wake of one that has already occurred, the state, the actors in the market, and every individual citizen are all "thrown" into the moral sphere and judged according to the way they put available TDs to work. Due to the very existence of a more or less sophisticated apparatus of TDs, just the possibility of a future disaster, let alone its actual occurrence, has a moralizing effect on the entire social system.

TDs are "in the moral" in the same way that scientists are "in the truth." To be "in the moral" does not necessarily mean to act morally (in the same way that a scientist may err and still be "in the truth"); it means that a certain attention to moral considerations becomes inevitable. And such attention becomes inevitable at the disaster site due to the mere fact that TDs are available and rescue and relief are possible. The very potential for rescue and relief turns disaster into a paradigm of a moral event and a unique place of morality. Disaster is always already a moral event and a moral place, but not because the duty to prevent it or to limit the damage it causes is placed over and above its political, economic, or religious meanings; on the contrary, disaster is a moral event due to the existence of TDs whose invention, maintenance, and operation are the business of the state, the market, and civil society at large. Disaster is a moral event precisely because (and to the extent that) all these agents have the means to intervene in its course or prevent its occurrence, and because its management is at stake in competitions and struggles among multiple social actors, who negotiate the proper criteria for the most efficient and hence worthiest ways to operate TDs — that is, to rescue and bring relief.

Here is a simple test for the morality of TDs: to avoid using them due to political or economic considerations is immoral. One may justify a failure to operate TDs or an improper use of them (in wartime, for example) with economic or political arguments, but not with moral arguments — unless the rescue or relief operation itself endangers other people's lives. Political and economic reasons that put limits on the use of TDs are often disguised as moral arguments. In other words, the "regime of justification" in effect at the disaster site is moral, governed by the imperative to save lives and not to forsake them.[7] Moreover, in and of themselves, when free of political manipulation, the instruments involved in TDs are color-blind. Differences of race, class, ethnicity, religion, language, gender, and so on cannot be articulated in the discourse of TDs. Such differences may be introduced only as exceptions to existing regulations or under some kind of disguise (for example, when regional boundaries overlap with ethnic or class differences). The imperative to care for life in distress sees no such differences. TDs care for life as such; they are concerned with what Agamben calls "bare life," life that exists prior to and outside of all political and cultural distinctions.[8] Their first and most urgent objects of concern are the body and the conditions that strip it of its social, juridical, and cultural protection.

In fact, it is the concept of life itself that has become blind to political and cultural distinctions. There is no life that is not worth living, no life whose abandonment is morally acceptable. [9] The universalization of the concept of life is an essential element in the ideology and technology of contemporary humanitarianism. This process is not self-evident and should be understood, at least in part, as a reaction to the hierarchical concepts of life proposed by various philosophical and political doctrines that emerged in the nineteenth century and were catastrophically implemented in the twentieth. Distinctions among different forms of life — based on biological, pseudobiological, anthropological, religious, or revolutionary principles — led to the disastrous distinction between life worth living and life whose abandonment and even elimination is permitted. Between universalist humanitarian ideology, which puts the rescue of human lives and the alleviation of human suffering first, and doctrines that accept the very possibility of a life not worth living, let alone explicitly advocate the abandonment of certain forms of life, there exists a clear *différend*.[10] There can be no common ground between those who are preoccupied with superfluous, preventable human suffering and those who are preoccupied with superfluous human beings who, under certain circumstances, may be eliminated.[11] The biological or social differences between forms of life that make a difference to the latter cannot be articulated in the discourse of the former.

AGAMBEN'S CRITIQUE OF HUMANITARIANISM

This *différend* divides the sphere of biopower and splits the interest in bare life. It imposes two distinct courses of action that introduce life into the political and exclude it from the sphere of law. It is this *différend* that Agamben rejects in his discussion of bare life in *Homo Sacer*. His critique of humanitarianism and the implied dismissal of an autonomous moral relation to bare life that is not always already part of the inclusive exclusion of the sovereign deserves our close attention.

For Agamben, the "inclusive exclusion" of bare life makes possible at one and the same time relief operations in the name of human rights and policies of elimination of a kind of life that is not worth living. The camp is the common ground where these two seemingly contradictory courses of action meet. This site, which has become "the fundamental biopolitical paradigm of the West," is a perfect combination of the sovereign authority to exclude or to abandon and the sovereign power to intervene, take care, offer relief to, or destroy any single individual or entire group.[12] It is the place where life has lost its political existence and the law has turned into an endless series of regulations that may be invoked or revoked ad hoc. The state of exception, a temporary suspension of the rule of law as a response to danger or as an act of revenge, has now become the rule, and it takes place prior to any particular danger and beyond any moral sentiment, revenge included. The exception is embodied in a well-demarcated space, outside the everyday life-world of the "normal" citizen, but constantly intruding on its social spaces. The exception has assumed a life-world of its own in which it is at once the ruling norm and the means of ruling. The state of emergency has become permanent, or at least a lasting aspect of everyday life.

Our interest in disaster should direct our attention to two seemingly opposed aspects of the camp. On the one hand, some camps create (or are formed intentionally in order to create) a disaster zone for their inmates. This is clearly the case in most totalitarian camps, but it may also be true of more benign sites, such as a hospital struck by an epidemic.[13] On the other hand, other types of camps open their gates to the survivors of disaster in order to provide relief and to help bring life "back to normal." Of the latter type, the refugee camp is the best example. In our contemporary world, refugees are often people who have been forsaken by the law in their countries of origin (either because the ruling power has failed to protect them or because it is seeking to destroy them). At the same time, they have usually not gained (and may never gain) such protection in the place where they are presently encamped. Refugees in a camp address a claim for protection to a sovereign of whom they have never been the subjects. They claim their human rights precisely because they have been deprived of their rights as citizens. The presence of millions of refugees at the gates of Western states, and sometimes in their midst, breaks "the continuity between man and citizen, *nativity* and *nationality*."[14] They create the cracks through which bare life appears at the heart of the political sphere of liberal democracies and is exposed as that sphere's "secret presupposition," thus putting "the originary fiction of modern sovereignty in crisis."[15]

For Agamben, the refugee camp has a critical revelatory power. It demonstrates a secret truth of liberal democratic regimes, forcing their ruling powers to expose the direct relation to life that lies beyond their juridical and political appearances and to deal directly and openly with a mass of living bodies, which, despite being deprived of rights and foreign to the nation, still demands the protection of power. Agamben identifies weakened models of the refugee camps in many demarcated areas inside the nation-state, not just along its territorial borders, but in its airports and in the ghettos of its main cities: to this list we might add workplaces employing daily immigrants who cross the border in the morning and return at night to their shanty towns on the other side.[16] These are closed sites that serve as buffer zones for separating and mediating between the bare life within and the political life outside, where the intrusion of bare life into the civilized city is controlled and channeled.[17]

The refugee camp embodies and articulates the difference and accelerates the separation between human and civil rights. "The rights of man that once made sense as the presupposition of the rights of the citizen are now progressively separated from and used outside the context of citizenship, for the sake of the supposed representation and protection of bare life," but the demand for protection repeatedly fails because of the opposition of the nation-state. The latter's refusal to accept refugees as immigrants and gradually to absorb them and grant them citizenship not only separates civil from human rights, but also openly and explicitly links bare life to the latter and disguises the biopolitical origin of the former.[18] In this state of affairs, humanitarian organizations that provide aid and relief to refugees, invoking the sanctity of their lives, act as a substitute for the political authorities and under their auspices, contributing to the reinstitutionalization of a false (ideological) distinction between the realm of bare life and the realm of politics. Humanitarian hyperactivity in the camps, where the law does not apply and aid is provided immediately and supererogatorily, regardless of nationality and particular interest, blurs — and thus helps reproduce — the biopolitical presupposition of political power, overshadowing the challenge to that power posed by the refugees and by the disaster that has forced them into exile.

Here Agamben adds significant weight and a new context to the arguments criticizing the contemporary humanitarian enterprise on the basis of the more or less tacit division of labor existing within the nation-state in the context of the ever-expanding neoliberal global economy.[19] Humanitarian organizations, in Agamben's words, "maintain a secret solidarity with the powers they ought to fight."[20] Regardless of their intentions, humanitarians actually help to diffuse the challenge created by the masses of refugees and to restore the local and global order of the nation-states and the global market. They depoliticize the disaster, obstruct understanding of its local and global contexts, and tend to represent its victims as passive objects of care, devoid of political will and organizational capacities — if they do not actually make the victims so.[21] Therefore, the problem with the contemporary, humanitarian form of TDs is not only that they may serve totalitarian and democratic regimes equally well; it is also that they directly contribute to the reproduction of the basic condition of political sovereignty: concealing the "originary" relation between the sovereign's violence and his subjects' bare lives; dissimulating the direct action of power over the subjects' bodies.

Following Agamben's line of critique, we must admit that TDs are moral technologies in precisely the same way that the disciplinary technologies described by Foucault are moral: although they lie "within the moral" according to contemporary conventions, from our critical point of view, they remain morally wrong. TDs may well be the locus of care for others in distress, but it is a kind of care that takes place only on the frontiers of the civilized world, in its "global borderlands," in the abandoned spaces where life is already forsaken, and the exercise of political sovereignty becomes ever more devastating.[22] By depoliticizing and sacralizing abandoned life, contemporary humanitarianism, according to Agamben, reaffirms the abandonment of life as the constitutive moment of political sovereignty.

THE MORAL RESIDUE

Despite the depth of his insightful analysis, Agamben does not give good reasons to drop the radical difference between the imperative to save and to provide relief and the license to abandon and to forsake that splits bare life as an object of moral and political interest. He fails to see the moral residue in the work of humanitarian organizations that cannot be reduced to the role they play in the political sphere, in the consolidation of a new world order, and in the reaffirmation of the basic principle of modern sovereignty. Like many other political theorists and sociologists, he fails to see this residue because he does not consider moral interests and, more generally, "the moral factor" to be real forces active in human reality.

Agamben can claim that contemporary humanitarianism merely reproduces the fundamental principles of the political — the sovereign exception that forsakes life, on the one hand, and the politicization of bare life, on the other — only because he conceives the extraordinary crises that call for exceptional humanitarian care as the other side of the sovereign exception. But these crises, which are never "natural" — in fact, they are always already politicized — are never a simple outcome of a sovereign decision on the exception. They, too, contain a residue — of untamed events, undercodified interactions, hybrid situations, and positions that evade the classifying power of the sovereign, or of any other authority. Agamben is well aware of the subversive potential of some of the crises that call for decisions on the exception, in particular the massive presence of refugees and their challenge to the basic categories of the nation-state. But he understands this challenge as a task to be undertaken, rather than as a part of an unfolding reality: "The concept of the refugee *must* be resolutely separated from the concept of the rights of man.... The refugee *must* be considered for what he is...a limit concept that calls into question the fundamental categories of the nation state...in order to clear the way for an overdue renewal of categories."[23]

The refugee is a limit concept indeed. This is not only because, like the sovereign, he is set apart at the threshold of the law, but also because his very presence separates the political from the moral. As a political noncitizen, he is outside the law; he does not enjoy the status of a juridical subject endowed with political rights. But he is also within the law to the extent that he becomes an object of concern for political authorities, especially when he camps in territories under their jurisdiction and his exclusion is legally authorized. At the same time, he is also an effect of a catastrophic event or of disastrous conditions, which he actually extends and introduces into the daily life of the civilized nation, being the embodiment and living presentation of the exceptional breach of order that the catastrophe has been or has created.

Indonesian soldiers line up to unload relief supplies from a C-130 cargo
plane at Banda Aceh airport six days after the devastating earthquake-
triggered tsunamis of December 26, 2005 (Bullit Marquez/AP Photo).

Usually the liberal sovereign (to whom I limit myself in this context) has no direct responsibility for this breach of order and for all the exceptions it entails. Even if the sovereign's policies generated the disaster, its coming into being could not be ascribed to or represented as the result of "a decision to make an exception" on the sovereign's part. The presence of refugees en masse means that an exception has been imposed on the sovereign or made for him. He is now called upon to make exceptions in response to an exceptional situation. He is required to make exceptional decisions relating to life that has been forsaken, decisions in which the further forsaking of life is always involved. But because humanitarians equipped with TDs are already present at the scene (if only as a mere potentiality, when they are denied access to it), exceptional response to the exceptional state of affairs has already been made, and it is made according to the moral imperative to save and to bring relief. Thus, thrown as they are at the threshold of the law and on the outskirts of the political order, refugees cast light on the sovereign's secret relation to bare life, as Agamben argues, but they also split this relation in two different, often opposing directions: a strictly moral one and a strictly political one. In our contemporary world, at least, the refugee is not just any other nomad, and his existence cannot be reduced to that of a stateless person, as Arendt had it.[24] Rather, the refugee is always already a double subject: a noncitizen of the sovereign state on whose soil he resides and a potential or actual subject (*subjectus*) and object of the humanitarian regime of discourse and action that would keep him alive.

The sovereign exception is coupled with another exception, from which it cannot separate itself and with which it cannot be entirely reconciled: the humanitarian exception, which should be made not for the sake of sovereignty and its political order, but for the sake of those excepted by this sovereignty and excluded from that order.

In an age of globalization, this transformation of the exception that the refugee embodies is reenacted in any large-scale disaster anywhere on the globe. Whether a calamity is defined as a "humanitarian crisis" or not, whether it is natural or man-made (and we know that such a distinction can no longer be maintained), it challenges sovereigns all over the world and forces them to make exceptions. In a globalized world, where images and information from faraway disaster zones reach every corner of the globe in no time at all and assistance may be transported within hours from anywhere on earth to stricken areas, there is hardly any large-scale disaster that is not also an event of deterritorialization. Postmodern catastrophes call for—and soon become scenes of—global intervention of all sorts: media coverage, humanitarian aid by governmental and nongovernmental agencies, pressure and assistance from neighboring countries, inspection by and assistance from bodies of international governance, and investigation and testimony collection by commissions of inquiry and interested members of the public worldwide. Most agents that respond to an emergency or try to take advantage of it interfere in the affairs of the sovereign in a limited and short-term way, but it is humanitarian intervention that calls into question the very foundation of political sovereignty. In a globalized world, no catastrophe is remote enough to be ignored, no refugee too much of a stranger to demand shelter and relief. From the humanitarian point of view, which is already anticipated by and integrated into the state apparatus, the presence of bare life in the disaster zone (where local sovereignty has become ruinous or is in ruins itself) or in the refugee camp (where local sovereignty is still oblivious to the new strangers) is not a license to exercise sovereign violence — rather, it is a call for sovereign protection. Catastrophes throw sovereignty into a space of exceptions; what they demand is the exceptional extension of the juridical order, rather than its suspension — a suspension that, when taken to its limit, may jeopardize the existing political order.

The split described here is not simply a clash between the state and its sovereign, on the one hand, and the nongovernmental organization and its global citizens, on the other. The split inheres in the sophisticated apparatus of TDs of the modern state itself. This apparatus is put to work within the state and outside its borders as an exemplary expression of the sovereign's right to proclaim exceptions and to make decisions about life and death. But, although by the beginning of the twentieth century the modern nation-state had taken on responsibility for the administration of disaster relief and although many governments in the West have at their disposal an apparatus of TDs much more powerful than that controlled by NGOs, it is not a simple *raison d'état* that dictates the operation of these governmental TDs. The scale of its TDs notwithstanding, the state, as I noted above, can only adopt, albeit partially and distortedly, the logic of care inscribed in the TD apparatus and exemplified in the practice of humanitarian organizations. When governmental TDs differentiate among forms and kinds of lives, they put external limits on the humanitarian operation, abusing the instruments at their disposal and exposing themselves to criticism and indignation. Even if TDs are treated like any other apparatus of power and disasters are conceived as external events to be mastered and manipulated for someone's benefit, those benefits come, at least in part, by playing by the rules — in this case, the moral rules. When a government invests in the stock market, risk analysis becomes part of political reasoning; this is precisely what happens to humanitarian considerations when a government invests in the aid industry — these considerations become part of the *raison d'état*. Like economic or diplomatic considerations, moral considerations count in the rationality of the state because they are considered independent of the state.

In other words, the point is not to designate a pure moral actor, but to recognize the independence that moral considerations have gained within the state apparatus due to the mere availability of TDs and the presence of the professionals who operate them.

This is clearly the case when catastrophes take place in weak states. The question of who owns and controls TDs then becomes crucial. In this sense, catastrophes demonstrate an important distinction between "strong" states that are capable of mobilizing a strong and sophisticated apparatus of TDs to handle their own disasters and to help other states, and "weak" states that lack the economic, technological, and organizational capacity to cope with large-scale disasters. In the contemporary, globalized world, these types of crises have become a chronic phenomenon in the weak states, and the intervention of humanitarian organizations, upon which those states are increasingly dependent, has become an important force contributing to the disintegration of their sovereignty. It is the very presence of a powerful apparatus of TDs that embody a clear moral interest that makes possible the transformation of the moral claim into political power.

The question of who owns and is capable of operating TDs is often a crucial one within the state itself, as the failure of the American rescue and relief agencies after Hurricane Katrina struck the Gulf Coast in 2005 made clear. On the eve of the catastrophe and during its first days, governmental agencies acted according to patterns that were well established in the United States — they provided safety nets for the rich and forsook the poor. This kind of policy is acceptable in American political culture as long as success and failure are ascribed, on the one hand, to individuals' gifts and commitments and, on the other, to the blind forces of the market. But when it comes to the blind forces of nature, forsaking the weak seemed unacceptable, and criticism of the government mounted. Why? Because catastrophes, like wars, seem to transform the arena of governmental action and responsibility. They are the business of the political sovereign, his most significant sphere of action, and the realm where sovereignty is established, tested, and contested. And it has been contested, not by a claim for alternative *sovereignty,* but by claims for a different *decision on the exception,* precisely those claims that characterize humanitarian concerns. In times of large-scale disasters, it is neither the market's nor God's invisible hand, but the sovereign's that is expected (since the turn of the twentieth century, at least) to distribute risks, redistribute losses, and administer disaster relief. In times of disaster, the very existence of a sophisticated state rescue apparatus means that responsibility for the fate of the poor rests on neither the poor nor their God, but on the efficiency of this same apparatus. And this efficiency is always already a moral matter.

The existence of such an apparatus is the privilege and sign of strong states. It functions as an integral part of biopolitics in general, and the occurrence of disasters as events to be predicted, avoided, and, if they are unavoidable, alleviated, is not only the objective of biopolitical mechanisms, but also an opportunity for expanding them and for strengthening their grip on the governed population. In strong states, large-scale disasters inevitably lead to a rapid augmentation of the deployment, activity, visible presence, and latent capacities of biopolitical apparatuses, as the attack of September 11, 2001 — and the more recent terror attacks in Madrid, in 2004, and in London, in 2005 — clearly demonstrated. Moreover, in a globalized world, where the "roots of evil" and agents of disaster cannot be contained within the boundaries of the nation-state, governmentally controlled TDs have been integrated into growing global biopolitical networks whose task is, on the one hand, the surveillance and capture of dangerous individuals — carriers of illegal drugs, bombs, or viruses — and, on the other hand, the monitoring of the condition of populations in danger. Of the many outcomes of these new biopolitical mechanisms, two should be singled out in the context of this discussion. First, strong states and international agencies can now mobilize an efficient rescue apparatus for the sake of endangered populations of weak states, which are usually more exposed to natural and political catastrophes and much less equipped to cope with them. Second, strong states are more interested in, and more capable of, the surveillance of certain citizens of weak states and those who find shelter there, because they are conceived as dangerous individuals, in fact, as agents disseminating disaster: terrorists.

Coming to the rescue of endangered populations before, during, and in the wake of large-scale disasters is a highly contested matter in the international arena. Even if no conscious political cynicism were involved, the moral cause would be thoroughly politicized due to the very presence of governments as major players whose actions and inaction have great effect on the suffering of many. The tension between pragmatic, political, or economic reasoning and moral reasoning (which in times of disaster and when the sovereign acts within his own state must be concealed or overcome) becomes manifest and shameless. But this tension is not a matter of an impotent "beautiful soul" facing the cynicism of power; it is, rather, the expression of rivalry and competition between state power and empowered groups of citizens, which are quite well equipped for their task and act outside the realm and logic of the state. The very presence of a powerful apparatus of TDs that embodies a clear "moral interest" makes possible the transformation of a moral claim into political power. Whereas the presence of governments at the site of a disaster politicizes a moral cause, the presence of humanitarian organizations in the international arena moralizes a political cause. It is here that the difference between humanitarian and political considerations becomes an overt contradiction.

Nongovernmental humanitarian groups that think and act globally run a course that, sooner or later, will be obliged to oppose that of governmental rescue and aid apparatuses. The contradiction is structural and rests on two opposing claims to the state of emergency and the exception to the rule. For the sovereign, declaring an emergency and suspending the law is a moment of self-constitution; for the humanitarian, it is a moment when the fate of the other becomes constitutive for the activity and attitude of the self.

THE TERRORIST AND THE HUMANITARIAN

In the background of this binary relation, the ghost of a third party is already hovering, waiting for our consideration. We have already encountered him in passing: the terrorist. He, too, takes a stand regarding the state of emergency — he seeks to bring it about or to force it on the sovereign. Whatever his political motives (and they may vary in ways that lead some people to make distinctions according to the nature of the terrorist's cause, but we must insist here on the similarities of tactics and practices), he is as indifferent to the law of the sovereign as he is to the moral concern of the humanitarian. When he acts, he is a rival to both. Indeed, in this triangle of relations to the state of emergency, each position, when thought of abstractly and according to its basic principles, negates the other two. Thus, for the humanitarian, it does not really matter what the political cause and origin of a state of emergency are. Whether the state of emergency has been declared by a disastrous sovereign or by a sovereign reacting to a natural disaster or to acts of terror, the humanitarian is concerned with bringing rescue and relief to the survivors, regardless of the political considerations of both the sovereign and terrorists. Not surprisingly, from the sovereign's point of view, the challenge posed by foreign humanitarian activists is not altogether different from that posed by terrorists. And it is not unrelated, either. Facing the threat of terror (even if this threat is imaginary or exaggerated), the sovereign nation-state is ready to suspend the law, along with the humanitarian apparatus that works on its margins, and, at the same time, it provides this apparatus with ample new sites and reasons to redeploy itself (as is the case of the United States in Afghanistan and in Iraq, Russia in Chechnya, and Israel in the occupied Palestinian territories). Humanitarian organizations, in turn, are often ready to suspend their condemnation of terrorism, a gesture which has become a cliché in the public discourse of the liberal states; they are ready to extend their work to populations that support or at least tolerate the new form of terrorism as long as their own neutrality is recognized and their immunity respected.

However, these causal links are quite contingent; the true affinity, perhaps even the common ground between the terrorist and the humanitarian is not causal, but structural, at least where the new form of globalized, international terrorism is concerned. The structural similarities between these two phenomena are striking (and embarrassing). Let us mention them briefly: transnational networks lacking a center (or having a center that is contingent and temporary); exemplary models of voluntary, heroic action that are quickly reproduced and distributed across the globe, breeding imitators and enjoying the admiration of large audiences that are not directly involved in the context where the model of action originated; the sacrifice and expenditure of resources taken out of regular cycles of commercial and political exchange for the sake of a goal that is portrayed as higher than the usual goals of everyday political or economic action; nomad practices and mobility that make it possible to land and sojourn for both short and long periods anywhere on the globe, combined with an in-depth interest in a particular locality, carefully chosen and meticulously studied; a special interest in bare life and a more or less systematic tendency to depoliticize the victims' bodies; a certain changing balance between spectacular and clandestine aspects of the operation; a certain indifference — in theory, if not always in practice — to the territorial and symbolic borders of the nation-state; and, finally, the use of religious discourse, which is not peculiar to terrorists, and even traditional philanthropic practices and organizations associated with religious institutions.

Let's take a closer look at these similarities and use them to understand better the place of global humanitarianism in the liberal nation-state and its relation to the political sovereign. Terrorists and humanitarian activists alike are interested in bare life, but in opposite ways. The humanitarian does not make explicit distinctions of skin color, race, ethnicity, or religion in his rhetoric, and when critics point out such distinctions in practice, he tends to reform his language and practices, or at least to make excuses. On the other hand, the terrorist makes an explicit distinction between friend and enemy in his rhetoric, but in practice, his enemy is analogous to the humanitarian's disaster: it designates an area, geographic and imaginary at the same time (America and its allies; Jews and their friends; the government and its collaborators), and targets anyone who happens to be within it. Attacks on tourist destinations (for example, Mombasa, Kenya; Kusadasi, Turkey; and Taba and Sharm el-Sheikh on the Sinai peninsula) demonstrate this clearly. Once a disaster site is targeted, the humanitarian works to save life, no matter whose — the only question (in principle) is where life is being forsaken. Once the enemy is declared, the terrorist's aim is death, it matters little whose — the main question is where lives can be effectively and easily taken. This difference between killing or forsaking life and bringing succor to forsaken life cannot be gainsaid.

Between the terrorist and the sovereign is a gray area inhabited by terrorist organizations seeking to establish a sovereign state and state terrorism that seeks to suppress dissenting movements. Between the humanitarian and the sovereign is a gray area inhabited by governmental and semigovernmental humanitarian organizations using TDs under the auspices of the sovereign and alongside other state apparatuses. But between the terrorist and the humanitarian is a gap, a void, that, despite all structural analogies, no existing practice can fill. Of course, some terrorist or so-called terrorist organizations operate philanthropic institutions, but this is accidental to their terrorist tactics; they do so because they are also political organizations that care for particular populations. There may even be — although this is certainly rare — some humanitarians who have adopted terrorist practices or lent their support to terrorist activities, but, from the humanitarian point of view, such activity, if it exists at all, is entirely accidental.

A CHALLENGE TO SOVEREIGNTY

In the postmodern arenas of large-scale disasters, contemporary refugee camps, and the rapidly multiplying scenes of international terrorism, there appear to be three related processes by which sovereignty is deconstructed: the monolithic, unified, and coherent concept of sovereignty is undermined by the multiplicity of agents that negotiate, compete, and fight over different types of exception making; a lacuna erupts at the heart of the usually ubiquitous mechanisms of biopower, which seem helpless at precisely the moment when they are most needed; and the territorial boundaries that spatially delimit sovereignty are constantly transgressed by streams of people, goods, and information flowing into and out of the disaster zone. But these processes could not take place without both the discourse and practice of humanitarianism and the disarray, anxiety, and death spread by terrorism. Indeed, both terrorism and humanitarianism need the active cooperation and mediation of electronic and print media, but the dreadful images and horrific stories would not make any difference without the new possibilities of action that have opened in these two opposite directions.

The terrorist and the humanitarian face the sovereign from opposite positions. They resemble each other in certain crucial aspects of their activity; their difference lies in the *direction* (and sense) of this activity, in its explicit goals and immediate effects. They both compete with the sovereign himself, never with each other, over the sovereign exception, the right and authority to forsake life, and the proper way of dealing with forsaken life. The two signify the opposite directions that the biopolitical apparatus of the modern state can take. On the one hand, there are moral technologies for the administration of disaster relief whose internal dynamic involves moving from the response to a catastrophic event and its consequences to an attempt to deal with the political conditions that make the catastrophe possible and that amplify its impact. On the other hand, there are disastrous technologies for the administration of life whose inner dynamic entails moving from response to disaster to the systematic production of disastrous conditions. Between the two, there are different areas of congruence and a considerable element of mutual imitation. In response to terrorist acts, the state imitates the terrorists, who, in turn, imitate the state; in response to large-scale disasters, the state imitates the humanitarians, who, in turn, often try to imitate and adopt the practices of a state apparatus.

Somewhere between the terrorist and the humanitarian, forsaken life imposes itself and demands a redefinition of the relationship between political rights and their exception and between the juridical order and its suspension or extension. It won't suffice to recognize the refugee as an abandoned body and forsaken life who "only as such is…made into the object of aid and protection."[25] Nor will it suffice to recognize the citizen as a body and locus of life that should be administered well in order to be protected from the unbearable randomness and cruelty of terrorist violence. The state of total abandonment that accompanies large-scale disasters, like the state of emergency imposed by terrorist attacks, and the state of total security sought after such attacks provides ample opportunities for biopower to extend and deepen its infiltration and colonization of the life-world and give it new legitimacy.

These extreme situations, which can no longer be considered exceptional, also challenge the sovereign by undermining his monopoly over the authority and power to suspend the law, make exceptions, and forsake life. At the same time, the accelerated intrusion of power into the daily life-world of the governed, which is justified by the need to "fight terrorism," is not simply or merely the effect of sovereign decisions. It is also, at the same time, a reaffirmation of the threat to this sovereignty, which continues to crop up behind the backs of the policemen, security agents, guards, and gatekeepers. The reach of this threat is as wide as the entire security network; the threat is present wherever sovereign power is present. Not only are the nation-state's borders being called into question here, but also, and perhaps mainly, its totalizing claim to the administration of life. In other words, what is being called into question is the authority of the sovereign to be the sole legitimate source of the decision to declare who should be abandoned, whose life can be forsaken, and which exception is the proper one. New relations between power and life are currently inscribed at the two ends of the spectrum through the two major, opposing forms of sacrifice and transgression in contemporary culture. The question ultimately concerns the authority of the sovereign to bring under his jurisdiction — precisely by suspending the juridical order — anything that lives or relates to the living, leaving no residue.

It should be noted that even when a functioning humanitarian nongovernmental apparatus is absent, the mere existence elsewhere — even the mere feasibility — of effective TDs (whose mobility now becomes crucial) turns life ruined by disaster or inside the refugee camp into a challenge to sovereign power. TDs' concrete embodiment of the moral imperative — to save as many lives as possible, to limit suffering and loss as much as possible — transforms every disaster, every refugee camp, anywhere on the globe, into a scene of confrontation and cooperation, and in any case into a zone of distinction, between the moral and the political. The same is true, in the opposite direction, for terrorism: even when an active terrorist infrastructure is lacking, the mere existence — even the mere feasibility — of disastrous terrorist activity turns "well-administered life" in the nation-state into life at imminent risk, to be forsaken at any moment, anywhere; this potential forsaking of life, which does not originate with the sovereign, is necessarily conceived as a threat to the sovereign nation-state, to any sovereign state around the globe. The moral, religious, or quasi-religious imperative embodied in the terrorist's deadly *mode of action* (for it is neither an apparatus nor a social institution) transforms any site within the social space into a possible scene of confrontation, tacit cooperation, and certainly differentiation between the anarchist element inherent in the ideology of terrorism and the *raison d'état*.

Humanitarian organizations widen the gap between the rights of man and the rights of the citizen, perhaps contributing to the exclusion of their clients from the public sphere of the liberal state and to the silencing of their voices.[26] But in doing so, they are not simply taking part in the depoliticization of disaster (as their critics rightly claim, although this is not always or necessarily the case); they are also placing the moral claim above and prior to the political or social bond and are ready to follow up on this claim, even when it transgresses the limits of the social bond. Terrorism, in turn, also widens the gap between man and citizen through the reaction it provokes from state power (closer surveillance of strangers; stricter forms of separation between citizens and aliens; easier limitation of suspected persons' rights; and so on). Wherever it is sensed as imminent, the threat of terror also tends to silence or at least flatten the political discourse. But it does something else, aside from contributing to the augmentation of the state and its biopolitical apparatus. Terrorism depoliticizes power by confronting us with an absolute enemy that is said to unite us all and that is portrayed as an extraterritorial element — a force that transcends the political sphere and that must be opposed, for its negation is a condition for the very existence of the social bond.

The depoliticization of the humanitarian claim, like the exclusion of the terrorist claim, may be in the short-term interest of both the sovereign and his two rivals. The humanitarians hope to gain better access to the places and victims of disaster by presenting the humanitarian space as apolitical; the terrorists seek to present a radical alternative to the political and avoid any kind of negotiation with the sovereign power. Power itself benefits from the depoliticization of disaster, for this enables it to deny its responsibility for the conditions that make disaster possible. Power also benefits from the depoliticization of terrorism, for this enables it to avoid coming to terms with the terrorists' demands and claims, their motivations, and the conditions that sustain them. In both cases, the primacy of the apolitical principle guiding both humanitarianism and terrorism may serve as a means of depoliticization, which helps to conceal and reproduce the biopolitical foundation of modern sovereignty, strengthens state power, and diminishes the universalist dimension of citizenship. But in both cases, what's at stake is the inevitably temporary suspension of the imminent political challenge posed by the sovereign's two rivals.

The terrorist's act impairs the state's capacity to administer its citizens' lives, but this is often merely a means toward an ultimate goal: the destruction of the state and the establishment of a radically different political order in its place. The humanitarian seeks, in principle, if not always in practice, to subjugate biopolitical apparatuses to the imperative of caring for others in distress. Implied in this claim — in principle, even if the implication is often debated and sometimes rejected in humanitarian discourse — is a further demand for the inevitably political transformation of the disastrous conditions themselves. This includes the elimination of the permanent state of emergency and the restoration of a civic dimension to the lifeworld of the stricken population. International terrorism ends and forsakes life in order to undermine the very possibility of citizenship within the existing political order, holding life itself in suspense until the coming of a radically new form of political bond. Global humanitarianism, or at least certain voices within it, speaks in the name of the humanity of forsaken lives and puts forward moral demands with political implications that create new forms of solidarity and challenge the boundaries of the nation-state and the way it constrains and nationalizes the idea, rules, and practices of citizenship.

This, I believe, is the subtext of the 1999 Nobel Prize speech of James Orbinski, the former president of Médecins Sans Frontières (MSF):

> Ours is an ethic of refusal. It will not allow any moral political failure or injustice to be sanitized or cleansed of its meaning. The 1992 crimes against humanity in Bosnia-Hercegovina. The 1994 genocide in Rwanda. The 1997 massacres in Zaire. The indiscriminate 1999 attacks on civilians in Chechnya. These cannot be masked by terms like "Complex Humanitarian Emergency," or "Internal Security Crisis." Or by any other such euphemism — as though they are some random, politically undetermined event. Language is determinant. It frames the problem and defines response. It defines, too, rights, and therefore responsibilities. It defines whether a medical or humanitarian response is adequate. And it defines whether a political response is inadequate.... For MSF, this is the humanitarian act: to seek to relieve suffering, to seek to restore autonomy, to witness to the truth of injustice, and to insist on political responsibility.... Ours is not to displace the responsibility of the state. The final responsibility of the state is to include, not exclude, to balance public interests over private interests, and to ensure that a just social order exists. Ours is not to allow a humanitarian alibi to mask the state responsibility to ensure justice and security.[27]

Everything is presented here in a nutshell: the irreducibility of the moral concern; the necessity to politicize humanitarian action — that is, to understand it in its proper political context and to take account of its political implication — without, however, taking any position regarding the stakes of the political game; assuming and addressing the state's responsibility to ensure justice and security and to protect every one of its subjects, without, however, speaking from the point of view of the state or its people; taking the position of a universal addresser whose sole legitimacy comes from the unbounded solidarity with the victims of power it claims to embody (but not to represent); the readiness to turn this unbounded solidarity with the victims into a challenge to the sovereign power that generates and fosters their plight or that blocks those who come to their rescue.

That in practice humanitarian action often finds itself entangled with the power it should oppose or challenge is obviously true, and the critique that has exposed this is abundant. The point, as I said above, is not that humanitarian actors are morally right due to their concern with the suffering of others, but that they are "within the moral." Thus, critical reflection that insists on deciphering their collaboration with the powers that generate disasters is not external to their discourse, but is one of its constitutive elements, and its efficacy may be compared to that of refutation in the sciences. The humanitarian "regime of justification" means that reflection on any course of humanitarian action must frequently go through and overcome the suspicion of collaboration; a course of action that fails the critical test should be abandoned. This is as close as one gets today to the existence of morality as a sui generis domain or a social sphere, with stakes, concerns, and interests of its own.

This paper is part of a research project funded by the Israel Science Foundation. I have greatly benefited from comments and criticism made on earlier drafts of this paper by Ronen Shamir, Michal Givoni, Yehuda Shenhav, Gil Anidjar, Michel Feher, and Ariella Azoulay. A different version of the paper was published as "Disaster as a Place of Morality," Qui Parle 16, no. 1 (2006).

1 Carl Schmitt, *Political Theology: Four Chapters on the Concept of Sovereignty,* trans. George Schwab (Cambridge, MA: MIT Press, 1985); Giorgio Agamben, *Homo Sacer,* trans. Daniel Heller-Roazen (Stanford, CA: Stanford University Press, 1998).

2 Daniel Panzac, *Quarantaine et lazarets: L'Europe et la peste d'Orient, XVIIe–XXe siècles* (Aix-en Provence: Edisud, 1986); Françoise Hildesheimer, *La terreur et la pitié: L'Ancien Régime à l'épreuve de la peste* (Paris: Publisud, 1990).

3 T.D. Kendrick, *The Lisbon Earthquake* (London: Methuen, 1956); C. R. Boxer, "Pombal's Dictatorship and the Great Lisbon Earthquake, 1755," *History Today* 5, no. 11 (1955), pp. 727–36.

4 Michel Foucault demonstrates this difference between the contingencies of a genealogy and the constraints of a structure in his study of disciplinary power and its "political technology of the body": *Discipline and Punish: The Birth of the Prison,* trans. Alan Sheridan (New York: Vintage, 1977).

5 On the humanitarian field, see, for example, Pascal Dauvin and Johanna Siméant, *Le travail humanitaire: Les acteurs des ONG du siège au terrain* (Paris: Presses de Sciences Po, 2002).

6 For the debate on humanitarian (military) intervention, see, for example, J.L. Holzgrefe and Robert O. Keohane (eds.), *Humanitarian Intervention: Ethical, Legal, and Political Dilemmas* (Cambridge: Cambridge University Press, 2003).

7 I am borrowing the concept of the "regime of justification" from Luc Boltanski and Laurent Thévenot, *On Justification: Economy of Worth,* trans. Catherine Porter (Princeton, NJ: Princeton University Press, 2006).

8 Agamben, *Homo Sacer,* pp. 4–9.

9 It is worth noting that the distinction between human life and the life of other animals has been recently called into question, as well, as the elimination of living species and the suffering of animals have become the object of much debate and political struggle.

10 I am using the term in the sense given to it by Jean François Lyotard in *The Differend: Phrases in Dispute,* trans. Georges Van Den Abbeele (Minneapolis: University of Minnesota Press, 1988).

11 See Adi Ophir, *The Order of Evils: Toward an Ontology of Morals* (New York: Zone Books, 2005), pp. 552–79.

12 Agamben, *Homo Sacer,* p. 181.

13 Here is but one quick example: in his book on Florence Nightingale's work of relief and nursing in the Crimean War, the historian Hugh Small writes, analyzing the causes for the high mortality rate in Nightingale's military hospital in Scutari, "In the five months before the Sanitary Commission arrived [in Scutari], between November 1854 and March 1855, Nightingale had not been running a hospital. She had been running a death camp." Hugh Small, *Florence Nightingale: Avenging Angel* (New York: St. Martin's Press, 1998), p. 88.

14 Agamben, *Homo Sacer,* p. 131.

15 *Ibid.*

16 Weakened in the sense that the virus in a vaccine is weakened.

17 Agamben, *Homo Sacer,* pp. 174–76.

18 *Ibid.,* pp. 132–33.

19 See, for example, Alex de Waal and Rakiya Omaar, "Doing Harm by Doing Good? The International Relief Effort in Somalia," *Current History* 92 (1993), pp. 198—202, and *Humanitarianism Unbound? Current Dilemmas Facing Multi-Mandate Relief Operations in Political Emergencies* (London: African Rights, 1994); Joanna Macrae and Anthony B. Zwi (eds), *War and Hunger: Rethinking International Responses to Complex Emergencies* (London: Zed Books, 1994); Alex de Waal, *Famine Crimes: Politics and the Disaster Relief Industry in Africa* (London: African Rights and the International African Institute and Indiana University Press, 1997); Pierre de Senarclens, *L'humanitaire en catastrophe* (Paris: Presses de la Fondation nationale des sciences politiques, 1999).

20 Agamben, *Homo Sacer,* p. 133.

21 See, for example, Barbara Hendrie, "Knowledge and Power: A Critique of an International Relief Operation," *Disasters* 21, no. 1 (1997), pp. 57–76; Jenny Edkins, "Sovereign Power, Zones of Indistinction, and the Camp," *Alternatives* 25, no. 1 (2000), pp. 3–25; B.S. Chimni, "Globalization, Humanitarianism and the Erosion of Refugee Protection," *Journal of Refugee Studies* 13, no. 3 (2000), pp. 243–63.

22 Mark Duffield, "Governing the Borderlands: Decoding the Power of Aid," paper presented at "Politics and Humanitarian Aid: Debates, Dilemmas and Dissension," seminar, Commonwealth Institute, London, 2001; available online at www.sussex.ac.uk/Units/CGPE/events/conferences/failed_ states/conference_papers/duffield.pdf.

23 Agamben, *Homo Sacer,* p. 134; emphases added.

24 Hannah Arendt, *Imperialism: Part Two of The Origins of Totalitarianism* (New York: Harcourt, Brace and World, 1968), pp. 149–70.

25 Agamben, *Homo Sacer,* p. 133.

26 *Ibid.,* pp. 131–33.

27 James Orbinski, "The Nobel Prize Acceptance Speech," Oslo, 1999, available online at www.doctorswithoutborders.org/ publications/speeches/1999/nobel.cfm.

Humanitarianism Reconfigured:
Philanthropic Globalization and the New Solidarity

Alex de Waal

Humanitarianism is a field with a short institutional memory, partly because its practitioners are often young and enthusiastic, partly because disasters are by nature different in every case. In little more than fifteen years, it has been transformed beyond all recognition. The period of the most rapid change was the early 1990s, when it seemed that every major crisis was the occasion for significant ethical and practical innovation.

At the close of the Cold War, international relief was already becoming big business, propelled to both size and prominence by a series of calamities, including ones in Cambodia and Ethiopia. But in each of those disasters, thoughtful humanitarians railed against the restrictions on their activities imposed by the politics of the Cold War. In Cambodia, relief agencies ended up feeding the Khmer Rouge and its supporters and captives, unable to operate legally inside a country whose government was not recognized. In Ethiopia, the government rendered millions of hungry people beyond reach because they lived in areas controlled by rebels. Barbara Harrell-Bond's paper "Humanitarianism in a Straitjacket" encapsulated this frustration.[1]

The end of the Cold War was an opportunity for humanitarians to escape these bounds. In the Sudan—then and now a laboratory for humanitarian experimentation—for the first time, a government allowed relief organizations to ship relief into rebel-held areas when Operation Lifeline Sudan was launched in 1989. The Ethiopian and Angolan governments followed suit. In Iraqi Kurdistan, in 1990, the coalition forces carved a "safe haven" out of a sovereign territory. The promise of a "new world order" had, it seemed, a humanitarian dimension. It was a bright dawn: the possibilities of using humanitarian resources and expertise to save lives and stop suffering seemed limitless.

But the view from the ground was more skeptical. Aid workers in the field, especially those familiar with local cultures or possessing inquiring sociological minds, recognized that the chief challenge of effective relief work was not getting access or resources, but providing suffering people with the capability to seek their own solutions. Aid could create as many problems as it solved, especially when delivered without sensitivity to

Internally displaced Somalis watch as food aid arrives for distribution at a camp in Wajid, December 4, 2005 (Antony Njuguna/AP Photo).

local requirements. From this vantage point, introducing new relief instruments was inherently problematic. Would the dismantling of sovereignty as a barrier to humanitarianism truly liberate poor and vulnerable people, or would it empower institutions that were not intrinsically accountable to the poor and hungry?

The drumbeat for a humanitarian intervention in Somalia in late 1992 and that campaign's success posed the issues sharply. Did the U.S. Marines who stormed up a Mogadishu beach in December 1992 represent the vanguard of the "humanitarian international" or the shock troops of philanthropic imperialism? It was, in fact, a false dichotomy: some humanitarians' dreams were indeed imperial. This was an early omen of how the field would confuse and conflate conventional political labels. However, when Operation Restore Hope in Somalia descended into the bloody debacle described in *Black Hawk Down,* the humanitarian agencies escaped the pressure for self-examination because the failure had so obviously been caused by the political and military errors of the United States and the United Nations.[2] The Battle of Mogadishu also seemed to illustrate the folly of a securitized philanthropy. In retrospect, it was only a temporary setback for that approach.

"HUMANITARIANISM UNBOUND"

The genocide in Rwanda and its aftermath threw the humanitarian dilemmas into the sharpest relief: with the end of the Cold War, humanitarians were no longer forced into playing a role strictly circumscribed by the political demands of Western governments. They were now allowed to operate in war zones and expand their mandates to include human-rights issues. Free of their straitjacket, humanitarian agencies could not only operate outside those old constraints, but also could set a real political agenda. "Humanitarian intervention" was emblematic of that ambition: using the hardware of the world's most powerful states to pursue philanthropic goals.

But, as I argued at the time, it was "humanitarianism unbound." There was a danger of hubris: the humanitarian agencies were shackled by other constraints, not the least of which were their own institutional self-interest and sociocultural precepts, which hampered their ability to analyze and respond to the human consequences of political crises.[3] Mixing the mandates of human rights, politics, and humanitarianism could lead to trouble, including expectations that could not be met. A striking instance of this was the disproportionate relief response to the flow of displaced people from Rwanda into eastern Zaire in 1994 in comparison with the neglect of the survivors of the genocide, a response that without doubt aided the *genocidaires'* efforts to regroup.

Should humanitarians return to their earlier, confined role, willfully blind to the political context of their actions? Or should they embrace their engagement with real politics and adopt an agenda of solidarity with the poor and oppressed? Many in the humanitarian world, as well as many of their critics, lean toward the latter, but it is remarkably difficult to do in a general way (as opposed to picking a few particular causes) while retaining the principles of neutrality and impartiality.

SIX CHANGES OVER A DECADE

There is no doubt that the Rwanda genocide and its aftermath generated intense self-scrutiny among humanitarian agencies. The issues were similar to those raised in Bosnia, except on a greater scale and with the humanitarians more clearly in the forefront of making critical decisions. As a result, at least six significant reforms were set in motion, shaping the changes that were already under way.

Deepening professionalization. In most respects, today's international humanitarians are more qualified and capable than before. A number of important sets of professional and ethical standards have been introduced and implemented through voluntary compliance. Agency staff members, broadly speaking, still see philanthropy as either a vacation or a vocation, and their motives are mixed, as always, but operational standards are undoubtedly higher in most fields. Most likely there is backsliding in some areas, for example, in command of local languages, and host-country professionals are still underrepresented, but the general trend is toward improvement.

Broadening mandates. In the early 1990s, it was still unusual for relief and development agencies to operate in conflict zones, to engage with issues of human rights and conflict resolution, and to call for international military intervention. It was also novel for human-rights organizations to concern themselves with relief and the well-being of populations in war zones. All of these concerns are now standard. While there remains a degree of operational specialization — Oxfam in water and sanitation, Médecins Sans Frontières in health, and so on — the blurring and intermingling of mandates has become routine, and international agencies have become more alike. Almost all receive government funding and work according to roughly the same professional and operational standards. Their staff members move seamlessly from one organization to another. Meanwhile, donors have themselves become more and more operationally active, and the boundaries between bilaterals, UN agencies, and NGOs have become even more blurred.

Democratizing the aid encounter. The difficulty of aid agencies' being accountable to the subjects of their concern was identified early on as a structural difficulty of international humanitarianism. Amartya Sen famously pointed out, with special reference to India, how democratic institutions can serve as a mechanism for timely response to or prevention of famine. How could the essentially domestic mechanisms of accountability be transferred onto an international stage? UN agencies and NGOs were answerable primarily to their donors — Western publics and governments — and poor and vulnerable people had little recourse should the organizations fail to provide relief or make terrible errors. What developed during the 1990s was not a formal mechanism of accountability, but an unprecedented transparency of international aid bureaucracies, including governmental donors and multilateral organizations such as the World Bank. Citizens of poor countries could influence these agencies not through direct representation, but through the NGO networks that had begun to permeate the decision-making processes of these bureaucracies. The aid encounter was becoming more democratic, albeit in a roundabout manner.

U.S. secretary of state Colin Powell (CENTER RIGHT) chats with the Sudanese vice president Ali Osman Mohammed Taha (RIGHT) after holding talks with the Sudanese rebel leader John Garang (CENTER LEFT) near the Kenyan town of Naivasha on October 22, 2003. Powell was meeting the Sudanese parties to push them to reach a comprehensive agreement to end the twenty-year civil war (Sayyid Azim/AP Photo).

Converging with security agendas. In the early 1990s, it was not clear whether humanitarians' flirtation with military intervention and other security issues (such as disarmament and demobilization) was a passing fancy or the beginning of a long-term relationship. Notwithstanding the misgivings over Somalia and Bosnia, the latter turned out to be the case. This trend was already noticeable in the second half of the 1990s and became much more marked after September 11, 2001.[4] It is now quite normal for NGO staff members to work in situations in which they require either their own armed guards or peacekeepers from the UN or a regional organization. It is salutary to recall that the International Committee of the Red Cross hired guards for the first time ever in Somalia in 1991.

The sustained dominance of the Northern NGO. The NGO of the global North or the international NGO looked like an expensive and cumbersome organization in the early 1990s, perhaps doomed to lose in competition with its Southern partners. In South Asia, this was noticeably occurring as local NGOs grew in strength and capacity. Was it just a matter of time before African NGO partners caught up? Thus far, that hasn't happened. This reflects the continuing dominance of Northern donor funds in the humanitarianism business. It may also reflect African relief professionals' preference for seeking work in established international organizations, rather than founding their own. This is particularly marked in the case of emergency activities in conflict situations, where security is a high priority: a staff member of an international agency has considerably more protection than someone working for a local NGO. Northern NGOs are also integrated into the networks that provide some influence and accountability over the donor apparatus. Meanwhile, Northern NGOs have changed their own administrative structure by becoming multinational and setting up confederal structures that in some cases include Southern partners on an ostensibly equal footing.

Emergence of a new solidarity politics. The model for "solidarity" NGOs in the 1980s was leftist: the best examples included the Sandinistas, the Eritreans, and the struggle against apartheid. These models were vanishing in the 1990s, to the regret of many on the left, who called nostalgically for a reinvention of solidarity. This has, in fact, happened, but in ways that were not anticipated. The most vigorous and powerful solidarity politics has come from religious constituencies within the right wing, which have mobilized around causes such as southern Sudan and HIV/AIDS — in the latter case with a distinct moral agenda. Christian morals are a powerful influence on aid politics. The left-leaning movement for solidarity with the developing world is represented by activists moving into government and politicians with genuine concern about world poverty. These individuals take a more top-down approach — perhaps because of their personal friendships with people who have become leaders. Evangelical churches have been a powerful influence and take their moral mission seriously. Strange alliances have arisen from this, as is symbolized by the missionary zeal of Tony Blair and George W. Bush and as is manifest in unexpected realignments on the situations in Iraq and the Sudan and the issue of HIV/AIDS. The "new solidarity" politics is confusing and multifarious.

EPISODES AND SCENES

The international humanitarian enterprise focuses its energy and innovations on certain key episodes and places, which garner high levels of attention and resources. It lends itself to an episodic analysis, a narrative with distinct scenes.

THE BIRTH OF THE NEW SOLIDARITY

The second Clinton administration took some remarkably strong positions on African policies. It backed regime change in the Sudan, supported the "frontline states" of Eritrea, Ethiopia, and Uganda, and quietly endorsed Rwanda's intervention in Zaire. It was motivated equally by horror at the human-rights abuses of the Sudanese jihadists and the Rwandan *interahamwe* and by enthusiasm for the "new leaders" of Africa, who were leftist liberation warriors with a sense of purpose. Senior members of Clinton's Africa team felt personal solidarity with the "new leaders" and brought a traditional leftist spirit of solidarity politics to the administration.

This had two repercussions for humanitarianism. One was a polarization of the debate over the Rwandan closure of the refugee camps in Zaire in November 1996 and the military incursion into the province of Kivu, which ended with the overthrow of President Mobutu and Laurent Désiré Kabila's accession to power in the country that he renamed the Democratic Republic of the Congo. Already, there had been a near-total breakdown in communication and confidence between the Rwanda Patriotic Front (RPF) and the international NGOs on account of the misshapen humanitarian response in 1994 and the continuing way aid flows assisted the genocidal forces in exile in Zaire. Uncritical solidarity with the RPF as it struck into Zaire helped deepen a tragedy that was, by this time, perhaps unavoidable. The developing disaster in what is now the Democratic Republic of the Congo became a dead end for humanitarian innovation and inspired an ever-inadequate effort to cope with the immense human tragedy of a disintegrating country.

The second humanitarian outcome was an initiative to move into rebel-held areas of the Sudan, aimed not only at assisting international organizations working there, but also at building up the capacity of the rebels themselves. This was also born out of a spirit of solidarity, not specifically with the Sudan People's Liberation Army (SPLA), but with the radical members of the Sudanese National Democratic Alliance. But very soon the programs were co-opted by individuals closely aligned with the SPLA, some of them influential in the United States Agency for International Development (USAID) and in due course by the SPLA itself. At the time, the SPLA was busy reinventing itself as the defender of Christian values against a Muslim onslaught — or at least was doing so in its selective propaganda offensive in the United States. What began as a program modeled on the solidarity assistance to the secular, leftist Eritrean and Tigrean liberation fronts was transformed into a vehicle for enabling the Christian lobbies in Washington to fund an opportunistic militarist organization that figured its best chance of success was donning a religious mantle. Some established secular NGOs received assistance for operations in southern Sudan, but most preferred to continue working through established UN-framed mechanisms, in part because their operations in areas under government control would have been jeopardized if they had worked too closely with the SPLA. American faith-based organizations were the chief beneficiaries of the new solidarity. This augured the spectacular growth of evangelical humanitarian agencies, mainly in the United States.

As the Clinton administration's Sudan policy came under increasing criticism, its architects turned to the religious right in Congress and various lobbying groups for support. After 2000 and the election of the Republicans — who rejected the regime-change policy in favor of seeking peace — the liberal solidarity leaders found themselves in the same lobby as the religious right, criticizing the peace effort as a sellout. They were joined by some members of the administration itself. In opposition were most of the State Department and many established NGOs, which may have disliked the Sudan's government, but which preferred a more conventional way of doing business.

INTERVENTION À LA CARTE

The events in Somalia and Rwanda were temporary setbacks in the trend toward using military intervention to resolve humanitarian and human-rights crises. The key was Bosnia: the Clinton administration finally bit the bullet and bombed the Serb positions around Sarajevo, a move that was praised by relief workers and human-rights activists. The next intervention was the dispatch of British troops to Sierra Leone. This, like the Bosnian action, was undertaken without a UN mandate. It was of uncertain legality and done in an almost surreptitious manner. Both interventions achieved their goals, bearing out the nineteenth-century writer and politician William Harcourt's view that "in the case of Intervention, as in that of Revolution, its essence is illegality, and its justification is its success."[5]

West Africa was the location of a series of exercises in ad hoc multilateralism. In Sierra Leone, the British provided special forces, logistics, communications, and funds for the UN and the West African force. In Côte d'Ivoire, a similar formula has been followed, with France in the lead. In Liberia, the U.S. briefly played a comparable role, albeit most of the time offshore — Nigeria has been the real power. This cluster of interventions shows how the geometry of intervention is changing; more attention is paid to local specifics, and responsibilities are parceled out to anyone willing to take them on. Obtaining a mandate at the UN Security Council is desirable, but can be bypassed, if necessary. What is important is the result.

Britain's Tony Blair was the prime mover in the Sierra Leone intervention. He interpreted the Labour Party's commitment to an "ethical foreign policy" in interventionist, almost missionary terms. Such an interpretation reflected impatience with a multilateral order that was seen as conservative and as protecting the privileges of abusive rulers at the expense of the rights of citizens and civilians.

The military intervention in Kosovo marked another precedent: a preemptive intervention to halt atrocities that were believed to be imminent. This was the boldest exemplar of interventionism, which reappeared in the Bush national-security doctrine. Despite the critiques of the actions of the United States in Kosovo and of its flawed justification for the Iraqi invasion, preemption has left its imprint on the politics of interventionism.

"MAKING POVERTY HISTORY"

While the boundaries between humanitarianism and military intervention were being blurred, a set of broad-based campaigns among Western publics was also bringing issues of poverty, disease, debt, and aid into national politics. Since Band Aid's inception in 1984, humanitarianism had possessed the power to embarrass political leaders, who were seen as stingy. By the late 1990s, those whose consciences had been awakened by the release of Band Aid's song and similar events were looking hard at the long-term structural causes of poverty and famine. Decades of public education by the World Development Movement, Third World First (later called People & Planet), Oxfam, and various church-based agencies were at last beginning to pay off. Jubilee 2000 was the first of several development campaigns that mobilized extraordinary numbers of people in Western countries. Other campaigns included mobilization around various HIV/AIDS issues, such as bringing down the prices of drugs, instituting fair-trade policies, and increasing aid. These have culminated, so far, in ONE (a "campaign to make poverty history") and the Live 8 concerts on the eve of the 2005 Group of Eight Summit in Gleneagles, Scotland.

Several of the most important humanitarian operations of the last decade must be seen in light of this new and sophisticated focus on the structural causes of poverty. The southern African crisis of 2002–2003 was widely seen as due, in part, to the effects of

Irish rock singers Bono (RIGHT) and Bob Geldof (LEFT) share a word with French president Jacques Chirac during a meeting on the sidelines of the G8 Summit at Gleneagles in Auchterarder, Scotland, July 8, 2005 (Michel Euler/AP Photo).

the HIV/AIDS epidemic. The Ethiopian food crisis of the same period was interpreted as a crisis of livelihoods. The Niger famine of 2005, coinciding with the G8 Summit, was seen in the context of the collapse of cotton production and pastoralism, partly due to unfair trade rules.

These campaigns originated in a coalition consisting of the liberal left, which was concerned with Third World poverty, and religious groups following an old tradition of church mobilization. Finding genuine converts in center-left governments in Europe, the campaigns were led to an extraordinary degree by elected politicians, but they also opened up aid decision making to a wide range of new, nongovernmental actors. Aid was becoming an important part of democratic politics in the West, and as such, it was being subjected to scrutiny as never before.

Despite their origins on the political left, these antipoverty campaigns found an extraordinary and unexpected groundswell of support on the right, especially among churchgoers. Although this is more marked in the United States, it is present in Europe, too. It is most clearly manifest among evangelicals, and NGOs with this support base — such as World Vision International and Samaritan's Purse — have been some of the fastest growing. President George W. Bush is perhaps the unlikeliest advocate of increased aid to Africa, especially for HIV/AIDS, but he has provided far more resources than his predecessor did. The aid comes with ideological strings, but the authentic charitable impulse cannot be doubted. The mechanisms that have emerged from these campaigns and the charitable political leadership are top-down and resource-driven and focus on the quantity of aid, rather than its quality. For the first time, many parts of the aid industry now have resources on the scale that they have long demanded, HIV/AIDS treatment, for example. This has echoes of the lifting of the sovereignty constraint fifteen years ago: it is a dawn of optimism. Those who have observed the problems on the ground and are concerned with the quality of aid, rather than its quantity, are skeptical and anticipate disappointments.

POST-9/11 INTERVENTIONS

The significance of the political right's "new solidarity" was minor until the September 11, 2001 attacks and the launch of the "global war on terror." Thereafter, this solidarity has become a determining factor in the trajectory of international humanitarianism. September 11 compelled the Republican administration to break its isolationism and to become the most interventionist U.S. government in recent history. Its motives are mixed and include national security, revenge, the interests of metropolitan capitalism (including the oil industry), libertarian ideology, and Christian evangelism. Humanitarian justifications for U.S. policies are brought in as ancillaries. Tony Blair, who has supported the same actions, has given them different justifications: humanitarianism and protection from weapons of mass destruction are higher on his list. This combination of explanations and exponents has thrown the critics of intervention largely off balance. The kaleidoscope has been rotated, and the old configurations no longer make sense.

Afghanistan was a relatively uncontroversial trial for intervention, because no one—especially on the left—was ready to speak up for the Taliban. The significance of the Afghan occupation is that, for the first time, humanitarian concerns became closely aligned with a pivotal national-security issue for the major Western powers. But Iraq was the key case. On the whole, support and opposition for the Iraq war followed right-left political allegiances, but this was more because people on the left opposed Bush and thought Blair had sold out rather than careful analysis of the pros and cons of the intervention itself. Four distinct positions exist among humanitarians and human-rights proponents.

A reflexive antiwar position. This stand has a fair chance of being vindicated because of the propensity of all armies to make blunders and commit crimes. As a result, events such as the torture committed at the Abu Ghraib prison can be conscripted post hoc to justify the stand taken earlier. The reflexive antiwar advocate argues that those who will the end should will the means and must therefore take some responsibility for the consequences of their initiatives. Another important aspect of this argument is that nations are entitled to self-determination, and an occupying power should not decide what is best.

Liberal democratic interventionism.[6] This is based on the idea that belief in liberty and human rights entails a duty to promote them where possible, and if that means overthrowing tyrants and thus abrogating the principle of states' sovereign independence and equality, so be it. This is the clearest instance of the politics of the "new solidarity": as part of our solidarity with the oppressed, we use our power—including military power—and influence to remove dictatorships. Whether driven by liberal internationalism, a belief in the transformative power of democracy, or religious sentiment, this new solidarity is becoming a revolutionary force in world affairs.

Multilateralist legalism. This view — which is that of the UN — holds that the perils of abrogating international law outweigh the potential benefits of violating the principle of states' independence and equality, even for a noble cause. The proponents of this stance include people who fear a new era of interventionism and those who fear it will hinder building multilateral security orders in Africa and elsewhere.

Consequentialism. It's justifiable if it works. The foundation of this approach is the claim that to do intervention, you must do it properly — its justification is its success. One can think that an intervention is a noble cause, but that it would be unforgivable to do it badly, which would include justifying it poorly and thus losing the support of international public opinion. Consequentialism, like utilitarianism, leads us to a hard look at principles. We must also look at opportunity costs: Iraq made intervention in Darfur much more difficult and the Liberia operation small and half-hearted. One consequentialist approach is to concede that an intervention is going to occur and then to support it in order to make it work as well as possible.

One significant fact for this discussion is that the established international humanitarian organizations have been outflanked by radical and conservative, left and right arguments. Meanwhile, the intervention and the resulting war have battered the agencies. Senior staff members of the UN and the major NGOs have been murdered, and all the organizations have been unable to fulfill their mandates in ways they consider safe and appropriate.

The core justifications for the interventions in Afghanistan and Iraq were security concerns: the threats posed by a millenarian, utopian, deterritorialized network and by a conventional aggressor dictatorship believed to possess nonconventional weapons. Humanitarian concerns were merged with, though secondary to, these hard political interests. But the nature of the intervention was in each case colored by ideologies and solidarities, giving each one a certain nobility of aim, if not necessarily of outcome. The place of humanitarianism in the shadow of these "just wars" is problematic.

HOMECOMING OF THE COMPLEX EMERGENCY

Until the occupation of Afghanistan, humanitarianism was a "soft" political issue. But even with the occupation of Iraq, it was still a foreign issue, affecting domestic politics only insofar as voters had a conscience about faraway suffering. This conscience could be considerable — the outpouring of charitable donations after the Indian Ocean tsunami demonstrated that the public did not suffer "compassion fatigue" — but the occupation of Iraq was still remote from Western voters' lives. This changed with two events in particular: the July 7, 2005 bombings in London and Hurricane Katrina, that brought awareness of the dimensions of a complex emergency home to Western voters in ways that focused on humanitarian and interventionist concerns.

The significance of the July 7 bombings is that the bombers, while having family origins in South Asia and northeast Africa, were brought up and radicalized in Britain. Terrorism and violent conflict were contributors to complex emergencies in other parts of the world, but in the summer of 2005, they suddenly became contributors to crisis in a Western capital. Hurricane Katrina was more dramatic still. It not only was a natural disaster, but also revealed many social and political pathologies in the United States, including the depth of poverty, its racial dimension, and the neglect of basic protections for the vulnerable. The breakdown of administrative and social systems in New Orleans warranted its description as a complex emergency, even though reports of looting and brigandage turned out to be somewhat exaggerated.

Hurricane Katrina challenged humanitarian agencies to become active in domestic American disasters. Residents of the stricken Gulf Coast remarked that the U.S. government responded more rapidly to foreign emergencies than to domestic ones. This may have been unfair, but certainly the level of professionalism of response was wanting in comparison with that of the actions mounted by local authorities and international agencies around the Indian Ocean.

For American political leaders, humanitarianism was now becoming not only a "hard" issue, but a domestic one, too. The philanthropic globalization of the 1990s was now coming home, and the same issues were arising in the home country. Foreign humanitarian failures were an embarrassment; domestic ones are a political disaster. The domestication of humanitarianism is still in its earliest days, and it is too early to predict what its trajectory will be. But the repercussions may be far-reaching.

THE SUDAN: ANOMALY OR AUGURY?

Immediately after 9/11, U.S. policy toward the Sudan was a striking anomaly. The Republican administration adopted a policy of conciliation and peacemaking toward a government that seemed to be a prime candidate for regime change. The "moderate" policy overrode vocal criticism from a left-right solidarity coalition, including liberal human-rights proponents, the Congressional Black Caucus, campus activists, and a powerful right-wing religious bloc. The Bush administration's approach was multilateral (albeit ad hoc) and incremental. It entailed cooperating with a government, and with individuals within it, that had proven links to terrorism, making symbolic gestures against genocide, and making democracy a low priority. It was Bush's most constructive engagement in the Arab-Muslim world.

The anomaly can be explained by specific factors: Bush's determination to distance his policy from Clinton's, the practical returns to counterterrorist cooperation with an intelligence service that had excellent files on al-Qaeda (having hosted it), and the assessments of the State and Defense Departments that the regime-change policy simply wasn't working. The Democrats had previously tried a neoconservative policy, and it hadn't worked. As Washington politics shifted, that failed approach was abandoned. Most assessments of the current situation in Iraq are that it isn't working and that a major policy reversal is in order. At minimum, the military and political costs of the Iraq conflict prevent the Bush administration from continuing to pursue revolutionary changes elsewhere in the world. From this perspective, we can perhaps see the Sudanese case as an omen: as the "new solidarity" politics overreaches, the United States and other Western governments will revert to Realpolitik.

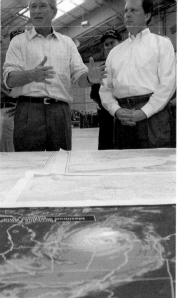

(LEFT) Residents wait to be rescued from the floodwaters of Hurricane Katrina in New Orleans on September 1, 2005 (David J. Phillip/AP Photo). (RIGHT) President Bush talks as Federal Emergency Management Agency director Mike Brown (RIGHT) looks on during a briefing on damage from Hurricane Katrina in Mobile, Alabama, September 2, 2005 (Susan Walsh/AP Photo).

The war and genocide in Darfur illustrate how these new alignments play out within the humanitarian community. Darfur has become the biggest issue for domestic activist mobilization in the United States since apartheid. There is more interest on campuses and in churches about Darfur than anyone might have imagined, and columnists regularly write exceptionally strong opinion pieces about it. The "new solidarity" has a grassroots movement and eloquent exponents. The mainstream human-rights organizations have modestly benefited from this, but they have not joined the chorus of calls for regime change and aggressive military intervention. Humanitarian agencies on the ground have been conspicuously quiet: the grassroots activism has almost completely passed them by. They benefit from aid budgets, but their programmatic activities are conventional and their advocacy muted. This is an extremely unusual case, one in which the portrayal of an African crisis has not been led by the established humanitarians. But it may augur the repositioning of those humanitarians as conservative players within the field.

IMPLICATIONS

The humanitarian arena is more complicated than ever before. It is visibly entangled with a far wider range of constituencies and political issues. The humanitarian international has influenced the agendas of certain big projects that have taken shape since 2000, such as huge increases in aid flows and revolutionary liberal interventionism. To some extent, it has been outflanked by these new projects and is treating them with caution or skepticism. But even if the campaigns to "make poverty history" through aid and to make intervention a norm overreach and fail, they will pull humanitarianism into new territory. One of the most interesting challenges will be the directions taken by the rapidly growing faith-based NGOs. Nourished by funds from American churchgoers and the U.S. government, evangelical agencies are rising to challenge their better-established, more secular brethren (including established church-based agencies such as Catholic Relief Services). Will they lose their distinctive faith-based identity as they adopt the professional procedures of mainstream organizations? Or will they chart a new course, cementing the radical new solidarities?

Relief technologies continue to improve. Aid from donors and lenders is more transparent and more open to civil society's influence than before. More Africans are involved as professionals. But organized humanitarianism continues to be dominated by Western organizations, which benefit from proximity to the sources of money. Philanthropic globalization is following the same broad trajectory as its economic counterpart: it is headquartered in the world's richest metropolitan centers and has a global reach. This globalization implies accountability to money and public opinion in metropolitan centers of the global North. Its accountability mechanisms are akin to those of a TV talk show with a studio audience, but at least African voices are in the audience, chiefly courtesy of NGO networks.

Humanitarianism remains a top-down enterprise as much as ever — that is, largely, but not entirely, driven by the perceptions and priorities of aid givers. This is perhaps inevitable, given that its subjects by definition are extremely vulnerable and have little power. However, moral righteousness has a powerful tendency to silence dissent and critique, because expertise often serves as its own justification. This is not always the case. In the last decade, humanitarians have shown a laudable capacity to examine and criticize themselves, even at times to excess. That is the most encouraging quality of the humanitarian business and its strongest guarantee for the future.

1 Barbara Harrell-Bond, "Humanitarianism in a Straitjacket," *African Affairs* 84, no. 334 (1985), pp. 3–14.

2 Mark Bowden, *Black Hawk Down: A Story of Modern War* (New York: Atlantic Monthly Press, 1999).

3 Alex de Waal and Rakiya Omaar, *Humanitarianism Unbound? Current Dilemmas Facing Multi-Mandate Relief Operations in Political Emergencies* (London: African Rights, 1994).

4 Mark Duffield, *Global Governance and the New Wars: The Merging of Development and Security* (London: Zed Books, 2001).

5 William Vernon Harcourt, *Letters by Historicus on Some Questions of International Law* (New York: Kraus Reprint Co., 1971), p. 41.

6 See, for example, Thomas Cushman (ed.), *A Matter of Principle: Humanitarian Arguments for War in Iraq* (Berkeley: University of California Press, 2005).

MOTIVES

STAKEHOLDER CLAIMS

PATENT

STAKEHOLDER ACTIVISM

questions by Michel Feher

Ever since the early 1980s, when the Reagan administration denied the claims of air-traffic controllers and the government of Margaret Thatcher defeated the representatives of British miners, times have not been good for trade unions. Over the past twenty-five years, their standing has been considerably damaged by the steady dismantling of the regime of collective bargaining, regulated markets, and Keynesian public policies that previously prevailed in Western Europe and to a lesser extent in the United States. Yet while undermining the capacity of labor organizations to protect the interests of wage earners, the reforms responsible for the demise of a welfare state committed to reign in capitalism have, in turn, generated new types of social mobilizations.

Among these challenges to neoliberal practices and doctrine are the various kinds of activism that gravitate around the notion of "corporate social responsibility." Their common premise is that corporations are not merely accountable to their shareholders, but also to a vast array of stakeholders: workers, consumers, suppliers, and, by extension, any group or individual affected by what a corporation does and how it operates. Corporate social responsibility thus pertains to the financial and commercial practices of a corporation, the working conditions of its employees, the environmental impact of its practices, and the quality and safety of its products.

To a large extent, the various movements engaged in stakeholder activism borrow both their rhetoric and their tactics from nongovernmental organizations involved in human-rights and civil-rights advocacy, humanitarian work, environmental activism, and consumer protection. At the same time, organizations such as Amnesty International, Human Rights Watch, Médecins Sans Frontières, Greenpeace, and Public Citizen are now focusing some of their resources and attention on issues pertaining to corporate social responsibility.

The recent surge of this multifaceted stakeholder activism, together with the fact that it parallels the growing disempowerment of labor unions, raises a series of questions that we ask Ian Robinson, lecturer in the Residential College's social science program and the department of sociology at the University of Michigan, and Mark Barenberg, professor of law at Columbia University, to address.

1   Judgments about corporate social responsibility vary greatly. Some denounce it as an oxymoron that sound business executives would be well-advised to treat as such — Milton Friedman famously declared that the only social responsibility of corporations is to make profits — or, conversely, as a public-relations strategy orchestrated by a hegemonic corporate world. Others see it as a valiant, albeit largely desperate attempt to curb corporate power and immunity at a time when labor organizations are weak and governments subservient to shareholders' interests. Still others take it as the appropriate framework for social mobilizations today, provided that a return to the welfare state of yore, let alone state socialism, can no longer be embraced either as a plausible or as a desirable response to neoliberal globalization. How would you assess the importance of, but also the historical conditions of, the emergence of corporate social responsibility and the stakeholder activism that it generates?

2   To what extent is the development of such activism a global phenomenon? Are some political cultures more prone to it than others, because they have a tradition of civil society "watchdogs," of rights-based activism, or of "moral reform" initiatives, for instance?

3   To what extent must this kind of activism be global? Are multinational companies its sole targets? How much does it rely on international networks of solidarity between different types of stakeholders, such as small producers in the Southern Hemisphere and socially conscious consumers in the North?

4   Corporate social responsibility attracts activists with very different political leanings: some simply want to help corporations be better citizens, while others perceive their actions as a way of conveying that "another world is possible." In light of these divergent perspectives, what do you think is the actual purpose of stakeholder activism, or, at least, which of its potential purposes is likely to prevail? Is it the moralization of capitalism, that is, an effort to persuade corporations that doing the right thing is at once good for society, good for their image, and thus good for business? Is it the restoration of public policies, nationally or at the international level, aiming at the regulation of markets and corporate governance? Is it the consolidation of a fair-trade sector, a niche where enlightened consumers and socially responsible producers would trade according to criteria other than the mere optimization of their financial interest? Is it an attempt to alter the current system of corporate governance, that is, to modify the balance of power between a company's shareholders and its stakeholders in favor of the latter?

5   Accordingly, who is the main addressee of stakeholder activism? Is it corporate executives, who should be persuaded to be more socially responsible? Is it national governments and international institutions, who should be pressured into defining and implementing mandatory norms of financial, commercial, environmental, and managerial conduct? Is it the socially responsible section of the (consuming) public, who should be enlisted to expand and consolidate the fair trade sector? Is it the shareholders of corporations, since the immediate target of most stakeholders' campaigns is the reputation of a corporation and thus the value of its stock?

6   Traditionally, social movements attempting to curb or check the power of capital owners have sought to limit, constrain, and regulate the realm of the market, either through collective bargaining or by extending the reach of fundamental rights. Stakeholder activism, however, tends to play more with the markets than against them. By launching campaigns that aim at altering the reputation of a brand and more generally at factoring social responsibility into a corporation's market value, its proponents seem at least as intent on modifying corporate strategies as on containing them. How would you assess the novelty, viability, and efficiency of their approach?

7   The growing prestige of corporate social responsibility has resulted in the creation of a new competitive market, that of agencies devoted to the definition and attribution of labels of corporate social responsibility. It has also encouraged international institutions to define their own ground rules and recommendations — such as the United Nation's Global Compact — although, for the most part, these guidelines are not mandatory. Do you see these developments as proof that stakeholder activism is taking hold, or conversely, as a sign that corporations are managing to control it and co-opt it for their own purposes?

8   The power and efficiency of stakeholder activism largely depends on the strength and viability of alliances between different types of stakeholders, such as suppliers, workers, consumers, environmentalists, and others. In light of these groups' often diverging interests, how do you assess the potential of such alliances?

9   Finally, how do you think the development of stakeholder activism is likely to affect the future of labor unions? Should the representatives of workers refashion themselves as one branch of a larger stakeholders' coalition in the making? Short of doing so, what can they learn or adopt from the skills and tactics of activists involved in corporate social responsibility? In return, how much of their own traditional agenda can they impart to the various groups engaged in stakeholder activism?

The Consumer Dimension of Stakeholder Activism: The Antisweatshop Movement in the United States

Ian Robinson

The concept of "stakeholder activism," as Michel Feher employs it, is very broad. Almost anyone can be considered a stakeholder if the criterion is that the actions of corporations have significant effects on their lives. Stakeholders can seek many types of change in corporate behavior: more respect for worker rights, improved wages and working conditions, sustainable environmental practices, and higher and more stable payments to primary commodity producers, among others. Stakeholders can seek such change by many routes, ranging from changes in public policy, to shareholder activism, to educating and organizing consumers.

So understood, it is impossible to do justice to the full range of possibilities encompassed by the concept of stakeholder activism in a single essay. Here, then, I focus on the pieces of this vast mosaic that I know best: U.S. social-movement efforts to expand worker rights and put an end to sweatshop conditions in the global apparel sector and the role (actual and potential) of consumers in this effort. Indeed, consumer education, organization, and mobilization play a critical role in the current strategies of this movement.

The following essay consists of four sections. The first section lays out the main forms that consumer-based strategies for fighting sweatshops have taken so far and asks why this type of strategy has reemerged in the last ten to fifteen years. The second section inquires into the market share that consumer-based strategies might reach under several different scenarios. The third section considers what sorts of changes would be required to maximize the potential extent of the market encompassing ethical apparel consumers and what would still remain undone, even if that happy scenario could be realized. The fourth section stresses the need to integrate consumer-based strategies with those designed to rebuild labor movements' political power and the capacity of democratic governments to regulate their economies effectively. I argue in this section that unions ought to support the consumer-based strategies in the various ways open to them and support as well the meshing of those strategies with other

Display experiment designed by University of Michigan researchers in a Michigan department store. Consumers were presented with two separate displays of ordinary athletic socks that were identical except for a label indicating that the socks in one display were produced under "good working conditions." After the price of the labeled socks was increased incrementally over several months, most consumers preferred to pay less for the unlabeled socks, but nearly one in four were willing to pay up to 40 percent more for the labeled socks.

approaches to ending sweatshop labor. The conclusion briefly addresses the question of what the experience and likely future of the antisweatshop movement implies for the larger questions concerning nongovernmental politics and new forms of social mobilization raised by the editor of this anthology.

WHY CONSUMER-BASED STRATEGIES NOW?

Feher suggests that stakeholder activism arises when the two principal means of regulating corporate power in twentieth-century labor markets — states and unions — are less able, or less willing, to perform that function effectively.[1] The experience of the antisweatshop movement in the United States, past and present, supports this hypothesis.[2] In the late nineteenth century, a powerful consumer-based antisweatshop movement emerged in the United States under the auspices of the National Consumer League's White Label Campaign (1898–1919). In the 1920s, too, unions in Seattle and other parts of the country sought to forge a synthesis of working-class consumerist and producerist strategies.[3] However, as unions gained enough power to end sweatshops in the late 1930s and 1940s through a combination of pattern bargaining and legislation, this and other elements of the consumer strategy for advancing worker rights faded away.[4] Consumer-based movements began to grow again, however, as unions proved unable, and governments either unable or unwilling, to prevent the return of sweatshops in the U.S. garment industry and their proliferation around the world.

In recent years, the regulatory capacity of governments and unions has been eroded primarily by increased international capital mobility and reduced tariffs, quotas, and nontariff barriers to trade. In the new context created by these changes, governments and unions worry that if they push too hard for improvements in worker rights or compensation, the companies at the top of the supply chain — brands such as Nike and retailers such as Wal-Mart — will source from other countries where unit labor costs are lower. The industry's exodus from the global North and shifts within the global South (from Mexico to Central America) suggest that this is no idle threat. In the neoliberal era, then, governments become less effective agents for eliminating sweatshops, and unions that do not knuckle under often find that contracts with employers are not renewed, their members lose work, and they lose members.

The second iteration of the antisweatshop movement was initiated in the early 1990s by critics who targeted companies particularly vulnerable to adverse publicity. These companies had two characteristics: first, heavy advertising investment in creating brands with high consumer recognition and status, investment that could be lost if consumers associated them with sweatshops; and second, market power due to their location at the top of supply chains and the high price premiums they were able to charge due to the popularity of their brands.[5] These brand-centered efforts against sweatshops invoked the (actual or potential) wrath of large numbers of individual consumers, whom activists claimed would care enough to alter their purchasing choices if sweatshop labor practices became widely known.

In July 1998, a second type of consumer-based strategy emerged, this one focusing on institutional, rather than individual consumers. Its first component was the campus-based student antisweatshop movement. Like the pioneers of the brand-centered approach, the students who launched this part of the movement had close ties with the U.S. labor movement. In fact, they first developed a national network, United Students Against Sweatshops (USAS), and a strategy for making their universities a tool for fighting sweatshops after participating in Union Summer.[6] Most of USAS's founding cohort did their Union Summer internships with UNITE!, the union representing apparel and textile workers in the United States and Canada.[7] In the course of this work, these students encountered firsthand the current challenges of organizing workers in this sector and began to see the value of supplementing traditional union organizing and bargaining with an institutional (that is, university) consumer component.[8]

Consequently, in April 2000, USAS launched the Worker Rights Consortium (WRC) with the support of unions, antisweatshop NGOs, and universities.[9] The role of the WRC was to investigate and report on worker complaints that university codes of conduct had been violated by plants supplying products to the universities. Where such violations were documented, the universities were expected to take the steps necessary to bring those suppliers into compliance with their codes. As of June 2006, 151 U.S. universities and colleges and three U.S. high schools were affiliated with the WRC.[10]

Efforts to use the purchasing power of other kinds of institutional consumers, including churches, school boards, and state and local governments, have also been underway for some years. In 2003, these efforts reached a new level of coordination with the formation of SweatFree Communities (SFC). Most of its founders came from Maine, Minnesota, New York, and Wisconsin. In February 2006, the governor of Maine, John Baldacci, called for the formation of a Governors' Coalition for Sweatfree Procurement and Worker Rights. However, in the last two years, SFC has made its greatest strides in California.[11]

Consumer-based strategies are not the only way — nor are they really the best way, if the goal is to ensure that *all* workers have the same basic rights and protections — to respond to the declining regulatory power of national governments and unions. An alternative response that goes to the institutional root of the problem is to modify the international institutions that determine the character of globalization in order to protect core worker rights and guarantee minimum international labor standards. If properly enforced, such provisions would cordon off core worker rights from competition and set a floor on competition based on differences in wages and working conditions. The European Union's "social chapter" is the strongest actually existing version of this strategy. NAFTA's labor "side deal" was advertised by supporters as a version of this strategy for North America, though it has proven much weaker that its EU counterpart. Many national labor federations in the global North and South, including the International Confederation of Free Trade Unions (ICFTU), have called for a version of this strategy, that is, a "social clause" protecting core worker rights, to be initiated within the province of the World Trade Organization (WTO).[12]

While in principle global institutional reform is a better response to the underlying problem of protecting workers, in practice, it faces a host of obstacles that render it impractical in the short to medium term.[13] Chief among these obstacles, global institutional reform requires the active support of many national governments to change the WTO's mandate, as well as to ensure that its new provisions are fully enforced. At present, such a social clause is opposed by many of the national governments of the North and South that would have to back it if it were to be implemented and enforced.[14] This does not seem likely to change soon.

In this political context, consumer-based strategies to alter corporate behavior become particularly attractive. Such methods can advance reforms while governments that oppose an effective social clause at the global level remain in power. Nor does this strategy require the same level of international cooperation in order to work: ultimately, no matter where brands and retailers source their apparel, they have to sell much of what they produce to the same rich Northern consumers. For example, enormous pressure can be brought to bear on Nike or Wal-Mart (and their suppliers) if most consumers of the United States insist that they respect core worker rights at all levels of their production chains. This is true even if consumers in the European Union and Japan do not do the same thing. As a matter of fact, consumer-based initiatives against sweatshops began in two of the global economy's three richest economic entities — the United States, Canada, and the European Union — at about the same time.[15] But the point here is that efforts in each place got off the ground with minimal international coordination.

My point about international coordination deserves elaboration. By their very nature, consumer strategies must be global in one important sense: since most of the apparel producers are in the global South and most of the consumers with substantial purchasing power are in the global North, both components have to be involved in the execution of this antisweatshop strategy. However, the extent to which Southern workers and their labor organizations are involved in the development and implementation of such a strategy can vary greatly. When the U.S. antisweatshop movement began, there was relatively little consultation with Southern unions.[16]

While unilateral action by Northern antisweatshop organizations is possible, a consumer-based strategy for ending sweatshops will be more effective if it is able to bridge the North-South divide, as well as divisions among regions of the consuming North. More North-South coordination would make Southern unions more central to the development and implementation of the strategy than they have been so far. Such coordination would be a positive development in antisweatshop programs of action, because union organization in the relevant Southern workplaces is the only truly effective solution to the challenge of successfully monitoring codes of conduct at factories.[17] Greater North-North coordination of demands, criteria and standards, labeling mechanisms and processes, and monitoring and enforcement strategies would more quickly move a larger number of companies in the desired direction, since it is easier for them to adapt to one new set of sourcing standards than to three or more. Moreover, greater coordination would increase both the costs of noncompliance and the benefits of compliance from the standpoint of corporate decision makers.

Coordination is increasing along North-South lines. Since the summer of 2005, United Students Against Sweatshops and the Worker Rights Consortium have been promoting a Designated Supplier Program (DSP) to replace the existing institutional approach to apparel consumption. The DSP commits participating universities to purchase a steadily growing share of the apparel that they license from factories maintained by the WRC. To make it onto the WRC's list of preferred apparel producers, factories must demonstrate to their satisfaction that the workers in that factory have a democratic organization, autonomous from state and employer control. In most cases, this will be a union, though a democratic and inclusive worker co-op could also meet this criterion. The factory must also pay its workers at least a living wage, as determined by the cost of living in the region where the factory is located. So far, thirty-one universities have formally considered participating in the implementation of the DSP; of these, twenty-eight have committed to a good-faith effort to implement the DSP principles.[18] The DSP system allots Southern worker organizations the key role in monitoring university codes of conduct and in the process significantly increases their bargaining power. Over time, the Designated Supplier Program aims at increasing the number of plants that have such worker organizations. In these ways, it contributes to increasing the participation of these Southern organizations in the transnational worker-rights networks being constructed.

In terms of the North-North dimension, there have recently been discussions about bringing together sweat-free labeling efforts in the EU and the U.S. While many obstacles to improved coordination remain, participants in these discussions are aware of the potential gains if these obstacles can be overcome.[19]

THE POTENTIAL SCOPE OF THE SWEAT-FREE APPAREL MARKET

What share of the world's consumers, and of the clothing produced for them, can the antisweatshop movement realistically hope to reach? A systematic answer to this question requires answers to three more specific questions. First, what share of the world's consumers care about such things, and what share of those that care are willing and able to pay attention to information about how products are made and (if necessary) to pay more for sweat-free products? Second, are ethical consumers confined to the global North for the time being, or can they also become a factor in the global South? Third, how do we reach all of those who would like to purchase sweat-free products, North and South, recognizing that existing mechanisms reach only a fraction of these consumers?

On the first point, survey data from representative national samples consistently show that a majority of U.S. consumers say they would be willing to pay more for apparel made under sweat-free conditions. The size of these studies' majorities seems to vary, as we might expect, with how much of a premium they are asked to pay for

Panicked garments workers descend from an eight-story building using cloths and bamboo in a Mirpur town near Dhaka, July 30, 1997, after a stampede triggered by a false fire alarm. At least twenty-three workers died and one hundred were injured (Sanjid Mosharrof/AP Photo).

sweat-free apparel.[20] Interestingly, however, most surveys show very little variation in support relative to family income.[21] One survey does find that — in contrast to what we know about those who purchase fair-trade products such as coffee — supporters of sweat-free apparel come disproportionately from lower-income, less-educated families.[22] I have found no countervailing evidence suggesting that richer families are more likely to support or pay more for sweat-free goods. Based on the U.S. survey evidence, then, we can expect either uniform, majority support for sweat-free clothing across all income strata or somewhat higher support among the lower- and middle-income groups.

Do such surveys overstate people's real level of concern and/or their willingness to pay more (if necessary) for goods made under sweat-free conditions? Some analysts have worried that they do, because most respondents probably think they know what the ethically appropriate response is, a response that costs them nothing.[23] I am a member of a team of researchers at the University of Michigan that has been working for several years now to assess people's willingness to "put their money where their mouths are." We are observing people's behavior in real-world consumption situations when they are presented with this kind of choice. We then ask them why they behaved as they did. In the working-class community department store in which some of our interviews have been carried out, we found that about half of those who met the cognitive preconditions of ethical consumption chose to pay the price premium for the sweat-free clothing.[24]

Can these U.S. results be generalized to consumers in the rest of the global North? Survey evidence bearing on this question is scant, but what there is suggests that there may be higher levels of ethical consumerism in other rich capitalist democracies.[25] We also know that the anisweatshop movement began somewhat earlier in Western Europe than it did in the United States and that other kinds of ethical consumer movements — for example, against bovine growth hormone and genetically engineered food — have been more powerful in Europe than in the United States, as well. This makes sense because, to reach anything approaching their full influential potential, ethical consumers must be organized and mobilized. They are ineffective influencers of corporate sourcing standards when acting as isolated monads. Most European societies are characterized by denser networks of organization (particularly on the left), including much higher union density levels. There are several reasons to expect, therefore, that there is a higher share of ethical consumers in most other countries of the global North — certainly, in Europe — than in the United States.

What of ethical consumers who live in the global South? If a substantial share of consumers in the global South are motivated to join the antisweatshop movement qua consumers, then the potential scope of consumer-based strategies is greatly increased. So far, Southern consumers have not played a substantial role in consumer-based strategies to eliminate sweatshop production, but I doubt that this is because few people in these countries care about the issue.[26] While only a small percentage of Southern countries' populations consume at levels comparable to the middle class of the global North, they still amount to very large numbers in absolute terms. Also, as we have seen with the United States, it is incorrect to think that only relatively well-off people care about sweat-free consumption.

Of course, equal concern is not the same thing as equal capacity to act on that concern, and low family income in the global South means something very different than it does in the United States. There is probably a threshold below which families simply cannot afford to spend anything extra for sweat-free goods, no matter how much they might like to do so. While low family income poses real constraints, its effect on purchasing decisions should not be overstated, for two reasons. First, we should not forget the important role of the *Swadeshi* movement (much of which revolved around textiles and apparel) in India's struggle for independence and the fact that Indians of all income groups participated in this movement.[27] This was possible at a time when most of India's people were poorer, at least in family income terms, than they are today. Second, it is not clear that much more must be spent to secure sweat-free apparel, provided that

Northern consumers are prepared to subsidize the costs of creating and maintaining the institutions needed to create markets for ethical apparel consumers.[28]

Against the lower family incomes of workers in the global South, we may note an additional motivating factor largely lacking in the global North: Southern working-class people perform most of the world's sweatshop labor. Thus, some portion of this group can be expected to support consumer-based activism out of solidarity with their fellow Southern workers, in addition to acting on other sorts of ethical motivations.[29] I assume that when multiple motivational factors all point in the same direction, people are more likely to act and/or to act more vigorously as supporters of sweat-free consumption. This dynamic could, to some degree at least, counteract the effect of lower income among consumers in the global South.

Summing up my analysis so far, while increased international capital mobility reduces the capacity of unions and governments to regulate corporate behavior, it does not have the same effect on efforts to organize and mobilize consumer purchasing power. Survey data, supplemented by more in-depth interviews with consumers at the point of purchase, suggest that (in the United States, at least) both conditions are met for a large plurality, perhaps even a majority, of all apparel consumers. This enormous, unfulfilled potential — relative to what seems possible via the alternative pathways of union collective bargaining and reforms to national or international regulations — is recognized by the antisweatshop movement and impels it toward consumer-based strategies for fighting global sweatshops.

REALIZING THE FULL POTENTIAL OF THE MARKET
FOR ETHICAL APPAREL CONSUMERS

How do we maximize this unfulfilled potential of consumer purchasing power in supporting antisweatshop strategies? Currently, individual consumers are used to threaten a small number of high-profile brands and retailers and institutional consumers are used to pressure suppliers of the clothing that they purchase. Neither strategy is capable of reaching most ethical apparel consumers. Most clothing purchases are made by individual consumers, not institutions, and most of the clothing that they buy does not bear a famous brand name for which a large price premium is paid. So the challenge is to reach this huge and as yet largely untapped pool of ethical consumers. If they can be provided with the information necessary to act on their ethical convictions, the scope of the consumer-based strategy can be greatly increased.

The first prerequisite for this quantum leap in the consumer-based strategy's scope and power is agreement among key actors on the criteria necessary to qualify as "sweat-free" and a widely recognized labeling system for clothing produced in factories that meet those criteria. With such criteria and labeling in place, customers who want sweat-free products can recognize them and pay extra for them, insofar as they are willing and able to do so. The designated-supplier approach advocated by USAS and the WRC provides a useful starting point. As we have seen, to be added to the list of designated suppliers, a supplier plant must meet two criteria: its workers must be organized into a union or some other form of democratic worker organization that has the power to bargain over worker compensation and working conditions, and its workers must be paid a living wage as determined by the cost of living in the place where the plant is located.

For several reasons, the criteria employed by the DSP would be excellent ones to adopt in this wider context. First, such criteria are already being used because many (though not all) antisweatshop organizations agree that worker organization is the key to making headway on the other work-related conditions. Second, they are very simple, making them easier to explain to people and easier to implement. Third, as already noted, the DSP approach creates its own solution to the problem of monitoring factories' compliance with codes of conduct: autonomous, democratic unions (or other worker organizations) in each workplace. Finally, this approach is the surest and most direct way to build unions that will become part of the political power base advocating changes in state regulatory policy, changes necessary to extend worker rights beyond the part of the market where ethical consumers hold sway.[30]

What does the consumer-based strategy for ending global sweatshops imply for the evolution of the global economic system? Feher distinguishes three possible directions in which the system might move: the "moralization of capitalism," the restoration of more effective regulation through public policy reform (national or international), and the consolidation of a niche sector of the market governed by ethical norms. Feher defines the moralization of capitalism as persuading corporations that "doing the right thing is at once good for society, good for their image, and thus good for business." On this definition, no change occurs in the basic motives governing decision makers in the firms operating in this sector, which remains some combination of increasing management income, increasing shareholder income, and increasing market share. What changes is the strategy for realizing these constant goals. Seen this way, government regulation, when effective, results in the moralization of capitalist firms.

I'd like to define "moralization" in a different way, as the internalization or incorporation of ethical principles into the goals and preferences of the top decision makers in a firm.[31] This definition distinguishes moralization from the restoration of regulatory power, where government regulation (like union collective bargaining) seeks to change the behavior of capitalist firms without altering their basic goals and preferences. The niche market envisaged in Feher's third scenario might be composed partially of moralized firms in this sense. Even if it were entirely composed of such firms, its market "niche" status implies that most of the sector is populated by firms that pursue traditional capitalist goals.

Which of these changes in trajectory will the antisweatshop movement bring about if it retains its current strategies, but expands them to their furthest limits? And how will such anticipated changes be affected if the individual consumer strategy is expanded in the ways that I outlined above, including improved labeling efforts based on clear sweat-free criteria and improved consumer information? Current strategies are contributing to the creation of a niche market in which companies respecting core worker rights are rewarded with high levels of customer loyalty from some fraction of the total population, as well as with higher initial profits. Two kinds of firms will likely populate this niche market: smaller firms started by people who wish to help ethical consumers get what they want (moralized firms), and larger firms (such as the big brands and retailers) that decide to participate in this niche market as part of their larger competitive strategy, but for whom this is a decision dictated by the conventional goals of the capitalist firm (that is, goals of increasing some combination of managerial income, shareholder income, and market share).[32]

I expect this niche market to expand for several reasons. Early entrants will make profits that are higher than the industry average because there will be relatively few producers and retailers in this niche. So competition will be less intense. As well, ethical consumers are willing to pay retail price premiums high enough to increase both wages and profits. Higher profits will encourage firms already in the niche to expand their sales through vigorous advertising designed to both increase the percentage of the consumers who are ethical consumers and increase the percentage of ethical consumers who buy from them, rather than from other ethical producers. Higher profits will also encourage new entrants. The more new entrants, the stiffer the competition, however, and the less that sales can be expanded to existing ethical consumers. Therefore, over time, the share of advertising expenditures devoted to increasing the number of ethical consumers will increase. If advertising is effective, it will increase the share of consumers participating in the niche market.

I see two types of limits to this expansion of niche market ethical consumption. The first limit consists in the fact that sweat-free clothing is offered to ethical consumers only in a limited range of venues: some brands and retailers will have some sweat-free lines, and people who are willing and able to shop in their outlets, as well as institutional consumers, will be able to buy sweat-free clothing through them. A few consumers are aware of Internet-based companies such as No Sweat and Justice Clothing that sell only sweat-free garments. But most nonbranded clothing is not sold through any of these channels and so will remain outside of this niche market, as will the bulk of consumer apparel purchases. Manufacturers wishing to enter this niche market can sell only so much of what they produce to brands and retailers (and through them, to individual and institutional consumers), and will have to sell the rest in the nonniche market for lack of direct access to ethical consumers.

The second limit on niche market growth is that firms whose underlying motivations have not changed (that is, have not been "moralized") seeking to enter the ethical-consumer segment of the market will claim to be sweat-free. These claims may take the form of simple assertions, or they may constitute more sophisticated efforts to debate the criteria that should be employed to define a product as sweat-free. Such a discursive shift—from denial that sweat-free is a legitimate category and/or efforts to suppress labeling to a growing number of capitalist firms claiming to be sweat-free—would appear to be a significant victory for the antisweatshop movement. Adding corporations and their advertising dollars to the chorus of those asserting the desirability of production processes that respect worker rights and that pay a living wage will increase the number of consumers who are aware of such issues and persuade others who were already aware of them that they should take such issues more seriously. This discursive shift should thus contribute to the number and share of ethical apparel consumers, other things being equal.

But the moment of discursive shift may also be dangerous for the antisweatshop movement, and other things may not turn out to be equal. Capitalist firms whose defining goals are unchanged will not wish to dismantle the supply chains that have proven so lucrative for them. When forced to concede the discursive point, they are likely to proceed in one of two directions. They may seek to water down the definition of sweat-free in order to convince ethical consumers that their current practices are ethical.[33] Or they may try to sow enough confusion about how sweat-free production should be assessed to convince ethical consumers that they do not and cannot know which companies they should support. Unless these strategic responses can be counteracted before they cause too much confusion, ethical consumers may find themselves back in a situation of ignorance, which means powerlessness qua market actors. In the worst-case scenario, disillusion might set in as consumers doubt the legitimacy and the motives underlying all such claims. This could result in the "demoralization" and demobilization of the consumer-based antisweatshop movement.[34]

If consumer strategies do not change, the movement will produce a relatively small ethical consumer niche market, with most consumers remaining in the traditional market characterized by "race to the bottom" dynamics. But if the movement is able to solve the problems noted above — reaching agreement on common criteria for awarding sweat-free status, a labeling system for signaling this status to consumers, and protecting these things from tactics of dilution and confusion — then it should be possible to reach all of the people who would behave as ethical consumers if this were practical for them. In that case, this niche market could eventually encompass a majority of the world's consumers, because no matter which retail clothing outlet consumers patronized, they could know at a glance which clothing on sale there (if any) had been made under sweat-free conditions.

Whether any of this would lead to the moralization of capitalism within this sector is less clear. Here we need to distinguish between apparel producers and apparel retailers (including brands). From the beginning, some of the retailers in this market were created by people whose primary allegiance is to the goals of the sweat-free movement, rather than to profit making, even though they are formally constituted as capitalist firms. Whether these retailers will survive the competition with firms driven primarily by the profit motive, once the latter begin to enter this niche market on a substantial scale, is an open question. I think that some ethical consumers will support the moralized firms out of loyalty to the critical role that they played at the outset of the movement, as well as in recognition of the moral difference that continues to exist between organizations

Illustration from *The Sweatfree Toolkit: How Your Community Can Help End Sweatshops* from the Global Exchange Web site.

whose bottom line is profits and organizations that are primarily committed to ethical principles. After all, the capacity to make this kind of distinction and the belief that it is important to act on that difference are part of what constitutes ethical consumers in the first place.

What of apparel-producing firms? There is a possibility that, over time, a growing share of the factories that manufacture clothing for ethical consumers will not be capitalist firms, but worker-owned cooperatives. The criteria of sweat-free production developed by USAS and the WRS support this as an acceptable alternative to capitalist firms in which workers have organized themselves into democratic unions. In some countries ravaged by neoliberal restructuring, formerly capitalist firms that closed while owing their employees back wages are being taken over by their former employees and run as cooperatives. In Venezuela, under Hugo Chavez, this process has gone an extra step, with the state actively supporting the creation of such a cooperative sector through financial aid and educational programming designed to promote the formation of mutually supportive networks of cooperatives.[35] Most stand-alone worker co-ops do not survive, but with this kind of state support, many more could. If the governments of several Latin American countries were to follow Venezuela's lead in this respect, they might find a place for themselves in the international division of labor where their apparel sector is geared toward supplying the sweat-free market.[36] In such a scenario, the share of worker co-ops in this niche's supply chain could rise to a high level quite rapidly.

INTEGRATING ANTISWEATSHOP STRATEGIES
AND THE ROLE OF ORGANIZED LABOR

What do these scenarios imply for the possibility of creating new national or supranational regulatory regimes to anchor what has been accomplished in the sweat-free niche market and thereby to generalize it to the rest of the market? Even in the most optimistic scenario, the sweat-free component of the global apparel sector will never expand to the point where its standards cover all workers in that sector. This is so for at least two reasons. First, short of regime change, some governments will not permit autonomous unions or worker co-ops to exist for political reasons. China is a prime example of this situation, though it is not the only one. Second, while we do not know how high the share of ethical consumers will rise relative to the total consuming population, it seems safe to say that it will never reach 100 percent. Thus, there is a need for state regulatory action if worker rights are to be protected in the rest of the sector. Of course, what is true for the apparel sector is also true for other sectors of manufacturing that have not yet produced an equivalent of the sweat-free movement and so do not yet have a sweat-free market niche (for example, the electronics industry).

Is this need for state action likely to be met? There are several reasons for optimism in the medium- to long-term future. Two of these reasons are endogenous to the development of the sweat-free movement. First, as both the number and percentage of ethical consumers grow, so does the number of citizens that sweat-free and union activists can recruit to support legislative change. I assume that these activists will take advantage of this opportunity, because they are well aware of the inherent limitations of the market niche approach. Moreover, as more firms commit themselves publicly to sweat-free production, there will be more corporate allies for this effort, or, at the very least, less explicit corporate resistance, since any such effort would immediately be publicized by the movement and used to discredit that firm's claim to be committed to operating sweat-free production processes.

The second endogenous factor holds if the DSP approach, currently confined to one type of institutional consumer, becomes the basis for labeling and marketing sweat-free clothing to individual consumers of unbranded clothing. If that happens, it will have a major positive effect on union formation in the global South, because it will give manufacturers wishing to produce for this market a positive incentive to tolerate worker rights, as against the very powerful negative incentives that they currently face. As the share of unionized workers in the apparel sectors of these countries grows, they will be able to expand their organizing efforts into other sectors, and they will also have increased political clout. Both of these changes will be conducive to moving governments to intervene more extensively and effectively to protect worker rights through regulation.

The other reason for optimism, if I can use that word in such a frightening context, is the fact that the current global economic system is moving toward ever greater regional integration at a time when, at the global level, it is highly unstable.[37] Indeed, the world economy is moving toward greater regional integration at the expense of global integration. That is, East Asian countries now do a larger share of their trade with one another than they did ten years ago, and the same is true of the countries of North America, South America, and the expanded European Union. The regionalization of the global economy makes the prospect of supranational labor regulation much better, because there can be social and political dimensions to regional integration that are impossible at the global level. This is so because the countries in a region typically have more in common with each other, politically and culturally, than they do with countries not in their region. This commonality, combined with the smaller number of countries that must be accommodated in a region, makes deals among key countries regarding the appropriate content of regional labor regulations much easier to achieve than at the global level.

Historical experience suggests that, contrary to neoliberal economic ideology, a strong social dimension is essential to the relatively stable and egalitarian functioning of capitalist market economies. The pressure to shift economic organization to the regional level will grow as the influence of neoliberal ideology wanes. Since regional integration is deepening, even under neoliberal globalization, it will seem "natural" to move to a continental form of world economic integration, in response either to the next economic crisis or to the evolution of political forces in the key countries that would have to cooperate to forge a regional economic bloc. If Karl Polanyi's analysis is correct, this regional form of integration will also be more social-democratic in that it will regulate capitalism with a view to promoting more rights-respecting production processes and more egalitarian distributive outcomes, at least in the countries with relatively high-quality democratic political processes.[38]

Moreover, this analysis suggests that in those regions of the world where relatively democratic states dominate, we will see the reconstitution of state-based labor regulation that could render the consumer-based antisweatshop movement obsolete for the second time in history. It also suggests that we can help to bring about that future more quickly — and perhaps also in more countries — by supporting current consumer-based strategies of the movement against sweatshop production.

What role should U.S. unions play in this effort? U.S. unions have actually already played an important role in the development of consumer-based antisweatshop strategies. They would be well advised to continue this support as the movement faces the new challenges outlined above, for two reasons. First, the shift away from neoliberal globalization toward a more social-democratic, regionally organized form of international economic integration will increase the economic and political power of the world's unions. If my analysis concerning the opportunities for labor organization and regulation opened up by the growth in ethical-consumer markets is correct, building the consumer component of the antisweatshop movement will aid the bargaining power, and hence the appeal to workers, of unions. Second, the discursive shift that the antisweatshop movement is bringing about by way of its apparel-sector activities benefits the cause of worker rights and union power in all sectors.

Organized labor in the United States has a long tradition of trying to convince its members to shop as ethical consumers. Initially, ethical consumption was framed as buying from union shops; later, as foreign competition began to take its toll on U.S. manufacturing jobs, this message was supplemented with an economic nationalist position. The logo of the AFL-CIO's Union Label Department currently reflects both tendencies, reading "Buy Union" and "Buy American." Today, U.S. unions have an opportunity to contribute to the creation of ethical consumers far beyond the boundaries of union membership by participating in the movement against sweatshop production. They can help ensure that the definition of "sweat-free" production includes workers' right to freedom of association, demonstrated by the existence of an autonomous and democratic union or a democratic worker-owned cooperative.

To maximize its influence within the movement and on the wider public, organized labor in the United States will have to abandon the "Buy American" rhetoric that privileges a product's national origin over worker rights.[39] Abandoning this rhetoric is desirable for other reasons, as well, not the least of which is that it improves labor's capacity to cooperate more effectively with workers and unions from other countries. Still, this kind of economic nationalism is deeply entrenched in U.S. manufacturing unions and in national identities and discourses more generally. It remains to be seen whether the U.S. labor movement will be able to make this important shift in its identity and corresponding discursive practice.

CONCLUSIONS

Ethical consumerism is a phenomenon far broader than the U.S. antisweatshop movement that I have focused on here. It has the potential to serve as an important weapon in the arsenal of many movements for social change, including those focused on promoting environmental sustainability and human development. The same kinds of considerations that prompted consumer-based strategies in the antisweatshop movement may well apply to these other movements. So we will likely see ethical consumerism become more central to the reform strategies of all of these movements for some time to come.

Those of us who seek a more just and ecologically sustainable form of economic and political organization should support the development and expansion of ethical consumerism. Not only does it offer an important way forward in this otherwise bleak era of neoliberal ascendancy, but it effectively hoists neoliberalism on its own petard by turning against it the shibboleths of consumer choice and the market mechanism at the center of the neoliberal ideal. The growth of this movement should thus contribute to weakening neoliberalism's ideological hold on the general public, even as it executes an end-run around the political power of the economic interests that champion this ideology.

The growth of ethical consumerism should also help to undermine the rational economic self-interest model of human motivation that has underpinned neoclassical economics for many years now. After all, if most consumers are not narrowly self-interested economic actors, even when they participate in competitive commodity markets, where in the world can they be expected to behave in such a fashion? If most people want — not only as producers and citizens, but also as consumers — economic processes and outcomes consistent with their understandings of fairness and justice, and if the current economic system does not meet these criteria, then there are enormous market failures and associated inefficiencies in the global market economy.

These inefficiencies — which are also injustices — will remain as long as governments and the social movements that help to keep them accountable lack the power to reform national and international institutions in ways that would bend market competition in these directions. I look forward to the day when national and international regulations will protect the core worker rights of all employees in every country. Meanwhile, we would do well to strengthen ethical-consumer movements where we can and to encourage them to cooperate with one another as much as possible while remembering that, no matter how reconstructed, markets can never offer more than a partial response to the demand for economic justice.

1   A similar hypothesis is offered in Michele Micheletti, *Political Virtue and Shopping: Individuals, Consumerism, and Collective Action* (New York: Palgrave Macmillan, 2003), who argues that groups turn to consumers and their market choices to achieve political goals (for example, regulating the behavior of corporations) when there are major obstacles to the effective exercise of political power by that group. These obstacles could take the form of a general problem (for example, an undemocratic or failed state), or a particular problem (the political marginalization or disenfranchisement of particular groups). She calls this "political consumerism."

2   The world's first large-scale consumer "boycott" (though this term for such an action would not be coined until 1880) directed against the worst form of sweated labor—slavery—fits Micheletti's thesis. In 1791, British abolitionists organized a consumer boycott against sugar produced on slave plantations. At the time, only a small fraction of the population had the right to vote, and a parliament dominated by proslavery interests refused to act on demands by a few of its members for an end to the British trade in slaves. Parliament's overwhelming rejection of action after a spirited debate led by Wiliam Wilberforce was the boycott's catalyst. Within a few months, in some areas, shop owners were reporting declines in sugar sales of one-third to one-half, and in just two years, British sugar imports from India increased ten-fold. Shops began running ads such as the following: "BENJAMIN TRAVERS, Sugar-Refiner, acquaints the Publick that he now has an assortment of Loaves, Lumps, Powder Sugar, and Syrup, ready for sale…produced by the labour of FREEMEN." See Adam Hochschild, *Bury the Chains: Prophets and Rebels in the Fight to Free an Empire's Slaves* (Boston: Houghton Mifflin, 2005), pp. 186–96.

3   See Dana Frank, *Purchasing Power: Consumer Organizing, Gender, and the Seattle Labor Movement, 1919–1929* (New York: Cambridge University Press, 1994), cited and discussed in Micheletti, *Political Virtue,* pp. 49–53.

4   On the first iteration of the U.S. consumer movement, see Monroe Friedman, *Consumer Boycotts: Effecting Change Through the Marketplace and the Media* (New York: Routledge, 1999). Micheletti, *Political Virtue,* pp. 42–51, contrasts U.S. political consumerism with that of Europe. She argues that the stronger labor movements of northwestern Europe led to greater stress on union and cooperative production as the focal point of political struggle, while in the United States, the relative weakness of the twentieth-century labor movement led to a longer and richer tradition of consumer-oriented strategies.

5   For example, Charles Kernahan's National Labor Committee made significant headway with Kathie Lee Gifford; see Lynne Duke, "The Man Who Made Kathie Lee Gifford Cry," *Washington Post,* July 31, 2005. Likewise, Jeff Ballinger's Press for Change tackled Nike; see Russell Mokhiber and Robert Weissman, "Nike Gets a Pass," *ZNet,* September 23, 2003, www.zmag.org/content/showarticle.cfm?ItemID=4235. These brand-centered tactics were articulated as a strategy for pressuring companies in many sectors by Naomi Klein in her influential book *No Logo: Taking Aim at the Brand Bullies* (New York: Picador USA, 2000).

6   Union Summer was (and remains) an innovative effort by the Organizing Institute, its supporting unions, and the AFL-CIO to connect university students with union organizing drives.

7   It might be argued that the fact that UNITE! and the AFL-CIO had important roles in launching this iteration of the consumer-based antisweatshop strategy undercuts the claim that such strategies arise in periods of union weakness. But the openness of AFL-CIO and UNITE! leaders to Union Summer and other innovative strategies was a consequence of their (accurate) perception that they were losing economic and political power and needed new strategies to counteract this decline.

8   See Liza Featherstone and United Students Against Sweatshops, *Students Against Sweatshops: The Making of a Movement* (New York: Verso, 2002).

9   See Alexander Gourevitch, "No Justice, No Contract: The Worker Rights Consortium Leads the Fight Against Sweatshops," *American Prospect,* June 29, 2001.

10 Four Canadian universities and one Canadian high school are also affiliated with the WRC. For a complete list of affiliates, go to the Worker Rights Consortium, www.workersrights.org/as.asp.

11 For an excellent overview of the current strategies and activities of SweatFree Communities, as well as perspectives shared by other actors attending their conference who are not part of SFC (for example, Europe's Clean Clothes Campaign), see SweatFree Communities, *International Conference 2006 Report,* www.sweatfree.org/docs/conferencereport2006.pdf.

12 Not all labor federations in the global South support the inclusion of a social clause. For a brief discussion of those who do and those who don't and why they differ, see Robert J.S. Ross and Anita Chan, "From North-South to South-South: The True Face of Global Competition," *Foreign Affairs* 81, no. 5 (2002), pp. 8–13.

13 Some would argue that consumer-based strategies are inherently superior, because they maximize individual consumer choice. According to this way of thinking, public policies, whether national or global, force choices (for example, whether or not to care about and pay for the protection of

worker rights) on some unwilling individuals. This is not the place for a full-fledged critique of this perspective, but I will briefly state the two main reasons why I reject it. First, people should not be able to choose whether it is legal for them to respect the basic rights of others, because history suggests that in such a system, many will choose to violate them. The conceptual point of basic human rights is that they are something that everyone should have; they are not a consumer good. Second, it is an illusion to think that the market provides real choices to all in this domain. The survey evidence (to be discussed at greater length later in this essay) suggests that there are millions today who would prefer to pay more for goods made via processes that respect worker rights but are unable to do this because they cannot distinguish clothing made in this way. Left to itself, the market does not supply this missing information; it could do so in principle, but it has not done so in practice, and it is worth thinking about why this is so. The primary reason is that it is not in the interests of the corporations that have benefited most from the existing system to see it dismantled, and they work vigorously to prevent the solution of this problem of imperfect information. The same corporate behavior is evident in the struggles around labeling genetically modified organisms, dairy products deriving from animals injected with bovine growth hormones, and the like. In all of these cases, the market fails due to imperfect information because the most powerful market actors want the information to remain imperfect, and (absent a powerful social movement) they have sufficient economic and political power to have their preferences prevail at the expense of millions of (unorganized) consumers.

14 The reasons for this opposition vary from the (unwarranted) fear that such a clause would facilitate Northern trade protectionism (advanced, for example, by recent Indian governments), to the ideological conviction that unions must be kept weak so that competitive markets can function effectively (the position of the current U.S. and Mexican administrations), to the (well-founded) belief that strong, autonomous unions can form the basis for a political challenge to the ruling party in authoritarian political systems (a concern of the current governments of Singapore and China, for example).

15 Europe's Clean Clothes Campaign, which now has affiliates in ten European countries, began in the late 1980s. See Sweat-Free Communities, *International Conference 2006 Report*, pp. 8–12 and 31–32. Discussions with sweatshop and worker rights activists indicate that a substantial antisweatshop movement has not yet emerged in Japan, the third largest of the rich Northern economies, after the U.S. and the EU. Why not? The kinds of explanations discussed at the outset of this essay — advanced by Feher, Micheletti, and me — do not give us much purchase on this question. Japan's labor movement is weaker than that of Europe, and neoliberal globalization has imposed at least as much economic restructuring on Japan as on Europe. So the structural conditions conducive to the growth of consumer strategies are present in Japan, probably to a greater degree than in the EU. So some other factor must be required, and it must be missing. What might this be? Some will find it tempting to appeal to national cultural explanations at this point, claiming that Japan's political culture is less rights-oriented or less internationalist. I doubt such national culture explanations in general and these specific claims about Japan in particular. But I don't have a good alternative. More research on this intriguing question would be welcome.

16 See Mark Anner, "The Dynamics and Unanticipated Outcomes of the Anti-Sweatshop Movement in the U.S. and Central America" (paper, Latin American Studies Association Conference, Miami, FL, March 2000); and Mark Anner and Peter Evans, "Building Bridges Across a Double Divide: Alliances between US and Latin American Labor and NGOs," in Deborah Eade and Alan Leather (eds.), *Development NGOs and Labor Unions: Terms of Engagement* (Bloomfield, CT: Kumarian Press, 2005), pp. 33–50; see also other essays in that anthology.

17 I recognize that this is a strong claim, and I cannot fully justify it here. The basic rationale is that codes of conduct cannot be enforced properly without continuous monitoring, given the powerful economic pressures to violate their codes that employers face. Even the elaborate scheme for "monitoring the monitors" proposed by Archon Fung, Dara O'Rourke, and Charles Sabel, in *Can We Put an End to Sweatshops?* (Boston: Beacon Press, 2001) offers no escape from this basic problem. The people who know the plant best, who are there every workday, and who have the strongest incentive to learn their rights and report violations are the workers in the plants.

18 Participating universities include all ten campuses of the University of California, Columbia, Cornell, Duke, and the University of Wisconsin–Madison. A few of these universities have hedged a bit on the democratic worker organization criterion, arguing that if workers clearly demonstrate an uncoerced desire not to have a union, the factories they work at should not be excluded from the list. It remains to be seen whether that position will be maintained, and if so, how absence of coercion will be determined. The three universities that have so far officially considered the DSP approach and refused to sign on (though they say they would like to keep talking about it) are the University of Michigan, Pur-

due University, and the University of Colorado–Boulder.

19 One such discussion, "Constructing Markets for Conscientious Apparel Consumers," occurred at a conference organized at the University of Michigan–Ann Arbor on April 1–2, 2005. A summary of the proceedings of this conference may be found on the Web site of the Labor and Global Change Program, University of Michigan, www.ilir.umich.edu/lagn/. These discussions have continued at the last two annual meetings of the SweatFree Communities coalition; for the most recent meeting report, see SweatFree Communities, *International Conference 2006 Report*.

20 Six national surveys have shown majorities ranging from a high of 86 percent, who said they would pay one dollar more on a twenty-dollar garment made under good working conditions (Marymount University Center for Ethical Concerns, 1999), to a low of 64.5 percent, who said they would pay five dollars more on a twenty-dollar garment not made in a sweatshop (University of Maryland Program on International Policy Attitudes, 2004). For more detail on these surveys, see Monica Prasad, Howard Kimeldorf, Rachel Meyer, and Ian Robinson, "Consumers of the World Unite: A Market-Based Approach to Sweatshops," *Labor Studies Journal* 29, no. 3 (2004), pp. 57–79.

21 I was able to obtain detailed cross-tabulations for the 1999 Marymount survey and the database for the 2004 University of Maryland survey. This enabled me to look at variation in stated willingness to pay more according to family income category. In both surveys, the variation was minimal: for the Marymount survey, 83.3 percent of the lowest income category (less than fifteen thousand dollars) and 86.8 percent of the highest income category (more than fifty thousand dollars) were willing to pay more; for the Maryland survey (using the same income categories that Marymount used), 67.1 percent of the lowest income category were willing to pay more, as was 67 percent of the highest income category.

22 Marsha Dickson, using her own nationally representative survey (547 participants), found that only 30 percent of participants who purchased No Sweat–labeled apparel had college degrees, while 41 percent of label purchasers did not; a plurality of these No Sweat–label consumers (40 percent) reported household incomes ranging from $25,000 to $49,999 (which is around the center of the U.S. income distribution). See Marsha Dickson, "Utility of No Sweat Labels for Apparel Consumers: Profiling Label Users and Predicting Their Purchases," *Journal of Consumer Affairs* 35, no. 1 (2001), pp. 110–16.

23 This question is raised by Kimberly Ann Elliott and Richard Freeman, "White Hats or Don Quixotes?: Human Rights Vigilantes in the Global Economy," in Richard B. Freeman, Joni Hersch, and Lawrence Mishel (eds.), *Emerging Labor Market Institutions for the Twenty-First Century* (Chicago: University of Chicago Press, 2005). See also Marsha Dickson, "Utility of No Sweat Labels," pp. 97–98.

24 There are three cognitive preconditions that must be met if people are to be considered as capable of choosing to be ethical consumers in the context of our in-store experiment. First, they must know what a sweatshop is and, thus, what is at stake in the apparel choice before them. Second, they must notice that one of the products they examine claims to be sweat-free. Third, they must also notice that the sweat-free product costs 20 percent more than one next to it, though very similar in style and quality, which makes no claim to be sweat-free. Our findings are summarized in Howard Kimeldorf, Rachel Meyer, Monica Prasad, and Ian Robinson, "Consumers with a Conscience: Will They Pay More?" *Contexts* 5, no. 1 (2005), pp. 24–29.

25 Michael Adams, *Fire and Ice: The United States, Canada, and the Myth of Converging Values* (Toronto: Penguin Press, 2003), pp. 76 and 160–61, defines "ethical consumerism" as "a focus on the perceived ethical and social responsibility policies and practices of companies from which [consumers] buy; consideration of labor policies, mistreatment of animals, etc.; desire to see companies be good corporate citizens in terms of these social concerns" — an attitude that Adams contends is more prevalent in some countries than in others. He finds that 24 percent of Americans embrace a cluster of values closely correlated with ethical consumerism, while 45 percent of Canadians adopt such values. As various iterations of the World Values Survey have demonstrated, Canada is closer to the United States on these kinds of personal attitudinal measures than Western Europe, where citizens tend to favor economic policies in which democratically accountable governments play a more substantial role in promoting social justice and economic development.

26 I am not aware of any survey data on how consumers in the global South feel about sweatshop labor and what they would be willing to do, as consumers, to change it. So this extrapolation from the U.S. data must remain conjecture at this point. But we can specify parallel evidence with respect to Southern attitudes concerning environmental issues. It is widely asserted, particularly by Northern economists, that most Southern workers care less about environmental quality than their Northern counterparts, because their incomes are lower. But the available survey evidence suggests that this is not true. For a review of this evidence, see Steve Brechin and Willett Kempton, "Global Environmentalism: A Challenge to the Postmaterialism Thesis?" *Social Science Quarterly* 75, no. 2 (1994), pp. 245–69; and Brechin and

Kempton, "Beyond Postmaterialist Values: National Versus Individual Explanations of Global Environmentalism," *Social Science Quarterly* 78, no. 1 (1997), pp. 16–25.

27 The *Swadeshi* movement asked Indians who supported Gandhi's demands for Indian independence from the British Empire to buy domestically produced goods despite the fact that they often cost more and (in some cases) were of lower quality. For a very interesting discussion of this movement and references to more detailed analyses, see Micheletti, *Political Virtue*, pp. 40–42.

28 This is so for two reasons. First, the contribution of labor compensation to final sales price for most clothing is very low, making it possible to double wages with very little effect on sale price, even if the additional labor costs are passed along entirely to the consumer. On this, see Robert Pollin, Justine Burns, and James Heintz, "Global Apparel Production and Sweatshop Labor: Can Raising Retail Prices Finance Living Wages?" (Working Paper 19, Political Economy Research Institute, University of Massachusetts–Amherst, 2002). Second, the brands and retailers that account for much of the price markup are (in many cases) making sufficiently healthy profits (think Nike and Wal-Mart) such that they could swallow the entire increase in labor costs in the form of marginally reduced profits. This could even become a demand of the antisweatshop movement if it were serious about expanding to include hundreds of millions of low-income Southern consumers.

29 There is surprisingly little research on the motives that underpin consumer participation (or nonparticipation) in the antisweatshop movement, though Dickson offers a number of interesting insights in "Utility of No Sweat Labels." The University of Michigan research team is also exploring this question. While our analysis remains very preliminary (we hope to publish a more sophisticated analysis soon), one relevant finding may be reported here: in 130 exit interviews with customers at a new American Apparel clothing store in Ann Arbor, Michigan, 71.5 percent of respondents stated that they would pay a premium above American Apparel's current prices if they could be sure that the clothing they were buying was sweat-free. When we asked them to tell us how much more in percentage terms they would be willing to pay for sweat-free clothing (relative to current prices), their answers ranged from 2 percent to 100 percent; the median among those willing to pay such a premium was 10 percent. Many of the people we interviewed expressed mixed motives for their ethical consumerism: 89 percent agreed that "better-off people like me ought to help people who are not doing as well" (motive: either charity or solidarity); 57 percent contended that "anyone who buys goods made in

a sweatshop is taking advantage of the workers and that's wrong" (motive: desire for "clean hands"); almost 53 percent claimed that "I feel a common bond with workers who make my clothes, and I get angry (or sad) when I think of their exploitation" (motive: empathy/solidarity); and almost 82 percent declared that "I feel it is an important part of who I am that I *actively* support efforts to improve the rights and conditions of disadvantaged people" (motive: ethical principles as an important component of personal identity). About 68 percent of this group agreed with all four of these rationales. We might anticipate that where multiple motives all point in the same direction, the commitment to act on those motives will be stronger.

30 Bama Athreya and I developed these arguments at greater length in our background paper for the April 2005 conference on conscientious consumption held at the University of Michigan–Ann Arbor. See, Ian Robinson and Bama Athreya, "Constructing Markets for Conscientious Apparel Consumers: Adapting the 'Fair Trade' Model to the Apparel Sector," (background paper, Constructing Markets for Conscientious Apparel Consumers, University of Michigan–Ann Arbor, March 29, 2005), www.ilir.umich.edu/lagn/Constructing-Markets.pdf.

31 This reflects my conviction that talk about moral or ethical behavior is ultimately about the motives or reasons for which decisions are made. An entirely self-interested actor may be induced, by some combination of threats and rewards made by the state, by unions, or by consumers, to behave in a fashion consistent with ethical principles. But in such a case, the proper bearer of the attribution "ethical" is not the self-interested actor, but the context — whether that means the institutions and regulations of the state, the power and demands of the unions, or the system of labeling that allows ethical consumers to effectively express their desire for goods made under proper working conditions — that induces the actor to behave in a way that others judge to be just. In other words, we should talk about just laws, or social-justice unionism, or ethical consumers, rather than about moral corporations, unless social-justice outcomes have substantial and independent weight among the criteria that determine corporate decisions.

32 The skeptic may ask whether there are really any moralized firms, as I have redefined that term, in this industry or in any other. The answer is yes, both in the manufacturing and the retail components of the apparel sector. On the manufacturing side, worker-owned co-ops are one such moralized component. Such co-ops typically care about worker rights and working conditions for the fairly obvious reason that the people who own the firm are those same workers. But

even where this is not the case, there are a few outstanding examples of capitalist firms that assign independent weight to worker rights and welfare. On the retail side, there are at least three retailers in the United States today — Justice Clothing, No Sweat, and Union Jean and Apparel — that exist primarily because their founders want to provide ethical consumers with sweat-free clothing.

33 A few years ago, this kind of problem began to emerge with the definition of "organic" foods in the United States, when agribusiness decided the time had come to enter this market. We may soon see a parallel problem in the fair-trade coffee sector, if one or more major roasters become interested in selling coffee labeled "fair trade," sourcing it from traditional coffee plantations. For overviews of developments in these sectors, see two essays by Laura T. Raynolds, "The Globalization of Organic Agro-Food Networks," *World Development* 32, no. 5 (2004), pp. 725–43, and "Consumer/Producer Links in Fair Trade Coffee Networks," *Sociologica Ruralis* 42, no. 4 (2002), pp. 404–24.

34 Within the antisweatshop movement, perhaps the most serious example of this problem to date is American Apparel. The critical question that this Los Angeles–based apparel manufacturer raises is whether a firm that pays wages and benefits above the industry average, but employs standard anti-union tactics to prevent the formation of a workers' union (in other words, violating core worker rights), can legitimately call itself sweat-free. In my view, it cannot, and it is critical that the definition of "sweat-free" make no concessions on this fundamental point.

35 See Camila Piñeiro Harnecker, "The New Cooperative Movement in Venezuela's Bolivarian Process," *Monthly Review Webzine,* May 12, 2005, http://mrzine.monthlyreview.org/harnecker051205.html.

36 Arguably, Cambodia has now settled on a strategy of producing for this market, though its firms are not worker-owned. See Don Wells, "'Best Practice' in the Regulation of International Labor Standards: Lessons of the US-Cambodia Textile Agreement," *Comparative Labor Law and Policy Journal* (forthcoming). Thanks to Don for sharing this fascinating paper with me in advance of publication.

37 This instability is the result of three deep-structural characteristics of neoliberal globalization that are not going to disappear unless an alternative model of economic regulation can be implemented at the global level. The political coalition of national governments needed to implement such an alternative does not exist, however, and is not likely to arise any time soon. The three basic sources of neoliberal globalization's instability are very high levels of international capital mobility and largely unregulated currency trading; a tendency to polarize income and opportunity in a way that is politically unsustainable in democracies; and a tendency to create a few winners and many losers at the level of national economies, as well. This last point deserves brief elaboration. In a unified global economy, there is one low-cost producer for any given commodity. In a world economy composed of five or six regional economic blocs, there can be five or six low-cost producers of every commodity.

38 In *The Great Transformation: The Political and Economic Origins of Our Time* (Boston: Beacon Press, 1944), Karl Polanyi implies that we have been in a situation like this once before. Let us hope that the disintegration of this, the second iteration of economic liberalism, does not give rise to the kind of fascism that followed the disintegration of the first. I am relatively hopeful on this point, since there is no communist system to legitimate the rise of a parallel fascism on the far right of the political spectrum and the countries experiencing the most traumatic economic restructuring in Africa and Latin America have already gone through fascist periods. Russia and China, particularly the former, are most worrying in this regard.

39 The incoherence of the current rhetorical pairing of worker rights *and* economic nationalism can be seen in the U.S. auto industry. The assembly-plant workers of the big three — one of which (Daimler-Chrysler) is now owned by a German firm — are all organized into the United Auto Workers (UAW). But (with the exception of a few joint ventures with the big three) all of the Japanese and European "transplant" assembly plants — Toyota, Honda, BMW, Mercedes — are nonunion, despite UAW efforts at organizing their workers. They remain nonunion because of sophisticated and effective anti-union policies. Meanwhile, every one of those companies' assembly plants in Japan and Germany is organized by the unions of those countries and pays their workers wages and benefits equal to or higher than those paid to UAW workers in the United States. So should U.S. trade unionists and ethical consumers be encouraged to buy the U.S.–produced, nonunion Toyota, or the Japanese-produced, union Toyota? Which option would put more pressure on nonunion firms in the United States to allow their employees to join the UAW? Which would make it easier to develop cooperative strategies with Japan's auto unions to bring pressure jointly on Toyota? Thanks to Steve Babson for providing me with this example, which he regularly uses in the labor education work he does with UAW members.

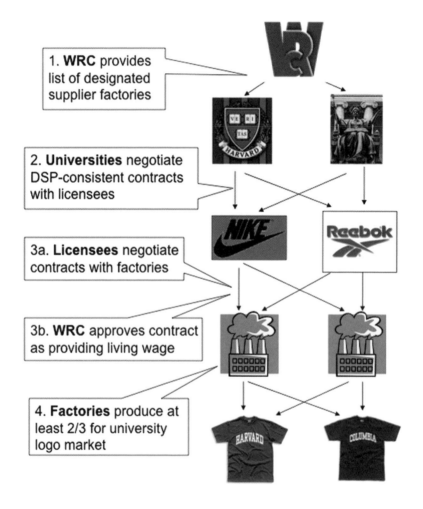

1. **WRC** provides list of designated supplier factories

2. **Universities** negotiate DSP-consistent contracts with licensees

3a. **Licensees** negotiate contracts with factories

3b. **WRC** approves contract as providing living wage

4. **Factories** produce at least 2/3 for university logo market

Diagram of the production and distribution of logo apparel under the Designated Supplier Program, United Students Against Sweatshops training kit, Columbia University.

Corporate Social Responsibility and Labor Rights in U.S.-Based Corporations

Mark Barenberg

In the mid-1990s, labor activists and media outlets in the United States publicized stories of horrendous working conditions in factories producing for global brands: child labor; machinery lacking safety guards; subpoverty wages; extreme overtime hours, often unpaid; seven-day work weeks; sexual coercion of various forms; and retaliation against those who participated in worker organizations. The stories focused on the production of apparel, footwear, and retail products. In these sectors, the supply chain extends from factories in Mexico, El Salvador, Indonesia, Vietnam, China, and other low-wage countries to U.S.-based retailers or manufacturers (the brands). The supplier factories are owned by corporations (the vendors) based in Hong Kong, Singapore, Taiwan, South Korea, and elsewhere. Although the factories are formally independent of the brands, the latter exercise strong and, in some cases, decisive control over the factories' operations.

In the face of bad publicity, the brands sought to protect their reputations through the device of "corporate social responsibility" (CSR). The central organizing concept of CSR is managerial responsiveness to the interests not only of investors, but of other stakeholders, as well as, in this case, the factory workforce. The voluntary "code of conduct" is its key institutional form, and the "labor monitor" or "social auditor" is its enforcement mechanism.[1] In its initial phases, CSR represented the substitution of technocratic, managerial methods and public-relations strategies for sovereign regulation, collective bargaining, and popular organizations and campaigns—at least in the United States and in the field of working conditions, to which this essay is confined. (CSR also extends beyond labor rights to environmental and human-rights matters.)

To date, CSR has largely deflected or captured the amorphous consumer, media, and political pressures that generated it. Yet a "double movement" through which labor and allied movements and public agencies in the global North and South attempt to wield CSR for their own purposes followed almost immediately upon the emergence of CSR.[2] Labor movements and public agencies adopted two alternative strategies: rejection of

CSR altogether on the ground that it displaces worker organization and democratic regulation and promotion of labor-centered monitors and public auditors whose practical work is intended to demonstrate the fundamental debility of corporate-centered labor monitoring.[3]

The labor movements succeeded in showing that in its present form, CSR could at best assist workers only in *particular* high-visibility factories and even then only under persistent pressure and vigilance by worker organizations in the South and grassroots campaigns in the North.[4] They showed that CSR could only protect workers' basic rights *systemically* if corporate managers agreed to four fundamental changes in the structure of global supply chains: stabilization of production in model factories (constraining the hypermobility of capital); joint responsibility of retailer/manufacturer and vendor/factory for meeting the cost of improved wages and working conditions; good-faith negotiations with legitimate worker organizations in supplier factories; and strengthening democratic, sovereign protection of workers' associational rights in global workplaces.[5] But full-blooded implementation of these changes would effectively revert to a regime of collective self-monitoring by workers overseen by public authorities, rendering CSR's self-monitoring by managers largely extraneous, except as a second-order compliance program of a traditional sort that predates CSR.

Both CSR and the ensuing double movement are very much embedded in the contingencies of the political and legal transformations that resurrected thoroughgoing laissez-faire in U.S. labor markets in the last quarter of a century. Whether CSR will ultimately stay on the managerial/technocratic path or instead be overtaken by worker-based and public-regulatory regimes depends on similar contingencies, not just in the United States, but in key U.S. trading partners, such as China. Market ideologies remain in the driver's seat in U.S. politics, even after the spectacular managerial scandals of the present gilded age. This is especially true for the ideology of labor markets. A progressive turn in CSR practices will occur only if, among other things, there is a reversal in the hegemony of competitive market ideology among political, managerial, and academic elites, including liberal legislators, intellectuals, and commentators.

A brief description of the five phases of CSR's history in the apparel industry in the United States will clarify the double movement between CSR and its critics. Then we will turn to the broader ideological and political contests that may determine its outcome.

Initially, in response to the exposés of working conditions in supplier factories, the brands relied on "first-party" staff to monitor the factories' compliance with their codes. That is, their own managers and employees did the monitoring. The most "progressive" brands created elaborate administrative structures reaching from CSR departments in their U.S. headquarters to regional and country offices overseas and to frontline personnel who did the actual factory inspections and reported up the managerial chain of command.[6]

There was an obvious conflict of interest in the brands' vouching for the labor conditions for which they now assumed some responsibility. For this reason, consumers and labor activists did not take managerial self-monitoring seriously, and CSR did not yet serve its key function of mollifying corporate critics, even if it showed modest success in reducing the most visible abuses in supplier factories, such as child labor and locked fire doors.

The brands therefore moved to a strategy of using "second-party" monitors to conduct factory inspections.[7] The second-party monitors were financial auditors such as PriceWaterhouseCoopers that took on the additional role of social auditing; consulting firms such as Intertek that specialized in supply-chain logistics, technical certification, customs clearance, and the like; and a plethora of firms that were newly established in order to cash in on the growing market in labor monitoring. But this outsourcing strategy suffered from the same flaws as first-party monitoring. Consumer and labor critics, as well as the media, were not convinced of the independence and competence of second-party firms chosen and paid by the brands.

In its third phase, CSR turned to trade associations of manufacturers and retailers such as Worldwide Responsible Apparel Production (WRAP) and to newly established consortia and "multistakeholder initiatives" composed of corporations and elite human-rights organizations such as the Fair Labor Association (FLA) and Social Accountability International (SAI).[8] These organizations "certify" second-party monitors and in some cases conduct their own monitoring to verify the work of second-party monitors. Yet again, the consortia and multistakeholder organizations were easy targets for activists, since retailers and manufacturers held controlling votes and veto power in the organizations' policy decisions, notwithstanding the repeated efforts by brands and their media enthusiasts to cast the consortia as "independent" monitors.[9] The corporations' limited commitment to labor rights was marked by the fact that it took significant political leverage (such as the Clinton administration's Apparel Industry Partnership) to create even these weak, corporate-controlled organizations, and even then, only the most progressive corporations and those most threatened by damage to the brand were willing to participate. A second indicator of the corporations' limited commitment was the fact that the multistakeholder consortia did not include the crucial stakeholder: namely, workers and their organizations. The latter refused to participate in organizations dominated by corporations and uncommitted to full disclosure of the information gathered in factory inspections.

In view of corporations' weak commitment to labor rights, U.S. unions and anti-sweatshop campaigners gave their support to the Worker Rights Consortium (WRC), a monitoring consortium that was fully independent of the industry. The WRC was the product of the student antisweatshop campaigns of the late 1990s, the largest and most effective student movement since the anti-apartheid and antiwar campaigns of the 1960s and 1970s.[10] The students sought to improve working conditions in factories producing collegiate merchandise, such as university caps and sweatshirts, and rejected corporate-controlled monitors such as the FLA. Once established, the WRC was governed by three constituents, each having equal voting power: university administrators; an advisory council composed of academics, labor-rights experts, and antisweatshop groups; and students. Neither corporations nor labor unions gave financial support to or held vetoes over the organization's policies, although two labor unionists were members of the advisory council. The WRC marked the fourth phase of CSR in the United States.

In its fifth and present phase, CSR is challenged by policy proposals that put it at risk of irrelevancy, at least in the apparel sector. In the private sector, the WRC is now implementing a Designated Supplier Program (DSP) intended to change fundamentally the operation of global supply chains, rather than to continue to chase footloose capital driven by labor arbitrage. A similar program is being pursued in the agricultural sector in an equally innovative experiment in labor-centered monitoring spearheaded by the Coalition of Immokalee Workers (CIW), a Florida-based organization representing workers who pick and pack produce for growers selling to fast-food chains and supermarkets. The CIW is seeking to hold fast-food companies (buyers) financially responsible for the wages and working conditions of the growers (suppliers) and to reward model growers with preferred purchasing by the buyers.[11]

The Designated Supplier Program and the CIW's preferred grower program respond to several problems revealed by the WRC's practical work.[12] First, even when rigorous monitoring succeeds in helping workers establish independent organizations, the latter are unable to bargain for significant increases in wages. This is due in large part to the brands' unwillingness to raise the unit price they pay to factories and growers for the goods they supply. On the contrary, many brands, most famously Wal-Mart, require their suppliers continuously to lower costs and prices. The message of corporate codes (telling factories and growers they must improve working conditions) is constantly undercut by the message sent by corporate pricing (denying factories and growers the additional resources necessary to fund such improvements, let alone wage increases).

Second, the pool of supplier factories maintained by industry sourcing departments has proven too large and variable for any monitor or combination of monitors to audit systematically and comprehensively. The WRC's monitoring protocols have been unusually effective, in part because they are highly labor-intensive. The WRC assembles teams of local advocates of workers and their communities, experts in labor law and occupational health and safety, and WRC staff. The teams engage in many days of high-trust interviews with workers off company property in confidential locations such as homes, villages, and restaurants. (This contrasts with corporate-controlled monitors, who typically undertake short, superficial interviews of workers in managerial offices during a one-day factory inspection.) The interviews and factory inspections are preceded by weeks or months of engagement with the workforce and the local community. They are followed by continuous contact with local accountability teams or, if present, with labor unions. These labor-intensive methods have set "best standards" in rigorous investigation and remediation of the most entrenched workplace abuses. But without the massive injections of resources that only public institutions, whether domestic or supranational, can provide, these methods cannot be scaled up sufficiently to match the large number of factories that are fundamental to the apparel industry's current structure.

Third, even the WRC's long-term engagement with local workforces is typically not enough to ensure continuous, tenacious monitoring of the kind that has proven necessary to induce brands and factories to remedy abuses. No external monitor in the North can maintain intensive local monitoring during the long periods of time between episodic, on-site audits. When monitors leave the scene, labor abuses reappear. The WRC quickly learned that it is necessary to find or create local accountability teams capable of providing detailed information about ongoing developments at the factory and applying continuous pressure on factory managers to implement remedial programs. However, long-term capacity for local monitoring proved unlikely to germinate unless the WRC's intervention was followed relatively quickly by the factory workforce's successful unionization.

Finally, when arduous monitoring and the building of local monitoring capacity succeed in improving factory conditions, brands and vendors very frequently remove their production from the model factory, sometimes quickly, sometimes gradually. The hypermobility of capital and the attendant suppression of workers' bargaining power underlies this and many other features of global labor markets.

The WRC's Designated Supplier Program responds to these four features of contemporary supply chains and the incapacity of CSR to address them.[13] The DSP requires brands to consolidate production in a small enough number of model factories to enable rigorous, labor-intensive monitoring of all factories. The brands are required to pay sufficient unit prices to enable factories to meet the cost of improved working conditions and nonpoverty wages. Factory workforces must be represented by unions or other legitimate representatives, and factory managers must engage in good-faith bargaining over terms and conditions of employment.

Taken together, these requirements fundamentally restructure global supply chains, rather than permitting corporations simply to overlay existing supply chains with CSR self-monitoring. As a result, the requirements have been aggressively opposed by brands and corporate-controlled monitors such as the FLA, even in the niche market for the production of collegiate merchandise. Nonetheless, these requirements have penetrated the collegiate market to some degree, as well as the agricultural sector supplying fast-food chains. But implementation of the requirements throughout global supply chains is hard to imagine in the present political environment. In the foreseeable future, Wal-Mart and other big retailers are unlikely to mandate that their suppliers pay a living wage and bargain with worker representatives, let alone assume financial responsibility for these and other improvements.

There are, however, modest developments in the public sector pointing toward the kind of political change that could disseminate the DSP beyond the university sector. Congressional representatives from the labor wing of the Democratic Party have

Farmworkers, students, and activists march to the corporate offices of Taco Bell, March 11, 2002, in Irvine, California, calling attention to the working conditions of Florida farm laborers who harvest tomatoes for the fast-food chain (David McNew/Getty Images).

introduced legislation that would require all contractors and affiliates of U.S. corporations to meet standards that, although not as rigorous as the DSP requirements, are a big leap forward. While there is no immediate prospect that these bills will pass, even stronger laws have been enacted at the city and state levels. Several big cities have begun experiments with using WRC-style monitoring as the method for enforcing their antisweatshop laws.[14] And as of this writing, three state governors have launched an initiative to create a multistate consortium devoted to procuring sweat-free goods to be monitored by an entity that, again, uses WRC protocols.[15]

The highly contingent politics surrounding CSR, the DSP, and city and state sweat-free laws make it difficult to predict if the developments toward the superfluity of corporate self-monitoring will prevail or if instead, the CSR industry will survive as either a sincere, albeit limited endeavor or as a necessary public-relations response to continued weak or moderate consumer pressures.

The experience of CSR's chief historical precedent — the "welfare capitalism" of the 1920s — may provide some lessons. Welfare capitalism promised improved working conditions and benefits, provided by enlightened managers. Although CSR responds to working conditions in overseas supplier factories as well as U.S. factories, welfare capitalism addressed working conditions only in domestic workplaces. Nonetheless, both promised the humanization of capitalism under the stewardship of corporate managers at a time when workers' collective organization was at a nadir.

Welfare capitalism grew from three social currents that have remarkably close analogues, if not direct descendants, in the genesis of CSR.[16] First, welfare capitalism drew heavily on the then-new arts of public manipulation — mass advertising and the public propaganda campaigns of the First World War. While some of the new worker benefits promised by welfare capitalism were real, corporate managers amplified their beneficence in mass communications aimed at consumers, owners, and political officials in order to fend off unions and government regulation. Likewise, the CSR departments in multinational corporations are closely connected to the firms' public-communications arms. The primary function of CSR, as already noted, is to avoid harmful media exposés, especially revelations about child labor, in order to maintain corporate reputations and preempt more costly interventions by consumers, investors, and political officials.

Second, the technocratic progressivism of the 1920s originated with the ethical consumer and antisweatshop campaigns of social elites such as the "white label" campaign of the National Consumers League of the 1910s.[17] CSR, too, is driven mostly by affluent, socially minded consumers in the North acting on their standards of ethical consumption.

The consumer-pressure movements of the Progressive Era failed. Campaigns that rely on actual or latent consumer boycotts are notoriously fragile. The effectiveness of consumer pressure depends on the public availability of fine-grained information about working conditions in specific factories, consumers' attentiveness to that information, and corporations' readiness to respond to consumer pressure by rigorously enforcing their codes in the most resistant factories, that is, the factories where workers' rights are most at stake. The Progressive Era consumer movements failed at each link of this chain. Government regulation and unionization, not consumer pressure and managerial self-regulation, accounted for the major gains against sweatshop production in the early twentieth century.

There are special problems in relying on actual or latent consumer pressure to achieve exacting enforcement of labor rights by CSR departments in the early twenty-first century. In the abstract, the best CSR departments have an interest in trumpeting their successes in monitoring workplaces and therefore in providing ample information about improvements in working conditions. In reality, the corporations' more powerful marketing departments aim to attach upbeat associations to their products and have no interest in drawing consumers' attention to the problem of sweatshops, even if highlighting solutions to those problems. The general practice of CSR is therefore to conceal information about problem factories (as well as about good factories) and not allow independent organizations or the public to evaluate the degree of remediation (if any) of those problems. The multistakeholder consortia, other than the WRC, have the same general policies of concealment.

Even the most vigilant consumers are therefore unable to make comparative (or absolute) assessments of the rigor of different CSR programs and are even less able to target their boycott threats surgically at corporations that are currently failing to remedy known violations of rights at particular factories. This is one important reason why the most promising forms of monitoring are backed not by diffuse consumer sentiment and managerial self-regulation, but by collective purchasers such as universities, cities, and states, which have continuous, attentive relationships with the brands, backed by institutional buying power.

Moreover, global corporations vest great power in their "sourcing" departments, whose primary interest is in maintaining access to their preferred supplier factories, regardless of poor working conditions. Since the sourcing departments are a profit center and the CSR departments are not, the latter find their best efforts constantly undermined by the former. Supplier factories have little worry of losing contracts with brands, even if frontline auditors find serious violations of labor rights. Even incorrigible factories understand that they'll be given another chance as long as they promise future compliance. For this reason, newly hired, well-meaning auditors are quickly demoralized. Their turnover rate is high, and their average experience and competence is low. These particular problems of contemporary CSR deepen the general defects of consumer boycotts in securing intensive, fine-tuned enforcement of rights by corporations.

Third, the welfare capitalism of the 1920s was the "progressive" technocratic response to workers' collective protests and organizing. In the 1910s and 1920s, engineers and managers associated with the Taylor Society turned scientific management from Frederick Taylor's retrograde vision of total worker discipline toward Otto Beyer's strategy of labor-management harmony.[18] The full-blown welfare capitalism of the 1920s was explicitly designed as a paternalistic, management-controlled substitute for labor unionism. According to some of its recent academic admirers, who are also leading supporters of CSR, welfare capitalism failed only under the unprecedented stress of the Great Depression. These proponents believe that without the Depression (and its New Deal political response), some variant of welfare capitalism, rather than collective bargaining, might have predominated in postwar labor policy and practice. CSR may therefore represent a return to the long-term, optimal norm in labor relations.

The most sophisticated proponents of welfare capitalism were steeped in a pragmatist philosophy of social cooperation wedded to state-of-the-art methods of industrial engineering. Likewise, the academic proponents of CSR reach back to the same pragmatist philosophy and weld it, not to Taylorism, but to Toyotist concepts of simultaneous engineering. In both cases, the actual or potential adversarialism of labor unionism turned many pragmatist intellectuals away from (and in some cases against) worker organization, belying the intellectuals' slogans of "industrial democracy" in the first era and "democratic collaboration" in the second. If social cooperation promises maximum gains for all stakeholders, what need is there of empowering organizations that threaten conflict in the name of redistribution? If decision making is ideally based on deliberative problem solving, what use is there for participatory organizations that might use power rather than conversation to come to decisions? Better to trust in managerial authority that manifestly remains in even the most "horizontal" and "collaborative" organizations, such as Toyota, however embarrassing this may be to the proposition that Toyota's frontline workers are citizens participating in a collaborative democracy.

This bias against worker organization is not just a matter of academic ideology, of course. In today's global supply chains, retailers and manufacturers own or contract with supplier factories in countries or export zones where workers' right of association is least protected. The brands are hardly likely to turn their supply chains into engines for re-creating the rights they have carefully sought to avoid.

For just this reason, the consultants and consortia that undertake labor auditing on behalf of retailers and manufacturers are notorious for failing to monitor the right of association effectively. They investigate whether there is "good communication" between labor and management, demonstrated by superficial practices such as suggestion boxes, which are taken as proxies for the protection of the workers' right of association.[19] These auditors are not likely to probe too deeply whether workers are subtly intimidated for trying to organize unions, even less likely to take the tenacious remedial steps necessary to reverse managerial retaliation, and less likely still to ask whether ostensible worker organizations are illicitly influenced by managers or corrupt political elites. They maintain that it is not their place to examine whether worker organizations are legitimately and democratically established, even though this is a fundamental component of workers' right of association in international and domestic labor law.[20]

Indeed, the primary function of corporate codes of conduct and labor monitoring, viewed as a regulatory regime, is to fill the void left by the steady decline of unionism since the 1970s. Their purpose is to legitimate supply chains in which workplace rights and standards have been trounced in the United States and in which supplier countries in the South try to keep brush fires of worker protest from flaring into broad-based, independent labor movements.

In this light, it is not surprising that the revitalized laissez-faire of U.S. labor markets is in some important respects mirrored in labor-market reforms in such critical host countries as China. Since the early 1980s, the Chinese government has increasingly abandoned the "iron rice bowl" of privileged incomes, welfare, and job security for urban factory workers. Formerly privileged urban workers have been replaced by temporary migrants from the countryside with almost no labor rights or contractual protection.[21] They must engage in low-level guerilla warfare with managers simply to get paid the low wages they've already earned — an indicator of a nearly Hobbesian state of pure labor market "flexibility." State-controlled unions are integrated into the "developmentalist" machinery of local governments, which are fully allied with investors and managers. Repression of wider protest and independent union organizing is

Web site banner from www.sweatfree.org.

swift and comprehensive. Companies such as Wal-Mart, therefore, enjoy maximally "flexible" labor markets in both their Chinese suppliers' factories and their retail stores and distribution centers in the United States. Labor rights and standards have been weakened throughout the transnational supply chain.

In the United States, unionism and other institutions protective of labor rights declined in the last quarter century for many reasons: intensified competition in both global and domestic markets; inhospitable macroeconomic policies; the shift from a manufacturing to a service economy and the attendant extinction of blue-collar communities; the split between residential and workplace life that came with suburbanization and corporations' deliberate dispersion of workplace sites from heavily unionized urban centers; the waxing of consumerist and identity-based cultures and the waning of producerist class consciousness; organized labor's adherence to Cold War foreign policies and their loss of élan in the eyes of antiwar progressives in the 1970s; the labor movement's decision that servicing existing members was more promising than organizing new ones and the attendant bureaucratic ossification of unions; and many more.

But without a doubt, one of the most important reasons for labor's decline is the quiet legal and political pulverization of labor rights in the last thirty years or, more accurately, the legal and political system's failure to protect workers against the unremitting onslaught of managers' campaigns to maintain union-free workplaces.[22] That failure encourages several of the other trends just noted, such as the unions' decision that new organizing is less cost-effective than servicing current members, the displacement of producerist by consumerist consciousness, and the quiet scorn of liberal elites for labor unions that have evidently retreated from the social mobilizing movement of earlier decades.

The core rights promised on paper by United States labor law are the right against discharge and other retaliation for engaging in union activity and the right to good-faith negotiation of terms and conditions of employment.[23] Employers' violations of these rights increased exponentially after the 1960s when Congress and the National Labor Relations Board limited the remedies for such violations to merely token sanctions.[24] As a result, surveys of workers show that they widely (and accurately) believe that they will face severe retaliation if they seek to unionize, and that if they should succeed in unionizing, they will meet across-the-board resistance to reaching a first collective contract. Many empirical studies conclude that employers' unfair labor practices and the government's failure to remedy those practices are responsible in significant part for the decline of unionism in the United States.[25]

The importance of these enforcement failures is demonstrated by the fact that unionization rates have remained high, indeed, have increased, among public-sector employees, even though their white-collar service jobs are the kind that are purportedly difficult to organize in the postindustrial economy. In the public sector, managers do not run the ferocious antiunion campaigns of their private-sector counterparts and, as a result, workers freely choose to organize in percentages equal to the 1950s high tide of private-sector unionism. A majority of workers in the private sector still express a preference for collective organization, but are unable to realize that preference in the face of managerial opposition.[26]

It is this constriction of labor rights in the private sector that accounts, in large part, for the re-creation of laissez-faire in U.S. labor markets, and that has established a domestic precondition for the United States' neoliberal global strategy. Without doubt, the U.S.-led liberalization of international product and capital markets further debilitated labor unionism, not just in the United States, but around the world. The prior crippling of the U.S. labor movement, however, was one of the political predicates of global liberalization.

The failure to enforce workers' rights is more than just a legal or administrative phenomenon. It is a reflection of the lack of political will to ensure the protection of workers' right of association. Surely the Reagan and Bush administrations' hostility to labor unionism was crucial. But for reasons too complicated to discuss here, the Democratic Party quietly allowed its most powerful liberal constituent to crumble in this way, rather than doing everything it could to shore it up.[27] The domination of the Democratic Party by President Clinton's probusiness Democratic Leadership Council and the party's

Web site button from www.sweatfree.org.

failure to support worker organizations and communities came back to haunt liberals in the 2000 and 2004 presidential elections. The Democratic candidates narrowly lost elections they would have easily won just twenty years earlier, when the labor movement could put swing states in the Democratic column.

Another marker of the seismic shift in party self-definition was the Clinton administration's promotion of the corporate-controlled Fair Labor Association and its concurrent failure to commit itself to all-out support for worker organization. That is, the rise of corporate codes of conduct and managerial self-monitoring in the United States is explained neither by "globalization" and "neoliberalism" at some abstract level nor by the ostensible propagation of analogous Pragmatist experiments in transborder regulation across many fields. The decline of unionism, the restoration of laissez-faire in U.S. labor markets, and the return of managerial self-regulation on a scale not seen since the welfare capitalism of the 1920s are the culmination of decades of contingent political and legal contests in the United States (as well as in supplier countries such as China). Whether CSR survives or gives way to a fundamental restructuring of global supply chains will turn — just like the fate of its precursor, welfare capitalism — on unpredictable domestic political contention linked closely with the resolution of severe imbalances in the global economy.

1   Ivanka Mamic, *Implementing Codes of Conduct: How Businesses Manage Social Performance in Global Supply Chains* (UK: International Labour Office and Greenleaf Publishing, 2004). This book is the report of a large-scale, multicountry research project on corporate codes and monitoring conducted by the research arm of the International Labor Organization (ILO). I was an independent expert on that project. Many of the conclusions in this chapter are based on the fieldwork for the project, although the conclusions are strictly my own interpretation of the evidence, not that of the ILO. My conclusions are also based, in part, on my participation in the monitoring activities of the Worker Rights Consortium.

2   The concept of the "double movement" is adapted from Karl Polanyi, *The Great Transformation: The Political and Economic Origins of Our Time* (Boston: Beacon Press, 1944).

3   Jill Esbenshade, *Monitoring Sweatshops: Workers, Consumers, and the Global Apparel Industry* (Philadelphia: Temple University Press, 2004).

4   Mark Anner and Peter Evans, "Building Bridges Across a Double-Divide: Alliances Between U.S. and Latin American Labor and NGOs," *Development in Practice* 14, nos. 1–2 (2004), pp. 34–47.

5   See the discussion below of the Designated Supplier Program of the Worker Rights Consortium.

6   See Mamic, *Implementing Codes of Conduct.*

7   For a good summary of first-party, second-party, and third-party monitoring, see Erin Burnett and James Mahon Jr., "Monitoring Compliance with International Labor Standards," *Challenge* 44, no. 2 (2001), pp. 51–73.

8   For an overview of these developments, see Kimberly Ann Elliott and Richard B. Freeman, *Can Labor Standards Improve Under Globalization?* (Washington, D.C.: Institute for International Economics, 2003), ch. 3.

9   Andrew Ross, *Low Pay, High Profile: The Global Push for Fair Labor* (New York: The New Press, 2004), ch. 1.

10 Liza Featherstone, *Students Against Sweatshops: The Making of a Movement* (London: Verso, 2002).

11 See the Coalition of Immokalee Workers at www.ciw-online. org.

12 I serve on the WRC Advisory Council and participated in several WRC factory investigations. The following paragraphs draw, in part, on that experience.

13 Worker Rights Consortium, "The Designated Suppliers Program: An Outline of Operational Structure and the Implementation Process," www.workersrights.org/dsp.asp.

14 Most notably, Los Angeles and San Francisco.

15 See Governor John Baldacci, State of Maine, "Formation of a Governors' Coalition for Sweatfree Procurement" (letter), February 28, 2006.

16 These elements of welfare capitalism are canvassed in Mark Barenberg, "The Political Economy of the Wagner Act: Power, Symbol, and Workplace Cooperation," *Harvard Law Review* 106, no. 7 (1993), pp. 1379–496; and Mark Barenberg, "Democracy and Domination in the Law of Workplace Cooperation: From Bureaucratic to Flexible Production," *Columbia Law Review* 94, no. 3 (1994), pp. 753–983.

17 Dana Frank, *Purchasing Power: Consumer Organizing, Gender, and the Seattle Labor Movement, 1919–1929* (Cambridge: Cambridge University Press, 1994).

18 Samuel Haber, *Efficiency and Uplift: Scientific Management in the Progressive Era, 1890–1920* (Chicago: University of Chicago Press, 1964).

19 For a diplomatic treatment of the fieldwork on this point, see Mamic, *Implementing Codes of Conduct.*

20 Fair Labor Association, "Issues and Comments on the Designated Supplier Program (DSP) Proposal," February 17, 2006. Available at the Worker Rights Consortium site, www.workersrights.org/dsp.asp.

21 Mary E. Gallagher, *Contagious Capitalism: Globalization and the Politics of Labor in China* (Princeton: Princeton University Press, 2005).

22 Barenberg, "Democracy and Domination."

23 *National Labor Relations Act of 1935*, U.S. Code 29, §§ 151–169, 8(a)(3) and 8(a)(5), as amended.

24 For recent evidence of this trend and analysis concluding that it constitutes a violation of international human-rights norms, see Human Rights Watch, *Unfair Advantage: Workers' Freedom of Association in the United States Under International Human Rights Standards* (New York: Human Rights Watch, 2000).

25 Barenberg, "Democracy and Domination."

26 Gallup Poll, "Labor Unions," August 8–11, 2005.

27 Matthew M. Bodah, Steve Ludlam, and David Coates, "The Development of an Anglo-American Model of Trade Union and Political Party Relations," *Labor Studies Journal* 28, no. 2 (2003), pp. 45–66.

Civic Think Tank

Peter Lurie interviewed by Gaëlle Krikorian and Emmanuelle Cosse

Peter Lurie is deputy director of Public Citizen's Health Research Group, a Ralph Nader-founded advocacy group in Washington, D.C. During his academic career, he worked on HIV prevention programs in the U.S. and abroad. At Public Citizen, he has sought to ban or relabel multiple drugs; to restrict the use of unsafe medical needles and candles with lead wicks; to prevent worker exposure to hexavalent chromium; and to reduce medical resident work hours. He teaches at the George Washington University School of Public Health and Health Sciences.

Can you tell us how Public Citizen began?

Public Citizen was founded in 1971. It started off as the Health Research Group, created by Ralph Nader and Sidney Wolfe. At the time, Ralph was already a very prominent figure, thanks to his work on auto safety, but he needed an umbrella organization. As for Sidney, he was a physician working for the National Institutes of Health (NIH). Sidney had heard about these IV fluids, made by the pharmaceutical company Abbott, that turned out to be infected with bacteria. When government officials learned about this, they decided that the doctors should be informed that the IV bags they were using might be infected, but they didn't force the company to take them off the market. Sidney was outraged and made a lot of noise about the issue. This episode got him to reevaluate his own life and to get in touch with Ralph. Together they decided that there was a need for an organization. Sid left the NIH, and that's how Public Citizen was formed.

Shortly thereafter, two new entities were added to the Health Research Group: the Litigation Group and the Congress Watch Group, which lobbies on Capitol Hill and which developed a spin-off group, called Global Trade Watch, specializing in globalization issues. Later on, more branches were created: a group working on tax reform that no longer exists, an anti-nuclear group called the Critical Mass Energy Program, and, most recently, under the influence of Joan Claybrook—who has been president of Public Citizen since the early 1980s—an entity specializing in car safety.

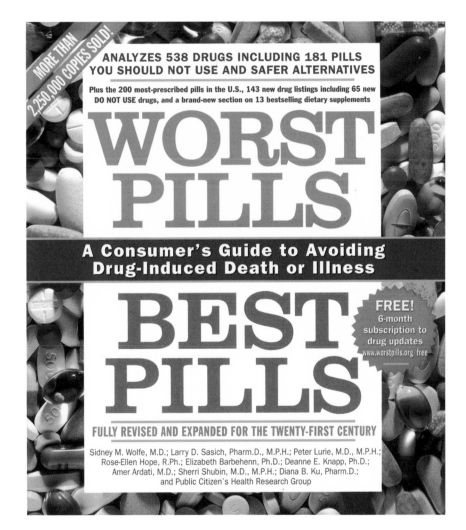

ANALYZES 538 DRUGS INCLUDING 181 PILLS YOU SHOULD NOT USE AND SAFER ALTERNATIVES

Plus the 200 most-prescribed pills in the U.S., 143 new drug listings including 65 new DO NOT USE drugs, and a brand-new section on 13 bestselling dietary supplements

MORE THAN 2,250,000 COPIES SOLD!

WORST PILLS

A Consumer's Guide to Avoiding Drug-Induced Death or Illness

BEST PILLS

FREE! 6-month subscription to drug updates www.worstpills.org/free

FULLY REVISED AND EXPANDED FOR THE TWENTY-FIRST CENTURY

Sidney M. Wolfe, M.D.; Larry D. Sasich, Pharm.D., M.P.H.; Peter Lurie, M.D., M.P.H.; Rose-Ellen Hope, R.Ph.; Elizabeth Barbehenn, Ph.D.; Deanne E. Knapp, Ph.D.; Amer Ardati, M.D.; Sherri Shubin, M.D., M.P.H.; Diana B. Ku, Pharm.D.; and Public Citizen's Health Research Group

Cover of *Worst Pills, Best Pills,* Public Citizen's consumers' guide intended to help patients "navigate the drug minefield."

What makes Public Citizen unique?

First of all, one of the most distinctive features of Public Citizen, ever since Ralph Nader founded it, is that we are active in the three branches of government — namely, the executive, the legislative, and the judicial branches. Other consumer groups in this country are active in one or more of these branches, but usually not in all three.

Ralph came from a consumer orientation that was about empowering consumers to make their own choices and forcing the government to make decisions that would protect consumers. Sid came from a research and clinical background. Their idea was that you could take your knowledge as a physician or as a researcher and transfer it into a form of advocacy in medicine, a field where there was no such thing. In law, there is quite a long tradition of public-interest activism, of lawyers who take civil action against large corporations. But not in health care. Structurally, medicine is about helping rather than battling — about working within the health-care system, rather than being adversarial. Many doctors certainly try to work things out in the interest of the patient, but even then, they tend to perceive their efforts as a continuation of their work as clinicians, rather than as activism in the realm of public health. Thus we can say that Public Citizen, and Sidney Wolfe, in particular, actually invented a field where physicians can be full-time activists devoting 100 percent of their time to the public interest.

Perhaps the weakness of public-health activism in the medical field also has something to do with doctors' attachment to their position of power vis-à-vis their patients.

That's right. Doctors become comfortable with the idea of being in charge. Some of their early resistance to the consumers' movement had to do with the fear that patients would feel too empowered — that they would refuse to take their medications, for example. If you were to give patients clear information about what their drugs do, they might make a choice, and it might not be the one you, as a physician, would think they should make. In fact, if you look back at the evolution of medicine in the last thirty years, that fear was well placed, though in most cases still in the overall interest of the patient. More and more, patients make their own choices. Such a trend has been tremendously accelerated by the Internet, where patients can get all kinds of information. Moreover, in this country, we unfortunately have direct-to-consumer advertising. So the patients learn certain biased information from the drug companies and bring it into the clinical setting, and the doctors resent it, which is partly understandable. If patients informed by drug companies' propaganda, start demanding a drug one can understand why physicians may be irritated. However, another part of the physicians' resistance to consumer empowerment is clearly about defending their authority.

You say that the identity of Public Citizen is that of a consumer group using the expertise of professionals. Yet, it seems consumers have no direct say in your policies.

Our group works like a quasi-democracy. We make clear what our position is, we advertise it clearly, we try to make sure everybody knows about it, and if some people don't like it, they don't have to support us. We don't want to be in the position of being ordered around, even by our members. For us, things happen too quickly, and a number of the issues involved are too technical. So there is no way that the consumers could directly elect us, for instance.

There are tensions within the consumer movement. There are people who literally want to be a voice for consumers in their consumption of particular products — *Consumer Reports,* for example. They rate things that you might buy; they help you to buy better, in some way. Others are more driven by social-justice issues and political concerns. Among the consumer groups, Public Citizen is the one that tends to take the hardest line, that attempts to be the most principled and political. We take no money from any industry or from the government, which enables us to remain unbiased. Thus, when we go to an FDA advisory committee and we say that we are representing the consumers, that doesn't mean that we've done a survey of lung-cancer patients to find out what it is that they want; it means that we have studied the data and are able, from a consumer's point of view, to stand up and explain what we think, untainted by some outside financial interest.

Although your legitimacy lies with the consumers whose interests you defend, your mode of operation is largely that of a think tank.

One of our most important contributions is certainly an intellectual one. Many of the people who work here are highly trained and produce sophisticated analyses of particular questions. So we are like a think tank, except that we have an activist orientation. There are obviously similarities between the work we do and what a lobby group working for the industry does. There are only a limited number of things that you can do, realistically speaking. It's not surprising or insulting that there might be an overlap of tactics. You can write a report or a letter to attack somebody, you can organize a protest, you can lobby, and you can block a doorway. Some parts of Public Citizen, such as the groups that lobby Congress, do a lot of community organizing. They articulate grassroots activism and think-tank work. In the health group, we sometimes organize physicians or medical students, but on a day-to-day basis, we have limited grassroots organizing activity. However, we have an important educational function. We produce written reports that are available to patients and two newsletters — one about general health-policy issues, sent to about forty thousand people every month, and the other, to which a hundred and fifty thousand people subscribe, is the only drug newsletter in the world for patients. Of course, there are other groups that write about drugs, and we use them (*Prescrire* in France, the *Drug and Therapeutics Bulletin* in Britain, the *Medical Letter* in the United States), but ours is particularly for patients.

We do educational work outside the drug area, too. We used to have a Web site that allowed patients to learn about their doctors — to know whether they had been disciplined by a state medical board or by the federal government. In addition, we are trying to bring models of what we call research-based activism into medical schools. One of our first research projects from those courses was about comparing the labels on cigarette packages

Protesters from Public Citizen assembled to heckle attendees at a lobbyist-sponsored fundraiser for indicted former House majority leader Tom Delay (R-Texas), November 17, 2005 (Tom Williams/Roll Call Photos).

internationally—what does Marlboro say in Senegal, in the United States, in France, and so on. It's the same product, so they should say the same thing, but it was easy to show that there are vast differences in the way people are informed. In every regard, developing-country residents were given less information. Thanks to a grant from George Soros, we have created almost twenty research-based activism courses, usually in medical schools, but also in public-health schools and in nursing schools.

For you, defending consumer rights is a matter of expertise and education. But, in many cases, it can also call into question matters of rules and practices. Does legal action play an important part in Public Citizen?

Our litigation group sues the government, not the corporations, except in rare cases. It's a strategic choice. Suing a corporation is a different kind of lawsuit. We don't do it for four reasons: first, suing a corporation may enable you to change that particular corporation or one aspect of its action, but it doesn't change the general picture; second, you need to have standing (the legal right to sue) for that kind of suit, and we often don't have it; third, the amount of work that goes into a lawsuit against a corporation is massive; fourth, the people who want to sue companies, such as the people who are going after Merck for Vioxx right now, have no problem being represented by other lawyers. What you usually don't find, however, are people who are willing to look at some obscure proceeding in some obscure government agency that is very important, but gets no attention. Usually, nobody but us is willing to go after that.

For example, when the FDA is deciding whether or not to approve a drug, it may sometimes hold an advisory committee meeting. Before the meeting, advisory committee members are given a large number of documents to review. These documents include what the companies have prepared in order to make their argument for their drugs and the FDA's review of the data given by the companies. Then, according to the law, there has to be an opportunity for public testimony during the meeting. However, it used to be that all this material wasn't available to the public prior to the meeting. We were expected to say something coherent during the public session when we didn't even know what the data were. So we sued the FDA, and we won. As a result, the data are placed on the Internet twenty-four hours before the meeting. That has completely revolutionized those committees — even if it would, of course, be better to have the data a week before the meeting. So, in practical terms, let's assume there is going to be an advisory committee meeting on a given Friday, and I would like to express my opinion. Thursday morning at eight o'clock, I will get on the FDA's Web site, put my finger on the refresh button, and keep pushing until eventually the data appear, so I can study them and prepare a statement for the next day.

These data are extremely useful for us, but we are not the only people using them. For instance, the people in Wall Street are also using them, because the FDA material, whether favorable or unfavorable to the drug, is likely to affect the stock price of the company. So, through public access, and thanks to our legal action, the whole thing is opened up, which is very healthy. Patients should know, we should know, journalists should know, Wall Street should know, everybody should know. And since the material put on the FDA Web site is available to everybody, advocates in other countries can use this information, too. As you can see, this is an example of a seemingly very obscure little detail that makes a very big difference.

A very large fraction of the government's actions, even if it's not obvious to most people, is really about the regulation of an industry. Thus, inevitably, the industry is going to try to protect itself, while we will attempt to promote a regulation that protects the public. For example, we do a lot of work in occupational health. We sued the government because it had failed to regulate hexavalent chromium — the chemical in that terrible Erin Brockovich movie. Hexavalent chromium causes lung cancer, and workers have been exposed to significant levels of it in this country. So we sued the government to force it to regulate the chemical, and we won. There was a hearing back in February. You can't imagine the number and variety of people who use hexavalent chromium and who showed up to protest the regulation. For instance, people who have to launder the clothes of the people who work in hexavalent chromium facilities and who might have to segregate the hexavalent chromium–contaminated clothing from other kinds of clothing were there to argue against the regulation because it will be hard for them to segregate the clothing. The polishers were there, and the welders were there, and the military was there to say that if the regulation goes through, money is going to be diverted from the military budget, which will cause a national-security crisis. And that is where we come in. We helped the government impose the regulation, and government officials were actually ecstatic to have us there. It is true that at the top level the administration never wanted to regulate this chemical. But the civil servants who are in charge of regulation wanted to regulate this problem. These people truly want us to sue them, and they are happy when we win.

So part of your relationship with governmental bodies is collaborative.

Officials are leaking documents to us all the time. They are usually lower-level people within government, people with scientific expertise, who are upset because their scientific judgment is being overridden at some higher level in government, very often for political reasons. They get upset, and they need somebody to put pressure on their superiors from another angle. Of course, there are also people in government who despise us or never have anything good to say about us.

Fundamentally, to us, it doesn't make a big difference if there is a Democratic or a Republican administration. We would criticize anybody. When Clinton came into office, for example, some groups were ecstatic, because they could finally get a telephone call returned. They thought they would have a tremendous impact, were making various kinds of compromises, and were excited to be at the table. To me, that was a completely wrong strategy. Most of those people got practically nothing for their efforts. In health care in particular, it was a disaster.

Does that mean that you situate yourself outside of party politics and prefer to consider yourselves experts whose work is primarily scientific?

To begin with, the legal structure for nonprofit groups requires us to be nonpartisan. But more importantly, at our level, the regulatory level, partisanship is not really an issue. Things are different for Public Citizen activists who work on the congressional level. But for us, what matters are the particular regulatory or administrative decisions, and much of that is really independent of party politics. The FDA is capable of approving a bad drug under a Democratic or a Republican administration. So nonpartisanship is particularly easy to sustain if you are working at the regulatory level. And the parties are making it easier for us by becoming more and more like each other. Both of them are so busy hustling up corporate cash that, in the end, they are both procorporate parties. And, in most regulatory settings, procorporate is going to be inimical to the interest of the public. Of course, I am not saying that the Bush administration doesn't have its own unique ability to do evil in the world.

But if I go back and I look at the things that we've done in the last ten years, the problems we are facing are there not because Bush is in the White House but, more fundamentally, because the governmental and regulatory system in this country is ill.

Aside from your work at the regulatory level, you have been very active on the issue of campaign finance reform.

Yes, campaign finance reform is a big part of what we do. It's a huge struggle, and it's at the root of much that is wrong in this country. It's very hard for the left to raise as much money as the right does from the corporations. The obvious source of cash, especially for the Republicans, is corporations. The obvious source of cash for the left is labor unions. But the labor movement is in terrible shape in this country.

What kind of relationship do you have with labor unions? Are the unions your allies?

The global trade group, Global Trade Watch, works very closely with labor unions. They work together to organize protests in Washington and elsewhere. For example, if there is a congressman who is crucial to a particular vote, who is a swing vote, we might work with a union and organize a protest in his district. On health, we work with unions in the occupational health area, to try get a chemical regulated or to get special needles on the market to prevent people from getting HIV or hepatitis C, and so on. With a doctors' union, as well as with a medical students' association, we are trying to reduce the number of hours that doctors are allowed to work at a hospital. In the occupational chemical area, we often sue together. They need us because they don't always have lawyers who have the proper expertise. On the other hand, in order to sue, you have to have what is called standing. Not just anybody can sue anybody; you have to have some direct level of involvement in the issue. You or the people who you represent must be people who would be affected by the regulation you are asking for. The unions have these people. So we sue together.

From what you are saying, it seems that, unlike other activist groups, the current political situation does not particularly influence you. It all seems pretty cut and dry.

We have been around for a long time. Public Citizen is an established organization. We own two buildings. That's the kind of stability that many nongovernmental organizations cannot even dream of, and I think it really helps to ensure the stability of our organization.

One of the big challenges for us is that the people who have been around since the beginning are getting to a point in their lives when they might wish to move on. We survived the first transition when Ralph Nader left. The next big question will be: can we succeed when other people, such as Sid Wolfe and Joan Claybrook, leave? Groups often fall apart during these kinds of transitions.

However, we have no problem finding issues to work on. It's basically endless. There will always be new drugs coming on the market; there will always be a new chemical left unregulated; there will always be people ready to sacrifice public health for corporate profit or government gain in some way.

Now, to go back to the political situation, obviously, in some fields, such as AIDS, the Bush administration has had a huge impact. In other areas, its impact is much less significant. You are always reacting to the political reality. But we're going to be in favor of campaign finance reform and of a national health-insurance bill no matter who is in power. These principles are unshakeable. The government can change, but we won't. We are grounded in principles and method. Our method is data analysis, advocacy, working in regulatory agencies, making an intellectual argument in an unbiased way. Once you're grounded in your method and your principles, things become very simple.

Another thing that is relevant, and that is at the heart of activism, is the ability to pick the right target, a target of the right size. Often, that means taking on something smaller than what you really want to take on. I think that what is extraordinary about, for example, Health GAP (Health Global Access Project) is that it took on something massive, international, and had a good amount of success with it. You have to admire people who are able to pull that off. But for most people, their activism has to focus on smaller issues. And there is a logic to this. I think that, in certain kinds of movements, there are people who are so ambitious they cannot identify the piece they can bite off. That can be counterproductive. You have to pick an issue that is not so small as to be irrelevant, so that when you win the world does change in some ways, but also not so large that you can't affect change. You have to find some kind of balance, for two reasons. First, as an activist, you have to want to win. If you don't want to win, you shouldn't be in the field. Second, psychologically, if you choose targets that you lose to all the time, you will eventually stop trying.

Also, in my experience, you can't seriously commit yourself to activism without getting increasingly involved in more and more technical issues. The AIDS movement is a good example of this. Initially, it was a movement about access to any effective drug; it started off with people saying, "You cannot have placebo trials, just give us any old drug." Today, the people who are interested in treatment are very technocratic, extremely knowledgeable, and frankly quite conservative. I say that admiringly; they think the data should be good.

So that seems to be the course of any serious movement: it is initially motivated by pure principles, but it lasts only insofar as it manages to thrive on the discussion of technical and minute arguments. At the same time, activists should not lose sight of what it is they are fighting for. That is why the initial grand phrases — such as Health GAP's slogan "Gore's Greed Kills" — are so important and memorable. They prevent you from forgetting that while you are seemingly arguing about technical details, you are still fighting for broader things.

One of my first battles, which started when I was still a medical student, was against St. Joseph Aspirin and other aspirin companies. We knew that children with chicken pox or the flu who took aspirin rather than paracetamol were much more likely to get a rare disease called Reye's syndrome. Thus, we simply wanted the company to write on the box, "Don't give this product to children with chicken pox or the flu." It turned out to be a long and tortuous battle: for many years there were no warnings on boxes. During those years, three hundred or so children a year were reported to get Reye's syndrome, and about a third of them died. Then, in 1986, we finally managed to force them to put the warning on the box. Now, Reye's syndrome has practically evaporated in this country. We were part of the reason why the warning is on the box. It is not the same thing as undermining the fundamental economic arrangements in the world. It's not the same thing as giving an effective malaria vaccine to people or treating people who have HIV. But there are a bunch of kids who don't have the disease. And I remember that sense that I had won something for the first time in my life. It was not the biggest victory in the world, but when you learn you can win once, then you learn you can win again.

In Nairobi on September 24, 2003, dozens of African activists infected with the HIV virus disrupted the Thirteenth International Conference on AIDS and STDs in Africa, demanding "less talk and more drugs" from their governments (photo by Gaëlle Krikorian).

A New Era of Access to Rights?

Gaëlle Krikorian

By all accounts, the Eleventh International Conference on AIDS, held in Vancouver in 1996, marked a decisive moment in the struggle against the epidemic. Scientific studies were then demonstrating the efficacy of antiretroviral medications which, when taken in combination or cocktails, would dramatically slow the disease's progress. While the HIV infection remained incurable, it was now possible to live with HIV/AIDS. The previously unthinkable prospect of eradicating HIV was suddenly on everyone's mind. "One World, One Hope" — the conference's slogan — epitomized this optimistic new era.

Not all participants, however, were equally enthusiastic about publicizing these data. Because the new treatment cost was on the order of $10,000 per patient per year, the announced therapeutic advances offered little hope to the 90 percent of the world's HIV/AIDS patients living in developing countries. Cynically questioning the universality of the good news, activists reformulated the conference slogan: "One World, One Hope — Big Joke."

The demand for access to medication for people with HIV/AIDS would soon go far beyond such cynical proclamations and find ways to make itself heard. The result was a complete reconfiguration of the international struggle against AIDS and the emergence of new alliances and divisions among the actors involved — NGO members, agents of nation-states and international institutions, and the employees of multinational pharmaceutical companies. The ensuing debate underscored the tensions involved in globalization and the relations between the global North and the global South. More importantly, the question of the rights of people with HIV/AIDS — posed on behalf of millions whose needs had never been heard — took on a new dimension.

ACCESS TO RIGHTS ON THE POLITICAL STAGE

The first public confrontations on this issue took place in Abidjan, Côte d'Ivoire, in December 1997 at the Tenth International Conference on AIDS and STDs in Africa. Along with the then-president of Côte d'Ivoire, Henri Konan Bédié, both President

Jacques Chirac of France and Hiroshi Nakajima, the executive director of the World Health Organization (WHO), were to speak during the opening session. President Chirac's entrance was met with an unusual honor guard. About twenty people with AIDS, primarily members of local organizations, lined the corridor leading to the amphitheater. Hoping to avoid any reaction from a rather agitated security police, they remained calm as the French head of state came forward. They silently brandished placards made of simple sheets of paper bearing various statements—"I do not want to die"; "The sick are all equal; they have the right to the same treatment"; "Access to medication for sick Africans"; among others. President Chirac came face to face with them as he was about to enter the conference room. He immediately approached the activists and, without the slightest hesitation, started to shake their hands. Still in total silence, he greeted them one by one, then proceeded to the podium. Under the watchful gaze of the guards and out of sight of the thousands of participants who were already seated, the protesters, quite dumbfounded, stood still a few minutes longer, then dispersed to take their places in the audience. Although timid, this confrontation marked a momentous occasion—one of the first times that people with HIV/AIDS from developing countries were able publicly to assert their right to medication and to deal directly with a head of state.

There is a certain irony in the fact that these demonstrators saw Jacques Chirac as the most suitable target for their symbolic action. Representing the rich nations, he was undeniably the most powerful of the political leaders present. Yet he was also the one head of state who was about to criticize most of the international organizations and health-funding sources and, alongside the activists, drag the debate about access to medication onto the political stage. On the heels of WHO director Nakajima's clichéd address, President Chirac launched into a long plea for poor countries' access to antiretrovirals, calling for international solidarity in the global struggle against HIV/AIDS:

> We have no right to accept that there are now two ways of fighting AIDS: treating those who are sick in the developed countries and only preventing further contamination in the South.... It would be shocking, unacceptable, and contrary to the most elementary kind of solidarity to witness and not react to the establishment of a two-speed epidemic. How can we continue to invoke human rights and human dignity in international forums if, at the same time, taking refuge in excuses, we accept the fact that millions of the sick remain deprived forever of the most effective therapies?... They tell us that the new treatments cost so much that their general application would be financially out of the question. Let's start by getting more mobilized.... [France] cannot act alone. It is essential that the other great industrialized countries join our increased effort. Here in Abidjan, before you, I want to make a solemn commitment to contribute my country's whole weight. And I hope that the next summit of what has now become the G8 marks a new stage in responding to the expectations of those who place a major part of their hope in the efficacy of our action. France urges its partners, notably European ones, to create a Fund for Therapeutic Solidarity.... More than ever, I am convinced that the fight against AIDS involves our

conceptions of humanity and of society. The expansion of the epidemic must be blocked. Our counterattack must be vigorous; it should not only be medical and scientific, but also resolutely political.[1]

Years later, French activists would continue to use the most edifying passages of this declaration to command their government to respect its commitments and to increase funding for the treatments of HIV/AIDS. But when he gave this speech, the French president was resolutely on the side of the sick. The next day, at a press conference, French health minister Bernard Kouchner, who had accompanied Chirac on the trip, invoked the duty of "therapeutic interference."[2]

Almost nobody really believed that the kind of equity for which Chirac's speech called for was achievable. But the few who did had already begun to take steps toward achieving it and were going to make a difference. The president of the Côte d'Ivoire joined in Chirac's appeal. During international meetings, his health minister, Maurice Kacou Guikahué, affirmed that "access to antiretrovirals [is] the condition *sine qua non* of the success of programs of structural adjustment in Africa."[3] Despite the cost, some governments began to consider the possibility of making these medications accessible to everyone. Although some called it "overly political," the conference received media attention. Latching onto the topic of treatment, the media in Côte d'Ivoire, as in other countries severely hit by the epidemic, transmitted a strong message to people with HIV. For those still ignorant of their HIV status (the very vast majority of people with HIV/AIDS in the world), the possibility of access could be groundbreaking, changing the way they thought about the disease and their lives. Indeed, the prospect of such access could motivate people who were previously unwilling or unable to face the grim consequences of testing to consider finding out their HIV status.

The reactions of representatives of the European Commission and the World Bank at the conference indicated that they considered this initiative a real "threat." They responded to Chirac's and Kouchner's speeches, as they did to demands from organizations of people with HIV/AIDS, by invoking "reality" and dismissing the declarations of the French officials as "utopian" and "demagogic." "A generation has been lost," acknowledged Bruna Vitagliano of the World Bank, but "the treatments are too costly" for Africans with HIV/AIDS.[4] More than ever, "the priority remains prevention," insisted Lieve Fransen, the head of AIDS programs for the European Commission.[5] These sharp reactions from the most important sources of funding for the fight against AIDS reveal what an extraordinary moment this was.

ON ALL FRONTS

After the effects of Abidjan the activists advocating access to HIV/AIDS drugs began infiltrating political spaces and making themselves heard. They vocalized their demands, even if they were violently rejected, in order to provoke confrontations. Fronts began to form and a set of oppositions crystallized.

One strong argument against distributing antiretrovirals related to underdevelopment. It was unthinkable to give pills to people without access to potable water to swallow them — that would be "putting the cart before the horse." As Daniel Tarantola of the WHO put it, "access to treatments [was] the tree hiding the forest."[6] The clichés came one after another, in newspapers and meeting rooms, from the WHO, government representatives, and NGOs — including those working on development, the fight against malaria, and even the fight against HIV. They believed that the logic of their arguments was based on common sense: antiretrovirals are the Rolls Royce of the fight against AIDS; developing countries must be furnished with clean water, roads, basic medications, palliative care, and so on before the drugs can be introduced. Asserting its expertise, the WHO lectured that access to health should be understood as a "pyramid" — first you lay the foundations, then you build on them, stone by stone.

Defenders of access to treatment retorted by calling attention to the urgency of the problem and the number of deaths — the inadequacy of a "business as usual" solution. For them, traditional methods had proven ineffective. It was disgraceful to focus on "palliative care" (accompanying the sick toward death), because it amounted to "palliating" the absence of treatment when treatment did exist. Because the epidemic was galloping along — every day there were more people with HIV, more people with AIDS, and more dead from the disease — they thought access to antiretrovirals should play the role of a "locomotive," driving a general strengthening of health systems. This implied not only a large-scale increase in financing for the fight against AIDS and developmental aid, but also a radical change in funding-source policies — for instance, the end of the World Bank's structural adjustments reducing and restricting expenditures in the health sector and the "all-prevention" approach it advocated in tandem with the European Commission.

But economists are stubborn. Mead Over of the World Bank continued trying to convince people of the efficacy of prevention, stressing the need to target prostitutes, the veritable "epidemiologic pumps."[7] When activists pointed out that, beyond the question of the availability of condoms, the challenge was to get people to use them — which is difficult when fatalism about an untreatable disease many prefer to ignore abounds — he replied that this exceeded his area of expertise and suggested they speak with a behaviorist.[8] This did not prevent him from publishing a series of booklets for the World Bank designed to "guide" the countries dependent on its funding in their strategies for fighting the epidemic — publications that carefully ignored the question of access to treatment.[9]

When numbers became the currency of debate, the confrontations became bitter. For the proponents of an exclusively preventive policy, it sufficed to multiply the number of people with HIV/AIDS in any Southern country by the cost of treating one patient for one year. The result — a figure higher than the country's gross national product — underscored the absurdity of the proposition. Armed with the art of calculation, all sides were counting their dead. Most of the NGOs and institutions engaged in the struggle against malaria argued that because malaria kills more Africans than AIDS — about a million a year — it should be a higher priority.

When the debate over access to antiretrovirals became more concrete, focusing on the specific conditions for its fulfillment, some sounded the alarm that the virus would become resistant to drugs if patients did not take them regularly. The antiretrovirals had to be taken consistently and at a fixed time, yet, stressed Andrew Natsios, director of the United States Agency for International Development (USAID), "many people in Africa have never seen a clock or a watch their entire lives."[10] The defenders of access to medication faced quite a challenge: How could they impress upon people the intolerable nature of the situation when it was widely known and accepted that a million people a year died from malaria, a preventable and treatable disease? Why should the highest international decision-making bodies — or public opinion — be especially moved by deaths due to AIDS, when deaths caused not only by malaria, but by famine, diphtheria, and tuberculosis were so common among these populations? The whole world deplores this situation, but, as the saying goes, "that's life" — and the principal problem is poverty.

Advocates of access to medication know they cannot just denounce the situation. Claiming the right to treatment in a context without even the most elementary of rights is not enough to shake things up. Anger and its expression might galvanize those already convinced, give them the energy to believe in their enterprise, but anger alone could not incite a sudden rise in consciousness or challenge international policies.

Still, a handful of people refused to tolerate the situation and declared it unacceptable. On the strength of this conviction, they turned to their governments to call attention to their moral duties and demand a reckoning. Invading political spaces, they opened a breach. Storming the fort on all fronts, activists appropriated various fields of rhetoric and expertise and reconfigured the terms of the debates. Among other things, it was necessary to deconstruct some arguments against access to drugs, exposing their inconsistencies and unveiling what really lay behind them: fatalism, racism, greed, and the assumption that the value of a life fluctuates according to its country of origin and is, in most cases, expendable. These efforts, exercised simultaneously, contributed to unsettling the established equilibrium and allowed a rethinking of reality.

Each year on December 1, World AIDS Day, the Joint United Nations Program on HIV/AIDS (UNAIDS) publishes statistics on the epidemic. By virtue of repetition, the litany of figures tends to become routine. One hears them, one repeats them, but the reality to which they refer dissipates with the string of calculations. So people with HIV/AIDS decided to confront the funding sources so fond of using abstract numbers with the faces of those who make up the statistics. Joining hands, organizations from the global North and South launched a simple campaign. People with AIDS would write letters and address them to those in power. Local HIV/AIDS NGOs would forward them by post or e-mail to colleagues in the North. They would photocopy and send them, in packets of thirty-five a week, to those responsible for the fight against AIDS at the European Commission, the World Bank, the WHO, UNAIDS, the Coopération Française, and USAID. The messages, which were often based on a model letter, were personal, their terms rudimentary, and the request always the same:

I am writing this letter to you to inform you of my situation and, mindful of your institutional responsibilities, to solicit your aid. I am infected with the AIDS virus. Living in _____, I do not have access to antiretroviral treatments. As you should know, this is a matter of life and death. You certainly have the power to procure for me the medications I need. Involved as you are in the struggle against AIDS, you cannot refuse to help me. My life is in your hands; I impatiently await your response.

Respectfully,

(Signature)

Among other things, this tactic responded to the Northern organizations' desire to transform their Southern colleagues' daily demands for help into a *political* act. Whereas some NGOs were advocating humanitarian resourcefulness — for example, gathering boxes of medication to ship to the South — others wanted a *political* answer, which would also permit their burden to be shared with those in positions of institutional responsibility. It was also a means to narrow the gap between the holders of the purse strings and the "reality on the ground." Because economic rhetoric was unavoidable, those arguing for access to HIV/AIDS medication agreed to play the game and insisted that the cost of treatment be weighed against the cost of inaction. As the World Bank began to state as of 2000, the epidemic is, in fact, very costly. The economic impact of the disappearance of the labor force and educated elites, long hospitalizations, absenteeism from work, and funerals is severe for countries as well as for individuals. Activists countered the logic of choices and oppositions (between AIDS and malaria or tuberculosis, between treatment and prevention) with the logic of public health and comprehensive care management. Prevention and treatment would reinforce each other and should not be separated; moreover, developing the capacity to treat people with HIV/AIDS would benefit the overall health-care system. They pointed out that AIDS, by attacking individuals' immune systems, fosters countless opportunistic diseases, including tuberculosis; by restoring or protecting people's immunity defenses, antiretrovirals would prevent some instances of these maladies.

In fact, from the start of the debate about access to medication, antiretrovirals were already available in developing countries. In each one of these countries, at least a few AIDS patients — the most affluent, of course — were receiving such treatment. Thus, while the terms of the public debate centered on the introduction of the drugs, the challenge was not to introduce them, but to control, broaden, and democratize access to them. The arguments of access could indeed be turned against them. To prevent anarchy in treatment and the counterfeiting of drugs or a black market devoted to them, the best strategy was to allow people access to these treatments, preferably for free. The challenge was formidable, but developing countries are not vast, desolate lands devoid of infrastructure. Existing hospitals and health-care centers, as well as networks of NGOs already involved in health care, encouraged hopes of broader access. Of course, this required rethinking social relations between the medical milieu and nonmedical actors, but, just as such a change had been viable in the North, it could be attempted in the South, as well.

The point then became to demonstrate the feasibility of access to antiretrovirals in poor countries. In 1997, UNAIDS launched pilot programs in Chile, the Côte d'Ivoire, Uganda, and Vietnam. With meager funding from Fonds de Solidarité Thérapeutique International, these programs were timidly established in 1998. The few who agitated for access to HIV/AIDS drugs — activists, doctors, experts from international agencies — mobilized their joint energies in order to prove that people with AIDS in poor nations could be treated properly and were just as disciplined about following therapeutic regimes as their rich-nation counterparts.

Finally, since the cost of the drugs posed so many problems, it seemed the right moment to question the cost itself. Having previously tried to secure price reductions from pharmaceutical companies, activists challenged even more forcefully the process by which these prices were fixed in the first place when faced with the disparity between final prices and poor countries' ability to pay. The multinationals were becoming the enemy of the sick — an enemy relatively easy to expose in the media. Their greed, power, and secrecy roused public anger. A reconfigured mobilization over access to drugs took shape on this new terrain.

RECONFIGURATIONS OF POLITICAL SPACE

After 1999, several NGOs — including Health Action International, the Consumer Project on Technology (CPTech), and Médecins Sans Frontières (MSF) — found a new line of attack in the struggle for access: they organized meetings on the theme of intellectual property and access to drugs. If the multinationals would not make their products accessible, other companies were in a position to manufacture generic versions. Brazil and Thailand had already adopted this strategy, with state-owned businesses producing certain antiretrovirals; and in India, private manufacturers were filling the breach. In 2001, the pharmaceutical company Cipla announced a three-in-one antiretroviral pill for under $300 per patient per year, which represented a 97 percent reduction from the average cost of $10,000 for antiretroviral combinations. With these new weapons at their disposal, proponents of access sounded their demands louder than ever. In the first place, the funding sources' calculations had to be revised. The economic argument lost its force. The WHO recognized that an "essential" drug is one that — like the antiretrovirals — helps patients survive, not just one that boasts a favorable balance between cost and efficacy.

Until then, information on the actual cost of manufacturing medications had been particularly opaque, which made it difficult to counter the drug companies' argument that they were unable to reduce their prices. Cipla's announcement, however, proved that it was possible to produce medication at extremely low costs. Meanwhile, financial reports on the pharmaceutical industry had never been so impressive. It was the most profitable industry in the world, with earnings that could make bankers and oil executives flush with jealousy. Embarrassing the industry by calling attention to its deceit and greed had become easy. Some of its corporate executives' public gaffes made it even easier. In France, for example, the director-general of the Syndicat National de l'Industrie Pharmaceutique (National Pharmaceutical Industry Association), Bernard Lemoine, declared in 2000, "I don't see why special effort should be demanded from the pharmaceutical industry. Nobody asks Renault to give cars to people who haven't got one."[11]

But the pharmaceutical industry had international law on its side. Its lobbyists had worked for almost thirty years to ensure, as part of the creation of the World Trade Organization (WTO) in 1995, the adoption of the Agreement on Trade-Related Aspects of Intellectual Property Rights (TRIPS), requiring all member states to respect drug patents. From then until either 2000 or 2006, depending on their level of economic development, all poor countries would be held to this standard. In all these countries, patents would protect the medications for at least twenty years, during which time the drug companies' monopoly would have the force of law on its side. The option of generic medications for people with HIV/AIDS in poor countries was now out of the question. A new battle began.

For activists, there were only two options: "abolish intellectual property wherever it kills" (the Act Up–Paris slogan) or adjust international law in order to circumvent patent protection. They chose to play both cards. Denouncing patents was one thing, but most NGOs knew that too extreme a position would prove ineffective in the short term. While it is important, at times, for activists to advance strong and intransigent demands — if only to build alliances with other antiglobalization movements — they must also know how to remain pragmatic. This approach came naturally to AIDS organizations. Their demands had always been urgent, made in the context of imminent peril; they would never enter a battle without aiming for at least a minimum of immediate concrete results. For AIDS activists, victories, however small, were always a question of survival.

But for the NGOs to call on the WTO to accommodate their demands required articulating some proposals. A galaxy of NGOs that were, in one way or another, all engaged with the issue of access to medication began to organize around this necessity. An international coalition emerged. Although informal, the coalition understood how to draw on the specific skills of each of its members; roles were distributed and knowledge and expertise identified. Some, like CPTech, had been working for years in the field of intellectual property and had amassed precise knowledge of how the pharmaceutical industry worked. Armed with experience and information, it offered a great deal of technical expertise and credibility on these issues. Others, such as MSF, had been confronted with the difficulty of finding medications adapted to the needs of populations they had served in developing countries. Thus, MSF questioned the international rules that restricted the availability of generic drugs and highlighted the inadequacy of research efforts aimed at discovering cures for diseases endemic to poor countries. Moreover, MSF has a powerful communication machine that, since its 1999 Nobel Peace Prize, has had a lot of authority in the eyes of official institutions and the media. Act Up, Health GAP, and others drew their legitimacy from the people with HIV/AIDS themselves.

Their public actions — against pharmaceutical laboratories, government representatives, and international institutions — caught journalists' attention and crystallized existing tensions. They maintained a sense of urgency by keeping the issue prominent, removing it from the field of traditional "humanitarianism" and giving it political resonance.

The South African activist group Treatment Action Campaign (TAC) knew how to use civil disobedience and the courts and thus became a prominent voice representing people living with HIV/AIDS in developing countries. Health Action International, expert in health issues and international lobbying, had long been involved in developing countries. The Third World Network (TWN), a lobbying group based in Southern countries, had shadowed the creation of the WTO and knew how to collaborate effectively with government representatives in developing countries. Oxfam, which runs an international program on development, put its communication skills and its expertise to work. The patients of the Thai Network of People Living with HIV/AIDS (TNP+) organized demonstrations and used the courts to defend the local production of medication. Still others joined what had become a real movement. Although the movement had relatively few members for such a large task, its desire and determination to succeed allowed it to overcome a number of the difficulties of collective action — for example, that such action needs to be flexible in order to accommodate its various allies and their different modes of operation, political backgrounds, and cultures. This peculiar nebula managed to give the illusion of power, of a multitude issuing from the four corners of the world. It developed an unnerving capacity to capture media attention as well as to articulate an expertise that would ultimately influence institutions.

The time for securing concessions or favors from the pharmaceutical companies had passed. Conflicts now took place on two axes. On the one hand, the NGOs involved had to defeat the pharmaceutical laboratories, both in the realm of morality and by finding ways to circumvent their influence, so that the right to affordable medication could take precedence over intellectual property. On the other hand, they had to maintain pressure on the funding sources: the World Bank, the European Commission, and rich countries in general.

In Pretoria, in April 2001, thirty-nine pharmaceutical multinationals that had sued South Africa to block legal loopholes favoring cheaper drugs were forced to abandon the lawsuit. South African AIDS patients who joined the suit alongside the government had won the battle with the support of their allies.

Some months later, in November 2001, the Fourth WTO Ministerial Conference took place in Doha, Qatar. The question of intellectual property and access to generic medications was on the agenda. The NGOs had spent months pressuring the secretariat of the WTO and mobilizing the media. In addition to putting pressure on Northern countries, these NGOs maintained direct links with delegations from some Southern countries.

After the 9/11 attacks, the international climate was tense and American diplomacy particularly restive. On the heels of discovering several contaminated letters, the Bush administration was especially worried about the threat of anthrax. Bayer, which held the patent on ciprofloxacin, the antibiotic used to treat anthrax, could produce it in great quantities, but demanded a relatively high price for its manufacture — between $1.75 and $1.85 per tablet. At a congressional hearing on October 23, 2001, Tommy Thompson, U.S. secretary of Health and Human Services, had said, "I can assure you we are not going to pay the price they are asking."[12] He explained that if Bayer did not lower its price, the government would suspend its patent and stockpile the generic version of the drug. This announcement was heard around the world. The United States was prepared to do for anthrax what it was trying to prevent developing countries from doing for AIDS. This episode provoked widespread anger and furnished the NGOs with a text-book case for their efforts to educate the media. Fifteen days later, when WTO member nations met in Doha, a bloc of more than seventy developing countries demanded the right to use flexibilities in the TRIPS Agreement to secure the right to generic versions of drugs before their patents expired. The debates were tense. But the developing coun-tries won the battle — the WTO adopted the Declaration on the TRIPS Agreement and Public Health. Albeit symbolic (since the declaration essentially clarified the interpre-tation of rights that already figured in the TRIPS Agreement), the victory was no less important. It marked the first time the WTO recognized that public-health imperatives might trump commercial interests. In its press release, Act Up–Paris proclaimed "People with AIDS 1, Drug Industry 0."[13]

Even though progress was less spectacular on the financial side, attitudes were slowly evolving. Between 2000 and 2002, an international consensus in favor of access to medication was finally achieved. The discourse of all relevant institutions had clearly changed. It had become impossible to deny the principle of the right to access and, in one way or another, everyone had to contribute. A massive increase in funding was approved. In April 2001, during the Summit of African Heads of State and Government on HIV/AIDS, Tuberculosis (TB), and Malaria, UN secretary-general Kofi Annan called for the creation of an international fund of $7 billion to $10 billion a year to fight these diseases. Some months later, the United Nations General Assembly held a special ses-sion on HIV/AIDS for the first time. The epidemic was increasingly presented as a question of "international security," and the media spoke of an "unprecedented will to control the epidemic." UN member states followed Annan, and this meeting eventually led to the creation of the Global Fund to Fight AIDS, Tuberculosis, and Malaria, which became operational in 2002.

The Group of Eight (G8) then became the activists' principal target. They wanted to push governments beyond declarations and promises to make appropriately large con-crete commitments. In different countries, national campaigns were launched. Taking advantage of upcoming elections to increase the pressure, some groups targeted presi-dential candidates. In 1999 and 2000, Health GAP tracked Al Gore in the United States; two years later, Act Up–Paris was on the heels of Lionel Jospin in France.

The activists' goals became more precise in 2002, when, during the Fourteenth Inter-national Conference on AIDS, the WHO announced its three-by-five initiative — plan-ning to treat three million people by the year 2005. Activists made this a media spring-board for pressing the only question that mattered: "Where is the [$]10 billion?"

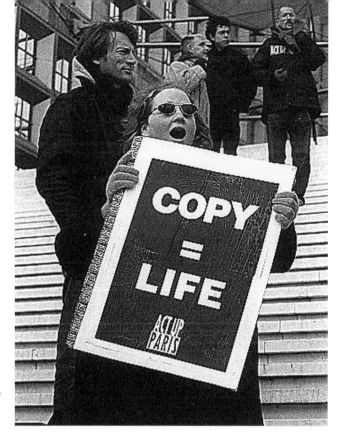

Act Up–Paris activists on March 5, 2001, the "global day of protest" against the forty drug companies that sued the South African government over its generic medicines plan.

On January 28, 2003, George W. Bush announced a U.S. government emergency plan against AIDS during his State of the Union address; on May 27, echoing the American activists, he said, "Every day of delay means eight thousand more AIDS deaths in Africa and fourteen thousand more infections."[14] While there was open diplomatic conflict with France (whose minister of foreign affairs solemnly opposed the military intervention in Iraq), and while antiwar demonstrations increased in most capitals, Bush invited Europe, Japan, and Canada to join him in a "great mission of rescue" and to "match their good intentions with real resources."[15] The next month, at the G8 meeting in Evian, he promised $15 billion over five years for AIDS relief in Africa. On the same occasion, Jacques Chirac announced that he was doubling France's annual contribution to the fight against AIDS in Africa to 150 million euros (roughly $190 million at the time).

AIDS became the key humanitarian card that Bush used to tout the United States as the "country of human rights." Since then, American funding has remained well below what was promised, but the United States continues to boast about taking charge of the fight against AIDS. While some are grateful that funds in this field are dramatically increasing, others worry that in some countries, 90 percent of the resources are of American origin. This money comes with strings attached. And the Bush administration's ideology, in its moral and religious conservatism, as well as in its economic liberalism, has lead to changes and reconfigured practices. Fighting the spread of the virus means preaching fidelity and abstinence, and drugs must be purchased from the multinationals, rather than from producers of generic versions. These billions of dollars impose the supremacy of a vision that the Global Fund — the sole instrument of full-scale multilateral funding that struggles to fill its coffers — can hardly counter.

CONCLUSION

In July 2004, the Fifteenth International Conference on AIDS in Bangkok, whose slogan was "Access for All," marked the return to a sort of equilibrium. The major conflicts over whether the fight against AIDS in developing countries would include access to treatment seemed to be settled.

However, the pharmaceutical lobby had reclaimed some ground since the Doha declaration of 2001 had affirmed the priority of public health over commercial considerations. Furthermore, the WTO was proving itself incapable of furnishing concrete guarantees of the availability of generic drugs. Moreover, while the battle raged, the number of people with HIV/AIDS doubled — there are over forty million today — and the impetus to extend access to medication lost some momentum. Nevertheless, it was undeniable that a movement was under way. From then on, it would be impossible to turn back.

Or at least that was what people thought in July 2004. Since 2005, the situation has blurred again. This time, it is not the activists who are stirring up the political space. The United States is trying to impose new norms — or, rather, old norms — by reviving practices presumed to be obsolete. It favors abstinence and fidelity over condoms, requires countries to sign bilateral commercial agreements that effectively deprive them of some of the intellectual-property flexibilities they had secured at the WTO, and — by exclusively financing the purchase of their products — guarantees the hegemony of multinational drug companies. In short, the United States is using all its means to short-circuit the existing multilateral arrangements — imperfect, but still more equitable than previous arrangements — in order to impose its unique worldview.

In an era in which U.S. policies are reconfiguring the terrain of the debate over global AIDS, activists will have to regroup and construct new strategies. Bush has reestablished the distinction between those who govern and those who are governed. The battle could begin again. Indeed it *must* begin again, so that the rights of people with HIV/AIDS — to exercise autonomy over their own bodies and private lives, to choose the products they consume, to participate in the ongoing construction of their countries and the world in which they live — are not lost to them yet again.

Translated by Susan Emanuel with Dorota Szymkowiak.

1   Jacques Chirac, Speech at the Tenth International Confer-
    ence on AIDS and STD in Africa, Abidjan, Côte d'Ivoire,
    December 7, 1997. French text available online at www.ely-
    see.fr/elysee/elysee.fr/francais/interventions/discours_et_
    declarations/1997/ decembre/discours_de_m_jacques_chi-
    rac_president_de_la_republique_lors_de_la_ceremonie_d_
    ouverture_de_la_xe_conference_internationale_sur_les_
    mst-sida_en_afrique-abidjan.1906.html.

2   Press conference, Abidjan, December 8, 1997.

3   Interview for the daily paper *Ivoir Soir,* "Les nouveaux trait-
    ements du sida seront vulgarisés" (The new HIV treatment
    will be popularized), July 30, 1996.

4   Press conference, Abidjan, December 8, 1997.

5   *Ibid.*

6   Intervention during a UNAIDS workshop, Abidjan, Decem-
    ber 6, 1997.

7   Comment made during a session at the Thirteenth Interna-
    tional Conference on AIDS in Durban, 2000.

8   Comment made by Mean Over during a meeting with Act
    Up–Paris's representatives in 1998 in Washington, D.C.

9   *Confronting AIDS: Public Priorities in a Global Epidemic,*
    World Bank/AIDS Economics, World Bank, 1997.

10 John Donnelly, "Prevention Urged in AIDS Fight: Natsios
    Says Fund Should Spend Less on HIV Treatment," *Boston
    Globe,* June 7, 2001.

11 Martine Bulard, "Apartheid of Pharmacology," *Le monde
    diplomatique,* January 2000. Available online at http://
    mondediplo.com/2000/01/12bulard.

12 Associated Press, "Government Threatens Bayer Patent Sus-
    pension unless Cipro Price Is Lowered," October 23, 2001.

13 Act Up–Paris, "WTO Declaration on TRIPS and Health: Peo-
    ple With AIDS 1, Drug Industry 0," press statement, Novem-
    ber 15, 2001. Available online at www.globaltreatmentaccess.
    org/content/press_releases/01/111501_APP_PS_Doha_decl.
    html.

14 George W. Bush, "Remarks by the President on the Signing
    of HR 1298, the U.S. Leadership Against HIV/AIDS, Tuber-
    culosis and Malaria Act of 2003," Washington, D.C., May
    27, 2003. Available online at www.whitehouse.gov/news/
    releases/2003/05/ 20030527-7.html.

15 *Ibid.*

Indian sex workers sing during their third state convention organized by the Durbar Mahila Samanwaya Committee, an Indian NGO helping sex workers enforce their rights, in Calcutta, India, May 27, 2005 (Bikas Das/AP Photo).

International Prostitution Policy
and Sex Workers' Rights in India

Svati P. Shah

Sex workers' informal and formal organizing has always been a part of the Indian grassroots political landscape. Stories of delegations of sex workers going to meet such nationalist leaders as Mahatma Gandhi and Babasaheb Ambedkar in the early twentieth century are common fare in larger narratives of the Indian Independence Movement.[1] Over the past fifteen years, a contemporary, progressive sex workers' rights movement has taken shape in India. This movement links prostitution with the concerns of labor rights in both formal and informal economic sectors. It began in places such as Kolkata, in the western state of Maharashtra, and, more recently, in the states of Kerala and Andhra Pradesh, initially as a response to HIV/AIDS. The infrastructure of the movement has grown from HIV-related interventions into nongovernmental organizations with large staffs and a reach that is often districtwide, statewide, and, with respect to policy issues, national. Alongside these funded organizations, a small, but significant coterie of nonfunded sex workers' collectives has also emerged. In this piece, I discuss how issues of HIV, sex trafficking, and livelihood have intersected in the international debate on prostitution, and I describe how two Indian NGOs have engaged this debate.

The first few cases of HIV infection in India were identified in 1986, in the southern city of Chennai, among male truck drivers and female sex workers.[2] The subsequent trajectory of HIV-related interventions in India followed from the identification of these two categories of people as "risk groups."[3] During this period in the United States, public-health research and media representations of HIV tended to characterize gay men, through the language of "risk groups," as inevitably diseased. The epidemic in sub-Saharan Africa and South Asia was contrasted with the American HIV epidemic in public-health literature and the media along the axis of sexuality through repeated assertions that HIV in the global South was infecting primarily heterosexuals. While activists in the United States and Europe struggled to separate gay male sexuality from HIV, the notion of "risk groups" in Asia and Africa lent itself to a historical tendency to conflate sexual commerce with disease, especially with respect to female prostitutes. In identifying epidemiological trends, most public-health and community-based advocates tried to emphasize the notion of "risk behaviors," rather than "risk groups," both within and outside of the United States. The identity-based definition of a "risk group," however, continued to organize priorities for targeted HIV prevention. In India, priority was first given to female, brothel-based prostitutes and soon was extended to all women, men, and transgendered people selling sexual services.

Juridical debates on prostitution intersect with discourses of HIV/AIDS prevention because the latter are imbricated with the question of the appropriate legal regulation of prostitution. Abolitionist and rights-based organizations have used both discourses on violence prevention and the HIV epidemic to argue variously for the criminalization, decriminalization, and legalization of all sexual commerce as ways to promote public health and to deal more effectively with HIV. Internationally, feminist debates on prostitution have prioritized the question of whether prostitution can be considered an economic solution to poverty, unemployment, and/or underemployment — and therefore — should be assessed as a labor-rights issue, or if prostitution always constitutes a violation of the seller's bodily integrity making it an activity from which people require "rescue and rehabilitation." This polarity functions in debates on prostitution in various policy and legal arenas, especially in the debate on trafficking in women and especially sex trafficking.[4]

Concerns about sex trafficking and HIV have been fueled by influential international donor agencies, including the United States Agency for International Development (USAID). The U.S. government has expressly devoted resources to antitrafficking work since the latter days of the Clinton administration. Under George W. Bush, antitrafficking work has become explicitly linked with the desire to abolish prostitution throughout the world via criminalization. Given the anti-immigrant overtones of the Bush administration's policies and its support for policies tightening and further regulating borders worldwide, concerns about trafficking should also be seen in relation to a broader anti-immigrant agenda. With respect to prostitution, the USAID has linked funding for NGOs that target sex workers to an "antiprostitution oath," which functions like the anti-abortion "global gag rule."[5] The "antiprostitution oath" is codified in the June 9, 2005 Acquisition and Assistance Policy Directive (AAPD) of the United States Leadership Against HIV/AIDS, Tuberculosis and Malaria Act of 2003:

> The purpose of this AAPD is to provide clauses to be included as new standard provisions for assistance agreements and contracts that include HIV/AIDS funds. These provisions: (i) permit recipients to not endorse or utilize a multisectoral approach to combatting [sic] HIV/AIDS, or to not endorse, utilize or participate in a prevention method or treatment program to which the organization has a religious or moral objection; (ii) prohibit the funds provided under the agreement to be used to promote the legalization or practice of prostitution or sex trafficking; and (iii) require recipients to agree that they oppose prostitution and sex trafficking.[6]

By influencing funding in this manner, this "oath" aims to direct the prostitution policies of all USAID's grantees toward criminalization. This oath was challenged in May 2006 in two U.S. district courts. While the presiding judge agreed that the oath violates the First Amendment rights of U.S.-based grantees, the ruling did not exempt subgrantees outside of the United States from signing the pledge.[7] This ruling affects groups using strategies that aim to decrease the stigma associated with prostitution, including unionization and self-regulatory boards and collectives of sex workers. These include several Indian NGOs that have succeeded in significantly reducing the incidence of HIV infection in their areas. Two of these organizations are the Durbar Mahila Samanwaya Committee (DMSC) in Kolkata and the Sampada Grameen Mahila Sanstha (SANGRAM) in southern Maharashtra.[8]

The DMSC grew out of a 1992 HIV/AIDS epidemiological study in some of Kolkata's red-light districts. This study led to establishing the STD/HIV Intervention Programme, more popularly known as the Sonagachi Project, named for the city's main red-light area, where the program works. The Sonagachi Project forms the core organizing space for the DMSC, which has been a registered NGO since 1995. The DMSC conducts a wide array of programs, including HIV prevention and condom promotion, literacy and livelihood training programs, and microcredit schemes, and organizes self-regulatory boards of sex workers. The DMSC has also helped put together several national conferences of sex workers and sex-worker advocates, each of which attracted at least three thousand participants.

In the international debate on prostitution, the DMSC has garnered much attention for its strategy of organizing self-regulatory boards composed of sex workers. These boards were first established to monitor and prevent human trafficking in red-light districts in Kolkata, and they now operate in surrounding rural areas, as well. These boards also function as intermediaries with local police and state authorities and work in conjunction with the DMSC to promote condom use through peer-based interventions.

The DMSC is also known for its widely disseminated *Sex Workers' Manifesto*, in which it defines the goals and functions of a sex-workers' rights movement. The manifesto links the need for HIV prevention among sex workers to the broader political goal of reducing the stigma associated with prostitution. In the manifesto, the DMSC says that:

> while promoting the use of condoms, we soon realised that in order to change the sexual behaviour of sex workers it was not enough to enlighten them about the risks of unprotected sex or to improve their communication and negotiation skills. How will a sex worker who does not value herself at all think of taking steps to protect her health and her life? Even when fully aware of the necessity of using condoms to prevent disease transmission, may not an individual sex worker feel compelled to jeopardise her health in fear of losing her clients to other sex workers in the area unless it was ensured that all sex workers were able to persuade their clients to use condoms for every sexual act?[9]

Indian sex workers listen to speeches during the May 27, 2005,
convention in West Bengal state (Deshakalyan Chowdhury/AFP/
Getty Images).

In seeing all these issues as interelated with more complex ideologies of sexuality, the DMSC advocates seeing prostitution as a potential livelihood option for people who are uneducated and vocationally unskilled. In turn, it argues:

> The kind of oppression that can be meted out to a sex worker can never be perpetrated against a regular worker. The justification given is that sex work is not real work — it is morally sinful. As prostitution is kept hidden behind the facade of sexual morality and social order, unlike other professions there is no legitimacy or scope for any discussion about the demands and needs of the workers of the sex industry.... What we advocate and desire is independent, democratic, non-coercive, mutually pleasurable and safe sex.[10]

The DMSC's efforts have resulted in significantly reduced rates of HIV transmission in Kolkata's sex industry, especially compared to HIV infection rates in cities such as Mumbai. The organization boasts a membership of over sixty-five thousand sex workers, and a strong base for advocating peer-based, collective models for addressing a host of health-related and other issues affecting sex workers.[11]

Like the DMSC, SANGRAM has mounted a formidable set of strategies to address HIV transmission among sex workers. In 1992, SANGRAM formed its first collective of sex workers through peer-based condom promotion. By 1996, this collective had grown and was formalized as the Veshya AIDS Muqabla Parishad (VAMP). SANGRAM and VAMP have prioritized the destigmatization of sex work as key to promoting condom use and reducing HIV/AIDS transmission. Over the course of their development, SANGRAM and VAMP have garnered significant international support, including grants from the Ford Foundation and the USAID. In late 2005, the USAID terminated SANGRAM's funding on the grounds that it was violating the "antiprostitution oath," based on an accusation by a conservative antitrafficking NGO that SANGRAM was interfering with its "rescue and rehabilitation" operations for minor girls. These "rescue and rehabilitation" operations, justified by abolitionists as the best way to "save" minor girls from being sexually exploited, are conducted as police operations in which brothels are raided and anyone who looks underage is taken to a government facility, where she is kept in custody as a ward of the state. There have been several major problems with this kind of operation: sex workers' rights have been violated; due process has not been respected when individual women and girls have been kept in custody; police and "rescuers" have forcibly entered sex workers' homes; women have been falsely identified as minors; and minors have been involuntarily taken from their families on specious evidence that they were trafficked or forced to engage in prostitution. More significantly, these raids have not been shown definitively to reduce the incidence of trafficking or sexual commerce.[12] Brothel raids do, however, sustain the criminality of prostitution and provide an incentive for sexual commerce to go underground.[13]

Following the termination of the USAID's support for SANGRAM, Meena Seshu, the founder and director of SANGRAM, responded to accusations that her organization was "preventing rescue and rehabilitation activities." The *Hindustan Times* reported:

Meena Saraswathi Seshu, director of SANGRAM, in turn, defends her organisation saying that it is strongly against child prostitution that is akin to child sexual abuse but feels that "a simplistic solution [such] as raid and rescue merely offered patchwork relief." She further states, "In 1991, before SANGRAM worked in this area, every brothel had minor girls in prostitution. Today, police and this organisation RI [Restore International] found thirty-five of whom thirty-one are in dispute. Why is it that organisations that work for the rights of women in prostitution and sex work are considered pro trafficking, which is a criminal offence or pro minors in prostitution when it is clearly child sexual abuse?"[14]

The SANGRAM case spurred a series of responses, including the lawsuit filed against the U.S. government charging that the "antiprostitution oath" violated the First Amendment. As I have noted, although the three U.S.-based plaintiffs won their case in two American district courts, these victories do not apply to grantees working outside the United States.[15] According to the Center for Health and Gender Equity:

> Public health, human rights, and faith-based advocates have been deeply concerned that the U.S. global AIDS "loyalty oath regarding prostitution" restricts programs from using best practices to prevent HIV/AIDS among sex workers and trafficked individuals. The prostitution loyalty oath requires that U.S. and foreign nongovernmental organizations receiving USAID funding must adopt a policy "explicitly opposing prostitution and sex trafficking" throughout their programs, regardless of funding source.[16]

Both the DMSC and SANGRAM belong to an array of organizations in India aiming to use best-practices approaches in dealing with issues related to health and human rights in various sex industries. Both organizations are notable for their creative use of the NGO structure, combined with the incubation of and partnership with local collectives of sex workers that conduct HIV-prevention and antitrafficking interventions. As the United States continues to shape immigration and prostitution policy through its funding priorities, the Indian sex-workers' rights movement will be key in demonstrating the efficacy of alternatives to criminalization and "rescue and rehabilitation."

1   Gail Omvedt, *Ambedkar: Towards an Enlightened India* (New Delhi, New York: Penguin, 2004).

2   Siddharth Dube, *Sex, Lies, and AIDS* (New Delhi: HarperCollins, 2000).

3   See, for example, Y.N. Singh and A.N. Malaviya, "Long Distance Truck Drivers in India: HIV Infection and Their Possible Role in Disseminating HIV into Rural Areas," *International Journal of STD and AIDS* 5, no. 2 (1994), pp. 137–38; and P. Pais, "HIV and India: Looking into the Abyss," *Tropical Medicine and International Health* 1, no. 3 (1996), pp. 295–304.

4   Texts that have recently articulated the debate on prostitution and trafficking include Kamala Kempadoo and Jo Doezema (eds.), *Global Sex Workers: Rights, Resistance, and Redefinition* (New York: Routledge, 1998); Rajeswari Sunder Rajan, *The Scandal of the State: Women, Law, Citizenship in Postcolonial India* (Durham, NC: Duke University Press, 2003); Lin Lean Lim (ed.), *The Sex Sector: The Economic and Social Bases of Prostitution in Southeast Asia* (Geneva: International Labour Office, 1998); Philippa Levine, *Prostitution, Race, and Politics: Policing Venereal Disease in the British Empire* (New York: Routledge, 2003); Bandana Pattanaik and Susanne Thorbek (eds.), *Transnational Prostitution: Changing Patterns in a Global Context* (London: Zed Books, 2002); and Ratna Kapur (ed.), *Feminist Terrains in Legal Domains: Interdisciplinary Essays on Women and Law in India* (New Delhi: Kali for Women, 1996).

5   On this subject, see www.globalgagrule.org.

6   United States Agency for International Development, *Acquisition and Assistance Policy Directive 05-04: Implementation of the United States Leadership Against HIV/AIDS, Tuberculosis and Malaria Act of 2003 — Eligibility Limitation on the Use of Funds and Opposition to Opposition to Prostitution and Sex Trafficking* (Washington, D.C.: n.p., 2005). Available online at www.usaid.gov/business/business_opportunities/cib/pdf/aapd05_04.pdf.

7   See www.genderhealth.org/loyaltyoath.php, accessed August 28, 2006.

8   Information about the DMSC and SANGRAM in this article is based on site visits, conversations and informal interviews, and attendance at major protests and events that each has sponsored. For an overview of each group, see www.durbar.org for further information on DMSC. For information on SANGRAM, particularly with respect to their encounter with the USAID prostitution pledge, see the Center for Health and Gender Equity Web site, www.genderhealth.org.

9   Durbar Mahila Samanwaya Committee, *Sex Workers' Manifesto* (Calcutta: n.p., 1997). Available online at www.cabiria.asso.fr/english/e_manifesto.html.

10 *Ibid.*

11 See www.india-seminar.com/2003/524/524%20communication.htm, accessed August 28, 2006.

12 Joanna Busza, Sarah Castle, and Aisse Diarra, "Trafficking and Health," *BMJ* 328 (2004), pp. 1369–71.

13 Svati Shah, "Seeing Sexual Commerce," *Cultural Dynamics* 18, no. 3 (November 2006).

14 Rema Nagarajan, "US Accuses NGO of Trafficking," *Hindustan Times*, September 29, 2005. Available online at www.hindustantimes.com/news/181_1504660,0005000.htm.

15 Center for Health and Gender Equity, "Prostitution Loyalty Oath: A U.S. Global AIDS Policy Restriction in Violation of First Amendment," www.genderhealth.org/loyaltyoath.php.

16 *Ibid.*

Biotechnology and Publicity

a profile of the Council for Responsible Genetics by Yates McKee

The sharp divide between a scientific inside, where experts are formulating theories, and a political outside, where nonexperts are getting by with human values, is evaporating. And the more it does, the more the fate of humans is linked to that of things, the more a scientific statement…resembles a political one. The matters of fact of science become matters of concern of politics.

—Bruno Latour, "The World Wide Lab"

Located amid the research universities and life-science corporations of Cambridge, Massachusetts, the Council for Responsible Genetics (CRG) is a nongovernmental organization that aims to "foster public debate about the social, ethical, and environmental implications of genetic technologies."[1] The CRG takes no general position on the technoscientific capacity to trace and intervene in the molecular structure of living beings. The organization neither celebrates biotechnology as an instrument that inherently advances human welfare nor demonizes it as the corruptor of an organic essence, whether defined in natural or social terms. Rather than merely expound upon the moral dilemmas such technologies pose for a universal humanity, the CRG draws critical attention to the specific practices of the public and private institutions that govern the development and application of these technologies in areas ranging from genetically modified crops to bioweapons research, genetic testing, and life patenting. According to the CRG, these governing agencies — universities, corporations, and various multilateral, federal, state, and local regulatory bodies — have been largely insulated from public accountability and civic oversight. This state of affairs is due in part to the power of technologically and biologically deterministic conceptions of society circulating in academia, policy circles, and the public sphere; the technical complexity of the scientific technologies and regulatory agencies in question; and the self-evident status of scientific expertise accepted by scientists, policy makers, and citizens alike.

With its four-person staff, a nine-person board of directors consisting of biologists, geneticists, public-health specialists, lawyers, and social scientists, in addition to an extensive informal network of scholars and activists in Boston and across the world, the CRG's

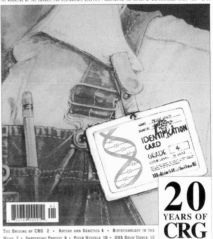

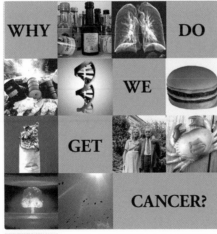

GeneWatch covers (CLOCKWISE FROM UPPER LEFT):
November/December, 2002; January/February, 2003;
September/October, 2003; March/April, 2006.

working methods comprise press releases, editorials, interviews, events, legislative consultation, partnerships with local political initiatives, and its bimonthly publication, *Gene-Watch*. The CRG neither equates its activities with the enactment of sheer technical expertise nor does it claim simply to demystify the latter in favor of popular moral wisdom; rather, the organization aims to translate scientific and policy analyses into terms that are accessible and resonant for legislators, media outlets, and a diverse nonexpert public (including consumers, farmers, patients, and urban inhabitants, among others) whose lives — in both the social and biological senses — are variously affected by genetic technologies as they are both implemented and governed. In keeping with the distinction once drawn by Michel Foucault between the "chief enemies" posited by 1960s militants — capital, the state, bureaucracy, and imperialism — and the specific power relations taken up by humanitarian, human-rights, and environmental movements since the 1970s, the CRG does not ideologically oppose in any simple sense the governing agencies whose practices it targets as sites of political concern.[2] This does not mean, however, that the organization renounces inscribing its activism in terms of two "grand designs" that it shares with certain other practitioners of nongovernmental politics discussed in the present volume: promoting a relatively autonomous civil society capable of analyzing and challenging governmental practices deemed to be intolerable from the perspective of individual liberties and public health, and questioning a set of concepts and policies that privilege technological development, individual initiative, private property, and profit making over concerns of ecological safety and the socially equitable distribution of public goods, services, and life opportunities, including access to scientific knowledge itself. The CRG lists its "central principles" as follows: "The public must have access to clear and understandable information on technological innovations. The public must be able to participate in public and private decision making concerning technological developments and their implementation. New technologies must meet social needs. Problems rooted in poverty, racism, and other forms of inequality cannot be remedied by technology alone."[3]

The roots of the CRG are to be located in the political and intellectual milieu of late-1960s Cambridge, Massachusetts, when faculty and students began to question the relationship of their research at the Massachusetts Institute of Technology (MIT) — research hitherto defined as "value-free" inquiry for the sake of knowledge alone — to governmental and corporate policies, most immediately with respect to the development of weapons destined for use in Vietnam. Announcing that "we no longer feel it is possible to remain uninvolved," they called upon their colleagues in Cambridge and across the United States to unite "for action against dangers already unleashed and leadership toward a more responsible exploitation of scientific knowledge [and] for turning research applications away from the present emphasis on military technology toward the solution of pressing environmental and social problems."[4] Such calls to action led to the inauguration of the Union of Concerned Scientists (UCS), with which numerous Cambridge biologists were involved, as well as more expressly left-wing organizations such as the nationwide Science for the People (SFTP) network, which for a time sought to bring scientists and technicians into contact with women's groups, community organizations, and labor unions.[5]

Yet a more immediate precipitating event in the emergence of the CRG was the 1976 formation of the Cambridge Experimentation Review Board (CERB), a novel oversight committee created by the Cambridge City Council in response to concerns voiced by a group of Harvard scientists about their university's plans to construct a high-level recombinant DNA (rDNA) laboratory in the middle of their densely populated township. Though the laboratory would conform to the research and safety guidelines for experimental gene-splicing established by the National Institutes of Health (NIH) in 1974, the Harvard plan was criticized for proceeding without public consultation and for failing to integrate any environmental impact and risk assessment procedures by specialists in fields other than microbiology (such as ecology, clinical medicine, and infectious diseases). The scientists had succeeded in pressuring the university's Committee on Research Policy to hold an open meeting on campus, which was attended by a city council member and a journalist, who brought the lab into the public sphere as an object of political concern and potential intervention. The city council itself held public hearings on the issue, but when the Harvard committee announced that it would proceed with the plans as originally laid out, the council voted to establish the Cambridge Experimentation Review Board, a panel composed of citizens to be selected by the city manager with the stipulation that none of them be experts in the field of microbiology. Bowing to the public scrutiny of the plan generated by the formation of the CERB, Harvard agreed to a four-month moratorium on its plans, during which the review board heard dozens of hours of testimony from advocates and critics of the project. Ultimately, the CERB issued a (nonbinding) resolution stipulating that the university adopt a more stringent monitoring and safety apparatus to guard against the potential release of experimental transgenic organisms into the socioecological system of Cambridge. Harvard voluntarily accepted this resolution, thus establishing a precedent for such research-and-development facilities in the future.

As CERB participant and CRG cofounder Sheldon Krimsky emphasized in a 1978 article for the *Bulletin of the Atomic Scientists*, the review board was by no means unassailable in conceptual, procedural, and political terms.[6] However, the CERB was nonetheless a remarkable experiment in a "politics of the governed." Rather than simply introducing a new set of themes into a preexisting political debate, it staged a new mode of interaction between municipal government, regulatory agencies, scientific expertise, and civil society. The key question animating the CERB, which was to have a formative effect on the CRG, concerned the accountability of governing agencies for the environmental risks that accompany the development of new technologies, in particular those pertaining to genetic experimentation. The CERB understood the implications of scientific research to extend beyond the context of the laboratory experiment and demanded that the public be defined not only as a generic beneficiary of scientific innovation, but also as a population exposed to potential biological and social hazards.

The Harvard lab controversy and the subsequent CERB process occasioned the formation of the Coalition for the Reproductive Rights of Workers and the Coalition for Responsible Genetic Research. Together, they formed a watchdog group that was to become the CRG in 1983 with the inaugural publication of *GeneWatch* magazine.[7]

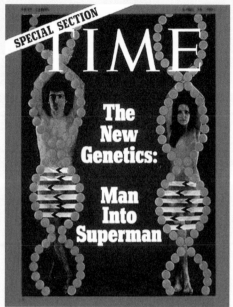

Time Magazine covers (CLOCKWISE FROM UPPER LEFT):
July 14, 1958; April 9, 1971; January 17, 1994; July 3, 2000.

Contemporaneous with, but not immediately implicated in the specific problematization of environmental risk assessment, public participation, and institutional accountability initiated by CERB, the SFTP-affiliated Sociobiology Study Group was established in Boston by Harvard biologists Stephen Jay Gould, Ruth Hubbard, and Richard Lewontin in response to their colleague E.O. Wilson's book *Sociobiology: The New Synthesis* (1975). In *Sociobiology,* Wilson extrapolated his analyses of animal populations, especially ant colonies, to patterns of human social organization and behavior by arguing that the latter are grounded in universal genetic programs of evolutionary selection, self-preservation, and self-propagation — to wit, "the survival of the fittest." According to the Sociobiology Study Group, Wilson and other writers, such as Richard Dawkins (author of *The Selfish Gene,* 1976), posited a "genetically determinist" model of life in general, declaring DNA to be the primary causal mechanism of both organismic development and social history. Sociobiology was thus charged with disavowing the extent to which the expression of particular genes depends on their articulation with contingent biochemical processes and ecological conditions that are irreducible to any internal program of an organism. Gould, among others, tracked the assumptions guiding sociobiology to eugenic concepts at the turn of the twentieth century in which appeals to sanguinary heredity legitimized the control, sterilization, and, in some cases, the eradication of populations considered to be evolutionarily inferior.[8] Their critique proved to be especially pertinent as sociobiological precepts increasingly began to inform discussions of issues such as psychometric testing (IQ), criminology, and welfare provision in the 1980s, epitomized by the success among policymakers and popular audiences alike of Richard J. Herrnstein and Charles Murray's *The Bell Curve: Intelligence and Class Structure in American Life.*

As the Sociobiology Study Group (the founding members of which went on to participate in various ways in the activities of the CRG) understood it, "genetic reductionism" is more than an ideologically dubious interpretation of biological processes that has been mapped metaphorically onto explanations of social life (the targeting of the "welfare mother" as a figure of parasitic "overbreeding," for instance). In its crudest versions, genetic reductionism unabashedly posited a natural foundation for historically inherited inequalities.

According to Richard Lewontin (who became a CRG board member), the cornerstone of "the DNA era" has been "the unjustified claim for special autonomous powers of DNA," a claim he opposed on scientific grounds:

> [T]here is no "master molecule," no "secret of life." The DNA is an archive of information about amino acid sequences to which the synthetic machinery of the cell needs to refer when a new protein molecule is to be produced. When and where in the organism that information is read depends on the physiological state of the cells. An organism cannot develop without its DNA, but it cannot develop without its already existing protein machinery.[9]

In other words, DNA is neither self-replicating nor autogenous; the hereditary traces encrypted within it are only ever activated in relation to other cellular and physiological systems that are themselves always marked by larger ecological systems, which are in turn affected by organismic activity, including human social activities such as those that generate potentially cancer-catalyzing pollution.[10] Criticizing the "dream" of the Human Genome Project — decoding the "essence" of human life through computational means — Lewontin contended that "an organism cannot be computed from its DNA because the organism does not compute itself from its own DNA."[11]

Lewontin's decentering, as it were, of the genetic code is not meant to reduce it to a mere "social construction." It suggests, rather, that the genetic code is constitutively marked by a certain trace of alterity that opens it beyond itself in a way that is incalculable.[12] This assertion of the irreducibility of the living organism to any inherent genetic code is the condition for a practice of "responsible genetics": it is only insofar as genes are never simply genetic, but depend for their activation and effectivity on contingent environmental and historical circumstances, that the unpredictable consequences of their technoscientific manipulability become a matter of political concern, one in which scientists, among others, are implicated and for which they have a certain responsibility.

According to Lewontin, this responsibility is disavowed by an exclusive fixation on DNA as the explanatory principle for life, a fixation that has effected a shift in the institutional, discursive, and practical parameters of scientific research itself. For instance, it has legitimized the reorganization of investment and funding priorities around the search for hereditary causes of a wide range of diseases and the development of genetically based cures for these afflictions. While many CRG-affiliated scientists have themselves been involved in such research, they have also sought to illuminate its relationship to broader ecological and epidemiological patterns, as well as to the state of the preventative health-care infrastructure in general, the concerns of patients' rights groups, private corporations, and federal regulators, and ethico-political questions concerning prenatal testing, genetic therapy, and the possibility of "genetic discrimination" being exercised by employers and insurance companies.

To take one recent example, geneticist and CRG executive board member Paul Billings testified at a 2005 congressional hearing on genetic privacy and confidentiality that "all people have the right to genetic privacy including the right to prevent the taking or storing of bodily samples for genetic information without their voluntary informed consent."[13] Significantly, Billings himself is an employee of thr Laboratory Corporation of America, a leading genetic testing company that has instituted policies against the discriminatory exploitation of its lab results by other corporations and institutions.

The genetic reductionism that the CRG has aimed to combat for the past twenty years thus has two related facets: an interpretation of biology that isolates DNA from the incalculable articulation of organismic physiology with historically overdetermined ecological-social networks; and an interpretation of the technologies capable of manipulating genetic material that isolates scientific research and development from a broader network of power relations and responsibilities.

With the CERB and the Sociobiology Study Group in mind, we can see that the origins of the CRG were marked by a concern with political technologies of risk assessment and

The Liability and Settlement Roundtable, first meeting of the Intergovernmental Committee for the Cartegena Protocol on Biosafety, Montpellier, France, December 2000: (LEFT TO RIGHT) Phil Bereano (Council for Responsible Genetics), Ambassador Philemon Yang (Republic of Cameroon), Yannick Jadot (Solagral), Willy de Greef (Syngenta Corporation), and Gurdial Singh Nijar (Third World Network).

a critique, both bioscientific and politico-ideological, of what Lewontin has called "the doctrine of DNA." Yet from the beginning, the CRG has supplemented and extended these questions with specific attention to the industrialization of biotechnology, especially in the fields of medicine and agriculture.

The CRG has been at the forefront of debates involving the development of genetically modified crop varieties by global corporations such as Monsanto. It has drawn attention to the ecological and economic implications of developing these crops for countries in the global South, as well as their ramifications for consumer health in the global North. For example, the organization participated in the meetings that drafted the 2003 Cartagena Protocol on Biosafety. As a supplement to the 1992 United Nations Environment Programme (UNEP) Convention on Biodiversity, the protocol was a treaty that, while lacking formalized enforcement mechanisms, could nonetheless be mobilized as a counterbalance to the stipulations of the World Trade Organization's (WTO) agricultural liberalization regime. Where, for instance, the latter empowers corporations and their member states to sue other governments for erecting "barriers to trade" if they require the labeling of genetically modified foods, the Protocol on Biosafety defends such labeling as a basic mode of protection for national food systems, small farmers, and consumers.

Along with the risks of transgenic accidents involving experimental crop varieties — such as the contamination of corn stocks destined for human consumption in fast-food chains such as Taco Bell by Aventis CropScience's StarLink corn, a Bt variety authorized for use only in noncomestible applications — the CRG's concern with biosafety also encompasses the deliberate extension of corporate privatization into agricultural systems. The latter are exemplified by Monsanto's so-called terminator technologies, which genetically engineer plants to kill their own embryos, thus requiring farmers to buy new Monsanto-produced seed and Bt crops (also designed to be pesticide resistant only in relation to chemicals sold by Monsanto) every season. Another facet of such corporate enclosure is the corporate patenting of local and indigenous farming techniques and practices, in particular, the patenting of small farmers' knowledge of the (economically profitable) properties of plant species such as the naturally occurring pesticide chemicals generated by the neem tree or the wound-healing properties of turmeric.

In the context of global trade negotiations, the CRG's efforts since the mid-1990s to combat the patenting of knowledges and techniques that pertain to the bio-intellectual heritage of the "genetic commons" resonates with the organization's long-standing critique of life patents. The latter were inaugurated by the 1980 U.S. Supreme Court decision in *Diamond v. Chakrabarty,* which allowed a corporate scientist to claim that a genetically engineered bacterium designed to eat oil spills was a form of constitutionally protected intellectual property and hence patentable. Since this ruling, which declared the bacterium to be a product of "human artifice," rather than a naturally occurring entity, numerous corporations and universities have used *Chakrabarty* as a pretext for their attempts to patent all varieties of organisms, cells, and genes — from Basmati rice, to the genetic archive of the Icelandic population; from cell lines pertaining to particular diseases such as breast cancer and Alzheimer's to the oncomouse, a transgenic mouse altered with human cancer cells to make it more susceptible to tumor formation, which is now sold en masse to research institutions for experimentation purposes.[14] The CRG does not, in principle, simply oppose any of these inventions or discoveries (whereas classical patent law has opposed them on the grounds that live organisms are not patentable inventions, a notion that has been unsettled by the technologies in question). What is at stake for the CRG, rather, is the ways in which such developments have been governed and the implications of the modes of governance for research and public health, such as the hampering of transinstitutional exchanges of ideas and materials between scientists working on the hereditary bases of a specific disease.[15]

To highlight these problems, in 1998, the CRG drafted a No Patents on Life petition, which prefigured the 2002 World Social Forum's Treaty to Share the Genetic Commons. Addressed to lay social movements, scientists, and policy makers, the CRG's petition opposes the ownership of living material:

> The plants, animals and microorganisms comprising life on earth are part of the natural world into which we are all born. The conversion of these species, their molecules, or parts into corporate property through patent monopolies is counter to the interests of the peoples of this country and of the world. No individual, institution, or corporation should be able to claim ownership over species or varieties of living organisms. Nor should they be able to hold patents on organs, cells, genes or proteins, whether naturally occurring, genetically altered

European demonstrators protest the patenting of umbilical-cord blood cells by the Biocyete Corporation. In 1999, the European Patent Office revoked the patent on the grounds that the therapeutic properties of the biological materials in question were common medical knowledge, rather than the exclusive "invention" of any single private entity (photo by Ricarda Steinbrecher).

or otherwise modified. As part of a world movement to protect our common living heritage, we call upon the Congress of the United States to enact legislation to exclude living organisms and their component parts from the patent system.[16]

Another arena in which the CRG has long been active is that of bioweapons, where, echoing the early claims of the Union of Concerned Scientists, it has consistently aimed to deconstruct the opposition between "offensive" and "defensive" research. The organization played a crucial testimonial and consultative role in the drafting of the Biological Weapons Anti-Terrorism Act of 1989, successfully pressuring the administration of George H.W. Bush to integrate the 1972 Biological and Toxin Weapons Convention (BWC) into U.S. civil law.[17] Since the 9/11 attacks, however, the provisions of this act have been increasingly sidestepped, with the federal government reorienting a considerable portion of its health-related research budget toward the purported threat of weaponizable pathogens such as anthrax, smallpox, and plague, a tendency codified in 2003 as Operation Bioshield.[18]

The implications of this budgetary reallocation have had immediate reverberations in the CRG's own urban milieu: in 2003, Boston University received a federal grant to build a level-4 bioterror lab, where exotic organisms will be cultivated, stored, and researched. The

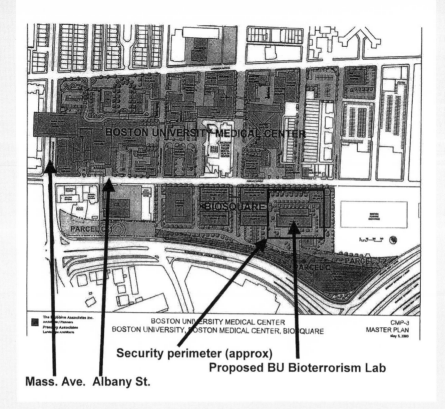

Alternatives for Community and Environment, map of proposed Boston
University bioterrorism laboratory, South End–Roxbury, Boston, MA
(www.ace-ej.org/biolabweb/backgroundinfopage.html).

lab is to be sited in the city's South End, a low-income black neighborhood that has historically suffered the effects of environmental racism and political marginalization. For three
years, the CRG collaborated with activists from the environmental-justice organization
Alternatives for Community and Environment (ACE) to reinstitute a CERB-type citizen's
review panel in which the skewed biodefense priorities of the Bush administration could be
considered in relation to a comprehensive environmental impact review, with special attention to the patterns of uneven risk exposure to which the population of the South End
has been subjected for decades.[19] Using a range of venues and media tactics, including
civil disobedience, city council meetings, legislative lobbying, and newspaper editorials,
the ACE/CRG alliance succeeded in transforming the unimpeachable federal-governmental
imperatives of biodefense into a site of substantial local political conflict. However, the
organizations were unable to defeat the lab plans entirely and are currently working to
pressure and modify the terms of the regulatory statute outlined for the lab by the Boston
Public Health Commission.[20]

Over its twenty-three year existence, the key paradigmatic innovation of the CRG has been to open a typically esoteric realm of technological research, development, and application to public legibility, scrutiny, and debate, thereby displacing, but not simply dissolving, the matters of fact of biotechnology into the realm of political concern. By aiming to articulate new forms of civic agency and governmental accountability vis-à-vis the social fact of DNA as a "quasi-object"[21] — a node in a sociotechnical network that is neither naturally given nor culturally constructed in any pure sense — the CRG occupies a unique place in the history of nongovernmental politics, bringing together a hitherto unaffiliated and heterogeneous range of analyses, sites, and constituencies. Such an articulation is performed in the council's Genetic Bill of Rights (2000), a remarkable document that at once receives and reinscribes the historical inheritance of human-rights discourse, exposing the latter to unforeseen environments, interactions, and mutations.

GENETIC BILL OF RIGHTS

ꞈEAMBLE

ꞈur life and health depend upon an intricate web ꞈ relationships within the biological and social ꞈorlds. Protection of these relationships must ꞈorm all public policy.

ꞈommercial, governmental, scientific and medical ꞈstitutions promote manipulation of genes despite ꞈofound ignorance of how such changes may ꞈect the web of life. Once they enter the ꞈvironment, organisms with modified genes ꞈnnot be recalled and pose novel risks to humanity ꞈd the entire biosphere.

ꞈanipulation of human genes creates new threats ꞈ the health of individuals and their offspring, and ꞈdangers human rights, privacy and dignity.

ꞈenes, other constituents of life, and genetically ꞈodified organisms themselves are rapidly being ꞈtented and turned into objects of commerce. ꞈis commercialization of life is veiled behind ꞈomises to cure disease and feed the hungry.

ꞈople everywhere have the right to participate in ꞈaluating the social and biological implications of ꞈe genetic revolution and in democratically guiding ꞈ applications.

ꞈ protect our human rights and integrity and the ꞈological integrity of the earth, we, therefore, ꞈppose this Genetic Bill of Rights.

1. All people have the right to preservation of the earth's biological and genetic diversity.

2. All people have the right to a world in which living organisms cannot be patented, including human beings, animals, plants, microorganisms and all their parts.

3. All people have the right to a food supply that has not been genetically engineered.

4. All indigenous peoples have the right to manage their own biological resources, to preserve their traditional knowledge, and to protect these from expropriation and biopiracy by scientific, corporate or government interests.

5. All people have the right to protection from toxins, other contaminants, or actions that can harm their genetic makeup and that of their offspring.

6. All people have the right to protection against eugenic measures such as forced sterilization or mandatory screening aimed at aborting or manipulating selected embryos or fetuses.

7. All people have the right to genetic privacy including the right to prevent the taking or storing of bodily samples for genetic information without their voluntary informed consent.

8. All people have the right to be free from genetic discrimination.

9. All people have the right to DNA tests to defend themselves in criminal proceedings.

10. All people have the right to have been conceived, gestated, and born without genetic manipulation.

1   CRG home page, "Who We Are," www.gene-watch.org.
2   On the distinction between "chief enemies" and "immediate enemies," see Michel Foucault, "The Subject and Power," in James. D. Faubion (ed.), *Power: Essential Works of Foucault, Volume 3* (New York: The New Press, 2000), p. 330.
3   CRG home page, "Central Principles," www.gene-watch.org.
4   Union of Concerned Scientists, "MIT Faculty Statement" (December 1968), available online at www.ucsusa.org/ucs/about/founding-document-1968-mit-faculty-statement.html.
5   To get a sense of the interdisciplinary research and advocacy carried out by Science for the People, see Rita Arditti, Pat Brennan, and Steve Cavrak (eds.), *Science and Liberation* (Boston: South End Press, 1980).
6   Sheldon Krimsky "A Citizen Court in the Recombinant DNA Debate," *Bulletin of the Atomic Scientists* 34, no. 8 (October 1978), pp. 37–43.
7   See Ruth Hubbard and Sheldon Krimsky, "The Origins of CRG," *GeneWatch* 16, no. 1 (2003). Also available online at the CRG Web site, www.gene-watch.org/genewatch/articles/16-2hubbard_krimsky.html. All further references to Gene-Watch articles include the location of their online versions on the CRG Web site.
8   Stephen Jay Gould, *The Mismeasure of Man,* rev. ed. (New York: W. W. Norton & Co., 1996), p. 20. The reissue includes a new introduction responding to *The Bell Curve,* by Richard J. Hernstein and Charles Murray (1994).
9   Richard C. Lewontin, "The DNA Era," *GeneWatch* 16, no. 4 (2003), www.gene-watch.org/genewatch/articles/16-4lewontin.html.
10 For further elaboration of this model of the "dialectical" coproduction of organism and environment, see Richard C. Lewontin, *Biology as Ideology: The Doctrine of DNA* (New York: Harper Perennial, 1992).
11 Lewontin, "The DNA Era."
12 Though Lewontin does not explicitly elaborate on the metaphors of "code," "script," "archive," and "information" employed in describing the model of DNA, his analysis of the historically, environmentally, and biochemically contingent "expression" of particular genes is resonant with Jacques Derrida's extrapolation of deconstructive analysis of "writing" as a trace-structure to the realm of "life in general": "The trace, where the relationship with the other is marked, articulates its possibility in the entire field of the entity... which metaphysics has defined as the being-present starting from the occulted movement of the trace. The trace must be thought before the entity." Jacques Derrida, *Of Gramma-*tolgy, trans. Gayatri Chakravorty Spivak (Baltimore: Johns Hopkins University Press, 1976), p. 47. Earlier in the book, Derrida writes, "It is...in this sense that the contemporary biologist speaks of writing and *pro-gram* in relation to the most elementary processes of information in the living cell" and references "the entire field covered by the cybernetic program," p. 9.
13 Paul Billings, "Standards for Privacy of Individually Identifiable Health Information," National Committee on Vital and Health Statistics, Subcommittee on Privacy and Confidentiality, January 12, 2005, available online at www.ncvhs.hhs.gov/050112p2.htm.
14 See former CRG staff member Matthew Albright's *Profits Pending: How Life Patents Represent the Biggest Swindle of the Twenty-First Century* (Monroe, Maine: Common Courage Press, 2002).
15 See Jonathan A. King and Doreen Stabinsky, "Patents on Cells, Genes, and Organisms Undermine the Exchange of Scientific Ideas," *Chronicle of Higher Education,* May 2, 1999. A copy of this article is available on the CRG Web site, www.gene-watch.org/programs/patents/undermine.html.
16 CRG, "No Patents on Life Petition," www.gene-watch.org/programs/patents/petition.html. For background on this campaign, see Rebecca Charnas, CRG, "'No Patents on Life' Working Group Update," www.gene-watch.org/programs/patents/update.html.
17 For a personal account of this legislative-consultancy process, see Francis Boyle, "Bio-Warfare and Terrorism," *Synthesis/Regeneration Online* 30 (Winter 2003), www.greens.org/s-r/30/30-12.html.
18 See "Special Biowarfare Issue," *GeneWatch* 17, nos. 5/6 (September–December 2004), www.gene-watch.org/gene-watch/archives.html.
19 See Alternatives for Community and Environment, "Background Information," www.ace-ej.org/BiolabWeb/Backgroundinfopage.html.
20 See Sujatha Byravan, "Biolab Oversight Crucial, Feasible," *Boston Globe,* August 27, 2006.
21 "Quasi-object" and "socio-technical networks" are terms developed by Bruno Latour; his inaugural example is drawn from a quotidian newspaper article about the "ozone hole": "The same article mixes together chemical reactions and political reactions. A single thread links the most esoteric sciences and the most sordid politics, the most distant sky and some factory in the Lyon suburbs, dangers on a global scale and the impending local elections or the next board meeting. The horizons, the stakes, the time frames, the

actors — none of these is commensurable, yet there they are, caught up in the same story." See Bruno Latour, *We Have Never Been Modern* (Cambridge, MA: Harvard University Press,1991), p. 1. While CRG analysts do not specifically cite his work, many of them are engaged with the discourse of Science, Technology, and Society, an academic quasi-discipline of which Latour is considered one of the founders and is especially strong at Harvard University and MIT.

WAYS

PRESENTATIONS

Members of the Action Against Hunger board of directors and board of advisors: (LEFT TO RIGHT) Alexis Azria, Harold A. Bornstein, Jessica Weber, Robert W. Rudzki, Anne-Sophie Fournier, Burton K. Haimes, Ketty Maisonrouge, Joseph G. Audi, and Wendy C. Weiler (photo by Jim Bulgatz).

Governance and Policies in Nongovernmental Organizations

Philippe Ryfman

Controversy over revenue sources is a recurrent theme in news coverage of nongovernmental organizations and one that is especially relished by politicians and the media. In some cases, NGOs themselves use this controversy to their advantage, or at least to assert their own identity. For example, the different branches of the transnational NGO Médecins Sans Frontières (MSF) are keen to emphasize the source of their funding both as a distinctive feature and as a publicity tool. Indeed, MSF is insistent on — and also vocal about — maintaining a particularly high ratio of private financing to public funds in its overall budget; the French branch (MSF-France) boasts the highest such rate (94 percent in 2005).[1]

The subject of financing also reveals an unexpected contrast between European — especially French — and American NGOs. In France, the tradition of generous public subsidies for the philanthropic sector is as old as the 1901 law that created the notion of freedom of association. However, this tradition does not really apply to development and humanitarian aid — and, to an even lesser degree, to human rights advocacy and environmental activism. In these sectors, private funds systematically outweigh public subsidies, as shown by the inquiries conducted every other year by the Commission Coopération Développement (CCD).[2] In the United States, on the other hand, which is supposed to be a paradise for private philanthropy, the most reliable evaluations indicate that at least 30 percent of public aid for development passes through NGOs.[3] Even if this is only a small percentage of the U.S.'s GDP, it still represents a considerable amount of public money allocated to NGOs of various sizes, including very large ones. Among the traditional recipients of federal funding, the Cooperative for Assistance and Relief Everywhere (CARE) occupies a choice spot: in 2003, it received 64 percent of its resources from the United States Agency for International Development (USAID), as well as another 13 percent from various other government sources. That same year, 85 percent of Mercy Corps's budget came from USAID, while the share of government funds at Catholic Relief Services (CRS) — in 2002 — amounted to little more than 50 percent. By contrast, the funding model of World Vision International (WVI) is decidedly geared toward private donors: the American branch announced in 2002 that 80 percent of its contributions were from private sources (individuals and companies).

Important as it is, the issue of NGOs' incomes and funding strategies should not be examined in and of itself. Rather, it must be contextualized as an element in a much larger problematic, namely, that of the *governance* of these organizations. To put it bluntly, the fact that an NGO is endowed with funding, human resources, and substantial material means proves rather inconsequential if, at the same time, the people in charge of this organization are incapable of setting up and implementing relevant programs that make good use of available resources and respond to actual needs. Observations on the ground show that governance, with respect to NGOs, is indeed a legitimate and crucial question — albeit one that still needs to be precisely delineated.

At issue is what might be called "nongovernmental policies" — in other words, the strategies devised by NGOs. In order to conduct their programs properly, these organizations need an appropriate and coherent mode of governance, for the latter conditions both the consensus among the members of the NGO and the standing of the NGO in the outside world. Meeting that second condition is all the more important because of the multiple pressures exerted on nongovernmental agencies, especially in the domains of humanitarian and development aid. First, these NGOs face increasingly demanding requests from the public institutions that fund them. Second, the security of their personnel in the field is steadily deteriorating, and they are constantly confronted by a wide array of forces — whether states, local governments, guerillas, or militias — that are intent on either confiscating the aid delivered by NGOs or inflecting its use to further their own agenda. Third, the NGO sector, at least in developed countries, is increasingly expected to be transparent and cost effective, as are other segments of society. This expectation has led to the proliferation of modes of oversight, such as audits and evaluations by public and private funding agencies. Media stories and public concern both testify to the intensification of the scrutiny to which NGOs are submitted. In Europe, in 2005, the medium-sized and larger humanitarian and development NGOs that accepted funds either from the European Union or from national governments were obliged to undergo an average of one audit per month. (These audits pertained both to the organizations themselves and to each of their programs.) And this trend is gaining momentum: in 2006, the number of these audits is expected to climb to about twenty, which amounts to almost two a month. Finally, the managers of humanitarian and development NGOs also face the pressure exerted by the stakes of their own work. In other words, being in command of managerial tools that enable them to control complex operations is not merely about satisfying donors: more than anything, it is about being able to provide assistance to impoverished or endangered populations that have a right to expect high-quality assistance.

In short, governance, far from responding only to internal preoccupations, exercises a direct influence on the policies and capabilities of a NGO. For example, bad governance choices may prevent an aid agency from being present in a particular location, when a more judicious decision might have allowed it to respond to an emergency. Moreover, a system of governance that is poorly adapted to the realities and expectations of the various stakeholders of an NGO — namely, its supporters, employees, volunteers, donors, and sympathizers — is liable to provoke "governance crises" that are detrimental to its operational capabilities, and sometimes its very survival. In such cases, the executive officers, employees, volunteers, and supporters of the NGO will have to devote considerable time and energy to trying to resolve the crisis — at the risk of wearing themselves out.

WHY GOVERNANCE?

With respect to NGOs, governance has a dual function: it counters the recurring accusation of opacity leveled at NGOs and it optimizes the ability of these organizations to fulfill their mandates. Such an approach is relatively new, especially for NGOs working at the international level. Until recently, these organizations have perceived governance as a notion that applies to their place and role in the context of what is called global governance, particularly within the framework of North-South relations.[4] This essay, however, discusses only "internal" governance, within the nongovernmental entity itself.

FROM ACCOUNTABILITY TO QUALITY

The way in which the operations of NGOs is examined, especially by the media, often leads to polemical assessments and accusations of amateurism, organizational chaos, or faulty accountability mechanisms. Politicians are also keen to criticize NGOs; for example, at the turn of this century, the Belgian foreign minister, Louis Michel (who later became the European Commissioner for Humanitarian Aid and Development), accused them of being totally opaque and unaccountable structures.

However, this is a crude generalization that corresponds less and less to the workings of humanitarian and development organizations, which are now bound by a series of obligations — bearing on their accounting, financial, publicity, and contractual practices. Various bodies are involved in overseeing the implementation of these obligations in France. For example, there is the Inspection Générale des Affaires Sociales (General Inspection of Social Affairs, a governmental inquiry service), as well as the Cour des Comptes, an independent court of auditors (equivalent to the General Accounting Office of the U.S. Congress), which oversees organizations that receive money from private donors. In Great Britain, the Charity Commission exercises uncontested and punctilious control over the philanthropic sector. Similarly, most developed countries require NGOs to make their accounts public, to nominate accounting commissioners, and to commission frequent audits. The requirements imposed by the principal public sources of funding have created a substantial (and rather remunerative) market for auditing firms. The European Commission verifies the use of funds granted to NGOs, and this practice is growing more detailed. Finally, the surge in self-regulatory initiatives should not be underestimated: in France, there is the Comité de la Charte de Déontologie des Organisations Sociales et Humanitaires Faisant Appel à la Générosité Publique (Committee for the Implementation of Deontological Standards), to which most significant organizations belong. Médecins du Monde's French branch (MDM-France) has a donors committee that functions independently of the organization's other structures. Auditing committees are beginning to take form within the Boards of Directors of aid groups such as Action Contre la Faim, France (Action Against Hunger, France [ACF-France]), while the position of internal auditor independent of financial management is gradually being created at various NGOs. In the United States, InterAction (the largest alliance of U.S.-based international development and humanitarian aid NGOs) requires its members to subscribe to common principles and protocols. These multiple mechanisms complement and reinforce the legal arrangements that already exist.

FULFILLING THE MANDATE THANKS TO GOVERNANCE

The true nature of an NGO's mandate is often misunderstood. Initially, there is a process whereby an NGO seeks to bestow legitimacy upon itself to appear, so to speak, legitimate in its own eyes.[5] However, the organization is soon led to attend to the sustainability of its self-conferred legitimacy: in other words, the mandate that the founders originally defined for themselves is in turn adapted and enlarged by their successors. Once established, this mandate is carried out by an agency whose proper functioning must be a top priority for the NGO's supporters, volunteers, employees, and donors. As Jean-Hervé Bradol, the president of MSF-France, writes: "We must be vigilant that the management of our significant resources does not take the upper hand over the purpose of our activities; we have to work on any faulty aspects of our interventions."[6]

Today, these principles and requirements for functioning are referred to collectively as "governance." The term became prominent in NGO circles around the turn of the millennium. In France, Coordination Sud — the central collective structure that brings together almost every French NGO working on development and humanitarian aid — proposed that its member organizations make governance a major theme for the coming years.[7] It gave no precise definition of the concept, but emphasized that the essential goal was to "secure over time the social mission of an NGO." Put explicitly: "It is a matter of fulfilling the mission that an NGO has chosen and thus of satisfying the ultimate beneficiaries of this mission in a permanent way. Everyone involved in the activity of the NGO in question is concerned with this issue."[8] What Coordination Sud seeks to "secure" comprises both the accountability of its members and the quality of the services they provide.[9]

In the United States, InterAction has developed, since 1992, a set of precise directives, entitled InterAction's Private Voluntary Organization Standards. As is the case with its French counterpart, the standards devised by InterAction enumerate the key obligations of its member organizations with respect to sustaining good governance and providing reliable, high-quality services to their beneficiaries.[10]

CORPORATE GOVERNANCE AND NONPROFIT GOVERNANCE

A TERM WITH MANY USES

Today, the word "governance" is pervasive in the language of international economics and politics. However, the fact that it is now commonly used does not necessarily imply that it is precisely understood.[11] In the first place, it refers to a mode of managing complex businesses in which vertical hierarchy gives way to a more horizontal, even egalitarian arrangement.

Historically, the concept comes from the business world: at the end of the 1980s, the question of "corporate governance" arose because of the deficiency of control mechanisms and the failures of some boards of directors. The latter had proved incapable of preventing several notorious bankruptcies, which had either been caused by or coupled with financial scandals due to inappropriate management. Great Britain was the pioneer country in the area of corporate governance: a commission presided over by Sir Adrian Cadbury was set up after scandals at Maxwell and BCCI, and Cadbury issued a report on the problem in 1992.[12] A series of scandals in which shareholders and employees found they had been cheated spurred reforms that can be associated with the advent of corporate governance. Gradually, a list of principles took shape, and certain rules were established. These principles and rules came to govern both the organization and the exercise of power within corporations. Publicly traded British companies were especially targeted. At first, these rules bore most particularly on relations among CEOs, boards of directors, shareholders, and personnel. By now, however, they also cover the modes of operation of boards of directors and of the various committees within these boards, the control mechanisms that a corporation must submit to, the obligations of executives to inform and be accountable to the shareholders of their company, and even the duties of executives to certain categories of stakeholders, such as employees, suppliers, and bankers.[13]

The rise of corporate governance was thus accompanied by the production of new norms, especially at the level of national legislations. In the United States, the point of reference is the 2002 Sarbanes-Oxley Act, which was both the outcome of a decade of reflection on and experimentation in corporate governance as well as the direct consequence of the fraudulent bankruptcies of the energy company Enron, in 2001, and the telecommunications company WorldCom, in 2002. In France, two important laws, the Nouvelles Régulations Economiques (New Economical Regulations Act), passed May 15, 2001, and the Loi de Sécurité Financière (Financial Security Act), passed August 1, 2003, similarly gave concrete and obligatory content to rules in the commercial sector.

Moreover, by the end of the 1980s, the English-speaking business world had elaborated a corpus of recommendations (a "Code of best practice" in Great Britain and "Principles of corporate governance" in the United States). These efforts at self-regulation do not contradict state regulation; rather, the rules developed by the public and private sectors constantly interact with each other.

The traditional (and initial) model of corporate governance is predicated on the "shareholder value" of a company, that is, on the idea that the main aim of a business should be to satisfy the requirements of its shareholders. The maximum satisfaction of the shareholders is envisioned as the optimized profitability that these shareholders can expect from their investment. However, this first model is being seriously challenged by another model, predicated on the "partnership value" of the company. According to this second model, besides the satisfaction of its shareholders, a company must take into account the interests of its various stakeholders, namely, its employees, suppliers, and subcontractors, but also local authorities, and so on. Governance, then, is a mode of organizing cooperation among these various parties, notably through the arbitration of any possible conflicts of interest.

When the notion of governance made its way into the philanthropic sector, especially in the realm of international humanitarianism, it became an object of intense debate. Eventually, however, the idea emerged that the "partnership value" model was suitable for nonprofit entities. It was difficult, though, to establish the list of an NGO's stakeholders. At the head of this list, obviously, are the recipients of the organization's aid programs: the populations, groups, or communities for whose benefit the group was formed and should be maintained. Then comes a first circle of internal stakeholders composed of the NGO's members, employees, members of the board, supporters, and volunteers, including the staff members employed in the field, whether they are expatriates or nationals of the country where the NGO is working. A second circle includes private donors (individuals, foundations, and businesses), sources of public money, partner organizations in the field, and the various networks to which the organization belongs. The third circle involves local communities, cities, and districts, as well as nation-states of the global North and South. Finally, suppliers, transporters, and various contractors form a last outer circle.

The perspective of governance does not merely serve to delineate this general framework. More importantly, it focuses on the regulation of the relationships among all these different circles and parties. As for the main issues that such a perspective raises, they include: first, the functioning and performance of the various modes of governance; second, the types of certification and evaluation that can be used to assess and improve the governance of NGOs; third, the emphasis that NGOs should, or should not, put on their nonprofit or philanthropic character, both in terms of their legal status and of the definition of their social mission; and fourth, the mission of the president of the NGO, as well as the mode of hiring and role of the members of the board.

NGO GOVERNANCE AND NONGOVERNMENTAL POLICIES

STRATEGIC PLANNING, INSTITUTIONAL DEVELOPMENT, AND QUALITY CONTROL

Improving internal procedures was the first aspect of NGO governance that received considerable attention. From the standpoint of the sociology of organizations, NGOs seem to conform to the "professional bureaucracy" model theorized by Henry Mintzberg: they are characterized by weak formalization, decentralization, departmentalization by function, and (relative) standardization of qualifications.[14] NGOs are also characterized by a number of — what is often referred to as — "postbureaucratic" features, such as the valorization of participative functioning, the reduction of hierarchical levels, and a network structure.

However, this model only imperfectly frames the growing complexity of the processes in humanitarian, developmental, and environmental organizations that are working at the international level. For these organizations often manage several dozen projects in as many countries at the same time. Accordingly, the trend among these NGOs is to develop gradually their strategic planning, which, in turn, facilitates their institutionalization. More than simply improving internal management procedures, such planning aims to modify the functioning of NGOs. For that purpose, NGOs may require the assistance of major international consultants, who put their expertise and command of business consulting at the service of the nongovernmental sector. The advice provided by these consulting firms largely relies on very elaborate "benchmarking" techniques, comparing NGOs, and on the construction of mathematical models. Resorting to this technology enables NGOs to harmonize the functioning of various departments, foster long-term programs, decentralize decision-making and structures, and thus strengthen autonomy at various decision-making levels. As in the commercial sector, NGOs are then able to establish four- or five-year plans, with interim revisions and adjustments.

Although apparently of internal relevance, the ensuing reorganization of NGOs is likely to have an impact on their policy. For instance, the adoption of a particular model of governance can persuade an NGO to reduce the number of its projects, as well as the number of countries where it intervenes, in order to concentrate its means on certain zones or themes. (In Europe, NGOs such as Concern and GOAL have chosen this strategy.) But a preoccupation with good governance can lead to many other decisions as well, such as increasing the number of locally based employees at the expense of expatriates, or aiming to become the NGO of reference in one particular domain at the expense of other activities.

There is also a growing concern with the quality of services provided by NGOs: quality-control approaches aim as much to improve the content, performance, and credibility of programs as to develop a culture of quality at all levels of the NGO.

Finally, issues such as that of clarifying the decision-making process within the NGO and the gender policy of the organization also affect nongovernmental governance.

Should NGOs be encouraged to certify their governance practices by submitting themselves to external auditors or to rankings established by funding sources or even by the media? Within the NGO community, this question is still an object of debate. Those opposed to any form of external certification or ranking stress that no method of selecting, labeling, or grading NGOs will be neutral. They also contend that any such attempt might not only harm an NGO's capacity for swift responses, but also stifle its inventiveness. In other words, the critics of external evaluation contend that the latter could subject NGOs to a web of restrictive and counterproductive norms.

Yet, opposition notwithstanding, these evaluations are gaining ground. Some initiatives even come directly from NGOs. For example, in 2004, five American organizations specialized in the sponsoring of children (Children International, Christian Children's Fund, Plan USA, Save the Children, and World Vision International) decided to have themselves evaluated by two independent agencies, both of which belonged to the auditing group Social Accountability International. These audits were conducted both on the ground and at the NGOs' headquarters. The outcome of this process was the delivery in July 2005 of a "multi-stakeholder" certification. This new certificate (which authorizes these NGOs to affix a special seal to their materials and documents) confirms the auditors' assessment that these organizations are operating in accordance with various directives — starting with the InterAction standards mentioned above. Until then, InterAction only required its members to provide annual self-certification of their adherence to its standards. However, as a result of the initiative of the five NGOs, InterAction plans to impose stricter certification procedures on its other members.[15]

VOLUNTEERS AND PROFESSIONALS

Among the most sensitive questions relating to nongovernmental governance are that of the apportioning of volunteer and salaried work within the structure of the NGO as well as that of the relative weight and influence of the organization's chairperson and its board in relation to its permanent structure (composed of professionals, whether they are salaried staff or paid volunteers).

The positioning (some even speak of "attractiveness") of NGOs, particularly with respect to private donors and public funding sources, owes much less than before to the presence of known and influential personalities on their board of directors, or to the charisma or celebrity of their leaders. By now, the professionalism of these nonprofits — even though civic commitments and activism presided over their creation — and its consequences in terms of performance and quality of its operations have become a more determining factor, particularly for international NGOs. However, as NGOs increasingly espouse professional standards and stake their "attractiveness" on their ability to meet them, their evolution necessarily raises the question of the place left for civically motivated volunteers in the process of governance.[16] At the organizational level, in particular, the way in which voluntary membership should be articulated within the permanent structure of the NGO is an issue that arouses intense and recurrent debates.

One way of resolving this issue is to follow the example of MDM-France, which relies on an original system of "dual command": operational activities are necessarily comanaged by paid staff members and volunteers, both at the headquarters and in the field; the "mission head," however, is required to be an unpaid volunteer from the organization. This singular form of governance manages to balance the exigencies of professionalism and civic commitment that are both equally essential to the NGO's standing, but it also generates at least latent tensions in the relations between volunteers and salaried staff members — tensions that can affect the NGO's decision to maintain or cancel specific missions. Thus, while dual command is a strong identity marker for MDM-France, it has also been the cause of crises of governance. (Both of these aspects manifested themselves in 2004, when the outgoing leadership team was defeated in elections to the board of directors, principally because it wanted to put an end to this dual command.)

Rather than balancing the relative power of staff members and volunteers, a number of NGOs specializing in development projects have gradually made members and staff almost identical, mingling the former with the latter. But in such a configuration, there is some risk that project policies will be dictated largely by the need to meet salary obligations.

Managing the tensions between the volunteer and employee levels of an NGO is thus a crucial and delicate dimension of nongovernmental governance. At ACF-France, for instance, the crisis of governance that culminated in 2002 with the resignation of the president, Sylvie Brunel, was largely the result of a confrontation between volunteers and employees. This crisis threatened Action Contre la Faim–France's very existence. The ensuing financial crisis had a direct impact on the number and extent of its field missions. It took about two years for the organization to recover.

EXECUTIVE OR NONEXECUTIVE PRESIDENCY?

The status of executive officers within NGOs is another crucial problem. Considering the constraints weighing on these organizations, and particularly on their leadership, the question often arises of whether all the managers of a NGO should devote themselves full time to their tasks and be paid accordingly. Such a question does not involve the directors, who always are on the NGO payroll, but the president and some board members who are in charge of strategic missions for the NGO. Should they not be remunerated — really, not just symbolically — in accordance with their level of responsibility? The French branch of MSF pays a salary to its president.[17] By contrast, the executive president of MDM-France has always been a doctor, involved in humanitarian work but who is not paid by the NGO and still practices medicine. Because of the heavy professional and personal constraints entailed by this arrangement, the mandate of MDM's presidents rarely exceeds two years, which is short in terms of governance. Other NGOs where the president is not salaried, such as Handicap International, conceive the presidency as a nonexecutive position. The president of Handicap International is indeed weak compared to the paid hierarchy.

Finally, a new configuration has been emerging in the last several years among European NGOs, one that is exemplified by the approach of Jean-Christophe Rufin who chaired Action Contre la Faim–France from 2003 to 2006. A well-known novelist in Europe, Rufin (previously a doctor) is also an analyst and an essayist writing about humanitarianism. He is thus very familiar with the humanitarian community. Rufin was not an executive president at ACF-France: he did not interfere in daily operational decisions, which were the responsibility of the general director. However, he acted as a moderator and facilitator, representing the NGO to the outside world and using his own reputation to shape that of ACF—or at least to reshape it in the wake of the crisis of governance mentioned above. Moreover, he also defined the main strategic orientation of ACF, in collaboration with the board of directors. In short, ACF under Rufin's presidency constituted an arrangement where the president put his or her personal fame at the service of the NGO.[18]

The adoption of this last model might lead some organizations to appoint a managing deputy chairperson or a deputy general director with broad powers, while the president or chairperson would be chosen for his or her prestigious reputation and professional accomplishments, even if the latter fell outside the NGO's area of specialization. What would be required of such a president would consist—to quote Fischer Howe—of "a strategic vision for the organization and the capacity to attract, motivate and guide all those involved in order to realize this vision."[19]

THE ROLE OF BOARDS OF DIRECTORS AND THE SOCIOLOGY OF MEMBERS

The last theme crucial to the field of governance is that of the mandate given to the members of the board—in other words, the role that the different stakeholders of the organization wish to see them play. Should the members of the board have a political function that would consist of defining the overall strategy of the NGO—of shaping its operational, campaigning, and lobbying policies? Or should their tasks extend to following up on briefs with directly operational implications, and even acting as the ultimate authority for the various departments and offices of the NGO?

While both models exist in Europe, in the United States, the dominant tendency seems to run toward a growing disconnection between the board and the permanent structure—a tendency that is consistent with the American philanthropic tradition. According to John Carver, a specialist in the governance of organizations (in both the commercial and the nonprofit sector) and advocate of this model, the function of board members is not to assist the paid staff or to be the ultimate supervisors within the NGO, but to represent the interests of the stakeholders of the NGO—starting with the beneficiaries of its activities.[20] To that end, the members of the board may take on the charges of overseeing the activities of the NGO and ensuring that it is fulfilling its social mission effectively.

A complementary question about the boards of NGOs relates to the recruitment and background of their members. Should board members be specifically required to possess prior knowledge or concrete experience (or both) in the specific domain of the NGO?

Before being elected to the board, should they have been practitioners of development, humanitarian aid, human rights, or environmentalism, for example? Or, on the contrary, is it preferable that they come from other areas and thus bring external viewpoints? Opinions on this matter vary, but in any case, it is worth considering whether directors should be trained once they have been elected (if only to facilitate their comprehension of the increasingly complex stakes of the NGO).[21]

CONCLUSION

In the deregulated, global, chaotic atmosphere at the start of the twenty-first century, nongovernmental culture is still in a phase of research and experimentation with respect to governance. In the future, however, governance will increasingly figure on NGOs' agendas and the outlines of what nongovernmental governance will be (and will not be) for the next two or three decades will gradually become clearer. On the whole, this trend is positive, in that it entices NGO executives to anticipate and prevent possible breakdowns and dysfunctions within their organizations.

Evolving in a transnational framework and strengthening their commitment to accountability with respect to their beneficiaries and contributors, both private and public, NGOs will be better equipped to respond to the numerous challenges they face. And they will indeed need to be well-equipped, considering what confronts them — from the human and material consequences of natural catastrophes to humanitarian crises resulting from armed conflicts, and from the struggles against poverty, malaria, and AIDS to those for access to water, education, health, and essential medications.[22]

Translated by Susan Emanuel with the author.

1 MSF-France, *2005 Annual Report* (Paris: Médecins Sans Frontières, 2006), available online at www.msf.fr/site/bibli.nsf/documents/rap280505msffin. Few European NGOs do likewise. Still, these private funds come, to a significant extent, from collections taken up by MSF's partners in countries other than France (the United States and Japan, for example), which remit a proportional share of the funds thus raised. The American branch (MSF-USA, which is institutionally attached to the French office) thus plays an important role in financing MSF-France, even though the latter's net contribution has been diminishing for several years.

2 The CCD, a joint authority composed of representatives of the French government and those of French NGOs, has done this survey since 1986. The most recent one (which covers 2002 and 2003) has the private-to-public ratio at 63 percent to 36 percent. Commission Coopération Développement, *Argent et organisations de solidarité internationale 2002–2003* (Paris: Ministère des Affaires Étrangères, 2005), available online at www.diplomatie.gouv.fr/fr/IMG/pdf/Argent_OSI_2005_B.pdf. In 1991, the figures were very similar: 65 percent to 35 percent.

3 Carol Lancaster, *Transforming Foreign Aid: United States Assistance in the 21st Century* (Washington, D.C.: Institute for International Economics, 2000).

4 See, for example, Laëtitia Atlani-Duault (ed.), *Les ONG à l'heure de la bonne gouvernance* (Paris: Colin, 2005), and *Revue Internationale des Sciences Sociales* 178 (2003), a special issue titled "Les ONG et la gouvernance de la biodiversité."

5 For an examination of some references for constructing the legitimacy of an NGO, see Philippe Ryfman, *Les ONG* (Paris: La Découverte, 2004).

6 Jean-Hervé Bradol, "Action sous pressions," *Messages MSF* 137 (2005), pp. 12–13.

7 The exceptions are MSF-France, which withdrew among a few other NGOs. Coordination Sud is the equivalent of InterAction in the United States, but it has fewer resources, of course, and its influence is more limited. The two coordinating bodies have begun to make connections with each other.

8 Coordination Sud and Cécile Ziegle (ed.), *Guide synergie qualité: Propositions pour des actions humanitaires de qualité* (Paris: Coordination Sud, 2005).

9 Such a concern translates into the NGOs' adopting and conforming to the "quality initiative" detailed in a publication of Coordination Sud, entitled *Guide synergie qualité: Propositions pour des actions humanitaires de qualité*. This document lists five interdependent objectives for the NGOs included in the collective structure: 1. Orientations must be defined, actualized, and widely communicated; 2. Responsibilities must be defined, actualized, and communicated; 3. Information must be honest, reliable, and available; 4. Internal functioning and external relations must respect and promote the values of the NGO; 5. Potential problems must be identified, evaluated, and treated so as to diminish the probability of their occurring and limit their nefarious consequences.

10 The most recent edition dates from May 2005.

11 Guy Hermet, Ali Kazancigil, and Jean-François Prud'homme (eds.), *La gouvernance: Un concept et ses applications* (Paris: Karthala, 2005); its "meaning was and remains variable… sometimes also very contrived."

12 Adrian Cadbury, *Report of the Committee on the Financial Aspects of Corporate Governance* (London: Gee, 1992).

13 See Jean-Jacques Caussain, *Le gouvernement d'entreprise: Le pouvoir rendu aux actionnaires* (Paris: Litec, 2005); Joseph A. McCahery, Piet Moerland, Theo Raaijmakers, and Luc Renneboog (eds.), *Corporate Governance Regimes: Convergence and Diversity* (Oxford: Oxford University Press, 2002); and Randall Morck, *A History of Corporate Governance Around the World: Family Business Groups to Professional Managers* (Chicago: University of Chicago Press, 2005).

14 Henry Mintzberg, *The Structuring of Organizations: A Synthesis of the Research* (Englewood Cliff, NJ: Prentice-Hall, 1979).

15 Ken Giunta, *Five NGOs Set New Standard in Accountability*, Monday Developments, August 8, 2005 (Washington, D.C.: InterAction, 2005), p. 6.

16 Domestic activities are very important at MDM compared to other NGOs, especially in the field of discrimination, which it addresses via its "Mission France."

17 More precisely, the president's salary is paid by Epicentre, a PVO (private voluntary organization) that is an integral part of the MSF-France group (which includes other nonprofits, the real estate company that owns MSF's office buildings, and the commercial company that produces its audiovisual materials). Epicentre's essential activity is epidemiological research and personnel training. The chairperson of MSF-France occupies a precise job at Epicentre, depending on his or her personal qualifications, and performs real work. Still, this job is not full-time, and the president is partly at the disposal of the parent PVO (MSF-France), which in turn pays Epicentre a prorated amount corresponding to the amount of time the president spends working for MSF. This particular arrangement is unique to MSF.

18 Typically, the inverse is often true, particularly in Europe, except in the UK: the chairperson becomes famous in his or her own right (at least as concerns the NGO's domain of

activity); he or she owes this renown to the organization and benefits personally from the organization's celebrity.

19 Fisher Howe, *The Nonprofit Leadership Team: Building the Board–Executive Director Partnership* (San Francisco: Jossey-Bass, 2004).

20 John Carver, *Boards that Make a Difference : A New Design for Leadership in Nonprofit and Public Organizations,* 2nd ed. (San Francisco: Jossey-Bass, 1997).

21 Ludovic Bourbé, Marie Perroudon, and Jacques Perrot (eds.), *La gouvernance des organisations européennes de solidarité internationale: L'exemple du processus décisionnel d'ouverture et de fermeture des missions* (Lyon: Bioforce, 2003). This study shows that out of forty-four European NGOs, only a quarter of them offered such training to their boardmembers.

22 Thérèse Delpech, *L'ensauvagement: Le retour de la barbarie au XXIe siècle* (Paris: Grasset, 2005).

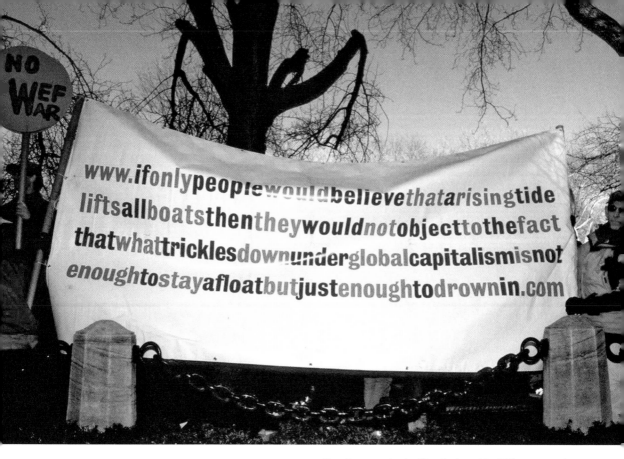

Boom! banner project by Oliver Ressler and David Thorne, as used in demonstrations against the World Economic Forum, New York, NY, January 2002.

Loose Bonds

Geert Lovink interviewed by Michel Feher

Geert Lovink is a media theorist and activist, Internet critic, and author of Dark Fiber *(2002),* Uncanny Networks *(2002), and* My First Recession *(2003). He has worked on various media projects in Eastern Europe and India. He is a member of the Adilkno collective, author of* Cracking the Movement *(1990) and* The Media Archive *(1992), and cofounder of Internet projects such as* The Digital City, Nettime, Fibreculture, *and* Incommunicado. *He is coorganizer of the tactical media festivals* Next Five Minutes. *He coinitiated recent conferences on the history of Web design, the critique of ICT for development, urban screens, Net porn, and creative industries research. Since 2004, he has been the director of the Institute of Network Cultures at Amsterdam Polytechnic (HvA) and associate professor in the media and culture department, University of Amsterdam. In 2005–2006, he was a fellow at the Berlin Institute for Advanced Study where he finished his latest Internet study,* Zero Comments *(2007).*

Let's start with the heroic beginnings of electronic networks. When did they appear and what was the political agenda — or, at least, what were the political hopes — of those who created them?

The history of the Internet is well-documented, yet an informed retrospective analysis of its concepts is still lacking. What we have seen thus far is a weak crossbreeding of academic postmodern cultural analysis and technology sales talk (note: not the technology itself). It is unfortunate that French philosophy has been misused in the context of our new media. What may have worked for painting and film failed dramatically in the case of the Internet. As a result, there is still no clear understanding, let alone a comprehensive study, of technolibertarianism, even though this philosophical sensibility dominated the 1990s. Because we are running after the facts, we now have to read Leo Strauss in order to understand the neoconservatives in power, but this latter group is a very different breed from the radical antistatist, promarket individualists of the 1990s. And understanding the political agenda of U.S. technohippies is not easy, especially for outsiders from Europe, Korea, or Nigeria. For it is not neoliberalism: Noam Chomsky, for one, is of no use in this context. For instance, the technopranksters fight for democracy, yet they fail to see the destructive nature of corporations. They love guns, but detest armies. They write free software while defending the freedom to spread Nazi propaganda. They define today's network architectures, but show no interest in conquering traditional positions of power. They do not like TV, yet they love multiplayer online adventure games. These are noteworthy and peculiar contradictions: the experiences that they inform should be mixed up neither with a neoliberal outlook nor with the good intentions of antineoliberal "media activists."

You claim that the electronic networkers of the 1990s became at once overly obsessed with state control and naively negligent of corporate infringement on their activities. Can you recount this "libertarian" turn of electronic networks politics? How does it relate to the simultaneous rise of the "third way" propounded by Clinton and Blair and of the dot-com economy?

Culturally speaking, early Internet culture has been shaped by young U.S.-American academics, mostly geeks and hackers. It is a white, male community of computer programmers that doesn't easily fit into the left-right schemes. The values of this hippie scene are surprisingly underresearched. Their key Web site, since 1998, has been Slashdot.[1] It's one of the most read sites on the Net. However, the scholarly literature about Slashdot looks only at its "open publishing" principles. The ways in which Slashdot diffuses its hard-core libertarian ideology by translating it into ostensibly technical issues remains an unreported factor in the global socialization of geeks. The key issue, to answer your question, is why the antiauthoritarian mentality of the 1960s and early 1970s focused its paranoid energies toward state control (the very state that financed them), whereas the critique of corporate domination was largely neglected. The IT world had become "libertarian" way before Clinton and Blair got in power, so I do not see a direct relation there. The only thing we could say is that by 1992–1993, a variety of forces had gained hegemonic status. I am reluctant to venture into a conspiracy theory, but books such as Paulina Borsook's *Cyberselfish* and Thomas Frank's *One Market under God* certainly give clues.[2] Richard Barbrook and Andy Cameron's famous essay "Californian Ideology," published in 1995, was part of the "*Wired* debate," but didn't add much insight.[3] For Barbrook and Cameron, as UK scholars, however, Blair policies were the exact opposite of the *Wired* ideology for the simple reason that for "third way" advocates there still is a role for a state, albeit a diminished one, whereas libertarians either are simply against state interventions and investments or refuse to admit that such interventions actually pervade the IT sector.

Mondo 2000, Wired's predecessor and competitor in the first months of 1993, had a more mellow, weird underground agenda and was at least open to progressive cultural issues. By mid-1992, Louis Rosetto, the publisher of *Wired*, had understood the Zeitgeist and suppressed any critical or intellectual concern. I witnessed this evolution from close up, because around that time, the *Wired* crew moved from Amsterdam, my hometown, to San Francisco. It meant quite a break, away from the cultural concerns of Old Europe, rapidly adapting the New Age agendas of people such as Peter Schwartz, Esther Dyson, Stewart Brand, and Kevin Kelly. Politically speaking, the magazine moved from alternative

CENTRALIZED
(A)

DECENTRALIZED
(B)

DISTRIBUTED
(C)

to conservative, with George Gilder and Newt Gingrich as its spokespersons. If one wants to dig into the archaeology of this metamorphosis, one should do a discourse analysis plus social-network analysis of the Technology, Entertainment, and Design (TED) conferences.[4] A key term here would be a comparison between progressive agendas predicated on the notion of change and the way in which these business gurus began styling themselves as "change leaders." Change, for them, meant to get access to money, which, in the United States, is in the hands of the "old" East Coast elites. Change in the 1990s was all about the merger of (venture) capital with technology. Obviously it was not social change that these people had in mind. They detested the power of the television networks, Hollywood, and Wall Street, but had little to say about the Microsoft monopoly and the unprecedented rise in power of global corporations.

Both the demise of the dot-com entrepreneurs and, even more dramatically, the advent of a new regime of global security after September 2001 mark the beginning of yet another phase in the short history of electronic networks. What do you see as the features and the main stakes of electronic network politics in the current era?

The dot-com crash, the corporate scandals around Enron and WorldCom, and 9/11 all came as a relief for the Internet as a whole. I am saying this with mixed feelings because I have often stated the opposite. The 2000–2001 events precipitated the sudden eviction of an aggressive business class that had become synonymous with the medium. These were often people who had moved into the Internet sector from other business backgrounds, and, luckily, they left as quickly as they arrived. We should not underestimate the size of this now-deceased greedy "virtual class" and the worldwide gold-rush atmosphere in which it came to be. What struck me was these people's lack of interest in the technical issues and even in the users of the technology. For them, the Internet was merely a vehicle to get rich quick. Once they left, we witnessed an interesting renaissance of the Net. Think of the rise of weblogs, wikis and Wikipedia, free software and open source, podcasting, Internet telephony (Skype), social networks such as Friendster, Orkut, and Flickr, and, yes, Google. Now investors look much more closely at what the hundreds of millions of users are actually doing online. Dot-com entrepreneurs had no time for their customers. Even though the Internet is said to move at the speed of light, the building of user communities needs time.

I understand what you are aiming at with your question, but we have to be aware that security and privacy concerns do not drive the Internet business. This goes back to the deep ambivalence of the geek coding class toward these issues. Hackers are concerned with privacy while admitting at the same time that there is no such thing. Remember: hackers write and fight viruses at the same time. They build the content filters for China to censor the Net and, at the same time, develop a program like Tor, which facilitates anonymous Web browsing.

For the sake of engaging you in a case study, how do you analyze the evolution of MoveOn.org, an entity initially constituted as a network of American citizens opposed

Types of networks from Paul Baran, *On Distributed Communications* (1964).

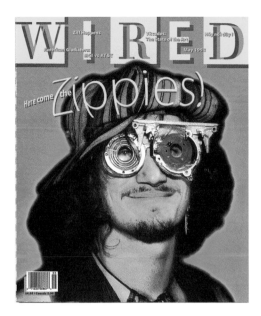

Wired (May 1994).

to the political exploitation of the Monica Lewinsky affair and now considered one of the most prominent agents of renewal on the left side of the U.S. Democratic party?

Over the summer, I read Joe Trippi's account of the Howard Dean campaign, *The Revolution Will Not Be Televised*.[5] The U.S.-American Internet campaign sphere is one that I am not intimately familiar with. To put it in friendly words: I do not have much in common with U.S. Democrats. What surprises me, however, is the efficiency and scale of such Web-based citizens' networks. What activists can learn from MoveOn.org is how one can set up and maintain large volunteer networks that can migrate from one campaign to the next. There is plenty of academic literature about the "learning organization." But how do we imagine a learning network? Social bonds are loose these days, and many campaigns have to start from scratch.

Electronic networks, insofar as they manage to sustain themselves without becoming networked organizations, are experiments both in sociality and in governance: at least, this is how your work invites us to look at them. So let me ask you, first, what you see as the distinctive features of network sociality — insofar as the network can neither be defined as a community nor reduced to a mere gathering site?

For the German theorist Christoph Spehr, the definition of free cooperation has to be negative. That's incredibly creative, to put negation center stage. For Spehr, we can speak of free cooperation only if members are able to leave the group voluntarily, without devastating consequences. I would like to say the same thing about network sociality. The absence of the social, the community, et cetera, is not something we should complain about. Loose ties are constitutional these days. We should stop reading them in terms of decline. If you want to organize the masses, you should both strengthen the ties in your neighborhood and, beyond that, prepare yourself for a sophisticated culture of indifference and noncommitment. Engagement comes in radically new ways. Networks are playgrounds; they are probes. A lot is happening — but please let's abandon all hope of recreating fixed social structures such as a party or a church. Networks are not the surrogates of nineteenth-century sociality. This T-shirt slogan says it all: "I Will Not Love You a Long Time." No more bonds meant to last until death do us part. Once we realize that, a whole new world opens up.

Second, regarding the governance of electronic networks, why do you think that organized networks are incompatible with the procedures of representative democracy, but have the potential to resist autocratic models such as those of the avant-garde party and the corporation? In other words, what do you see in the self-government of electronic networks that could foreshadow a postrepresentative democracy?

Networks need no outside representation. In the large world out there, network members have a multitude of memberships. They are not primarily concerned with formal relationships. This may sound like an adolescent gesture, as if networks haven't grown up and refuse to play by the rules of the adult world, dominated by institutions. That's one way of looking at it. But, of course, such a complaint itself is a fraud, because it is full of immature resentment. We're facing two contradictory tendencies here: networks are gaining importance and their numbers are rising exponentially; however, their culture remains deeply informal. They are pervasive and invisible at the same time. Conspiratorial thinkers and Jesuits would not see this as a contradiction, but in a world that claims to be open, accountable, and transparent, it is. The level of commitment shown by members of networks remains generally low. Their involvement can be passionate, but it often is topical and temporary. What Ned Rossiter and I have written about "organized networks" is rather speculative and starts with a simple question: Do networks need incorporation in order to fully operate in today's society? NGOs went through that process of incorporation, but, thus far at least, networks did not. If we take the network seriously as a form of social and political organization, and we should, then we should expect some form of legal and financial incorporation. The other issue is internal power relations. Networks claim to be open and egalitarian, but very often they are not.

1 See http://slashdot.org.

2 Paulina Borsook, *Cyberselfish: A Critical Romp Through the Terribly Libertarian Culture of High Tech* (New York: PublicAffairs, 2000); Thomas Frank, *One Market under God: Extreme Capitalism, Market Populism, and the End of Economic Democracy* (New York: Doubleday, 2000).

3 Richard Barbrook and Andy Cameron, "Californian Ideology" (1995), in Peter Ludlow (ed.), *Crypto Anarchy, Cyberstates,* *and Pirate Utopias* (Cambridge, MA: MIT Press, 2001), or see www.hrc.wmin.ac.uk/theory-californianideology.html for multiple versions of the essay.

4 See www.tedmed.com/history.html.

5 Joe Trippi, *The Revolution Will Not Be Televised: Democracy, the Internet, and the Overthrow of Everything* (New York: Regan Books, 2004).

Human Rights, Testimony, and Transnational Publicity

Meg McLagan

In the period between the end of the Cold War in 1989 and the events of September 11, 2001, human rights became the dominant moral narrative by which world politics was organized. Inspired by the momentous political and cultural transformations taking place at the time, from the fall of the Berlin Wall to the spread of global communications technologies, promoters of human-rights discourse optimistically predicted that a transnational public sphere dedicated to democratic values would emerge. (We now know, of course, that such predictions were wrong, as early post–Cold War hopes gave way to the harsh realities of contemporary globalization.)

In order to help create the transnational public sphere they envisioned, international human-rights activists deployed a number of strategies, among them the production and circulation of testimonies by victims of rights abuses.

A testimony is a first-person narrative in which an individual's account of bodily suffering at the hands of oppressive governments or other agents comes to stand for the oppression of a group. Rooted in the Christian notions of witnessing and of the body as vehicle of suffering, testimony is a deeply persuasive cultural form that animates and moves Western sensibilities. Although testimony has long played an important part in rights advocacy (dating back to abolitionism), its use grew in the 1990s, when testimonies proliferated in multiple genres and arenas, from written texts to film and video documentaries to live performances and face-to-face encounters at activist meetings, NGO forums, and governmental hearings.[1] This essay explores this phenomenon, focusing on the role of several mediated forms of testimony, such as "cine-testimonials" (testimony on film or video) and online testimony, in activists' attempts to construct a transnational public.

While media are recognized as being critical to the general diffusion of human-rights norms and values, especially in the post-Second World War period, relatively

The Nakamata Coalition, comprised of ten tribal groups in the Philippines, is learning to harness digital technology to defend its members' rights in one of the poorest and most remote places on earth. From the film *Seeing is Believing: Handicams, Human Rights and the News*, codirected by Katerina Cizek and Peter Wintonick (www.seeingisbelieving.ca/press/stills).

little scholarly work exists that adequately addresses their role in the making of contemporary human-rights claims.[2] This neglect can be attributed to two things: first, a tendency to treat human rights as "something out there" waiting to be realized legally or philosophically, rather than as a flexible and expansive category through which politico-ethical claims are made and sociopolitical transitions are accomplished; second, a tendency to overlook the fact that media are not merely conduits for social forces and do not simply express social realities, but possess a logic and power that is itself constitutive of thought, identity, and action. One implicit aim of this essay, therefore, is to counter rights legalism by demonstrating the centrality of media (and cultural production) to the human-rights movement.

To render something public once meant submitting it to the critical judgment of others; in recent years, publicity has gained new meanings — making something public is the result of a "bewildering array of spatial and technical mediations." As Arvind Rajagopal notes,

> the effect of the means and modes of reproduction, whether analog or digital, electronic or mechanical, and the space of an event, whether in a shopping mall, a crowd, [or] a city square, or, for that matter, in a broadcast image or a Web site, all shape the experience of publicity in significant and different ways. The kinds of visibility a public event has are not secondary to its being public; rather, they condition the forms of publicity mobilized.[3]

The taxonomy of testimony proposed in this essay underscores Rajagopal's observation that analysis of public texts, events, and practices must be form sensitive. Testimony can work through the enumeration of facts, as well as through emotionally laden narratives of suffering; each entails a different kind of signification. Although human-rights activists often deploy both kinds simultaneously, the larger point is that testimony is not a transparent genre or practice, as the following discussion of its mediation in various forms demonstrates.[4]

Analysis of the relation between human-rights testimonies and transnational publicity thus involves bringing aesthetic questions about formal semiotic properties and generic conventions to bear on considerations about how testimonies generate action outside the textual event itself. In this essay, I argue that human-rights testimonies can be understood as a form of political communication, that is, a means through which ethical arguments or claims are made and collectivities are hailed and potentially persuaded and mobilized.

TESTIMONY AS DOCUMENTARY EVIDENCE

The discovery and representation of information on human-rights abuses through specific forms of realism is central to most human-rights work. Indeed, human-rights activists and organizations are first and foremost "collectors, filterers, translators, and presenters of information regarding human rights violations."[5] The underlying assumption is that the circulation of such information generates political action, whether it be through direct pressure on governments or corporations to change their policies or through the mobilization of individuals on a grassroots level. Although the naive epistemology about exposure and revelation upon which this belief is based has been challenged in recent years by situations in which knowledge has actually failed to produce action—most notably the war in Bosnia, the genocide in Rwanda in 1994, and, more recently, the American occupation of Iraq—it nevertheless remains a guiding principle of traditional human-rights politics.[6]

In the early years of Amnesty International USA, activists devoted a huge amount of their energies to gathering specific data about violations, which they analyzed according to human-rights principles and put in the form of written reports. These "thick rivers of fact" were circulated to governments and the press as evidence of their claims.[7] Activists' reliance on "documentary rhetoric"—realist forms of representation and conventions of documentation—presents a problem in that abuses are never clear-cut; there are always contradictions between human-rights classifications of violence and how violence actually plays out on the ground.[8] In order to manage the instability of the category on which their claims are based, human-rights activists formulate their reports using abstract universal discourses and a particular style of journalistic realism. In his writing on human-rights reports, Richard Wilson notes that the genre presents information as if it were simply factual and transparent; claims are supported with numerous references to how sources are checked, to international human rights standards, and to previous reports.[9] By presenting their findings in this way, NGOs are able to appear credible (and their information objective), and in so doing, they "cultivate a veneer of independence and impartiality in the international arena, which helps legitimize their assertions about the need for human rights norms."[10] In recent years, this orthodox insistence on revelation and documentation has come under considerable pressure, for instance in the context of truth commissions, which some have argued enable a process of forgetting—rather than the prevention of forgetting—crimes against humanity and human-rights violations.

Seeing Is Believing: Handicams, Human Rights, and the News, a documentary film directed by Katerina Cizek and Peter Winotick, is an instructive look at the role of digital video in documenting human-rights abuses around the world.[11] Filipino political scientist Alex Magno sets up the broader framework of the piece with his observation that video cameras are simply part of a long line of new communications technologies or "small media" that have played a critical part in various political revolutions around the world, from audiocassettes in Iran in 1979 to faxes in China in 1989 to e-mail and text messages in the Philippines in 2001.[12]

Gillian Caldwell, the executive director of the New York–based human-rights media organization Witness, elaborates on Magno's point, underscoring the importance of video images gathered by activists as visual evidence of human-rights violations. Drama is provided by the story of a Filipino activist named Joey who works closely with a coalition of indigenous people's groups known as the Nakamata Coalition. First Joey is shown training members of the coalition to document their struggles with local plantation owners over land in Mindanao; then coalition members take the camera themselves to record a meeting with some officials. The practice of documenting oral transactions on video has emerged as an important one for indigenous people who view such transactions as contractually binding within their own societies. By videotaping discussions about land claims, for instance, nonliterate activists create records they can use when agreements between parties break down.[13] Soon after the coalition training process finishes, violence breaks out, and the camera provided by Witness is there to record it all.[14]

At the heart of this film is a theory of truth and transparency that is premised on two things: the authenticity of experience (I was there, I witnessed it, therefore it is true) and a commitment to gathering and displaying visible evidence. Yet as countless writers on documentary photography and film point out, the truth status of images has always depended on critical contextualization. Images do not create meaning without framing, a point perhaps most starkly illustrated by the various readings of the video footage elicited by the prosecution and the defense during the trials of the police officers charged with beating Rodney King.[15] Ilan Ziv's documentary *Consuming Hunger* further underscores the need for contextual information to educate audiences about what they are actually seeing.[16] Although the transparency attributed to video evidence parallels that attributed to legalistic realist forms such as written human-rights reports, human-rights testimonials on film (or "cine-testimonials") can be distinguished

Video still of Los Angeles police officers beating Rodney King, March 3, 1991, in Los Angeles, California, from an amateur video shot by George Holliday (CNN via Getty Images).

by the use of explicit framing devices that supplement images with specifically targeted information aimed at provoking change.

What happens when the documentation is done not by the victims of human-rights abuses but by the perpetrators? Such was the case with the now-iconic photographs of detainees taken by U.S. soldiers at the Abu Ghraib prison in Iraq in 2003. These low-resolution images, made with the near-ubiquitous cell-phone cameras then carried by many Americans in Iraq (which have since been forbidden by the army), were not just the means through which humiliation and abuse were revealed, but also a part of the abuse itself. Or as Allen Feldman put it, "The photographs of American soldiers humiliating and terrorizing Iraqi detainees are not incidental documentary records or a recreational pastime of the jailors, but central to the meaning of the war and occupation"; they are part of America's war of "visual dominance."[17] Of course, it is ironic that this "inconvenient evidence" emerged and circulated globally, given the Bush administration's "highly controlled visual strategies," which were used to sell the war and then to prevent the American public from seeing images of Iraqi civilian casualties or of dead American servicemen and women in coffins.[18]

TESTIMONY, AFFECT, AND ETHICAL ARGUMENT

In *Argument and Change in World Politics: Ethics, Decolonization, and Humanitarian Intervention,* Neta Crawford explores the consequential role of argument in world politics. Her theory focuses on the place of ethical arguments in fostering changes in long-standing practices of oppression, such as colonialism, slavery, and forced labor: "Ethical arguments concern how to act in a particular situation so as to be doing good, assuming that the good has been defined through cultural consensus or meta-argument."[19] They operate through an assertion that an "existing normative belief or moral conviction ought to be applied in a particular situation."[20] She points out that assertions that slavery was not "natural" and contradicts Christian principles, for instance, were persuasive because they were emotionally appealing — they played on and resonated with audiences' underlying ethical and moral beliefs.

The use of testimony by abolitionists can be seen as an early precursor of the use of testimony by human rights activists since the Second World War.[21] Like slave narratives, human-rights testimonies are important vehicles through which ethical arguments are made. They use symbols, images, and accounts of individual experiences of suffering to engage their audiences affectively and to persuade them of a cause's moral worth.[22]

The body (and its pain) is a necessary medium in human-rights work, because it is what people have in common with others. Testimony is premised on the belief that pain is universal.[23] This belief in the universality of pain and its effectiveness as a tool for creating solidarity is underscored by researchers who have found that torture is the easiest human-rights issue on which to campaign.[24] Testimony creates an intersubjective space for exchange in which identification with a suffering "other" can take place. Through our identification, we become connected to a political project and can be moved to action. As Alison Brysk notes, "A message can foment change by creating an alternative reality, transferring daily experience to a different realm in which it is valued and thus opening the recipient to consider a new social order."[25] In this sense, human-rights testimonies are performative — they make ethical claims on viewers and listeners and cultivate potential ethical actors in the global arena.

This observation is perhaps best exemplified by the video *Testimony: Annie Lennox in Conversation with Palden Gyatso*.[26] Produced and directed by Annie Lennox, the well-known Scottish singer from the Eurythmics, the video documents the testimony of Palden Gyatso, a monk from Tibet who was imprisoned after the Chinese takeover in 1959. A large portion of the half-hour program is devoted to Gyatso's tale of his arrest and mistreatment by Chinese authorities over the years, including torture with an electric cattle prod made in Britain. At one point, Gyatso pulls out several torture instruments that he brought with him from Tibet. (It is never explained how the monk managed that.) He leans forward and demonstrates to Lennox the way the thumb cuffs work. Lennox, for her part, leans forward too, watching and listening attentively. In this moment, testimony functions as a kind of intercultural technology, bringing together individuals from different worlds through the medium of pain.

Testimonial documentaries thus work on an affective level by exposing audiences to stories of pain with which they cannot help but identify on the basis of the embodiment or corporeality they have in common. They also work on another level of signification, one that reinforces the first. As "a discourse about the world," as Bill Nichols puts it, documentaries show us situations and events "that are recognizably part of a realm of shared experience, the historical world as we know and encounter it, or as we believe others to encounter it."[27] The experience of documentary "can be a force unto itself and move us beyond itself, toward that historical arena of which it is part."[28] In other words, engagement with documentary can extend "beyond the moment of viewing into social praxis itself."[29]

How is this effect achieved? The answer begins with the exceptionality of documentary's referentiality and the materiality of the indexical bond that exists between the photographic image and the object in the historical world to which it refers. What is seen on film can seem "to bear indexical links to another world with autonomy and specificity of its own,"[30] although, as the Rodney King video proves, even "raw" video footage doesn't guarantee a particular meaning. This sense of a referential link creates a sense of awe that makes it easy to forget that the film is a system of signs, not a direct, unmediated duplication of reality. The result, Nichols suggests, is a constant oscillation between the duplication of reality and the reality of the duplication. The tendency to forget that the filmic reality remains a construct, an approximation and re-presentation of a profilmic reality to which it does not grant truly direct, unimpeded access, however, is what gives viewers of realist documentaries such pleasure: for the time being, their knowledge of this fact is suspended, and they can surrender themselves to the immediacy of the reality on-screen.

Much has been written about "resemblance" in the documentary aesthetic. One strand of documentary theory in recent years has tried to recuperate realist film by making an argument for the politicizing potential of documentary based on its "aesthetics of similarity."[31] Jane M. Gaines, for example, uses the term "political mimesis" to describe the process whereby a sensuous link is formed between bodies represented on-screen and bodies in the audience.[32] Here she is building on the work of the film theorist Linda Williams, who writes about film genres that "make the body do things" through a kind of involuntary mimicry of the emotion or sensation of the body on-screen; for example, "horror films make us scream, melodrama makes us cry, and porn films make us come."[33] According to Gaines, realist political documentaries work by performing a mimesis; that is, they produce emotion in the spectator in and through conventionalized imagery of struggle. Through an indexical identification with the characters on-screen, then, spectators are "poised to intervene." As she is careful to point out, however, shared cultural and historical values, and not the indexical image alone, are what lead viewers to sympathetic action. In other words, political mimesis is possible because an audience experiences the same set of political, historical, and cultural forces. Realism, then, is a device that, through the process of political mimesis, acts on a politicized audience, extending the community of activists.

I suggest that human rights testimonies on film and video achieve their representational efficacy through the process of political mimesis Gaines describes. By producing and circulating these texts, activists explicitly seek to create intersubjective spaces through which processes of political mimesis can occur and sympathy can be evoked and performed.[34] It is in this sense that a transnational "witnessing public" is constituted around human-rights trauma through testimony.[35]

TRANSNATIONAL PUBLICS AND THE BRANDING OF HUMAN RIGHTS

The global spread of electronic and new digital technologies over the last two decades has transformed the ways social movements organize their relationship to publicity.[36] Human-rights activists have been in the forefront of the creation of a new kind of media activism, one that not only makes sophisticated and innovative use of techniques of celebrity and publicity through a wide range of forms, including older analog media, such as print, photography, and film, and through new digital media, such as the Internet, digital video, mobile-phone photography, and video blogs, but that also involves the creation of new organizational structures that provide a kind of scaffolding for the production and distribution of these media. Indeed, a whole new arena of social practice has emerged around human-rights media, from organizations that provide media training to activists, such as Witness, the SPIN Project, and the Digital Freedom Network, to those that provide outlets for distribution, such as the International Human Rights Watch Film Festival and MediaRights. These organizations help activists channel their messages to their intended audiences, whether those audiences are found in classrooms, watching home videos, in movie theaters, on the Internet, or in official forums, whether governmental (for instance, congressional), intergovernmental (such as the United Nations), or nongovernmental. In providing the means for the production and distribution of human-rights media, these new organizational forms are contributing to the creation of a new circulatory matrix or platform through which testimonies can summon witnessing publics.[37]

This aspect of the human-rights movement builds on a long history of pioneering work by Amnesty International, which was the first group to attempt to "brand" its organization through the creation of a logo in the 1970s. The explosion of rights-oriented digital media in the second half of the 1990s represented an expansion of this kind of image politics, with human-rights activists self-consciously deploying complex rhetorical strategies borrowed from advertising. Before the creation of the World Wide Web, political activists used the Internet to connect to each other via e-mail, newsgroups, and chat rooms; the "virtual politics" carried out online was a largely logocentric affair.[38] Since then, as it has become faster, easier, and cheaper to send visual data electronically, there has been a seismic shift in the political use of networked computers. Today, activists of all stripes recognize the necessity of having a presence online—well-designed Web sites are now assumed to be key "portals" into activism, especially by members of the younger generation, who take the existence of the technology for granted. In the case of human-rights Web sites, information and testimonies are increasingly presented not in a gritty, realist, documentary style, but embedded in such objects as Flash graphics and supplemented by downloadable MP3 audio files—strategies that pivot not on the emotional identification discussed above, but on different forms of signification.

The significance of this shift in relation to age and generation was brought home to me in my teaching a few years ago when I asked students in an undergraduate class on human rights to pick out their favorite human-rights Web sites. I was interested in what students thought about the sites' organization and aesthetic strategies, as well as what conclusions they might draw about the sites' potential efficacy as tools to promote human rights. One of sites we explored together was www.stoptorture.org, a project of Amnesty International. On the bottom of the screen were the words "Click here to stamp out torture."[39] Absurd as the proposition that one simple click could stop such a practice might appear to me, none of my students seemed to question the claims of sites promising visitors this kind of fast and easy activism. The point was underscored when we looked at the site of Group 133, a local Amnesty International group based in the Boston area that was responsible for organizing a campaign to free fourteen Tibetan nuns imprisoned by the Chinese for demanding their homeland's independence. Group 133 launched the site www.drapchi14.org in December 2001. I was initially interested in the site after reading something about its innovative use of MP3 files. While in prison, the fourteen young women managed secretly to make a tape recording of songs calling for Tibetan independence; the tape was smuggled out of the Drapchi prison and eventually landed on the desk of Robert Barnett, the cofounder of the now-defunct

Tibet Information Network, in London.[40] After removing the names of the women on the tape in order to protect their identities, Barnett made the tape available to human-rights groups interested in the nuns' situation, including Group 133.

Drawing on Amnesty International's "prisoners of conscience" model, Group 133's Drapchi 14 campaign was designed to publicize the nuns' situation and, in so doing, to win their release. In an interview, one of the group's organizers, Carl Williams, adopted a marketing metaphor to describe what they were doing: "If you want to use the marketing term 'branding'…to get a person's name out there makes it much more difficult to torture or kill that person," Williams told the *Boston Herald.*[41]

Williams's comment about branding prisoners of conscience raises an interesting set of issues that are worth spelling out briefly. First, what does it mean for human-rights advocates to articulate their politics using an advertising term or commercial idiom? Like the subjects of countless human-rights documentaries, the individuals represented on the Drapchi 14 site are victims whose stories of suffering are meant to provoke readers' identification and to stimulate political action. Yet the way they are represented — that is, through the techniques of celebrity and advertising — transforms their meaning. Or does it? Could there be different ways of interpreting or decoding the relationship between form and content such that what strikes one generation as the "aestheticization of politics" strikes another as a new way to reconcile political goals and capitalist aims using a pervasive and influential medium? For those who have grown up in the post-1970s era, one marked by the growth of social marketing, is this mode of political communication simply taken for granted? Do teenagers and people in their twenties simply possess a different aesthetic, as Lev Manovich suggests in his writing on the use of Flash software in Web design, than that of previous generations, who located gritty politics in realist representation?[42] Indeed, can the continuing evolution of technological and aesthetic strategies and the consequent production of new political forms be mapped in terms of generational shifts?

More work needs to be done on the link between the emergence of new commercial venues in which human-rights testimonies circulate — for example, in the Benetton commercials on MTV — and their forms of signification. Clearly, encountering testimonies in such contexts challenges our sense that such material belongs in the so-called rational public sphere where citizens deliberate on political issues. The question is how and whether deeply moral and politically contested issues can be meaningfully expressed in commercial culture using commercial language. Given that it is our language, how do we effectively suffuse it with meanings that resist the rhetoric of advertising, which is designed specifically not to tell the truth or to convey complex or contradictory ideas? Does the option to "click here" merely position us as consumers who are choosing between predetermined possibilities online, or is it a meaningful way of taking "action"?

A second issue linked to the idea of branding victims of human-rights abuses is efficacy. In *No Logo: Taking Aim at the Brand Bullies,* Naomi Klein examines some of the

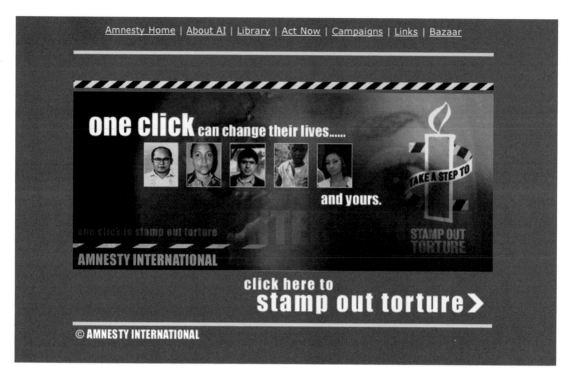

Stoptorture.org entices visitors with the promise of direct action
through the phrase: "Click here to stamp out torture."

limits and contradictions of what she calls "brand-based politics," by which she means antiglobalization activism that focuses on individual companies, such as Nike, Shell, McDonald's, and Starbucks.[43] Klein notes that although targeting popular brand-name corporations has been successful, these sorts of campaigns can have unintended and contradictory consequences (for example, companies often end up spending more time and money on publicity than on internal reform, or people decide they must consume more ethically and don't do much else). Similarly, by focusing a campaign on individual sufferers of human-rights abuses who have been branded in a certain way on these sites, activists run the risk of freeing certain people, but not necessarily achieving the long-term effect they desire—forcing governments to change their practices. For example, China released well-known members of the Drapchi 14 on the condition that they leave the country.[44] This is part of a much broader Chinese policy toward dissidents that enables the government to quiet Western criticism of its poor human-rights record without actually having to make major changes. Once the individuals are released, the pressure on the Chinese government is usually lessened, and attention is focused else-where. Thus, although activists are always extremely happy to be able to secure the freedom of individual dissidents, there are clear limits to the usefulness of deploying publicity in this manner.

CONCLUSION

I began by noting that human-rights activists often deploy various genres of testimony simultaneously, each of which circulates in a particular arena, reaching a particular audience. I want to conclude by suggesting that we think about this practice in terms of activists' use of different "registers" to construct political issues. These registers feed off and at times clash with one another in interesting and productive ways. For instance, logocentric and realist forms of documentary evidence and testimony continue to play a fundamental role in the work done by human-rights lawyers; they remain power-fully persuasive to congressional committees, international legal bodies, and nongov-ernmental organizations that seek to influence policy, rather than mass audiences. Human-rights documentary films and videos, although they rely on a similar concept of visible evidence, are visual media and, as such, have a capacity to generate emotion in audiences through evocative storytelling and affective imagery. Activists use this form to mobilize new publics around individuals who function as "nodal points" in a transna-tional network of identification and solidarity.[45] Through victims' on-screen narratives or testimonies, witnesses are situated as potential ethical actors who might intervene in the situation that produced the suffering that is on display.

Finally, new media refashion prior media forms, such as writing, film, and photog-raphy, and this process of "remediation" upends old ideas about subjects and partic-ipants, producers and texts, that underpin theories about how media work.[46] In the case of human-rights Web sites, instead of occupying just one position, readers occupy multiple, shifting positions (voyeur, consumer, activist). How does this plural position-ing square with the argument made above that human-rights media offer one subject position, that of the witness with an ethical responsibility? Understanding the ways digital activism might reshape the possible horizon of identities and actions that can be produced is critical to making sense of the new arenas of practice and publicity that are emerging around human rights.

1 The spread of human-rights testimonies also contributed to a more general cultural trend that led Renata Salecl to describe the 1990s as "the decade of testimonies." See Renata Salecl, "Why One Would Pretend to Be a Victim of the Holocaust," *Other Voices* 2, no. 1 (2000). Available online at www.othervoices.org/2.1/salecl/wilkomirski.html. See also Geoffrey Hartman, "Tele-suffering and Testimony in the Dot Com Era," in Barbie Zelizer (ed.), *Visual Culture and the Holocaust* (New Brunswick, NJ: Rutgers University Press, 2001), pp. 111–26.

2 See Meg McLagan, "Introduction: Making Human Rights Claims Public," *American Anthropologist* 108, no. 1 (2006), pp. 191–95, and Mark Philip Bradley and Patrice Petro (eds.), *Truth Claims: Representation and Human Rights* (New Brunswick, NJ: Rutgers University Press, 2002).

3 Personal communication. Thanks to Arvind Rajagopal for sharing his thoughts on "publicity and its careers" with me.

4 See Ann Cvetkovich, *An Archive of Feelings: Trauma, Sexuality, and Lesbian Public Cultures* (Durham, NC: Duke University Press, 2003), p. 167, for a discussion of this point in relation to trauma theorists' claim that testimony is an "impossible genre, an attempt to represent the unrepresentable."

5 Margaret E. Keck and Kathryn Sikkink, *Activists Beyond Borders: Advocacy Networks in International Politics* (Ithaca, NY: Cornell University Press, 1998), p. 3.

6 See Thomas Keenan, "Publicity and Indifference: Media, Surveillance, 'Humanitarian Intervention,'" in Thomas Y. Levin, Ursula Frohne, and Peter Weibel (eds.), *CTRL [SPACE]: Rhetorics of Surveillance from Bentham to Big Brother* (Cambridge, MA: MIT Press, 2002), pp. 544–61.

7 Kenneth Cmiel, "The Emergence of Human Rights Politics in the United States," *Journal of American History* 86, no. 3 (1999), pp. 1231–50.

8 Wendy S. Hesford and Wendy Kozol, "Introduction," in Hesford and Kozol (eds.), *Just Advocacy?: Women's Human Rights, Transnational Feminisms, and the Politics of Representation* (New Brunswick, NJ: Rutgers University Press, 2005), pp. 1–29.

9 See Richard Wilson, *Human Rights, Culture and Context: Anthropological Perspectives* (London: Pluto, 1997).

10 See Ann Marie Clark, *Diplomacy of Conscience: Amnesty International and Changing Human Rights Norms* (Princeton, NJ: Princeton University Press, 2001), on the role of Amnesty International USA in the formation of international human-rights norms.

11 Katerina Cizek and Peter Wintonick, *Seeing Is Believing: Handicams, Human Rights, and the News* (New York: First Run/Icarus Films, 2002).

12 For more on this topic, see Annabelle Sreberny-Mohammadi and Ali Mohammadi, *Small Media, Big Revolution: Communication, Culture, and the Iranian Revolution* (Minneapolis: University of Minnesota Press, 1994), a seminal study of "small media" during the Iranian revolution. See also Craig Calhoun, *Neither Gods nor Emperors: Students and the Struggle for Democracy in China* (Berkeley: University of California Press, 1994), on the importance of faxes and CNN during the events in China in 1989, and Vincente L. Rafael, "The Cell Phone and the Crowd: Messianic Politics in the Contemporary Philippines," *Public Culture* 15, no. 3 (2003), pp. 399–425, on the use of cell-phone text messages during the uprising against President Joseph Estrada in the Philippines in 2001.

13 See Faye Ginsburg, "'From Little Things Big Things Grow': Indigenous Media and Cultural Activism," in Richard G. Fox and Orin Starn (eds.), *Between Resistance and Revolution: Cultural Politics and Social Activism* (New Brunswick, NJ: Rutgers University Press, 1997), pp. 118–44, for more on the use of video in indigenous communities.

14 For more on Witness, see Sam Gregory, "Transnational Storytelling: Human Rights, Witness, and Video Advocacy," *American Anthropologist* 108, no. 1 (2006), pp. 195–204.

15 For more on the use of video in the Rodney King trials, see Allen Feldman, "From Desert Storm to Rodney King via ex-Yugoslavia: On Cultural Anaesthesia," in C. Nadia Seremetakis (ed.), *The Senses Still: Perception and Memory as Material Culture in Modernity* (Chicago: University of Chicago Press, 1996), pp. 87–108; Avital Ronell, "Video/Television/Rodney King: Twelve Steps Beyond the Pleasure Principle," *Differences* 4, no. 2 (1992), pp. 1–15; and Bill Nichols, "The Trials and Tribulations of Rodney King," *Blurred Boundaries: Questions of Meaning in Contemporary Culture* (Bloomington: Indiana University Press, 1994), pp. 17–42.

16 Ilan Ziv, *Consuming Hunger* (Maryknoll, NY: Maryknoll World Video Library, 1988).

17 Allen Feldman, "Abu Ghraib: Ceremonies of Nostalgia," *Open Democracy*, October 18, 2004. Available online at www.opendemocracy.net/media-abu_ghraib/article_2163.jsp.

18 On "inconvenient evidence," see Brian Wallis, *Inconvenient Evidence: Iraqi Prison Photographs from Abu Ghraib* (New York: International Center of Photography, 2004). On the Bush administration, see Wendy Hesford, "Staging Terror," *The Drama Review* 50, no. 3 (Fall 2006). It is even more ironic that the U.S. military appears to have had an easier time controlling professional journalists than the civilian personnel and contractors working for it. See Peter Howe, "Amateur Hour," *The Digital Journalist*, June 2004, www.digitaljournalist.org/issue0406/howe.html, and Susan Sontag, "Regarding the

Torture of Others," *New York Times Magazine,* May 23, 2004.

19 Neta Crawford, *Argument and Change in World Politics: Ethics, Decolonization, and Humanitarian Intervention* (Cambridge: Cambridge University Press, 2002), p. 24.

20 *Ibid.*

21 See the discussion of abolitionism as an early form of transnational advocacy in Keck and Sikkink, *Activists Beyond Borders,* pp. 39–78.

22 Meg McLagan, "Affective Politics" (manuscript).

23 See Elaine Scarry, *The Body in Pain: The Making and Unmaking of the World* (New York: Oxford University Press, 1985), in which she argues, contra Stanley Cohen and others, for the difficulty of translating pain across the membranes between bodies.

24 See Stanley Cohen, *States of Denial: Knowing about Atrocities and Suffering* (Cambridge: Polity, 2001), and "Government Responses to Human Rights Reports: Claims, Denials, and Counterclaims," *Human Rights Quarterly* 18, no. 3 (1996), pp. 517–43.

25 Alison Brysk, "'Hearts and minds': Bringing Symbolic Politics Back In," *Polity* 27, no. 4 (1995), p. 560.

26 Annie Lennox, *Testimony: Annie Lennox in Conversation with Palden Gyatso* (n.p.: Television Trust for the Environment, 1998).

27 Bill Nichols, *Representing Reality: Issues and Concepts in Documentary* (Bloomington: Indiana University Press, 1991), p. x.

28 *Ibid.,* p. xvi.

29 *Ibid.,* p. x.

30 Bill Nichols, *Ideology and the Image* (Bloomington: Indiana University Press, 1981), p. 238.

31 Feldman, "From Desert Storm to Rodney King."

32 Jane M. Gaines, "Political Mimesis," in Jane M. Gaines and Michael Renov (eds.), *Collecting Visible Evidence* (Minneapolis: University of Minnesota Press, 1999), p. 90.

33 Linda Williams (ed.), *Viewing Positions: Ways of Seeing Film* (New Brunswick, NJ: Rutgers University Press, 1995), cited in Gaines, "Political Mimesis," p. 90.

34 Nichols, *Blurred Boundaries,* p. 13.

35 Meg McLagan, "Principles, Publicity, and Politics: Notes on Human Rights Media," *American Anthropologist* 105, no. 3 (2003), pp. 605–12.

36 See Meg McLagan, "Spectacles of Difference: Cultural Activism and the Mass Mediation of Tibet," in Faye D. Ginsburg, Lila Abu-Lughod, and Brian Larkin (eds.), *Media Worlds: Anthropology on New Terrain* (Berkeley: University of California Press, 2002), pp. 90–111, for an analysis of new forms of mediated activism.

37 See Meg McLagan, "Circuits of Suffering," *Political and Legal Anthropology Review* 28, no. 2 (2005), pp. 223–39, for an exploration of these new political practices and spaces.

38 Meg McLagan, "Computing for Tibet: Virtual Politics in the Post–Cold War Era," in George E. Marcus (ed.), *Connected: Engagements with Media* (Chicago: University of Chicago Press, 1996), pp. 159–94.

39 Clicking on the link leads to the home page of Amnesty International's Stop Torture campaign, which includes images of several recent victims of torture and a brief paragraph stating Amnesty International's position that freedom from torture is a fundamental human right. At the bottom of the page is a space where people can enter their e-mail addresses if they want to receive updates and appeals for action. This site is no longer available online.

40 One example of this is the case of Ngawang Sangdrol, a nun detained at the age of thirteen for participating in independence demonstrations in Tibet. The best known of the Drapchi 14, she arrived in the United States in early April 2003 after being released from prison on parole by the Chinese for medical reasons. See www.savetibet.org for more information on her reception in the United States. See also Steven D. Marshall, *Rukhag 3: The Nuns of Drapchi Prison* (London: Tibet Information Network, 2000), and the accompanying CD-ROM.

41 Christopher Cox, "Marketing Human Rights: Amnesty International Group Tries New Tactics in Support of Political Prisoners," *Boston Herald,* January 3, 2002. Available online at www.tibet.ca/wtnarchive/2002/1/3_4.html.

42 Lev Manovich, "Generation Flash," available online at www.manovich.net/DOCS/generation_flash.doc.

43 Naomi Klein, *No Logo: Taking Aim at the Brand Bullies* (New York: Picador USA, 2000), pp. 421–38.

44 For more on the campaign, see www.drapchi14.org/drapchi14/.

45 Diane Nelson, "Indian Giver or Nobel Savage: Duping, Assumptions of Identity, and Other Double Entendres in Rigoberta Menchu Tum's Stoll/en Past," *American Ethnologist* 28, no. 2, (2001), pp. 303–31.

46 Jay David Bolter and Richard Grusin, *Remediation: Understanding New Media* (Cambridge, MA: MIT Press, 1999).

The Architecture of Strategic Communication

a profile of Witness by Meg McLagan

In today's globally mediated world, visual images play a central role in determining which acts of violence are redeemed and which get recognized.[1] Human-rights activists in the global North understand this fact and in recent years have built a formidable transnational communications infrastructure through which "local" actors' claims are formatted into human-rights "issues."[2] This new infrastructure is organized fundamentally around the need to internationalize. Whether an indigenous group on a remote island or a minority group in a city, any group wishing to broaden its reach must rely on strategies that will enable it to circumvent governments, armies, corporations, or other entities that are violating its rights and to connect with supporters abroad. Witness is one of the best-known and most successful nongovernmental organizations involved in this process. Based in New York City, it provides equipment, training, and support to activist groups around the world to help them use video in their human-rights advocacy campaigns.

FROM DOCUMENTATION TO STRATEGIC COMMUNICATION

In 1988, English musician Peter Gabriel joined Amnesty International's Human Rights Now! global concert tour, which was celebrating the fortieth anniversary of the United Nations Universal Declaration of Human Rights. Following the tour, the Reebok Human Rights Foundation was created, and Gabriel was asked to join the board. At the foundation's annual meeting, he proposed that the organization begin an initiative to supply human-rights activists with video cameras. Motivated by "the experience of meeting many survivors of human-rights abuses, and listening to their stories," he describes how

> there was no way I could walk away from their requests for help. Some were living in fear, being regularly threatened and harassed, some had witnessed their family being murdered, and some had suffered terrible tortures.... However, in many ways what shocked me most was that many of these human rights abuses were being successfully denied, buried, ignored

Cover from Witness organizational brochure, 2005 (design by Lippa Pearce).

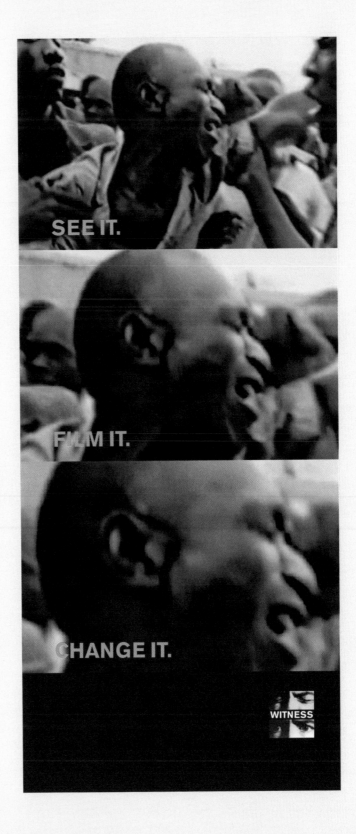

and forgotten, despite many written reports. But, it was clear that in those cases where photographic film or video evidence existed, it was almost impossible for the oppressors to get away with it.[3]

Gabriel's recognition of the power of visual evidence, compared with the written enumeration of facts, was in keeping with the growing interest in visual evidence shown by transnational NGOs in the North such as Amnesty International. During the 1970s and 1980s, these NGOs had become convinced that media and cultural production were central to the construction of human-rights issues in the public sphere.

Witness's embrace of small-format portable video cameras can also be understood in the context of a long history of communications technologies that have played a critical part in various political movements around the world: from audio cassettes in Iran in 1979, to faxes in Tiananmen Square in 1989, to e-mail and text messaging in the Philippines in 2002. When Witness was created, there was widespread optimism about the potential for such "small media" to reshape the world along more democratic lines. Witness's initial mission reflected this optimism, aiming to give video cameras to the "frontline defenders of human rights, who witnessed what was happening as it happened" so that they could document abuses on tape and demonstrate to the world the validity of their claims against their government. Indeed, at that time, video cameras did make a difference in places where states engaged in flagrant violations of rights in public gatherings such as Tiananmen Square in 1989.

Eventually, however, the notion that giving people cameras would enable them to capture images of human-rights abuses was revealed to be naive, not only in terms of the mechanistic assumptions about revelation and exposure, but also in terms of how video advocacy actually works. Local activists needed training in order to know how to create effective visual representations that would fit into preexisting mass-media protocols and generic storytelling conventions. As Sam Gregory, program manager at Witness, relates: "Activists needed training to operate cameras, and they needed strategic guidance on where the audiences were for the video they shot, and how to incorporate video into their attempts to influence those audiences. They needed support through the process of production and post-production, and in the implementation of distribution and advocacy plans with the finished video."

Witness responded to this need by refocusing its work on providing production and communication services. Rather than simply getting cameras into people's hands, Witness began to invest energy in all phases of support, from equipment provision to technical and tactical guidance during documentation, editing and postproduction support, and distribution and outreach. In other words, it became a full-service organization for thirteen to fifteen "core partners" each year, training them how to frame the visual evidence they were gathering into a visual argument for change. In so doing, Executive Director Gillian Caldwell recast Witness as a human-rights organization that leverages media, moving away from its former image as a media charity organization.

Over time, as more groups contacted the organization seeking assistance, Witness began to offer short-term support to those groups that didn't qualify for intensive collaborative partnership, but still needed help. This component of Witness's work was designated as the "seeding video advocacy" strategy. By dividing its time this way, the organization was able simultaneously to build capacity and to concentrate most of its efforts on those groups for whom video could really make a difference in a specific period of time.

This move away from a form of 1990s technophilia, and from a model of change based on the transparency of media and abuse revelations, to brokering relations between partners, audiences, and decision makers was critical to Witness's success in subsequent years. In essence, what Witness does today is help groups construct issues as "rights issues" and assist in the internationalization process through the strategic use of video. In other words, Witness aids the work of issue formatting by bringing an issue into a human-rights framework. For those struggling against injustice, the advantages of doing so can be significant, enabling them to initiate or to engage with a set of rights-related mechanisms, which in turn offer new platforms for action.

One of Witness's biggest successes in recent years was its work with Mental Disability Rights International (MDRI), a Washington, D.C.-based group involved with documenting conditions in psychiatric facilities and mental-retardation facilities around the world. After receiving information that egregious abuses were happening at the Neuropsychiatric Hospital in Asunción, Paraguay, MDRI and local activists contacted Paraguay's minister of health in order to gain access to the hospital and gain permission from the director of the hospital to videotape conditions in the facility. With help from Witness, MDRI then edited the footage into a video that was submitted, along with an emergency petition, to the Inter-American Commission on Human Rights (IACHR), asking for intervention on behalf of the 460 inmates. As a result of this appeal, the commission approved urgent measures to protect those in psychiatric institutions from human-rights abuses, a precedent that is now used in other countries. Meanwhile, MDRI and Witness brought the issue to the public by streaming video over their Web sites and by contacting CNN en Español to do a follow-up story, which aired in late 2003. The story caught the attention of Paraguay's president, who fired the hospital's director and created a national commission to reorganize the mental-health services in Paraguay. Of note in the MDRI example is the way in which Witness helped MDRI frame the issue of mental disability in terms of human rights, using different strategies addressed to different audiences. Video footage was used as documentary evidence of abuse and addressed to an intergovernmental body, then retooled for an investigative TV report addressed to the Paraguayan public. This retooling of media, a form of product differentiation, is one of the hallmarks of the emergent rights-oriented communications infrastructure. Drawing on approaches from the world of advertising and marketing, it involves the creation of specialized messages that are adapted to particular contexts and target specific decision makers, publics, elites, and grassroots audiences.

Witness's evolution into a kind of service organization that provides professional advice on how to use media to translate an issue into rights discourse, and that brokers information and contacts between various parties, has put it at the cutting edge of contemporary media practice. Witness's adoption of innovative techniques that facilitate the embedding of video into larger campaigns of action has enabled it to move beyond the implicit call to

A Duty to Protect, produced by AJEDI-Ka with assistance from Witness, explores the issue of child soldiers in the Congo.

action located in the text itself, instead creating conditions for the formation of specific publics around a problem or issue.

In a larger sense, Witness's work also exemplifies the way in which publicity has become the structuring principle of activist politics. By nesting texts within activist contexts, strategically linking production and circulation, and relying on community-based forms of circulation, Witness has been able to extend the reach and effectiveness of the projects it supports.

DIGITAL TECHNOLOGIES AND THE TRANSFORMATION OF THE POLITICAL AUDIENCE

The proliferation of new digital communication channels and formats, as well as the increased blurring of boundaries between media consumption and realms of social life that are conventionally understood as separate from it (such as politics), are part of the emergent "media ecology" that is reshaping both domestic and international activism. Important lessons about some of the characteristics of this new media landscape can be gleaned from writings on the current state of independent media in America.[4] For example, we are entering a period of unprecedented media flexibility as a result of the emergence of a global digital platform for media of all kinds. Similarly, writings on the recent spate of political documentaries (such as Michael Moore's *Fahrenheit 9/11,* among others) contain valuable insights into the role of digital technologies in creating new circuits through which change-oriented media can move, and around which campaigns can be organized.[5] These new pathways enable the circumvention of mass media gatekeepers, while facilitating the formation of transnational networks of diverse social actors who use technologies such as e-mail, electronic mailing lists, and cell phones to exchange information and coordinate action.[6]

As I have already suggested, human-rights groups trained by Witness take a strategic approach to communication that is quite sophisticated. In describing how Witness works with its partner organizations, Gregory describes how they start with a desired goal and work backwards, designing an advocacy strategy tailored to meet that goal: "In our process of working with locally-based human-rights groups we start with their goals for advocacy. From this we identify which audiences have the potential to influence this advocacy and in what sequence these audiences need to be persuaded, and then identify what format of video will work for that audience, bearing in mind the organizational and environmental constraints facing a given human rights group."[7]

Witness has been remarkably successful in teaching groups how to engage in this form of "smart narrowcasting," which consists of "personalizing messages to specific groups and individuals or entities, and reaching them through specialized communication."[8] Their differentiation of audiences and the formats and strategies needed to reach them is not unlike the new distribution model, which connects audiences directly to filmmakers and activists, that political documentarians, such as Robert Greenwald, have pioneered.[9] Dubbed the "upstairs/downstairs" model, it involves targeting core audiences and selling directly to those audiences, a strategy that has enabled filmmakers to bring a guerrilla style of filmmaking to the masses. Grassroots organization MoveOn.org and other progressive organizations such as *The Nation* magazine have promoted and sold DVD versions of Greenwald's films on their Web sites.[10] After selling thousands of copies and demonstrating its commercial value, Greenwald's film *Uncovered: The Truth About the Iraq War* was picked up by a distributor and released theatrically. Political documentaries like *Uncovered,* including *Outfoxed: Rupert Murdoch's War on Journalism* (another Greenwald film), Michael Moore's *Fahrenheit 9/11, The Corporation* (a film by Mark Achbar, Jennifer Abbott, and Jeff Bakan), and *Soldier's Pay* (by David O. Russell, Juan Carlos Zaldivar, and Tricia Regan), have found similar success by relying on grassroots marketing and publicity techniques and viral networking to reach audiences and eventually mass-media distributors. These promising new distribution paths have become possible with the development of powerful digital tools such as DVD, digital projects in theaters, and the Internet.[11] The cross-platform approach of the upstairs/downstairs model, with its simultaneous focus on grassroots and elite audiences, underscores a shift toward increased specialization, diversification, and sophistication by activists and media makers in recent years.[12]

The emergence of effective and innovative production, distribution, and exhibition strategies by human-rights advocates such as Witness offers productive ways to reconceptualize media as part of an ongoing process of issue creation, rather than conceiving of media as a collection of static texts. By charting the itineraries of digital media, such work also provides us with a window onto the process of public making, that is, the process of summoning witnessing publics.

FROM NONCOMMERCIAL TO COMMERCIAL SYSTEMS

The development of a global digital platform and the subsequent profusion of media forms and structures have created new possibilities, upending the categories we use to organize our lives as activists, audiences, citizens, and producers. One of the most intriguing aspects of Witness's work is the way in which it has taken advantage of the noncommercial platform to launch its political messages and material into the commercial system. Instead of focusing on setting up an entirely alternative media system that exists parallel to mainstream media, as the media collective Indymedia (Indymedia.org) has done, Witness and other human-rights media groups have begun crossing boundaries that are traditionally conceived of as separating these realms. For instance, Witness has availed itself of opportunities to broaden its reach by making agreements with national broadcasters to use footage from Witness partners. Thus, the ABC network was allowed to use footage depicting human-rights abuses of mentally ill patients in Mexican hospitals, footage that aired on the network's flagship news magazine show *20/20* in 2000.

To further its role as conduit and mediator of relationships between its partners and various audiences/users, Witness spends more time now on the front and back ends of productions, that is, on its strategic function as a power broker during the conception and distribution of films. It has also improved its training with regard to storytelling and the emotional and empathic aspects of video so that its partners might in turn produce material that communicates more readily across cultural borders.

Witness's work thus puts it at an intersection of multiple professional worlds, including those of human rights (where it primarily places itself), strategic communication, news media, and entertainment media. This latter category has become more important to Witness over the years insofar as the organization has been approached about branded programming by entertainment networks such as the National Geographic Channel and Oxygen Media. This development in turn has raised a set of questions about repurposing content and engaging with mainstream commercial media in America. (At one point Witness was even approached about participating in a human-rights reality TV show.) The strong demand for content from satellite and cable television venues and Web portals has had to be balanced with the organization's original concern with training local people to speak for themselves and to local audiences and decision makers.

CONCLUSION

As communications media have changed dramatically in the fifteen years since Witness was founded, the organization has continually "challenged the paradigms of traditional media content creation by incorporating the latest technologies" into its work.[13] This continues to be true as the organization prepares to launch their new Video Hub in 2007, where anyone with footage of human-rights violations can upload a video, which can then be used to advocate for change. The Hub will directly contribute to Witness's mission by enabling individuals to upload documentation via their computers, PDAs, and even cell phones. The decision to launch a participatory Web site — a single online platform — puts Witness in the position of acting as a facilitator in making, aggregating, organizing, and disseminating human-rights videos. Following MoveOn.org's example, Witness is poised to use video as a key tactic in fostering participation in advocacy campaigns around specific human-rights issues. How this new initiative will develop remains to be seen, but it does seem clear that Witness is well on its way to becoming a premier human-rights media clearinghouse, as well as a central hub in a globally networked human-rights community.

1   Material for this profile was drawn from two of my previously published essays: Meg McLagan, "Circuits of Suffering," *Political and Legal Anthropology Review* 28, no. 2 (2005), pp. 223–39; and Meg McLagan, "Introduction: Making Human Rights Claims Public," *American Anthropologist* 108, no. 1 (2006), pp. 191–95.

2   For an analysis of this phenomenon, see McLagan, "Circuits of Suffering."

3   Peter Gabriel, "Foreword," in Sam Gregory, Gillian Caldwell, Ronit Avni, and Thomas Harding (eds.), *Video for Change: A Guide for Advocacy and Activism* (London: Pluto Press, 2005), pp. x–xi.

4   Andrew Blau, "The Future of Independent Media," *Deeper News* 10, no. 1 (Sept. 2004), www.gbn.com/independentmedia.

5   Much of this research has been collated by the Center for Social Media at American University and is available on their Web site, www.centerforsocialmedia.org.

6   Lance W. Bennett, "New Media Power: The Internet and Global Activism," in Nick Couldry and James Curran (eds.), *Contesting Media Power: Alternative Media in a Networked World* (New York: Rowman and Littlefield, 2003).

7   Sam Gregory, "Transnational Storytelling: Human Rights, Witness, and Video Advocacy," *American Anthropologist* 108, no. 1 (March 2006), p. 198.

8   Simon Rosenberg, "Where We Are," Archive of New Democrat Network and NDN PAC, www.newdem.org/partyfuture/whereweare.html.

9   Michael Fox, "Truth or Faction: The Year of the Political Documentary," *Inside Indies,* October 22, 2004, www.pbs.org/independentlens/insideindies/infocus/truthorfaction.

10 Robert Boynton, "How to Make a Guerrilla Documentary," *New York Times Magazine,* July 11, 2004.

11 Peter Broderick, "Maximizing Distribution," *DGA Magazine,* January 2004.

12 For more on this shift, see Martin Shaw, "Western Wars and Peace Activism: Social Movements in Global Mass-Mediated Politics," *Crisis/Media* (Delhi: SARAI Reader, 2004), pp. 42–51.

13 Video Hub Detailed Overview, pdf, available at www.witness.org (accessed June 29, 2006).

Fred Askew, *Special Registration* (2003).

"Eyes and Ears": Aesthetics, Visual Culture, and the Claims of Nongovernmental Politics

Yates McKee

Photographically displaced and dismembered, an anonymous hand stages an offering that trembles between presence and absence, memory and oblivion, luminosity and darkness: a paper triangle bearing the words "Mohammed Maddy 44 years old Egyptian DISAPPEARED in the USA." "See…here it is — I hold it toward you," the hand seems to say, but it does not simply present an object to view or convey a message to be read; rather, it impresses upon the unspecified others to whom it is addressed — on us, for example — an obligation to bear witness to what is not simply visible or, rather, what interrupts the imperatives of exposure, transparency, and information traditionally associated with the public sphere. Marked with a safety pin, the triangle is a kind of name tag that has been detached from the body it would help to identify properly. But it also betrays a strange relay between naming and identification — "Mohammed…Egyptian" — and the ways in which bodies are made to register in both a perceptual and an institutional sense. While singular, the proper name and the absent body of which it is a placeholder have a certain exemplarity: it is not just any name that appears, but a name of a specific type, intimating that the body has gone missing not by accident, but as the result of a structured — if obscure — practice of selective surveillance, profiling, or targeting; it did not simply disappear, it was disappeared. Like the triangular form of the name tag, this verbal modulation echoes other times and spaces, other missing bodies, other memorial conjurations in the face of other "special" measures undertaken in the name of national security and public order.…

In "Confronting Governments, Human Rights" a short statement written in 1984 in conjunction with a campaign aiming to publicize and intervene in the plight of the second wave of Vietnamese "boat people" being victimized by pirates in the international waters of the South China Sea, Michel Foucault set forth some general reflections on the contemporary proliferation of activist projects carried out by "an international citizenry" whose claims were not legitimized by governments, political constituencies, or

even ideological programs in the typical sense, but rather by a "certain shared difficulty in accepting what is happening." Motivated by an intolerance for specific ways
of governing — whether by the policies of governments rejecting the refugee's claims
for asylum or by negligent inaction, such as that perpetrated by the governments and
intergovernmental agencies standing silent in the face of refugees' consequent exposure to piratical violence — the "duty" of this unauthorized, nongovernmental citizenry
was "always to make an issue of people's misfortune, to keep it in the eyes and ears of
governments — it is not true that they are not responsible. People's misfortune must
never be a silent remainder of politics. It founds an absolute right to rise up and address
those who hold power."[1]

This duty and right to address governing agencies, to hold them accountable for
the external costs or collateral damages of their calculations and decisions, implicitly
involved for Foucault an aesthetic dimension — "to make an issue of people's misfortune, to keep it in the eyes and ears of governments." While Foucault affirmed what
he called in an earlier discussion of the Polish Solidarity movement "the importance
of political affect," suggesting that "the role of the governed is to take offense and
put passion into their actions,"[2] he also cautioned against an understanding of activism that would assume "a theatrical role of pure and simple indignation."[3] Making a
political issue out of "what is happening" would involve more than simple exposure and
denunciation, he wrote. It would involve rendering visible and audible the grievances of
those affected and doing so by means of specific techniques and policies — demands for
occupational safety by unions, reproductive autonomy by feminists, and effective legal
representation by prisoners' groups. Only thus might these grievances become sites of
concern and potential modification, not only for the governing agencies theoretically or
practically responsible for them, but also for affectively invested, open-ended publics
capable at least of exerting pressure on such agencies, if not of calling into question the
bases of the latter's claims to authority altogether.

The challenge posed by Foucault was thus how to mobilize civic passions against
practices deemed "intolerable" without assuming a horizon of satisfaction for such passions that would base itself in an ultimate moment of transparency, liberation, or transcendence that would exist beyond the condition of being governed in some form or
other. He called, in other words, for a politics of "the governed" who are determined to
act as such — capable of both constraining and displacing the monopoly of vision and
hearing, appearing and silencing, speech and action, arrogated to themselves by governing agencies. Initiating new rights and claims, such a politics would be bereft of — but
not unmarked by — the reassuring sights, sounds, and spaces projected by the great
narratives of liberalism (the surpassing of the state by the spontaneous action of civil
society) and socialism (the reconquest of the means of production by the proletariat
from the bourgeoisie). While complicating these great narratives, Foucault by no means
resigned himself to a myopic pragmatism that would leave the conceptual assumptions
and operational parameters of a given mode of government intact — "A reform is never
anything but the outcome of a process in which there is conflict, confrontation, struggle,

resistance.... It is a matter of making conflicts more visible, of making them more essential than mere clashes of interest or mere institutional blockages. From these conflicts and clashes a new relation of forces must emerge whose temporary profile will be a reform."[4]

The agencies and modes of government have of course mutated and multiplied since "Confronting Governments, Human Rights" was written, as have the identities, claims, and tactics of the nongovernmental activists seeking to pressure, reform, or displace them. (Foucault's immediate references were to organizations such as Médicines du Monde and Amnesty International, whose paradigmatic targets of censure were dictatorial, genocidal, or negligent nation-states, rather than private corporations and multilateral intuitions.) Drawing on a range of visual artifacts, including some emerging from the margins of what is known as "contemporary art,"[5] the purpose of the present text is to stage some general methodological questions concerning the aesthetic techniques, forms of expression, and modes of self-presentation pertaining to certain nongovernmental political actors over the past decade or so, providing what I hope will be a useful supplementary lens through which the diverse images appearing throughout *Nongovernmental Politics* might be seen as more than mere illustrations of the texts they accompany.

From the outset, it is important to emphasize that "aesthetic techniques" will here be understood not as mere ornamental embellishments layered on a set of preexisting political objectives or, in a slightly different register, as secondary means for the accomplishment of ends that would exist outside the sphere of means, mediacy, or media.[6] Following the post-Foucaldian insights of Jacques Rancière, this text will suggest that the "politics of aesthetics" is not a matter of mere "aestheticization"—for example, the reduction of questions of substantial political concern to a pleasurable play of sensory effects and formal conventions—but rather "a delimitation of spaces and times, of the visible and the invisible, of speech and noise, that simultaneously determines the place and the stakes of politics as a form of experience. Politics revolves around what is seen and what can be said about it, around who has the ability to see and the talent to speak, around the properties of spaces and the possibilities of time."[7] In this view, aesthetic techniques (including but far exceeding "art" as a specialized set of perceptual and conceptual experiments) do not simply introduce new elements into an arena whose rules are agreed upon in advance—a scenario that would reduce politics to what Foucault called "mere conflicts of interest or mere institutional blockages." Rather, such techniques have the potential to interrupt and to reconfigure what Rancière calls "the partition of the sensible," which "parcels out places and forms of participation in a common world by first establishing the modes of perception within which these are inscribed."[8] This includes, paradoxically, those whose part in society is that they "have no part," the surplus or remainder of the population whose grievances do not register as such for the agencies that govern them.

If we accept this expansive sense of the aesthetic as being synonymous with the demarcation of who or what can be seen or heard as political, as well as when and where, and for whom and in what ways, the analytical protocols of "visual culture" may prove useful in examining the specifically image-based dimensions of the general field of appearances and disappearances to which Rancière insists that we attend. Drawing on the vocabularies of art history, anthropology, and film theory, this mode of analysis challenges the idea of "culture" as either a bounded set of agreed-upon values or a rarefied class of artifacts, understanding it instead as an unstable network of signifying practices, technical apparatuses, and institutional power relations that hail subjects in multiple, overlapping, and often contradictory ways.[9] Visual cultural studies thus shares important affinities with recent neo-Gramscian social-movement research that has emphasized concepts such as "ideological hegemony" and "cultural contestation" in order to challenge both the narrow formalism of political science — for example, an exclusive focus on the activities of electoral parties and nation-states within taken-for-granted arenas of conflict, interaction, and negotiation — and the rationalism of resource-mobilization theory, which assumes the motivational structure of political actors to consist of the maximally efficient attainment of finite material interests, rather than of attempts to "redefine the meaning and limits of the political system itself."[10]

Brought together, these modes of analysis suggest the need for a double sense of vision, one that treats vision as a metonym for perception, cognition, and aspiration in general *and* that takes account of the specific configurations of visuality enabled — but never completely determined — by the various image-based technologies through and to which nongovernmental political actors address themselves.

Yet if vision acquires an inflated metaphorical privilege because of the centrality of technologies such as cameras, camcorders, television, satellites, the Internet, and PowerPoint presentations in contemporary politics, it is only insofar as they prevent vision from ever simply being itself. It is not that these technologies distort the immediacy typically associated with the optical faculty; rather, they magnify and exacerbate the general point that every visual artifact and experience is always already marked by an unforeseeably mediated network of histories, interpretations, and contexts that, strictly speaking, are not visually evident as such.[11] In this sense, every image is a kind of text that requires both looking and reading, or rather looking *as* reading, regardless of whether an image contains or is accompanied by text in the narrow sense of the word. This axiom runs in the reverse direction, as well, which is to say that every text is a kind of image; that words and the contexts in which they appear are always marked by certain graphic qualities that can be quite significant politically, whether one considers the typography of a protest banner, the architecture of a Web site, the design of a television advertisement or a press release, the layout of an NGO's annual report prepared for a foundation, the highlighted terms of a slide show presented to a congressional committee, or the bringing to light of an incriminating government document.

It might also be argued that every image and every text has a certain acoustic dimension, as well, whether or not it involves an audio-visual technology per se: images and texts address, call out to, and make claims on others, the most elementary interpellation being that they should be looked at, read, and responded to at all, whatever their intended meaning or destination may have been.

With this synaesthetic contamination of the visual, the textual, and the acoustic in mind, the task of visual culture studies is to read image-texts as faithfully as possible in terms of their strategic motivations, formal qualities, and technical conditions while attending to the errancies of use, meaning, and appearance that haunt them at every moment. Such an attention to image-texts implies a double imperative: that researchers, activists, and specialized cultural producers of all sorts (journalists, videographers, filmmakers, media strategists, graphic designers, interface architects, publishers, celebrities, artists, curators, and performers, among others) take images seriously as a force to be reckoned with, while also not taking the effects of images for granted, as has been the case in the canonical activist paradigm of "mobilizing shame."

As Thomas Keenan has noted, the presupposition of this paradigm is that governing agencies should be approached as psychological beings susceptible to feelings of embarrassment and humiliation whose dirty deeds may be exposed to the watchful

HOLDING A MEDIA EVENT

(Adapted from Salzman's "Making the News" and SPIN Project Materials)

What is a Media Event?

- An activity intended to generate news coverage. They often involve gimmicky visuals, playful stunts, props, etc.

Hints

- Determine if your event is newsworthy. The more of the following characteristics it has, the more likely it will get coverage:

  + *Novelty*
  + *Conflict*
  + *New data, symbol of a trend*
  + *Simplicity*
  + *Humor*
  + *Prominent figure involved*
  + *Action*
  + *Bright props and images*
  + *Local impact*

- *Holidays, anniversaries.*
- Build your media event—site, speakers, visuals—around your message and slogan.
- Make it fun. If you don't look like you want to be there, why should the press?
- Don't be afraid to employ stunts. Sexy and trendy events take precedence over long range things with the media.
- Consider timing. Is your event competing with other things? It is best to stage an event Monday through Thursday, 10 A.M. though 2 P.M.
- Find an effective location. Consider the following questions when choosing a location:

  + *Is the site convenient? Reporters are busy and won't travel far for an event.*
  + *Is your site too commonly used for media events? Try to find a unique location, if possible.*

- *If your event is outdoors, do you have a backup location? A little rain or bad weather won't ruin an event, but severe conditions will. Also consider if it is possible to postpone it if the weather is very bad.*
- *Do you need a permit? Check with the local police department.*
- Arrange to have photographers take pictures of your event.
- Display large banners or signs with the message you want to communicate.
- The event should last 15 to 45 minutes.
- Distribute information about your issue and organization at the event.
- Remember equipment. Will you need a megaphone, podium, or portable microphone?
- Have spokespersons ready to be interviewed.
- Find out which reporters attended the event. Follow up with the no-shows.

"Holding a Media Event," from Global Exchange, *The Sweatfree Toolkit: How Your Community Can Help End Sweatshops* (2005).

gaze of public opinion, thus forcing the agencies in question to alter their behavior.[12] Without simply dismissing the concept altogether—"shame" remains an important politicizing term in the vocabulary of many organizations and movements—Keenan finds its underlying assumption problematic in that it posits an automatic "if/then" relay between visibility and exposure, on the one hand, and ameliorative or preventative action, on the other. Haunted by episodes in which such a relay proved to be far from guaranteed—the racist-paranoiac acquittal of the Los Angeles police officers captured on videotape brutalizing Rodney King,[13] the dubious narrative of "ancient ethnic hatreds" underpinning the position of humanitarian neutrality adopted by the Western powers in the face of the extensively publicized Rwandan and Bosnian genocides,[14] the initial success of the Bush administration in framing the torture techniques on display in the Abu Ghraib photographs[15] as the actions of "bad apples" isolated from a larger chain of command and accountability—Keenan insists that the indispensable imperatives of monitoring, watching, and witnessing governmental abuses and evasions be supplemented by a detour through what he refers to as "aesthetic categories."

This call implies both a general acknowledgment that evidence itself is not self-evident—the difficulty of effectively "making an issue" out of the practice of a governing agency, rather than simply revealing it to the presumably morally sensitive "eyes of the world"—and a vigilant attention to the specific conditions, mediations, and tactics of such issue making. Keenan associates "aesthetic categories" with forceful acts of seeing and projecting, reading and writing, hearing and speaking, attuned to what Walter Benjamin recognized as the "thoroughgoing permeation of reality with technical equipment."[16] This general exposure of life to technologies of reproduction and dissemination neither alienates the perceiving subject from an authentic experience of publicity nor consummates such an experience in a moment of communicative immediacy. While new media open new times and spaces of public action, they also remove the grounds of certainty to which the proponents of such action might have once appealed.

Keenan's critique of the axiomic link between images and responsible, effective publicity resonates with a certain aesthetic awareness developed by many practitioners of nongovernmental politics over the past decade, for whom terms such as "framing" and "storytelling" (rather than the simple transfer of information) have become increasingly important in the development of both policy analyses and publicity campaigns. While affirming that nongovernmental political strategies in the litigative or legislative realms often—though not always—need to be supplemented by discursive and audio-visual tactics designed to persuade or to outrage a generalized "court of public opinion," such emphases should not be confused with a reduction of politics to a matter of rhetorical acumen alone.

This is a charge that has been leveled at George Lakoff's influential "cognitive framing" paradigm, the aesthetic implications of which are indicated in a summary provided by sympathetic critics at the Boston University Movement/Media Research and Action Project (MRAP):

APPENDIX: AUDIOVISUAL COMPONENTS

All video is made up of combinations of visual and audio elements. Think creatively and expansively about different kinds of sound and images. What will make this story visually interesting? Can you tell your story using different combinations of visuals and audio components? What will have most impact on your audience? What do you have access to given security, budget and time constraints? Can you make a virtue out of necessity?

Some kinds of visuals and audio to think about:

1. Visuals
* Visual and audio documentation of events happening – People *doing* things, without commentary.
* Landscapes, locations and inanimate objects that are part of the story.
* Interviews – One or more people answering questions, posed to them by an interviewer on or off-camera who may be edited out of the final film.
* Conversations observed – People aware of the presence of a camera, but not being interviewed directly.
* Conversations or people talking to each other, with the camera unobtrusive or hidden.
* Re-enactments – Factually accurate recreations of scenes that could not be filmed, or are in the past. Remember that there may be credibility problems with this in the human rights context, particularly if the reasons are unclear to the audience why a scene could not be filmed, or needed to be re-enacted.
* Expressionistic shots – Often symbolic or artistic, to represent a concept or provide visuals where you do not have access to the location, e.g. in historical interviews.
* Manipulation of imagery via slow-mo, fast-forward, motion-capture etc.
* Still photos or documents – Either static or shot with the camera panning/tracking or zooming in or out.
* Text including on-screen titles, headlines, and graphics – Used for creative and informational purposes, including subtitles for foreign languages. These are usually added in the editing.
* Library, news and archive footage –This could be from a professional archive, but also personal memorabilia, and possibly material from other films. Remember footage from a commercial source is usually expensive and complicated to get permission for.
* Blank screen – Causing the viewer to reflect on what they have just seen or heard, prime them for what is next, indicate a change of sequence or location, or to emphasize sounds.

2. Audio or Sound Elements
* Interviewee – You can use audio only, or audio from a picture-and-sound interview with audio only used, or both picture and audio used.
* Conversations – Either recorded with the participants' knowledge or unobtrusively/secretly.
* Narration – Could be a narrator, the filmmaker or a participant.
* Synchronous Sound – Sound shot while filming.
* Sound effects – Individual sounds shot while filming, or at a later point.
* Music – This is usually added in editing.
* Silence – The absence of sound can indicate change of mood or place, or cause the viewer to refocus on the screen.

"Appendix: Audiovisual Components" from Witness, *Video For Change: A Guide for Advocacy and Activism* (2005).

A frame is a thought-organizer. Like a picture frame, it puts a rim around some part of the world, highlighting certain events and facts while rendering others invisible. Like a building frame, it holds things together but is covered by insulation and walls. It provides coherence to an array of symbols, images, and arguments, linking them through an underlying organizing idea that suggests what is essential…we do not see the frame directly, but infer its presence by its characteristic expressions and language.[17]

Critics such as MRAP have argued that such an attention to hearts and minds, narratives and norms, scripts and symbols, visions and values, must be considered in relation to the organizational resources, technological interfaces, institutional platforms, and spatiotemporal decisions involved in the construction of political claims. Exemplary in this regard are the funding, training, and brokering activities of Witness, an organization whose apparently straightforward injunction—"see it, film it, change it"—is belied by its complex partnerships with other NGOs to develop the practical, conceptual, and formal skills of hand-held videography as an integral dimension of human-rights advocacy work in a variety of institutional registers. It stresses the importance of "paying attention to your audience and to the stories that will engage that audience. A film to 'rally the troops' will require a different approach than one required to persuade a committee of impatient, time-pressed, and skeptical legislators."[18]

In its emphasis on the careful articulation of technics, tactics, and poetics, an organization such as Witness compels the student of visual culture to ask the following open-ended questions of the image-texts that appear throughout *Nongovernmental Politics*: Who or what produces an image-text? How, when, and where is it (re)produced? Who sees it under what conditions, and in relation to what contexts of interpretative and institutional reception? How do different aesthetic techniques envision and address their publics? How do they envision and address the targets of their demands? At what scale, in what arenas, and at what level of specificity do aesthetic techniques operate? What rhetorical styles, iconic figures, affective tones, and historical resonances are mobilized in one context and not another? How do different aesthetic practitioners engage the tension between the Gramscian imperative sounded by Chantal Mouffe in her discussion of the capacity of artistic practices to "mobilize the passions" through popular-democratic identifications, on the one hand, and a Foucauldian attention to the specificity of governing agencies and techniques and modes of subjectification, on the other?[19] How do different nongovernmental activists theorize the capacities of an aesthetic technique to reach a targeted governing agency—including those who deliberately avoid high-profile media visibility for fear of jeopardizing their fragile relationships or negotiations with the agencies whose behavior they aspire to modify? What forms of technological expertise, equipment, and infrastructure pertain to an aesthetic technique, and how do these elements condition the composition, distribution, circulation, and archiving of image-texts?[20]

All of these questions are pertinent, for example, to the photograph that appears at the beginning of this article. In its compositional technique of dismemberment and anonymization, the photograph echoes at a formal level the aesthetico-political predicament addressed by the outstretched hand and the triangular placeholder it holds forth—how to make disappearance appear as such, which is to say, as an intolerable governmental practice premised on the dismembering of particular subjects from the realms of both legal protection and public memory.

Crucial to the task of re-membering these subjects is the use of the word "disappeared" itself, which evokes a reference to a crucial moment in the history of human-rights activism: *desaparacido* was of course the name given by civil-society movements to persons detained, tortured, and assassinated by Latin American military governments in the 1970s and 1980s. Such governments operated under permanent states of

Mothers march with silhouettes of the disappeared (photograph by Gerardo Dell'Orto, 1988, from Marguerite Guzman Bouvard, *Revolutionary Motherhood: The Mothers of the Plaza de Mayo* [1994]).

emergency in which the suspension of civil liberties and the mobilization of exceptional forms of violence were legitimized with reference to the putative threat of Communist subversion. Through rituals of mass witness bearing in public spaces, groups such as the Madres de los Desaparecidos in Argentina sought to mark the memory of their missing loved ones as a gap in national memory generated by governmental denial, secrecy, and impunity.[21]

Similarly, the triangular form of the name tag in the photograph indicates another debt to the image-based archives of human-rights discourse. In the concentration camps of the SS, the uniforms of prisoners other than Jews were marked with inverted triangles that were color coded according to the "type" of prisoner in question. Gay men, for instance, were required to wear pink triangles, a signifier reappropriated by gay-liberation activists in the 1970s and most famously in the pioneering visual culture of Act Up in the late 1980s and early 1990s, referred to by Douglas Crimp as the group's "Demo-Graphics," where the triangle functioned simultaneously as a historically inflected identity claim and a call for mobilization against governmental indifference to — and thus complicity in — the emergent AIDS crisis: "Silence = Death."[22]

Though obviously different in terms of the specific power relations it aims to address, the name tag imparted by the photograph can still be considered a kind of demo-graphic technique, conjuring the memory of Act Up's own gesture of historical reactivation: less well known than either the yellow stars or pink triangles were the blue triangles affixed by the SS to the prison uniforms of "foreigners," who, like Jews, had been required to register with the state in the years preceding their incarceration and eventual murder. This resonance is further marked by the title that supplements the photograph, which articulates the latter's particular relation to a certain kind of abstraction or universality — Special Registration. The title refers to an actual U.S. government program undertaken in the aftermath of 9/11 while at the same time alluding to the necessity of mobilizing "special" aesthetic techniques — both the photograph qua formal artifact and the triangular name tag itself — in order to make this governmental practice "register" as a site of political demands, rather than simply as a police operation legitimized by the unassailable imperatives of security.

The photograph forms part of a series by Fred Askew documenting a demonstration held by civil-rights activists and community groups, including the Blue Triangle Network, which designed and distributed the name tags. The demonstration was held at 26 Federal Plaza in Lower Manhattan on November 22, 2002, the deadline for the National Security Entry Exit Registration System (NSEERS), which required that the male citizens of twenty-four Muslim nations living in the United States present themselves in person to the Immigration and Naturalization Service to be interviewed, fingerprinted, and photographed.[23]

Askew's photograph appears, among other places, on the Web site of the Visible Collective, a network of cultural producers dedicated to addressing the aesthetic and cultural conditions of post-9/11 carcereal governmentality, both within the United States and in its global "archipelago of exception," from Guantánamo Bay to Abu Ghraib. Among their projects is *NaHnu Wahaad (But Really, Are We One?),* an ongoing memorial database marking the names — and absence of names — of those "disappeared in America" that has been displayed in a variety of presentational formats at museums, community centers, and online.[24]

Trevor Paglen uncannily echoes the Visible Collective's database in *Missing Persons* (2006), a project that operates at the intersection of conceptual art, investigative journalism, and experimental geography. The project, portions of which are reproduced in the current volume (pp. 50–55), consists of a dossier of semifabricated documents all sharing the same format: printed in the upper left-hand corner of each page are the name, address, and phone number of corporations with nondescript names such as "Premier Executive Transport," below which are listed the governmental agencies with which such corporations would be required to register in order to conduct their activities, such as the Federal Aviation Administration. The documents are devoid of any other information, the blank field of the page marked only by a signature in the lower right corner pertaining to an authorized representative of the company in question, such as might be inscribed on a flight log or a business license. Each signature is repeated in two different documents, and each time it is evident from the script that a different hand has signed for the "same" individual—an individual, as it turns out, who does not otherwise exist as a legal subject who might be held responsible for the actions of the entities on whose behalf it signs.

Participants in the semiconspiratorial subcultural world of "planespotters"—people who obsessively monitor obscure, though often publicly available FAA data—first drew the attention of journalists and human rights groups to these documents. They then began in 2004 to track the anomalous flight patterns of civilian aircraft traveling between various airports in the United States, Europe, the Middle East, and most suspiciously, Guantánamo Bay. Though it cannot be positively proven, the signatures located and publicly reproduced by Paglen appear to pertain to the network of shell corporations allegedly set up by the CIA to practice "extraordinary renditions," in which terrorism suspects are apprehended without due process and transported in secret to unnamed locations across the globe where interrogation techniques officially repudiated by the United States can be used with impun-ity.[25] Rather than straightforwardly presenting such information, Paglen's project delineates precisely the legal and perceptual "black hole" in which this officially nonexistent practice takes place and the precarious evidentiary traces it leaves behind, which are meaningless without the sort of reformatting and recontextualization performed by *Missing Persons*. The "missing persons" in question thus form an uncanny couple: the fabulous realization in language of a *unreal* subject such as "Tyler Edward Tate" shows up as the precondition for the derealization of a *real* subject as a "ghost detainee."[26]

For Paglen, the extraordinary practices and spaces of U.S. sovereignty require extraordinary or even extraordinarily banal visual techniques that index their own encounter with governmentally enforced unseeability. Supplementing the semifictive documents of *Missing Persons* is a pair of somewhat blurry photographs of unremarkable structures in Kabul. One, situated at the dead end of a tree-lined residential street, is marked with a spray-painted sign reading "STOP"; the other, set against a barren hillside, is surrounded by a single strand of barbed wire. By themselves, these images convey little if any positive information; what is crucial is that they document, from the relatively safe physical distance afforded by a supertelescopic lens, the "actual" coordinates of the quasi-governmental, officially unacknowledged "black sites" to which terrorist subjects are rumored to be rendered.

Another kind of "black site" shows up in a project by the Speculative Archive entitled *In Possession of a Photograph*. Here, a series of spectacular touristic images of architectural landmarks such as the Brooklyn Bridge are retrieved from the Google Image search engine and coupled with black voids of the same size. These voids mark instances, both pre-9/11 and post-9/11, in which "suspicious persons" have been interrogated

Governor's mansion, Austin, Texas
Kamran Aldar, 2003

Dr. Ching-Kuang Shene
http://www.cs.mtu.edu/~shene/DigiCam/Gallery/
Travel/Austinmansion.jpg

Brooklyn Bridge, New York
Gharoub al-Abrash Ghalyoun, 1997

unnamed photographer
http://www.emediawire.com/prfiles/2005/07/06/
258826/CelebrationBrooklynBridgeNewYorkCity.jpg

Shell Chemical facility, Geismar, Louisiana
unnamed persons, 2004

courtesy Shell Chemicals Ltd
http://www.chemicalstechnology.com/projects/ptl/
images/ww82403_highres.jpg

and/or detained for attempting to photograph these same sites. The project thus speaks simultaneously to the paranoiac temporality of preemption, which strives, in the words of the 2002 *National Security Strategy,* to "eliminate threats before they have emerged," and the way in which this temporality underwrites the uneven exposure of different populations to surveillance.

In their attention to archival hauntings, missing bodies, and black holes, the paradoxical aesthetics of disappearance articulated by this cluster of practices resonates with Judith Butler's call for a "critical image" that "must not only fail to capture its referent but *show* that failing." She associates this with the ethico-political task of post-9/11 "cultural criticism," which would "interrogate the emergence and vanishing of the human at the limits of what we can know, what we can hear, what we can see, and what we can sense."[27]

Though addressing an entirely different set of governmental agencies than those discussed above, a similar emergence and vanishing of the human is staged by documentarian Fred Lonidier in his project *N.A.F.T.A. (Not A Fair Trade for All), Getting the Correct Picture.* This documentary installation includes a series of "counter-portraits" produced in collaboration with workers struggling to form an independent union from 1997 to 1998 at the Han Young factory (a subcontractor of the Hyundai corporation) in Tijuana, Mexico. Mimicking the format of police mug shots, photographs show each worker against a wall from the neck up. But rather than distinguishing the physiognomic features of criminal subjects,[28] in these portraits, the workers' faces are obscured by grotesque monster masks and accompanied by captions identifying the workers with pseudonyms such as "son of Frankenstein."

At one level, this gesture recalls Marx's account of the capitalist factory transforming the laboring body into a "crippled monstrosity"[29]; however, rather than illustrating a general thematic of alienation or dehumanization, the photographs register the specific dangers to which workers are exposed when attempting to organize independently. The monster masks, which in one sense efface the identities of the workers, paradoxically enable them to show up in public as political subjects. Their appearance as monsters is thus both a form of protection from surveillance by governing agencies and a way of making visible the fact of that surveillance itself, which is to say, the risk of being disciplined, fired, imprisoned, or in some extreme cases, disappeared if identified by management or union officials.

The stakes of publicizing this continued risk of reprisal were especially high in the case of Han Young, which was the first such effort at mobilization since the ratification of NAFTA and its side agreement on labor, which obliged the Mexican government to recognize formally the right of workers to organize outside the "corporatist" parameters of the official unions.[30] The masks thus become an ambivalent index for a specific transformation in the mode of governing the interactions of state, capital, and labor. NAFTA lessens restrictions on capital, but in principle increases the accountability of the

The Speculative Archive, *In Possession of a Picture* (2005–present).

Fred Lonidier, installation detail from *N.A.F.T.A.*
(Not A Fair Trade for All) (1999).

government to guarantee certain rights that were not considered pertinent within the top-down model of industrial relations during the era of import substitution. This "in principle" is often denounced as mere neoliberal window dressing for corporate exploitation, but it has also been a precarious point of leverage and resignification for human-rights groups and unions struggling to maximize the accountability of governments to the universal values they purport to uphold.[31] The "monstrosity" of the workers thus not only speaks to the anxiety that their activities may induce among employers (the exhibition in which these images appeared was shut down under pressure from a coalition of industrialists concerned about protecting the "business image" of the city)[32] but also to the incalculable future of labor movements themselves when faced with a new form of governmental rationality that at once intensifies the dynamics of exploitation and opens the possibility of new rights claims — not against "capital" as such, but with respect to the biopolitical conditions of work: saftey, health, wages, hours, and so on.[33]

Approaching Lonidier's photographs in terms of the precarious relationship between governmentality and rights complicates, though does not simply negate, the iconography of anticaptialist resistance that has emerged in the aftermath of the demonstrations against the World Trade Organization in Seattle in 1999. The latter is epitomized by *We Are Everywhere,* a dynamically designed "activist anthology, agitational collage and direct action manual" that weaves together stories and images from a variety of Northern and Southern movements into a collective portrait of "global anti-capitalism."[34] For the Notes From Nowhere editorial collective that produced the publication, the potential for self-organization in this "movement of movements" is best captured in the colorful theatrics displayed in situations of collective protest and civil disobedience described by one of the editors in terms of "direct action": "a rejection of politics which appeals to governments to modify their behavior in favor of physical intervention against state power in a form that prefigures an alternative."[35] It is on the basis of this creative immediacy that carnivalesque street revelers in Genoa and NGOs in the Narmada Valley supposedly coalesce into a global "we."[36]

While it is important to question the antigovernmental imaginary conjured by a project such as *We Are Everywhere,* it nevertheless remains crucial to attend to the specific visual and performative repertoires of the activist practices in question. The point is not cynically to isolate them from one another, but to caution against allowing a spectacular opposition between impassioned bodies of the "multitude" and the ominous riot gear of "empire"[37] to overshadow the need to attend to other sites, styles, techniques, and rhythms of nongovernmental politics, not only on the antineoliberal left, but also among liberal and right-wing activists, as well.

Ironically, the concept of "direct action" as theorized in *We Are Everywhere* disavows the extent to which, beginning in earnest with the Civil Rights movement and formalized by Greenpeace in the 1970s, the extraordinary performative tactics often deployed by nongovernmental activists are by and large designed as photo opportunities or media events. Such tactics unsettle any firm opposition between the physical

Notes from Nowhere, cover of *We Are Everywhere* (2003).

spaces and structures in which they intervene and the pages and screens on which they show up as images, whether this be a banner drop on a nuclear reactor or a human chain formed around an abortion clinic. Aiming to put intolerable governmental techniques in the "eyes and ears" of both the general public and the governing agencies themselves, these actions inherently expose themselves to reproducibility, dissemination, and recontextualization beyond their immediate points of intervention.

Such spatiomediatic interventions can take a number of forms: sometimes these involve temporary or mobile architectural structures such as Médecins du Monde's installation of dozens of tents around the entrance to the Pompidou Center in Paris to address not only the city government's neglect of the needs of the homeless population but its tolerance of homelessness as such. Likewise, the Women on Waves campaign uses its photogenic seafaring vessels not only to provide extraterritorial abortion services to women living in nations where the procedure is illegal, but also to subject these nations to international and domestic scrutiny regarding their criminalization of abortion itself.

Often both intersecting with the discourse of direct action and exhibiting affinities with the principle of "mobilizing shame" are the notions of "adbusting" and "tactical media." Loosely inspired by the Situationist principle of *détournement,* or the diversion of established technologies, circuits, and cultural elements from their officially authorized functions and meanings,[38] these concepts were first theorized in places such as *Adbusters* magazine and Naomi Klein's *No Logo* (1999).[39] Operative early on in the visual tactics of the environmental and antisweatshop activists surveyed by Klein, these concepts consider the public brand image of a governing agency (especially, but not limited to, corporations familiar to consumers such as Nike or Shell) to be a primary site of political vulnerability and thus a point of intervention and leverage for activists. Most often, this has meant negatively inflecting or re-marking the iconic resonances of a brand for a media outlet, consumer, or shareholder in relation to a set of overt claims that criticize the agency in question, such as the Killer Cola campaign targeting Coke's toleration of anti-union violence in Colombia: "Murder...It's the Real Thing."

In other cases, prankster-activists such as the Yes Men have not simply defaced, but have meticulously impersonated the visual identity of corporate spokespersons to such an extent that they have been misrecognized by consumers, experts, and media outlets, thus giving them a temporary platform from which to criticize the practices of the entity they claim to represent, usually through a kind of Brechtian exacerbation of official claims. The logic of such projects is to gain visibility for an issue not only by disseminating critical information, but also by forcing a public response, defense, or explanation from the agency whose image has been hijacked—a response that can often prove more incriminating than the initial intervention.

Combining both digital and architectural *détournement,* another project along these lines is Nikeplatz, a seamlessly rendered public-information center installed at

Home page, www.killercoke.org.

the central plaza in Vienna announcing that the space was to be sponsored and redesigned by Nike, replete with a massive monument in the form of the corporation's iconic "swoosh."

Exacerbating the public disrepute already associated with the corporation for its attempts to evade responsibility for the abusive labor practices of its subcontractors, Nikeplatz addressed the increasingly unaccountable abrogation of public-service provisions by the state and the ideology of corporate citizenship that has accompanied the privatization of spaces, infrastructures, and goods of all kinds.

Such tactics operate primarily in a negative mode to create a moment of spectatorial estrangement or disidentification from a familiar figure, object, or image, reframing it as the locus of relations, processes, or practices open to conflict and thus to transformation. Yet it would seem just as important to examine critically the counterpoint to overtly antagonistic forms of address, that is, the "positive" identifications constructed by NGOs themselves, as well as the visual design and marketing of products and programs they may advocate, coordinate, or distribute, whether in collaboration with or as an alternative to those of governing agencies. Such strategies include fair-trade campaigns, for instance, or the array of emergency shelter and life-support technologies developed by the field of "humanitarian design,"[40] examples of which were displaced from their immediate points of application in a remarkable media event staged by Médicines Sans Frontiers in Central Park in September 2006. Timed to coincide with the global press attention focused on the annual meeting of the UN General Assembly, the organization set up a para-architectural exhibition entitled "A Refugee Camp in the Heart of the City," replete with tents, latrines, and medico-nutritional distribution equipment. The exhibition was staffed by experienced MSF aid workers — some of whom were former camp residents — who led guided tours through the "camp," detailing the functional operations of such emergency spaces and evoking, to the extent that it is possible, the experiential conditions of camp life for refugees themselves. Rather than simply advertising their work as a viable "solution" to humanitarian crises that a generically sympathetic public might be moved to support, a crucial interpretative role of the MSF tour guides and media spokespeople was to draw attention to the fact that "there are no humanitarian solutions to humanitarian problems." As Nicolas De Torrente put it in an interview on National Public Radio concerning the exhibition:

> If we are [at a site of humanitarian emergency], as an independent humanitarian organization, it is already a sign of failure…people support us so much, and they tend to think "more, more, can you go there, help here "…but what we want to point out to the people is that if we are there it's a sign of failure, that there are people who are theoretically responsible to respond to these crises, and that they are not responding properly…that's why we need to educate our donors and supporters…good intentions are not enough.[41]

Though the exhibition sought to publicize the plight of thirty-three million refugees around the world, its message implicitly synergized with the demands made by the Save Darfur Now: Voices to End Genocide rally being held contemporaneously in

Nikeplatz (www.nikeground.org), Karlsplatz, Vienna (2003)
(Eva and Franco Mattes, 0100101110101101.org).

MCKEE   345

Médecins sans frontières, *Refugee Camp in the Heart of the City*,
Central Park, New York, NY, September 9, 2006.

Central Park — an event whose visual signature was the proliferation of blue hats, code
for a demand that the Bush administration and Kofi Annan support the immediate
deployment of UN peacekeeping forces to the Sudan with a Chapter Seven mandate to
protect civilians.[42]

The aesthetic techniques considered thus far typically imagine a general public of consumers, citizens, or even investors unengaged with the internal processes of activism
and advocacy. Yet as Meg McLagan has stressed in her work on the mediatization of
human-rights testimonials, a high-profile visual artifact such as a film screened on public television or at a festival must be understood in relation to a more subtle range of
other, more specific activities, arenas, and circuits.

    Though they have received less theoretical attention than, for instance, the semi-
otic conventions of civil disobedience, adbusting, or documentary film, another crucial
set of aesthetic techniques to consider in both the operations and the claim making of
nongovernmental organizations is those often referred to as "information design" — the
translation of various kinds of evidentiary data sets, often of a technical or quantitative nature, into visual patterns, arrangements, figures, and formats that are cognitively

accessible to nonexpert audiences. Statistical graphs, tables, charts, diagrams, timelines, blueprints, maps, and specialized scientific images are among the materials addressed by information design, a term whose conceptual underpinnings are a matter of dispute. For Edward Tufte, author of the canonical treatise *Envisioning Information,* the founding premise of information design is that the form in which data is presented crucially shapes its content and the way in which it is received, judged, and used.[43] Yet what flows from Tufte's basic aesthetic insights concerning figure-ground relations, the layering, differentiation, and arrangement of elements, and the use of color and typography is a transcendental imperative to optimize and clarify "communication," a term whose value he takes to be self-evident. While he recognizes a dimension of "persuasion" in information design, he neutralizes its political dimension by taking consensual "problem solving" as the telos of the public sphere to which he calls upon designers to contribute their skills.

Tufte's emphasis on the implications of the often taken-for-granted visual forms in which data are inscribed and organized thus needs to be supplemented with questions about who or what is authorized to produce data in the first place and how visual information is mediated before, during, and after becoming an element in the articulation of a political claim. This means understanding specific visual-informational artifacts in relation to the stories that they implicitly or explicitly tell and that are told about them in the different institutional, technical, and discursive conditions that mark their appearance, whether the artifact is a demographic chart presented at a congressional hearing, a dossier of forensic evidence shown by a lawyer at a war-crimes tribunal, an urban plan criticized by a housing-rights organization at a city council meeting, or the animated models of climate-change data deployed by environmentalists.

It is from within the discourse of architecture that some of the most innovative responses to these problems have emerged. A number of designers have recently developed spatial information design techniques that do not simply aim to "envision" preexisting information, but that make critical claims in their own right concerning both the formal and political dimensions of mapping itself. Such projects question the self-evidence of physical territory, suggesting that the future of spaces is inextricably bound up with the conflicting ways in which they are marked, framed, and interpreted through technologies of virtualization.

One important example of such innovation in visual information design can be found in the maps developed by architect Eyal Weizman in collaboration with the Israeli human-rights organization B'Tselem, which detail the precise territorial strategies of the Israeli state in its deployment of settlements across the West Bank. Weizman color codes geographical data in such a way that actually existing settlements, which take up only around 2 percent of the West Bank and appear relatively randomly dispersed on a typical map, show up as nodes in a much wider and longer-term set of topographic, infrastructural, and administrative mechanisms designed to fragment and control the territory as a whole. These include hilltop developments, bypass roads, remarkably expansive municipal boundaries, and, most recently, the so-called security fence.

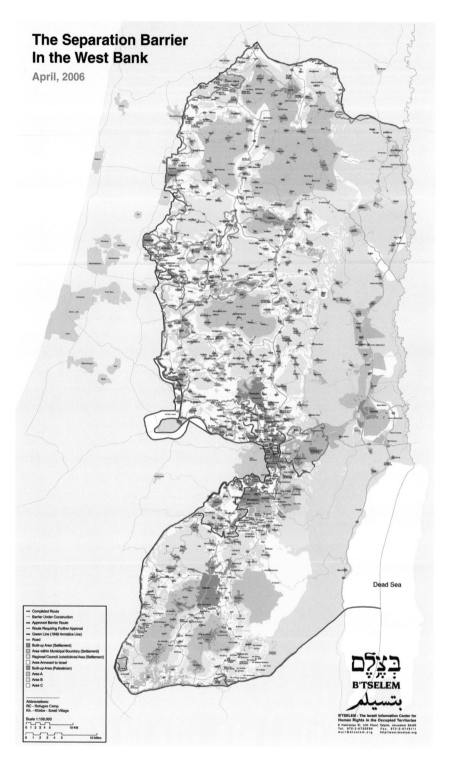

The Separation Barrier
In the West Bank

April, 2006

B'teselem: the Israeli Information Center for Human Rights in the
Occupied Territories, annotated map of the separation barrier in the
West Bank, April 2006.

While these maps have been important for B'Tselem in articulating their claims that West Bank settlements violate Israel's own obligations as an occupying power under international humanitarian law, Weizman (along with Rafi Segal, the partner in his architecture firm) also intended for them to appear in an exhibition entitled *The Politics of Israeli Architecture,* which was selected by the Israel Association of United Architects (IAUA) to represent Israel at the World Congress of Architecture in Berlin in 2002.[44] However, the exhibition was canceled, because it became clear to the IAUA that the exhibition not only represented politics as an external theme, but actually located the institutions of architecture and planning themselves—typically considered a matter of aesthetic embellishments and technical procedures—at the heart of the "civilian occupation" of Palestinian territory.[45] The exhibition, which ultimately traveled to the United States, called for architects to take responsibility for their witting and unwitting proximity to governing agencies and for the discipline itself to shift its priorities from the design of buildings and structures within intolerable conditions to the critical spatial analysis of those conditions in public concert with the Israeli and Palestinian human-rights movements.

Another example of such activist cartographic techniques are those employed by the Justice Mapping Center (JMC), an affiliate of the Open Society Institute's After Prison Initiative, which introduced the Million Dollar Blocks into the debates surrounding criminal-justice reform in the United States. Invented by policy analyst Eric Cadora, the Million Dollar Blocks is simultaneously a rhetorical figure, a visually dynamic index, and a technical unit of sociospatial analysis that correlates data on state prison expenditures with the block-by-block residential origins of incarcerated individuals, as well as the racial and class compositions of the neighborhoods in question.[46]

Detouring the Geographical Information Systems (GIS) software used by the Justice Department to visualize crime patterns, Cadora cartographically collated incarceration and residential data sets—some of which had never been extracted from public archives—making visible the highly uneven concentrations of criminal-justice spending in particular areas and populations of U.S. cities. General patterns of disproportionate incarceration have long been decried by prison activists, but the Million Dollar Blocks is framed in terms of positive governmental investment, which is to say, the channeling of techniques, energies, and resources in the pursuit of a particular objective: reducing crime and increasing the security and welfare of the population. Yet Million Dollar Blocks analysis also works on a temporal axis, tracking the high recidivism rates of formerly incarcerated people who return to their neighborhoods, thus questioning, on the state's own terms, the rationality and efficiency of its modes of investment. Rather than calling for governmental disinvestment, then, the Million Dollar Blocks opens a speculative debate about reinvestment in the lives and environments of individuals reentering the realm of citizenship following imprisonment. Assuming that its own stated purposes and aims are not well served by its current modus operandi, what other modes might governmental investment take in neighborhoods with high rates of crime, incarceration, and recidivism, especially when these data are layered onto other

Spatial Information Design Lab, Million Dollar Blocks (2006): (LEFT) prison
expenditures by census block in Brooklyn, NY, 2003; (RIGHT) thirty-one men,
two blocks, $4.4 million, Brownsville, Brooklyn, NY, 2003.

(BELOW) Planning scenario at the Spatial Information Design Lab's Architecture
and Justice exhibition, Architectural League, New York, NY, 2006.

spatiovisual patterns pertaining to economic inequality and governmental neglect in areas such as job training, health care, and housing?

As suggested above, the meaning and force of the claims built into the technical, formal, and aesthetic operations of an informational artifact such as a Million Dollar Blocks map cannot be assessed apart from the specific contexts in which it is seen, interpreted, and used. Though Cadora's maps have received attention from numerous legislators concerned first and foremost with the inefficiency of their own budgets, they have not circulated widely outside the domain of expert policy analysis until recently. With this limitation in mind, a partnership has been established between Cadora and the experimental architect Laura Kurgan under the rubric of Columbia University's Spatial Information Design Lab with the goal of rearticulating justice mapping in new public formats and in relation to new data sets pertaining to what the designers refer to as a permanent cycle of mass migration between poor New York neighborhoods and the upstate municipalities that warehouse them.[47]

The inaugural event in this collaboration was an exhibition at the Architectural League of New York (October 2006) in which the original graphic and analytic procedures of the Million Dollar Blocks were deployed as a large-scale environmental interface designed to function as both a pedagogical display for a general public engaged with architecture and urbanism and, more importantly, as a surface of interaction, projection, and debate during specially arranged "scenario-planning" meetings between an expanded arena of stakeholders in criminal-justice reform, including community groups, advocates for the rights of (ex)-prisoners, researchers, journalists, designers, planners, and government officials.

Complicating prominent tendencies in contemporary art, theory, and activism that call for a radical confrontation with the world system of "empire,"[48] the aesthetic techniques of designers such as Weizeman and Kurgan address what Foucault called "power relations, and not power itself."[49] Their objective, in other words, is to "attack not so much 'such and such' an institution, or group, or elite, or class, but rather a technique, a form of power."[50] Thus, they do not oppose what Foucault called the "'chief enemy'" — capital, the state, imperialism — but rather the "immediate enemy": the "how" of governmental techniques that act upon and attempt to channel the actions of populations, such as infrastructural planning and criminological mapping. While those who employ these practices do not "expect to find a solution to their problem at a future date (that is, liberations, revolutions, end of class struggle),"[51] they also do not acquiesce to a merely technical reformism or renounce inscribing their endeavors into a grand design that might imagine alternatives to the large-scale geopolitical and economic dynamics that drive the permanent states of emergency to which residents of Bethlehem or Brooklyn are exposed. Instead, they supplement the militant impulse of "being-against"[52] with the difficulties of being governed — and of endeavoring to act as such.

1   Michel Foucault, "Confronting Governments, Human Rights," translated in full by Thomas Keenan in "The 'Paradox' of Knowledge and Power: Foucault on the Bias," in Keenan, *Fables of Responsibility: Aberrations and Predicaments in Ethics and Politics* (Stanford, CA: Stanford University Press, 1997), p. 157. Reprinted in James Faubion (ed.), *The Essential Works of Michel Foucault, 1954–1984, Volume 3: Power* (New York: The New Press, 2000), p. 474.

2   Michel Foucault, "The Moral and Social Experience of the Poles Can No Longer be Obliterated," in Faubion (ed.), *Essential Works: Power*, p. 471.

3   Foucault, "Confronting Governments, Human Rights," p. 157.

4   Michel Foucault, "So Is It Important to Think?," Faubion (ed.), *Essential Works: Power*, p. 457.

5   "Contemporary art" encompasses the relatively elite transnational network of discourses, institutions, and publications involved in the training, accreditation, and funding of professional artists and the circulation, exhibition, interpretation, and in some cases marketing of the aesthetic phenomena they create. More specifically, the phrase refers to the work of artists engaged with the institutionally validated histories of the formally innovative and politically ambitious European avant-gardes of the early twentieth century (Constructivism, Dada, Surrealism) and the reactivation of these legacies after the Second World War, especially in Europe and the United States. For the authoritative survey of these histories, see Yves-Alain Bois, Benjamin H.D. Buchloh, Hal Foster, and Rosalind Krauss (eds.), *Art Since 1900: Modernism, Antimodernism, and Postmodernism* (London: Thames and Hudson, 2005). In the past ten years, the networks of contemporary art have become both increasingly globalized, as indicated by the proliferation of biennials in Latin America, Asia, and Africa. Especially since the 1999 demonstrations against the World Trade Organization in Seattle and the 9/11 attacks, this globalization of contemporary art has in many cases involved an increasing porosity between professional artistic practices and the expanded networks of activist counterpublicity pertaining to antineoliberal and antiwar movements. For a sense of the tensions and possibilities of this conjuncture, see Julian Stallabrass, *Contemporary Art: A Very Short Introduction* (Oxford University Press, 2004); Okuwi Enwezor (ed.), *Documenta 11, Platform 5: Exhibition Catalogue* (Ostfildern-Ruit: Hatje Cantz, 2002); Gregory Sholette, "Dark Matter: Activist Art and the Counter-Public Sphere," *Journal of Aesthetics and Protest* 3 (Fall 2003), available online at www.journalofaestheticsandprotest.org/3/sholette; and Yates McKee, "Suspicious Packages" *October* 117 (Summer 2006), pp. 99–121.

6   This is an allusion to what Giorgio Agamben calls "means without ends" — "the sphere of pure means or gestures (i.e. means, which, while remaining such, are freed from their relation to an end) as the properly political sphere." Cited in Keenan, *Fables of Responsibility,* p. 189.

7   Jacques Rancière, *The Politics of Aesthetics,* trans. Gabriel Rockhill (London: Continuum, 2004), p. 21.

8   *Ibid.,* p. 22.

9   For a critical survey of this fifteen-year-old quasi-discipline by one if its originators, see W.J.T. Mitchell, "Showing Seeing: A Critique of Visual Culture," in Michael Ann Holly and Keith Moxey (eds.), *Aesthetics, Art History, and Visual Studies* (New Haven: Yale University Press, 2005), pp. 231–50. Along with canonical art-historical paradigms of iconological analysis pioneered by Erwin Panofsky, Roland Barthes' semiological account of the "rhetoric of the image," and psychoanalytic theories of fantasy, desire, and identification, the key sources for this concept of "culture" are the synthesis of Antonio Gramsci's theory of hegemony and Louis Althusser's theory of ideological interpellation by Raymond Williams in *Marxism and Literature* (Oxford: Oxford University Press, 1977) and the supplementation of the latter with Foucauldian thematics of discipline and subjectification by Stuart Hall in texts such as "Cultural Studies: Two Paradigms" (1980), in Nicholas Dirks (ed.), *Culture/Power/History* (Princeton, NJ: Princeton University Press, 1995), pp. 520–38. Conspicuously absent from Mitchell's reading list is the work of Gyorgy Kepes, the Bauhaus-trained editor of the *Vision and Values* series (New York: George Braziller Publishers, 1963–72) and founder of the Massachusetts Institute of Technology's Center for Advanced Visual Studies (est. 1967), both of which enabled pioneering exchanges between the arts, the humanities, the sciences, and the policy disciplines regarding the relations between media, technology, and environment.

10 In a discussion of the coemergence of civil society activism and neoliberal restructuring in postdictatorship Latin America, Sonia Alvarez, Evelina Dangino, and Arturo Escobar write, "Cultural contestations are not mere 'by-products' of political struggles but are instead constitutive of the efforts of social movements to redefine the meaning and the limits of the political system itself…when movements deploy alternative conceptions of woman, nature, race, economy, democracy, or citizenship that unsettle dominant cultural meanings, they enact cultural politics." "Introduction" in Sonia Alvarez, Evelina Dangino, and Arturo Escobar (eds.), *Cultures of Politics, Politics of Cultures: Reenvisioning Latin American Social Movements* (New York: Harper Collins, 1998), p. 7. For critical surveys of social-scientific paradigms

of social movement research, see Alison Brysk, "Hearts and Minds: Bringing Symbolic Politics Back In," *Polis* (Fall 1995), pp. 559–89, and Clifford Bob, "Globalization and the Social Construction of Human Rights Campaigns," in Alison Brysk (ed.), *Globalization and Human Rights* (Berkeley: University of California Press, 2002), pp. 138–47.

11 As Mitchell writes, "Visual studies entails a meditation on blindness, the invisible, the unseen, the unseeable, and the overlooked." "Showing Seeing," p. 236.

12 Thomas Keenan, "Mobilizing Shame," in "And Justice for All? The Claims of Human Rights," Eduardo Cadava (ed.), special issue, *South Atlantic Quarterly* (Spring 2004), pp. 434–49.

13 See Judith Butler, "Endangered/Endangering: Schematic Racism and White Paranoia," in Robert Gooding-Williams (ed.), *Reading Rodney King, Reading Urban Uprising* (New York: Routledge, 1993), p. 17.

14 See Michel Feher, *Powerless by Design: The Age of the International Community* (Durham, NC: Duke University Press, 2000).

15 See Mark Danner, *Torture and Truth: America, Abu Ghraib and the War on Terror* (New York: New York Review of Books, 2004). In its meticulous situating of the Abu Ghraib photographs in relation to the extensive archival trail of official Bush administration documents (both public and classified) pertaining to the treatment of prisoners in the "war on terror," Danner's book exemplifies the interpretative work required for effective human-rights activism; it shuttles between textual reading and visual witnessing, rather than presenting the images as self-evident documents of torture.

16 Walter Benjamin, "The Work of Art in the Age of Mechanical Reproduction," in *Illuminations*, trans. Harry Zohn (New York: Shocken, 1968), p. 234. According to Samuel Weber, this "permeation" neither alienates the perceiving subject from an authentic reality nor renders the latter immediately accessible as a terrain of practical intervention, effecting instead an ambivalent "un-securing" of the spatiotemporal coordinates of politics itself. See Samuel Weber, "Mass Mediauras, or: Art, Aura, and Media in the Work of Walter Benjamin," in *Mass Mediauras: Form Technics Media* (Stanford, CA: Stanford University Press: 1996), pp. 76–107.

17 A major voice in the left-liberal public sphere who has been a consultant for the likes of Howard Dean, Lakoff is the director of the Rockridge Institute at U.C.-Berkeley (www.rockridgeinstitute.org), which is devoted to "revitalizing progressive discourse by reframing progressive policies in ways that speak to shared American values." William Gamson and Charlotte Ryan, who direct the Movement/Media Research and Action Project (MRAP) (www.mrap.org), criticize Lakoff for his privileging of the intellectual who "reframes" an issue in the public sphere while remaining blind to issues of resource mobilization, unequal institutional access, and on-the-ground organizational strategy that social movements deal with on a day-to-day basis.

18 Witness, *Video For Change: A Guide to Advocacy and Activism,* p. 3.

19 In the course of an interview with Thomas Keenan, Rosalyn Deutsche, and Branden Joseph that begins by affirming that "artistic and cultural practices are absolutely central as one of the levels where identifications and forms of identity are constituted" and that "every form of artistic practice either contributes to the reproduction of the given common sense — and in that sense is political — or contributes to the deconstruction or critique of it," Chantal Mouffe explains that "what makes people act politically is what I've called 'passions.' Collective identifications have to do with desire, with fantasies, with everything that is not interests or the rational. Instead of thinking about politics as a place where we should all get together and try to find the rational solution… politics needs to speak to people about their passions in order to mobilize them toward democratic designs." "Every Form of Art Has a Political Dimension," *Grey Room* 2 (Winter 2001), p. 123. Tony Bennet provides a crucial discussion of the tension between the different understandings of power posited by post-Gramscian analyses such as Mouffe's, on the one hand, and governmentality studies, on the other. The latter has accused the former of hypostasizing terms such as "hegemony," "common sense," "identification" — however contested or heterogeneous — as reductive explanatory schema for understanding the constitution of the political field. Scholars such as Mitchell Dean insist on the specificity of modes of government, which is to say, the technologies, apparatuses, and forms of expertise than enable particular fields of conduct to open and modes of personhood to become operational — and contestable. Bennet suggests that such a Foucauldian approach should be taken to the study of "the cultural" itself — that is, inquiring into how governing agencies constitute the specificity of the field of "culture" as site of expertise, programming, intervention, and education and how the targets of such measures are encouraged and trained to imagine themselves as subjects of culture. See Tony Bennet, "Culture and Governmentality," in Jack Z. Brantich, Jeremy Packer, and Cameron McCarthy (eds), *Foucault, Cultural Studies, and Governmentality* (Albany: State University of New York Press, 2003), pp. 47–63.

20 The Independent Media Network (www.indymedia.org) is a crucial point of reference in this regard. For the political

claims built into its formal architecture, see Dorothy Kidd, "Indymedia.org: A New Communications Commons," in Martha McCaughey (ed.), *Cyberactivism: Online Activism in Theory and Practice* (New York: Routledge, 2003), pp. 71–96.

21 See Diana Taylor, *Disappearing Acts: Spectacles of Gender and Nationalism in Argentina's "Dirty War"* (Durham, NC: Duke University Press, 1997).

22 Douglas Crimp and Adam Rolston, *AIDS Demo Graphics* (Seattle: Bay Press, 1990).

23 See Rachel Meerpol (ed.), *America's Disappeared: Secret Imprisonment, Detainees, and the "War on Terror"* (New York: Center for Constitutional Rights/Seven Stories Press, 2005). Incidentally, this volume contains a harrowing testimonial by Mohammed Maddy — the man memorialized in Askew's photograph — a ticket taker at JFK airport who after six months of incommunicado detention in New York and New Jersey prisons was deported to Egypt on the basis of a minor visa infraction (pp. 171–78).

24 See http://disappearedinamerica.org.

25 See A.C. Thompson and Trevor Paglen, "The CIA's Torture Taxi," *San Francisco Bay Guardian,* December 20, 2005.

26 On the extralegal status of the "ghost detainee," see Human Rights Watch, "The CIA's Long Term 'Ghost Detainee'" (2004), www.hrw.org/backgrounder/usa/us1004/.

27 Judith Butler, *Precarious Life: Powers of Mourning and Violence* (New York: Verso, 2004), p. 159.

28 On the intersection of state archives, photographic surveillance, and pseudoscientific criminological assessments of the link between physiognomic traits and social deviance, see Allen Sekula, "The Body and the Archive," in Richard Bolton (ed.), *The Contest of Meaning: Critical Histories of Photography* (Cambridge, MA: MIT Press, 1989), pp. 343–88.

29 "While simple co-operation leaves the mode of the individual's labor for the most part unchanged, manufacture thoroughly revolutionizes it, and seizes labor-power by its roots. It converts the worker into a crippled monstrosity by furthering his particular skill as a forcing-house, through the suppression of a whole world of productive drives and inclinations…. not only is the specialized work distributed among different individuals, but the individual is himself divided up, and transformed into the automatic motor of a detail operation." Karl Marx, *Capital: Volume 1,* trans. Ben Fowkes (London: Penguin, 1976), p. 481.

30 The exemplarity of the Han Young struggle is explicitly addressed by the editors of the *New York Times* in "Mexico's Vulnerable Workers," August 11, 1997. On the crisis of Mexican corporatism, see Julie Tiechman, "Economic Restructuring, State-Labor Relations, and the Transformation of Mexican Corporatism," in Gerardo Otero (ed.), *Neoliberalism Revisited: Economic Restructuring and Mexico's Political Future* (Boulder, CO: Westview Press, 1996), pp. 149–66.

31 See David Bacon, "Testing Nafta's Labor Side Agreement," *NACLA* (May 1998).

32 Julie Light, "University Professor's Photos Draw the Wrath of Border Industrialists," April 29, 1999, www.corpwatch.org/article.php?id=697.

33 In 2000, the Han Young worker's struggle ended in defeat. Despite successfully coordinated publicity and litigative actions by unions on both sides of the border, the subcontractor dismissed its employees and moved its operations to a different town several miles away from Tijuana in which independent labor organizers presented less of a threat. See Heather Williams, "Of Labor Tragedy and Legal Farce: The Han Young Factory Struggle in Tijuana, Mexico," *Social Science History* 27, no. 4 (2003), pp. 525–50.

34 Notes from Nowhere (ed.), *We Are Everywhere: The Irresistible Rise of Global Anti-Capitalism* (New York: Verso, 2003), jacket cover.

35 These are the words of Notes From Nowhere member David Graber in "The New Anarchists," in Tom Mertes, (ed.), *The Movement of Movements: Is Another World Really Possible?* (New York: Verso, 2004), p. 203. On "prefiguration" as the microtopian realization of ideal social arrangements through "direct democracy" in the context of the antinuclear mobilizations of the 1980s, see Barbara Epstein's "The Politics of Prefigurative Community: The Non-Violent Direct Action Movement," in Stephen Duncombe (ed.), *The Cultural Resistance Reader* (New York: Verso, 2002), pp. 333–47.

36 For an extended critique of *We Are Everywhere,* see McKee, "Suspicious Packages," pp. 99–121.

37 Here I am referring, of course, to the primary world-historical antagonism of the post–Cold War world envisioned by Michael Hardt and Antonio Negri in *Empire* (Cambridge: Harvard University Press, 2000) and *Multitude: War and Democracy in the Age of Empire* (New York: Penguin, 2004). The importance of these books cannot be overestimated for understanding the anticapitalist and antistatist iconography of groups such as Notes From Nowhere.

38 See Guy Debord, "A User's Guide to *Détournement,*" at www.bop.org/SI/detourn.html. Geert Lovink and David Garcia reactivated the implications of *détournement* for post–Cold War activism in their 1997 manifesto "The ABC of Tactical Media," available online at www.nettime.org/Lists-Archives/nettime-l-9705/msg00096.html.

39 See www.adbusters.org and Naomi Klein, *No Logo: Taking Aim at the Brand Bullies* (New York: Picador USA, 2000).

40 See Architecture for Humanity (ed.), *Design Like You Give a Damn: Architectural Responses to Humanitarian Crises* (New York: Metropolis Books, 2006).

41 Brian Leher Show, WNYC-FM, New York, September 9, 2006. www.wnyc.org/shows/bl/episodes/2006/09/19.

42 For documentation and other publicity materials related to this event, see www.savedarfur.org/content.

43 Edward R. Tufte, *Envisioning Information* (Cheshire, CT: Graphics Press, 1990).

44 See the "Maps" page of B'Tselem's Web site: www.btselem.org/English/Maps/Index.asp. It is important to note that Weizman and B'Tselem are by no means the first to insist on the centrality of cartographic techniques in both the implementation of and resistance to the Israeli occupation. See, for instance, Edward W. Said's cartographic analyses in "Palestinians Under Siege," in Roane Carey (ed.), *Resisting Israeli Apartheid* (New York: Verso, 2001), pp. 28–42.

45 The exhibition catalogue was published as Rafi Segal and Eyal Weizman, *A Civilian Occupation: The Politics of Israeli Architecture* (London: Verso, 2003).

46 See Jennifer Gonnerman, "Million Dollar Blocks: The Neighborhood Costs of America's Prison Boom," *The Village Voice,* November 16, 2004, available online at www.villagevoice.com/news/0446,gonnerman,58490,1.html.

47 See the Spatial Information Design Lab home page at www.arch.columbia.edu/SIDL/.

48 Exemplary in this regard would be the large-scale wall diagrams entitled *World Government* designed by the French Marxist collective Bureau d'Etudes, whose activities intersect in various ways with the *We Are Everywhere* project: http://utangente.free.fr/index2.html.

49 Michel Foucault, "The Subject and Power," in Faubion (ed.), *Essential Works: Power,* p. 339.

50 *Ibid.,* p. 331.

51 *Ibid.,* p. 330.

52 "Today, the generalized being-against of the multitude must recognize imperial sovereignty as the enemy and discover the adequate means to subvert its power." Hardt and Negri, *Empire,* p. 210. Though Hardt and Negri cite Foucault's work on disciplinary power, they remain invested in a ontology of self-organized antisystemic subversion that has little immediate purchase on the specific discursive and aesthetic techniques of criminal-justice reform, for instance. An important counterpoint to my argument is to be found in the documentary videos and theoretical diagrams concerning the Prison Industrial Complex created by the artist Ashley Hunt, an affiliate of the Critical Resistance network: http://ashley-huntwork.net/.

WAYS

REGISTERS

How do **you** say A2K?

Access to Knowledge • Acesso ao Conhecimento • Dostep do wiedzy • Acceso a los Conocimientos • Acceso al Conocimiento • Accès au savoir • 知识获取 • Sifuna ulwazi • Πρόσβαση στη Γνώση • Adgang til kundskab • Adgang til viden • Ona Ọgbọn ati Oye • Zugang zu Wissen • Доступ до знань • الوصول الي المعرفة • Доступ к знаниям • Toegang tot Kennis • Klíč k vědění • Tilgang til kunnskap • Waniko yeruzivo • Достъп до Знания • Pristup znanju • Приступ знању • Пристап до знаење • Accès à la connaissance • U swikelela ndivho • კოდნის ხელმისაწვდომობა • Teacht ar eolas • Rok no and • Accesso alla conoscenza • БИЛИМ АЛУУГА ЖЕТИШӨӨ • Arivukkaana Vaaipu • Komunikimi me dijen • জ্ঞানের রাজ্যে প্রবেশ • Denumata Praveshaya • Katamelletso ho Tsebo • Dostop do Znanja • Ukufinyelela ulwazi • ការចូលញាកំណេះ៩៩ • Gye nyansa • Kuva nemukana wekuwana ruzivo • Kufinyelela Elwatini • Teisė žinoti • Toegang tot inligting • ການເຂົ້າສູ່ຄວາມຮູ້ • Njira ya tsopano yopezera chidziwitso • Hebbaade gàndal •Hunes e mand • Accès aux connaissances • Dugg buntu xamxam • Puleleho tsebong • Monyetla wa ho ithuta • Ukufikeleleka Kulwazi • Ukufinyelela Olwazini • Kufikelela kutiva • Okufuna okumanya

How do you make it happen? WIPO/IIM, June 20–22, 2005 Be There!
www.tacd.org • www.cptech.org/a2k

Nongovernmental Generation of International Treaties

James Love interviewed by Gaëlle Krikorian

James Love is the director of the Consumer Project on Technology. He was formerly senior economist for the Frank Russell Company, a lecturer at Rutgers University, and a researcher of international finance at Princeton University. He is the coauthor with Tim Hubbard of "Paying for Public Goods," in Code: Collaborative Ownership and the Digital Economy *(2005).*

What are the main problems with the current regime of intellectual property, especially for those social and economic agents — such as AIDS patients, librarians, practitioners of peer to peer exchange — who have good reason to object to monopoly practices?

The current system has three major disadvantages. First, by eliminating competition, it fosters high prices and deprives the less privileged of products that result from research — whether medical drugs, diagnostic tools, books, or new technologies. Second, by being secretive about what is happening in the field of research, systems privileging intellectual property rights work to hinder the exchange of information and ideas that nourishes researchers. Finally, by responding to the private sector's logic of profitability, the current regime promotes research that is far removed from the most urgent needs of many populations. When the market value of an invention constitutes the principal motive for research, there will always be more depilatory creams — but not treatments for tropical diseases — more video games inspired by Harry Potter — but not printers for the visually impaired.

The World Trade Organization (WTO) has already dealt with some of these issues. What do you think about how things have been handled?

In the area of health care, we have had some success. When the WTO was founded in 1995, it adopted an agreement on Trade-Related Aspects of Intellectual Property Rights (TRIPS), which standardizes the level of intellectual property protection for all the member states. Activists, governments of developing countries, and certain international institutions called attention to the major problems that this agreement created in terms of poor

Poster promoting the Access to Knowledge (A2K) movement initiated
by the Consumer Project on Technology.

countries' access to medications, and of stimulating research that responded to the needs of particular populations. These objections were first presented to the World Health Organization (WHO), and became the subject of an international campaign. As a result, in 2001, WTO adopted a declaration called "TRIPS and Public Health," which granted nation-states the right to infringe on patent monopolies. However, this victory at the level of international organizations scarcely produced any concrete changes in the national institutions that handle intellectual property rights. So we had to look toward the World Intellectual Property Organization (WIPO).

Why WIPO in particular?

WIPO is the United Nations' agency that deals with questions about intellectual property. Beyond providing technical assistance, WIPO has pursued a unique mission: to secure protection of intellectual property and to promote the idea that this protection is good, everywhere and for everyone. Property rights' owners lobby the secretariat of WIPO, which protects not only their interests but also those of the American, Japanese, and European governments, all governments ideologically committed to strengthening intellectual property. WIPO is like a machine that manufactures international norms. Once a treaty is adopted, it aids countries — that is to say, developing countries — with technical assistance and advises these governments on how to modify existent legislation and apply the new set of procedures. In principle, the secretariat should maintain neutrality; however it uses the assistance provided to impose its own orthodox line. Despite its considerable power, nobody contested WIPO for a long time. So we decided to get involved. We wanted to get a better grasp on how WIPO functioned so that we could effectively modify its procedures.

From this perspective, our first task was to get inside the organization. In certain respects, we were dealing with a multilateral and open institution — more open than the WTO, for example. NGOs can get access to WIPO's negotiations and may speak during meetings. However, until very recently, the only accredited NGOs that participated were those representing owners of property rights! Indeed, when we started to get involved, WIPO met us with resistance. At first, the secretariat would not allow us to attend the Committee on Patents as observers; our only recourse was to join the delegation of a member state or of an accredited NGO. Then the United States blocked us. We had created an organization called the Civil Society Coalition, which facilitated accreditation for small NGOs. American authorities discovered that Act Up was a member of this "coalition" and quickly invoked security issues in order to block us, arguing that Act Up was well-known for using highly disruptive tactics. Nevertheless, despite several such episodes, little by little we forced WIPO to become more open and to modify its practices. This progress owes a lot to the protests of the southern NGOs, especially in Brazil.

That was the first phase of your strategy: to penetrate the institution. Once you did this, what was your objective?

We were then able to assess what WIPO had done and to contest its politics. But we did not stop there: we also developed a positive vision of what the institution could be and of what role it might play. This constructive approach caught both the secretariat and the governments off guard, since they believed that NGOs were systematically opposed to treaties of any kind. Instead of denouncing WIPO or calling for its radical transformation, we looked for small ways to influence the organization. We formulated proposals that addressed issues that were secondary and unsatisfactory elements of WIPO's existent treaties — including the exceptions they allowed. For example, we requested that a special treaty be drawn up protecting the rights of the blind and another that guaranteed a minimal set of rights in the field of long distance learning.

So you began by targeting the specific needs of certain categories of people?

We wanted to see if, through small initiatives, WIPO might then move toward making some fundamental changes. For example, numerous products and services were inaccessible to the blind because they were not adapted to their special needs. Consequently, it was necessary to make clear that the visually impaired needed special treatment in copyright law — or more precisely, that this exceptional treatment, which already exists in the United States and Europe, should be ratified at the global level. For many years, the intellectual property rights' holders have been really aggressive. In 1996, even before member states had legislated on this, WIPO had already ratified two treaties that guaranteed international protection of their rights. At that time, there was not even *one* treaty protecting the rights of consumers in the digital environment. So it wasn't a question whether we should first address the rights of the blind or of librarians — even if some cases were obviously more urgent than others. What mattered most was that WIPO be positioned to solve the problem of some consumer constituency in such a way that it would obtain the same legitimacy as intellectual property rights' owners.

At the same time that we were intent on establishing a set of exceptions that would together take into account the rights of consumers, we also wanted to make WIPO aware of innovations in the legal and technological spheres, such as the free software movement and the Open Access Publishing Movement. The goal was to try and show how less intellectual property protection would be more equitable for information users and more productive for researchers.

So you tackled three interconnected tasks: drawing WIPO's attention to specific problems, showing it how these problems could be solved, and finally fostering the development and recognition of alternative modes of protecting intellectual property rights?

One of our goals was to move WIPO into the present so that it would think about issues in terms of new technologies, new opportunities, and new knowledge goods. In 2003, we proposed that WIPO organize a meeting on collaborative efforts to create public goods. Seventy experts — Nobel Prize winners, scientists, law professors, and economists — supported this initiative by signing our proposal. The WIPO secretariat initially accepted it, which surprised a lot of people. It was all very positive. But then Microsoft and the U.S. Patent and Trademark Office (USPTO) intervened, and the meeting was canceled. This intervention shocked many people who, up until that point, had not paid much attention to these debates. In preventing the meeting, the director of the USPTO implied that WIPO had a partisan and nonobjective position, one that aimed only to strengthen the protection of intellectual property. We then decided to take this on ourselves. In the fall of 2003 there was a big meeting in Lisbon on the WIPO program organized by Transatlantic Consumer Dialogue and Consumers International. Numerous experts from the global South attended as did representatives from the European Commission and the U.S. government. We invited representatives from the industry as well as from NGOs and, despite its refusal to host the meeting, WIPO sent several representatives from the copyright and patent section.

You managed to make WIPO attend your meeting and to integrate it into your program?

By inviting WIPO, we wanted to express our desire to include it in the debate — and also our own determination not to be excluded from it. A follow-up meeting that was devoted to access to essential learning tools took place in New York in the spring of 2004. Given the success of the WTO's campaign for access to medicines, we wanted to gauge the chances of similar results in other international forums. We tackled the issues of textbooks, academic journals, databases, software, and tools for long-distance education. During the debates, participants began to reflect on the possibility of launching a broader campaign. It became apparent that access to essential learning tools was too narrow a focus. Our concern was larger than this: it was about access to knowledge.

So things took on new proportions....

Right. In September 2004 we had a conference with the title "The Future of WIPO." We rented a hall across the street from the WIPO office and invited hundreds of people. Some famous speakers came, including Larry Lessig, Richard Stallman, Jamie Boyle, Yochai Benckler, and Bernt Hugenholz. WIPO sent speakers to participate in almost every panel. Many governmental delegations were present, even representatives from the private sector, including Shira Perlmutter from AOL Time Warner, Eric Noehrenberg from the International Federation of Pharmaceutical Manufacturers and Associations (IFPMA), the world syndicate of the pharmaceutical industry, and Hugh Hansen from Fordham University. For a good number of the WIPO delegates, this was a decisive moment. Some weeks earlier, Argentina and Brazil had in fact already introduced a resolution calling for major changes in WIPO's so-called "development agenda." This resolution mentioned various measures that we were to discuss at our meeting — the Creative Commons Web site,[1] free software, Open Access Publishing, even the idea of a treaty on access to knowledge.

This initiative from Brazil and Argentina aroused intense debate in WIPO. Despite the opposition of a certain number of northern governments, a southern bloc was set up to demand that WIPO address developmental issues. Did you have contact with the members of this coalition before the meeting in September 2004?

We had intense exchanges. During the meeting on the future of WIPO, various experts decided to issue a declaration. At the end of a complicated drafting process, we finally reached a strong and precise statement. It did not circulate publicly, but people passed it along in their networks, and it was very successful. Five hundred people signed it: Nobel Prize winners, European deputies, members of governments, famous writers. The text described the crises that existed in the field of access to and innovation of knowledge. Naturally, it was critical of WIPO, but it also invited the institution to play a positive role. It sketched alternative economic models to the current regime of excessive privatization and exclusive rights; it proposed new ways for inventors to work, new modes of sharing and circulating information — all inscribed in a coherent legal framework. The declaration had a considerable effect on the parties involved in debates about WIPO's "development agenda." The delegates from southern countries were satisfied and felt they had good intellectual support; the northern countries' delegates were impressed by the number of prestigious signatures. This certainly contributed to the fact that the initiative already proposed by Brazil and Argentina and presented to the general assembly of WIPO was then incorporated into the agenda of the institution's working program.

It seems evident that a movement is created, then grows and diversifies, and is finally internationalized. But due to the very heterogeneity of its components, one might easily imagine that it would also be riddled with tensions and conflicts.

I think that since September 2004, a real social movement has emerged. It is true that a very heterogeneous set of actors has worked together so far, but there have been remarkably few conflicts — partly because we all felt committed to the same large, international coalition, but especially because of the working method we had adopted. When the Argentinean and Brazilian governments requested that WIPO establish a treaty on access to knowledge, they still did not have an idea of what the treaty's concrete content should be. So, we decided to work collaboratively with Third World Network (TWN) and the International Federation of Librarian Associations and Institutions (IFLA) to organize an initially closed meeting in Geneva in February 2005. Seventy people spent two days working together to figure out what a treaty on access to knowledge should look like concretely. Before the meeting, the participants had been encouraged to submit proposals that were then debated during the sessions. This group was also very eclectic: alongside the independent scientists who were experts representing their governments — mostly from the global South — there were also representatives from companies such as SISCO, IBM, and Verizon, as well as NGO members and activists from the free software movement, among others. Despite their differences, there were no major conflicts among the participants, and everybody grappled with the details of all the proposals. Apart from the enthusiasm we all felt, this exercise allowed people to shed their customary roles — whether criticizing globalization, defending national interests, or protecting property rights. We held a follow-up meeting in London in May 2005, during which the treaty project was reviewed article by article. Our editorial committee then prepared a second draft. That is where we are today: in the next few months, we will have a session to finalize the draft.

You insist on the heterogeneity of your coalition — the A2K movement (access to knowledge) — and you stress that this diversity is an essential source of your success. Given these conditions, how does one analyze the way this social movement is structured in political terms? Do the different groups agree pragmatically to put their ideologies aside, to ignore their disagreements in order to focus on their common goal? Or does the solidarity emerging out of this collaboration alter slightly their traditional political polarities?

The question of the relation between intellectual property and political ideology is extremely interesting. With the Transatlantic Consumer Dialogue, we had a meeting in March 2006 in Brussels on this very theme. As you know, this is not a new question: during one of our first campaigns in the United States, in 1996, we perceived that the alliances that were created did not correspond to the usual split between the left and the right. Among those who (like us) were contesting the current legislation, one of the most determined critics was the president of the Chamber of Commerce. In his testimony to Congress, he attacked the regulation for being incompatible with free competition and innovation. In Europe, debates on software have also led to unusual positions. On both sides of the Atlantic, it is not necessarily left-wing politicians who are on our side. In a general way, when politicians of the left or the right pose as defenders of employment at the local or national level, they are inclined to maintain that it is their duty to protect local or national innovators by strengthening their intellectual property rights.

Consequently, it would be too hasty a move to presume that debates on intellectual property rights are going to divide people according to their commitment or hostility to the notion of private property. The emergence of a vast economic sector that can cheaply copyright raises issues that did not exist fifty or a hundred years ago. Larry Lessig speaks of a "remix" culture: you record a product created by someone else and you "remix" it to create something entirely new. This metaphor from the music world describes what is happening on a larger plane, in the domains of texts, data, and medical research. This is what happened with the fixed dose combination treatment for AIDS. Several molecules that are associated in a certain way were constituted into a new product, a new invention. Such a process will surely modify the very notion of intellectual property. This can perhaps be understood from the perspective of distributive justice, which takes you back to the good old opposition between right and left, but questions of freedom and innovation will still intervene, which complicates things. It is precisely because it is urgent to think about this complex and unprecedented situation that we organized a debate on the relationship between intellectual property and political ideology.

So during the meeting in Brussels what happened? People are not used to openly discussing ideology as it relates to intellectual property. On the contrary, they are usually encouraged to put their personal beliefs aside. Did participants acknowledge and explain their political strategies?

Usually, ideology is below the surface, but nobody acknowledges it; people prefer to pretend there is no ideology or politics. At this meeting, it was on the table the whole time.

Over the course of the two days, a lot of balancing had to be done. We had participants who favored software patents and ones who opposed software patents; we had fervent defenders of a strong patent system and people who preferred no patent system at all. We had more skeptics and critics than we had supporters. And we saw that the traditional left versus right marker was not a good indicator of what position people would adopt.

One part of our conference concentrated on the more practical parts of politics: what are the positions of political parties? How do intellectual property rights' owners try to influence public opinion, and what is the role of NGOs as compared with that of drug manufacturers' trade associations or software companies? The other part focused on ideology in more theoretical ways.

It was surprising to me how little people, before they came to the meeting, had thought about how to formulate the relationship between political strategies and intellectual property. There was quite a bit of discussion about the way IP [intellectual property] lobbying operates, but there is so much more to explore. For example, there is the issue of how owners of rights fund academics and NGOs, hire public-relations firms, and even create their own NGOs. In this case, examining debates about tobacco control or about climate-control regulation and environmental policy would be really informative. There are some truly interesting stories about how companies devote significant sums of money to try and shape public opinion. Exxon, for example, found people that claimed that global warming was not a problem. Tobacco companies manufactured a whole pseudoscience suggesting that smoking is not harmful. Drug companies produced propaganda about the relationship between patents and the invention of new medicines. In fact, the International Policy Network, which is industry funded, recently published a so-called "civil society report" to which pharmaceutical companies readily refer. That kind of activity plays an important role — a lot of people are taken in and fooled by it.

Once you have fully explored the most obvious ways that ideology plays itself out in the field of intellectual property — through political parties, lobbies, or strategies — what will be the next step in developing this debate even further?

The most interesting thing would be to raise people's consciousness about how their views on intellectual property are much more ideological than they are aware of. The reason innovations in pharmaceuticals are rewarded by high prices is more an ideological than practical matter. It's not so much right-left ideology as it is the ideology of what constitutes property and how property should be controlled. There is a tendency to identify something that you do as something that is your property — for instance, a book that you write, a song that you perform, an idea or an innovation that you come up with. And it seems natural to people that you would want to control that. To understand this is a starting point for comprehending the particular way we think about what knowledge goods are. Since we think of them as property, it is also quite natural to think of their management in terms of private control, setting prices, and so on. With physical property, when someone uses something that comes from someone else, you have the image of someone taking something from someone else and keeping it so that its original owner doesn't have it anymore. But with knowledge, the situation is different. Two people can share the same thing at the same time. It is a funny concept. We identify so much with physical goods that it makes it hard for us to imagine how different it is in the area of knowledge goods. And it is different in very important ways. With knowledge goods, there are rarely cases of ideas or inventions that are unique to the person who comes up with them. They are usually influenced by the culture and the environment in which this person lives, the community he or she is a part of, the ability to share information among people, and so on.

So wanting to create a system that allows this progression to take place is important. It raises several questions: what is the definition and what are the boundaries of ownership? What can you own, how deep can it go, and how long can it last? How far can control extend?

So, you want people to reflect on their own relationships with the notions of creation, ownership, and access?

We are trying to make people more self-conscious of their emotional attachment to different concepts of ownership and control of information. The first step is to make them more aware of the hidden things — the anxiety they have and the analogies they make in their minds that drive their decisions regarding intellectual property. We have ideologies that act as filters. It is a way of not thinking about things. In a way, it makes our lives simpler, more predictable. It also hinders independent thinking. With intellectual property, people are on autopilot. They are deeply influenced, but the ideology they have about intellectual property is very often too hidden for them to understand or question.

At the same time, more and more people agree that this model doesn't serve them well. They are unhappy with the outcomes of the deep-ownership, deep-control model. There is no access to medicine, there is a lot of misappropriation of software, it is impossible to make documentary films in the United States, and so on. This is also why people are now interested in questioning at very deep levels the notions around this issue and why we had this meeting. Even though there were vast differences of opinion on outcomes, there was a surprisingly positive feeling as the discussions proceeded. But one meeting, of course, is just a start, and we have to do it again. Our intention is to repeat this dialogue in the United States, probably in 2007. In a way, discussions such as these open onto a new field that is just emerging.

Translated by Susan Emanuel and Blake Ferris.

1   Inspired by free licenses, Creative Commons offers (at no cost) flexible copyright contracts to disseminate all kinds of creations. See: http//www.creativecommons.org.

Dilemmas of Home Improvement:
Can Clean Energy Technology Mediate
Civic Involvement in Climate Change?

Noortje Marres

On the Internet, there are several Web logs, or blogs, that are dedicated entirely to people's practical attempts to improve the energy efficiency of their homes. These blogs show pictures of the efforts involved, such as a group of men dragging an old boiler over a roof, or a set of solar panels barely fitting into a small urban garden.[1] Interestingly, some of these Web sites also present notes on the science and politics of global climate change, as well as reports of public events treating this issue. Indeed, it is not too far-fetched to say that such blogs present domestic practices around energy technologies as a way for citizens to address the issue of climate change. As such, these blogs must be seen against the backdrop of a broad range of innovative projects centered on citizen involvement in climate change that have emerged in recent years. Many of these projects, which are initiated not only by private individuals, but also by NGOs, governments, and businesses, focus on people's private energy use, and many of them rely on the World Wide Web as a public platform.

The blogs are interesting for a variety of reasons, including the connections they establish between domestic practices and the larger issue of global politics. In the context of the proliferation of publicity campaigns around climate change that focus on private energy use, it is possible to problematize such initiatives on a number of grounds. We can ask whether such practices reformat civic involvement in climate change as a consumption practice, transforming public concern about one of today's major issues into a matter of buying the right kind of "green" products. This kind of criticism is difficult to counter in some respects, especially because it seems obvious that climate change requires an institutional solution: the cause of the problem — the vast increases of global CO_2 emissions since the Industrial Revolution — clearly cannot be alleviated by private individuals' domestic efforts alone. However, at the same time, it can be argued that domestic engagements with energy technologies fulfill a number of important conditions for citizen involvement in politics that more conventional formats for such involvement fail to provide.

A Londoner's back garden renewable-energy project, *Rowan Langley's Journal*, November 2005 (http://rowanlangley.livejournal.com).

In raising such concerns, these projects open discussions about the relative merits of "lifestyle" politics versus established forms of civic behavior, such as participation in elections and public debates and membership in civic organizations. But domestic energy projects are certainly not just about this. Because domestic energy use is now actively promoted by major institutions as a prime location of citizen involvement, it raises questions about the forms of politics by which climate change is (and is not) addressed in societies at large. Moreover, in social and political theory, arguments have been developed that problematize the idea that it is simply a matter of "choice" whether citizen involvement in politics is enacted in traditional locations, such as public meetings, or with technological practices. In research on the politics of technology, it has been argued that technological practices constitute a principal location in which power relations in our societies take shape. I would like to explore these various problems and promises of domestic energy use as a location for citizen involvement in climate change. More specifically, I will take these practices as an invitation to reconsider theoretical understandings of what constitutes citizen involvement in politics. In doing so, I will pay special attention to the World Wide Web as a site for such involvement — although I should make it clear from the start that, in this instance, technology will not "solve" the tricky problems involved.

CLIMATE CHANGE COMES HOME

Today, people can pursue an impressively wide range of activities to do something about climate change. Besides more conventional civic behavior — such as voting for green parties, belonging to environmental organizations, and participating in public debates on the issue — people can participate in the broad spectrum of alternative formats for citizen involvement that has developed.[2] Internet-based projects seek to involve users actively in the project of "communicating" the issue, inviting people to devise "innovative" publicity strategies, such as, wearing T-shirts with slogans and installing solar panels in visible places.[3] In other cases, people are asked to take on the role of "environmental witness" and to send in personal pictures of tangible evidence of climate change for publication on the Internet, in what amounts to a public archive of images of garden flowers blooming too early in the year, people enduring the heat wave of 2003, or ski slopes without snow.[4] Thus, campaigns promoting citizen consumers to reduce their energy use can be seen as only one element in a broader range of projects that seek to redefine the means of civic involvement in more creative and concrete terms. However, these campaigns occupy a particularly prominent place in this spectrum. In European countries such as the Netherlands and the United Kingdom, the government, businesses, and NGOs have all launched such projects in recent years.[5] Framed as a way for people to make a measurable contribution, they entice citizen consumers to tackle the prime cause of the phenomenon and to reduce their "personal CO_2 emissions." Thus, a substantial number of brochures and Web sites encourage people to calculate their output of greenhouse gases using special gadgets; to take practical steps such as using energy-efficient light bulbs, switching to "green energy" packages, and enrolling in tree-planting schemes for frequent fliers; and to make bigger technical interventions, such as installing heat pumps and wind turbines.[6] Indeed, given the proliferation of this type of project, one could conclude that presently the domestic setting constitutes the prime location for solving the problem of climate change.

Commentaries on these alternative forms of citizen involvement frequently note that there is something odd about the marked focus on individuals as actors who can make the "crucial" difference with respect to climate change. After all, there is good reason to hold industry primarily responsible for the phenomenon. Private households and private car use together amount to only 25 percent of Europe's greenhouse gas emissions — as was pointed out by a BBC report on a campaign called "You Control Climate Change," launched by the European Union.[7] Indeed, it is difficult not to find this project absurd, or at the very least its title. Attempting to raise everyday practices to the status of an important site for action, the project also has the express goal of informing citizens about the practical steps they can take to curb CO_2 emissions with slogans such as "Turn down. Switch off. Recycle. Walk." Not surprisingly, the European Commission does not use quite the same language in its communications to the industries responsible for much of the remaining 75 percent of greenhouse gas emissions. Indeed, it is common knowledge that European governments have consistently failed to enforce significant emission reductions for industries. The turn to "small" citizens as the actors that can set things right where "big" government and business cannot is thus in some respects difficult to take seriously.[8] However, projects such as these certainly cannot be dismissed as "daft," considering that "market-led," "technology-driven" approaches to climate change have recently emerged as dominant strategies for addressing the problem in Europe, as well.[9] The articulation of climate change as an issue to be tackled by responsibly consuming citizens can thus be viewed as a development aligned with the shift from government regulation to market investments as a prime policy format for climate change. There are, therefore, good reasons to interpret the framing of citizen involvement in climate change through energy use as just one element in a broader "marketization" of climate change.

Furthermore, climate change has been depoliticized. We appear, then, to be moving toward a situation in which the fate of climate change is being decided in locations where the business transaction, not the political trial of forces — for example, public controversy among representatives of interested parties — constitutes the dominant form of interaction. However, there are several reasons to question this neat conclusion. To begin with, the focus on people's use of electricity, gas, and petrol can be interpreted in political terms. These practices can be seen as aligned with strong traditions of environmentalism in lifestyle politics and, more specifically, the "do-it-yourself" ethic, according to which normative engagement with environmental issues must be directed at the activities in which one participates. The adoption of these traditions by governments and businesses certainly modifies their critical potency, that is, their capacity to disrupt established social routines, as the French sociologists Luc Boltanski and Eve Chiapello have argued convincingly.[10] But this does not make the normative requirements they place on the environmentally aware any less relevant. In addition, from the more conceptual perspective of social and political theories of technology, the shift to domestic energy technologies as a prime location for civic engagement in climate change is an intelligent move. Technological arrangements have been described by Langdon Winner and Bruno Latour, among others, as important locations of politics insofar as they constitute the material means by which social life is organized.[11] Indeed, it is thus possible to infer that technologies deserve recognition as political instruments that exist alongside, and in association with, more standard institutional and discursive tools. Such arguments also lend support to a more common sense inference: the dependency on dirty energy technology, namely oil, gas, and mining, explains the nonpolitics of climate change; that is, the continued absence of drastic interventions to bring down levels of CO_2 emissions effectively. The use of clean energy technologies that rely on wind, solar, and biomass is, therefore, a good place to start addressing the matter.

The emergence of domestic energy practices as a crucial location for citizen involvement in climate change, then, opens up the following problematic. On the one hand, it can be argued that the rise to prominence of these practices may have the effect of channeling civic energies away from conventional political processes: citizen bodies pressuring governmental organizations (advocacy), which are then compelled to impose constraints on powerful economic actors (regulation). But domestic practices of energy use cannot qualify as a full substitute for such "politics of pressure." Such practices do not have the capacity to impose requirements for the reduction of greenhouse gas emissions on powerful economic actors.[12] On the other hand, practices of domestic energy use have specific benefits as a form of civic involvement in environmental issues. These practices can no longer be considered radical in the classic sense of trying things outside the mainstream. But other valuable features, such as the fact that they enable people to address climate change by means and competences that are constitutive of their own ways of living, are undeniable. These practices thus invite a set of partly contradictory judgments. However, I would like to argue that the above considerations—the critique of marketization and the appreciation of the do-it–yourself ethic—far from exhaust the positive possibilities afforded by domestic energy technologies as sites for citizen involvement. Indeed, the ways everyday practices here come to mediate civic involvement in politics—or, rather, in issues—make some things visible that can enrich theoretical understandings of civic involvement more broadly understood.

THE POLITICS OF TECHNOLOGY AND THE POLITICS OF ISSUES

The perspectives discussed above cannot fully account for practical efforts to address climate change for one reason in particular. These perspectives are insufficient if the normativity of these practices is considered. The critique of the "marketization" of issues that require a political solution locates the values that these practices enact in the *institutional configuration* that they help to implement. The tradition of lifestyle politics tends to locate normativity in the "life forms" that material-social practices help to realize. These practices entail a specific way of life in that they enact particular divisions of roles among actors and foreground particular objects and languages. However, these practices' normativity also derives partially from the issues they seek to address. These issues transcend both the institutional configuration and the ways of living to which the practices belong. Social theories of the politics of technology deserve special attention in this respect, because they have demonstrated that the normativity partly resides in the technologies upon which the practices rely. These theories underscore that practices mediate normative programs that have been formulated elsewhere. That is, they make evident that technologies cannot be understood as mere means to implement certain "formats" in practice, as the critique of marketization seems to suggest. And neither can technological practices be viewed as life forms unto themselves, which for practical purposes can be considered free from contamination by larger societal programs. Technologies themselves make a crucial difference in the type of normative action they ultimately facilitate. As such, this perspective clarifies how technological practices may come to mediate an issue such as climate change.

Social theories of the politics of technology such as those of Winner and Latour mentioned above extend the work of Michel Foucault.[13] Taking up his accounts of the disciplinary effects of technological arrangements such as school buildings, these theories focus on the ways technologies constrain human actions. In doing so, they demonstrate that technologies provide powerful instruments for enrolling people in normative projects, in building institutions or markets. However, in making this point, they also warn against reducing these practices to this function. Thus, another sociologist who has contributed to this now-classic line of work, Madeleine Akrich, has described how in the 1980s the installation of electricity meters in homes in the Côte d'Ivoire in part constituted a state-building exercise. Because the government of Côte d'Ivoire had few resources at its disposal for involving individuals as citizens in the state, the national electricity grid became an important means for turning them into political subjects. As people were enlisted as consumers of electricity, Akrich writes, they were also enrolled as subjects of a nation-state in the making.[14] Here we encounter a variation of the critique that was discussed above: domestic energy technologies may be used to extend a particular political-economic formation, such as the nation-state or the market. It is, however, significant that Akrich's study makes it clear that technological practices cannot be regarded merely as the means for enrolling users in institutional configurations. Like other authors who seek to extend the Foucauldian approach, such as Judith Butler in *Bodies that Matter*, Akrich emphasizes the inherent creativity of practice.[15] Practices have a way of resisting the neat normative programs that have been built into technologies. Thus, the energy meters that Akrich studied also provided users with opportunities to tinker with these devices. Sabotaging the meters, some succeeded in tapping unregistered electricity, thereby evading the enlistment that the technologies were supposed to bring about while getting electricity. The notion of the resistances of practice is crucial, and I will return to it below. However, while Akrich complicates the more straightforward critique of technological politics that understands it as the implementation of institutional programs in society, her perspective, too, is limited in its view of the normativity of technological practices.

The post-Foucauldian approach to the politics of technology was developed in the 1980s and has recently been reconsidered by sociologists, who have pointed out that this approach is not sufficient today.[16] This is because such an approach does not really consider what happens when engagements with technology are explicitly framed as performances of citizen involvement in politics, as is the case with energy use today. The politics of technology that is discussed in studies such as Akrich's can be characterized as clandestine, in the sense that the project of state building she describes is covert — it hides behind the overt project of providing people with energy. Nevertheless, when technological practices are more openly defined as sites of politics, as when domestic energy technologies are framed as ways for citizens to get involved in climate change, such an analysis of hidden programs no longer suffices. In such cases, a third element enters the scene: an issue. That is, technological practices are articulated as ways to address public affairs. But this dynamic cannot be very well described from the standpoint of theories of the politics of technology. This is because, from this perspective, the normativity of practice depends on the success with which a normative program is implemented or resisted in practice. The normativity that may enter technological practices by virtue of the issues that they address or fail to address — environmental, economical, political, and so on — cannot be recognized from this vantage point. When we consider that technological practices mediate substantive political issues, an important question arises: To what extent do they succeed in doing so? Thus, the question of whether these technologies enlist or fail to enlist actors can no longer be the overriding concern.[17] We must now also ask to what extent these practices "work" as a way of engaging the issue — in our case, the environmental problematic of an overheating, melting world.

Regarding the question of how we should appreciate the role of issues in practices of civic involvement, we would do well to turn to the work of the classic American Pragmatists John Dewey and Walter Lippmann. Writing in the 1920s, these authors developed an issue-oriented approach to practices of public involvement in politics. While this approach has since been extended by others, the work of Lippmann and Dewey remains particularly solid.[18] In *The Public and Its Problems*, Dewey proposed that political outsiders — that is, average people — only become actively concerned with politics when they are personally affected by issues beyond their immediate control. For Dewey, issues are therefore an indispensable condition for the involvement of citizens in politics. Moreover, according to Dewey, practices of citizen involvement in politics are also principally dedicated to finding a way to settle such issues. In making this argument, Dewey extended Lippmann's claim that civic participation in politics cannot be understood as a fulfillment of an abstract duty, such as the duty to be an active member of a political community. Indeed, it was Lippmann who first proposed that the emergence of problems that *institutions cannot solve* provides a principal condition for the public to get involved in politics.

While the Pragmatists are not always interpreted in this way, such emphasis on issues as occasions for citizen involvement in politics may prove particularly useful for our purposes.[19] It may be useful in making sense of civic practices that, like the one under discussion here, deviate from the more established formats of participating in debate and voting.[20] The Pragmatists' point that people get politically involved because they are implicated in issues opens up the possibility of valuing civic practices in terms of their capacity to enable people to act on their concern about issues.

From an issue-oriented perspective, domestic practices around energy technologies may then "work" as civic practices, to the extent that they provide a way for people to act on their concerns about climate change and, perhaps, to address the issue. Such practices enable a performance of citizenship in the sense of giving active and concrete expression to the circumstance of being personally affected by an issue that is beyond one's control. Also, because citizen involvement here takes on the form of concrete interventions, the enactment of citizenship foregrounds the overriding importance of tackling the issue itself. The issue-oriented perspective then makes it possible to appreciate practical approaches to the performance of citizenship without having to apply a "closed-world" perspective. The notion of lifestyle politics risks bringing with it a retreat of politics from larger societal platforms into the intimacy of domestic practice, reducing it to an activity that is mainly concerned with the inevitably small-scale life forms enacted. However, from the issue-oriented perspective, people's engagements in concrete efforts to address an issue may be understood as a performance of civic concern for an issue that transcends these very practices. The issue-oriented perspective on civic involvement, then, allows us to extend the post-Foucauldian approach to the politics of technology in the following way.

As mentioned above, a crucial contribution of post-Foucauldian approaches to the politics of technology is their emphasis on the formative roles that technological practice plays in the enactment of normativities. Practices may produce specific mediations — that is, transformations — of the normative programs that technologies embody. Combining this insight with the Pragmatists' point that civic involvement in politics should be understood as an issue-oriented activity makes it possible to approach technological practices as sites of civic involvement in two ways. First, we can now see technological practices such as those around domestic energy use as significant contributions to the performance of civic concern for an issue. Just as technologies make a difference in the enactment of normative programs, we can now ask what difference they make in the articulation of an issue. Thus, it becomes important to determine what the particular affordances of technological practices are for enacting civic engagement in an issue — affordances that may compare favorably or at least interestingly with other formats of civic involvement. The second insight of the post-Foucauldian approach to the politics of technology is the notion that the politics of technology is an ontological politics. The normative effects of technology intervene materially and physically in everyday life. The politics of technological practices of civic involvement may be approached in similar terms. Where technological practice serves as a site for the enactment of civic involvement, we can observe a break with epistemic approaches to citizen involvement. The performance of citizenship is often defined in terms of ideas (expressing views, advocating values, and so on). Technological practices, on the other hand, enable a civic involvement that is more physical. We can now ask to what extent technological practices allow a concrete enactment of civic concern for issues, which themselves may also be understood in physical and material terms. Practices of civic involvement may thus be said to operate on the connections, at least some of which are physical in nature, that constitute the issue in question. I will now examine these perspectives on technological practices of civic involvement in relation to domestic efforts to address climate change.

DO-IT-YOURSELF CLIMATE-CHANGE POLITICS ON THE WEB

The proposal that technological practices mediate concern about climate change requires an important addition: to realize this, practices must be explicitly articulated as such. This is because the connections that link these practices with citizenship and with the issue of climate change are not self-evident. Therefore, domestic practices around energy technologies could, in principle, also be defined as "leisure," "a good way to save some money," or simply "maintenance work." The links must thus be actively established, even if it would be an exaggeration to say that there is nothing "civic" about domestic energy technologies in themselves or that they have "nothing" to do with climate change. (That would be to deny the physical, institutional, and normative connections that are already arising in practice between energy use and climate change and responsibilities that must accordingly be taken.) This indeed seems to be the "catch" with regard to alternative formats of citizen involvement: it is never self-evident that such practices indeed qualify as instances of civic engagement with issues. They must be actively formulated as such.[21] This articulation of the technological practices with concern for climate change is now facilitated by the World Wide Web.

Generally speaking, the Internet can be seen as an increasingly important technical arrangement for the performance of citizenship that functions alongside or as an integrated component of existing machineries such as, public opinion research, media debates, elections, citizen consultations, protest events, and so on. Considering this, social theorists such as Nikolas Rose have argued that Internet technology is in part constitutive of contemporary forms of citizenship.[22] Notions of "active" or "entrepreneurial" citizenship that also play their part in publicity campaigns around climate change must then be understood partly as artifacts of the rise to prominence of interactive media, or at least as developments reinforced by these technologies.[23] I would like to emphasize that information and communication technologies such as the Internet facilitate or reinforce not only specific framings of the civic subject, but also particular forms of civic involvement. Indeed, the Internet can be held partly responsible for the articulation of citizenship as an engagement with issues. Whether it is because of the interactivity of the medium, the intimate location of computers in the home, or the fact that the Web can be understood as an extension of whole assemblages of personal recording technologies, from cameras to Xerox machines, is hard to decide. But Web sites and online discussion forums frequently serve as platforms for presenting personal activities publicly. As such, they facilitate the "enunciation" of all sorts of situated practices as personal attempts by user-citizens to "do" issues in their own way. One way to document such enactments of citizen involvement is to locate and visualize "issue networks" on the Web.

Hyperlinks among Web sites can be used to connect sites that publicize a common issue, and such networks can be located and visualized with the aid of link-analysis software. Locating climate-change networks on the Web is one way to document how domestic energy technologies are being framed as practices of citizen involvement in the issue. It may render visible the connections among practices of home improvement, climate change, and citizenship that are being established in this informational domain. We have seen above that many Web-based projects frame domestic energy use as a site for citizen involvement in climate change. So it doesn't come as a surprise that this practice figures quite prominently in climate-change networks on the Web. (Indeed, this can be taken as another indication of the extent to which civic concern about climate change has recently been reformatted as practical concern about personal energy use.) In order to examine these relationships in more detail, I located two climate-change networks, one Dutch and one British. (I found that a national approach was most common in climate-change campaigns that focused on practical action by citizens.)[24] Quite impressively, when compared with the amorphous networks that one finds in many other cases, both these networks turned out to provide an answer to one question in particular: What can I (an average person) do about the climate? Even the most cursory glance at the Web sites gathered in these networks yield the following answers:

DUTCH DO-IT-YOURSELF CLIMATE-CHANGE NETWORK

www.duurzameenergie.org/ (consume green energy)

www.duurzaam-beleggen.nl/ (invest in environmentally sustainable businesses)

www.energieprijzen.nl/ (compare prices for gas and electricity)

www.europeesecolabel.nl/ (buy green products certified by the EU)

www.klimaatkaart.nl/ (compare the climate policies of Dutch municipalities)

www.senternovem.nl/duurzaaminkopen (buy green products)

www.thebet.nl/ (students can make a bet with the local government or a business that they will reduce their emissions)

www.voetafdruk.nl/ (calculate your ecological footprint)

www.chooseclimate.org/flying/ (calculate the warming effect of air flight)

www.goingcarbonneutral.co.uk/ (read about the efforts of the Cheshire village of
    Ashton Hayes [pop. 1000] to become England's first carbon-neutral village)

www.greenbuildingstore.co.uk/ (buy green construction materials)

www.msarch.co.uk/ecohome/ (take a virtual tour of the eco-home of Gil and Penney
    in Nottingham — and learn about their architectural services)

www.sustainablehousing.org.uk (buy an environmentally friendly house)

Many of the approaches articulated in these networks are decidedly practical and "domestic" in their orientation. As one site puts it: "ODE [Organisatie voor Duurzame Energie, or Organization for Sustainable Energy] shows what normal people can do to generate and use sustainable energy."[25] Crucially, however, this type of reduction of an important public affair to a "domestic affair" cannot, in the context of these networks, be interpreted as an evasion of the political complexities that climate change presents. These networks disclose a host of connections between energy practices in the home and other elements that constitute the issue of climate change, such as melting glaciers and criticisms of CO_2 emission-trading schemes. These networks thus display the associations through which domestic energy practices may become "normatively charged" with the issue of climate change.

In these networks on the Web, we can observe how domestic practices are being pulled into the climate-change "subsystem": comparisons of electricity and gas contracts, tips on how to install a solar water-heating system, and an online store for ecological building materials here appear as elements in "professional" climate-change networks that connect the United Nations Framework Convention on Climate Change to the World Wildlife Fund and several other big international nongovernmental organizations that have been campaigning and lobbying for climate change for about fifteen years. More specifically, these networks link the practical to the natural, connecting domestic energy use with visual presentations of the effects of climate change on nature around the globe: shrinking ice caps, disappearing species, and extreme weather phenomena. Finally, on the surface level of these networks on the Web, domestic energy practices appear not in opposition to, but in connection with other formats for civic involvement in environmental issues: a campaign to vote for green parties in local elections in the Netherlands, a petition against nuclear energy, as well as public information on the attempts of organizations to enact political pressure, whether in the form of protest, advocacy, or legislature.

Another way of putting it is that these climate-change networks on the Web are heterogeneous networks. They are not predominantly government or business or NGO networks, as I have found in other cases. They do not represent pure versions of policy networks, advocacy networks, or green-market networks. As they tie together the heterogeneous elements listed above, these networks show that climate change indeed qualifies as an issue. They constitute a tense tangle of elements that had few social connections with one another only a few decades ago: the fate of icebergs, coastal regions, and flowers and insects living in northern European parks is linked to increases in energy consumption and the lack of a capacity to enforce emission reductions.[26] To the extent that domestic energy use is explicitly involved in this tangle of connections, such practices can be said to mediate the issue of climate change. To work with clean energy technologies in the home is also an indirect way to engage with melting glaciers and governments' failure to do something serious about them. As long as such connections remain active, the reduction of climate change to a green market cannot be established as given.

Climate-change networks on the Web also make visible other affordances of domestic practices around energy technology that render it resistant to being reduced to "mere" consumerism. These relate to the particular ways such practices mediate the issue of climate change. First, technological practices constitute material practices. Textual and visual presentations of practices of "home improvement," such as those presented by the blogs mentioned in the introduction, make it clear that concrete efforts to address climate change must deal with the refusal of matter—pumps, electricity cables, garden soil, and digging machines—to comply with "neat ideas." "At last we are underway with our heat pump system. The instruction manual says: dig trench, lay pipe, pressure test and backfill. But it ain't that easy."[27] Accounts like these not only make it clear that technological practices in the home do not exhibit the "passivity" that is associated with consumerism; they also make a more general point. Concrete attempts to do something about the climate cannot be reduced to pure normative formats—those of managerial problem solving or, for that matter, ideologically consistent behavior. Indeed, these displays present actual efforts made in the certain knowledge that they may not solve the issue. As such, these practices can also be read as comments on the discursive commitments made by "big" players to invest "substantial" resources. The normativity of domestic energy practice, then, does not reside only in the idea that "small is beautiful." Rather, accounts of material practices are much more effective at documenting the difficulties of addressing the issue than discourses of "problem solving." In this sense, the framing of citizen involvement in climate change as a technological practice can be seen as an important strategy for resisting the reduction of climate-change policy to "market solutions."

Second, the articulation of climate change happens on the level of the associations that make up everyday life. As climate-change networks on the Web help to make clear, one of the important achievements of recent definitions of climate change has been to establish continuities between issues of big politics (how effective are emission-trading schemes?), natural phenomena (mountain snowcaps are melting), and domestic practices (energy efficiency in the home). In these networks on the Web, as I have said, we can watch how people are pulled into a political-economic-environmental-cultural affair, and a major one at that. What is important about the insertion of domestic practices in this respect is that they provide a way to involve people in the issue by way

Dutch climate-change network on the Web,
located and visualized with the aid of Issuecrawler,
February 22, 2006 (www.issuecrawler.net).

of people's social, physical, and technical personal "attachments." Concrete elements
that make up everyday life and that can be appreciated as such are here brought into
"material" continuity with important public affairs, highlighting specific connections
among them. The text circulating in climate-change networks on the Web also provides
an indication of this. Querying the British climate-change network on the Web with
the aid of the search engine Google, the text fragments returned by the engine give a
rough, but clear sense of the practicalities of "home improvement":

> in the second session, the focus was in the kitchen and also the utility room where there
> is a condensing combi boiler....

> A good symbolic moment as we throw out our oil boiler. Our biggest single contribution
> to reducing our carbon emissions....

British climate-change network on the Web,
located and visualized with the aid of Issuecrawler,
February 22, 2006 (www.issuecrawler.net).

In re-plumbing use narrow-bore pipework and keep the run between the boiler and appliance as short as possible.

Put screw-in aerators or low-flow heads in....[28]

The language is specific, concrete, and personal, and as it circulates among climate-change Web sites, it equally comes to speak of an engagement with a "big" issue. In this way, these networks on the Web show people evading the usual requirements for performances of political citizenship: dissociating from everyday life and rising to the level of a general, abstract, or intellectual concern with the "common good." But the turn to domestic practices cannot be dismissed as a withdrawal into a private universe of alternative practice, because these networks establish a host of connections between practice and issue. Climate-change networks on the Web thus make it clear that domestic

"Heat Pump — the Commitments," *The Greening of Hedgerley Wood: The Diary of One Family's Attempts to Save CO2,* August 2005 (www.hedgerley.net/greening/?p=48).

engagements with climate change have the capacity to resist simply reducing this explosive issue of political economy to a modest effort to "be good" and to "contribute."

CONCLUSION: STICKING WITH THE DILEMMA

Although domestic energy practices can be valued as positive interventions in climate-change politics, they do not solve the dilemmas raised by the displacement of climate change to the home setting. The problem remains that more conventional political efforts by citizens may be weakened by the rise to prominence of material practices as locations of citizen involvement. As civic energies are invested in concrete domestic efforts, practices of building pressure on powerful actors who can intervene in energy economies with rather more "substantial" means may suffer. Indeed, my appreciation of technological practices of personal energy use may make matters worse. This problematic cannot be said to be resolved in climate-change networks on the Web — in an appeal, for instance, to the "conjunctive logic" of networks. It would be a mistake to celebrate networks as a form of organization that makes possible a politics of the "and…and": a politics in which material practices of home improvement and other forms of political participation, such as public debate, are not in tension with one another, but only enrich one another. Such an observation ignores the circumstance wherein displacements of issues are to a degree exclusive in their effects: where the action shifts to domestic settings, other locations may grow quiet. Nor do climate-change networks on the Web appear to address seriously the tension between the rise to prominence of domestic approaches to climate change and the need to tackle the issue. I have not found any indication in these networks of a focused controversy around "civic consumption" as one of the principal formats of climate-change policy. Thus, the conclusion that there is "not enough politics" in these networks may well be justified and necessary. The slogans "think positive, say positive, do positive" that characterize domestic engagements with climate change diffuse the confrontational approach necessary for the rise of the power politics of climate change. In this essay, I have concentrated on appreciating what is gained by displacing the issue of climate change to the home. The diagnosis of a "shortage" of politics fails to appreciate the capacity of home improvement to enable civic involvement in the issue. Because attempts to address climate change take the form of material and concrete practices, they may favorably reconfigure the terms of engagement with the issue. It is now a little less inconceivable that the demand for such concrete engagement can be joined with more "political" engagements.

1 *The Greening of Hedgerley Wood: The Diary of One Family's Attempts to Save CO2,* www.hedgerley.net/greening; rowan-langley's Journal, http://rowanlangley.livejournal.com/.

2 To name two examples, local branches of the Dutch NGO Mileudefensie have been organizing "klimaatcafes" since the beginning of 2005, and the British NGO coalition Stop Climate Chaos maintains a live calendar of public meetings organized in different municipalities in the UK.

3 See www.climatechallenge.gov.uk/ for the communications initiative on climate change launched by the British Department of the Environment in December 2005 .

4 "In Pictures: Your Changing World," *BBC News,* http://news.bbc.co.uk/2/shared/spl/hi/picture_gallery/05/sci_nat_your_changing_world/html/1.stm.

5 As the references above make clear, I will focus on these countries, because I know them best.

6 See below for references to such projects.

7 Alix Kroeger, "Europeans Urged to Act on Climate," *BBC News,* May 29, 2006, http://news.bbc.co.uk/2/hi/europe/5026094.stm.

8 It may be tempting to see such campaigns as a form of performance art, and perhaps one should. A recent project undertaken by art students in London summarizes the situation quite elegantly. In a ludic reference to the UN treaty that failed to enforce the reduction of greenhouse gas emissions, the group adopted the title "Do It Yourself Kyoto." It has developed a gadget for measuring energy use in the home, which is advertised on the Web as making it possible for "individuals [to] take responsibility for climate change, rather than leave it solely in the hands of governments and big businesses," *Nesta Creative Investor,* "Awardee Story," 2002 (updated 2005), www.nesta.org.uk/ourawardees/profiles/5111/index.html.

9 See the full text of the speech by Tony Blair in "Prime Minister: 'Concerted International Effort' Necessary to Fight Climate Change," *Directgov,* February 24, 2003, www.number10.gov.uk/output/Page3073.asp; and the letter by the director of the Dutch environmental organization Natuur & Milieu found in Mirjam de Rijk, "De milieumarketing van Minister Brinkhorst" (The Environmental Marketing of Minister Brinkhorst), *Volkskrant,* June 24, 2005.

10 Luc Boltanski and Eve Chiapello, *The New Spirit of Capitalism,* trans. Gregory Elliott (London: Verso, 2005).

11 Langdon Winner, "Do Artifacts Have Politics?" in *The Whale and the Reactor: A Search for Limits in an Age of High Technology* (Chicago: University of Chicago Press, 1986), pp. 19–39; Bruno Latour, "Where Are the Missing Masses? The Sociology of a Few Mundane Artifacts," in Wiebe E. Bijker and John Law (eds.), *Shaping Technology/Building Society: Studies in Sociotechnical Change* (Cambridge, MA: MIT Press, 1992), pp. 225–58.

12 In this respect, it is remarkable how little explicit mention is made of the economic reliance on oil in reports on clean-energy technology and climate change — an issue that is closely tied to the argument in favor of imposing binding emissions-reduction targets on industry.

13 Here I focus on just one theoretical perspective on the politics of technology. It is a particularly important one, because — unlike many other approaches — it assigns technology a formative role in the production of political effects. That is, it grants technologies themselves normative agency in the performance of politics, as will be discussed below. However, it should be noted that it is disputable whether the "politics" of technology in all cases deserve that name. As I will also discuss below, it may be better to recognize that for a technological practice to qualify as a site of politics, it must be actively articulated as such.

14 Madeleine Akrich, "The De-Scription of Technical Objects," in Bijker and Law (eds.), *Shaping Technology/Building Society,* pp. 205–24. A second example that Akrich gives is that of a development project providing households with solar-powered lamps in the Côte d'Ivoire. In Akrich's description, this project involved the attempts of French development organizations to introduce their vision into energy-consumption practices. Akrich thus indicates that technology may facilitate the transportation across practices of various scripts: a script of development designed in France and one a state building devised by the government of the Côte d'Ivoire.

15 Judith Butler, *Bodies that Matter: On the Discursive Limits of "Sex"* (New York: Routledge, 1993).

16 Andrew Barry, Michel Callon, and I have all highlighted the importance of "issue formation" for the transformation of technology into an object of politics. This point is not necessarily a critique of the post-Foucauldian approach, however, because sociological studies of issue making focus on a different kind of practice, namely, ones in which technology is explicitly politicized. The effectiveness of the politics of technology described by Akrich resides precisely in the fact that it remains implicit. See Andrew Barry, *Political Machines: Governing a Technological Society* (London: Ath-

lone, 2001), and "Public Knowledge and Demonstration: Politics and the Pipeline," unpublished MS, 2004; Michel Callon, "Europe Wrestling with Technology," *Economy and Society* 33, no. 1 (2004), pp. 121–34; Noortje Marres, "No Issue, No Public: Democratic Deficits after the Displacement of Politics," PhD diss., University of Amsterdam, 2005.

17 A similar criticism can be made of approaches that seek to give a positive spin to the concept of technological politics. Some authors, such as the Dutch philosopher Peter-Paul Verbeek, interpret the notion that technology exerts a formative influence on social life in constructive terms. Peter-Paul Verbeek, "Artifacts and Attachment: A Post-Script Philosophy of Mediation," in Hans Harbers (ed.), *Inside the Politics of Technology: Agency and Normativity in the Co-production of Technology and Society* (Amsterdam: Amsterdam University Press, 2005), pp. 125–46. Technological practices then become important sites of moral intervention, because this is where social roles are distributed among actors. Such an approach extends the insight that the "personal is political" and that is associated with the notion of "do-it-yourself" to the idea that the technologies of everyday life may carry a positive normative charge. (This point is missed in certain other understandings of the politics of technology: it is sometimes argued that we must focus on the processes of decision making about technologies in order to ensure that their normative consequences are morally and politically sound. Such arguments do not really acknowledge that situated practices determine what normativities, exactly, technologies enact.) However, this constructive approach, too, largely ignores how the issues that are addressed in technological practices inform their normative charge.

18 John Dewey, *The Public and Its Problems* (1927; Athens, OH: Swallow Press, 1991); Walter Lippmann, *The Phantom Public* (1925; New Brunswick, NJ: Transaction, 2002). There are various ways to conceptualize the role of issues in public involvement in politics, such as those focusing on agenda setting. But the Pragmatist perspective stands out in this respect, because it makes particularly strong claims. (Here, issues are considered indispensable for involving publics.) Also, especially in the case of Dewey, the Pragmatist approach to civic involvement is an ontological one. This is particularly valuable for the case under discussion here: the mediation of citizen involvement by material practices.

19 Dewey's arguments in favor of participatory democracy, that is, the involvement of citizens in public debates, tends to overshadow his more "abstract" theory about issues as occasions for the formation of publics. As for Walter Lippmann, he is widely recognized as a democratic skeptic, so people

rarely turn to his books for positive arguments about how publics can become involved in politics.

20 This is so even if their approach may enrich analyses of established practices, as well.

21 Nevertheless, once we understand citizen involvement as a practice of enacting concern with issues, it becomes clear that something similar may apply to established formats for the performance of citizenship. When people participate in elections, it cannot be assumed as a matter of course that they are enacting civic involvement.

22 Nikolas Rose and Carlos Novas, "Biological Citizenship," in Aihwa Ong and Stephen J. Collier (eds.), *Global Assemblages: Technology, Politics, and Ethics as Anthropological Problems* (Malden, MA: Blackwell, 2005), pp. 439–63.

23 The medium is also used as an example of the "technological revolution" that climate change requires. Thus, the BBC reported, "Tony Blair has called for a 'technological revolution comparable to the internet' to slow global warming": "Blair Demands Green 'Revolution,'" *BBC News,* March 29, 2006, http://news.bbc.co.uk/2/hi/uk_news/politics/4854886.stm.

24 As starting points for locating these two networks, I chose the Web sites of Dutch and British NGOs that deal with climate change and the practical steps people can take to address it. (Generally speaking, NGOs are most reliable for disclosing issue networks, because, unlike governmental organizations, they often provide hyperlinks to other organizations.) The networks were located with the aid of a program for network location, visualization, and analysis on the Web called Issue Crawler. Issue Crawler is a server-based tool that enables locating networks on the Web on the basis of link analysis, that is, by analyzing which pages link to other pages as a way to determine the relative importance of Web pages within a given network. Issue Crawler is developed and hosted by the Govcom.org Foundation in Amsterdam. See www.govcom.org. For more information on the methods and techniques of issue-network mapping, see Noortje Marres and Richard Rogers, "Depluralising the Web, Repluralising Public Debate: The Case of the GM Food Debate on the Web," in Richard Rogers (ed.), *Preferred Placement: Knowledge Politics on the Web* (Maastricht: Jan van Eyck Akademie, 2000), pp. 113–35; and Richard Rogers and Noortje Marres, "Landscaping Climate Change: A Mapping Technique for Understanding Science and Technology Debates on the World Wide Web," *Public Understanding of Science* 9, no. 2 (2000), pp. 141–63.

25 This slogan was translated from the Dutch on the home page of the Organisatie voor Duurzame Energie (Organization for Sustainable Energy), www.duurzameenergie.org/.

26 In this respect, it is noteworthy that less than ten years ago, it was still assumed that climate change, as a natural phenomenon, could be made visible only by complex climatological models. Because the effects of climate change are now noticeable in the "park across the road," it could be said that climate change has been transformed from an "epistemic" into an "ontological" phenomenon. This shift provides much of the context for the practices discussed here.

27 "Heat Pump — the Commitments," *The Greening of Hedgerley Wood: The Diary of One Family's Attempts to Save CO$_2$,* August 3, 2005, www.hedgerley.net/greening/?p=48.

28 These fragments were found with the aid of a program called Google Scraper. This script makes it possible to use Google to query only the Web sites in the issue network for terms. Google Scraper was developed by Koen Martens and Erik Borra of Sonologic.nl. See http://tools.issuecrawler.net.

Martin Khor addresses the NGO symposium coinciding with the WTO
ministerial conference in Seattle on November 29, 1999.

The Lobby That Came in from the South

a profile of Third World Network by Gaëlle Krikorian

The origin of the Third World Network (TWN) lies in a 1984 seminar that brought together NGOs from Asia, Africa, and Latin America. Organized in Malaysia by the Consumers Association of Penang (CAP), a particularly active critic of national and international modes of governance, the seminar culminated in the creation of TWN — a new entity that would first, forge links and alliances with organizations active on the ground, and second, make their positions heard by institutions and in international negotiations.

The question of world governance, particularly in the field of international trade, occupies a central place for TWN. TWN maintains that the current system is essentially biased, favoring the interests of developed countries and of multinationals that not only take advantage of developing countries, but also jeopardize their sovereignty. TWN advocates the revision of rules governing international trade so that trade would become a more equitable and sustainable instrument of development, and not merely an end in itself. TWN articulates this principle when the organization responds to solicitations from their NGO partners. TWN has, furthermore, prompted networks of mobilization to emerge around specific themes: genetic engineering, biodiversity, the World Trade Organization (WTO), intellectual property, deforestation, international financing, access to medical drugs, employment, and so on. In Asia, for example, the issue of tropical forests involves not only the consequences of deforestation policy on the environment (its effect on biodiversity, increased soil erosion) but also the social repercussions for different populations: inhabitants of the forests who are witnessing their disappearance; inhabitants of rural zones whose water reserves are being polluted by sediments; and those settled in towns suffering from flooding caused by the growing volume of water flows brought about by the absence of vegetation.

Sharing information and collective analysis of situations allows TWN to map the problems experienced by different populations as well as to identify their causes. The network aims to establish a link between the damages wrought and their sources — whether they result from national or international policies or the conjunction of the two. TWN is equally committed to drawing connections between local movements and the various arenas where policies are being elaborated. One of TWN's prime targets is the World Bank and its so-called "structural adjustment" programs. The World Bank's policy does not change from one country to another; thus its effects are similar, turning it into an adversary of choice.

TWN privileges campaigns against governmental or multilateral bodies rather than against private enterprises. This, however, does not preclude some of TWN's partners from pursuing such a strategy. TWN lays no claims to possessing a specific ideological vision and it eschews partisan political debates. As Martin Khor, TWN's spokesperson, has said, the network "is not hostile to multinationals, the market, or the State."[1] TWN tries to influence both government policies and national and international laws and regulations, including World Bank projects and bilateral European programs and WTO or World Intellectual Property Organization (WIPO) treaties. In each case, TWN selects its targets according to the negative effects they are believed to engender. Once a diagnosis is made, TWN's goal is to put pressure on the responsible institutions by exposing and explaining the harmful consequences of their projects, policies, or regulations in order to protect the affected populations as well as the standing of the countries in question. In this regard, TWN, in alliance with other groups, has succeeded in inflecting the World Bank's policy on forests.

First conceived as a particular branch of the Consumers Association of Penang, TWN has gradually become autonomous and has built its own infrastructures. Two offices in Asia and Africa employ about twenty-five people; a third in Latin America (established within a larger organization) has five to seven employees; and now a fourth in Geneva has three salaried employees. TWN's regional secretariats maintain permanent contact with NGOs and partner movements, which, while they do not have the status of institutionalized members with direct structural control, collaborate with them to develop strategies.

The creation of a base in Geneva, the capital for lobbying international institutions, required a considerable economic investment — in the office itself (the cost of a single staffer in Geneva is the equivalent of ten or twenty in a regional office) as well as in the individuals involved (the majority of activists worked in their own native countries and were reluctant to leave and relinquish local involvement). For TWN, this is a conscious choice that Khor calls "a costly, but necessary sacrifice: local intervention alone is not sufficient, because the policies pursued locally are the fruit of national decisions — and also the consequences of the actions of foreign and international actors." TWN thus finds itself in a relatively unprecedented position for an organization coming from the South: it can intervene in international debates and negotiations as well as lobby representatives of the United Nations or of permanent missions based in Geneva on a daily basis.

Such lobbying relies on research to underscore the difficulties activists encounter on the ground, to problematize the causes of these difficulties, and to formulate possible solutions. The group seeks to mobilize opinion — above all, among an informed public and experts — originating in both governmental and nongovernmental worlds. Its activity is thus organized around the appropriation, production, and dissemination of knowledge, which contribute in turn to the network's credibility.

Consequently, TWN's publication output is an essential part of the network that nourishes different types of support systems. Apart from the minutes of meetings in which TWN participates or whose proceedings it follows, which are disseminated in ad hoc letters, TWN produces two magazines — the monthly *Third World Resurgence* and the biweekly *Third World Economics* — as well as a daily bulletin, *SUNS,* which is devoted to trade and development. TWN also regularly publishes books and articles.

Sales from these publications partially fund the group. Other sources of funding include subscriptions by the NGOs that are affiliated with TWN and support from various charitable foundations and UN agencies. Credible funding sources are critical because governments, and in particular the Malaysian government, are prone to discredit NGOs by accusing them of being beholden to foreign interests.

From the beginning of TWN to the present, relations between Southern NGOs and their governments have evolved considerably. Khor recalls that, even a few years ago, it was still impossible for Southern NGOs to communicate with the governments of their own countries: "Many of the leaders were veritable dictators. Since then, the forms of government have diversified, which has opened up possibilities." When, fifteen years ago, TWN asked for the first time to participate in a United Nations meeting, the UN, taken by surprise, asked the government of Malaysia to rule on the request. Malaysian authorities responded by organizing a meeting with the TWN's representatives and, as a result of these discussions, the two parties realized that it was actually possible for them to have a dialogue. Beyond the Malaysian case, NGOs and governments of the South have developed new modes of relating to each other that include recognizing the right of the citizen to speak to his or her government.

Over the years, TWN has gained the trust of a growing number of governmental agents in countries of the South. One of TWN's strengths today lies in its capacity to hold workshops and symposiums on specific subjects, which are not only organized jointly with national and international institutions, but also involve experts from NGOs. Gradually, the network has also developed a system of briefing meetings for country representatives prior to major conferences or summits of nation-states. Offering its expertise to delegations from developing countries, it helps fill lacunae that result from a lack of financial and human resources. This advisory and informational work helps to reinforce collaborative relations between NGOs and governments and to legitimize the organization's status as an expert. In addition, TWN has been consulted on multiple occasions by various governments to assist in preparing legislation and policies, especially on biosecurity, ecological diversity, and genetic resources. As a strategy, lobbying leads to providing valuable technical assistance. It not only constitutes a way of influencing the formation of the southern countries' positions but, because it benefits from the support of civil society, it simultaneously strengthens those positions, especially with respect to rich countries.

Translated by Susan Emanuel.

1   Quotes from Martin Khor are from an October 2005
    interview with the author.

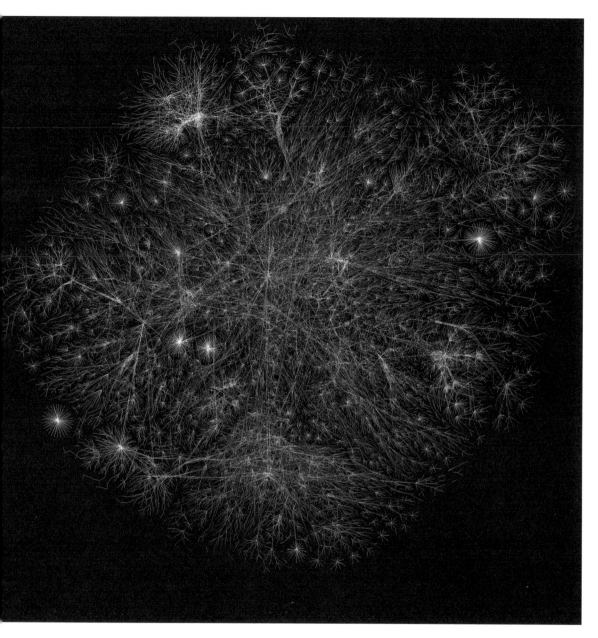

This model of the Internet was created to make a visual representation
of a space that is very much one-dimensional, a metaphysical universe
(courtesy of Barrett Lyon, OPTE Project, www.opte.org).

The Case for Communication Rights:
After the World Summit on the Information Society

Soenke Zehle

Many observers of the United Nations World Summit on the Information Society (WSIS) anticipated that any attempt to address the existence of "digital divides" within the global network economy in terms of human rights to education, information, and knowledge would be difficult, if not impossible. And indeed, WSIS was not a development summit: issues central to what, for lack of a better term, is still referred to as the "global South" were marginal, and its agenda became even narrower as the WSIS proceeded.[1] So for some, WSIS was a failure, merely another costly, yet inconsequential intergovernmental jamboree. For others, however, WSIS marked a legitimacy crisis that may even be considered a turning point in the way we speak about the information society more generally. The reemergence of "communication rights" as an infopolitical umbrella concept seems to have both contributed to this crisis and delineated, if perhaps only provisionally, the terrain of contemporary transnational mobilization around communication and information concerns.

The media activist Seán Ó Siochrú has described WSIS as a conjuncture or conflictual encounter between two infopolitical visions rooted in the 1970s: that of an information society organized around the principles of a neoliberal technomanagerialism, driven mainly by government and corporate actors, and that of a communication society realizing the post–Third Worldist agenda of gaining a comprehensive set of material rights to communication, driven mainly by nongovernmental or civil-society organizations and corresponding social movements. Whereas the information society perspective has focused mainly on the role of information, the Internet, and the existence of "digital divides" between the centers and peripheries of the global network economy, the communication society perspective includes broader issues of media diversity and ownership, as well as a comprehensive critique of the ever-expanding regime of intellectual property rights that restricts new forms of collaborative creation. Conceptually, the former is rooted in the technodeterminism of postindustrialism and corporate-driven IT development facilitated by the privatization of state-owned telecoms; the latter builds on the Third Worldist agenda of a "New World Information and Communication Order"

(NWICO) and contemporary efforts to revive the concept of communication rights.[2]

Although "no human rights standard has been adopted to address communication as an interactive process," Cees Hamelink — initiator of the People's Communication Charter and one of the key proponents of the concept and agenda of communication rights — contends that

> this omission could be remedied by the adoption — as part of the existing human rights standards — of the "human right to communicate." This right is perceived by its protagonists as more fundamental than the information rights presently accorded by international law. The essence of this right would be based on the observation that communication is a fundamental social process, a basic human need and the foundation of all social organization. The right to communicate should constitute the core of any democratic system.[3]

Combining a broad set of infopolitical demands under the umbrella of communication rights, the Campaign for Communication Rights in the Information Society (CRIS) was launched in 2001 by the Platform for Communication Rights, a coalition of individuals and organizations already involved in policy advocacy around global media and communication issues.

Unlike previous international initiatives addressing information and communication, WSIS was to adopt a "multistakeholder" approach, breaking with the intergovernmental logic of previous summits to reach out to nonstate actors. A CRIS seminar, Communication as a Human Right in the Information Society, quickly recruited additional organizations to the campaign and attracted the attention of the WSIS Secretariat, UNESCO, and the International Telecommunication Union (ITU). In addition to creating a series of background documents meant to broaden the WSIS agenda, CRIS activists also worked with the Civil Society Division of the WSIS Secretariat to develop mechanisms for civil-society involvement.[4] Sobered by the initial WSIS "Preparatory Committee" (PrepCom), a presummit gathering of official delegates failed to include civil-society organizations in key negotiations, CRIS nevertheless decided to maintain a stance of skeptical engagement vis-à-vis a process that seemed to develop according to the standard logic of yet another intergovernmental summit, notwithstanding official pronouncements regarding the value of multistakeholderism and its celebration as a postsovereign paradigm.[5]

With origins in market-oriented international communications policy and task force reports, the initial agenda of the WSIS paid little attention to social-justice concerns.[6] Hosted by the ITU, which was looking for a new institutional mandate after its role as a global regulator had been compromised by technological advances and policy initiatives like the World Trade Organization (WTO) Telecommunications Agreement, the summit was predestined to neglect human-rights issues related to information and telecommunication technologies.

According to the media activist Alan Toner, CRIS wanted "to bring together governments and NGOs disaffected by the neoliberal paradigm, initiate concrete projects that could have a more enduring impact in areas such as spectrum allocations policy, and to develop a more radical declaration on the 'information society' that will counter the asinine production of the 'official summit'," and do so by organizing a transnational advocacy campaign to establish its collective identity as a new stakeholder in global communications governance.[7] The campaign was ambitious in that its use of the phrase "communications rights" was meant to aggregate existing organizing efforts around communications and information issues, an objective that would make the campaign capable of consolidating and sustaining itself as a collective actor outside the organizational dynamic of WSIS.[8] Yet save for a few critical comments about the charter-based approach of the CRIS campaign, the concept of communication rights failed to resonate with a surprising number of media activists, making me wonder what it means to "speak rights" in an infopolitical forum such as WSIS and whether the idiom of rights was not only a choice of tactics, but also a major fault line separating key infopolitical milieus.

For its advocates, the emphasis on communication rights could both revisit and transcend the Cold War split between the two major human-rights covenants: one that stresses mainly procedural political rights, another mainly material socioeconomic rights.[9] Yet what separates these two human rights covenants is not only their conceptual difference — procedural versus substantive rights — but also the de facto judiciability of their respective claims.[10] The almost exclusive focus of the institutional human-rights apparatus on procedural political (first-covenant) violations implies that, somewhat paradoxically, communication-rights claims, understood mainly in terms of material rights, are likely to remain outside the dynamic and institutional grammar associated with a politics of rights, a grammar regarded with suspicion by many media activists and network-culture theorists.

This, in turn, suggests that when approaching the communication-rights agenda, one could shift attention from the possibly contradictory outcomes if communication rights were indeed codified, ratified, and enforced in terms of what it means to "speak rights" in transnational policy forums such as WSIS.[11] To approach human rights as an idiom, that is, as a way of speaking, involves dealing with implicit (cultural, ethical, and social) "grammars" that order or structure desires for freedom, justice, liberation, and respect before these "rights" can become intelligible as claims, entitlements, or charges of violation. To claim a right is to position or produce oneself as an autonomous, rights-exercising individual within an institutional matrix connecting rights holders, rights protectors, and rights violators. The question of what human rights "do" is related to the question of what it means to acquire and employ the idiom of human rights in the articulation of claims and in defining the identities of claimants.

But where human-rights advocates interpret such a juridification of social-justice concerns as a form of empowerment, critical analyses of the politics of representation and its constitutive limits offered by network-culture theorists have engendered a corresponding suspicion regarding this process of judicial self-subsumption. They recommend caution in the face of the (bureaucratic) implications of an institutional commitment to a politics of rights, and express concerns that rights-based approaches accelerate the general trend toward a professionalization of social change.[12] From this perspective, a politics of communication rights might seem quite alien to network-culture approaches that have explored the constitutive limits of a certain public-sphere model of communication and that are unable to see how or even why new rights could possibly repair a mode of public communication they see as having already exhausted itself.[13]

Recourse to rights seems to make sense only in the larger context of a politics of representation, including the adjudication or judiciability of violations, and "speaking rights" is in turn framed by various institutional sites of articulation, that is, a complexly structured scene of speaking to which the articulation of grievances shifts. Participants in this scene include parliamentary commissions, human-rights organizations, local and international courts, intergovernmental agencies, framing the conversation among actors allied to their respective mise-en-scènes, architectures, and even aesthetics of justice. (Think, for example, of court wigs and the general order of the court, or recall the enormous effort by the United States to reconstruct the buildings of the Nuremberg Tribunal in order to underwrite its claims to legitimacy.) "Speaking rights" is also in turn framed by the institutional practices associated with the enforcement and protection of rights. The common implications of such a grammar are also frequent criticisms.[14]

On the other hand, the grammar of human rights might also be understood differently, as an element of a tactical reappropriation that makes more sense within a network-culture context than as part of a standard approach to rights-based politics. One might revisit the notion of communication rights, perhaps along the lines suggested by Paolo Virno, who outlines a rights-based politics no longer aimed at the state as the anchor of its institutionalization, but performed in terms of the risky reinvention of democracy outside the "grammatical" constraints of a statist public sphere. Virno's conception of the "right to resistance," which precedes the alienation of natural rights in a foundational act that gives rise to state sovereignty and civil society, suggests that "state" and "rights" can indeed be uncoupled; as rights become unhinged from their exclusive association with liberal (statist) forms of individuation, they open up to a different social space and praxis of communicative constitution.[15] Similarly, Étienne Balibar has also associated a politics of rights both with constituted and constituent power, a politics of rights which always produces an excess of power that is available above and beyond state sovereignty.[16]

This is an interpretation that does in fact resonate with the communication-rights approach. As far as I understand it, the notion of communication rights takes as its point of departure the assumption that Article 19 of the Universal Declaration of Human Rights—freedom of expression—captures the essence of democratic communication as it has been commonly understood, that is, in terms of a clear-channel problematic that also underwrites the relation between sovereignty and its subjects, but is considered inadequate to the postsovereign communicative socialities that characterize the network society. While some CRIS members, Hamelink among them, continued to stress the need to institutionalize new rights, rather than merely to invoke them in the process of movement building, others have emphasized that tactical uses of a phrase such as "communication rights" can fashion a language of solidarity and facilitate cooperation among existing, yet separate, infopolitical efforts. As a strategy, it appealed even to Geneva03/We Seize!, a smaller anti-WSIS campaign initiated by activists from the autonomous corners of network-culture mobilization, who were rooted in the 2003 European Social Forum. While We Seize! decided to position itself deliberately outside the organizational dynamic of WSIS, it maintained connections to CRIS and acknowledged the usefulness of its dialogic definition of communication rights, both in addressing the complexity of the contemporary dynamic of collaborative creation and in articulating a corresponding critique of the existing system of intellectual property rights.[17]

This, in any case, is how I have come to interpret the emergence of communication rights in the context of WSIS: as an example of tactical media shifted to the forums and terrain of transnational policy making, calling for a corresponding shift in analytical emphasis from the institutionalization of rights to the material effects produced by the mobilization around rights-based claims. CRIS seemed to exemplify this possibility, especially because its inclusive strategy stressed the tactical appropriations of the idiom of rights, which could broaden the agenda of transnational communications and information governance and shift it from an apolitical infrastructuralism toward a social-justice agenda, rather than the possible institutionalizations of the demands grouped loosely under the umbrella of "communication rights."

Because the area of global communication and media governance had not seen many campaigns of similar scope, CRIS attracted a wide array of social-movement researchers who offered critical assessments of its agenda and organizational dynamics.[18] While CRIS members were widely credited with facilitating and coordinating civil-society involvement in the WSIS process, the notion of "communication rights" was not widely used beyond the campaign membership, and CRIS no longer exists as a transnational advocacy campaign. The CRIS agenda, however, survives, inviting speculation regarding the implications of such a tactical reappropriation of the politics of rights and its resonances with other forms of infopolitical mobilization.

Discounting such a tactical politics of (communication) rights might end up underestimating the extent of the legitimacy crisis engendered by the sustained mobilization of communication-rights issues. Any social transformation begins with the delegitimation of the way things are, and, as it turns out, even simply "speaking rights" in the context of WSIS was no small matter. CRIS also showed that despite the universalizing implications, human rights can still be used to invoke and retrieve the complex legacy of specific anticolonial and Third Worldist perspectives, perspectives that continue to inform contemporary visions of a different information and communication order. In its publications, CRIS encouraged a rehistoricization of the apolitical, technodeterminist idioms of contemporary communications and information governance.[19] The limits of such an approach would have appeared, of course, had CRIS succeeded in consolidating itself as a collective actor. It would have had to choose whether specific demands should be advanced in terms of individual entitlements or broad collective rights and to struggle with the complexity of how to arrive at a mandate for specific interventions in governance regimes related to its agenda.[20] At best, however, and its failures notwithstanding, CRIS contributed to the delegitimation of the information society as we know it. Future infopolitical efforts will have to take it from there.[21]

1 The only initiative directly related to development concerns was the so-called Digital Solidarity Fund, see www.dsf-fsn. org. Toward the end, virtually the only agenda item left was the question of Internet governance. To address this question, WSIS had already created a Working Group on Internet Governance (WGIG), which produced a series of reports and engaged in substantial exchanges with civil-society organizations in an Internet Governance Caucus. After WSIS failed to resolve key Internet governance issues, the UN Secretary-General initiated an Internet Governance Forum (IGF) in 2006. See www.wgig.org; www.net-gov.org; the archive of the Internet governance mailing list, https://ssl.cpsr.org/pipermail/governance; and the Internet Governance Project (IGP), www.Internetgovernance.org. For the IGP, see www.intgovforum.org and "A Development Agenda for Internet Governance: Calling for a Framework Convention on the Internet," *IT for Change* (August 15 2006), http://itforchange.net.

2 Seán Ó Siochrú, "Will the Real WSIS Please Stand-Up? The Historic Encounter of the 'Information Society' and the 'Communication Society,'" *Gazette — The International Journal for Communication Studies* 66, nos. 3–4 (June–July 2004). On postindustrialism, also see Armand Mattelart, "Post-Industrial Scenarios," in *The Information Society: An Introduction,* trans. Susan G. Taponier and James A. Cohen (London: Sage, 2003), pp. 73–98.

3 Cees Hamelink, "Human Rights for the Information Society," in Bruce Girard and Seán Ó Siochrú (eds.), *Communicating in the Information Society* (Geneva: UN Research Institute for Social Development, 2003), p. 121.

4 See http://comunex.net/wsis.

5 For an optimistic assessment of multistakeholderism, see Wolfgang Kleinwächter, "A New Diplomacy for the 21st Century? Multi-Stakeholder Approach and Bottom-Up Policy Development in the Information Society," in Daniel Stauffacher and Wolfgang Kleinwächter (eds.), *The World Summit on the Information Society: Moving from the Past into the Future,* UN ICT Task Force Series 8 (2005), pp. 110–13, www.unicttaskforce.org.

6 See www.itu.int/wsis/index.html.

7 Alan Toner, "Disassembly Language: Unzipping the World Summit on the Information Society," *Mute* (July 3, 2003), www.metamute.org/en/Dissembly-Language.

8 Seán Ó Siochrú, "A Transnational Campaign in Media and Communication: What Needs to be Done?" European Social Forum, Paris (November 13, 2003), http://sos.comunica.org.

9 The legal anthropologist Rosemary J. Coombe offers an account of this controversy in her "Intellectual Property, Human Rights and Sovereignty," *Indiana Journal of Global Legal Studies* 6 (1998), pp. 61ff:

Although economic, social, and cultural rights have been juridically marginalized in comparison to civil and political rights, both in terms of the institutional frameworks developed for their implementation and in terms of their judicial interpretation, failure to monitor the violation of economic, social, and cultural rights has less to do with the legal obligations established by the CESCR than with political problems of resolve. The idea that there are two categories of rights originated in the 1966 United Nations General Assembly adoption of the two discrete Covenants: one dealing with civil and political rights and another dealing with economic, social, and cultural rights. This twofold division originated in a controversial 1951 decision of the United Nations General Assembly. The States of the Soviet Bloc are widely believed to have championed economic, social, and cultural rights, while Western nations put emphasis on the civil and political rights that guaranteed civil liberties. However, even this dichotomy is misleading. "International second-generation rights" in fact have Western origins in: President Roosevelt's "Four Freedoms Address" in 1941, his proposal for an "Economic Bill of Rights" in 1944, and the American Law Institute's draft international bill of rights that same year. According to Philip Alston, the Cold War "changed what was a rational and balanced debate between 1944 and 1947 (culminating in the adoption of the Universal Declaration) into a struggle that encouraged the taking of extreme positions and prevented objective consideration of the key issues raised by the concept of economic and social rights." Ideological conflict created the perception of two discrete kinds of rights. The decision to divide the two sets of rights into separate covenants was predicated on a number of assumptions, many of which are now considered questionable. Civil and political rights were believed to be "absolute" and "immediate," whereas economic, social, and cultural rights were considered more "programmatic" — they could be and would have to be realized gradually; hence, they were not viewed as rights in the same sense. Similarly, civil and political rights were deemed "justiciable" in that they could be more easily applied by courts and other tribunals, whereas economic, social, and cultural rights were more political in nature. In retrospect, it appears that these assumptions were overstated, misleading, or mistaken and that there are substantial similarities pertaining to State obligations with respect to both groups of rights. In fact, of the almost 120 States that have ratified the CCPR, only two — the United States and Haiti — have failed to also ratify the CESCR, and overall, more States have ratified the latter. While resistance to particular rights may be found in many societies, the tendency in both Western and non-Western societies has been toward a greater integration of the rights that are internationally recognized.

10 For a survey debate on these second-covenant or economic, social, and cultural (ESC) rights, see the issue of *Human Rights Quarterly* 26, no. 4 (2004), with contributions from Mary Robinson (UN high commissioner for human rights from 1997 to 2002), Leonard S. Rubenstein (executive director of Physicians for Human Rights), and Kenneth Roth (executive director of Human Rights Watch).

11 Some human-rights organizations criticized the umbrella strategy because it could have compromised existing human-rights provisions. See Article 19, "Note on the Draft Declaration on the Right to Communicate Prepared by C. Hamelink" (January 2003), www.article19.org/pdfs/analysis/hamelink-declaration-the-right-to-communicate.pdf. The interest in reflecting on policy processes such as WSIS and the mobilization of communication rights in relationship to the politics of rights more generally originated in an ongoing collaborative research project, the "incommunicado research network" (see http://incommunicado.info). The term "incommunicado" generally refers to a state of being without the means or rights to communicate, especially in the case of incommunicado detention. The incommunicado project takes up the question of what a "normal," nonexceptional state of a communicative being actually implies.

12 While network-culture skepticism regarding the way a politics of rights affects the dynamic of organizational transformation resonates with the ongoing debate over the (lack of) accountability of nongovernmental actors, it is precisely the adoption of rights-based approaches that is often promoted as a key element of new accountability strategies. For an account of the ambivalence of many NGOs vis-à-vis rights-based approaches, see Emma Harris-Curtis, Oscar Marleyn, and Oliver Bakewell, "The Implications for Northern NGOs of Adopting Rights-Based Approaches," *INTRAC Occasional Papers Series* 41 (November 2005), www.intrac.org.

13 Tiziana Terranova, "Communication Beyond Meaning," *Social Text* 80, no. 22 (Fall 2004); see also her *Network Culture: Politics for the Information Age* (London: Pluto, 2004).

14 See David Kennedy, "The International Human Rights Movement: Part of the Problem?" *Harvard Human Rights Journal* 15 (Spring 2002), pp. 99–125, or the introductory chapter of his *The Dark Sides of Virtue: Reassessing International Humanitarianism* (Princeton: Princeton University Press, 2005) for a nearly exhaustive list.

15 Paulo Virno, *A Grammar of the Multitude,* trans. Isabella Bertoletti, James Cascaito, and Andrea Cassonsee (New York: Semiotext(e), 2004). See also Virno's writings collected at Generation online, www.generation-online.org/p/pvirno.htm.

16 Étienne Balibar, "What is a Politics of the Rights of Man?" in *Masses, Classes, Ideas*, trans. James Swenson (New York: Routledge, 1994), pp. 205–25, 242–45.

17 For archives of We Seize!, see http://geneva03.org. However limited it may have been, this exchange was significant in its own right, because as social-movement researchers have noted, there is a general lack of democratic relationships between formal and informal modes of activism in transnational movement networks. See Catherine Eschle and Neil Stammers, "Taking Part: Social Movements, INGOs, and Global Change," *Alternatives: Global, Local, Political* 29, no. 3 (June–July 2004).

18 See, for example, Pradip Thomas, "The Communication Rights in the Information Society (CRIS) Campaign: Applying Social Movement Theories to an Analysis of Global Media Reform," *International Communication Gazette* 68, no. 4 (2006), pp. 291–312.

19 Such a rehistoricization is also visible, for example, in the coupling of communication rights with the right to development. On the right to development, see Arjun Sengupta, "On the Theory and Practice of the Right to Development," *Human Rights Quarterly* 24 (2002), pp. 837–89, as well as Alan Brouder, "The UN Human Rights Council and the Right to Development," *Policy Papers on Transnational Economic Law* (May 2006), and Andrea Cornwall and Celestine Nyamu-Musembi, "Putting the 'Rights-Based Approach' to Development into Perspective," *Third World Quarterly* 25, no. 8 (2004), pp. 1415–37. The contradictory conduct of the newly constituted UN Human Rights Council — one of the arenas where the right to development has resurfaced — suggests, however, that an assertive "global South" may not in fact be as supportive of communication rights as activists hoped. For updates on the general relationship between NGOs and the Human Rights Council, see www.globalpolicy.org/ngos/ngo-un/hrcindex.htm.

20 Milton Mueller, "Communication Rights in the Information Society: Democratization of Communication as Social Movement?" Organizational Case Study, Research Project "Civil Society, WSIS, and the Globalization of Information and Communication Policy" (2005), http://dcc.syr.edu/ford/tnca.htm.

21 See, for example, the campaign for a change in the mandate of the World Intellectual Property Organization, www.cptech.org/ip/wipo/da.html.

Southern Views on the Political Economy of Information

Parminder Jeet Singh interviewed by Soenke Zehle

Parminder Jeet Singh is cofounder and executive director of IT for Change in Bangalore, India. IT for Change attempts to address the ideological biases of market-driven approaches to information and communication technologies. It affirms the possibility of cooperation among the agents of the global South to sustain the application of new technologies in ICT-related areas of development in equitable and empowering ways.

Can you give a quick overview of IT for Change and your own involvement in the info-development debate?

IT for Change was born out of the excitement over new technologies at the turn of the century and the manner in which the debates and practice of information and communication technologies (ICT) for development seemed to supplant traditional development ideologies — which accent equity, social justice, and empowerment — with new formulations emphasizing efficiency and pragmatism. The promised gains of applying new technologies to various activities of development came with a strong ideological bias that was detrimental to the objectives of development. So we felt it necessary to question the notion of ICT for development, or ICT4D. We at IT for Change were always very clear, however, that such a questioning would not be merely an intellectual critique of existing ICT4D discourse and practice, but would attempt to present constructive alternatives as well; we agreed with the basic premise of the ICT4D enthusiasts that the new ICTs, in their appropriate application, offer transformative possibilities for development. We therefore have tried to straddle the difficult aims — with their subtle, but often strong incompatibilities in organizational terms — of doing both research and advocacy as well as field projects in the ICT4D area.

How does the "Bangalore experience," the rapid development of a local IT industry that effectively placed Bangalore at the core of the national network economy, affect the

Indian employees work at a call center in the southern Indian city of Bangalore, June 26, 2003. India's call centers provide cheap English-speaking workers and high-speed telecoms to provide customer service for companies around the world (Reuters).

way you think about the political economy of the information society and the agenda of infopolitical activism?

When a group of development professionals from different fields got together in 2000 to give birth to IT for Change, the "Bangalore experience" was in the back of our minds, because everything related to IT was so magnified in Bangalore. The new material and ideological strength that the IT phenomenon brought to the Indian middle class in many ways formed the basis of its final disavowal — backed by an unprecedented self-confidence — of the real "development status" of India and its poverty-ridden majority. Indian politics had become disproportionately influenced by the agenda of this resurgent middle class, and economic growth policies were being shaped in a manner that put development priorities — again, of equity, social justice, and empowerment — on the back burner.

With origins in the market-oriented international policy and task force reports that have been adopted by many donors and that have come to define ICT for development on the ground, the initial agenda of the World Summit on the Information Society (WSIS) was characterized by the marginalization of human-rights perspectives. Yet you have also described WSIS as a key event, in that it affected the legitimacy of the information-society visions outlined in initiatives such as the Digital Opportunity Task Force (DOT Force), the Digital Opportunities Initiative (DOI), the International e-Development Resource Network, the Global Digital Opportunity Initiative (GDOI), and even the UN Information and Communication Technologies Task Force. In your view, does this legitimacy crisis merely affect ICT4D-related initiatives, or does it extend to the entire regulation regime of the network economy?

Globalization and its hyperpowered version in the networked economy have relegated global and national policy spaces to the status of enablers of the market. This phenomenon is much greater and stronger for the information society than the process of co-optation that is part of the neoliberal development agenda. However, while developing countries have been able to create some conceptual basis to oppose the dominant agenda in policy arenas such as those of the World Trade Organization (WTO) and the World Intellectual Property Organization (WIPO), and to even put alternative agendas into effect with some success in the arena of information society (IS) discourse, these countries had almost completely acceded to the dominant formulations of the North. The WSIS meeting, despite its limited visibility, success, and impact, helped break down that so-called consensus. Now that the dominant "win-win" IS discourse has lost its legitimacy, there is perhaps a way to build alternative theoretical conceptions of the information society and network economy, especially for the global South. To dislodge the unfair policy regimes that buttress the network economy globally is a much larger and much more difficult project. However, alternative South-based formulations of the information society can certainly provide some ammunition for achieving this.

What do you expect from the Access-to-Knowledge (A2K) Treaty or the development mandate for WIPO? What other kinds of campaigns are you aware of that take advantage of this legitimacy crisis?

The World Intellectual Property Organization has been an important arena for strong South-South alliances. The development agenda at WIPO constitutes a good starting point for similar campaigns within information-society debates, since some of these debates are critically linked to WIPO issues. Attempts to build a development agenda concerning Internet governance have recently gathered momentum, with members of civil society consulting with governments of developing countries on this issue. Recent developments at the WTO have also shown the strength of such alliances. Civil society has also used this legitimacy crisis to organize itself at new levels globally: the World Social Forum is one example.

When you and your colleagues at IT for Change discussed WSIS in the broader context of what you call "a Southern view" of the political economy of the information society, you stated that "WSIS can be seen from two very different vantages. One, as a process that was unable to confront the neoliberalization of the development agenda within the UN and could even be blamed for taking such a trend further; and two, as the probable beginning of a more legitimate discourse on IS that brought to the table issues of human rights in the IS, on the one hand, and of the central role of public policy and community processes in shaping the IS, on the other."[1] What do you think is gained by reframing the agenda of infodevelopment within a politics of rights? Does the language of rights offer a way to reclaim information and communication technologies as public infrastructures, for example, with corresponding implications for public policy? To what extent would such claims be at odds with the assumption that ICTs are mainly economic infrastructures that create and maintain competitive advantages within the global network economy? Could a politics of communication rights both address and resolve this tension? Finally, does such an emphasis on rights necessarily reaffirm the role of the "developmental state" as a central actor in development regimes, or can it be used to articulate other, postnational or transnational visions?

Infodevelopment today is mostly premised on virtues of self-interest, competition, and "win-win" situations packaged in uneasy ways as part of a developmentalist and NGO culture. Its practice mostly takes the form of building or plugging into the dominant neoliberal socioeconomic system. Access to ICTs and their innumerable possibilities is not considered a universal resource of civilization that societies and communities can claim and use for their own agendas of self-determined growth and development. So the current ICT4D paradigm mostly offers capabilities and possibilities to establish a neoliberal socioeconomic system as the default global system. In order to counter this, it is important to reclaim the basic building blocks of ICT4D or information-society discourse. Casting the ICT4D agenda in terms of the politics of rights attempts to rebuild new sets of opportunities and challenges in the information age from a people-centered and community-centered vantage point.

In my opinion, a rights-based formulation of ICT4D or the information society can be compared to the status of education in our society. Education basically serves to develop competitive advantages between people and between social groups, and a rights-based approach to education is a widely accepted formulation. Education, though a factor of economic productivity, is considered an issue of equal access to opportunity for all. Additionally, education is seen to have a significant role in human and social development in dimensions other than economic. Access to ICTs can also be a significant opportunity equalizer for participation in economic systems, as well as have significant noneconomic human and social implications. On both these counts, a rights-based approach to ICT4D is the appropriate starting point for building an alternative vision of ICT4D or a development-oriented information society.

However, it must be stated here that the communication-rights movement is still in its infancy, and it may need to evolve both in terms of its substantive content, where a greater South-based orientation is required, as well as in its form, which must cultivate closer alignments with other rights-based social movements on the ground, both in the North and in the South.

On the issue of whether an emphasis on rights promotes a necessarily statist political idiom, I think the conception of rights has a dynamic interplay with the evolution of the society-state relationship, as well as across the local-global spectrum, the latter becoming increasingly relevant in the information society. The concept of rights is certainly broader than a statist political idiom. However, it is undeniable that the state still plays an important role in our social organization, and we are not close to any alternative that can radically alter this arrangement. The relationship between development and the state is an important subject that requires constant assessment.

Often based on the example of the growth of mobile telephony, the private sector has successfully positioned itself as the "natural leader" in the development of information and communication infrastructures, attributing technological breakthroughs almost exclusively to private-sector innovation, successfully maintaining the separation of ICT4D from traditional development actors and agendas, and taking an ever-greater role in ICT-related decision-making, policy, and standard-setting processes that stress the autonomy of the economic realm. You argue that we should not accept such a valorization of an "autonomous" transition to an information society, but rather reaffirm the public nature of core infrastructures for connectivity, software, and content. Can you elaborate on this?

The phenomenon of mobile telephony occurred in the context of a mature application — carrying voice over distance — and added mobility of use. Its demand is spontaneous and does not require building complex processes for constructing and delivering value. The information society, on the other hand, is a much more complex phenomenon, requiring new technosocial systems be built in many different areas of social activity. These systems also have social, legal, and political aspects that have to evolve over time, often with deliberate design and initial social investments. E-governance and new platforms for linking distributed small-scale economic activity are just two such technosocial systems that need considerable social investments. The private sector either does not have the incentive to put in sufficient upfront investments for such systemic changes or, if they do step in, they will produce systems with built-in biases and inequalities of opportunity.

It is therefore important in times of such wide-scale systemic changes, which the emergence of an information society implies, that the public sector make core infrastructural investments to build appropriate technosocial systems that will provide fair opportunity to all. Such infrastructure implies connectivity, basic software, and content, as well as contextual applications and services for areas and sectors that are not addressed adequately by markets. In fact, the very nature of much of the information-society infrastructure, with its antirival properties, means that a public-goods approach makes the best economic sense, as well.[2]

You have described the emergence of Internet governance (IG) as a key issue in terms of its global relevance, but also as a crucial terrain for the contestation or affirmation of neoliberal assumptions regarding global public policy. In your own contributions to the debate, you have stressed the relationship between governance issues and a politics of rights, especially the right to development. What are the infopolitical stakes in the Internet governance controversy? Given that many nongovernmental actors use a politics of individual rights to defend the current IG arrangement for fear of governmental interference, does the idiom of communication rights offer a way to reframe the debate itself? And how does the status of IG relate to the affirmation of the public nature of core communication infrastructures?

The stakes in the Internet governance debate are twofold. First, in terms of process, IG represents one of the first major issues that is both inescapably global and inescapably urgent — something that has to be dealt with right away and on a continuous basis. It therefore provides an important starting point for setting up the context and politics of a new global governance paradigm and for an increasingly integrated global community. Second, on a more substantive note, the Internet is increasingly becoming the common infrastructure relative to which most civilizational systems play out, including commerce, governance, social interactions, organizational processes, entertainment, education, health, and so on. The approach to Internet governance will have implications for all of these areas. It therefore is important to assert early on the rights-based, public nature of the Internet, and to oppose the purely commercial infrastructure where everything plays by the rules of the market — which, being global, is unencumbered by policy constraints beyond the very basic neoliberal ones favored by the entrenched market players, such as intellectual property rights (IPR).

Regarding the question of whether a politics of individual rights ends up defending the current IG arrangement, it is certainly important to extend the rights debate beyond negative rights to positive, socioeconomic rights. However, these rights, in terms of IG, have not yet been fully conceptualized, and this challenge needs to be addressed most of all by South-based development actors. Civil-society advocates from the North, who are most concerned with negative rights, often attempt to limit IG debates and policy making to the "logical layer" of Internet architecture: allocation of domain names, managing the root server, and such. However, from a prodevelopment perspective, it is important to assert that applications, content, and infrastructural layers, as well as appropriate principles for Internet governance based on a rights-oriented and public goods-oriented approach, need to be developed.

To what extent does the shift from state-led development projects to piecemeal, solutions-based approaches that rely on autonomous, bottom-up initiatives — built merely on a "win-win" participation of all stakeholders, to the exclusion of systemic transformations — relate to the civil-society renaissance more generally?

To the extent that much initial ICT4D activity came through donor-driven initiatives with various NGOs as key players, ICT4D has considerable civil-society dominance at the field level. But I would not associate it with a civil-society renaissance. At the level of global networks, new ICT possibilities have certainly given a fillip to the process.

You have suggested that we start speaking of an "Information Society for the South," rather than ICT4D, because the latter does not capture systemic issues of institutional and structural transformation that are required to capitalize on the development opportunities available today. Is the notion of an "antirival commons" a way to arrive at a definition of development in the age of peer-to-peer computer networks, open-source software, and wireless public connectivity projects?

I wouldn't call it an attempt to arrive at a new definition of development. Development must continue to be defined in terms of its objectives, which are in a constant state of evolution. In this respect, there isn't such a strong discontinuity with the advent of the information society. However, IS, with its new arenas of antirival commons for many significant IS resources, does give a radically new context to development. For new and important IS resources that have a very important role in most activities in the IS, such as connectivity, software, and content, appropriate public policies can ensure that development does not suffer the constraints that are classically associated with physical resources.

You have also interpreted the neoliberalization of ICT4D in terms of a lag in state organizational innovation, a tremendous gap in the extent to which corporate and state actors have mastered the network form. What role do civil-society networks have in demonstrating the possibility of new forms of global governance and preventing market-based ideas from continuing to fill this vacuum?

Whereas state actors have indeed not mastered the network form to any significant extent, civil society has been moderately successful in adopting the network form; its failure to confront neoliberalism comes more from perennial structural problems of civil-society legitimacies. Globally networked CS is still to be learned, and one hopes that the process will concern how we use the network form to establish and enhance legitimacies, rather than just seeking, as economic players do, the progressive aggrandizement of those who are already closely linked while further marginalizing those on the periphery. These legitimacies will come from lateral linkages across CS networks, but more importantly from grassroots movements and organizations. With increasing use of the new information and communication technologies by the latter, the possibilities for such legitimizing networks do exist.

As is evident in virtually all ICT-related policy debates, the North is unlikely to promote an alternative vision of infodevelopment. But if it is the role of South-South alliances to reaffirm the traditional emphasis in development on equality and social justice, who will take the lead? What are key examples of new forms of South-South cooperation or innovative realignments between nonstate, state, and suprastate actors?

I see a great opportunity in civil-society actors building South-South alliances to reaffirm equality and social justice. But again, issues of legitimacy and exclusion haunt such attempts, and one expects a move toward greater lateral and horizontal linkages, as well as more effective processes of accountability and transparency. Many South-based governments have taken parochial stands on the information society (for example, IT powerhouses such as India have focused primarily on the business issues involved), mostly because the battle lines have not been clearly demarcated in arenas such as the WTO and WIPO. However, governments mostly act when issues are fully ripe, and IS issues will soon surface with much greater strength and regularity than most are prepared for. Some South-South alignments between governments have gained strength around the WTO and WIPO, and as more IS issues arise, alignments will form in this area as well, likely between both state and nonstate actors.

These comments are considerably forward-looking, and I am unable to give any great examples of South-South cooperation at present. The expected processes cannot be linear and will proceed through considerable contestations among civil-society players at different levels, among different governments, and between state and nonstate players.

1   Anita Gurumurthy and Parminder Jeet Singh, *Political Economy of the Information Society: A Southern View* (Montevideo, Uruguay: Instituto del Tercer Mundo, 2005), p. 12.

2   The concept of "antirival" goods plays off the notions of "rival" goods (which, if consumed by one consumer cannot be consumed by another) and "nonrival" goods (which, if consumed by one consumer can still be consumed by another—parks are a classic example), goods that tolerate "free riders." Antirival goods actively encourage and, in fact, thrive on "free riders." The term "antirival" goods was coined by Steven Weber in *The Success of Open Source* (Cambridge, MA: Harvard University Press, 2004).

The Refugee-Media Nexus

Amy R. West interviewed by Soenke Zehle

Amy R. West writes on human-rights and development issues pertaining to refugees, asy-
lum seekers, internally displaced persons (IDPs), and HIV/AIDS communities in Africa,
the Caribbean, Europe, and the United States. Most notably, she has written two the-
matic reports for Article 19's Global Campaign for Free Expression and has presented these
reports at the World Summit on Information Society (WSIS) in Geneva (2003) and in Tunis
(2005). Article 19 is a human-rights organization with a specific mandate that focuses on the
defense and promotion of freedom of expression and freedom of information worldwide.
The organization believes that all people have the right to freedom of expression and access
to information and that the full enjoyment of this right is the most potent force for achiev-
ing individual freedoms, strengthening democracy, and preempting repression, conflict, war,
and genocide.

Contemporary political philosophy has rediscovered "bare life," an existence outside
the community of civic and human rights that is often associated with the experience
of displacement, exile, and migration, and with the camp as a paradigmatic space of
exception and manifestation of new modalities of governance. What is the origin of
your own interest in refugee networks, your emphasis on marginality, vulnerability, and
even despair? Do you see a relationship between refugee research as a human-rights
concern and such research as a conceptual challenge to the way we think about agency,
communication, media, and politics?

To answer your last question first, there are both competing and intersecting relationships
between refugee research as a human-rights concern and research that addresses refugees from quite another angle — that of refugees as an organized group providing a challenge to the law, politics, and social norms that address marginalized groups in theory, but
that often exclude them from the collective global table in practice. The question for me
tends to be: do refugees identify more with the framework of legal and political systems
they may have adhered to before their refugee experience, or over time do they identify

Main village road in Eastern Cape Province, South Africa, 2005
(photo by Amy R. West).

more with a new identity because they no longer have recognized claims to their previous identity? Are refugees prone to engage with other marginalized groups the longer they are left to exist outside the international legal and political systems of once-functioning, stable societies, and what does this mean to regional stability in an age where extremists, insurgents, and rebel groups, also perceived as among the marginalized, are looking to increase their numbers? This perhaps leads to an entire discussion concerning the strength and potential of informal groups and the capabilities of those frustrated and disgruntled by a status quo existence that does little to promote respect for and the participation of the disenfranchised in decision making.

The best approach to either perspective — concerns for human rights or a focus on conceptual challenges to the legal, political, or communication frameworks that societies depend on — is not to ignore or favor one over the other. There must be room for looking at both sides of the refugee equation and accepting the fact that refugees are stakeholders in international policy decisions. International law and international agencies speak of the provision of certain basic needs and the protection of the dignity of people, but a generous application of the law is often lacking with regard to various marginalized groups.

Are refugees set apart from us, or are they connected to us? This is a fundamental question. Refugee research easily defaults to defining and categorizing hordes of human beings as ceaseless masses, flows, or waves. Those who survive are so-called victims, decimated by conflict, ethnic cleansing, and the destruction of home, family, and livelihood. Media pictures focus on images that reinforce refugees as the most destitute and miserable of populations, barely ever capturing the resourcefulness and organization that dominates camp life. After a time then, refugees become for us a lump sum. We fail to see individual faces, and we speak about them, not to them.

It is amazing to me that the world has traditionally believed refugees to be weakened human beings, resigned to temporary limbo, people without contributions and devoid of resources, the most pitiable of people, at the complete mercy of humanity's goodwill. Certainly there are numerous human rights issues involved in how a refugee comes to be a refugee, as well as in the questionable treatment and protection of refugees in camps, in repatriation, or in the resettlement process. But are refugees weak? There are dangers in this line of thinking. To disrespect and underestimate the survival instinct and ingenuity all human beings possess by drawing thick lines between "us" and "them" is wrong and exacerbates destructive gaps between ethnic, religious, gender, and class differences. A favorite journalist of mine, Fergal Keane, quotes a poem by an Ulster writer, Michael Longley, in his memoirs: "All of these people, / alive or dead, / are civilized."

To address your initial point, indeed "bare life" could afford to be rediscovered by more than just contemporary political philosophers. Imagine the effects on policy making if each of us were made to walk in the shoes of those for whom decisions about security and development hold direct consequences in the most immediate way! Indeed, themes of marginalization and vulnerability pepper my work. I would argue against the use of your word "despair," however. People find themselves in desperate circumstances, but I have met and interviewed very few people in my life who have crossed over the line from losing hope to actual despair. Generally, another avenue — with positive or negative consequences — is chosen before this occurs.

As for the origins of my interests in refugees and other displaced populations: I heard someone once say we need to be people of passion in our professional pursuits, harnessing what affects us personally in positive ways. Certainly what moves the individual can motivate him or her to focus professionally on a particular area. For me, suffering is actually the "barest" component of life, the common denominator that defines what we are all capable of enduring, on the one hand, as well as meting out, on the other. This perspective on the world motivates me professionally to try to understand others who suffer. One of my core beliefs is that human beings are not immune to irrelevance, invisibility, even extinction. Everyone will experience, at one time or another in life, displacement, exile, or migration of some kind. This is maybe the greatest hope, then, for refugees or other marginalized groups: that more of the world existing outside of these marginalized realities will identify with even a small piece of the experience that exists for them. This would go a long way toward tempering the legal and policy decisions being made on behalf of these people.

One of the themes in your research is that dominant ideas of how communication takes place obscure the central role played by direct, informal systems of communication and information. But rather than celebrating this informality, you warn against the security implications of governmental actions that restrict refugees' access to official information. Can you say more about how you frame and approach your media-related research in refugee camps?

I do celebrate the informal or creative ways in which people communicate. I would not wish my statements to contradict this. Direct communication, when you look someone in the eyes, speak to a person, rather than to a machine, and interact in real time is what builds understanding, emotional connection, respect, and cohesion. The more physical distance between people, the harder it is to be moved by them or to connect with them. Refugees, displaced populations, and various groups on the margins of society — I am thinking of those infected with HIV/AIDS living in places where they cannot reveal their status or receive the care and support essential to maintaining a particular quality of life — especially need direct contact and communication. Can you imagine being ostracized, in addition to suffering violence, economic devastation, and disease, without the ability to communicate with family, friends, the leaders you once trusted, or the people who say they can protect you? Can you fathom being stripped of your rights and not being expected to adhere to any responsibilities? Or worse, being expected to be responsible one-sidedly, without knowing what that responsibility entails, and receiving nothing in return for that responsibility? People have a right to information, and when they don't have access to it, they will do whatever is necessary to find their own access points and trusted sources to inform them.

I don't believe I contradict myself by warning of the security implications involved in restricting refugees' access to official information. I believe that we will act on something when it is in our best interests to do so. Certainly international organizations, governments, and those working to resolve conflict and develop postconflict regions should find it in their best interests to look at the security risks of not providing factual information to traumatized people and abetting the spread of rumors. People in emergency situations need information on what is happening, where family members are, how long a crisis will last. Deprive people of this information and they will stop at nothing, even opposing the agenda of those trying to protect them, to find out what they need to know. Cut them off from the more official channels of communication and they will start to use and trust another channel. There is no telling whether alternate channels will promote stability or incite instability. The longer an emergency lasts, the more urgent the need for information becomes. There is food, clothing, shelter, and health care to think about. If food does not arrive, why not? If soap is not handed out on the designated day, why not?

Those who are traumatized are sensitive to the slightest change in the wind. They trusted stability before and were disillusioned, so why should they trust the hands they do not see, barely know, and can rarely address? Within this context, NGOs and the UN High Commissioner for Refugees (UNHCR) must work doubly hard to communicate and build respect with refugees. The least that can be done is to have a physical presence on the ground that builds relationships and communicates effectively with refugees in order to make sure refugees know their rights and responsibilities, receive information on what is happening in their home country, as well as in the host country, and are able to connect with relatives.

My research pertains more to information and communication systems than to media, to be honest. I seek to frame such an approach by looking at history, the law, and the context of people's lives. I address human rights, particularly the fundamental rights everyone has to freedom of information and expression.

Refugee researchers suggest that the structural category and status of "being a refugee" does not really translate into a political identity. Refugee networks that meet common expectations regarding a minimum degree of institutionalization in order to be considered "organized" seem to be the exception — and where there is no organizational structure, there is no sustained articulation of political agency. Or is there? What has been your own experience of forms of networking and self-organization among refugees, both inside and outside camps? Do you think that perhaps the desire to stress the existence of individual and collective agency below the standard thresholds of institutionalized self-organization ends up romanticizing conditions of marginality and vulnerability?

Those who would suggest that "being a refugee" holds no possibility of political identity, in my opinion, do so to dismiss the importance and stake refugees have in society. Of course refugees are political. To believe otherwise almost supports their marginalization. Refugees are capable of supporting one rebel group over another, swaying policy decisions in the host or home country, and maintaining instability in a region if they so choose. Individuals in general organize themselves in family units, communities, gangs, rebel groups, nations, religious denominations, and so on. Throw individuals together in a crowded space and they will organize themselves somehow. A more nefarious example of political identities and organization is al-Qaeda. Just because those of us on this side of the gap do not understand the informal structures in which marginalized groups operate — oftentimes paralleling a more formal framework on which we are growing more and more dependent — does not mean there is a lack of political agency, identity, or organization.

My own experiences researching in the refugee camps in western Tanzania, working with asylum seekers in the greater Boston area, interviewing Haitian exile communities in France, Canada, and the United States, and interacting with Zimbabwean migrants in South Africa undoubtedly support the fact that displaced people inside and outside refugee camps organize and network. There are very few ethnic groups or nationalities among the numerous ones that I have encountered that do not build a human infrastructure — social, cultural, political, or economic networks — amid their displacement. People organize in all sorts of ways. When the distance from the home country is great, refugees or asylum seekers organize around the news they hear — from contact with those back home or through contact with other sources — and share this among those in the network. For example, the Somalis have developed informal banking systems; political leaders in exile have rallied support among their exile communities in order to challenge governments back in a home country; and there are those who transport valuables or property for friends and family between home and host countries.

Children gathering for an HIV/AIDS workshop in a remote village in KwaZulu-Natal, South Africa, 2005 (photo by Amy R. West).

When the distance from the home country is just the camp border, certainly the same organization takes place. In refugee camps, people have been known to organize the distribution of food cards. I don't know if this has changed in recent years, but the card was able to serve more than one person, so while one person left the camp to sneak back across the border, someone else was being fed in his place. Within a camp, there is often an elected leadership that comes to office through popular vote. Refugees are said to be protected by international organizations, but the protection forces leave the area at nightfall. Thus, refugees must form their own security systems, which they do, and this extends to a system of justice when a perpetrator of a crime is caught. Zimbabwean migrants in South Africa organize themselves with regard to information. There is so little accurate information leaking out of Zimbabwe right now, but people have organized — both white farmers and black farm workers — to glean information on what is happening to the economy, families, and politics at home. Zimbabweans even have a system of crossing over the gated border at night and traversing the Limpopo River. They organize to hand deliver messages or they collect money to help an individual travel back into Zimbabwe for a funeral so that he or she can return to bury the dead. The price of gas in Zimbabwe and the disintegration of the transport sector means one person's return home could take weeks, sometimes months, to travel, for example, from a place such as Musina on the border into Matabeleland and back.

I don't think marginalization or vulnerability is romantic, do you? But regarding the romanticization of marginality, I think that both those of us who research it and those who are in it, that is, the marginalized themselves, can do just that. Perhaps the latter do so when they want to excuse responsibility — I am thinking of the mind-set of a rebel who chooses that option. For the former, maybe it is just healthy for those of us researching or analyzing refugees and displaced people to check ourselves. I think glorifying conflict or an emergency situation in which people are suffering is patronizing, to say the least. I do not conceptualize the marginalized as below any threshold. I see the marginalized as existing parallel to us. The Millennium Development Goals talk of closing gaps between the rich and the poor, the developed and the developing. Those gaps threaten to become chasms if we don't value and understand both sides of the gap. It's in the interests of our own established institutions and frameworks that we do so.

Can you imagine if we wake up one day to find that the world has shifted, someone has pulled the plug on electricity, the information and communication technologies (ICTs) we depend on for national security, identification, bank accounts, information, and communication are useless? What if nothing that extreme happens, but we wake up one day to discover several airplanes have been hijacked and flown into the major economic and defense centers of a country, or entire cities are inoperable because young people have organized themselves in the streets through the use of cell phones, or protracted refugee camps full of victimized people are destabilizing entire regions of the world? It is worth considering that one day the most marginalized in society will be organized enough to marginalize the rest of us. Far better to communicate with, assist, and meet the needs of the marginalized than to keep them at a distance, dismiss them, or underestimate the creativity born of desperation.

Certainly the newest and most rapid advances in ICTs are amazing, but these should never make passé direct person-to-person conversation in real time, the reflection and emotion that once was embodied in handwritten letters or the still-relevant utility of radios. What's more, those who do not have access to computers, electricity, and/or the knowledge or know-how to operate high-tech machines are obliged to find other ways to communicate. And they will, because communication is essential to human beings. I often talk about relevance and context. There are places in the world where ICTs do not meet a direct and urgent need.

While the concept of "being a refugee" is rarely considered in terms of a political identity, dedifferentiating media coverage, often aggravated by the natural-catastrophic metaphor of "flows," continues to lump refugees together and reduce the heterogeneity of their constituent identities to the single status of refugee. In the UK, media projects such as the Institute of Race Relations (IRR), Refugees, Asylum Seekers, and the Media (RAM), or the Exiled Journalists Network (EJN) work to criticize this and offer alternative coverage. How important is this kind of work in relation to the on-site, hands-on development or humanitarian work you describe? Do you see a relationship between crude, even racist, media coverage in the treatment of different refugee populations by international agencies and their implementation partners?

I would say there is room for developing everyone's perspective on refugees, IDPs, and other marginalized groups. Certainly the wider population needs more understanding of refugees and internally displaced populations, and media projects that educate and inform people about refugees and IDPs are enormously critical. I might even say that those in media have more capacity and ability to influence a broader spectrum of the population by responsibly reporting on refugees in-depth than even those of us writing human-rights, development, or academic reports on this issue. Displaced populations are not just a narrow field of interest; while it's promising to see that the number of refugees has been reduced around the world (though this can change in a heartbeat), the fact that internally displaced populations number over twenty-five million is disturbing. As more countries shut their borders to refugees, this number will skyrocket, thus raising a host of unsettling questions about the international community's ability to protect IDPs.

Is it racist media coverage, or are there racist policies — and subsequent consequences — being exposed by media? I am sure there is enough of both in the world. I do believe that there are differences in how refugee populations are treated. This needs more exploration, though, and I try not to engage in finger-pointing without hard evidence. An anecdote to this end, however, is provided by a Burundian I met who had been living in a refugee camp for at least eight years, a former government official and a distinguished gentleman with popular support at home in Burundi who was esteemed by those living with him in the camp. He asked me what I thought about the fact that refugees in Kosovo received better food than Burundian refugees. He listed for me what they ate, based on a BBC radio report he followed with great interest. He also told me he heard how much more the UN was spending per refugee in the Balkans than in the Great Lakes region of Africa. There

Refugees awaiting food and soap provisions, Ngara, Tanzania, 2001
(photo by Amy R. West).

was a remarkable difference. I apologize that I do not remember the numbers. I would like to think I understand the economics of purchasing power parity, but spending time in a refugee camp in Africa raises a question or two about the process behind budget decisions for funding refugees in the Balkans, for example, and funding refugees in Africa. I am sure there is no refugee camp in the world that is Club Med, but some are in worse shape than others. I don't know, to be honest, whether this is a challenge to the UN or to the member countries whose purses support one disaster area over another.

You have said that the UNHCR is officially committed to research, yet suspicious of researchers who actually investigate on the ground. You noted that in open contradiction of the UNHCR mandate, refugees in all of the camps you visited were not aware of their rights under international law, did not know their responsibilities, and had no idea which UNHCR representatives were in charge of their particular camp. How does this lack of awareness of international law relate to the agenda and demand for communication rights? What do communication rights mean from the perspective of the marginal, vulnerable individuals and communities that are at the center of your research?

The guarantee of the freedom of both information and expression can be found in the Universal Declaration of Human Rights, the International Covenant on Civil and Political

Rights, and the African Charter on Human and Peoples' Rights, to name a few. I believe strongly in freedoms of information and expression. I believe people need to be able to communicate in their mother tongue and participate in the decision-making processes that affect their lives and livelihoods. I don't believe that the marginalized are excluded from the tenets of international law. There are rights and responsibilities for every individual. And "everyone" means everyone.

Your analysis that key international actors are well-connected to global communication networks, but disconnected from local stakeholders characterizes not just the refugee policy of international agencies such as the UNHCR, but dominant approaches to the role of ICTs in development more generally. You argue that development should "affirm the creative capacity communities possess to express, communicate, and evolve their own knowledge base" — a definition similar to the one offered by Amartya Sen — yet you observe that this is not what is taking place.[1] Thus, you insist on "the need to reboot the ICT-development machine," as the subtitle of your Article 19 report puts it. What makes it a machine, and why does it have to be rebooted? How would you describe the impact of the introduction of ICT as a development concern on the language and visions of development more generally?

In my writing, I warn of the consequences of embracing ICTs as a panacea and endorsing either directly or indirectly the idea that informal means of communication are useless, or defunct, or hold worth only for those who are poor or disenfranchised. Does being developed mean we are connected only by wireless grids or electrical wires? I find this thought deeply disturbing.

I would defer to Graham Hancock and his incredibly courageous book *Lords of Poverty* to answer your question about whether development is a machine that needs rebooting. "Machine" is defined in many ways: it is any mechanical or electrical device that transmits or modifies energy to perform or assist in the performance of human tasks, an intricate organization that accomplishes its goals efficiently (for example, "war machine"), a group that controls the activities of a political party ("political machine"), and a device for overcoming resistance at one point by applying force at some other point.[2] The way technology is being applied to solve development issues, especially its perceived utility in furthering the Millennium Development Goals, is machinelike. There is the belief that through connectivity there will be an effective connection. Yet is it possible that the more communication and information devices exist, the less individuals have human interaction? I wonder.

Information and communication technologies hold enormous potential and need to be utilized in sustainable development. However, applying a technology means examining what the capacity and need are, if development and not despair is to be promoted. What is the use of ten computers in a remote village in Eastern Cape, South Africa, where there are no tarred roads, no electricity or running water, no plugs to plug in the computer, and no one who has even operated a computer before? These computers will sit in that community and gather dust or be pulled apart and the pieces sold for bits of money to put food on someone's table. Juxtapose that with a township in KwaZulu-Natal, South Africa, that is given ten cell phones for community-based health-care workers who do home visits from one shack to another and then text messages into a hospital to chart antiretroviral and TB treatment progress. Efforts need to be coordinated and contextualized. If we don't see the difference in utility and effectiveness or listen to what people truly need, then development is indeed a machine whereby we input certain things based on what is believed to be the desired outcome. In a way, it's mass production without any variance or consideration with regard to regional, cultural, and social realities. Surely we can use technology more intelligently than this in our development strategies.

Information efforts as different as the Association for Progressive Communications (APC), Africa ICT Policy Monitor, the Highway Africa News Agency, and Russell Southwood's Balancing Act emphasize African issues and perspectives in the general ICT debate. Do you think that such an "Africanization" of development discourse is what needs to occur? Or do you see other ways to make explicit and challenge the assumptions that characterize and frame standard ICT development (ICTD) approaches?

Yes, perspective from Africa is needed. But from Africans, and I don't just mean the elite of Africa, who get to show up at meetings such as WSIS and are no more in touch with reality than a lot of the people sitting in nice offices in Geneva or New York. Have you seen average African citizens at WSIS standing up to talk about how computers have completely revolutionized their communities? Maybe if they came to WSIS, they would talk about how computers *won't* revolutionize their communities. Or what about South African nurses having a microphone at WSIS to talk about why they need Nokia to invest in them so that they can use cell phones to relay text messages from a remote location to a central hospital and how that will help them in the fight against HIV/AIDS?

I choose to focus on Africa because that is a region I have spent considerable amounts of time studying and working in, not because I default to Africa as the central development concern. If, alternatively, I had experience living and working in Asia, Asia would be my focus. I suppose I am guilty of not focusing enough on my own country, for there certainly are serious human-rights and development concerns in the United States that need addressing. My writing reflects where I have collected my research. Certainly Africa, in and of itself, regardless of my engagement with the continent, provides serious fodder for the ICTD debate. From country to country, the development terrain changes on the continent, yet within countries such as South Africa there are enormous gaps between those with and those without access to information and communication.

To take one example, look at prevalence rates for HIV infection in sub-Saharan Africa. A country such as South Africa has the largest number of HIV-infected individuals living within its borders; HIV/AIDS is at the level of a national crisis, with averages of a thousand people dying a day in one province alone. You can drive by cemeteries that are overflowing with the dead, and space to bury the dying is in seriously short supply. South Africa makes a valid case study for analysis of how certain ICTs can best be used to meet immediate and dire needs concerning HIV/AIDS education and information. The failure of information and communication systems that have not been used effectively to educate people about risky sexual behavior, facts about HIV infection and transmission, violence against women, treatment and care support, and basic health and nutrition practices must be addressed. One cannot say that the potential of ICTs—lauded at WSIS —in the struggle against HIV is inconsequential in a country such as South Africa. More can be done and is not being done to apply ICTs to a direct need there.

You have discussed Bush Radio in Cape Town—"the mother of community radio in Africa" and now one of about a hundred community radio stations in South Africa alone—and predicted that low-cost technologies such as radio will continue to remain more relevant than computers or television. Organizations such as the World Association of Community Radio Broadcasters (AMARC) have done much to connect local projects in a global network and raise radio-related issues in WSIS and other international policy forums, but you suggest that the radio has been sidelined in the general ICTD discussion, because latest-tech projects are shifting funding away from community-media initiatives. What should be done about this?

I just think international organizations and NGOs should use radio more in education programs and in spreading information to the general population, especially with regard to law programs for refugees, to inform them of their rights and responsibilities, and with regard to HIV/AIDS, to give them facts about infection, best practices for treatment and care, and so on. There is no end to how community-based organizations can develop radio programming to inform and educate those living even in the remotest of areas. Radios are proven to be effective, especially in remote areas and among highly illiterate populations. We shouldn't discard what works. And I think that ICTD does need some rearticulation, because most of the people working on and promoting ICTs so far seem to be techies and engineers. This sudden idea that ICTs can help connect everything (e-government, e-health, e-education) has been a bit of a disaster, since there aren't an overwhelming number of development experts standing up and lauding how ICT is helping health, education, and even relief efforts in different places. I would say there is still a huge disconnect between those trying to sell ICT for development and those who would use or presumably benefit the most from information and communication technologies.

1   Amy R. West and Audrey N. Selian, *Experiencing Technical Difficulties: The Urgent Need to Rewire and Reboot the ITC-Development Machine* (London: Article 19, 2005), p. 8.
2   For further definitions of "machine," see Die.net's online dictionary at http://dict.die.net/machine/.

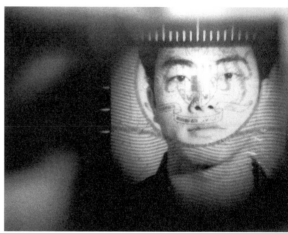

Olivier Aubert, *Border Police, Paris* (1999). The *Bureau des fraudes documentaires* (Fraudulent Documents Department) examines all false documents and classifies them according to the type of fraud. In this case, Chinese immigrants tried to enter France with Korean and Japanese passports that were stolen in Europe, Africa, or Japan and then sent to China where the smuggling networks use them repeatedly.

Between Testimony and Expertise: How Immigration Policies Challenge the Humanitarian Ethic

Estelle d'Halluin

During the past twenty years, the right to asylum has gradually eroded in Western countries. After the Second World War, the ideal of defending human rights and freedom — defense of the "right to have rights," to use Hannah Arendt's expression — was made concrete in an international convention on the protection of refugees: the Geneva Conventions of 1951. Widely ratified by Western European countries, these conventions were applied liberally until the 1980s. Factors such as postwar reconstruction and economic growth, as well as the logic of the Cold War, favored the reception of refugees whose numbers were gradually decreasing. During this period, the exile enjoyed a certain prestige and was not yet suspected of "fraudulence." But asylum gradually lost its legitimacy in Europe as economic and social conditions deteriorated. Increasing unemployment and xenophobia led governments to restrict, if not to eliminate, the immigration of laborers. At the same time, demands for asylum in Europe increased, and a discourse that criminalized refugees developed. Thus, starting in the late 1980s, the reception of refugees was gradually subordinated to a logic of controlling migratory flows; and policies designed to limit the flow of asylum seekers were put in place at the national and European levels.[1] France is no exception in this construction of what is referred to as "Fortress Europe." Although asylum seekers are not accused of being "scroungers" in France (as they are in the British tabloids), they are still widely suspected of being "false refugees" and "frauds."[2] In this new context, only a minority of refugees, having succeeded in proving their legitimacy, can benefit from France's "generosity."

But this evolution did not destroy support for refugees in Europe: today a network of organizations under the name of the European Council on Refugees and Exiles is engaged in this very cause.[3] In France, during the 1970s, several new organizations joined those already defending foreigners and trying to improve the conditions for arriving refugees (health care, housing, legal aid, and so on). Long left to private initiative, this reception was gradually institutionalized. The state began to finance and organize it within a legal framework administered by various organizations. Nevertheless, the disequilibrium between the means set up for their reception and the precarious situation of a growing number of asylum seekers made initiatives from organizations working on the margins of public agencies even more necessary. French asylum policies, therefore, are marked by a double evolution. On the one hand, asylum seekers have more and more difficulty proving their right to protection before administrative authorities. On the other hand, the basic and humanitarian needs of asylum seekers are gradually being recognized as a right, so that the state has begun to provide financial support through nonprofit organizations.

These organizations, especially the medical and humanitarian nongovernmental organizations, have been increasingly caught in the vise of policies of control, on the one hand, and support for humanitarian action, on the other. Little by little, the state has recognized the value of NGOs' medical assistance to exiles. But it has also solicited these organizations' medical skills in implementing asylum procedures. In effect, these humanitarian associations have been confronted with a new demand: to gather exiles' testimony and to evaluate it, by judging the compatibility between the alleged acts of violence and the observable physical and psychological repercussions. Medical doctors, psychiatrists, and psychologists produce medical certificates for the asylum seekers who, in turn, attach them to their case files in order to corroborate the accounts they give to the authorities granting the right to asylum. Medical professionals have therefore been placed in the position of experts — "specialists whose judgment is objectified as an essential piece of evidence in a case file that authorities then judge according to their own criteria to arrive at some practical options."[4] Through a history of one of these NGOs, the Comité Médical pour les Exilés (Comede), I propose here to examine how this demand to provide expert knowledge has disrupted the organization's practices and ethics both as medical professionals and as political activists.

In 1979, several members of organizations that aided the exiled population in France joined together to create Centre d'orientation médicale (Comed) — a center that provided medical information and facilitated asylum seekers' access to the health-care system in the Paris region.[5] At that time, lack of information and administrative delays made it difficult for asylum seekers to secure social protection. It could take several months for exiles to become part of the French system of health care, unemployment, and pension coverage once the application for asylum was submitted. Comed's goal was to alleviate this problem by providing information to exiles and directing them to the correct agencies. A provisional and transitory office that did not provide care itself, Comed nevertheless became a permanent agency for granting medical, psychological, and social care. When the organization incorporated in 1982, it was renamed the Comité Médical pour les Exilés (Comede), thus formalizing its function as a free clinic.[6] In the field of health care, it can take pride in having been in the avant-garde of agencies fighting discrimination: Comede opened a reception center for recent immigrants seven years before Médecins du Monde set up its first center for those in need.[7] Comede's 2004 annual report provides a good overview of the organization's activities: in over 25 years, Comede received 81,562 patients and provided 405,535 consultations for medical, psychotherapeutic, nursing, and social services.[8] Aware of the changes in the organization's structure and of the crises in the evolution of collective action during this period, Comede's members insisted on a continued commitment to the humanitarianism central to the organization's history, despite the fact that its structure had undergone numerous changes.

However, Comede does not consider itself to be on the margins of the political order. It aspires to change this order, at least in its own field of activity. It intervened in politics primarily by testifying publicly (in colloquia, newspapers, journals, and the like) about the health problems and social conditions of exiles, in order to raise consiousness about these issues and to improve the situation for incoming immigrants. An article published in the journal *Migrations santé* in 1986 emphasized that the organization's goal was to "lobby the public authorities and associate itself with any initiatives that aim to modify regulations for the sake of better protecting this population, in terms of social benefits and health care."[9] From the outset, members of Comede favored active participation in shaping public policy, a kind of activism that "engages institutions."[10] Comede contributed to public debates and was active in changing legislation concerning ailing foreigners' right to Aide Médicale de l'Etat (State Medical Aid) and Couverture Maladie Universelle (Universal Health Coverage).[11]

Soon, however, Comede's doctors called as expert witnesses, both by asylum seekers and by government administrators. Over the years, this type of work has become more central to the organization's identity and intervention — without reducing its emphasis on the humanitarian imperative to guarantee health coverage for at-risk exiles. In 2001, Arnaud Veïsse, director of Comede, expressed concern about this evolving role in an article published in the journal *Vacarme*.[12] Serving as expert witnesses introduces a tension between the organization's basic humanitarian focus — its function of providing care to exiles and testifying about their condition — and the bureaucratic requirements it has increasingly confronted as legal restrictions on the right to asylum have tightened over the last two decades. How has this organization managed to integrate this demand into its activities? How have its members negotiated their medical practices and their activist and professional identities in their new role as experts? Have the organizational adjustments arising from the increased demand for their services inflected their practices toward a rationalization and a technicalization that contradicts the empathy characteristic of Comede's original, humanitarian purpose?

THE ENCOUNTER BETWEEN THE POLICY OF PROOF AND THE POLICY OF TESTIMONY

"Since Comede was first formed, we have been confronted with the administration's demand for medical certificates. This very quickly led OFPRA (Office Français de

Protection des Réfugiés et Apatrides — the French Office for the Protection of Refugees and Stateless Persons) to perceive our organization as providing medical expertise."[13] This is how, in 2002, Comede's medical coordinator framed the issue of expertise within the organization. Comede's medical expertise might thus appear as the result of a productive encounter between the necessity for doctors to testify about their treatment of ill exiles and the search for probative elements by both the OFPRA and the CRR (Commission des Recours des Réfugiés — the Refugee Appeals Board), the two organizations that grant refugee status to foreigners requesting asylum in France. OFPRA does so first, after an interview with a protection officer; CRR does so in cases of appeal, after a public hearing before a three-person tribunal.

One might consider the "policy of testimony" — to borrow the agents' term — characteristic of the second age of the French humanitarian movement.[14] Comede members' willingness to provide testimony is not unlike the position adopted by emergency medical organizations created in the 1970s (such as Médecins Sans Frontières and, in 1980, Médecins du Monde),which refused to adopt the policy of silence embraced by humanitarian associations such as the Red Cross. "Treat, then denounce": this was the movement's new credo, which grounded their public interventions in the doctors' firsthand experience treating victims. Comede's doctors, therefore, thought that by granting medical certificates they were testifying directly about the effects of torture and the experience of their exiled patients. Nevertheless, the form their testimony took was inscribed within a set of medical and political exigencies, and was directed only at affecting changes at the administrative level. It thus differed from public denunciations, which could potentially mobilize public opinion.[15]

This testimony accorded with the policy of proof required by the 1951 Geneva Conventions in France. During the interwar period, obtaining asylum membership in a community officially recognized as persecuted (for example, the Armenians of Turkey) was sufficient. Following the Second World War, the universalism of the Geneva Conventions did not challenge state sovereignty, since it allowed nation-states to retain the power of organizing the selection of asylum seekers. Thereafter, most European states created their own individual procedures, which became even more fastidious when economic crises made foreigners "undesirable." In France, for example, asylum seekers are individually subjected to a truth test. This proves difficult for many foreigners, who are often exhausted by an arduous voyage, struggling with the host countries' language and bureaucracy, and unable to furnish the necessary documents. Furthermore, they have to appear before government institutions — where today a climate of suspicion reigns.[16] As Gérard Noiriel has remarked, governments and their agencies have progressively limited the debate on the right to asylum to bureaucratic considerations: using the excuse of insufficient documentation, they justify the eviction of a large number of "false refugees." This strategy allows them to appear rigorous in their requirements.[17] Since the end of the 1930s — a prosperous decade for France — as the number of requests for asylum increased, the government has become increasingly selective about granting asylum status. In France between 1980 and 1990, the rate of granting asylum went from 80 to 20 percent. If 1974, the year the borders were closed, was a turning point in the history of labor migration. Then 1989, when sixty thousand people applied for asylum, marked the establishment of a set of procedures that discouraged individuals from seeking asylum. Since the 1990s, the rate of granting asylum status has varied from year to year, fluctuating from 15 to 20 percent.

This is the context for understanding the practice of medical certification, which some have perceived as the "mother of all proofs," the real "evidence," as one CRR judge has described it.[18] Within institutions responsible for granting refugee status, however, many people are more suspicious about the value of the medical certificate in substantiating an application's credibility: the certificate is "one index among others"; it "sheds light" on the case.[19] By all accounts, asylum seekers' case histories and interviews remain the crucial pieces of evidence and provides "the final verdict." And yet, at the same time, asylum seekers and their lawyers value the medical certificate because it can at times function to "draw the attention," or "dissolve the remaining doubts of certain judges."[20] For this reason, over the past twenty years, these organizations have witnessed an increased demand for medical certificates. This phenomenon is not peculiar to France: in Sweden, England, the Netherlands, and Canada, doctors and psychologists are increasingly asked to inform the judgments of the suspicious authorities that grant asylum status.[21] In a legal and administrative framework in which institutions call into question the truth of asylum seekers' accounts, the body has become the site where the subject's veracity is tested — or, rather, the site where it is tested by a third party, the doctor, who is supposed to be both impartial and knowledgeable.[22]

This form of medical expertise does not follow a formal, written legal procedure. Thus, the various participants have turned freely to the medical organizations specializing in the treatment of ill exiles, which are perceived as highly competent due to their vast experience with this population. These organizations have rapidly gained credibility and garnered a major share of the work in providing expert testimony. Therefore, since its creation, Comede has steadily increased the number of medical certificates it grants to asylum seekers. In turn, its members have had to redefine their areas of competence and their role in this social game; they have also had to decide which choices and practices were ethical when administering medical certification. The introduction of this type of specialization has prompted transformations in the organization's distribution of work. The evolution of Comede's role in this respect can be divided into three phases.

THE FIRST PHASE OF EXPERTISE: THE EMERGENCE OF A "PROBLEM"

The first phase corresponds to the first decade of Comede's existence, when the organization essentially offered the services of volunteer medical and paramedical personnel, who — in their own words — were "much more militant in their souls" than the later generation.[23] Medical certification was, at that time, only a peripheral activity. Following the thirteen thousand consultations provided in 1985, Comede granted fewer than two hundred certificates. In her 1985 study, Anne Guillemette Simonot-Sault remarked on the extreme heterogeneity of the certificates Comede produced.[24] The medical practitioners seem to have been quite autonomous in deciding how they would use their expertise and how they would present the cases in their reports. Still a peripheral activity, certification was only a minor problem that did not require rethinking the organization's work. Comede's archives testify to this: they contain documents on the specific pathologies encountered, the proposed treatments, and the patients' access to care. Certification was just one of the means for testifying to the experience of exiles.

Nonetheless, practitioners began to express concern about being interpolated as experts. During a colloquium organized by Amnesty International in March 1985, the president of Comede stressed the difficulty doctors confront when

> OFPRA demands so-called objective elements of proof. In many cases, the description of lesions does not permit us to assert definitely whether they are due to torture or not. And how can you prove subjective elements?... How can you supply proof of the suffering of people who often cannot even "say" what they have undergone?... There is an ambiguity between what the lawyers ask for — "proof" — and the role of the doctor — which is to care for patients. A perversion seems to exist at the level of the right to asylum since they are being asked for "proof" of torture, whereas the reasons why they left their countries ought to be sufficient in and of themselves.[25]

Reflection on the practical and ethical problems raised by certification thus emerged during the 1980s, raising questions that would henceforth be on the agenda. The first question addressed a technical matter: how could the complex suffering and lived experience expressed by the patient be transcribed into scientific language? The second question related to policy. The medical certificate attested to the effects of violence, and therefore superseded the criterion of "fear of persecution" set forth in the Geneva Conventions. Fear of being persecuted no longer sufficed; the threat had to be actualized, and its trace verified. In 1986, during a colloquium in Lyon, a psychotherapist from Comede expressed the fear that "this contributes to thinking that the actual fact of having been tortured constitutes the sole valid criterion for being granted the status of refugee."[26]

THE SECOND PHASE OF EXPERTISE: THE CREATION OF AN ETHOS

The second phase took place between two "institutional crises," in 1988 and 1998. Members of Comede refer to this period as the phase of the organization's "professionalization." In 1988, an audit requested by some members of Comede's administrative council concluded that it was necessary to create a position for a director who was neither a doctor nor a healthcare provider and to restructure the organization so that it could better meet patients' needs and secure additional funding. Marked by power struggles, personality conflicts, and different visions of the organization's mission, the general assembly of April 1989 concluded — after ten hours of stormy debate — with the "victory of the majority of the council, which had requested the audit and hired the director."[27] In the restructuring that ensued, the division of labor and the specialization of tasks were reorganized and positions for a coordinating doctor and an administrative head were created. At the same time, available subsidies were diversified and solidified, notably through growing support from the government's Direction des Populations et des Migrations (Populations and Migrations Directorate), Fonds d'Action Sociale (Social Action Fund), and Direction Générale de la Santé (General Health Directorate).

During this period, an ethos regarding certification and guidelines for writing certificates began to emerge. The demand for certificates (which had grown at the end of the 1980s) stabilized at between five hundred and six hundred per year. In 1990, in cooperation with the ethics center of Lyon — Centre Droit et Ethique de la Santé — a working group started to reflect on this issue of medical certification.[28] The group articulated its project around, on the one hand, producing an ethical and political position on the social function of the certificate and, on the other, formulating a template for the medical certificate.

The ethical and political position of Comede was clarified in an article, "Torture et mythe de la preuve" (Torture and the Myth of Proof), published in 1992 in *Plein droit*, the journal of GISTI (Groupe d'Information et de Soutien des Immigrés — Group for Information and Support for Immigrants).[29] This journal was widely circulated among people working with foreigners. The article took up questions that had been posed in the organizations first phase, but also stressed other dimensions surrounding the issue of medical expertise, most notably, the reduction of the importance of the victim's words in deference to those of the doctor. Moreover, the article addressed how the relationship between caregiver and patient was being perverted by the administrative instrumentalization of both the doctor and patient. Finally, concern was raised about the performative effect of the certificate: while in certain instances it seems to have worked in the applicant's favor, in others, OFPRA's or the CRR's rejection letter noted that the certificate had no "probative value" given that no study had yet been done on this subject.

If one considers Comede as an actor participating in the more general network of asylum procedures via its provision of expertise, its position vis-à-vis the social system — whose dysfunctions are known — might be characterized, in Albert O. Hirschman's terms, as "critical loyalty."[30] Of course, the possibility of boycotting the certification process has been brought up several times in the past, but loyalty to the system is maintained even today. The consequences of defecting are judged as too harmful and the organization still hopes it can improve the system by their taking a stance. Members publicly denounce "the perverse opinion that asylum should be granted only to those who have actually undergone torture," as well as "the deficiencies in the exercise of the defense law by reason of the overload and speed of procedures." Furthermore, refusing to perform certification has not been considered by Comede, "not only for the sake of codes of practice, but above all to preserve the essential therapeutic relationship between doctor and patient."[31] In the absence of this documentation, patients' chances of obtaining refugee status are significantly reduced. Beyond the difficulties pertaining to this field of expertise, members stress the medical certificate's social and therapeutic functions: "Rehabilitating the word of the victim signifies that the doctor means to transcribe something of the exile's story. Taking these words seriously already has a therapeutic function. By addressing the certificate to the relevant administrative bodies, claimants transmit their stories to the social body."[32] During this second phase, it was possible to attribute both functions to the certificate, because the doctor often still proposed certification when treating each patient and could take the time necessary to prepare the certificate.

In addition to establishing an ethos, Comede formulated guidelines about preparing the certificate that testify to an effort to regularize practices within the institution. Concretely, the doctor was supposed to conform to a model: to retrace the patient's history *briefly,* to listen to his or her complaints, to note physical and psychological symptoms, and to produce an impartial judgment on their compatibility with the alleged facts. But practices were hard to standardize, which may be explained by Comede's parallel structure. At that time, it had twice as many employees as it does today, most of whom were volunteers working one or two half-days per week. Their vague attempts at autonomy made it more difficult to impose institutional norms for both treatment and certification. Logisitical planning fell to a group of militant doctors who were almost exclusively devoted to certification and sometimes imposed a very rigorous conception of it. Consultations were thus solely centered on this activity; they could last for as long as three hours, focusing primarily on the patients' autobiographies. Also, at the time, certificates were often more lengthy documents, providing an in-depth account of the patients' case histories and the emotions that emerged during the interview. Such conditions allowed doctors to still envision medical certification as part of a "policy of testimony."[33]

THE THIRD PHASE OF EXPERTISE: THE STANDARDIZATION OF PRACTICES

According to the members of Comede, an "institutional crisis" between 1995 and 1998 caused a profound modification of their work. After that crisis, all doctors both provided health care and served as experts. Tasks were prioritized, new positions were created, and only salaried staff members were recruited. The organization returned to its medical vocation. These changes were due to internal restructuring, but they also responded to the state's increased control over the organizations it finances. Such changes have proven an essential condition for the normalization of practices within Comede. Many of the current personnel declare themselves "less militant than the preceding generation" and define themselves primarily in terms of their professional skills, to the point that one of the doctors stated that "if you want to keep focused on medical care, you have to leave activism behind."[34]

However, at the very moment when Comede was reasserting its medical vocation, increased demand for its expertise compelled its doctors to make new adjustments in the organization of their work. Since there was always a consensus that humanitarian activity took precedence, it became necessary to limit the time and number of consultations devoted to certification without compromising medical care during the process. Various attempts were made to include the provision of expertise, but they were always limited. Exiles therefore developed their own strategies for obtaining a form that they believed was invested with a certain power in the eyes of the French authorities. Moreover, the number of individuals aspiring to obtain this certificate, which doctors agreed to provide during the consultation, continued to grow. The waiting period for an appointment was so long — more than three months — that expert medical care for new patients was regularly suspended for several months at a time. This situation was a source of inequality among patients and generated many tensions between the doctors and the clientele. As the sociologist Everett C. Hughes has noted, this type of tension is typical of professions where the provider deals on a daily basis with situations its clients view as emergencies.[35]

In this context, the increased demand for certification made expertise an "urgent" issue. In the first and second phases discussed above, the doctor could offer the patient a medical certificate only after several consultations, once a relationship of mutual knowledge and trust had been established. In the current phase that kind of case has become rare. Now the doctor, often solicited in emergency situations, has limited time for consultations if he or she wants to see all his or her patients for the day. In order to establish a correspondence between physical scars and acts of violence, for example, the doctor must pose a series of short questions designed to reconstruct the scene of violence and place it in the context necessary for the certificate. Doctors are aware of the perverse effects of the current configuration: "the asylum seekers," writes one doctor, "can put pressure on the doctor when they come in a crisis situation to obtain 'proof.'… The claimants' anxiety is matched by the doctor's when he or she finds it impossible to take the necessarily long amount of time to conduct a full examination. In their haste, doctors risk reproducing a 'police' interrogation that reactivates the victims' suffering."[36] The process of biographical explanation is all the more necessary under the circumstances so that Comede's doctors do not fail the claimant by producing a certificate whose account differs from ones written for other institutions. The necessity of presenting a clear and precise report leaves doctors with the impression that they have "become the police."[37] Indeed, how is it possible to avoid turning the consultation into a police interrogation that operates according to the logic of a detective investigation (establish facts; gather clues, evidence, or confessions), thereby moving away from the logic of a clinical interview more attentive to the patient's sufferings? In a 2003 article in *Plein droit,* Comede's director, Arnaud Veïsse, underlined the risks of reactivating trauma in such interviews. Veïsse quotes the United Nations' manual for the investigation of torture, which warns investigators about how traumatic reactions can be produced when exiles remember torture during physical and psychological examinations.[38] The constraints of providing expertise here collide with Comede's humanitarian mission and with the campaign for awareness about the trauma suffered by exiles that it has launched in other venues (seminars, publications, and so on).

Recently, the form of the medical certificates has become more standardized. A quantitative survey of five hundred certificates randomly selected every five years has consistently shown a uniformity. Less space is given to the patient's complaints and account of violence; the clinical report on observed scars has become more precise. All subjective evaluation is avoided. Banished from certificates are phrases that used to emphasize the clarity, coherence, and precision of the patient's story, that described the patient's tears or broken voice, or made judgments such as, "The veracity of the alleged facts can be believed." The ideal form of the certificate seems now to be consensual. This evolution relates to an increase in the number of claimants, combined with a drop in the amount of time allotted to each one, which leads to a gradual depersonalization of the process and sometimes makes the doctors feel they are doing the "stereotypical work" of administrative regulation. There is also a strategic dimension: in focusing on the examination and description of scars, rather than on the restitution of the patient's subjective experience, doctors confine themselves to their fields of competence as both doctors and jurists.[39] It is difficult today, given these conditions, to see the medical certificate as a record of testimony about the exile's complex experience; for some doctors, it amounts to a "macabre accounting for scars."[40]

Doctors realize how, for many of the patients who urgently solicit their expertise, the effects of routinization and the lack of time to get beyond the purely factual often strip the expert evaluation of the therapeutic dimension referred to in the statements Comede made in the 1990s. The doctors no longer invoke a "policy of testimony," although such testimony is still made in other places, such as the life stories of patients published in Comede's journal, *Maux d'exil* (Ills of Exile). The doctors continue to offer their expertise solely out of a loyalty attentive to the problems that might ensue if they stopped. If Comede did not participate in the certification system, asylum seekers might have to exhibit their bruised bodies during the public hearings of the CRR; there is a substantial risk that other experts, unscrupulous and less favorable to the refugees, would take Comede's place. In addition, not consulting Comede's doctors would lessen opportunities to address medical problems. The positive social function of the certificates is mentioned less often now that participants in the process feel caught up in the increasingly technical logic of a certification process that must often be performed quickly.

Ultimately, the daily practice of doctors makes manifest the contradictions inherent in the French management of asylum according to a dual logic of compassion and repression.[41] The left hand of the state finances the health center, while the right hand uses expert testimony "to separate the wheat from the chaff." The organizational and moral tensions that Comede's doctors feel acutely thus seem to arise less from their adjustment to new working conditions and ethical positions than from their reactions to the evolving policies of asylum at the national and European levels. The more the logics of selectivity and the control of immigration flows are tightened, the more these doctors' margins of maneuver will be restricted — whether in terms of their capacity to furnish humanitarian aid or their ability to modify policy through their individualized help as experts. The constraints weighing on the process of obtaining refugee status now seem to have been internalized by the exiles themselves, since the form of self-presentation associated with the application for asylum — proving one's status as the victim of political repression by stripping the body bare — sometimes takes precedence over any concern for the exiles' physical and psychological condition.

Translated by Susan Emanuel.

1   Michelle Guillon, Luc Legoux, and Emmanuel Ma Mung (eds.), *L'asile politique entre deux chaises: Droits de l'homme et gestion des flux migratoires* (Paris: Harmattan, 2003).

2   For an overview of the way asylum seekers are depicted in the tabloids see Louise Pirouet, *Whatever Happened to Asylum in Britain? A Tale of Two Walls* (New York: Berghan Books, 2001), and Jean-Pierre Lafon, "Dérives du droit d'asile: État des lieux," *L'Express,* January 10, 2002. Lafon is a senior civil servant in the Ministry of Foreign Affairs.

3   See the council's Web site: www.ecre.org. See also the list of the Web sites of various European organizations at www.forumrefugies.org/pages/liens/liens.php?cat=AE.

4   Robert Castel, *La gestion des risques: De l'antipsychiatrie à l'après-psychanalyse* (Paris: Minuit, 1981), p. 124.

5   The groups were the Service Oecuménique d'Entraide (Cimade), the Groupe Accueil et Solidarité, and Amnesty International.

6   I would like to thank the Comede members and the people I interviewed in other institutions for their cooperation during this study. Dider Fassin and I performed an ethnographic study during which we spent two periods of four months with Comede; we observed medical consultations and staff meetings, interviewed personnel, and studied the group's archives. This article summarizes and extends the analysis in Didier Fassin and Estelle d'Halluin, "The Truth from the Body: Medical Certificates as Ultimate Evidence for Asylum Seekers," *American Anthropologist* 107, no. 4 (2005), pp. 597–608. In the present essay, I concentrate on a single group, tracing Comede's institutional evolution and the tensions that resulted from it.

7   Didier Maille and Arnaud Veïsse, "Des difficultés des exilés à accéder au système de santé en Ile-de-France: Les demandeurs d'asile et la CMU—Comment intégrer le système de santé?" *L'observatoire du droit à la santé des étrangers,* June 2000, www.odse.eu.org/article.php3?id_article=5.

8   Comede 2004 annual report, p. 4, www.comede.org/.

9   Patrick Le Courtois, "Comede," in *Migrations santé* (1986), pp. 56–58.

10 On this subject, see "Militantismes institutionnels," special issue of *Politix* 18 (2005).

11 French universal healthcare (the Couverture Maladie Universelle law of July 27, 1998) offers health insurance at no charge to people who earn less than €542 a month. Asylum seekers are automatically covered for free, as are legal immigrants, under certain conditions: financial eligibility, successful completion of a medical examination, and continuous residence in France for more than three months. Out-of-status foreigners benefit from the minimal protection of Aide Médicale de l'Etat (State Medical Aid).

12 Arnaud Veïsse, "Les salles d'attente de l'universel," *Vacarme* 17 (2001), available online at www.vacarme.eu.org/article203.html.

13 Interview with the head doctor at Comede, November 6, 2002.

14 Didier Fassin and Estelle d'Halluin, "Témoigner en Palestine: La qualification psychiatrique des violences de guerre," in Marc Le Pape, Claudine Vidal, and Johanna Siméant (eds.), *Crises extrêmes: Face aux massacres, guerres et génocides* (Paris: La Découverte, 2006).

15 Luc Boltanski, *Distant Suffering: Morality, Media, and Politics,* trans. Graham Burchell (Cambridge: Cambridge University Press, 1999).

16 Patrick Delouvin, "The Evolution of Asylum in France," *Journal of Refugee Studies* 13, no. 1 (2000), pp. 61–73.

17 Gérard Noiriel, *Réfugiés et sans-papiers: La République face au droit d'asile, XIXe–XXe siècle* (Paris: Hachette, 1998).

18 Interview with a judge delegated by the United Nations High Commissioner on Refugees (UNHCR) to the CRR, August 2002. The UNHCR was created in 1950 by the General Assembly of the UN and given the mandate of coordinating international action to protect refugees and to find solutions to the problems of refugees everywhere. One out of three judges on CRR committees is a delegate representing the UNHCR.

19 Interviews with members of the OFPRA and the CRR.

20 Statements by lawyers in the course of a conference on asylum, Terra (a scientific network, http://terra.rezo.net/article289.html), Paris, March 1, 2004.

21 According to interviews in Montreal and London, as well as discussions recorded during a workshop of the European network of health centers for victims of torture, Paris, March 2006.

22 Fassin and Halluin, "The Truth from the Body."

23 Interview with a nurse from Comede, Feb. 7, 2003.

24 Anne Guillemette Simonot-Sault, "Déclarations de torture: Les problèmes du constat médical," M.D. diss., Université Claude Bernard—Lyon I, 1985.

25 Gabrielle Buisson-Touboul, "L'action du Comede contre la torture," Amnesty International Colloquium, March 22-23, 1985, from the Comede archives.

26 From a speech given by Miguel Olcese entitled "Colloque d'éthique de santé," Lyon, January 1986, from the Comede archives.

27 Interview with the former Comede director, November 5, 2002.

28 This center was created by Dr. Nicole Lery as a unit of the Hospices Civils de Lyon in order to handle staff conflicts linked to ethical questions and other more general ethical problems. Asylum seekers around Lyons often come to this center for medical expertise.

29 Elisabeth Didier, "Torture et mythe de la preuve," *Plein droit* 18–19 (1992), pp. 64–69. Available online at www.gisti. org/doc/plein-droit/18-19/torture.html. GISTI was created in 1972 by students at the Ecole Nationale d'Administration, along with lawyers, magistrates, social workers, and activists. Their investment in the issue of immigration came from a growing movement to include the problem in national debates after May 1968. Using something akin to impact litigation, GISTI helped change the legislation on immigrants' rights in France.

30 Albert O. Hirschman, *Exit, Voice, and Loyalty: Responses to Decline in Firms, Organizations, and States* (Cambridge, MA: Harvard University Press, 1970).

31 Patrick August, in a speech on exile, the environment, and health entitled "Exil, environnement et santé," colloquium given by the monthly journal *Passages,* Paris, April 8, 1992, from the Comede archives.

32 Didier, "Torture et mythe de la preuve."

33 Patrick Lamour, "Accueil medico-psycho-social des demandeurs d'asile," at the Santé et Publics Démunis conference, Besançon, France, May 16–18, 1994, from the Comede archives.

34 Interview with a Comede general practioner, October 28, 2002.

35 Everett C. Hughes, "Work and Self," *The Sociological Eye* (New Brunswick, NJ: Transaction Books, 1984), p. 346.

36 Didier, "Torture et mythe de la preuve."

37 Interview with a Comede general practitioner, January 9, 2003.

38 UNHCR, *Manual on the Effective Investigation and Documentation of Torture and Other Cruel, Inhuman and Degrading Treatment or Punishment* (Geneva: United Nations, 2001); Arnaud Veïsse, "Les lésions dangereuses," *Plein droit* 56 (2003), pp. 32–35.

39 Interview with a general practitioner, October 23, 2002.

40 Interview with a Comede general practioner, July, 31, 2003.

41 Didier Fassin, "Compassion and Repression: The Moral Economy of Immigration Policies in France," *Cultural Anthropology* 20, no. 3 (2005), pp. 362–87.

SITES

BORDERS

2006 Immigrant Mobilizations in the United States

Claudio Lomnitz

The spring of 2006 was a season of stunning mass protests in the United States. Sparked by indignation against the 2005 House of Representatives' Border Protection, Antiterrorism, and Illegal Immigration Control Act (HR 4437), more than three million "illegal aliens" and their supporters marched across U.S. cities, with demonstrations of over 100,000 in San Jose, Phoenix, New York, Chicago, Washington D.C., Los Angeles, Dallas, and Chicago. These rallies were the largest in recorded history for the cities of Los Angeles (650,000–700,000), Chicago (400,000–750,000), Dallas (350,000–500,000), Phoenix (100,000–250,000), and San Jose (100,000).[1] If we interpret the marches as a form of labor protest, they constitute the largest mobilization of workers in the history of the United States.[2] If we interpret them as civil-rights protests, they were the most important since the 1960s.

The immigrant movement of 2006 was built on the sutured gash that unites the United States with Mexico and the rest of Latin America. In addition to their sheer scale, the rallies were marked by three unusual features. The first of these is the hybridity of their form, that is, the way in which aspects of mass political protest common in Central and South America were melded with characteristic U.S. political concerns for influencing voting behavior. While multigenerational mass demonstrations of the kind staged in 2006 are a preferred form of political expression in Mexico, they have been rather exceptional in the United States. It is true that massive, peaceful rallies have occurred in relation to national crises such as the Vietnam War, the Iraq War, and the 2004 Republican Convention (at which George Bush was nominated for reelection), but they only rarely have been an instrument of protest for a specific group of people. Louis Farrakhan's Million Man March in October 1995 offers some points of comparison, but this rally was styled as a singular movement, concerned as much with the spiritual atonement of African-American men as with protesting the Right's curtailment of social programs important to black Americans.[3]

Thousands of demonstrators gather in downtown Los Angeles during an immigration protest on May 1, 2006. Rallies in Los Angeles were the largest in the city's history. Overall, the pro-immigration rallies of spring 2006 were the largest in U.S. history (Stefano Paltera/AP Photo).

A volunteer from the Minuteman Project stands near an American flag placed in the barbed wire fence that divides the U.S. from Mexico, April 4, 2005, near Naco, Sonora. The U.S.-Mexico border is the longest existing political boundary between a rich and a poor nation. For the past few decades, it also has stood as the border between the United States and Central American migrants, who cross Mexico to get to the U.S. Until the 1880s, this divide was a frontier rather than a border. Since then, the vast frontier has developed border zones that are sites of intense traffic. Millions of trucks cross the U.S.-Mexico border each year. Legal and illegal goods, documented and undocumented people, and investments flow across, with money changing hands. As a rhetorical gesture, this fence needs to be understood in this context (Scott Olson/Getty Images).

Rather, the more festive, multigenerational, peaceful, and massive march typical of 2006 has its clearest counterpart in Mexican political life. In the United States, voting and related practices, such as writing letters to congresspeople and signing petitions, have been the favored forms of political expression. In Mexico, on the contrary, voting has had either a competitive or a supplemental relationship to street demonstrations. Collective bodily presence in public spaces has been a key form of democratic expression there. Mass rallies in the United States also have not received the same level of media coverage as their Mexican counterparts, which can be watched regularly in the United States on the Spanish-language networks. At the same time, Latinos in the United States have been systematically read by U.S. political experts as "apolitical" because of their low level of electoral participation (though this trend has been reversed somewhat in recent elections, with the dominant U.S. political parties courting Latino voters). Importantly, then, the very form of the 2006 U.S. immigration rallies suggests a new degree of transnational cross-fertilization at the level of political forms.

Indeed, the choice to stage a string of mass rallies on May 1, International Workers' Day, which originally commemorated the 1886 Haymarket Riot in Chicago, but is not widely observed in the United States, further registers this cross-fertilization of methods of political protest. Moreover, the rallies in the United States were widely publicized by the Mexican media, and were accompanied by a Mexican movement to boycott U.S. products for the day. The hybrid form of these immigration protests, which were informed by both transnational and American patterns of political action, was thus concomitant with efforts to generate political pressure on both sides of the U.S.-Mexico border.

THE POLITICS OF VISIBILITY

The politics of visibility espoused by the 2006 immigrant movement suggests parallels between the situation of the illegal immigrant in the United States and that of the citizen in Mexico. In addition to their hybridity, the second important feature and effect of these simultaneous or closely coordinated nationwide demonstrations was public recognition of the presence, and opinions, of millions of people who had until recently been spoken for by governments and policy makers, a process that parallels the politics of democratic recognition that began in Mexico with mass mobilizations in 1988, and which continues to this day.

Until the 2006 rallies, public discussions about Mexican immigrants in the United States comfortably relied on their physical absence from the public sphere, an invisibility that was guaranteed by their status as "illegals," by their lack of citizenship, and indeed, by their incipient knowledge of U.S.-style democratic politics. Thus the "immigration problem" was discussed by anti-immigrant critics and immigrant supporters alike, confident that the immigrants themselves could not or would not speak up in public. Now, however, as the national media reported, Mexican immigrants were taking time off work and banding together in small groups on the main streets of small-town America.[4] Their presence as a national force could no longer be ignored.

(TOP) Purépecha men, from the Cherán region of Michoacán, jump over a fence near the Texas border. The governor of Arizona has said that if you build a fifty-foot fence, immigrants will build a fifty-one-foot ladder. But border fences have had a material effect on migration patterns, pushing workers to cross in desert regions, leading to a growing numbers of deaths in the desert. Since the enforcement of border fences, hundreds of migrants have been dying in the crossing every year. Most estimates calculate that about half of the United States' undocumented workers enter the country legally through official ports of entry, either with temporary visas or with false papers (Nicholas Olson/Getty Images).

(BOTTOM) This wall is a precursor to the seven-hundred-mile barrier that was approved by Congress. Wall-building initiatives are a dimension of current electoral politics in the United States, and both major parties are split as to how to view them. Republicans have been unable to gain internal consensus on developing a migrant-worker program that would involve legalizing the nation's twelve million illegal workers, but they have found it politically expedient to invest in a wall along the U.S.-Mexico border (Spencer Platt/Getty Images).

Until 2006, the absence of illegal immigrants in the public sphere as an organized and outspoken group contrasted starkly with their ubiquitous presence in the workplace and in communities throughout the country. Yet in the past decade, immigrants from Mexico (and Central and South America) have been singled out as a social group in various ways: in terms of the growing importance of Latinos as a national voting block (an importance underlined in the 2006 marches by signs that read "Today We March, Tomorrow We Vote"); as a "market niche" possessing considerable clout, which is coveted and courted by corporations; and as users of public goods and services, including schools, hospitals, and even jails, whose (cultural and linguistic) needs must be accommodated. In short, there was a sharp disjunction between how politicians and industry cultivated the powerful presence of Latinos in social and economic life and their scanty presence in the public sphere as a group with organized interests, despite recent political gains for Latinos.

The public voice of Mexicans and Central Americans, in particular, was generally limited to those who had acquired citizenship, or at least green cards. Illegal immigrants showed themselves to be a collective primarily at soccer matches or at Cinco de Mayo parades, which in the United States has become for Mexicans what Saint Patrick's Day is for the Irish. Yet these forms of public visibility entailed some risk: flying the Mexican flag, for instance, which garnered illegal immigrants (and even legal immigrants, given the underrepresentation of this minority in public affairs) a measure of collective visibility, has been the privileged butt of anti-immigrant attacks, along with other affirmations of national and cultural difference, such as the use of Spanish in public forums. Reactions to public manifestations of Mexican solidarity include the 1986 approval of Proposition 63 in California, which made English the official language of the state, and Harvard professor Samuel Huntington's well-publicized nationalist diatribe against Latino immigration (developed into the 2004 book *Who Are We? The Challenges to America's National Identity*), in which he repeatedly recalled the 1998 Gold Cup soccer match played in Los Angeles, during which the U.S. national team was booed while the Mexican national team was acclaimed.[5] Bearing such reactions to Mexican flag waving in mind, Linda Chávez, a Mexican-American media figure who was nervous as the 2006 mobilizations began, warned Latinos not to bear the flags of their native countries during the rallies so as not to generate backlash from U.S. voters and their representatives in government.[6] And indeed, the televised image of illegal immigrants taking to the streets by the thousands, waving U.S. flags interspersed with Mexican and other flags, had a chilling effect on a portion of the U.S. public, an effect that is possibly not so different from the shudder that was manifest in segments of public opinion when Rosa Parks refused to sit in the back of the bus in 1955.

DILEMMAS OF THE RIGHT

The rallies of the spring placed the Right, and especially the Republican Party, in a real quandary as to how to respond to these protests of support for immigrants hailing from south of the U.S. border. Ironically, this political dilemma was in part due to the

(LEFT) A Minuteman (or Minutewoman) clutching an American flag, in a soulful gesture of resolute defense. The question of violation, represented sometimes as rape, is present in the more emotional appeals against immigration. The Southern Poverty Law Center has documented hate speech among border vigilantes that features references to immigrants' "lack of respect toward American women" (Chris Hondros/Getty Images).

(BELOW) Anti-immigrant sentiment has increased substantially since 9/11. Mobilizations by the Minuteman Project, a border vigilante group, have rarely brought out more than three hundred protesters to a rally. However, the force of their protests has carried beyond their numbers, in part because, as the woman on the left announces with her green sign, "Illegal = NO Rights" (Mandel Ngan/AFP/Getty Images).

(ABOVE) The festive quality of the pro-immigration marches on April 10, 2006 (LEFT: Boston; RIGHT: New York) contrast with the sullen looks and occasional despair of anti-immigrant mobilizations (Joe Raedle/Getty Images; Michael Brown/Getty Images).

(LEFT) The immigration debate is also a contest over the flag and over the nature of the nation. Anti-immigrant nationalists such as Samuel Huntington have argued that America is a nation of settlers rather than of immigrants, and that it is an Anglo-American culture rather than a melting pot. Pro-immigrant sentiment emphasizes that the United States is a nation of immigrants (Chip Somodevilla/Getty Images).

success the Republicans had in courting the Latino vote during the 2004 elections, when George Bush garnered a whopping 40 percent of their vote. Bush's election victory, which has had momentous consequences for the world, also had a positive effect for Latinos in 2006: it kept the Republican Party from reacting as a united block against Latino immigrants.

In addition to this grimly pragmatic consideration, immigration experts generally agree that the prospect of effectively enforcing the proposed criminalization of illegal immigration from Mexico is slim. The deportation of eleven million people would be disastrous for the American economy, impracticable for its law enforcement agencies, and calamitous for Mexico's stability; building a wall on the border would damage the U.S.'s already tattered international image beyond repair; and creating a national identity card system is expensive and presents a series of challenges to states' rights (and the evidence from France is that it is far from foolproof). As a result, the politics of anti-immigrant legislation are situated between the electoral alliances that are needed by the Republican Party and the economic and political costs of vigorously enforcing anti-immigrant proposals and bills. Within this frame, the politics of recognition and empowerment of illegal aliens seems likely to continue, while it is also true that it is likely to emerge forcefully only in special conjunctures, rather than as a continuous form of organizing and expression. Ugly anti-immigration expression is practically guaranteed in the United States, given the political preoccupations that have been legitimated by its security state. At the same time, electoral and economic factors conspire to provide such expression with cyclical or wavering governmental support. In such a climate, a corresponding wavelike structure of reaction from immigrants seems likely.

IDENTITY POLITICS AND INTERNATIONAL POLITICS

The third innovation of the mobilizations of 2006 is its implication for the connection between U.S. identity politics and international politics. The international policies that followed the September 11 attacks have been so unpopular in Latin America that anti-Americanism is threatening to turn into a hegemonic discourse where both the right and the left converge. In this context, the emergence of an ethnic/racial conflict within the United States is an especially delicate issue for U.S. diplomacy, and such a possibility has consistently softened the response of the federal government to the immigrant mobilizations.

At the same time, one of the most interesting dimensions of this form of nongovernmental politics is the indistinct identity of its subject-participants—in other words, its destabilizing effect on the categories of U.S. identity politics. While it is clear that the most important single presence in the rallies was Mexican, it became equally evident that the label of "Latino" or "Hispanic," an ethnic category promoted by the U.S. Census Bureau, has become useful for grassroots movements. The rallies of the spring were composed of illegal aliens from every corner of the world, as well as "Latinos"

(ABOVE) Increased patrolling and the militarization of the border have flourished in tandem with a widespread humanitarian concern for saving migrant lives. A confluence of institutions that claim to be interested in protecting migrant lives, including organs of the Mexican federal government, state and local governments on both sides of the border, NGOs, and local ranchers, provide water to immigrants and organize rescue parties (courtesy of Humane Borders).

(RIGHT) Maps for would-be migrants show distances measured in days by foot, in order to discourage them from their desert crossing (courtesy of Humane Borders).

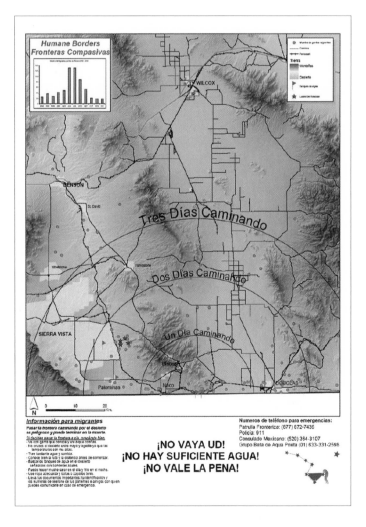

A Minuteman project for a border fence. In October 2006, Congress approved a $2.3-billion project to build a seven-hundred-mile wall on long stretches of the U.S.-Mexico border. After promoting the bill in Congress, senator Jeff Sessions (R-Alabama) tried to diminish the effect that the edifice might have on international opinion by declaring that "good fences make good neighbors." Congresspeople defending the project against those who compare it to the Berlin Wall emphasize the fact that the latter was built to keep people in, while the wall along the U.S.-Mexico border is being built to keep people out (© Let Freedom Ring, Inc., 2005; used with permission; design by Vollmer Associates).

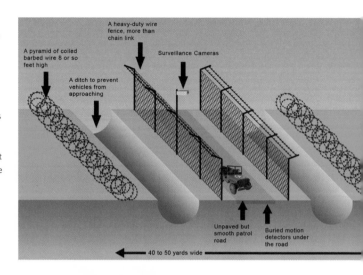

A pyramid of coiled barbed wire 8 or so feet high

A heavy-duty wire fence, more than chain link

Surveillance Cameras

A ditch to prevent vehicles from approaching

Unpaved but smooth patrol road

Buried motion detectors under the road

40 to 50 yards wide

Border anxieties have led to more walls, which have led to several thousand migrant deaths. The border itself has now become a site of commemoration and protest, with special masses and rallies held each year on the Day of the Dead. The individualization of dead migrants has also arisen as a new phenomenon. Undocumented immigrants today are beginning to find their names, places of origin, and biographies in the press — sadly, sometimes in the form of a eulogy (Nicholas Roberts/AFP/Getty Images).

who are legal residents or citizens, and friends and sympathizers of immigrants who are not ethnically marked as "Hispanic."

Indeed, the mass rallies of 2006 were simultaneously a transnational-local production, spearheaded by more than six hundred registered hometown associations formed by Mexican migrants in the United States; a class production, mobilized by union organizations; a national minority production, spurred forward by civic associations of so-called Latino civil society, such as the National Council of La Raza; a church-based organization, including both Catholic and evangelical Protestant church groups (whose growth in the United States has been fueled by migrants); and a mass-mediated mobilization publicized by the Spanish-language media in the United States and in Mexico. (In the United States, there are three national television networks that broadcast in Spanish, over three hundred radio stations, and about seven hundred Spanish-language newspapers.) The mobilizations were also an international production, taking inspiration from Mexican democratic politics, and drew on cross-national media products such as the 2004 film *A Day Without a Mexican,* directed by Mexican filmmaker Alfonso Arau, which developed a theme from a popular National Public Radio broadcast that imagined what a single day without Mexican workers in the United States would be like.

Ultimately, then, the confluence of these organizational resources and the multiple references for political organizing that are implied by them suggest that the current immigrant movement may be sounding the death knell of organized labor's traditional hostility to illegal immigration. Such a posture not only has been relevant to the major labor confederations, but has also fueled ethnic tensions between blacks and Latinos, and has generated tensions between "Chicanos" and "Mexicans," as well: César Chávez's United Farm Workers, for instance, favored forms of labor regulation that implied immigration control.[7]

1 For data on individual marches and other pertinent data on the mobilizations of the spring of 2006, see Jonathan Fox, "Mexican Migrant Civic Participation in the United States," August 15, 2006, Social Science Research Council, http://borderbattles.ssrc.org/Fox/index2.html.

2 Ruth Milkman suggests that there is a strong overlap between community-based organizations, worker centers, Change To Win (CTW) unions, and the mobilizations of 2006; the AFL-CIO has moved quickly to forge alliances with Mexican workers and worker centers since the mobilizations. See her "Labor and the New Immigrant Rights Movement: Lessons from California," July 28, 2006, Social Science Research Council, http://borderbattles.ssrc.org/Milkman/.

3 By far, the closest U.S. precedent to the 2006 rallies was the 1994 mass protest by California Latinos against Proposition 187, a ballot initiative designed to deny public services to undocumented immigrants.

4 See, for example, Randal C. Archibold, "For Latinos in the Midwest, a Time to Be Heard," *New York Times,* April 25, 2006.

5 Samuel P. Huntington, *Who Are We?: The Challenges to America's National Identity* (New York: Simon and Schuster, 2004), p. 242.

6 Linda Chávez, "American Dreams, Foreign Flags," *New York Times,* March 30, 2006.

7 From 1958 on, César Chávez opposed the Bracero Program, a guest-worker system, and pressed local merchants and planters to hire only local residents. Similarly, in 1969, five years after the Bracero Program had concluded, he organized a march through the Coachella and Imperial Valleys to the U.S.-Mexico border to protest growers' use of undocumented migrant labor.

The Migreurop Network and Europe's Foreigner Camps

Claire Rodier

Founded in 2002, Migreurop is a network of activists and researchers from several countries of the European Union and the Maghreb whose objective is to identify, bring to light, denounce, and combat the policies used by European authorities to marginalize so-called "undesirable" migrants and asylum seekers. The network emerged from the mobilization of several activists around the creation of the Sangatte refugee camp in northern France. For three years, from 1999 to 2002, Sangatte exemplified policies designed to assemble, confine, and sequester foreigners, thereby eluding — partially or completely — supervision by democratic institutions. For this reason, the administrative detention of migrants — "camps for foreigners" in Migreurop's terminology — constituted a primary axis of Migreurop's work, and the network produces a regularly updated map, *Camps for Foreigners in Europe.*[1]

What the network understands by "camp," however, far exceeds the image of isolated detention centers located in geographically strategic areas. Today in Europe, camps for foreigners range from prisons — such as those in Germany and Ireland — to makeshift detention centers. The latter include centers in the Greek isles hastily set up to house passengers from capsized or intercepted refugee boats attempting to make landfall, Italy's *centri di permanenza temporanea ed assistenza,* France's *zones d'attentes* and *centres de retention,* and the *centres fermés* for asylum seekers in Belgium. To retain a narrow definition of the camp as a lockdown facility would therefore obscure a large part of the current situation.

The diversity of administrative mechanisms and technical-humanitarian restrictions that aim to regroup migrants requires one to move beyond a narrow understanding of camps as sites of physical confinement and to consider all sites where foreigners are marginalized as "camps." These sites can take many forms and sometimes bear little resemblance to the classic picture of a holding center surrounded by barbed wire.

An African immigrant stands in the temporary housing area in the Spanish enclave of Melilla, October 7, 2005 (Samuel Aranda/AFP/Getty Images).

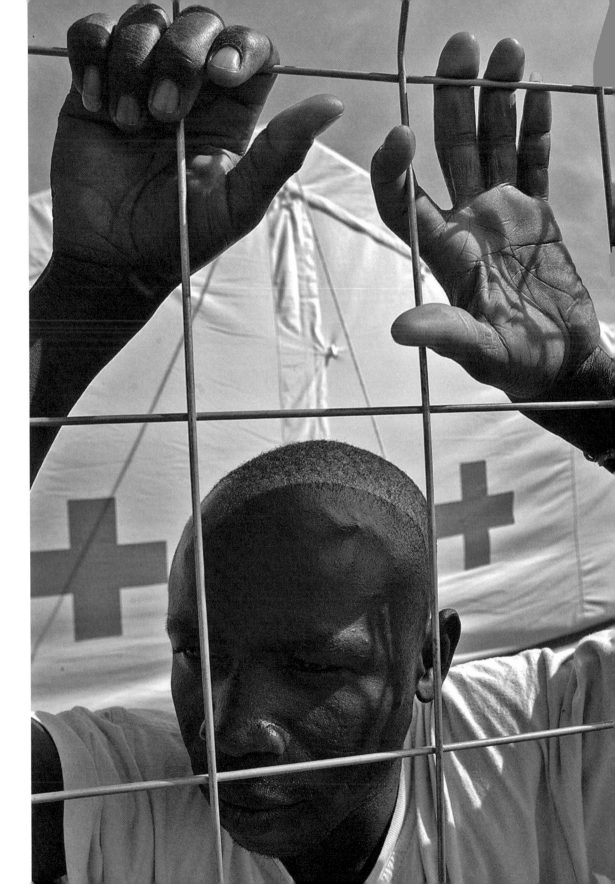

Some "open" reception, transit, or lodging centers, for instance, have the apparent objective of providing assistance and shelter. Yet this poorly masks the fact that their occupants—migrants and asylum seekers—have no choice but to remain there. This is the case in both Germany and Belgium, where the application for asylum and the disbursement of a survival allowance depend on the refugee's consent to being placed in a reception center not of his or her own choosing. Even further, given the enforced wandering of migrants who, in some countries, are explicitly dispersed in order to avoid the development of new geographical concentrations of settlers, can we not see the complex forms of marginalization of foreigners that exist in Europe? Can we not assimilate the interdiction of foreigners from areas where they are considered a nuisance to an unofficial house arrest?

Indeed, police harassment and a foreigner's obligation to be invisible function as barriers, delimiting areas set aside for foreigners. Accordingly, the camp as a specific type of facility becomes a process that symbolizes the enforced wandering and perpetual movement of migrants and exiles whom European societies do not want to welcome or see in their territory. Understood in this broader sense, the expression that Migreurop has chosen—"The Europe of Camps"—seems the best way to characterize the mechanisms of exclusion that, under the guise of immigration policy, have gradually been implemented not only within EU territory, but also in non-European regions along its borders.[2]

The diversity of confinement centers for foreigners in Europe led Migreurop to examine the informal concentration of foreigners along the borders of Europe. Via police cooperation with its close neighbors, the EU has moved to outsource the management of migrant flows to adjacent countries. These states are charged with interrupting, at all costs, refugees arriving at the borders of EU territory. The migrants find themselves trapped and often must endure long months of illegal and miserable treatment, as in the case of the migrants from sub-Saharan Africa who were forced to hide in Moroccan forests while waiting for a chance to enter Spain. The public was suddenly made aware of the hardships faced by this particular group when, in 2005, more than ten individuals were fatally shot while trying to enter Ceuta and Melilla, Spanish enclaves on Moroccan soil.[3] Today, buffer camps have increasingly formed along the EU's borders, such as those in Morocco, Algeria, Libya, Ukraine, and Turkey. This phenomenon is part of the policy of "externalization" pursued by the EU through its border-control policies, a trend that is at the heart of Migreurop's concerns.[4] In this essay, I analyze how the process of externalization has expanded since the end of the 1980s as well as present the ripostes Migreurop has launched against these trends in immigration policy. Given that countries on the edge of Europe are dependent on European interests, such trends have not only made it increasingly difficult for migrants to cross borders, despite the rules of international law—especially the right to political asylum and, more broadly, the principle set forth in the Universal Declaration of Human Rights recognizing the right of all individuals to "leave any country, including his own."

Barbed wire on top of fence   Two parallel fences

3 metre high fence

Immigrants use makeshift ladders

(TOP) On September 27 and 28, 2005, some seven hundred sub-Saharan migrants managed to cross the border fences separating Spain's North African enclave of Melilla from Morocco (*Melilla Hoy*).

(BOTTOM) A worker repairs a barrier in Melilla, October 3, 2005 (Rafael Marchante/Reuters).

CAMPS FOR FOREIGNERS, TOOLS FOR THE EXTERNALIZATION OF EUROPEAN MIGRANT POLICY AND BORDER CONTROL

In EU member states, confinement has become a routine means of managing migrant flows and asylum seekers in their own territories. This policy has been at the forefront of media attention since 2000, when the EU moved to externalize migrant policy in the form of "transit centers," which would remotely manage migrant flows and asylum applications outside the borders of the EU. That this policy was advocated by a British proposal in 2003 is hardly surprising. On January 27, 2003, Prime Minister Tony Blair provocatively announced that, in order to address the problem of mass immigration from Eastern Europe and elsewhere, he was prepared to act in a radical manner at the international level. If necessary, he would rethink what he believed was an outdated agreement: the European Convention for the Protection of Human Rights and Fundamental Freedoms.[5] That year, Blair forced this subject onto the agenda of the Council of Europe, which brings together leaders from the twenty-five EU member states. Amid controversy, a project to establish camps outside Europe was added to the European Commission's work program, where it was gradually modified and, with the assistance of the United Nations High Commission for Refugees (UNHCR), repackaged as a program to protect migrants. During the summer of 2004, the interior ministers of Germany and Italy supported the project. Despite opposition, it became part of the EU's five-year action plan for liberty, security, and justice (the so-called Hague Program) adopted in November 2004.[6] Not surprisingly, proponents of externalization policies almost never use the term "camp." However, as we will see, all the players, each in its own fashion, have endeavored to delineate what this term actually designates.

The concept was not new. As early as 1986, the Danish government had proposed a management system for asylum applications that would have set up UN-administered regional processing centers for the systematic detention of asylum applicants who had illegally entered the country. A few years later, the Netherlands managed to introduce a project to create reception and processing centers for asylum seekers into the agenda of the EU's 1994 Intergovernmental Conference. These processing centers were to be located in transit countries near the borders of applicants' respective countries of origin.[7] The Netherlands and Denmark, moreover, were ardent supporters of the British externalization proposal that was debated in 2003 by the EU fifteen.

Actually, the same approach has already been practiced for many years in non-European countries. For example, in the United States, "boat people" sailing from Haiti were intercepted and detained at the Guantánamo naval base in Cuba and aboard a U.S. Marine Corps ship moored off the coast of Jamaica. The Haitians intercepted at sea were detained while their applications for asylum were subjected to preexamination. Some won admission to U.S. territory, but a greater number were turned away.[8] More recently, a Mexican "migrant holding center" (MHC) was opened with American support near the Mexico–U.S. border. Its purpose was to assist Mexicans "who hope to satisfy the conditions necessary to enter American territory."[9] Similarly, in 2001, Australia launched an asylum program known as the "Pacific Solution." Under this program, operational management of candidate processing was outsourced to microstates in Australia's geopolitical zone of influence, with the creation of remotely funded camps in island nations overseen by the International Organization for Migration (IOM) and the UNHCR.[10]

THE BRITISH PROPOSAL FOR "TRANSIT PROCESSING CENTERS"

The 2003 British proposal, titled "New International Approaches to Asylum Processing and Protection," made direct reference to the Australian system and was a last-minute addition to the agenda of an informal conference of the EU ministers of interior and foreign affairs in March of that year.[11] The British proposal assumed that the asylum system was in crisis due to the abuse of the asylum route by "bogus" refugees seeking to bypass the rules of economic immigration and thus compromising the viability of the international protection regime. The proposal featured two components: the creation, under the supervision of international organizations, of security zones in the reception countries, called "regional protection zones," where asylum seekers whose candidacy was rejected and who were unable to return immediately to their countries of origin could be placed; and the creation of "transit processing centers" (TPC) along the routes traveled by asylum seekers headed for Europe. Following an attempt to cross European borders, migrants would be sent to facilities where asylum applications would be processed prior to any admittance into the EU. The link between the current asylum system (in which asylum applications are examined within EU member states and processed according to the national laws of the country in which the request is made) and the two components of the British proposal is as follows: asylum seekers arriving in the EU would be sent to a TPC in a country such as Albania, Bulgaria, or Romania.[12] Individuals officially recognized as refugees would be transferred to an EU country, eventually according to a quota system corresponding to the capacities and needs of the reception states, while the rest would be returned either to their country of origin or to a country within the protection zone in the asylum seeker's region of origin.

The project, which put forward regions in Turkey, Iran, Iraq, Kurdistan, northern Somalia, and even Morocco as potential protection zones, was finally shelved during the Thessaloniki Council of Europe in June 2003 when it failed to receive support from a number of member states (in particular, Sweden and Germany). Yet the idea still lives on. The UK has even been invited to initiate "small-scale experiments" in this direction with the assistance of certain countries such as Australia. In its concluding remarks, the Thessaloniki Council of Europe "invite[d] the Commission to explore all parameters in order to ensure more orderly and managed entry in the EU of persons in need of international protection, and to examine ways and means to enhance the protection capacity of regions of origin," noting that "a number of Member States plan to explore ways of providing better protection for the refugees in their region of origin, in conjunction with the UNHCR."[13] Explicitly solicited by the council, the UNHCR and the European Commission are, in fact, at the heart of this debate.

In 2001, the UN High Commissioner for Refugees (UNHCR) celebrated its fiftieth anniversary, using the occasion to launch a campaign of international consultation to explore new forms of international refugee protection. Starting with the assumption that the 1951 Geneva Convention Relating to the Status of Refugees, of which it is the trustee, was no longer suitably adapted to current patterns of population movement, the initiative's main thrust was to assure "more equitable burden and responsibility sharing."[14] Ruud Lubbers, the high commissioner at the time, spelled out this approach in a 2002 address to representatives of the fifteen core EU member states at the Copenhagen Justice and Home Affairs Council meeting, during which he announced the creation of the Convention Plus program, designed to respond to "a major concern today," namely, "secondary movements of refugees."[15] ("Secondary movements" refers to the transit of refugees through a third country while en route from their country of origin to a destination country.) Among the solutions proposed by Convention Plus were agreements to define the respective roles and responsibilities of destination countries, transit countries, and even refugees' countries of origin, as well as a functional international system of responsibility sharing permitting refugees to obtain protection and assistance as close as possible to their region of origin. This initiative can be understood as an attempt to halt the flow of refugees through the transit countries that they traverse during their flight from their home countries.

It is important to note that asylum applications in the EU have declined greatly in the last decade, a trend that has been both continuous and spectacular.[16] Thus, in this context, the objective and solutions proposed are worrisome insofar as they are concerned less with protecting refugees than with securing the borders of Western countries. Lubbers appeared to confirm just this when he specified to the European ministers that "with a greater emphasis on ensuring lasting solutions in regions of origin, the numbers of refugees requiring settlement in European countries will be lower, and the need to integrate these people into your societies will be easier to explain to your citizens."[17]

The rhetoric of the UNHCR's 2002 Convention Plus might be summed up in the single phrase "to receive refugees elsewhere to better protect them." This idea, in turn, can also be understood as the direct precursor of the 2003 British proposal's guiding principle. In fact, by the end of March 2003, the two programs increasingly seemed to be promoting the same approach. While denouncing the "bogus refugees" supposedly responsible for the majority of asylum applications — "real refugees" remained in their regions of origin — Tony Blair also endeavored to convince his counterparts that it was necessary to develop "proposals for better international management of refugees and asylum seekers."[18] These statements echoed Lubber's presentation to the EU ministers responsible for immigration issues in which he argued that the asylum system was being distorted due to "economic migrants [and nonrefugees] abusing and clogging up [Europe's] asylum systems."[19] The British proposal to create transit camps to process asylum applications outside of Europe was in turn supported by UNHCR staff. The latter offered to help EU member states determine whether or not individuals were in need of international protection and to set up a streamlined and coherent European system for receiving and examining asylum applications in order to process them more rapidly, thereby lightening the burden on the national systems. For Lubbers, this system would involve the detention of asylum seekers in closed centers, eventually set up on the territory of certain future member states, those that would enter the EU as part of the 2004 expansion of the Union, and that at that time constituted its eastern border.[20] While the UNHCR programs were concerned only with asylum applications deemed "abusive" — those considered "manifestly unfounded," according to the official formula — the British proposal sought to transfer all asylum seekers to external camps. Nevertheless, in accepting both the principle of externalization and the recourse to the detention of asylum seekers, the UNHCR made a fundamental contribution to the legitimacy of camps as a tool of asylum management in Europe.

The UNHCR position was confirmed in the European section of Convention Plus, published as a working paper in June 2003.[21] Even though the UNHCR's program was presented as a counterproposal to the British proposal, it in fact adopted its overall architecture, with the exception of the external nature of the detention centers recommended by the British. A few months later, while the European Commission, as we will see, sought to buy time, the UNHCR once again relaunched the idea of centralized management in "European processing centers" of asylum seekers believed to be "bogus." The UNHCR emphasized the advantages of a collective management of persons denied asylum, potentially including detention, because it would make deportation easier: "rejected asylum-seekers from the same country of origin can be held together (and if likely to abscond, detained) before deportation and returned more easily as a group."[22]

On January 22, 2004, testifying in Dublin at an informal Justice and Home Affairs Council meeting of the twenty-five EU leaders, high commissioner Lubbers agreed that national asylum procedures in EU countries were overloaded and once again recommended "the establishment of EU reception centers where the claims of certain categories of asylum-seekers can be processed by experienced teams of asylum assessors and interpreters drawn from across the EU."[23] In particular, Lubbers argued, it would be useful to create "a collective EU system to promptly return those asylum-seekers judged not to be refugees or in need of other forms of international protection. This system would be based on readmission agreements to be negotiated by the EU as a whole with the countries of origin."[24] The Hague Program, adopted by the Council of Europe at Brussels on November 4 and 5, 2004, also linked the UNHCR to externalization programs: "a separate study, to be conducted in close consultation with the UNHCR, should look into the merits, appropriateness and feasibility of joint processing of asylum applications outside EU territory.... The Council of Europe...invites the Commission to mobilize existing Community funds to assist Member States in the processing of asylum applications."[25] These recommendations had been concretized in advance when, a month earlier, one million euros, cofinanced by the commission at 80 percent and by the Netherlands at 20 percent, were released for "pilot projects" in cooperation with the UNHCR, in order to aid Mauritania, Morocco, Algeria, Tunisia, and Libya in developing "a national system of asylum." Even if the vocabulary has changed and "camps" are no longer mentioned, the objectives remain the same.[26]

THE EUROPEAN COMMISSION: EUPHEMISMS AND ABSTRACTIONS

The British proposal upset established conventions in the European Commission by forcing a discussion of the notion of camps at a time when it was struggling to harmonize member states' asylum regulations. However, externalization was far from being a new component of European immigration and asylum policies. It was already one of the measures stipulated in the Tampere Program, which emerged after the 1999 summit meeting of European heads of state in Finland.[27] The Tampere Program was comprehensive in its approach and included a section discussing relationships with third countries, countries of origin, and transit countries. This section was intended to be a complement to the "internal section," which was dedicated to setting up a consistent and Europe-wide regime for border management and the reception of migrants and refugees within Europe. Shortly thereafter, however, the external section became the main priority action item, a change that mainly resulted from the member states' inability to agree on a common asylum policy. The EU "relationships with third countries" evoked in the Tampere Program thus gradually came to designate the exportation of migratory management to these countries and a concomitant transfer of asylum responsibilities.

In a December 2002 statement, the European Commission proposed to "integrate migration-related concerns…into the external dimension of the Community's action."[28] It placed an item on the 2003 budget to fund "an analysis of the legal, financial and practical questions related to…Transit Processing Centres in third countries" (facilities destined, one surmises, to receive asylum seekers) with the aim of "reducing secondary movements to EU Member States" and of creating "processing, reception and protection capabilities, including as regards persons returned from the EU."[29] Even if this formulation is less direct than that of the British proposal, it is easy to see beyond the euphemism: the Union was prepared to invest in creating camps outside its borders to handle foreigners whom it wished either to keep from entering its territory or to expel.

The terrain was thus prepared when, in March 2003, the commission, in response to the "crisis of the asylum system" and amid controversy over the British proposal, called for research into new approaches, including a "genuine policy of partnership with third countries and relevant international organisations," and advocated "stronger involvement of third countries in reception and transit."[30] This program would thus lead to the "consolidation of protection capacities in the region of origin" of refugees through the "treatment of protection requests as close as possible to needs" — in other words, the creation of deterrent mechanisms in "cooperation" with third countries, which were asked to detain refugee candidates in order to prevent them from reaching Europe.[31] As such, the European Commission's and the UNHCR's externalization of European border management policies and creation of camps for asylum seekers masqueraded as an effort to improve refugee protection. According to two statements by the commission, the EU henceforth committed itself to this double logic and — in the name of implementing a more accessible and equitable asylum system — it called for enhancing the "protection capacity of a third country in the region of origin" with a view to "improving access to durable solutions."[32]

FROM EXTERIOR ASYLUM CAMPS TO "VOLUNTARY IMMIGRATION CAMPS"

The same attitude is evident in the multiyear program for asylum and immigration policies adopted in November 2004 in The Hague by the twenty-five EU heads of state.[33] Extending the notion of externalization beyond the domain of asylum, the five-year plan, known as The Hague Program, devoted considerable attention to the external dimension of asylum and migration. Emphasis was placed on the need for the union to support so-called "third countries" through close partnerships designed to improve their ability to manage migratory movements, protect refugees, and prevent and fight illegal immigration. From this perspective, the plan emphasized that "policies which link immigration, development cooperation, and humanitarian assistance should be coherent."[34] Regarding the issue of asylum, it was proposed that a study was necessary to evaluate "the merits, appropriateness and feasibility of joint processing of asylum applications outside EU territory."[35] The plan also envisaged reinforcing cooperation along the southern and eastern borders of the EU so that border states could provide adequate protection for refugees and better manage immigration.

Up to this point, the official justification for setting up camps outside the EU's own borders had relied principally on the argument of protection — to deter "bogus" refugees and help "true" refugees avoid the pitfalls and dangers along the routes of exile. The Hague Program, by introducing the issues concerning the dimensions of immigration to Europe, responded to an apparent contradiction between concerns long voiced by the commission: the European economy needs foreign workers, while member states want increased border security. Since the late 1990s, the European Commission had argued for renewing the call for labor immigration on the condition that it was adapted to the needs of labor markets in member states. This return to "utilitarian immigration" was bluntly summed up by Romano Prodi, president of the commission at the time: "We need migrants, but migration should be selective, controlled and directed to the right places" (*scelti, controllati e collocati*).[36] The European Commission used the same argument in 2003, specifying that labor immigration presupposes a simultaneous deterrence of undesirable immigration through financial and law-enforcement cooperation with origin and transit countries.[37]

(FOLLOWING PAGES) Map of foreigners' camps: inventory and analyses on the policy of detention of foreigners from www.migreurop.org.

Foreigners' camps in Europe
and in Mediterranean countries

Methodological Note
Migreurop network has an extended definition of "camps" that covers a large variety of places.
On this map, however, we have chosen to show only detention centers or " closed camps "
The locations where migrants are detained and deprived of their freedom of movement.
The camps are classified as follows :
Blue - for people awaiting permission to enter the territory, primarily those wishing to apply for asylum (asylum seekers) or immigrants refused entry and waiting for an examination of their situation. After this examination, the person held may be admitted to the territory or rejected and returned to the port/border.
Orange - for people who have been arrested in an illegal situation in the territory of a state and are awaiting deportation.
Red - most of these places are used to detain both types of people, and may also serve as identification/screening centres.

We have also included certain exceptions : e.g the open camps in Ceuta and Melilla where freedom of movement is primarily subject to administrative
constraints. These open camps symbolise the externalisation of borders.
In some cases, we have also included certain national particularities: e.g in Germany and Ireland, prisons are often used for detaining migrants.
In other cases, some of the camps shown on the map are places where migrants gather informally without being directly placed under the control of the authorities :
- To the South of the Mediterranean: migrants waiting for and organising their passage to Europe.
- In European countries such as France or Italy : an old train station in Rome (where migrants are awaiting admission), Calais in France (where foreigners wait to cross the Channel to reach the United Kingdom).

- Country of European Union and out of Schengen space
- Country of European Union and Schengen space
- Candidate Country to the European Union

- ● Closed camp
- ☐ Open camp
- ☐ ● migrants waiting for admission
- ☐ ● migrants about to be deported
- ☐ ● mixes of the two abovementioned functions of examining admission and deportation
- ◥◣◥ informal camp
- ○ informal places located in the suburbs of big cities in Southern or Eastern Mediterranean countries

North Sea

IRELAND

UNITED KINGDOM

Channel

Atlantic Ocean

FRANCE

SWITZ

PORTUGAL

SPAIN

Tanger

Alger

Rabat

Casablanca

Fès

Tu

TUNISIA

MOROCCO

ALGERIA

© Migreurop 2005

0   200   400   600   800   1000 km

Fond cartographique : PHILIPPE REKACEWICZ

MAURITANIA

MALI

Tamanrasset ○

Notes :
* For France, the map shows only the zones d'attentes (waiting zones) used for detaining foreigners entering the territory.
** In Germany, prisons are shown since they are the main detention places of migrants.
*** Migrants subject to removal orders are often detained in special sections of prisons. There are 23 such places in Switzerland which can not be all shown on this map : Appenzell, Bâle (2), Bern, Chur, Dornach, Einsiedeln, Gampelen, Glarus, Granges, Mendrisio, Olten, Saignelégier, Schaffhausen, Schüpfheim, Sissach, Solothurn, Sursee, Thônex, Widnau, Zug, Zürich (2).

Migreurop don't have datum for Egypt, Syria and Tunisia [countries at the South and East of Mediterranean Sea] and Byelorussia, Bosnia-Herzegovina, Macedonia and Montenegro. For Russia, only information, of European report of Andrea Gross, are on the map.

Datums : European Committee for the Prevention of Torture and Inhuman or Degrading Treatment or Punishment / UNHCR http://www.unhcr.ch / Gross Andrea (2000) Arrival of asylum seekers in european airports, European Council / Germany : Initiativen gegen abschiebehaft-Berlin / Austria : Asylkoordination Österreich / Belgium : Mrax / Denmark : http://www.coe.int/T/F/Com/Presse/Actualita/ Spain : APDHA / Estonia : Legal information centre for human rights / France : ministère de l'Intérieur français / Greece : Articles de presse (http://www.enet.gr/online/online) / Hungary : Hungarian Helsinki Committee, helsinki@mail.datanet.hu / Ireland : Irish refugee council / Italy : Storie in gabbia, supplément à Il Manifesto du 31/5/03, http://www.migranti.net/pages/inserto_CPT.pdf / Latvia : The latvian centre for human rights and ethnic studies / Lithuania : rapport de M. A. Gil-Robles, commissaire aux droits de l'Homme sur sa visite en Lituanie (2004) http://www.coe.int/T/f/commissaire_d.h/ Luxemburg : http://www.cpt.coe.int/documents/lux/2004-12-inf-fra.pdf / Malta : jrsmalta@waldonet.net.mt ; http://www.sept.off // Netherlands : www.autonoomcentrum.nl / Poland : JRS / Czech R. : http://www.mvcr.cz/suz/uvod.html, Sandrine Carton (2003) "L'institutionnalisation de l'asile en Europe centrale : l'exemple tchèque. 1990-2003", Paris I / United Kingdom : http://www.barbedwirebritain.org.uk/ Slovakia : Jesuit Refugee Service (JRS) / Slovenia : JRS / Sweden : Migration Board, www.migrationsverket.se/english/maps and addresses / Switzerland : Organisation suisse d'aide aux réfugiés, www.sfh-osar.ch, Office fédéral des réfugiés, Office fédéral de la statistique, Conférence des directrices et directeurs des départements cantonaux de justice et police / Gross Andrea (2000) Arrival of asylum seekers in Europeans airports, Council of Europe. Bulgaria : Bulgarian Red Cross, Bulgarian Helsinki Committee / Croatia : Croatian Red Cross, Croatian Law Centre / Rumania : Bénédicte Michalon - Migrinter-CNRS / Serbia&Montenegro : Groupe 484, Gracanicka 10, Belgrade / Ukraine : Ukrainian State Committee

Thus, the reinforcement of barriers to migration and the externalization of its management cannot be deemed incompatible with the selective opening of borders, and camps would play a crucial role in attaining both objectives. The same idea was explicitly promoted by Italy and Germany in August 2004, in response to the massive waves of migrants landing on the Sicilian coast. Using the pretext that tragedies could be avoided during illegal attempts to enter Europe and criminal activities committed by human traffickers or smugglers could be reduced, the plan, according to the former Italian minister of European affairs, proposed to establish centers dedicated "simultaneously to humanitarian assistance [and to] furnishing information so that candidates for immigration can come in contact with the work world and obtain information regarding the skills in demand."[38] This project — which said little about how its objectives would be accomplished — stirred up considerable debate when, at the end of September 2004, it was discussed by the twenty-five EU ministers in charge of immigration.[39]

A SEMANTIC FREE-FOR-ALL:
FROM "RECEPTION POINTS" TO "REGIONAL PROTECTION ZONES"

Although the use of the term "camp" has been rejected ("We have decided never to use this word again," declared António Vitorino, former European commissioner in charge of justice and internal affairs) — and has been exchanged for a grab bag of politically correct alternatives — the concept is still ubiquitous, even if it remains quite vague, alternately mixing the issues of asylum and immigration.[40] In 2004, the German minister of the interior, Otto Schily, contemplated the creation of "reception centers" in Mediterranean states and the Ukraine, where candidates for immigration would be evaluated according to European directives concerning not the right to asylum, but the potential benefits of their admission: "Due to financial and logistical assistance, individuals whose requests are rejected will be immediately returned to their countries of origin."[41] France was reputed to be hostile to the idea: "Transit camps are a false good idea," asserted the then minister of the interior Dominique de Villepin. However, Villepin also suggested "providing specific resources to North African countries by creating 'reception points'" where migrants and asylum seekers would be brought together for a short time, enabling the repatriation of "bogus" asylum seekers to their countries of origin, a program that could be managed, "at low cost, since the transfer would be made by bus, not by plane."[42] For their part, the Italians and Germans once more presented their proposal to create "European immigration centers" in order to gather candidates outside European borders as part of a comprehensive plan to fight illegal immigration, provide development assistance to "source" countries in sub-Saharan Africa, and render the processing of asylum applications in transit countries "more humane."[43]

While there has been no winner in this semantic melee, migrants are the big losers. As the EU continued its discussions in the fall of 2004, various alliances began to take shape. Italy, which had previously argued for lifting the EU weapons embargo on Libya, began openly negotiating bilateral agreements on technology cooperation to fund the creation of holding camps for migrants trying to reach its shores from Libya.[44] As for the European Commission, at the end of 2004, it funded a pilot project to explore the feasibility of outsourcing immigration procedures to countries in the Maghreb, Libya, and Mauritania. Then, at the beginning of 2005, it moved to secure substantial European resources to "allocate funds to strengthen hosting and protection capacities on the ground[,] which…seems less costly than providing reception in refugee centres set up in EU Member States."[45] After North Africa, the commission planned to develop the same type of activities in the countries of the Great Lakes region of Africa and along the eastern border of the EU, notably in the Ukraine, Moldavia, and Belarus. Officially presented in September 2005, the plan was to link the establishment of "regional protection zones" near departure countries from which refugees leave in search of initial asylum to transfer programs designed to bring negotiated contingents of these refugees from the countries of first asylum to EU countries.[46] The plan reconciled the stipulations of the Geneva Convention Relating to the Status of Refugees with the immigration needs of Europe by setting up a filtering system in which camps would most probably be the key component.

However, as members in this new partnership, the countries selected as holding zones for refugees prior to the issuance of EU visas were far from being "safe" with regard to the protection needs they are intended to meet. According to the NGO Human Rights Watch, the Ukrainian authorities subject asylum seekers and migrants to unacceptable treatment and to numerous abuses: prolonged detention, physical and verbal violence, and, in some cases, forced deportations back to their countries of origin, where they risk torture and persecution.[47] In the case of Belarus, the EU is aware of, and has regularly expressed concern over, Belarus's repeated human-rights violations.[48] Even if one were to consider these countries safe — which is obviously not the case — the very concept of regional protection zones is problematic, since very often asylum seekers are fleeing countries with porous borders. Consequently, the asylum seekers are in danger not only in their countries of origin, but also in neighboring countries and, in a more general sense, throughout the geographic zone of influence of the countries they have left.[49]

It would be naive to see a contradiction between these disturbing facts and the EU's planned cooperation with these countries, since the policies were not adopted on the basis of their ability to "allow refugees access to protection" in the first place. This is the official objective. However, these countries have clearly been targeted because of their geographical location and their capacity to serve as buffers protecting Europe from undesirables and not on the basis of their ability to guarantee protection to migrants. When the former criterion is prioritized, "fundamental" rights are relegated to the background, and this has become ever more frequent when the rights of foreigners are at stake. Eclipsed by law-enforcement imperatives, human rights frequently become incidental.[50] This trend has been gathering momentum ever since the European countries implemented their immigration policies at the end of the 1980s. With the externalization of the procedures applied

Spanish soldiers patrol along the barrier that separates Spain's
North African enclave of Ceuta from Morocco in Castillejo, northern
Morocco, October 3, 2005 (Anton Meres/Reuters).

to migrants and refugees and the multiplication of detention and holding centers outside the EU's borders, contempt for human rights risks becoming routine.

INFORM THE PUBLIC, DENOUNCE THE POLICIES, FIGHT THE TREND

On the one hand, some of the public is convinced of the inanity of a migratory policy that detains individuals whose only crime is attempting to cross a border. On the other hand, the principle of the externalization of border control is far more popular, and it is difficult to influence public opinion on this issue. This is the case, first of all, because — barring a few exceptions, such as the shipwrecks of "boat people" in the Strait of Gibraltar or in the Mediterranean, or the suppression of migrant "assaults" on Ceuta and Melilla — the effects of externalization occur in "distant" lands, unwitnessed by many Westerners. No one knows how many migrants on their way to the European "El Dorado" have perished in the Sahara, victims of starvation and thirst on the most dangerous routes through Algeria, Libya, or Morocco. Furthermore, as we have seen, externalization often masquerades as protection: outsourcing of migrant processing is justified in the name of improved safety for migrants. Thus, EU policies are disingenuously represented as efforts to keep migrants out of the clutches of traffickers or from undertaking perilous journeys. Finally, certain aspects of externalization are accepted, supported, or even encouraged by those who supposedly defend victims of these policies. We have already discussed the ambiguous role played by the UNHCR concerning externalization programs. Finally, as the rights of migrants and refugees on European territory have eroded, certain NGOs, in the name of pragmatism, have adopted an attitude that creates other types of obstacles to generating public debate over the question of externalization.

This is the case with the asylum process. At the same time that some NGOs were criticizing the attempts to tighten the minimum criteria for granting asylum applications — measures that resulted in a drop of approximately 30 percent in the number of asylum seekers allowed to settle in the EU in under three years — the same groups were contributing to efforts to "enhance protection capacity" in third countries through ad hoc grants earmarked for such projects. As such, these NGOs are principally protecting the EU and its efforts to offload its asylum responsibilities onto non-EU countries. It is the same story with immigration policy. European funding is channeled through NGOs that have agreed to help develop programs aimed either at organizing the repatriation of migrants stopped during their journey or at discouraging those who have not yet set out. Naturally, this is all done in the name of improving the management of migrant movements, something that is meant to benefit everyone (except the migrants themselves): the EU thus rids itself of undesirables, the countries of origin negotiate financial or political deals with destination states in exchange for accepting deportees, and finally, the NGOs involved in these activities sometimes compromise their missions in exchange for institutional recognition and funding, which are increasingly sought after as the humanitarian sector becomes more professionalized.[51]

FIGHTING THE CURRENT TREND TOWARD PRAGMATISM

Such "pragmatism" is in fashion not only in the NGO community, but beyond it. Over the past decade, several think tanks have followed the EU's lead in migration policy. Not surprisingly, partisans of a principally economic approach to the issue champion utilitarian conceptions about the admission of foreign workers into the EU labor market which are similar to those of the European Commission.[52] It is more startling, however, that academic specialists in this domain have remained relatively quiet as the EU proceeds to dismantle the juridical foundations of the right to asylum through a series of texts adopted from 2001 to 2005 — texts that many observers believe weaken the rights accorded refugees by the 1951 Geneva Convention.[53] This silence can be explained as follows. First of all, a close intellectual relationship exists between the relatively small number of experts in Europe involved and the drafters of the European Commission proposals debated by the member states. Second, the silence partially results from an excessive "Europeanism." Given the xenophobic climate that prevailed in several member states during the late 1990s, having EU institutions be responsible for migratory policies seemed the best way to dedramatize and rationalize the discussion. This approach sometimes led to excessive confidence in the European political project surrounding these questions, even though the orientation of these programs quickly became apparent.

As the EU prepares to export these programs, it is disturbing to note that the risks of externalization are not discussed in either academic milieus or during meetings of experts. One example of this passivity lies in the lack of imagination among legal specialists when confronted by the blatant human-rights violations that are openly being committed on the borders of Europe. All this takes place as if the national and international juridical frameworks forming the legal basis of EU institutions — which are supposed to guarantee respect for these rights — lose their force once violations occur outside EU territory or when the victims are foreigners. Certain member organizations of Migreurop, in fact, were the only ones that filed complaints with the European Court of Justice of the Council of the European Union against the commission's failure to act when Italy openly violated EU principles in 2004 and 2005. Italy's decision to deport several hundred migrants to Libya without individually identifying them denied the migrants their right to apply for asylum and exposed them to inhuman and degrading treatment, thus violating the Convention for the Protection of Human Rights and Fundamental Freedoms.[54]

DECODING AND "NETWORKING"

Consequently, rather than addressing the public at large, Migreurop dedicates part of its activity to decoding the often disingenuous migration policies of the EU and its member states in order to convince informed groups or others potentially receptive to its work, such as activists, of the validity of its analyses. To bring its message to the latter, Migreurop participates in several activist gatherings while simultaneously reaching out to

academics and NGOs by participating in and organizing colloquia and educational seminars. Publishing articles in NGO journals or academic publications is another way that
the group disseminates its policy analyses. Most of these articles are simultaneously
made available on the Migreurop Web site.[55] The growing role that migration issues
play in the concerns of activist and labor movements has made this milieu an important
place to pass on information and to multiply Migreurop's contacts both within and outside Europe. Migreurop has taken part in the European Social Forum since 2002 and was
present at the World Social Forum held in Bamako in 2006. At these events, the network
was able to develop links with groups in the Maghreb that confronted the effects of
the EU partnerships discussed above, as well as with associations of African deportees,
which include victims of deportation programs to Mali, Algeria, and Morocco organized
by European countries.

TURNING PUBLIC OPINION AGAINST THE CREATION OF CAMPS ON EUROPEAN BORDERS

To address the public at large, Migreurop's strategy has been to raise the visibility
of camps and to inform the public of their existence. The map *Foreigners' Camps in
Europe* — which includes camps at its borders — was first distributed during the European Social Forum held in Paris in November 2003. Since then, it has been included
in approximately forty publications and translated into three languages. The map has
become the network's calling card and is regularly updated with information furnished
by its correspondents. The successive versions of the map show an increasing number
of dots, representing the multiplication of migrant camps and demonstrating the dramatic expansion of the practice of holding migrants in detention centers. Between the
lines, it also shows the growing number of links that the network is developing with
new partners. It has been an important tool for the campaign launched by Migreurop
in 2004, when the proposals submitted by Rome and Berlin placed the issue of migrant
camps on the EU's agenda.

In addition to an article entitled "The EU Slips toward Inhumanitarianism: Germany
and Italy Propose Refugee Camps Outside European Borders" published in three Italian dailies and in Belgium and France, the network also launched a "European Appeal
against the Creation of Camps at European Borders" signed by some three hundred
associations and more than one hundred elected European officials, including a significant number of European Parliament members.[56] The signatories of this petition
rejected both the idea of border camps and the externalization of European migration
and asylum policies and demanded that "rather than shifting the responsibility for refugee protection on[to] other countries," the EU should "improve access" to its territory
for people who need protection.[57] This gesture of resistance was probably one of the
factors that led the European Parliament to adopt a resolution firmly condemning Italy's
mass expulsion of migrants to Libya, a country not particularly known for its respect of
human rights in general and those of migrants in particular. In Libya, migrants are often

imprisoned or deported a second time. In this way, Migreurop takes part in the "official" political discussion when it can exploit openings to get its message across.

This was not the case at the beginning of 2006. In response to the "assault" of migrants who were being held in Morocco within the walls of the Spanish enclaves of Ceuta and Melilla and to the thousands of migrants from Mauritania and Senegal that spectacularly came ashore on the coast of the Canary Islands, the governments of the global North and the global South joined forces to stem the arrival of migrants they deemed undesirable. Many summit meetings are planned to bring together ministers from transit and destination countries with the explicit goal of stopping the movements of migrants at their source. A concept formally reserved for totalitarian countries, "illegal emigration" has entered the political discourse on the two sides of the Mediterranean and has been placed in the service of this objective. Aside from violating the principle according to which "Everyone has the right to leave any country, including his own, and to return to his country" (Article 13 of the Universal Declaration of Human Rights), the criminalization of emigration threatens to expand the marginalization of "undesirables" to a global scale, transforming rich countries into fortresses and the rest into vast detention centers from which the poor are forbidden to leave. This is a vision that Migreurop rejects, and in the summer of 2006, it planned a Euro-African meeting of NGOs to allow the voices of civil society in the Maghreb, sub-Saharan Africa, and Europe to be heard.

Translated by Blake Ferris.

1   The map *Foreigners' Camps in Europe* produced by Migreurop inventories migrant detention centers or "closed camps" in Europe and in Mediterranean countries. See Migreurop, "Camps in Europe and Elsewhere," www.migreurop.org/rubrique45.html (in English and French), for maps, analyses, and inventories of camps.

2   On the use of the term "camp" to designate detention centers for foreigners, see Migreurop, "Derrière le mot camp," November 16, 2004, www.migreurop.org/article880.html.

3   Migreurop, "C'est l'UE qui fournit les armes," (op-ed), *Libération,* October 12, 2005. Available on the Migreurop Web site as "Ceuta et Melilla: L'UE déclare la guerre aux migrants et aux réfugiés," October 12, 2005, www.migreurop.org/article887.html.

4   The term "externalization" began to be popularized in 2003, notably by Migreurop, and was borrowed from economics to designate certain aspects of the EU's immigration and asylum policy.

5   The Convention for the Protection of Human Rights and Fundamental Freedoms, also known as the European Convention on Human Rights (ECHR), is an instrument of the Council of Europe (and not of the EU) and was ratified by more than fifty countries. Established by the convention, the European Court of Human Rights is responsible for ensuring compliance with its stipulations, and its decisions must be respected by the signatory states. The court's decisions have given rise to considerable jurisprudence in the area of the protection of human rights, including substantial jurisprudence concerning the rights of migrants. For Tony Blair's comments on the ECHR see Prime Minister's Official Spokesman, press briefing, Prime Minister's Office (Downing Street), January 27, 2003, www.pm.gov.uk/output/page1321.asp.

6   Presidency Conclusions, Council of Europe (Brussels), November 4–5, 2004, 14292/04, http://register.consilium.europa.eu/pdf/en/04/st14/st14292.en04.pdf.

7   Gregor Noll, "Visions of the Exceptional: Legal and Theoretical Issues Raised by Transit Processing Centres and Protection Zones," *European Journal of Migration and Law* 5, no. 3 (2003), pp. 303–41. Available online at Open Democracy, www.opendemocracy.net/people-migrationeurope/article_1322.jsp.

8   Gilles Danroc, "États-Unis: le retour des refoulés," Plein Droit 18–19 (October 1992), www.gisti.org/doc/plein-droit/18-19/etats-unis.html.

9   Facility announced by Luis Ernesto Derbez, Mexican minister of foreign affairs, AP dispatch of February 17, 2005.

10 Amnesty International, "Offending Human Dignity: The 'Pacific Solution,'" August 25, 2002, http://web.amnesty.org/library/index/ENGASA120092002.

11 This proposal was attached to a letter that Tony Blair sent to Costas Simitis, then titular president of the EU, on March 10, 2003. A copy of Blair's letter and his proposal, "New International Approaches to Asylum Processing and Protection," is available at Statewatch, www.statewatch.org/news/2003/apr/blair-simitis-asile.pdf.

12 In the current asylum system, the responsibility of an EU member state for examining an asylum application is set out in the regulation known as Dublin II.

13 Presidency Conclusions, Council of Europe (Thessaloniki), June 19–20, 2003, www.eu2003.gr/en/articles/2003/6/20/3121/. For the French version of these conclusions see Migreurop, "Le Sommet européen de Thessalonique, 19–21 Juin 2003," July 23, 2003, www.migreurop.org/article42.html.

14 Erika Feller, "'The 1951 Convention in its Fiftieth Anniversary Year': Statement by Ms. Erika Feller, Director, Department of International Protection, UNHCR, to the Fifty-second Session of the Executive Committee of the High Commissioner's Programme," UN Department of International Protection, 2001, www.unhcr.org/cgi-bin/texis/vtx/admin/opendoc.htm?tbl=ADMIN&id=429d71382.

15 Ruud Lubbers, "Statement by Mr. Ruud Lubbers, UN High Commissioner for Refugees, At an Informal Meeting of the European Union Justice and Home Affairs Council" (Copenhagen), High Commissioner's Office, September 13, 2002, www.unhcr.org/cgi-bin/texis/vtx/admin/opendoc.htm?tbl=ADMIN&id=3d92deeb6. For Migreurop's collection of documents relating to the UNHCR and its Convention Plus initiatives, see "HCR and 'Convention Plus,'" n.d., www.migreurop.org/rubrique50.html.

16 The statistics of the UNHCR show that "the number of asylum applications lodged in Europe and the non-European industrialized countries [has] declined sharply," particularly since 2001. In 2004, the number of asylum seekers recorded in the European Union fell 19 percent, compared with the preceding year, which had already seen a large decline in such applications. See UN High Commissioner for Refugees, Population Data Unit/PGDS, *Asylum Levels and Trends in Industrial Countries,* 2004 (Geneva: UNHCR, 2005), p. 3, www.unhcr.org/cgi-bin/texis/vtx/home/opendoc.pdf?tbl=STATISTICS&id=422439144&page=statistics.

17 Ruud Lubbers, "Statement by Mr. Ruud Lubbers, United Nations High Commissioner for Refugees, At an Informal meeting of the European Union Justice and Home Affairs Council," (Veria), High Commissioner's Office, March 28, 2003, www.unhcr.org/cgi-bin/texis/vtx/home/opendoc.htm?tbl=ADMIN&id=3e8480244&page=ADMIN.

18 Blair, "New International Approaches."

19 Lubbers, "Statement," March 28, 2003.

20 *Ibid.*

21 UN High Commissioner for Refugees, "UNHCR's Three-pronged Proposal," working paper (Geneva: UNHCR, 2003), www.statewatch.org/news/2003/jul/unhcr2.pdf.

22 UN High Commissioner for Refugees, "A Revised 'EU Prong' Proposal," working paper (Geneva: UNHCR, 2003), p. 3, www.unhcr.org/cgi-bin/texis/vtx/home/opendoc.pdf?tbl=RSDLEGAL&id=400e85b84.

23 UN High Commissior for Refugees, "UNHCR Warns EU of Looming Asylum Problem, Proposes Remedies," press release, January 22, 2004, www.unhcr.se/se/News/pdf/22janeup.pdf.

24 *Ibid.*

25 Presidency Conclusions, Council of Europe (Brussels), p. 18.

26 On the funding of these asylum systems, as well as their relationship to transit centers and camps, see, for example, Liza Schuster, "The Realities of a New Asylum Paradigm," working paper WP-05-20 (Oxford: University of Oxford, 2005).

27 While this program was initially slated for completion on May 1, 2004, it was not actually finalized until December 1, 2005, with the adoption of a highly controversial directive on the procedures applicable to asylum seekers.

28 Communication from the Commission, "Integrating Migration Issues in the European Union's Relations with Third Countries," COM (2002) 703 final, December 3, 2002, http://europa.eu.int/eur-lex/lex/LexUriServ/LexUriServ.do?uri=COM:2002:0703:FIN:EN:PDF.

29 European Commission, Directorate-General Justice and Home Affairs, *Call for Proposals 2003,* budgetary line item "Cooperation with Third Countries in the Area of Migration," B7-667, http://ec.europa.eu/justice_home/funding/cooperation/content/b7_667_call_2003_en.pdf.

30 Communication from the Commission, "Communication on the Common Asylum Policy and the Agenda for Protection," COM (2003) 0152 final, March 26, 2003, pp. 6 and 3, respectively, http://europa.eu.int/eur-lex/lex/LexUriServ/LexUriServ.do?uri=COM:2003:0152:FIN:EN:PDF.

31 *Ibid.,* p. 3.

32 Communication from the Commission, "On the Managed Entry in the EU of Persons in Need of International Protection and the Enhancement of the Protection Capacity of the Regions of Origin," COM (2004) 410 final, June 4, 2004, pp. 4 and 1, respectively, http://europa.eu.int/eur-lex/lex/LexUriServ/LexUriServ.do?uri=COM:2004:0410:FIN:EN:PDF.

33 Presidency Conclusions, Council of Europe (Brussels).

34 *Ibid.,* p. 22.

35 *Ibid.,* p. 18.

36 Romano Prodi, Ansa (Italian press agency), September 11, 2000, quoted in Alain Morice, "'Choisis, contrôlés, placés': Renouveau de l'utilitarisme migratoire," *Vacarme* 14 (Winter 2001), http://vacarme.eu.org/article68.html.

37 Communication from the Commission, "Communication on Immigration, Integration and Employment," COM (2003) 336 final, June 3, 2003, http://europa.eu.int/eur-lex/lex/LexUriServ/LexUriServ.do?uri=COM:2003:0336:FIN:EN:PDF.

38 Philippe Ricard, "Rome et Berlin veulent créer des centres d'accueil hors de l'Union pour les candidats à l'immigration," *Le Monde,* September 3, 2004.

39 On the period discussed here, see the section "La politique des camps: Chronique européenne," in Jérôme Valluy, "La nouvelle Europe politique des camps d'exilés: Genèse d'une source élitaire de phobie et de répression des étrangers," *Cultures & Conflits* 57 (Spring 2005), http://conflits.org/document1726.html.

40 Antonio Vittorino, quoted in Alexandrine Bouilhet, "L'Europe financera des 'centres' de réfugiés à l'extérieur de l'Europe," *Le Figaro,* October 2, 2004.

41 Georges Marion, "En Allemagne, le projet du ministre de l'intérieur est critiqué," *Le Monde,* September 30, 2004.

42 "Débat confus sur la politique d'asile européenne," *Le Monde,* October 1, 2004. For more Villepin commentary, see Bouilhet, "L'Europe financera des 'centres' de réfugiés."

43 Alexandrine Bouilhet, "Désaccord européen sur les camps pour immigrés," *Le Figaro,* October 18, 2004.

44 Claire Rodier, "L'Europe et l'externalisation: La Libye en première ligne," in Franck Düvell (ed.), *Politiques migratoires, grandes et petites manoeuvres* (Lyon: Carobella ex-natura, 2005).

45 Franco Frattini, quoted in Claire Rodier, *Analysis of the External Dimension of the EU's Asylum and Immigration Policies: Summary and Recommendations for the European Parliament* (Brussels: Directorate-General for External Relations, 2006), p. 15, www.europarl.europa.eu/meetdocs/2004_2009/documents/dt/619/619330/619330en.pdf.

46 Communication from the Commission, "Communication on Regional Protection Programmes," COM (2005) 388 final, September 1, 2005, http://europa.eu.int/eur-lex/lex/LexUriServ/LexUriServ.do?uri=COM:2005:0388:FIN:EN:PDF.

47 Human Rights Watch, "Ukraine: On the Margins — Rights Violations against Migrants and Asylum Seekers at the New Eastern Border of the European Union," November 30, 2005, http://hrw.org/reports/2005/ukraine1105/.

48 UK Presidency of the Council of the EU, "Declaration by the Presidency on Behalf of the European Union on

the Anti-Revolution Bill in Belarus," December 2, 2005, www.eu2005.gov.uk/servlet/Front?pagename=OpenMarket /Xcelerate/ShowPage&c=Page&cid=1107293561746&a=KArticle&aid=1132599454714.

49 Gil Loescher and James Milner, "The Missing Link: The Need for Comprehensive Engagement in Regions of Refugee Origin," *International Affairs* 79, no. 3 (2003), pp. 583–617, www.ecre.org/eu_developments/debates/missinglink.pdf.

50 Editorial, "Des droits fondamentaux bien encombrants," *Plein Droit* 64 (April 2005), www.gisti.org/doc/plein-droit/64/edito.html.

51 See Michel Agier, "La main gauche de l'Empire: Ordres et désordres de l'humanitaire," *Multitudes* 11 (January 2003), http://multitudes.samizdat.net/La-main-gauche-de-l-Empire.html.

52 European Commission, "On an EU Approach to Managing Economic Migration," green paper, COM (2004) 811, January 11, 2005, http://ec.europa.eu/justice_home/doc_centre/immigration/work/doc/com_2004_811_en.pdf.

53 Pirkko Kourula, director of the UNHCR's Europe Bureau, is of the opinion that the European directive on asylum procedures adopted in December 2005 "could even erode international standards of refugee protection far beyond the EU."

See UN High Commissioner for Refugees, "UNHCR Says EU Directive May Trigger Downgrading of Asylum Standards," December 2, 2005, www.unhcr.org/cgi-bin/texis/vtx/news/opendoc.htm?tbl=NEWS&id=4390762c4. Kofi Annan, secretary-general of the UN, similarly argued that "the asylum system is broken" in an address to the European Parliament. See Kofi Annan, "UN Secretary-General Annan Addresses European Parliament," European Parliament, January 29, 2004, http://europa-eu-un.org/articles/sk/article_3178_sk.htm.

54 The details of the procedures are available in French at Groupe d'information et de soutien des immigrés (Gisti), "L'Union européenne doit faire respecter les droits fondamentaux," June 14, 2005, www.gisti.org/doc/actions/2005/italie/tpi.html.

55 The Migreurop Web site is www.migreurop.org.

56 See Migreurop, "Dérive inhumanitaire de l'UE (The EU Slips toward Inhumanitarianism)," October 15, 2004, www.migreurop.org/article884.html. For a list of documents pertaining to Migreurop's European campaign against camps, including "Against the Creation of Camps at European Borders," see www.migreurop.org/rubrique196.html.

57 Migreurop, "Against the Creation of Camps," October 12, 2004, www.migreurop.org/article959.html?lang=en.

Woomera Detention Center Good Friday breakout, March 29, 2002:
(1) About one thousand protesters make their way to the outer
perimeter fence to let the prisoners know that people are there to
support them. Soon after arriving at the fence the protesters notice
that the three-meter fence topped with razor wire is not the barrier
that it might seem. (2) In fact, the fence comes down easily. And
there are no state or federal police present. (3) Protesters move closer
to the detention camp. They can now see and hear the detainees.
(4) The next layer of fences proves an even easier barrier to cross.
One detainee manages to escape and is greeted by the protesters
(photos by Pip Starr, www.rhproductions.com.au/womera1.htm).

Exceptional Times, Nongovernmental Spacings, and Impolitical Movements

Brett Neilson and Angela Mitropoulos

At the border, politics risks exposing itself to the impolitical, to a sense of movement beyond its conventional sociopolitical definitions, and to an expression of the political without a sovereign tone. One might say that it is this risk — which is also to say, this chance for a life otherwise — that a migratory politics seeks out. And yet, just as the prospect for movement seems to become ever more limited, such limits are reinforced by nostalgic repetition no less than through the proliferation of borders.

In late April 2003, around five hundred people traveled to the newly constructed Baxter Detention Centre in the South Australian desert for a three-day protest. At the time, Baxter held some three hundred detainees, including migrants from Iraq and Afghanistan. The decision to build this highly fortified structure had been made just days after an earlier action, exactly a year before, in which some fifty inmates had escaped from the detention center at Woomera. In retrospect, it is no exaggeration to claim that the events at Woomera in 2002 and the September 2000 protests against the World Economic Forum in Melbourne were the most significant local expressions of the congeries of nongovernmental actors that, at the turn of this century, composed the so-called movement of movements. Not only did the images of the Woomera 2002 protest circulate globally, but the whole pattern of dismantling fences and escape would be echoed in distant locations, including the action against Italy's Bari Palese detention center in July 2003. At Bari as at Woomera, the camp would be closed after the protests. Yet between the protests at Woomera in 2002 and those at Baxter in 2003, little would remain the same. Not only would the new camp involve advanced technologies of surveillance, biometrics, and isolation, but during the intervening period, there would occur an increased militarization of the policing of protests, paralleled by the Australian government's willing participation in the war in Iraq.

Despite these shifts, the protest at Baxter was explicitly organized as a repetition of Woomera; just as, it might be noted, an antisummit protest in Sydney in 2003 was billed as a repetition of the one in Melbourne in 2000. What, then, is this urge to repeat in nongovernmental politics? Why this inclination to, as some put it, complete unfinished work or, as others insist, to return to the site of a prior achievement? Perhaps the very iterability of protests, which would cast any given protest as a constitutive index of "the movement of movements," was already put into play through the calendrical, quasi-serialized codifications of J18, the international day of protest on June 18, 1999; S11, the protests at the World Economic Forum in Melbourne on September 11, 2000; and so on. Even in Genoa, after the bloodbath perpetrated by the Italian state during the protests at the G8 economic summit in July 2001, there would be the compulsion to return *un anno dopo*. Nevertheless, as with Hollywood, the sequel is inevitably disappointing. So, too, with Baxter in 2003: smaller numbers, harsher policing, electric fences, constant and futile maneuvering, debates about organizational form divorced from the issues at hand, the absence of surprise, and the evolution of police control. The point here is not to dismiss the demonstration out of hand; it had its own logic and point of intervention, not least in the attempt to breach the isolation of those interned at Baxter. Yet it is undeniable that the convergence marked the end of, as some might say, a particular "cycle of struggles," perhaps due to the very inclination to engineer a cyclical recurrence.

From this point on, it became clear that nongovernmental struggles against the camps had been absorbed by an antiwar mobilization that, with the actual deployment of troops in Iraq, would become increasingly bound to nationalist agendas. To some extent, this was a continuation of tendencies that had already beset the diverse factions opposed to Australia's border controls: ethical posturing would outweigh a regard for political effect; the fracture between pro-civil society and antineoliberal activists would be accentuated; and the question of labor (as a question of the role of the camps in the formation of labor markets) would be all but subtracted from the ensuing polemic. In one sense, these were local manifestations of a wider recomposition due to the regime of global security imposed after September 2001. Even so, they unfolded as a result of specific events related to Australian migration policy and with changes that were made tangible with the appearance, in August 2001, of a red ship on the horizon.

Before we detail the events surrounding the Norwegian freighter *MV Tampa*, let us backtrack to note that the Woomera breakout in 2002 was not the first time detainees had escaped from camps in Australia. Indeed, the camp is a constitutive feature of Australia as such, which began its existence in the form of British penal colonies, with reserves for the internment and forced labor of the continent's Aboriginal peoples. Since the time of these first missions and prisons, the figure of the fugitive has tapped into deep anxieties about the possibility of establishing political control over a land deemed to be *terra nullius*: empty, godless, and unsusceptible to the kind of cultivation that, most clearly in the writings of John Locke, provided the basis for landed property and sovereign possession.

The deeply racialized character of the camp and its constitutive place in Australian history are thus critical points of departure for any analysis of recent struggles against the camps. Many of the original convicts of the penal settlements were Irish, regarded at the time as a different race from the British, who had been deported from Britain under the policy of transportation, as it was then called. Following the end of transportation in the mid-nineteenth century, the camp remained an institution not only of Aboriginal internment, but also of indentured labor, drawn for the most part from China and the Pacific Islands. In 1940, a shipload of over twenty-five hundred people fleeing Germany, many of them Jewish, were sent by the British to be interned in the Australian Outback for the duration of the war. Four years later, the escape of some four hundred Japanese prisoners of war from a camp in Cowra resulted in a machinegun massacre that left 234 dead and 108 injured. This history of racial confinement, which continued in more or less institutionalized forms during the entire period of the so-called White Australia policy (1901–1973), hangs over the current internment regime. Almost immediately after the establishment of the first of these more recent facilities at Port Hedland in 1992, there ensued a long series of riots and breakouts that culminated, most notoriously, with the escape of five hundred people from Woomera in June 2000 and a prolonged hunger strike of thirty-nine detainees (five of whom sewed their lips together) at Curtin in August 2001.

In any consideration of nongovernmental politics surrounding the camps, it is paramount to recognize the importance of the struggles conducted by the detainees themselves. Too often their actions are excluded from the political field, perhaps because they do not accord with the imperatives of civil dialogue or public debate which, in the liberal democratic imagination, are held to delineate the sphere of political relations and expression. Indeed, criminalization and incarceration remove the bodies of those who are interned from the domain of public space and, in so doing, show how the ideal of rational dialogue and communicative exchange that supposedly undergirds this sphere is founded not on reason, but on force. To put this more emphatically, when this sphere is imagined as national in foundation and extent, the tendency to attribute political action to citizen-activists, but not to migrants, serves merely to reaffirm the boundaries of a state that, in turn, seeks to reinforce itself through the exercise of migration controls.

Therefore, it is not only the struggles of detainees that need to be understood as politically significant, but also the momentum of migration as such. To understand these transnational trajectories as strategies undertaken in and against the workings of the global political economy is neither to homogenize all motives for movement nor to romanticize them as necessarily transgressive. Undoubtedly, the motives for migration are varied and shaped by disparate factors. Moreover, as numerous studies have shown, reasons for migration are irreducible to aggregate economic forces of push and pull, demography, and so on. At the same time, migratory movements have a definite effect on aggregate economic performance, which is one reason they are subjected to such stringent geopolitical control. As Yann Moulier Boutang argues, the attempts of capitalists to control the mobility of workers form an enduring thread in modern economic history.[1] The current system of borders and camps is one in a long line of means for controlling this mobility, building on techniques such as slavery and indenture. The attempt to violate or evade the border, whether conceived in this frame or not, is thus a politically significant act. Involving complex relations between heterogeneous agents, not all of whom act for beneficent reasons, it signals a politics of potentiality, or of *what might be,* despite existing geopolitical divisions and territorializations.

To be sure, there is also a procapitalist politics that advocates the erasure of borders under the auspices of free-trade protocols that ease the circulation of goods and capital around the globe according to a logic in which labor is a commodity like any other. And yet, the contemporary world is marked by a system of control that promotes the free passage of money and other commodities while increasingly scrutinizing and restricting the movement of human bodies and their labor, precisely because it is this potential that distinguishes labor from all other commodities. And so, as a kind of mirror of the capitalist version of a borderless world, much of the nongovernmental politics developed within the initial wave of protests after the WTO actions in Seattle contested this neoliberal order as a struggle against capitalist free trade without posing the question of migration in terms of the specificity of labor in the world of commodities. The famous victory against the Multilateral Agreement on Investments was won — first in 1998 and then again at the WTO meetings in Cancún in 2003 — on the basis of a nationalist rhetoric that asserted the right of elected national governments to adjudicate investments in their area of sovereignty.

Therefore, without denying the analytical importance of the concept of neoliberalism, it should be noted that this framework tends to depict those who suffer the consequences of capitalist globalization in the global South as mere victims, denying them a position as active social subjects within current processes of global transformation. Moreover, such an account distinguishes the state from capital so as cheerfully to offer the former as either the ground for or principal agent of resistance to the latter — as if the operations of the world market do not presuppose differential labor markets and vice versa. To stress the active role of migrants in the contemporary global order redresses this oversight, signaling the importance of opposing the operations of capital from something other than a nation-statist position whose terrain is the management and administration of the flow of things.

Questioning the existence of the border as such is thus not to accede to neoliberal free-trade orthodoxies but, instead, to contest the exercise of sovereign power as much as the power of the market, to the extent that they are inseparable. It would simply be incorrect to suppose that capitalism, left to its own devices, would lead to the erasure of borders. The current world system involves increasingly flexible means for policing labor mobility, often resulting in the displacement of borders (outward or offshore) from the territorial boundaries of the state. This is complemented by a multiplication of microborders within the supposedly homogeneous space of the state. In metropolitan contexts, incidents such as the revolts in the French banlieues or the "riots" at Sydney's Cronulla Beach (to name just two episodes of urban unrest that unfolded in late 2005) result from the supposed transgression of borders that divide the metropolitan space according to more or less racialized criteria. In both cases, the upshot was to reinforce these borders through emergency laws and police lockdowns and to block the movement of people to certain parts of the city where they were deemed not to belong.

Moreover, we would suggest that there remains a crucial sense in which the self-managed exploitation that post-Fordist forms of work solicit depends on the border. The border and its various techniques of racialization function here as ways to distinguish those who can manage their own exploitation from those who must be exploited (or worse) by direct coercion, conditioning the experience of work in and through this persistent threat and/or identification. Or, to put it another way, the rationalization of violence that defines the border remains pivotal to the utopia of contractual freedoms that post-Fordism is said to comprise.[2]

In any case, questioning the eternity of the border or its necessity as it is posed in antineoliberal analyses that distinguish state and capital is to refuse both the antipolitical fetishism of a world ruled by uncontrollable economic forces and the unrealizable dream of a politics that would "once again" master the world. Politics is not determined by what lies beyond its borders, but remains limited only by what it is. In other words, to question the eternity of the border is to declare an end to the "end of the political." There is a need to acknowledge that at stake in every politics of border control is an attempt to control the borders of the political. In the case of struggles surrounding undocumented migration, the very notion of movement fractures along a biopolitical or racialized axis: between movement understood in a political register (as political actors and/or forces that are more or less representable) and movement undertaken in a kinetic sense (as a passage between points on the globe or from one point to an unknown or unreachable destination). To keep these two senses of movement separate not only denies political meaning to the passages of migration but also fails to think through the complexities of political movement as such — not only the incompleteness and risk of every politics but, more crucially, the kinetic aspects of political movements that might be something more or other than representational.

In this sense, the depoliticization of migratory movements, their presentation as being bereft of political decision and action, functions as a means by which politics is bound to a sovereign space and recapitulates its bearings. Nevertheless, it is in this nexus of movement as politics and movement as motion that the nongovernmental struggles concerning undocumented migration take shape, primarily as challenges to the demarcations that define politics as always, inexorably, national and/or sovereign. In the most felicitous moments of these struggles, these two senses of movement meet and become indistinct.

As is often commented of the 2002 Woomera protest, it is unclear who pulled down the fences: the detainees on the inside or those on the outside, even if it can be said with some certainty that those on the inside initiated the escapes. At stake here is not merely some ethos of collaboration that observes that force was applied to both sides of the barrier, back and forth, to bring the fences down. More radically (and disturbingly, for constituted powers), there is a certain elimination, however provisional, of inside and outside, of the lines between the interned migrant and the civil dissident, between motion and politics. Perhaps this is why the techniques of control instituted at Baxter in 2003 aimed, above all, at keeping those inside separate from those outside. Indeed, the very siting of the camps in remote locations has been premised on the political necessity of just this division. By 2003, however, the technologies of decomposition and partition introduced by the state had already far exceeded any routine efforts at crowd control, extending way beyond Australian territorial boundaries and involving new methods of excision and exclusion.

How to conduct the struggle against border control when power violently intervenes to separate and disavow the connection between the two senses of movement? That is the question that has haunted nongovernmental politics in addressing the issue of the camps in the past five years. It is a condition marked by a constant deferral of the state of emergency or, better, by the fact that an emergency cannot be formally declared when it has already become the norm. The arrival of the *MV Tampa* in Australian waters in August 2001, just weeks before the obliteration of the Twin Towers in New York City, is the iconic event that marks this turn. Carrying some 436 migrants rescued from a sinking boat, the freighter was refused entry to Australian waters and then stormed by crack special troops (the same unit that would soon be deployed in Afghanistan and Iraq). The aesthetic impact of a floating red hulk on the horizon facilitated the televisual modulation of mass sentiment as the government pressured its Pacific neighbors, Nauru and New Guinea, to establish internment camps for the *Tampa*'s passengers in return for monetary payments.

That sovereignty should be up for sale is no surprise. Nor is it shocking to learn that Nauru, a former money-laundering haven for the Russian mafia, would eventually change its constitution to allow for the long-term detention of the *Tampa*'s passengers. But just as these people were hurriedly ushered to a makeshift camp in Nauru to avoid a writ of habeas corpus that sought to release them, the Australian parliament passed new border legislation that, among other things, excised key territorial outposts from the so-called "migration zone." While formally the right to seek asylum remains, these laws remove the ability of migrants who arrive on certain islands and reefs to seek asylum. Which particular islands, reefs, or territories might be excised is a matter of ministerial decision whose force can be retrospective. Combined with the redoubled effort of border policing known as Operation Relex and the offshore camps on Nauru and New Guinea's Manus Island, these procedures formed the cornerstone of Australia's new border technologies that, in many ways, would become its primary export in the subsequent "war on terror."

What matters here are not simply the deaths and deceptions that, in the final months of 2001, would come to characterize the long season of repulsing boats from Australia's shore, including the drowning of those aboard the *SIEV X* and the so-called "children overboard" affair. Despite extensive investigative journalism, the circumstances behind these operations — and, in particular, the extent of complicity between Australian and Indonesian police — remain obscure. There can be no doubt, however, that the Australian government used these moments to indulge in the most sly electoral chicanery, among other things by doctoring photographs to create media images that reinforced race-laden slanders about migrants throwing children from a sinking ship (a vessel quite possibly sabotaged by Australian forces). The pursuit of this deception, however, which many campaigners (both governmental and nongovernmental) would take up, left unquestioned the regime of border control as such.

At stake in uncovering and protesting the alteration of truth — as if only this, and not the collective purchase of affect, is what matters in contemporary representative politics — was some notion of the proper or civilized way to turn back migrants, and not the practice of border policing itself. This points to a division at the very heart of the struggles against Australia's migration policies. On the one hand, there are those who advocate what we might call "gentle detention" or "gentle rejection," that is, the notion that border policing remains a necessary means of controlling population and labor flows in today's world. Adherents of this view tend to hold a number of common assumptions. Most pointedly, they believe that the status and fate of undocumented migrants should be decided by the rights-giving state. They tend to campaign around issues presented as scandalous, such as the detention of children or, more recently, the increasing internment of citizens identified by immigration officials as racially other or, in one particular case, mentally disabled. Finding its major expression in groups such as the Refugee Action Coalition (RAC) or ChilOut (Children Out of Detention), this "gentle detention" position is often framed in explicitly nationalist terms: for instance, through claims that Australia is sullying its ostensible former reputation as an upholder of human rights, or through the affective vector of national shame. Finally, those who hold this position exhibit a tendency to appeal to transcendent moral imperatives and to fashion arguments against internment in registers more often ethical than either political or economic.

On the other hand, there is a much smaller network that, as with European no-border groups, calls unequivocally for the abolition of the camps and the erasure of borders as such. Here, the emphasis is on the role of migration controls in the contemporary neoliberal global order, such as the constitution of distinct zones where labor attracts different costs, the patrolling and elimination of populations that resist proletarianization, and the distribution of capitalist speculation and labor competition through geographic demarcations. Moreover, the scandalous internment of citizens or children is regarded as the inevitable, rather than accidental outcome of the camps — in other words, its institutional manifestation.

In Australia, these no-border positions began to emerge around the time of the September 2000 protests against the World Economic Forum in Melbourne. While they developed in tandem and often in direct dialogue with European analyses subscribing to an "autonomy of migration" position, they have assumed a specific character that in many respects is an index of Australia's position and history as an outpost of empire — in the South, but not of it.[3] There are at least three aspects to this character: opposition to the explicitly nationalist demeanor of rights-based migrant advocacy in Australia; attention to the colonial heritage of penal confinement (which makes racism a salient and unavoidable issue); and, perhaps most importantly, concern with the nature of the border regimes that have emerged in and beyond Australia since the time of the *Tampa.*

It is perhaps unnecessary to reiterate here the conflicts between rights-based "refugee" activism in Australia and no-border positions. Suffice it to say that there have been a number of skirmishes, both in the shape of RAC criticisms of actions such as those at Woomera in 2002 and more theoretical debates (some of which we have participated in) conducted in small journals.[4] The terms of these disagreements are similar to disputes in other parts of the world. Those who hold to a rights-based position tend to see the idea of a borderless world as dangerous and idealistic, venturing a decline into anarchy and petty fortresses. Those who hold the no-borders position accuse their antagonists of equivocating on whether the camps should be abolished and reproach them for brushing aside the analysis of global capitalism while blindly adopting the logic of statist and sovereign arguments under the pretext of safeguarding the concept of rights. Some of this debate has turned on whether the discourse of refugee advocacy strikes a sovereign tone in conferring propriety to the conditions and classifications of migration policy ("refugee," "immigrant," and so on). It is worth noting that the persistence of the demand to "free the refugees" has become somewhat incongruous at a time when an increasing proportion of those who are interned in Australia are undocumented migrants who overstay or contravene the conditions of their visas and who make no claims for refugee status.

Arguably, rights can be conceived of outside the normative logic of the state, by emphasizing their use as "strange attractors" in political struggles or their relation to invented practices that traverse the borders erected by standard critiques of civil society as a neoliberal notion. Thus, some liberal/civil society activists understand their struggle as tactical: a series of incremental claims that aim gradually to persuade their addressees that what appear to be abuses of the rule of law are in fact symptoms of the bordered world. Linked to this is a tendency to consider the no-border position as merely rhetorical and heuristic, a ruse to expose contradictions within rights-based advocacy, rather than a serious attempt to eliminate the camps and borders. No-border struggles are viewed by such civil-society activists as a kind of radical gesture, at once intransigent and idealistic, rash and counterproductive. Yet it is precisely this impolitic aspect, we suggest, that makes the no-border position coherent and powerful. In making a claim that is seen as outrageous and unacceptable, at least to a certain sense of the political, no-border perspectives expose this sense for what it is, revealing its grounding in a tradition that takes political fact as value, equates power with the good, and understands justice as reducible to law and calculation. At stake here is not the surreptitious reimposition of an alternative border on the political, its determination by what is apolitical or antipolitical. Rather, at stake is the refusal of any valorization of the political — that is, the refusal of the autolegitimating logic of modern politics, both in its contractual and representative moments, as well as its politico-theological modes of legitimation.[5]

Whatever the complexity of these relations, the disagreements between civil society and no-border perspectives attest to the fact that the space of the nongovernmental is divided. The schematism of this division is to some extent a caricature of complex and nuanced positions. However, there remains an acute sense in which the very existence of the border obliges a similarly sharp political decision: *either it should be there or it should not*. Such a decision, by affirming the border, however gently, can mime the sovereign decision, thus leaving the nongovernmental to exist in the shadow of the state and its exceptions. Or, the border can be refused, thereby enacting an opening, a break for freedom that places the nongovernmental outside the affective and tangible strictures of the existing international state system.

To be sure, these alternatives do not present a fork in the road. They intermesh and clash as much as they diverge — no more so than at the border itself. But where is the border? The question has been chewed over enough with respect to European borders, particularly in the context of EU integration and constitutional debates. However, Australia presents quite a different geographical and political situation. As modernity's original gulag continent, and notwithstanding the Internet and jet travel, it remains surrounded by a kind of moat: vast expanses of ocean that stretch to all points of the compass, replete with a matching affective map. In a technical sense, policing these borders is a more feasible proposition than blocking mountain passes, scrutinizing road and rail crossings, or rolling out electric fences. The exclusion of islands and reefs from the "migration zone" has been one method of preemptively blocking migrant passages. Almost paradoxically, this preemption functions in a post hoc or "just-in-time" manner.

Consider the case of fourteen Kurdish migrants from Turkey who, in November 2003, landed on Melville Island, one of the Tiwi Islands to the north of the city of Darwin. Upon learning of their arrival, the Australian government rushed legislation through the lower house to excise retrospectively almost three thousand islands around the main continent, including Melville Island, from the "migration zone." This was done with full expectation that the upper house, which the government did not control at the time, would overturn the legislation, as it had similar regulations introduced twice in the previous year. Nonetheless, the minister for immigration, Amanda Vanstone, boasted that the migrants would never be able to seek asylum in Australia since, on her advice, even if the regulations were struck down, they would "be valid for the time period during which they were valid."[6] An exception was thus declared, not only in a spatial sense — through the excision of the islands and the placing of the migrants beyond the rule of law — but also in a peculiar temporal sense. In other words, the laws would function only in the time of the future anterior.

The challenge, then, confronting the nongovernmental struggles against Australia's border regimes — and, we would argue, against the global organization of border controls — is how to operate not only in the space, but also the time of the exception. In this latter regard, the strategy of repetition so rigorously pursued at Baxter 2003 (and elsewhere) begins to fail. The logic of return and iterability cannot possibly deactivate the time of detainment that is so crucial to the institution of the border emergency. It is perhaps not only war that, as Gertrude Stein once noted, "makes things go backward as well as forward,"[7] but the very sense of the exception itself. The exception suspends time in an attempt to correlate and confine, both preemptively and post hoc, the aleatory moment of border crossing—the encounter with difference, if you will—for which no amount of control can prepare.

Such a peculiar temporality pertains not only to the sovereign mechanisms by which the emergency is declared, as in the case of Melville Island. It also inflects the daily experiences of migrants whose lives are held up, formally and informally, through border technologies. Lan Tran, who arrived in Australia from Vietnam via a camp in Malaysia, remarks:

> For me, my ordeal has become an adventure because over the years it has lost its element of danger and profound sense of uncertainty of what the future may hold. From where I'm speaking *right now,* I am *at one point in that future of my past.* I can see from my experience that the ordeal wasn't the journey itself. It was how we were received by the community at large. And that is an ongoing process. I am conscious of *now and again,* beyond my experience as a Boat Person, a refugee, an Australian citizen living in Australia. I am Asian and because of that I would have to continually justify my place in this society through a full admission of *my history that was elsewhere.*[8]

Although Tran exists "beyond" her experience as a "Boat Person," what she describes here is nothing less than a process of "detainment," of living in the future of her past. It is the same insistence on the future anterior that animates the sovereign decision and finds its material embodiment in the physical experience of detainment or incarceration. And just as one might say that there is *no going back* for those who experience such detainment, no return to origins or possible repatriation for those who have risked their lives at sea and cut their ties with a "history that was elsewhere," so it is also *impossible to go back* to Woomera, to the joining of the two senses of movement in that moment of escape. By far, a more creative action in this regard was the so-called Flotilla 2004, which involved a group of protesters traveling on a boat from Sydney to the offshore camp on Nauru. Tracked by satellite communications and blog entries, it involved diverse groups along the way and, importantly, declared that closing the camps was a method, not just an aim. The notion of setting protest in motion, or of rejoining the two senses of movement in time, distinguished this action from the merely spatial maneuvers of Baxter. As it happened, however, the removal of the boat by force from Nauru, which paralleled the forceful interdiction of boats from Australia's waters, imposed a spatial division similar to the one enforced at Baxter: the violent partition of movement from movement.

By the time of the flotilla, nongovernmental struggles had largely been absorbed by an antiwar campaign that culminated on February 15, 2003; from that point on, the movements never could quite recompose themselves, even in the form of further antiwar protests. There are, of course, good reasons to see border-policing regimes as an integral part of the ongoing global war, most notably in the centrality of internment camps to the operations of war and in the importance of the preemptive logic of racialization to the configuration of the enemy and the distribution of violence. However, these links were never made in an antiwar campaign that, at a certain point, swept away the entire trajectory of radical movements from 2000 to 2002, primarily under the seduction of swelling ranks, however fleetingly. Indeed, the unprecedented turnouts at initial antiwar protests were stoked by prevalently nationalist agendas — with slogans such as "Bring our troops home" and "Don't follow the USA" — that were in no way immune to the sovereign imperatives that animate the border-control regime. The prevalent disposition of the antiwar protests inclined to the civic nationalism that favors "gentle" detention and rejection — while not entirely overlapping with it — quickly collapsed under the weight of the nationalist imperative to "support our troops" once Australian forces entered Iraq.

In Europe the adoption of issues concerning precarious labor facilitated a degree of recomposition of the protest movements, beginning with the Euro May Day protests of 2004. In Australia there was no comparable articulation. A diffuse campaign around the issue of job security reassembled some elements of the flagging antiwar movements in Europe and, in some instances, forged productive (if tense) links with no-border groups, but Australians were unable to organize despite the introduction of industrial relations "reforms" in which the issue of job security is certainly relevant. One reason for this failure is the entrenchment of a centralized trade-union culture in many sectors of the social left — one that, it should be noted, no longer possesses the material base for compulsory, centralized bargaining that formed its foundation in the early twentieth century.

Nonetheless, and notwithstanding the difficulties that confront nongovernmental politics with regard to the Australian camps, there is something exemplary about the development of these political positions, if only because they operate in the most difficult of circumstances and confront methods of control replicated elsewhere. It is no secret that Tony Blair's proposal of March 2003 to establish transit-processing centers outside EU borders was inspired by the precedent of Australia's Pacific Solution, composed of offshore internment camps. By the end of the same month, Italy, Spain, and the Netherlands had endorsed a version of the Blair proposal; by October, Italy had already begun to send migrants to camps in Libya financed by the Italian government to prepare them for deportation. But this exportation of the Australian detention model should not be taken as license to imagine that struggles in this part of the world might offer advanced or particularly effective strategies of resistance and escape. To the contrary, it is in Australia that the defeat of such struggles has been most brutal. Nationalism is no less dangerous when it is mediated by shame than by pride. And the expression of activist enthusiasm for locally or nationally based struggles can all too quickly develop into an affective statist position, particularly insofar as it grounds itself in the dialectical process of national shame — which, perhaps, explains something of its compulsion to repeat.

Indeed, the urge to repeat has structured the logic of much nongovernmental politics in the last three years, particularly politics that seeks to relaunch the mobilizations that seemed so promising at the turn of the millennium. Moreover, this urge to repeat inflects the way nongovernmental movements understand the operations of sovereign power and its relation to contemporary governmental forms, as an anachronism or return of what is past in present time. Yet the time of repetition cannot be remapped onto the linear time of chronology or progress. This much we have known since Marx's lesson on tragedy and farce, not to mention Kierkegaard's discussions of anamnesis and movement. The kind of retrospective preemption that has come to characterize current border regimes does not merely interrupt history presented as chronology. It is not simply the return of an anachronism — the reappearance of sovereignty in governmentality — but also a temporalizing strategy that structures the potential of persons to act politically. We have described this temporal ordering as the separation of movement from movement or, in other words, as the sundering of the potentiality of kinesis (bearing in mind that Marx described labor power as *potentia*) from the sphere of action that has traditionally constituted the political. Here, the errancy of movement extricates the differentialities of *potentia* and of the political from the time of detainment and the laborious tempo of repetition.

If there is one thing that ought to be heeded in the Australian experience, it is how the institution of the camp, with all its implications for the control of labor under global capital and the policing functions of global war, builds on the colonial experience of racialized internment. The persistent specter of racialized difference is visible as emergency conditions are matched by a "colonialization" of the world's metropolitan centers: the appearance, if one may be excused redundant terms, of the Third World in the First World and of the First World in the Third. If, as Achille Mbembe writes, the colony is "the site where the violence of the state of exception is deemed to operate in the service of civilization," the peculiar insistent appearance of the colonial camp in the metropolitan context (think of Milan's Via Corelli or Roissy's ZAP 3) must be conceived of against the rhetoric of a civilizing mission that haunts the making of the world as war.[9] If alternative ways of being in the world are to be derived — and what else is politics if not the creation of the world on the cusp of human relations — there must be some understanding of how colonialism insinuates itself into the emergency and vice versa.

Neither optimism nor pessimism are useful substitutes for working through this problem. Nor, as we have suggested, are mere repetition and displacement good strategies for dealing with technologies of detainment that play themselves out across time and space. Moreover, it remains to be asked whether iterability, in a political-economic register, is perhaps nothing more than the kind of interchangeability that constitutes the indifference of commodities. In any event, to seize the moment for what it might be, to rejoin movement and movement, there must be an encounter with the contingent and the other, in other words, with the cut of difference. This can occur only in the fluid and transsubjective space that defines the very sense of what it means to experience the world, in the dimension prior to the partition of meanings and relations where the coappearance of the divisions might be glimpsed in their incipiency and untimeliness.

In this sense, what is unrepeatable about Woomera in 2002 was precisely what was important about it: the very context of the detainment of time. In other words, it was exceptional insofar as it marked a tangible proximity to the other of politics, which cut through the ossified senses and divisions of the political and of movement. How this event came to be seen was a surprise, as much to those who were there to protest as to the authorities. Proffering neither succession nor iterability, this event represents a kind of total risk. Yet it is not a risk that can be shirked or deferred. Rather, it must be followed at precisely that point or moment where *now* meets *not now,* and *here* meets *there,* where the experience of indistinction erases the affective and geopolitical borders of politics, and with them the camp. This is the impolitical imperative of the times and the disjunction through which time can flow. To go looking for guarantees steeped in nostalgic reminiscences because the times seem so grim only avoids an engagement with what has changed and how one might respond to such change. More deeply, it gives up on the promise of a migratory politics against which borders are fashioned.

1   Yann Moulier Boutang, *De l'esclavage au salariat: Économie historique du salariat bridé* (Paris: Presses Universitaires de France, 1998).

2   See Angela Mitropoulos, "Under the Beach, the Barbed Wire," *Mute,* February 7, 2006, www.metamute.org/en/Under-the-Beach-the-Barbed-Wire.

3   For an example of this direct dialogue, see Sandro Mezzadra and Brett Neilson, *"Né qui, né altrove* — Migration, Detention, Desertion: A Dialogue," *Borderlands E-journal* 2, no. 1 (2003), www.borderlandsejournal.adelaide.edu.au/vol2no1_2003/mezzadra_neilson.html.

4   See, for instance, *Arena Journal,* vols. 65, 66, and 68 (2003–4); and *Overland,* vols. 166–69 (2002).

5   On the impolitical tradition in political thought see Roberto Esposito, *Categorie dell' impolitico* (Bologna: Il Mulino, 1988).

6   Australian Immigration Minister Amanda Vanstone, quoted in Meaghan Shaw, "Islands Excised to Head Off Boat," *The Age,* November 5, 2003.

7   Gertrude Stein, *The Autobiography of Alice B. Toklas* (London: Penguin, 1966), p. 2.

8   Lan Tran, panel discussion led by Anne-Marie Medcalf, Boat People Symposium, Centre for Research in Culture and Communication, Murdoch University, Perth, Western Australia, Oct. 15, 1996. Our emphasis. Available at www.mcc.murdoch.edu.au/ReadingRoom/boat/panel1.html.

9   Achille Mbembe, "Necropolitics," trans. Libby Meintjes, *Public Culture* 15, no. 1 (Winter 2003), p. 24.

Naval Battle

a profile of Women on Waves by Élise Vallois

Rebecca Gomperts, the founder of Women on Waves (WOW), describes the creation of the organization as a coincidence. Gomperts is a woman, a doctor from the Netherlands, and an experienced abortion practitioner. On a mission in Mexico as the doctor aboard Greenpeace's ship, Gomperts confronted the harsh reality of women suffering from illegal abortions. The organization, Women on Waves, was born of that experience.

Traditionally, women deprived of the freedom to get abortions in their native countries go abroad for the procedure. But with WOW, the movement is reversed. WOW offers a way to overcome legal restrictions by extending the borders of the Netherlands: they use a ship. Because abortion laws in Europe vary, WOW is committed to allowing women to benefit from the most permissive abortion laws possible. Women, who otherwise would not have had this opportunity, can thus terminate unwanted pregnancies legally.

The operation is ingenious. WOW charters a mobile clinic ship under the Dutch flag; WOW's ship crosses the sea to a country where abortion is illegal or where the laws are extremely restrictive. Women seeking abortions board the ship; it then sails for international waters outside the territory where the country of embarkation exercises sovereignty. Dutch law applies on board, so that women — who so desire — can have completely legal abortions performed before the ship docks.

ABORTION AT SEA

In practice, though, the organization performs only a limited number of abortions. There are two main reasons for this. First, the Dutch government has granted WOW only a seriously limited right to provide for the voluntary termination of pregnancy. Although Dutch law authorizes abortions until the twenty-fourth week, Women on Waves does not have the right to practice abortions after the sixth week. Why? Medical abortion up until the sixth week is considered a customary procedure; however, it is necessary to obtain official authorization to terminate a pregnancy beyond that point. Although Women on Waves follows all the stipulated legal conditions, it took the organization a year of negotiations and lobbying

Barco da moral & dos bons costumes

"Ship of Morals and Nice Uniforms," one of the many cartoons in the Portuguese press depicting Women on Waves's trip to Portugal in the summer of 2004 and the reaction of the Portuguese authorities (*Expresso,* September 9, 2004).

to convince the Dutch government that WOW should be granted the right to prescribe and administer the abortion pill. After this victory, WOW then filed a suit to obtain permission to perform abortions between the sixth and the twelfth weeks: the case went before the Dutch Supreme Court, which ruled definitively in December 2005. WOW won this case, but is still awaiting the Dutch Ministry of Health's inspection and approval. The second reason why WOW performs a small number of abortions is practical: the high cost of renting the ship. For this reason, the organization, which is financed exclusively by individual gifts, currently limits its field of action to Europe: it went to Ireland in 2001, to Poland in 2003, and to Portugal in 2004.

Although the ship's mobile clinic is WOW's basic initiative, it is also part of a larger strategic engagement. Even if, for example, all the Portuguese women who wanted to board WOW's ship in 2004 could have done so, the legal issues surrounding the question of abortion in Portugal have still not been satisfactorily or definitively resolved. WOW also seeks to address such restrictions. The practice of safe and effective abortions thus constitutes only one aspect of Women on Waves' activities.

The Women on Waves ship *Borndiep* stayed in international waters twelve miles from Figueira da Foz, a small holiday town in Portugal, from August 28 until September 9, 2004. The ship was blocked from entering Portuguese national waters by two Portuguese warships (www.womenonwaves.org).

GIVING WOMEN CONTROL OVER THEIR BODIES

More generally, WOW's second goal is to publicize women's situations and thus to persuade the public of the need for comprehensive legislation legalizing abortion. From this perspective, WOW's Web site, www.womenonwaves.org, plays an essential role. It serves both as a platform for the organization's information campaigns and as a site for listening and dialogue. Almost fifty thousand people visit the site each month; volunteers respond to around ten questions a day. One can learn how to terminate a pregnancy up to the ninth week by means of simple medications, how to protect oneself against sexually transmitted diseases, and so forth. Since 2004, three visitors out of four have been Portuguese, a sign that the site complements the shipboard campaigns.

Beyond acting as an intermediary and fielding questions on its Web site, WOW distinguishes itself through its determination to carry out activities in close collaboration with feminist organizations in the countries concerned. More precisely, the WOW ship never goes anywhere uninvited. Gomperts calls this "extra solidarity." The campaigns that precede and accompany the ship's arrival are assiduously publicized and are well covered by the media. Local activists can therefore use this attention to make their demands better heard. As such, WOW envisions itself as providing tools to further its partners' missions.

WOMEN ON WAVES AGAINST THE PORTUGUESE ARMADA

In partnership with several Portuguese organizations, Women on Waves appealed to the European Court of Human Rights and the European Commission to condemn the actions of the Lisbon government during its 2004 campaign. The government sent in battleships almost immediately when WOW's ship entered Portuguese territorial waters. It is not difficult to imagine how shocked WOW was by this violent reaction. Was the organization such a threat to the Portuguese government that it had to simulate war? Or, was this aggression a manifestation of the Portuguese government's humiliation over its own failings—notably vis-à-vis its commitments to the European community? The fact remains, however, that WOW was not a foreign invader and it did not violate any laws. Quite the contrary: as with this instance, WOW is always careful to act only within the law, despite the constraints such punctilious legalism imposes.

Moreover, WOW does not believe that its actions contravene the domestic affairs of the visited countries. According to Gomperts, WOW merely allows women to exercise their right to have an abortion. She holds the right to be universal regardless of the principle of territorial sovereignty that some of WOW's opponents use to deny that right. WOW works to obtain the possibility of choice for women. Governments that scorn the right to abortion are, in fact, interfering harmfully in women's lives.

Not only did the Portuguese armada's intervention call attention to the specific issue of abortion, it also forefronted the question of women's rights in general. While boats chartered by commercial companies can travel freely, territoriality and its borders are reasserted when a boat that bears the flag of feminism—demands permission to dock. Ironically, the Portuguese government's simulacrum of a naval battle worked in WOW's favor. The media coverage of WOW's campaign, as it were, capsized the battleships. It still remains to be seen how Portuguese abortion laws will be modified by WOW's campaign.

Translated by Susan Emanuel.

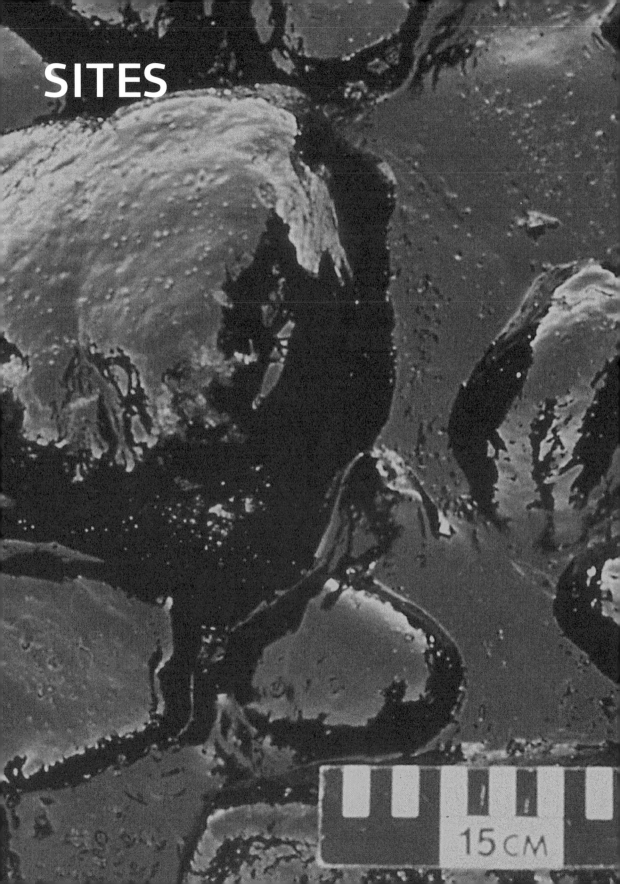

DISASTER ZONES

Bhopal: Unending Disaster, Enduring Resistance

Bridget Hanna

On March 23, 2006, fifty survivors of the Bhopal gas disaster and subsequent water contamination trudged into New Delhi and requested a meeting with the prime minister of India, Manmohan Singh. The Bhopal disaster had occurred in 1984, when the Union Carbide Corporation (UCC) pesticide plant leaked forty tons of methyl isocyanate (MIC) into the city of Bhopal, exposing half a million people to the toxic gas. The fifty survivors, several in their eighties, had walked all the way from Bhopal, sleeping on the side of the road and covering over five hundred miles on foot. Their demands were chillingly simple: a commission to administer their relief and medical care, the provision of safe drinking water, and the active prosecution of those criminally accused of being responsible for the disaster, which has killed at least twenty thousand people to date.[1] They also demanded environmental remediation of the factory, a national day of mourning for the victims, and the disaster's inclusion in school curricula. Finally, they wanted the prime minister to pursue — and blacklist, if possible — the corporation liable for the disaster, Union Carbide Corporation USA, owned since 2001 by the Dow Chemical Company.

These demands were not new. Most of them had been on the survivors' agenda since at least 1991. But this time, three survivors, three Indian activists, and two international supporters of the survivors — all on an indefinite hunger strike — were granted a meeting with the prime minister after waiting twenty-seven days. On April 17, Prime Minister Singh granted all of their demands, with the caveat that the government would do nothing "extralegal" in pursuit of the UCC or its current parent company, Dow Chemical.

It had been over twenty-one years and five months since the disaster occurred. Why would it take twenty-one years to meet such basic demands? And how could the Bhopal movement suddenly be strong enough to win its demands, twenty-one years after the disaster, when most people around the world believe it to be ancient history?

Hadjra Bi and other women at a protest against Dow Chemical in Bhopal (Sambhavna Documentation Center).

Contrary to popular belief, the situation in Bhopal has gotten worse, not better, over the past two decades — especially the problem of water contamination. The deteriorating environmental conditions, combined with delayed justice and ambitious, but bungled, government rehabilitation efforts, have given survivors a political education to go along with their anger and suffering. With every passing year that issues remain unresolved in the Bhopal case, the stakes are heightened for its eventual resolution. All involved — the victims of chemical exposure, the government of India, and the corporation — understand that their continued survival or legitimacy may hang on the final outcome of the Bhopal problems.

The first half of this article, Disaster and Governmental Interventions, covers the basic aspects of the disaster and its aftermath. These two sections outline the historical facts and controversies, but pay particular attention to the role of the Indian government — including its convoluted relationship with the UCC and the United States government — and to the logic of its relief efforts in Bhopal. Then, Survivors' Movements looks at the evolution of the survivors' movement in Bhopal and their progressive politicization and articulation of rights, developed in relation to the combination of official negligence, corruption, and governmental patronage that they have endured. Finally, Impacts discusses the Bhopal crisis as a stimulus for the formation of new networks, alternative activist formats, and expanded targets for activist intervention. In sum, I show how the constellation of government, corporate power, and development projects have laid the groundwork for a marginalized group of people from central India to form the center of a political movement that incorporates their daily crises into a powerful international critique of the chemical industry and the corporate system.

DISASTER

In the late 1960s, the UCC built a small factory at the edge of the city of Bhopal, India. It formulated the carbamate pesticide Sevin for sale on the Indian market and imported its most hazardous components, phosgene and MIC, in small batches. In 1972, company engineers proposed upgrading the facility so that they could also produce these hazardous ingredients on-site and thus increase the factory's output of Sevin. The plans for the upgrade were drafted by Union Carbide USA and vetted by, among others, the company's future CEO, Warren Anderson.

HAZARDOUS PRODUCTION

The technology proposed for the upgrade was inferior to that used in the UCC's American operations, and the proposal detailed inherent risks in this plan that could have been mitigated "had proven technology been used throughout."[2] The UCC designers also noted that the proposed waste-disposal system — solar evaporation ponds — posed the "danger of polluting subsurface water supplies."[3] In addition, highly unstable MIC

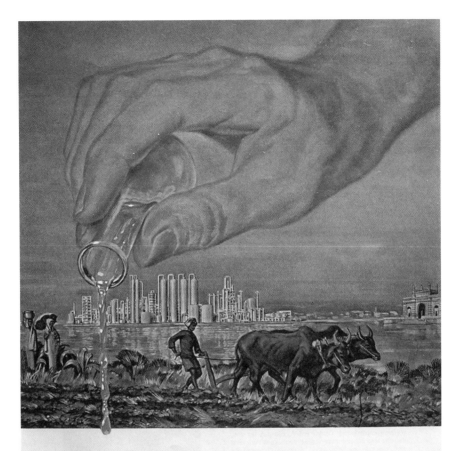

Science helps build a new India

Oxen working the fields . . . the eternal river Ganges . . . jeweled elephants on parade. Today these symbols of ancient India exist side by side with a new sight—modern industry. India has developed bold new plans to build its economy and bring the promise of a bright future to its more than 400,000,000 people. ▶ But India needs the technical knowledge of the western world. For example, working with Indian engineers and technicians, Union Carbide recently made available its vast scientific resources to help build a major chemicals and plastics plant near Bombay. ▶ Throughout the free world, Union Carbide has been actively engaged in building plants for the manufacture of chemicals, plastics, carbons, gases, and metals. The people of Union Carbide welcome the opportunity to use their knowledge and skills in partnership with the citizens of so many great countries.

A HAND IN THINGS TO COME

UNION CARBIDE

WRITE *for booklet B-5 "The Exciting Universe of Union Carbide," which tells how research in the fields of carbons, chemicals, gases, metals, plastics and nuclear energy keeps bringing new wonders into your life.*
Union Carbide Corporation, 270 Park Avenue, New York 17, N. Y.

Advertisement for the Union Carbide Corporation
(International Campaign for Justice in Bhopal).

was to be stored in an unnecessarily large tank — constructed despite internal objections — in part because UCC policy provided pay incentives to the board for producing larger infrastructure elements.[4]

Bhopal is the capital of Madhya Pradesh ("middle province"), a lush agricultural state sometimes referred to as the "breadbasket of India." The UCC viewed India, especially Madhya Pradesh, as the next big market for Sevin. At the time of the Bhopal disaster, the government of the Republic of India, a young democracy, was struggling with the desire to industrialize and to attract foreign investments and the need to manifest independence and autonomy from foreign interference. A few years earlier, the Indian parliament had passed the Foreign Exchange Regulation Act (FERA), which aimed to increase state control over foreign business ventures. The act reduced the amount of equity that a foreign corporation could provide to any given project in order to dilute foreign ownership of Indian-based firms. The bill also strongly encouraged the transfer of proprietary production technology to Indian firms, rather than just the formulation and sale of products, in order to lay the groundwork for eventually nationalizing such technologies.

In the case of the Bhopal plant, however, the UCC wanted to retain control of both the project and the technologies they had invented. While FERA did not allow foreign corporations to be majority stakeholders in such projects, an exception was made for the UCC on the grounds that it was bringing in "special technology." In order to retain their 50.9 percent stake in the undertaking, the UCC cut the cost of construction from 28 million to 20 million dollars, primarily by using substandard technology and cheaper materials.[5] Although the UCC claims its plant in Bhopal was built to the same safety specifications as its American facilities, when it was finally constructed, there were at least eleven significant differences in safety and maintenance policies between the Bhopal factory and its sister facility in Institute, West Virginia. For example, the West Virginia plant had an emergency plan, computer monitoring, and used inert chloroform for cooling the MIC tanks. Bhopal had no emergency plan, no computer monitoring, and used brine — a substance that may dangerously react with MIC — for its cooling system. The Union Carbide Karamchari Sangh (Workers' Union), a union of Bhopal workers that formed in the early 1980s, recognized the dangers at the factory, but their agitation for safer conditions did not produce any changes.[6]

"GREEN REVOLUTION"

The economic rationale for the construction of the Bhopal factory was the demand for pesticides engineered by the "green revolution," a massive, internationally sponsored shift in agricultural practices. The "green revolution" was set in motion in India (and in other developing nations) during the 1960s and 1970s by an alliance of governments, multinational corporations, and world development and trade agencies. Under the banner of the eradication of food shortages, the "green revolution" purposefully disrupted the small-scale, manual, multicrop, organic agriculture that had developed in India over thousands of years in favor of large-scale, monocrop, chemically and mechanically maintained agriculture.

Unfortunately, the "green revolution" did not succeed in eliminating hunger, and by the late 1970s many had already become disillusioned with its promises. The economic, political, and health toll of these often unsustainable initiatives quickly became apparent. Most of these costs were borne by peasant farmers, who were displaced from their small plots of land when mechanized agriculture began to demand huge land holdings. In Madhya Pradesh, the peasant population migrated to cities such as Bhopal, settling densely on the outskirts in illegal squatters' colonies (*bastis*) and doing day labor to survive. Though usually tolerated by the government as potential labor pools and vote banks, these settlements were not entitled to state services such as sewage, piped water, or roads, and could be demolished at the whim of an official. Additionally, most of those who lived there did not possess citizenship documents—such as birth, marriage, or death certificates—which would later become crucial to proving the right to state services. Few who lived in the *bastis* had ever received much in the way of services from the government.

The UCC factory was on the Kali parade grounds outside Old Bhopal. Old Bhopal was the traditional Muslim center of the city, while wealthier New Bhopal, in the hills on the other side of the Upper and Lower Lakes, had arisen after 1956, when Bhopal was made the capital of Madhya Pradesh. When the UCC decided to upgrade the Bhopal facility from formulation to production, they violated the municipal zoning regulations due to their proximity to human settlements and major infrastructures, such as the train and city bus stations. However, when the municipal administrator served notice to the UCC, requiring them to relocate outside the city boundaries, they did not move. Instead, the administrator was suddenly transferred from his post, and the issue was dropped.[7] Meanwhile, the *bastis* kept growing, filling in most of the available land on the outskirts. Although the Kali parade grounds had been farmed for many generations, the population had never been so dense. By 1980, when production at the UCC's factory finally began, the slums had expanded to meet the walls of the new factory, and the government had granted many residents their one crucial document: a *patta*, which gave them rights to the land on which they lived.

Although the safety of the plant was the responsibility of its operators, the safety of the city was the responsibility of the Indian government. Without transferring all responsibility to the state, it is important to note here that the Indian government repeatedly violated its own laws—from FERA to zoning restrictions, to ensuring comparable safety standards—in their dealings with the UCC. None of the early indications of problems at the plant—including repeated complaints of worker injuries, the 1981 death of Mohammed Ashraf, employed in the Bhopal MIC unit, letters from concerned citizens (sent to the local and national government, and to the UCC's offices in Bhopal, Bombay, and its U.S. headquarters in Danbury, Connecticut), and the huge fire that raged through the alpha-naphthol unit in 1982—prompted the government to take any regulatory action.[8] Amnesty International's report on the disaster on its twentieth anniversary notes that they were "unable to find evidence that the central or state government took adequate steps to assess the risk to local communities or the environment, or to press Union Carbide to review safety mechanisms."[9] Instead, politicians looking for votes happily granted *pattas* to illegal residents next to the factory, never informing them that it posed an immense hazard.[10] This close and legally slipshod relationship between the UCC and the Indian government set the stage for the disaster.

THE GAS LEAK

Sevin failed to perform as well on the Indian market as had been hoped. By May 1982, the factory received a damning report from the safety audit team sent from the United States. The huge new factory ceased production by the middle of 1984, when the UCC was reportedly shopping it around for sale. None of the plant's six safety systems, including the refrigeration system for the MIC, which must be kept at 0 degrees Celsius, were functioning. Some had been turned off to save money — 30 dollars per day in the case of the refrigeration system. At midnight on December 3, 1984, while most of the city was sleeping, a rupture disc failed on a forty-ton tank of MIC, which escaped the tank as a low, poisonous cloud that then drifted south. Over half a million people lay in the path of the gas, which traveled most thickly over the slums closest to the factory, thinned out slowly over Old Bhopal, and finally began to disperse above the lake toward New Bhopal.

The number of people who died that night, like the number of chronically ill and genetically damaged, continues to be a contested and highly politicized issue. Very few of those closest to the factory were likely to be carrying identifying documents; many were itinerant and would not have been accounted for in a census; and large numbers were summarily buried in mass graves or cremated immediately. The government has legitimized only the documented and registered individual deaths, a process that required an autopsy and registration with the police. The current official death toll is therefore less than 7,000 total, of which 3,000 died in the immediate aftermath. Estimates based on the number of burial shrouds and wood for cremation purchased in the aftermath bring the estimate of immediate deaths as high as 10,000.[11] Amnesty International confirms that 7,000 people died immediately, with 15,000 additional deaths to date, and at least 100,000 chronically ill.[12] Over twenty years later, 4,000 registered gas victims continue to seek treatment at government hospitals every day, according to the state government's annual reports.

GOVERNMENTAL INTERVENTIONS

In the immediate aftermath of the gas disaster, American personal-injury lawyers flocked to Bhopal, signing up victims by the thousands. They uniformly promised gigantic rewards, often took the victims' only documents with them, and sometimes hired local goons to "recruit" clients. In part to stem these unscrupulous practices and

(LEFT) This haunting image from 1984 of an infant being buried after the disaster has become emblematic of Bhopal but may no longer adequately represent its complexities (Raghu Rai/Magnum Photos).

(RIGHT) Bodies lying in the street on the morning of December 4, 1984 (Prakash Hatvalne).

in part to expedite the legal process, India passed the Bhopal Gas Leak Disaster (Processing of Claims) Act of 1985. This act appointed the government sole representative of and negotiator for all gas victims in *parens patriae*. Legally, this labeled the victims "juridically incompetent," a status usually reserved for the very young or the mentally ill. In fact, most of the gas victims did not have the resources or even the language (in this case, English) necessary to fight the legal battle for themselves, but the Bhopal act included no provisions for victims to communicate with their sole representative, the government, and no recourse for remedying poor representation. The government, assuming the legal role of a parent in relation to the gas survivors, robbed them of their legal right to pursue the UCC individually while technically establishing their right to be provided for, and advocated for, by the government.

FORUM NON CONVENES

In 1985, the Indian government took their case against the UCC to the Second District Court of New York, arguing, poignantly, that "the interests of justice required the case to be tried in the United States on the grounds that [India's] own legal system was backward and procedurally outmoded, lacking any class action device or other provision for representative suits, burdened with the legacy of colonialism, and subject to massive delays caused by endemic docket backlogs."[13] At a moment when American legal justice seemed applicable to Bhopali survivors, the Indian government strategically confessed that its own infrastructure — legal, and as it would turn out later, medical, scientific, political, social, and economic — was unable to grasp or adequately address the ramifications of this catastrophe.

The presiding judge in the case, Judge John F. Keenan, however, summarily dismissed the government's argument to try the case in New York on May 12, 1986, on the basis of *forum non convenes,* literally, "inconvenient forum." As Rajan Sharma, a legal expert on Bhopal and the primary litigator in a current civil case brought against the UCC/Dow on behalf of several Bhopal survivors (under the Alien Tort Claims Act) has written, Keenan's "decision rested, in part, on the notion that trying the case in the U.S. courts would amount to 'yet another instance of imperialism' imposing foreign legal standards upon a developing country with 'vastly different values,' different levels of 'population' and 'standards of living.'"[14] The message from Keenan's court was unambiguous: American courts are for American citizens. The accusation of criminal acts committed by Americans abroad would not function to bestow American-style rights on their victims. The representatives of the Indian government went home with a new agenda: damage control. From then on, the fate of the Bhopal victims would be directly tied to India's reputation as a corporate-friendly and investment-friendly market.

LEGAL COMPROMISES

In 1989, the Indian Supreme Court approved a "full and final" settlement between the UCC and the Indian Government for 470 million dollars in the civil litigation over the Bhopal disaster. The government had previously estimated the damage at 3 billion dollars.[15] The settlement was based on an estimate of 300,000 people affected by the gas, although the amount would eventually be disbursed to over half a million who could prove victimhood (approximately 500 dollars per person for lifelong injury or disability on average). No stipulations for treatment, research, or economic rehabilitation for the thousands who had lost the ability to work were included in the agreement. In addition, the court quashed the criminal charges of culpable homicide against the UCC, its former CEO Warren Anderson, the UCC's Indian subsidiary, and all seven Indians implicated in the disaster. The UCC's stock rose in response to the dual victories — over half the settlement was covered by their insurance. No survivor representation or testimony was accepted in the case, and news of the deal caused an immediate uproar among observers worldwide. Survivors flooded into New Delhi and protested on the steps of the Supreme Court, and women's unions from Bhopal spontaneously entered and trashed the UCC's Delhi offices in a rage.

In 1991, in response to a revision petition challenging the settlement filed by survivors and support organizations, the Supreme Court revisited the settlement issue. Rather than increasing the amount payable by the corporation, the Supreme Court instead stipulated that if the amount was deemed insufficient in the future, the government of India would make up the difference. Under the guise of a generous revision, the government established explicitly, for the first time, its own structural motivation to shortchange the survivors and downplay the long-term consequences of gas exposure. Although it was jettisoning the possibility of further financial remedy from the corporation, the Supreme Court succumbed to public pressure and reinstated the criminal charges against the UCC, Anderson, and the accused from India, unable to justify their dismissal. This move crucially reactivated the possibility of criminal justice for the survivors of the disaster. These two capitulations to the protests of the gas victims and their supporters — reinstating warrants and accepting governmental responsibility — were perhaps due to the influence of the leftist Janata Dal party, which was briefly in power in India in the early 1990s and had made rectifying the settlement one of their central platforms. The political will to accept government responsibility for the disaster has since been lacking.

As of 2006, warrants remain outstanding for both the UCC and its former executive, Warren Anderson, who was arrested in Bhopal in 1984, released after posting less than 2000 dollars bail, and has never returned. An investigation by Greenpeace and the British newspaper *Daily Mirror* found Anderson living in New York in 2002; in 2003, India finally delivered the arrest warrant for Anderson to the U.S. Department of Justice. Nearly one year later, despite the joint extradition treaty between India and the United States, the Justice Department declined to extradite Anderson. Meanwhile, India's Central Bureau of Investigation (CBI), charged with prosecuting the case, has repeatedly tried to dilute charges against all of the accused. Survivors' groups succeeded in preventing the CBI from reducing the charges against Anderson and the UCC from culpable homicide to criminal negligence, but failed to prevent the same reduction of charges against the Indians accused, who are finally, twenty-one years later, beginning to testify in the slow-moving Bhopal court. The government has failed to hold anyone accountable for this man-made disaster, and those in Bhopal commemorate this failure yearly with fiery effigies that bear the names of the accused and the governments that protect them. The lack of criminal justice in the Bhopal case, while certainly not the most pressing issue, may be the most demoralizing one to a community that will never be the same.

Although the legal response to the disaster in India has fulfilled the government's own negative expectations, it has not always been clear whether this failure is strictly legal or the result of a political reluctance to irritate the UCC or the American government. The combined effect of these legal and political failures has been to demonstrate India's inability and unwillingness to protect its citizens from foreign and corporate interests. Willing to treat survivors as children via *parens patriae,* the government has failed to care for them. Obliged to charge the guilty, the government has failed to criminally prosecute a single individual or corporation successfully. Instead, it has attempted to cover for the corporation by grappling with the crisis itself. To protect the UCC, the Indian government promised to facilitate a social-welfare and rehabilitation project that it is loath and poorly equipped to execute effectively. Uninterested in protecting the vulnerable, the government has been even less interested in the difficult work required to heal them.

COMPENSATION

In her excellent 1995 book on the Bhopal issue, *Critical Events,* the anthropologist Veena Das discusses the processes that led up to the civil settlement, including the Bhopal Act and the technologies of medical categorization used to identify the health effects of the disaster. One of the dynamics she identifies is the manner in which the government employed the legal process to transform the Bhopal victims from "sufferers" into "malingerers." In her analysis, the government's rhetorical monopolization of the poverty and acute suffering of the survivors became a way to rob them of their rights by declaring them *non sui juris* (without the legal capacity to act for themselves). According to this thinking, the victims needed a more expedient resolution to their problems than what they could achieve individually because of their poverty and illness. Yet via a circular logic, their poverty and their outsider status in the proceedings were repeatedly used to cast suspicion on their injuries.

Das notes that in this case, the suffering of the survivors was transformed into something that they thought they deserved or were inventing in reference to their pre-existing suffering and medical conditions, such as tuberculosis or malnutrition, which made codification of their "new" symptoms difficult. MIC was known at the time to be the most potent pulmonary and sensory irritant among industrial isocyanates, and what little else was known suggested that exposure to MIC could cause chronic respiratory, corneal, and immune problems, with potential carcinogenic and second-generation effects. The science, however, did not yet exist for victims to "prove" the causal relation between their specific symptoms and MIC. As Das points out, the government claimed that "the subjective symptoms did not correspond with the known objective indices of disease.... In effect, victims were responsible for the fact that their disease was not understood by modern medicine."[16] This suspicion and lack of knowledge was combined with a flawed system of medical categorization, one which lacked any framework for conceiving of the total toxic insult to a person's system or the long-term dangers of exposure to MIC. In fact, those who did not have evidence of having received medical treatment during the chaotic weeks of the crisis itself were considered "uninjured," despite the facts of their condition in 1989.[17]

The inability of the government or scientific community to understand or to diagnose the collective condition of the gas victims allowed the transformation of the victims' right to justice into the rights of the "greater good of greater numbers."[18] Das quotes the attorney general of India, defending the Bhopal Act against a challenge by petitioners and survivors' groups that contested its constitutionality: "'When rights are curtailed, permissibility of such a measure can be examined only upon the strength, urgency, and preeminence of rights and the largest good of the largest number sought to be served by curtailment…. If the contentions of the petitioners are entertained…rights may be theoretically upheld — but ends of justice would be sacrificed.'"[19] In this case, it appears that the "greater good" was not the good of the survivors, but the good of those who stood to gain from India's soft stance on corporate crime. This entrenched position became clear when, upon revisiting the settlement in 1991, the Supreme Court noted that the government's categorization system had been inadequate, the numbers low, and their understanding of MIC's potential effects severely limited. And yet the court still refused to adjust the settlement amount.

It was on these terms — amid accusations of false claims and invented symptoms — that the Supreme Court drafted the guidelines by which compensation would be disbursed to the survivors after 1991. The process they developed was overly bureaucratic, founded on suspicion, and plagued by corruption. Praful Bidwai, an investigative journalist in India, contended at the time of the distribution of funds that the compensation guidelines were "flawed by a fundamental confusion about what is being compensated. In tort law, the principal damages are paid for injury or discomfort caused by (past) civil wrong, such as negligence. Loss of earnings is a second, consequential factor. Further, if a disability arises and necessitates fresh expenditure or loss of earnings, that is yet another factor."[20] Rather than awarding the (already inadequate) settlement money to the victims, the compensation process required each victim to prove his or her own suffering and medical problems, despite the poor understanding even among professionals about the etiology of gas exposure. Obtaining this proof often required victims to present significant bribes to medical officers. This exchange, quoted in Kim Fortun's book *Advocacy after Bhopal*, is representative:

> *Judge*: You have been categorized as "C," which entitles you to 25 thousand rupees in compensation. Do you accept?
> *Plaintiff*: Sir, I have already spent that much on medicines.
> *Judge*: Do you wish to contest?
> *Plaintiff*: Sir, do what you think is fair.[21]

Analysis after the fact found that most people received the minimum amount of compensation or less than the amount required by the government guidelines for each gradation of injury, and that those closest to the factory received less on average than denizens of certain wealthier neighborhoods farther away. There was no recourse for survivors denied compensation due to the onerous documentary requirements, and by the end of the compensation process — in the mid-1990s — the government had given away less than half the money. It sat on the rest — attempting to use it for several pet projects — until a court order in 2003 confirmed that it belonged to the victims.

MEDICINE

A survey found that despite the intention of tort law, much of the compensation money was eventually used to cover medical expenses. Medical care was guaranteed free to survivors by the government, though not to their children born after the disaster. However, in part because of the near nonexistence of scientific literature on MIC exposure, the health-care system does not seem to have advanced in treatment since 1984. Patients report poor quality of care at the government hospitals and are often forced to buy the medicines that legally should be provided free of charge. Meanwhile, Bhopal has seen a proliferation of hospital construction: as of 1994 it had 1.25 beds per thousand persons, exceeding the World Health Organization standard of 1.0 bed per thousand.[22] But despite the proliferation of certain kinds of infrastructure, there is still no official treatment protocol for gas exposure. Most of the treatment remains symptomatic because of official disinterest and a poor understanding of disease etiology. Many doctors perceive gas syndrome as an imagined (or invented) symptom of poverty, despite the consistent excess mortality and morbidity in badly affected areas.

In 1985, twenty-four long-term medical studies were initiated by the government-affiliated Indian Council of Medical Research (ICMR) to document the effects of the unprecedented exposure. These studies potentially could have provided a precise picture of symptom and disease trends that constitute gas exposure, and would have been able to predict damage in the second generation. However, by the late 1980s, a number of the studies had already been quietly closed; the last study was ended prematurely in 1992, against the protests of its chief investigator and just as evidence of second-generation effects was emerging. A technical report was released in 2004 asserting that more research was necessary. The ICMR clinical and toxicological studies have yet to be published.

CONTAMINATION

The UCC knew even before it built its production facility that its design posed the "danger of polluting subsurface water supplies in the Bhopal area" and that in order to prevent this, "new [disposal] ponds [would] have to be constructed at one to two year intervals."[23] Furthermore, even before the solar evaporation ponds were constructed, the formulation plant had been indiscriminately burying chemical waste all over the site. Residents were complaining of cattle deaths and damage to crops even before the disaster, and the UCC's own documents show that they knew of leaks from their disposal ponds as early as 1981. Internal correspondence from April of that year notes that "continued leakage from the evaporation pond [is] causing great concern," but the UCC never warned the community.[24] Evidence has emerged since then, including evidence disclosed in several studies by Greenpeace, that confirms that dangerous chemicals and heavy metals were disposed around the site. One Greenpeace research team tested the drinking water of nearby communities and found that high levels of contamination made well water in the area unsuitable for drinking. Substances that exceeded World Health Organization and Environmental Protection Agency standards included carbon tetrachloride, chloroform, trichloroethane, tetrachloroethane, dichlorobenzenes, and heavy metals. The Greenpeace researchers concluded in 1999 that the presence of these contaminants is "undoubtedly due to the long-term industrial contamination of the environment surrounding this plant. Long-term consumption of water, contaminated by chemicals that have been found in this study, could cause significant health damage."[25]

In 1991, survivors and activists presented the government with information that there were dangerous substances indicated leaking from the factory. In fact, the Madhya Pradesh State Research Laboratory produced reports between 1991 and 1996 stating that water near the factory was "unfit for drinking," but they declined to warn the residents, release their reports, or act on their findings.[26] Meanwhile, a government agency, the National Environmental Engineering Research Institute (NEERI), produced several reports on the factory site, all of which were rife with methodological problems and omissions.[27] One of these, funded by Eveready Industries India Ltd. (one of the subsidiaries formed in India by the UCC split), famously and groundlessly asserted in 1997 that contamination would take twenty-three years to reach the ground water.[28] Even Arthur D. Little, the UCC's consulting firm, commented internally that NEERI's weaknesses included ignoring standard sampling processes and also expressed serious doubts as to the validity of NEERI's conclusions based on the inferior quality and misinterpretation of data. However, internal correspondence indicates that the UCC chose to work with NEERI because they expected to have "an opportunity to participate and put forward our views during the progress of study, and try to protect company's interest."[29]

In 1994, in response to a petition by Ian Percival submitted in December 1993, the Indian Supreme Court allowed Union Carbide USA to sell its 50.9 percent share in its Indian subsidiary, Union Carbide India Limited (UCIL), despite the fact that the Indian government had declared the UCC to be an absconder from justice in 1992 and had frozen its assets. Then, in 1998, UCIL, under its new name Eveready Industries India Limited (EIIL), handed over the factory premises to the Department of Industries.[30] During this time, the contamination was spreading north from the factory at an estimated rate of 300 to 700 meters per year, and by 2006 it had extended a minimum of three kilometers away from the factory. In total, an estimated 20 thousand people live in the contaminated area, approximately 90 percent of whom have no other source of drinking water. According to a small study by the Sambhavna Trust, 50 percent of residents of the affected *basti,* Annu Nagar, suffer from "a multitude of symptoms," most commonly "abdominal pain followed by giddiness, pain in chest, headache and fever."[31] The 1999–2004 Fact Finding Mission on Bhopal found bioaccumulation of toxins in vegetables and breast milk. Lead, mercury, nickel, volatile organic compounds (VOCs), hexachlorocyclohexane (HCH, formerly known as benzene hexachloride, or BCH) pesticide, and halo-organic compounds were found in soil, water, vegetables, and breast milk samples from ten residential sites close to the plant.[32]

Nongovernmental organizations struggled for years to build up the documentation and momentum necessary to motivate the government to address the water-contamination issue. Finally, in May 2004, the Indian Supreme Court ordered that clean, piped water be supplied to the affected communities. However, the municipality never

Residents fill buckets from one of the contaminated wells near the
Union Carbide Corporation factory. They know the water is unsafe, but
have no alternatives (Sambhavna Documentation Center).

supplied more than 10 percent of the water necessary — less during the monsoon — and
only provided water by tanker, rather than piping it in. Although the ongoing civil suit
on behalf of gas-affected Bhopal residents in the New York court has pushed the Indian
government to clarify their position on the contamination issue (caving to activist pressure and a hunger strike in 2005, they sent a letter to the court agreeing that the UCC
could be compelled to clean up the factory in India), they still have not chosen to register official support for the lawsuit.

The environmental and contamination issues in Bhopal have been ignored and marginalized for as long as possible because they disrupt an official discourse about Bhopal
as an event that was "fully and finally" ended with the 1989 settlement. Like the process
of neglecting or marginalizing medical research and the victim's access to it, the official
narrative of the contamination has been at the mercy of the flawed presentation of
data and expertise controlled by the government and influenced by the corporation.
This lethal combination of negligence and deceptiveness by both parties has occurred
at the expense, again, of those living in Bhopal, who by and large do not have access

to these scientific discourses. Yet it may be that this double insult and the victimization of a new generation has made explicit the consequences of irresponsible development that the Bhopal situation illustrates. Today's activists, both in Bhopal and abroad, have experienced a renaissance — both of protest tactics and of techniques for scrupulous documentation and collection of data to counter the official numbers.

SURVIVORS' MOVEMENTS

To date, over 1.2 billion rupees have been spent on rehabilitation projects for gas-affected persons in Bhopal (approximately 41 million dollars, if taken at the average 1994, rather than the 1984 or 2006 rate of exchange).[33] In total, according to government reports, 274 million rupees have been spent on environmental rehabilitation, 457 million rupees on social rehabilitation, 258 million rupees on economic rehabilitation, 173 million rupees on administrative expenses, and 59 million rupees on other associated expenses. But of the hundreds of millions spent on income-generation projects, today these projects employ fewer than 200 people and are profitable ventures for the proprietors of them. Hundreds of millions of rupees have also been spent on housing projects, but thoughtlessness and carelessness have plagued these ventures. For example, homes for gas widows were constructed as blocks of four-story apartments on the far edge of town, but many widows, chronically breathless, cannot manage the stairs, much less afford to get into the city. Over 2.6 billion rupees (approximately 86.7 million dollars) have been spent on "free medical care," yet the victims are as sick as ever. Hospital wards lie empty for lack of staff, expensive, never-used machinery is commonplace (purchased on commission, of course), and none of the hospitals keep records of their patients for long-term tracking and monitoring. The Supreme Court Hospital Monitoring Committee, formed in 2004 as a result of activist pressure, made a recent surprise visit to a Bhopal hospital and was unable to locate a single doctor in an hour and a half of waiting.

RIGHTS AND REHABILITATION

Add these failed attempts to the failures of compensation, research, and criminal justice and a vivid picture of the official attitude toward Bhopal emerges. The stated goals of initiatives on behalf of the gas victims have remained unrealized. Efforts have been uniformly plagued by lack of oversight and accountability, characterized by thoughtlessness or premature termination. Corruption, lack of transparency, an unwillingness to communicate with or listen to the needs of the survivors, and the lack of an overseeing body — such as the demanded National Commission on Bhopal — has allowed for the misuse of much of the money earmarked for relief and has contributed to the failure of the government as the guardian of the survivors.

According to a survey conducted by the Indian Council of Medical Research, 68 to 86 percent of those affected by the gas came from a very depressed socioeconomic class, a large percentage of whom were Muslims and low-caste persons. In general, the very poorest neighborhoods were hit the hardest. This fact had complex consequences. On the one hand, these poor communities suddenly had a special right to health and were allotted previously unavailable social guarantees. The Supreme Court has agreed that for Bhopal victims the right to health care equals the right to life, and the right to life is guaranteed in Article 21 of the constitution. On the other hand, these poor communities' initial exposure to the gas was because of their vulnerability. The government then exploited this assumption of their lack of power when it became their representative, via *parens patriae,* a status that means they are *by definition* marginalized, disenfranchised, and "unfit" to articulate their own needs. Thus, once again, their "right" to treatment, compensation, and justice was translated by its executors as charity for the undeserving poor, much in the same way that their suffering was described in the Indian legal case. Discrimination and lack of education from all quarters contribute to this attitude toward the gas victims. Professor Suroopa Mukherjee characterizes the attitude of bureaucrats and doctors in the wealthier, unaffected part of Bhopal — who are the service providers for the victims — as follows: "'A large section of this population has become lazy and greedy. We cannot get domestic help in Bhopal because that section of society lives on the dole. NGOs and activists back them. They take to the streets and voice their complaints. Every gas victim in Bhopal is a politician who takes advantage of a corrupt system.'"[34]

Certainly there have been some false claims, but statistics on registration and compensation show that it is likely more real claims were excluded. It has been clearly established that the Indian government was willing to subvert its own laws by allowing the UCC to build the factory, to betray its own legal system by settling with the UCC and instantiating the Bhopal Act, and to risk the lives of tens of thousands in order to avoid confronting the contamination issue and the question of corporate liability. This failure to protect Indian gas victims, alongside the development of a dysfunctional welfare system, has damaged, politicized, and educated the Bhopal survivors, whose movements — troubled, but increasingly powerful — have grown to demand far more than their health.

WOMEN'S WORK

Amnesty International notes in its report on Bhopal that "it is clear that the gas leak radically altered the social fabric and economics of everyday life, and entrenched existing poverty and social disempowerment."[35] After the gas disaster, those workers who survived did not have the physical strength or endurance to do the type of hard labor that most had done previously. The victims and their families began to go hungry.

Bhopal had almost no tradition of political organizing or union work prior to the disaster, particularly within the *bastis,* and certainly not among women, many of whom were confined to their homes. Immediately after the disaster, relief and political efforts were therefore dominated by outside (Indian) activists who had the training and resources, not to mention the energy, to fight the necessary battles. The survivors asked for jobs. In 1985, the Madhya Pradesh government created thirty-eight income-generation projects to employ gas-affected women. (Men were not offered employment by the government, ostensibly because many of them had been driven to alcoholism by their losses or their sudden physical inability to provide for their families.) These workshops trained women in printing, the production of leaf cups and plates, leatherwork, sewing, and crafts.[36]

In 1986 however, the government closed these workshops, claiming they were no longer necessary, although nothing had changed materially in the situation of the survivors. (It took several more years before they won any interim relief.) Six hundred women in one facility organized and successfully agitated for the reopening of the workshops, obtaining jobs for 2300 women.[37] The organization these women formed, Bhopal Gas Peedit Mahila Udyog Sangathan (BGPMUS), or the Bhopal Gas-Affected Women Workers' Organization, would became the largest organization of female gas survivors in Bhopal, with membership in the tens of thousands. Around the same time, Champa Devi Shukla, a Hindu, and her Muslim co-worker, Rashida Bi, began to agitate for better wages and conditions at their government workshop, which employed one hundred women. This agitation led to the creation of the Bhopal Gas Peedit Mahila Stationery Karamchari Sangh (BGPMSKS), or Bhopal Gas-Affected Women Stationery Workers' Union.

The BGPMUS and the BGPMSKS, though rarely working together and occasionally at odds, grew to become the core of rights agitation for Bhopal survivors.[38] Women, chosen for the governmental employment schemes on the basis of their traditional roles — in other words, because of the cultural taboo against women drinking alcohol, among other reasons — took small steps out of these roles when they began working in the factories. Many of these new heads of household had never left home unaccompanied by a man or without a veil.

These women-led organizations formed the bases through which survivor-activists could ferment a variety of claims, such as their right to adequate compensation, medical care, and rehabilitation — and in some cases, personal-rights claims, such as the right to move about without a burka. The strategies of the unions included protests against government action and inaction and weekly meetings that helped keep the focus on the story of the gas disaster, as well as on economic rights (income generation). They also provided a face and a base for establishing a survivor perspective in the global conversation about Bhopal and about industrial disasters in general. However, like many of India's poor, as Fortun notes in her work on Bhopal advocacy, "most Union women never expected to be provided for by the state in a positive sense. Nor, however, did they expect a relationship with the state by way of the negative. Insufficiency could be lived quietly. Asphyxiation could not."[39] Rights, particularly rights guaranteed by the state, were not something presumed by the survivors. But beginning with their rights as laborers, women responded to the progressive promises and

Rashida Bi and Champa Devi Shukla address the women in their union, Bhopal Gas Peedit Mahila Stationery Karmachari Sangh, at a meeting in their stationery producing workshop in 2004 (Sambhavna Documentation Center).

failures of the government by identifying and demanding their rights—as gas survivors, Indians, and humans. Eventually, through the unions and the education provided by their contact with government bureaucracies, outside activists, and other chemically affected communities, their demands expanded from labor to rehabilitation, justice, compensation, medical care, safe environment, and, finally, to global corporate accountability.

However, the path has been necessarily indirect. Women activists in Bhopal not only had to overcome obstacles of health, socioeconomic status, and lack of information, but also had to deal with basic issues of gender rights. The BGPMUS took on a male convener, Abdul Jabbar, because his gender granted him more freedom of movement. He was also literate, and so he became their representative, framing their meetings and directing protests—the first of the many layers of translation and mediation that the women's message would often have to pass through to reach its target.[40]

Although the Bhopal survivors' movement is not exclusively made of women, its pre-dominately female composition has framed its techniques. In India, male police officers cannot touch women. A separate police force of female officers is required to subdue a women's protest physically, and these officers are often not as rigorously trained or quick to use violence as their male counterparts. Similarly, female protesters have been consistently underestimated in terms of their ability to cause damage. Their strength and spontaneity, in fact, have become legendary. A knack for overwhelming the police, comfort with the aggressive edge of "nonviolence," an ability consistently to surprise, and an eye for the visually symbolic — in particular, gendered symbols and weapons — are all characteristic of their techniques.

Spontaneously walking 700 kilometers is one example. On June 1, 1989, seventy-five women from the BGPMSKS began walking from Bhopal to Delhi. They were demanding regularized factory salaries and wages in the stationery workshop where they had been trained to produce paper products. They had just discovered the stipulations of the Factories Act and the Minimum Wages Act, and were determined to receive their legal due for their work. Having failed to secure jobs at the legal pay rate, they decided to walk to Delhi to meet the prime minister, Rajiv Gandhi.

They didn't know where Delhi was or how to get there. They decided to go, although they had not arranged for food and shelter along the way. They did not have the where-withal to notify either the press or the prime minister's office of their journey. When they arrived in New Delhi, after a long march filled with hardships, they did not have funds to stay there and did not know how to contact the prime minister. After making inquiries, they were told that the prime minister was away for the weekend and would then be traveling for ten days. Suresh Pachauri, the minister from their own state, came and assured them if they returned home, matters would be resolved. He promised to take care of their case personally and get their demands met. With the minister's assurance, the women decided to return home.

The promises were not kept. A while later, Gandhi visited Bhopal to address a public meeting. The women forced their way in, despite attempts by the police to stop them. They interrupted the meeting and told the prime minister their grievances and their story. In the end, they were victorious. Today, these one hundred workers earn salaries of around 2000 rupees each (about 50 dollars) on a fixed basis in the paper press. In this case, the survivors walked to Delhi with no support and no media attention. They had no channels through which to gain access to those in power. It was only through their trademark forcefulness and with a bit of luck that their demand (simple enforcement of the law) was met. Their experience and reception contrast starkly with the 2006 *padyatra,* or protest, that many of the same women joined.

Other examples echo these dynamics. After the announcement of the government's 1989 settlement with the UCC, hundreds of people jumped illegally onto trains bound for New Delhi and spontaneously trashed the UCC offices in rage. A witness describes policemen running from crowds of women armed with chili pepper and jumping on passing buses to escape. As I've noted, on each anniversary of the disaster, survivors and activists burn effigies of the corporation, the government, or Warren Anderson, or some combination thereof. Bhopali activists have been twice sued by Dow for "disrupting business" by protesting outside their Mumbai offices. Hunger strikes have been levied effectively by activists seeking attention to gas victim's demands. And as they have organized, Bhopal's victims have purposely relabeled themselves. They are now *survivors.*

The BGPMVS met every Saturday in a park off Hamida Road to retell their stories. They had not been able to tell them in court, and so weekly they told their stories to each other, sharing and solidifying the injustice of their ordeals and expounding on theories of responsibility. In the speeches they gave each week, they connected their experience to global systems and powers, as Brian Mooney has discussed in his dissertation "The Bhopal Disaster: Discourse and Narrative in the Ethnography of an Event." But what would happen once the civil-compensation case ended? Mooney quotes a survivor he spoke with during the period when the government was dispensing the UCC compensation money who, in discussing fading graffiti that said "Hang Warren Anderson," noted that "the graffiti is fading—we're fading."[41] Mooney attributes this sentiment to the palliative effect of the compensation money, and, temporarily, perhaps, this was true. The government succeeded in closing most of the workshops that served as the BGPMVS bases once the compensation was disbursed.

However, the UCC settlement was a huge blow to both morale and organization. Some interim relief had been procured as a result of activist work, criminal charges were crucially reinstated in 1991, and the government was forced to pledge support to the survivors in lieu of the corporation. But despite the creative and energetic work of survivors groups, the most important battles seemed to have been lost during that period. Since 1996, however, the stakes seem to be slowly changing as a new configuration of Bhopal activists has emerged. When the legal battle appeared to be over, the government and the corporation consolidated their positions and attempted to forget all about it. The government unceremoniously stopped counting gas deaths in 1992, although evidence shows that approximately twenty persons still die each month as a result of exposure. The UCC, on the other hand, slowly evaporated. Although their Indian assets, including the factory site, had been attached by the Bhopal District Court pending the resolution of the criminal case, Justice A. M. Ahmadi (who later became the trustee of the Bhopal Medical Trust, set up by the UCC) allowed the UCC to transfer their shares in 1994. Having disposed of its assets, the UCC then split its Asian sections into several subsidiaries under different names and finally, in 2002, the parent company in the United States was absorbed as a fully owned subsidiary of the Dow Chemical Company.

On the ground, this period was a time for regrouping, strategizing, and often for disagreeing. The faces of the movement began to shift: the pitched and creative protests that the organizations were known for needed much greater infrastructural support once the civil case in India was closed. The survivors' organizations and their support groups began to change in the face of the continuing need to generate new and alternative protest formats, scientific and medical data, and media messages. The use of new technologies for networking, the involvement of new generations of activists in India and abroad, and, of course, the continuing and increasingly inexcusable crisis on the ground — now including water contamination — would all become crucial to this evolution.

NETWORKS

Hundreds of outsiders, individuals, and organizations arrived to help with relief work in the chaos of the immediate aftermath of the gas disaster. Confusion ruled the day. Doctors had no information about how to treat the thousands of victims filling the hospitals, and no one knew for certain how far the gas had traveled. The UCC refused to release the studies they had done on MIC's effects on living systems. Immediately, the divisions between relief, justice, and research work became treacherous. What was most important, and who got to decide?

INFORMATION AND TRANSLATION

As I have mentioned, most of the first initiatives for justice and rehabilitation were spearheaded by middle-class, leftist Indian activists from outside Bhopal. In terms of class and background, these activists had more in common with the government functionaries or corporate officers they were fighting against than they did with the poor and working-class victims for whom they were fighting. Some had their own political agendas. They frequently miscommunicated with, stereotyped, and discriminated against the victims. The organizations that immediately formed to advocate for the victims were rarely comprised of victims or had them in positions of power. All of the groups formed by activists and led by volunteers who were not gas-affected collapsed within two years due to political disagreements and internal conflicts, including the most influential group, known as the Morcha.

However, these activists were fluent in the many idioms of this truly international disaster. They were capable, crucially, of engaging on the many fronts on which the Bhopal battle was fought: in at least two countries; with many types of expertise; against corporate, governmental, and media targets; in several languages, particularly English; and using the concepts and terms of science, medicine, technology, and law. The Bhopal Group for Information and Action (BGIA) formed in 1986 to address the contradictions inherent in having outsiders speak *for* the survivors.[42] Formed from the wreckage of Morcha, it searched for ways to assist the nascent survivors' groups with translation, research, and documentation needs, and was conceived of as a volunteer organization of activists that could interpret and mediate between Bhopal and the rest of the world.

The normal differential in power between a large multinational corporation and poor communities such as the *bastis* in Bhopal is huge. However, the technological aspect of this unprecedented chemical exposure made the divide much more radical in the case of Bhopal. No one knew what the consequences would be for long-term health. It was expected that doctors and scientists would determine the scope of the damage, but neither the Indian government nor the UCC had any interest in producing a balanced assessment, and the private sector could not take up the slack for such a large problem. Survivors would need to develop their own experts, and the BGIA did its best to facilitate this. Its activists tried to bridge (though always inadequately, in its own estimation) the legal, research, and media divides between the survivors and the objects of their activism: the Indian government and the Dow/UCC. But neither the UCC nor the government has appreciated having activists capable of doing this work. In 1986, for example, they arrested three BGIA activists for tape-recording the proceedings of a (public) meeting of doctors on the status of health in Bhopal. The activists were accused of being "Carbide agents," and all of the medical and legal documentation their offices had collected was confiscated and destroyed. Despite many setbacks such as this, their consistent intervention, particularly in the legal realm, has been crucial.

INTERNATIONAL ALLIES

The BGIA (although not the only support group) became, over the years, the primary contact and entry point for international activist involvement in the Bhopal issue. International involvement, however, dates back to the disaster. Around the world, people were shocked, not only by the suffering in Bhopal, but also by the potential parallels to it in their own backyards. The slogan "We all live in Bhopal," coined by George Bradford in 1985, attempted to universalize the implications of Bhopal — we are all responsible for Bhopal, and we are all (potential) victims of "a Bhopal." Fortun notes that the environmental legislation and regulatory requirements enacted in the United States in the late 1980s were often referred to as "Bhopal's Babies," legislation that made industrial manufacturing in the United States safer as a result of the Bhopal disaster's lessons.[43] Foreign actors, moved by both the specific and the universal elements of the story, offered connections to a wider network, access to communication technologies, and resources. Mostly consisting of a small core of committed individuals from the United States and the UK, they have worked over the years to create alternatives to the national and international legal and medical infrastructures that have chronically failed to accommodate the realities on the ground.

The convening of a Permanent Peoples' Tribunal (PPT) session on Industrial and Environmental Hazards and Human Rights in 1992 was one such effort. It was an attempt to address the inadequacy of the legal response to the Bhopal disaster, by providing an alternative forum for the articulation of justice. In the PPT session, survivors could finally testify about their experiences. In the medical arena, as a result of PPT recommendations, the International Medical Commission on Bhopal (IMCB) was formed, visiting Bhopal in 1994 just as the government was prematurely closing the studies begun by the ICMR. The IMCB was a group of independent doctors who attempted to assess the scope of the damage ten years after the gas leak. Its investigations highlighted the inattention of groups like the World Health Organization to the world's worst industrial disaster. The medical commission issued its report in 1994 noting, among other things, that "Bhopal's current, hospital-based delivery of health care is inappropriate for the chronic nature of the disease," which necessitates consistent and accessible community-based care and monitoring, rather than crisis based hospital infrastructure.[44] However, due to internal conflicts and the overwhelming scale of the problems, the IMCB soon disbanded. While it flagged the inappropriate nature of the health-care work being done in Bhopal, as a nongovernmental group of volunteers, it did not have the resources or power to correct the problem.

The International Campaign for Justice in Bhopal (ICJB), a coalition of survivors and local and international activists, emerged in its current form in the late 1990s — though several more diffuse and smaller international networks with similar names had existed over the years. There are several crucial differences, however, between the ICJB and its predecessors. First, the ICJB formalized an internal structure that included survivors' groups, a refreshing inversion of the earlier history of the movement, when activists of all kinds struggled with the problem of how to represent those on the ground. The ICJB thus consists of groups and individuals abroad who coordinate with four

The Permanent People's Tribunal, convened in Bhopal in 1991, was one of the first major international efforts to provide alternative forums for justice in Bhopal (Sambhavna Documentation Center).

survivors' groups in Bhopal, with the BGPMSKS as convener. Another crucial difference is the ICJB's ability, over the last ten years, to finally raise funds to pay for several full-time international campaigners, allowing it to work more quickly than groups depending on weary volunteers. While the ICJB, in its many forms, has always been important to Bhopal, these two innovations, along with the expanding technological opportunities provided by the Internet, have increased the organization's impact and effectiveness.

The ICJB maintains an unbending anticorporate stance in accordance with the wishes of the survivors' groups, which has impeded some efforts at collaboration with more moderate corporate-reform groups. Part of developing this network has been reaching out internationally to many different types of organizations. This has meant making connections with other grassroots and labor groups. (One of the ICJB's predecessors, the International Coalition for Justice in Bhopal, organized a tour by several survivors of the disaster through Japan, Holland, Ireland, and the United States — a "toxic tour" of meetings with other affected communities.) It has also meant allying with trade unions in many countries and creating networks of chemically affected groups in Asia. More recently, it has meant forging alliances with some very high-profile advocacy groups, such as Greenpeace and Amnesty International.

While entry into each of these networks has positively affected the ability of the Bhopal survivors to reach different audiences, it has also reframed their issues in some cases. Greenpeace, for example, concentrates on the water and soil contamination problem (where its work has been crucial), rather than on health, justice, or economic rehabilitation, in order to fit the organization's environmental aims. It has also come into conflict with campaign groups because its centralized command structure and overriding concern with media representation has at times prevented its representatives on the ground from participating in actions that the survivors considered crucial and pressing. Similarly, Amnesty International interprets Bhopal as a human-rights issue. Though its research is excellent, its interpretation of the legal and humanitarian violations that constitute the disaster weighs heavily on analyses of the international agreements and human-rights treaties to which India is signatory, and on the official channels that are only one aspect of the work done by the activist groups. Bhopal is both an international issue and a local one, and as such, the relationship between the Bhopalis and these international advocacy groups is mutually beneficial and also inherently fraught with the problems of translation, differing priorities, and issues of representation that we have examined. What is more important, cleaning up the factory, criminal justice, or economic rehabilitation? Is the Bhopal disaster best served by a rhetoric of pure victimization, the face of a dead child being buried (long the archetypal image of Bhopal), chants of "flames, not flowers," (as some chant), or by a photo of women warriors on a campaign to "jhadoo maro Dow ko" (hit Dow with a broom)?

Today, the ICJB campaigns on both local issues — contaminated water, police brutality, court battles — and global issues such as corporate accountability, environmental standards, and the safety of others affected by Bhopal. It is bolstered by a burgeoning student movement called Students for Bhopal (SFB), made up of about seventy chapters in the United States and close to twenty more around the world. The SFB functions as an arm of the ICJB, but many of its activists are younger than the gas disaster, newly incensed that the Bhopalis have been waiting their whole lives for justice. SFB's work includes campaigns to force universities to disinvest from Dow Chemical and agitation at Indian embassies in the United States. Another crucial network that supports the ICJB is the Association for India's Development (AID), a lively network of students and professionals of Indian origin with seventy chapters in the United States and twenty more around the world. A recent example of a joint ICJB campaign was, Neend Udaoo (Drive Sleep Away), which involved women from various communities in Bhopal banging on pots and pans outside the homes of uncooperative local officials at night while international allies in other time zones woke officials with phone calls at odd hours. (There were even accounts that female supporters abroad were calling the homes of bureaucrats at night and giving the wives of these uncooperative officials false impressions about their marital fidelity.)

International support gave the survivors' groups and the BGIA the leverage to create the 2006 *padyatra,* the march from Bhopal to Delhi, a protest on many fronts and with widespread impact. Fax actions, relay hunger strikes, active Web sites with rich online archives, connections to many other movements, and the aggressive student campaign are just some of the tools that have supercharged the work of the survivors' groups. Daily blogging and photo updates from volunteers walking alongside the *padyatris* allowed thousands around the world to track the daily troubles and victories of the marchers. Meanwhile, the message they brought to other contamination-affected communities along the march route was a global one, calling attention to the rights of these communities in the face of corporations such as Coca-Cola and Hindustan Petroleum. One American in Texas, Diane Wilson (famous for her own environmental battles), launched an indefinite hunger strike in April to put pressure on the Indian prime minister. And when Bollywood superstar Aamir Khan visited the Delhi protest site to show support, Champa Devi Shukla took Khan to task for his sponsorship of Coca-Cola, given the corporation's behavior in the state of Madhya Pradesh. (Shukla had lost her husband and both her sons to the gas; one daughter also became paralyzed, and her granddaughter was born with no palate or upper lip.) On April 15, 2006, the Calcutta *Telegraph* reported that Khan was "tak[ing] up the [pollution] issue with Coke" as a result of his conversation with Shukla.[45]

CORPORATE ACCOUNTABILITY

On February 6, 2001, the UCC became a fully owned subsidiary of the Dow Chemical Company, the largest chemical company in the world. However, this did not diffuse the campaign to get the UCC to take responsibility for the Bhopal disaster. Rather, this merger strengthened the Bhopal movement by uniting it with a growing network of other groups victimized by Dow. Bhopalis now stood in solidarity with the Agent Orange victims of Vietnam (including U.S. veterans), with Nemagon victims from Nicaragua, and with dioxin-affected communities at Dow's headquarters in Midland, Michigan, just to name a few. This has opened new frontiers for Bhopal, as well as for other groups. Lawyers have challenged Dow over Bhopal by filings with the U.S. Securities and Exchange Commission, alleging that Dow misrepresented the UCC's liabilities when it purchased UCC. Shareholders have introduced resolutions at the Dow annual general meeting calling for it to resolve the Bhopal liabilities (the resolution received 6.3 percent of the vote in 2006). Activists have delivered "Bhopal water" to the homes of Dow trustees and have developed a knack for humiliating both Dow trustees and CEOs. In at least three recent cases, officials have resigned within weeks after being humiliated. Most recently, Harold Shapiro, a Dow board member and Princeton faculty member, resigned the day after his university office was deluged with faxes implicating him personally in the suffering of the Bhopalis.

The recent accomplishments of the *padyatris* and their allies are highly significant. Their demands in 2006 are not all that different from those the survivors' organizations and the BGIA made to the government in the wake of the 1991 settlement review. But their ability to exert pressure on the government and to provide the necessary data to back up their claims has finally become significant enough — fifteen years later — to guarantee their victory. The momentum of a number of important victories won since the ICJB regrouped has also been very important, and many of these victories have significance beyond Bhopal, in the greater realm of corporate accountability. In January 2005, the Bhopal court issued a summons to Dow USA (whose subsidiaries do business in India), asking why it could not present the absconder, the UCC, to the Bhopal court. Activist pressure in 2005 motivated the Indian Oil Company (a state-owned industry) to cancel a multimillion-dollar technology purchase contract with Dow that summer. The Indian Oil Company justified its withdrawal on the grounds that Dow had misled it: the proprietary technology in question had not been developed by Dow, but rather by the absconding corporation, the UCC. Autonomously, on the twentieth anniversary of the Bhopal disaster, the Yes Men, a media-activist duo, impersonated Dow on the BBC international television news channel, taking full responsibility for Bhopal, causing temporary panic and lasting anxiety among shareholders and corporate officials, and helping reinstate Bhopal as a contemporary concern, particularly in the United States.

Dow appears to be very threatened by the ICJB. The company is the largest user of the ICJB Web site (www.bhopal.net). It pays Google for advertising links to any Internet reference to Bhopal, sending users to www.bhopal.com, the corporation's version of the Bhopal events. In 2003, Dow conducted a drill outside one of its New Jersey factories in which peaceful Bhopal protesters turned out to be "terrorists" who stormed the factory and were subsequently "killed" by the police, a maneuver that earned them the *Multinational Monitor*'s facetious Lawrence Summers Memorial Award.[46] In 2004, Dow hired the public-relations firm Burson-Marsteller to assist it in coping with the Bhopal issue.

The UCC's Web site (which disappeared at the time of the merger) suddenly reemerged, along with a specious identity as a semiseparate entity. Primarily a vehicle for "Union Carbide's" statement about Bhopal, it simultaneously functions to deflect attention from Dow and to reiterate their position that Bhopal is long over. As they state, "In the wake of the release, Union Carbide Corporation worked diligently to provide immediate and continuing aid to the victims and set up a process to resolve their claims. All claims arising out of the release were settled sixteen years ago at the explicit direction and with the approval of the Supreme Court of India."[47] An article in *Forbes* magazine titled "Dow's Pocket Has a Hole" commented: "Is there no end to the legal liability a corporation incurs for making chemicals? There probably is no end, indeed, and the sickly stock price of Dow Chemical, at 26 dollars down 13 percent so far this year, is testimony to the problem. Dow made the mistake in February 2001 of buying Union Carbide, the company that owned 51 percent of an operation in India that suffered a catastrophic poison gas leak in 1984 in Bhopal."[48]

Just as Bhopal has haunted its survivors, so too, it seems, will it continue to haunt the corporation(s) that caused it. Although Prime Minister Manmohan Singh — even as he granted his recent bonanza of requests to the survivors — refused to pursue any "extralegal" options in going after Dow or the UCC, many legal options remain open, not least the criminal prosecution of the UCC in the Bhopal courts. Meanwhile, government officials have reported that they have been in conversation with Dow on the subject of the UCC factory. Dow officials, concerned about legal liability, do not want to pay for the cleanup of the UCC site as a result of any legal pressure, but have expressed interest in paying for the cleanup via a nongovernmental organization or foundation of some kind as a "charitable gesture." Survivors' groups say that's fine, as long as Dow is paying for the cleanup. Meanwhile, the U.S.-based Cherokee Corporation wants to clean up the site with corporate donations and World Bank funds in what may be a preliminary strike against the possibility of a precedent-setting action in which UCC/Dow might be forced to follow the principle that the "polluter pays" — a precedent that wouldn't be good for any multinational corporation. Cherokee, known for similar cleanup operations in the United States, teamed up with the chairman of the Madhya Pradesh Pollution Control Board, Dr. P. S. Dubey, and brought him to Duke University in June 2006 to discuss Cherokee's plans for Bhopal. In addition to the pollution control board's obvious neglect of the contamination issue in Bhopal, the BGIA and survivors' groups have also unearthed evidence of Dubey's improper financial dealings and his conduct during a botched "cleanup" effort in 2005 (which churned chemical waste into the air and sent dozens of local residents to the hospital), evidence that illustrates Dubey's general indifference to the health of survivors. The ICJB learned of Dubey's appearance at Duke University from the Association for India's Development network, and a team of activists arrived in time to heckle Dubey for his neglect and poor performance. (By the end, Cherokee was distancing itself from its star, while in Bhopal, the BGIA had already approached Dubey's boss about why he wasn't at work.) With confrontations like this flaring up all around the world, the stage is set for the next big battle, and the Bhopal survivors may yet curb global corporate misbehavior. However, the question is no longer "Will there be a cleanup?" but rather "Will Dow and the UCC be forced to accept liability for the site?"

In 1992, the Indian government stopped counting gas deaths, and in 1996, the Sambhavna Trust Clinic and Documentation Centre opened.[49] Its first project was to begin what it called "verbal autopsies," which commenced recording oral histories from family members about the circumstances of the decline and death of their loved ones. This was the first of many ways in which Sambhavna challenges the obfuscatory techniques employed by the government in the wake of the disaster. Satinath Sarangi, the BGIA activist who founded Sambhavna, had organized many clinics, particularly in the immediate aftermath of the disaster. None lasted more than a few months either because of government intervention and arrests, as in a few cases, or more generally, because they depended on volunteer labor and had no consistent funding source. Funding has always been a thorny issue in Old Bhopal, a neighborhood victimized by the only foreign entity (UCC) that ever significantly invested in it. Taking government money would be counterproductive to producing alternatives to the government models, and corporate or foundation money usually comes with invisible strings (not to mention the distrust with which such funds are regarded by many of the Bhopalis that could be served by them).

Fortuitously, in 1996 Sarangi met a British adman who had been working with Amnesty International. He said he could raise money from ordinary, newspaper-reading people in the UK through fundraising ads. Sarangi said he would use the money to start Sambhavna, and he put together a trust for that purpose. The idea behind Sambhavna is that medical care must be connected to initiatives in community health, research, and documentation, because community involvement and information are necessary if exposure is to be *healed,* rather than simply treated. The trust, responding to the unscientific, unsympathetic, and palliative treatment that survivors received in government hospitals, presents alternative care and measures the outcomes of treatment. Patients (affected by gas and water contamination) can choose between rational allopathic treatment, traditional Indian Ayurvedic treatment, or yoga and *pranayama* (yogic breathing techniques) as forms of treatment. A thorough registration process allows the clinic to track the health of their patients (since, as we have noted, shockingly, none of the government hospitals or the corporate hospitals keep accessible records of their patients), as well as the efficacy of different treatments for different complaints. Nearly 16 thousand people have so far registered, and many receive long-term care at the clinic, which is within walking distance of the most severely affected *bastis.*

As Sambhavna treats more patients, as more patients come to prefer Sambhavna's treatment to the government options, and as the clinic's documentation refutes claims

राजश्री 10324

यूनियन कार्बाइड के जहरीले रसायनों से पीडितों के लिए

स्वास्थ्य पुस्तिका
HEALTH BOOK
FOR PEOPLE POISONED BY UNION CARBIDE'S CHEMICALS

सम्भावना ट्रस्ट क्लिनिक
SAMBHAVNA TRUST CLINIC

बाफना कालोनी, बैरसिया रोड
भोपाल (म.प्र.) – 462001

Bafna Colony, Berasia Road,
Bhopal (M.P.) – 462001

☎ : 0755-2730914, 2743157

The Sambhavna Clinic tracks the health of each patient with the goal of improving the long-term quality of life, and provides each patient with a copy of their medical reports.

that the crisis has ended, its existence increasingly challenges the government's standards of care.[50] Also, in part because of their use of a fundraising model that depends on connecting with individuals through published appeals, the clinic has developed an international following and volunteer base. International volunteers of all stripes bring skills to the clinic and take away a passion for the issues it raises and the people it serves.

In 2004, Champa Devi Shukla and Rashida Bi of the BGPMSKS were awarded the prestigious Goldman Award (known as the "Green Nobel prize") for their activism. With their prize money, they established the Chingari Trust, a foundation to sponsor the medical or surgical care of children born to parents exposed to gas. The trust awarded fellowships to woman activists fighting corporate crime, and has a scholarship program for gas-affected children. Along with six other organizations, the trust also sponsors a people's museum to commemorate the disaster. Joined in the trust by Sambhavna and a number of other support and survivors' groups, Bi and Shukla finally have the opportunity

Rashida Bi and Champa Devi Shukla won the Goldman Award in 2004, putting Bhopal activism back on the map internationally (Goldman Foundation).

to take a leadership role in pursuing economic and social rehabilitation, as well as in commemorating the Bhopal disaster and its survivors. Memorialization has been a charged issue for a long time: government neglect has competed with the occasional delirious plan conceived by the state to turn the factory into a disaster amusement park. (The latest ideas include encasing the UCC plant in glass, with human dummies operating it.) The survivors want memorialization, but on their own terms. Having finally won a concession from the prime minister in April 2006 that requires that survivors be included in any belated commemorative projects, perhaps they'll finally get the memorial they want, even if it is twenty-two years too late.

CONCLUSION

The UCC brought in technologies and chemistries that even they admitted were unproven and poorly understood. These technologies were installed in India in contravention of Indian laws because the Indian government wanted foreign corporations to raise the bar on technological development in India under pressure from the World Bank, the U.S. government, and U.S. corporations that were driving the so-called Green Revolution. Disaster struck because both the Indian government and the UCC were willing to treat safety as a dispensable concern in the Bhopal factory project. The aftermath became long, grueling, and explosive because neither party was willing to establish any precedent that might change or challenge the priorities that caused the disaster. Although the government stated at the time that their response to Bhopal would constitute "a model for future disasters," it has in fact been exemplary only in its ability to avoid the problem.[51]

What is particularly painful and disappointing about Bhopal is that an astute pessimist, familiar with the situation on the ground, could have foreseen it all: the disaster; the refusal of the United States to resolve it legally; the limitations of the Indian judicial system; the victims being robbed of legal power; the Indian government's selling out to the UCC; and the neglect and suspicion that have characterized the relief efforts. It is a sad, appalling story, but it is not a terribly surprising one. Around the world, it is most often the poor and the powerless who suffer as a result of industrial accidents or environmental contamination, and most of their stories will never be heard. Those in Bhopal have been lucky, at least, that the magnitude of the disaster was undeniable and that Indian democracy requires that justice must appear to have been done. Surprisingly, the Bhopalis have managed to expand the definition of the disaster imposed by the government and corporation, and their movement for justice has become, nearly twenty-two years later, "a sure-footed and able-bodied movement in the prime of its youth, poised with the stamina required to carry on the fight until justice is done."[52]

Bhopal activism, at its best, has centered on representing Bhopal as a continuing disaster that challenges truisms about poverty, health, justice, and the tolerated parameters of corporate behavior. Effective campaigns aside, however, Bhopal remains in crisis. Initiatives such as those carried out by Sambhavna and the PPT can function only as examples and possibilities; they cannot replace functioning international and national structures. The prime minister's recent promises are the best sign yet for a lasting resolution to Bhopal's problems, but they are still only promises. Bhopal groups have struggled to prevent the elimination of their tenuously evolving rights by developing broad-based support across borders and by constantly challenging the Indian government both to stand up to its proclaimed responsibility to the gas survivors and to place some of that responsibility on Dow/UCC, where it belongs. In this long, sad story, hope is greater than ever before that both of these possibilities will be realized.

Bhopal is both exceptional and exemplary, sadly reflected (on differing scales) in the experiences of millions of people worldwide. It is therefore crucial to understand the problems that have become explicit in the varied responses to the Bhopal gas disaster, because a sophisticated balancing of these tensions remains necessary to the conception of permanent solutions. First, the inadequacy of government and corporate responses helped stimulate a now global discourse of rights within (particularly female) survivors' groups, transforming their own sense of entitlements and enabling them to focus their resilience, savvy, and rage on global targets that embody injustice and impunity. Second, in attempting to surmount, under great duress, the extremity of the structural inequalities that constituted (and, it could be argued, caused) the disaster, survivors and activists have found themselves alternately caught within these structural frameworks and singularly liberated to change and subvert them through democratic processes. The problems and rewards of translation between cultures and classes, and the subversion of legal and scientific bodies have marked Bhopal as a locus for global innovation in communication, community health, and activism. Finally, Bhopal survivors and activists have refigured the terms of engagement on both chemical and corporate issues, forcibly and constantly refuting government and corporate efforts to define the continuing catastrophe as a discrete "event," and effectively strengthening and rearticulating demands against Dow and the UCC precisely at the moments when they attempt to dissolve their responsibility and liability.

The recent capitulation of the Indian government to all of the substantive demands for support and services put forth by the 2006 *padyatris* may mark the end of a period of denial about the costs of development in India, a period that began well before the gas disaster, when the UCC planned its "unproven" factory and the landless Bhopalis swelled to meet its walls. Although this article has focused mainly on the relationship between the Indian government and survivors of the Bhopal disaster, the story of the corporate and international pressures that helped cause the chemical and environmental disaster in Bhopal is an equally important one, but one that remains to be told. Corporations continue to be poorly regulated and are characteristically opaque, while the underlying aims of the World Bank and the U.S. government are also difficult to track in a country such as India. Tracking them has not been my purpose here, but neither has it been to lay the final blame for this continuing tragedy at the doorstep of the Indian government alone. Instead, I have tried to note the interactions between the government and its constituents that have arisen from the Bhopal disaster and to point out both the opportunities and limitations that activists face in attempting to put pressure on corporations or governments beyond their own borders.

Bhopal illustrates the consequences of a model for progress and a global system in which governments prefer picking up the (potentially endless) costs of remediating an industrial disaster rather than taking action against its perpetrators. As a result of activist pressure, the Indian government seems finally to be acknowledging that development has a cost and that they will end up paying for it if they cannot adequately regulate foreign actors. It remains an open question whether the activism around Bhopal, the tenacity of the survivors, or the outrage of their supporters can bring about a sea change in international justice, environmental policy, or corporate accountability. Similarly, whether the Indian government will continue to turn a blind eye toward multinational corporations at the expense of the poor or vulnerable is also an open question, although a question suddenly clearly visible to everyone, including the prime minister. Dow Chemical, meanwhile, poised to accelerate a major expansion of its operations in India, is encountering a bit more resistance than the UCC found when it arrived many years ago. Regardless of Dow's enormous power as the largest chemical company in the world, the Bhopal survivors will ensure that from now on, nothing goes unnoticed about its actions in India and beyond.

Many thanks to Satinath Sarangi for all his help on this article. For more information about the Bhopal campaign, please visit www.bhopal.net.

1   Amnesty International, *Clouds of Injustice: Bhopal Disaster 20 Years On* (London: Amnesty International Publications, 2004), p. 12. A complete copy of the report is available in PDF online at http://web.amnesty.org/library/Index/ENGA SA200152004?open&of=ENG-IND.

2   UCC, internal memorandum (excerpt), December 2, 1973, UCC 04206. Many excerpts from UCC documents, which were obtained and published during the discovery phases of law-suits brought against the UCC, and documents seized by the Central Bureau of Investigation (CBI) from Union Carbide India Ltd. are available online at International Campaign for Justice in Bhopal, http://bhopal.net/oldsite/poisonpapers.html and www.bhopal.net/oldsite/citations-full.html.

3   UCC, internal memorandum (excerpt), July 21, 1972, UCC 04129.

4   Joshua Karliner, *India: Setting the Record Straight. A Conversation with Edward A. Munoz, former Managing Director of Union Carbide India, Ltd,* VHS. (Oakland, CA: CorpWatch, 1994). Transcript of the interview available online at Corp-Watch, www.corpwatch.org/article.php?id=11735.

5   Himanshu Rajan Sharma, "Proof from Carbide Itself: Interview with Himanshu Rajan Sharma, U.S.-based Attorney," *Frontline* (India), December 21, 2002. Available online at www.frontline.in/fl1926/stories/20030103003809800.htm. Sharma is the U.S.-based attorney representing Bhopal plaintiffs in a suit brought against the UCC in the Southern District Court of New York.

6   Amnesty International, *Clouds of Injustice,* p. 44. See also T. R. Chouhan et al., *Bhopal, the Inside Story: Carbide Workers Speak Out on the World's Worst Industrial Disaster,* new ed. (Mapusa, India: Other India Press; New York: Apex Press, 2005).

7   See Rajkumar Keswani, "Bhopal, Sitting at the Edge of a Volcano," in Bridget Hanna, Ward Morehouse, and Satinath Sarangi (eds.), *The Bhopal Reader: Remembering Twenty Years of the World's Worst Industrial Disaster* (New York: Apex Press, 2005), p. 14.

8   Suketu Mehta, "Bhopal Lives," *Village Voice,* December 3, 1996.

9   Amnesty International, *Clouds of Injustice,* p. 5.

10 Kim Fortun, *Advocacy after Bhopal: Environmentalism, Disaster, New Global Orders* (Chicago: University of Chicago Press, 2001), pp. 161–62.

11 Dominique Lapierre and Javier Moro, *Five Past Midnight in Bhopal: The Epic Story of the World's Deadliest Industrial Disaster* (New York: Warner Books, 2002), p. 376.

12 Amnesty International, *Clouds of Injustice,* pp. 1 and 12.

13 Himanshu Rajan Sharma, "Catastrophe and the Dilemma of Law," *Seminar* 544 (December 2004), p. 21.

14 *Ibid.*

15 Amnesty International, *Clouds of Injustice,* p. 61.

16 Veena Das, *Critical Events: An Anthropological Perspective on Contemporary India* (Delhi: Oxford University Press, 1995), p. 155.

17 *Ibid.,* p. 162.

18 *Ibid.,* p. 159.

19 *Ibid.,* p. 158.

20 Praful Bidwai, quoted in Claude Alvarez, "Ten Years Later," in Chouhan et al., *Bhopal, the Inside Story,* p. 126.

21 Fortun, *Advocacy after Bhopal,* p. 45

22 Ingrid Eckerman, *The Bhopal Saga: Causes and Consequences of the World's Largest Industrial Disaster* (Hyderabad, India: Universities Press, 2005), p. 151.

23 UCC 04129.

24 UCC, telex, April 10, 1982, UCC 01736. A copy of this telex can be viewed online at International Campaign for Justice in Bhopal, www.bhopal.net/oldsite/excerpts.html.

25 Iryna Labunska, Anjela Stephenson, Kevin Brigden, Ruth Stringer, David Santillo, and Paul Johnston, *The Bhopal Legacy: Toxic Contaminants at the Former Union Carbide Factory Site, Bhopal, India, Fifteen Years After the Bhopal Accident* (Exeter, UK: Greenpeace Research Laboratories, 1999), p. 23.

26 Amnesty International, *Clouds of Injustice,* p. 24.

27 BGIA, *Interim Application before the High Court of Madhya Pradesh,* Writ Petition no. 2802/2004, August 11, 2005.

28 NEERI, *Assessment of Contaminated Areas Due to Past Waste Disposal Practices at EIIL* (Nagpur, India: NEERI, 1997), UCC 01099-01100.

29 C.K. Hayaran to A. Chakravarti, February 14, 1995, "Re: Disposal of Sevin and Naphthol Tar Residues Lying at Our Plant," UCC 02148, Sambhavna Trust Documentation Center, Bhopal, India.

30 The proceeds of this sale were used to set up the Bhopal Memorial Hospital Trust in the UK. Eventually these funds went toward building a huge, lavish specialty hospital in Bhopal, on the far outskirts of town. According to Vibha Varshney, "Sick Berth," *Down to Earth,* May 31, 2006, p. 42, the Bhopal Memorial Hospital and Research Centre, "built specifically for Bhopal gas victims…has become a centre for systematic discrimination against them"; it also has a reputation for money laundering that benefits senior doctors and trustees and for poor treatment of all of its other employees.

31 Sambhavna Trust Clinic, "Findings of Survey of Annu Nagar (Groundwater Contaminated), 2003," in Hanna et al., *The Bhopal Reader,* p. 156.

32 Ravi Aggarwal and Amit Nair, *Surviving Bhopal: Toxic Present, Toxic Past* (New Delhi: Fact Finding Mission on Bhopal, 2002). A PDF of the full report is available online at Fact Finding Mission on Bhopal, www.bhopalffm.org/Environment.htm.

33 The translation of these figures directly into dollars is complex, because the exchange rate has varied tremendously over the past twenty-two years. Currently, the exchange rate is about 46 rupees to a dollar, which would make the total amount spent approximately 26.6 million dollars. However, in 1984, the rate averaged 10 rupees to the dollar, and in 1990, about 20 rupees, with inflation climbing steadily since then. The figure given here is therefore likely much larger, because most of the money was spent during the late 1980s and the 1990s. However I do not have a definitive breakdown of these numbers.

34 Suroopa Mukherjee, "Twenty Years After: Anger and Denial on the Streets of Bhopal," *InfoChange Agenda,* December 2004, InfoChange News and Features, www.infochangeindia.org/agenda1.jsp.

35 Amnesty International, *Clouds of Injustice,* p. 18.

36 Satinath Sarangi (BGIA), in discussion with author, 2005–2006.

37 Fortun, *Advocacy after Bhopal,* p. 219.

38 There are, however, other important groups, such as Bhopal Gas Peedit Mahila Purush Sangharsh Morcha, led by Syed M. Irfan, a gas survivor, and Bhopal ki Aawaaz, a small organization of children orphaned by the disaster and led by Shaheed Noor, a gas orphan. Today, both of these organizations work with BGPMSKS and the ICJB, while BGPMUS primarily works autonomously.

39 Fortun, *Advocacy after Bhopal,* pp. 224–25.

40 For more on this topic, see Brian Mooney, "The Bhopal Disaster: Discourse and Narrative in the Ethnography of an Event," PhD diss., University of Michigan–Ann Arbor, 2002.

41 *Ibid.,* p. 167.

42 The processes and difficulties of translation between survivors and advocates is addressed in fascinating detail in Fortun, *Advocacy after Bhopal.*

43 *Ibid.,* p. 15.

44 Birger Heinzow, M.D., "Report of the International Medical Commission on Bhopal (1994)" in Hanna et al., *The Bhopal Reader,* p. 139.

45 "Enter: Aamir the Activist," Calcutta *Telegraph,* April 15, 2006, available online at www.telegraphindia.com/1060415/asp/frontpage/story_6102578.asp.

46 The *Multinational Monitor* explains the award as follows: "In a 1991 internal memorandum, then–World Bank economist Lawrence Summers argued for the transfer of waste and dirty industries from industrialized to developing countries. 'Just between you and me, shouldn't the World Bank be encouraging more migration of the dirty industries to the LDCs (lesser developed countries)?' wrote Summers, who went on to serve as Treasury Secretary during the Clinton administration…. 'I think the economic logic behind dumping a load of toxic waste in the lowest wage country is impeccable and we should face up to that…. I've always thought that under populated countries in Africa are vastly under polluted; their air quality is vastly inefficiently low [sic] compared to Los Angeles or Mexico City.' Summers later said the memo was meant to be ironic." See *Multinational Monitor,* "Lawrence Summers Memorial Award," available online at www.multinationalmonitor.org/mm2006/012006/front.html#LARENCE.

47 Union Carbide Corporation, Bhopal Information Center, www.bhopal.com (accessible via the "Bhopal Information" link at www.unioncarbide.com).

48 Phyllis Bergman, "Dow's Pocket Has a Hole," *Forbes,* March 13, 2003, p. 34, available online at www.forbes.com/forbes/2003/0331/078.html.

49 "Sambhavna" means "hope" or "possibility."

50 For example, a study by Sambhavna on the health of the children born after the disaster to gas-affected parents found significant growth retardation in boys. Boys were found to have smaller upper bodies and developmental difficulties, while girls had increased incidences of hormonal disorders. See Nishant Ranjan, Satinath Sarangi, V.T. Padmanabhan, Steve Holleran, Rajasekhar Ramakrishnan, and Daya R. Varma, "Methyl Isocyanate Exposure and Growth Patterns of Adolescents in Bhopal," *Journal of the American Medical Association* 290, no. 14 (2003), p. 1857.

51 Claude Alvares, "Ten Years Later," in Chouhan et al., *Bhopal, the Inside Story,* p. 133.

52 Nityanand Jayaraman, "Twenty Years Later," in Chouhan et al., *Bhopal, the Inside Story,* p. 158.

The Yes Men in Bhopal

Andy Bichlbaum, Mike Bonanno, and Satinath Sarangi
interviewed by Bridget Hanna

*Under the name the Yes Men, Andy Bichlbaum (**AB**) and Mike Bonanno (**MB**) have conducted a series of culture jamming activities, practicing what they call "identity correction." Pretending to be powerful people and spokespersons for prominent organizations, they use their new identities to express ideas that demonstrate the atrocities of many corporate and governmental organizations. The Yes Men have posed as spokespeople for the World Trade Organization, McDonald's, Dow Chemical, and the United States Department of Housing and Urban Development. Some of their exploits have been documented in the film* The Yes Men *and in the book called* The Yes Men: The True Story of the End of the World Trade Organization.

*Satinath Sarangi (**SS**) was finishing his PhD in metallurgical engineering in 1984 when the Union Carbide Corporation gas disaster occurred in Bhopal. He arrived two days later to assist with relief work and has never left. He played a crucial role in the founding of the survivors' support organization the Bhopal Group for Information and Action, and in the 1996 founding of the Sambhavna Trust Clinic, which provides free medical care to survivors and those affected by water contamination. Sambhavna also undertakes community health work while researching the long-term effects of the Bhopal gas exposure. Sarangi continues to provide medical and legal support for the people of Bhopal.*

On December 3, 2004, the twentieth anniversary of the Union Carbide Corporation (UCC)'s gas disaster in Bhopal, India, a spokesperson on the live television news program *BBC World* announced that Dow Chemical Company (now the owner of the UCC) was finally taking full responsibility for the catastrophe. The spokesman, Jude Finesterra, stated that $12 billion had been set aside for the victims and for site remediation. He told the news anchor that the UCC would be liquidated; Dow would fund any medical or scientific research on the effects of the gas; and the corporation would finally release its own scientific studies on methyl isocyanate, the gas that had leaked. Around the world, incredulous activists celebrated and Dow corporate officials panicked, stupefied. In Bhopal, there were tears of joy, celebration, and relief…for about an hour. Jude Finesterra (whose name alone should have given the BBC pause) was not a spokesman for Dow. He was a spokesman for the Yes Men.

The disaster in Bhopal, an issue as pressing twenty years later as it was in the immediate aftermath of the disaster, is unique. Not only was it the worst industrial accident in history but it has been fol-

lowed by a nearly unbelievable legacy of suffering and injustice. The Yes Men's hoax was also unique in the history of anticorporate activism. Their seven-minute television statement caused a temporary $2 billion drop in Dow's stock price, and, on the other side, had the potential to cause disappointment and frustration among the long-suffering survivors in Bhopal, who had no idea what was happening.

How did the Dow hoax happen? What were its implications in Bhopal? How has it changed the possibility of corporate accountability? On March 3, 2005, the Yes Men (Andy Bichlbaum and Mike Bonanno), Satinath Sarangi, and Bridget Hanna discussed the hoax for the first time.

How did each of you get involved with the Bhopal issue?

SS: I came to Bhopal a day after the disaster, in December 1984. Since then, I've been involved with a wide range of activities, mainly with the survivors' organizations. I've been involved with relief work, publicizing the situation in Bhopal, trying to get information from outside Bhopal to Bhopal people, doing research and documentation, and taking legal action. For the past eight years, I have been with the Sambhavna Clinic, which provides free care to Bhopal survivors and victims of contaminated groundwater. Along with survivors' organizations, I remain active in the campaign for justice in Bhopal.

AB: Well, for a number of years, we [the Yes Men] were involved in an anticorporate activism Web site called rtmark.com. We sponsored, encouraged, and publicized actions that had to do with exposing corporate misdeeds. As part of doing that, we started putting up these fake Web sites. One thing led to another, and we ended up with a Web site for George W. Bush [www.gwbush.com], a fake campaign site that got a lot of attention. And then somebody approached us with gatt.org, the fake WTO site that got more attention. Finally, some environmentalist friends we had met at a conference approached us with an idea to do a Web site about Dow, and that's how dowchemical.com [a satire of www.dow.com] — and eventually dowethics.com [after www.dowchemical.com was taken over by Dow] — happened. So one thing just led to another, and then we were doing this particular action.

MB: One interesting thing about this is that neither Andy nor I, as United States residents, had heard that the disaster site in Bhopal had not yet been cleaned up — at least not until these environmental activists approached us and said, "Let's put up a site against Dow." We became interested in it — with our history of anticorporate activism — because it's the biggest and most dramatic example of corporate misdeeds out there. It's the largest industrial accident in history. Since it still hasn't been cleaned up and people still haven't been adequately compensated, it's symbolic of a much larger problem. It [the Web site] was directly about getting Dow to accept some responsibility for Bhopal.

So the hoax came about when someone at the BBC carelessly mistook dowethics.com for the real Dow Chemical Company site and sent an e-mail to that site asking for Dow's comments on the twentieth anniversary of the Bhopal disaster. Mike and Andy, what were you thinking when you originally got the e-mail?

AB: Well, when we originally got the e-mail from the BBC, we immediately contacted the friends we'd been working with on dowethics.com for a while, and we strategized about what to do. We examined two choices; one was the one that we ended up taking, and the other was a much more brutal kind of truth telling. We thought that we would go on TV and say, from Dow's perspective, what they were really about. So it was either to say, "We're going to do everything right; we now understand that we should do this, that we should compensate people," or to say, "We have no obligation to the people; we only care about our shareholders. We're a company; our only obligation is to profit, so why would we do anything for the people in Bhopal?"

We decided together with our friends that the approach we actually ended up taking would make more waves, because Dow would have to go on record and deny it, and that would create a lot more media attention. The overall goal of this was to get media attention for the Bhopal anniversary in the United States, where, of course, most people still didn't know what was going on. A lot of people don't even know what Bhopal was. And many who do don't realize that the [factory] site still hasn't been cleaned up, that people still die from contamination of groundwater, and so on. So the idea was to get as many articles in the U.S. press as we possibly could. We all thought this was the best way to do it, to force Dow to really respond.

For a little while there was even some talk about contacting people in Bhopal and alerting them. But then a kind of communal decision arose, where we decided that this would be risky if somehow it got leaked. It would endanger the entire thing. So we decided, for better or for worse, not to do it.

What happened once you got to the newsroom to give the report? What was surprising?

MB: In a way, the whole thing was surprising. Initially getting the invitation, and then going, and then having it go out live — it was all surprising, the whole time. As far as the reactions went, we had anticipated that we would cause people some amount of grief, but we'd imagined that it would be minimal, because they'd make the correction quite quickly. So we went ahead with it anyway, because we decided that our goal as activists was to get attention for the issue and not to make friends, let's say.

So it was just shocking to see the whole thing unfold and to see that it went on [the air] and Andy was able to say the entire thing — he was able to say everything we wanted to say. They let the piece run on longer than they had initially said. They said it would be four or five minutes, but it ended up being six and a half to seven minutes. He explained everything that we would like to do if, in a parallel universe, Dow was actually to do the right thing.

So it was surprising that they didn't, halfway through the broadcast, just cut it off, once they realized it wasn't true. Afterward it was really interesting to see the responses. We went on an emotional roller coaster. We were initially extremely happy that it had gone off well — Andy performed really well. He nailed everything, basically. Then, when we got home, we started reading the reports. We started feeling like shit, about, oh, two or three hours later, when we saw the effect it was having in Bhopal.

But then, after about two days, we started feeling better again when we saw the results in the U.S. media and actually got to tally how many stories made it into newspapers [in the United States] as a result of the hoax that probably wouldn't have been there otherwise.

SS: One major impact I think it had was educating people within Dow's international global network. During our meetings with Dow officials in Europe and in other countries, we were shocked to find that these officials did not know anything about the disaster in Bhopal. Even the senior officials of Dow were surprised to know that Union Carbide, with which Dow had merged, was still absconding from a warrant in the criminal case in Bhopal. For these officials, it must have been a revelation about their own company. People must have called them up and tried to find out if what they had heard was true. This would have happened all over the world.

Satinath, can you tell us the story of what was happening on the ground in Bhopal?

SS: Well, we had had our anniversary march to the factory. Thousands of people were there, and the effigy [of Dow Chemical] was just burning down.

Suddenly, the BBC crew that had been there all day came running toward me. They came closer, with their cameras rolling, and told me that BBC correspondents had spoken to a Dow representative and that Dow had promised to give some $12 billion to Bhopal survivors to settle all liabilities once and for all.

I just couldn't believe it at first. And then when it sank in, which was only a fraction of a second after, I couldn't hold back. I started crying. It was the hugeness of the amount that made this so different. It was so massive, you could think of so many things to do, so many possibilities.... At that moment, all I could think about was that if this had been done a long time ago so much suffering would have been avoided. That was the most intense thing I was feeling. But I also felt how many possibilities were now opened up in Bhopal, like good health care and proper cleaning of the toxic contamination. With so much money, Bhopal would be a completely different city.

By then, a crowd of local activists had gathered around us. Because the conversation with BBC reporters was in English, they could not understand what was going on, but they figured out that it was momentous and they were eager to know. In Hindi, I told them what the BBC reporters had told me. They ran to tell others. There was much screaming, crying, hugging — people not knowing what to say, people trying to figure out how much $12 billion was in rupees, people wanting to know more. Meanwhile, because the BBC people were filming us, other media people came running toward us. All this was happening around us for about an hour. Up until then, we did not know [that it was a hoax].

The BBC reporters said that they wanted to do live interviews with lots of people and began setting up their equipment. After some time, they came back to us and said, "No, no, it's a hoax," and "Our people have checked; Dow has refused." So that was when it all came crashing down.

But when we realized it was a hoax by the Yes Men, we were no longer unhappy. Particularly when the activists and leaders of the survivors' organizations found out why it had been done and the impact it had had, I don't think there was any anger left.

MB: Well, firstly, we just really want to apologize. And please pass it on to anybody else that was there with you. We really didn't intend to put you through that, even if it was for only a few hours. Do you have anything to add to that, Andy?

AB: Satinath, you mentioned that you weren't *that* disappointed when you found out that it was a hoax. Are you just being polite?

SS: No, no. Firstly because it was too good to be true, so I was kind of suspicious. It was all very sudden when the BBC guys said [that], and the rational part of my mind was suspended. Once I knew it was a hoax, I imagined how much trouble Dow would have all over the world. Also, it wasn't like the news had reached a lot of people in Bhopal.

Still, for a few days afterward, there was a lot of speculation as to who could have done this. And then there were people who said pretty terrible things about the Yes Men, not knowing who they were or why they had done it. Later, the whole story came out in the newspapers as to how this was part of a subversive activity, and then there was a much wider appreciation.

Our big worry was the Bhopal Medical Appeal, because we raise all our money through newspaper advertisements in England, and we thought that if our potential donors read this — because this ad also goes out around the time of the anniversary — they would think, "What's the point of giving or donating more money?" It didn't really affect [fundraising], because these people also soon found out about it. But it was a close call.

Has this experience changed your ideas about what you're doing or might do in the future?

MB: Well, if opportunities like this come along [again], we would certainly take them. We felt like this was probably our most successful project to date, in terms of being able to focus attention on an issue that we cared about. As for where we take it in the future — well, with this thing, we want to follow it up and keep working on the issue of Dow Chemical and [its] negligence in Bhopal.

But these sorts of pranks are only part of what we do; the other part is making media about the pranks that we then show to a different audience. We are going to be pursuing this with the Dow work as well.

What does it take to do this kind of anticorporate activism?

MB: Well, the two methods that we had, that were choices in this Dow project, were: one, showing that another world is possible and laying out some simple steps to achieving that other world; and two, shocking people into realizing how awful the consensus is. We couldn't act on either of them if other kinds of activism didn't exist there.

For example, there are people who are thinking specifically about alternative models for say, running economies or governments. We rely on those organizations to figure out what it is that we want to propose. That's why with this Dow thing we ended up working with other activists who had been working on the issue for a long time — because we needed their guidance in proposing a solution.

AB: The core of it is that the work that we are doing is a kind of education rather than real hard-core activism. The real hard-core stuff is being done by people on the ground who are fighting with their bodies or with their minds, changing laws or doing research that provides people with all kinds of tools to become more active. What we're doing is sort of popularizing these issues — like with our film about the WTO stuff. It's not even popularizing the issues, it's just sort of getting people interested in the issues.

SS: To me, this was a clear case of how these two different kinds of activism really need each other. Because if you leave aside the few hours of disappointment and all, I think that this was a very positive example in terms of education, and convincing people of the importance of this issue and inspiring people to become agents of change or to get involved.

Andy and Mike can be examples for lots of people of what you can do with a smart text and a borrowed jacket. So these are things that show people the different range of activism that you can do, that can be subversive as well as fun.

For more information, see the following Web sites: www.dowethics.com (the Yes Men's parody of Dow Chemical's www.dow.com); www.bhopal.org (the Sambhavna Trust Clinic and the Bhopal Medical Appeal); www.bhopal.net (the International Campaign for Justice in Bhopal); and www.theyesmen.org (the Yes Men's Web site, which includes a video of the Dow hoax).

Timor-Leste: Ground Zero

a profile of the Haburas Foundation by Philippe Mangeot

For anyone who believes that only the rich care about the environment, the Haburas Foundation will prove a serious counterexample. Based in Dili, the capital of Timor-Leste, Haburas was founded in 1998 by Demetrio do Amaral de Carvalho, a leader of the underground resistance during the Indonesian occupation. At the time, the country was still controlled by Jakarta's military junta, but the fall of Suharto on May 21, 1998 rekindled hopes for independence. "Within the resistance, we began to think about how to rebuild the country," recalls de Carvalho. "During the twenty-four years of the Indonesian occupation, more than two hundred thousand people were killed. The Indonesians razed East Timor's indigenous cultures, destroyed its housing stock, and ravaged the natural environment — the very resources upon which the country's future depended. So in imagining how to rebuild Timor-Leste, we not only wanted to focus on environmental problems. We also had to think about human-rights issues, political issues, development issues; and about how to interconnect issues in human rights, politics, development, and the environment. The Haburas Foundation was born of that mandate."[1]

In 2002, Timor-Leste gained its independence and a constitution was secured that contained no fewer than four articles stipulating the necessity of assuring environmental protection and explicitly framing this as vital to the nation's collective interests. The inclusion of these provisions was Haburas's first major victory. With members of parliament, Haburas fought to ensure that principles of environmental justice became integral parts of the founding document of the world's newest state. According to de Carvalho, "the country had become a 'ground zero,' and there was a risk that environmental issues would be systematically overlooked. It was thus necessary to inscribe environmental protection into the constitution as a fundamental principle that future policies would have to respect."

Quite quickly, Haburas came to see itself as a pressure group whose relationship with national authorities was both critical and supportive. Its mission was facilitated by the relationships that had been forged with members of this new ruling class during the resistance. Nonetheless, given that Timor-Leste is one of the world's poorest counties, Haburas's focus on the environment is still quite remarkable. In the months prior to their departure

Planting trees in Fatucama. In 2003, Haburas planted one thousand trees in addition to planting native grasses for erosion control. For his efforts in East Timor, the director of Haburas, Demetrio do Amaral de Carvalho, won the 2004 Goldman Environmental Prize (courtesy of Haburas).

in 1999, the Indonesian troops and their militias destroyed three-quarters of East Timor's infrastructure. During the United Nations' assumption of temporary authority, some of the country's infrastructure was rebuilt, but today, an entire economy still awaits reconstruction. "We continually have to show," says de Carvalho, "that there is no contradiction between the urgent need to rebuild the economy and the protection of natural areas. On the contrary, sustainable development in Timor-Leste can only be achieved if it is based on environmental policies." In a country where peasants who barely make enough to survive are the majority of the population, it is clear that the future lies in the rationalization of agriculture. In a territory where the beaches and the coral reefs are visited by at most two hundred tourists a month, all agree that tourism is a sector ripe for development. But what kind of agriculture and what kind of tourism? "The government," says de Carvalho, "seems to have learned nothing from the experience of other small countries in the global economy. It has developed intensive agricultural projects, and we already know the damages they can do: the majority of farmers risk losing their renewable resources. While we do need to promote some form of ethical tourism, one sensitive to the country's cultural specificity and its natural riches, if we aren't careful, Timor-Leste could fall prey to the corporate purveyors of mass tourism. Could we be in the midst of exchanging one kind of colonial dependence for another?"

Instead, according to Haburas, the key to independence lies in enabling the Timorese to reappropriate their environment. This is why the scope of the foundation's actions has gradually widened. De Carvalho explains: "The goal is no longer merely to mobilize opinion. We must also get involved on the ground to restore the devastated environment and to promote methods of natural-resource management that will not accumulate future debts."

In Tetum, the traditional language of Timor-Leste, *haburas* means "to make green and fresh." Alongside its lobbying work, the NGO organizes reforestation campaigns that bring together hundreds of volunteers recruited from the restoration areas. Timor-Leste's rainforest has suffered considerably during the years of military occupation. The rainforest was the resistance movement's base of operations as well as the place where it was systematically pursued. De Carvalho clearly remembers the fires started by napalm attacks in the jungle where his family had found refuge. But the forest also suffered under colonial mercantilism, which overexploited resources such as sandalwood. Today, the damage continues; the majority of citizens live on less than a dollar a day, and many of them subsist by cutting and selling wood for fuel. "It does not make much sense to outlaw tree cutting when it is a condition of survival for many people," says de Carvalho. "That is why we have emphasized education about environmental and development issues. We work with local communities, and together we identify the problems they face and come up with solutions. If one village has rich resources of bamboo, we train the villagers in ways to use bamboo lucratively. It is always a question of building up community skills."

One way this strategy works is though the revitalization of traditional practices, starting with Tara Bandu, a form of customary law. According to de Carvalho, "All the members of a community agree to protect a given area for a given period, as long as it takes for it to recover." Prohibited by the colonial Indonesian administration, this "traditional ecological wisdom" had been all but forgotten — "We are trying to revive it and to teach people about it."

For his work with local communities, de Carvalho was awarded the 2004 Goldman Environmental Prize, a kind of ecological Nobel awarded each year to environmental activists around the world. The honor bestowed on de Carvalho also benefited the small NGO he directs: Haburas became a much more influential organization than its relatively modest staff (fifteen permanent employees) and average annual budget (about $125,000) had previously permitted. Conferred with a newfound legitimacy and publicity granted by the reward, the Haburas Foundation was, furthermore, in a position to represent the people of Timor-Leste with whom it works so intimately. Depending on the situation, this double legitimacy allows Haburas the possibility either to criticize the government of Timore-Leste or to lend it crucial support.

The toughest battle Haburas faces today concerns a proposal to construct a hydropower plant located on Lake Iralalaru, in the eastern part of the country. According to

Haburas and the Australian experts it has commissioned to review the project, the plant would destroy the surrounding wetlands and destabilize neighboring populations. Haburas has developed a plan to counter the government's designs: the creation of Timor-Leste's first national park which, Haburas believes, would become a major destination for the eco-tourism the foundation hopes to develop.

In Timor-Leste's dispute with Australia over the definition of maritime borders, how-ever, Haburas has been a strong ally of the government. The stakes are enormous, since the borders will determine control of the undersea oil and gas fields that lie between the two countries. In 1989, Indonesia ceded the majority of these resources to Australia in exchange for Canberra's recognition of the annexation of East Timor. Consequently, Australia is currently exploiting petroleum and gas resources whose entire revenues, were maritime borders to be redrawn in conformity with international standards, would belong to Timor-Leste. For several years, Timor-Leste has been renegotiating the borders, but the Australian government has delayed resolving the matter. In September and October 2005, Haburas and twelve other NGOs united to demand that the borders be redefined accord-ing to international law. The initiative was a costly one. In November 2005, the Austra-lian Agency for International Development (AusAID) suspended funding allocated for an environmental education program in Timor-Leste schools, explaining that the NGOs had "overtly criticized Australia."

Haburas's stake in the conflict is twofold. According to de Carvalho, "not only do we think it is outrageous that Australia is earning millions of dollars from operations in the disputed zones while the Timorese are tossed a few crumbs. But it is also clear that as long as rights to these areas remain in dispute, environmental questions will not be given proper attention." It should also be added that Haburas's tactical alliance with the government will end as soon as the battle is won. Haburas will then have to exert pressure on the gov-ernment of Timor-Leste to ensure the protection of an ecosystem threatened by petroleum extraction.

This two-tiered strategy aptly characterizes Haburas's approach. At the same time that it maintains its historical proximity to the country's political ruling class, it also remains faithful to its criticisms of government policies. Asked whether he has ever considered a conventional political career — a real possibility for a former captain of the resistance — de Carvalho responds in the negative: "As far as environmental issues are concerned, the NGO route was both the least expensive and the most rewarding." Can we hold onto the dream that one day a Timorese Green Party will exist? Is this the plan? "No, it is just a possibility."

Translated by Blake Ferris.

1   Quotes from Demetrio do Amaral de Carvalho are from a
    November 2005 interview with the author.

Monochrome Landscape (Green)

a project by Laura Kurgan introduced by Yates McKee

The green field that spreads across the following two pages is characterized by a tension between the dense organic patterns that mark its surface and the rectilinearity of the space of the page. The space is not only cut off from that which surrounds it; it has also been cut through by a sinuous swath of reddish-brown, a trail that cleaves the verdant density of the pictorial terrain from within. Yet this bisection is something other than a formal investigation of fields and lines as such; green is a color traditionally excluded from the realm of modernist abstraction on account of its referential association with the natural world, and thus, the supposedly outmoded conventions of landscape aesthetics as opposed to technoscientific conditions of modernity. And indeed, the bisected field is marked by an uncanny intensity of detail that exceeds any mechanical regularity or reductive gestalt. What we discern are the singular, constituent treetops of a forest canopy, viewed from an aerial perspective whose extreme altitude is suggested by the slightest of cloud formations appearing in the top left-hand corner of the image. The latter detail is a clue that the image is a satellite photograph, a visual fragment cut out from the spatiotemporal continuum of history by an inhuman eye-in-the-sky. The photograph thus speaks to a certain cutting, violence, or even destruction, transforming a singular area of the Earth's surface into a mobile set of digital signals capable of being recomposed in an infinity of future contexts and formats, including the following two pages of the present volume. This formal structure of the cut echoes a more specific practice of cutting that shows up within the image — the cutting down and cutting through of forest cover. But who or what is the agent of these various cuts, and what are the conditions of their public appearance?

In 2000, the local offices of the NGO Global Forest Watch (GFW) announced its suspicions that French timber companies had begun to cut illegal logging trails into the rapidly disappearing old-growth forests of southern Cameroon, areas protected by that nation's nascent sustainable-yield forestry legislation. Monitoring such corporate violations in dense, remote jungle terrain is an inherently difficult task. In 2001, experimental architect Laura Kurgan took an interest in the reports of the GFW; extending her long-standing exploration of the unforeseen aesthetic and political possibilities presented by "post-military" spatial-information technologies, Kurgan channeled the budget for a museum installation project into "tasking" the commercial Ikonos satellite to produce an extremely high resolution (one meter per pixel) surveillance photograph of an eight-kilometer by eight-kilometer sector of the rainforest area where the GFW suspected illegal logging was taking place.[1] The result was the environmental crime scene that appears in the following two pages, which provides a powerful supplement to the textual, photographic, and carto- graphic data-projection techniques used by environmental monitoring organizations such as the GFW to make their claims about the activities of corporations and/or governments.

But if the bird's-eye view of the satellite is often associated iconographically with a sense of omnipotence and mastery, here it is revealed in its precariousness. On the one hand, it presents an ultraprecise rendering of environmental phenomena, to such an extent that it becomes possible to count the individual trees threatened at certain coordinates at a certain moment in time. On the other, it releases this singular *locus* into heterogeneous spaces and times of archivization, dissemination, interpretation, and potentially, legal deci- sions and protective interventions.

Staging a set of structural couples — preservation/destruction, landscape/data, site- specificity/displacement — Kurgan does not simply celebrate this newfound technology of global environmental surveillance as an end-in-itself. Through a kind of abstractionist withdrawal from thematic communication, the image insists on remaining to some extent enigmatic or open-ended; not in order to cast doubt on the documentary and testimonial claims of an organization such as the GFW, but to sustain, as it were, the *political* question of who can claim the mandate of sustainability when a particular ecosystem is marked as a site of dispute and negotiation between corporations, multilateral intuitions, NGOs, and export-dependent, revenue-desperate states such as Cameroon, as well as frequently over- looked stakeholders such as migrant forestry workers and the fourth-world peoples whose livelihoods depend on sylvan ecologies that are all-too-often (un)marked as pristine and uninhabited. Kurgan's work does not pretend to resolve or even explicitly comment upon such tensions; but by unsettling the self-evidence of "forest watching" it perhaps opens onto a political ecology of resource management that would no longer take the meaning of environment for granted, nor the common humanity typically called upon to protect it in the interests of generations-to-come.

1 For a discussion of the full series of Kurgan's *Monochrome Landscapes* see Geoffrey Batchen, "The Forest for the Trees" *Aperture* 178 (Spring 2005), pp. 26–33, as well as Kurgan's own Web site at www.lo0k.org. For ongoing GFW reports on logging in Cameroon, see www.globalforestwatch.org

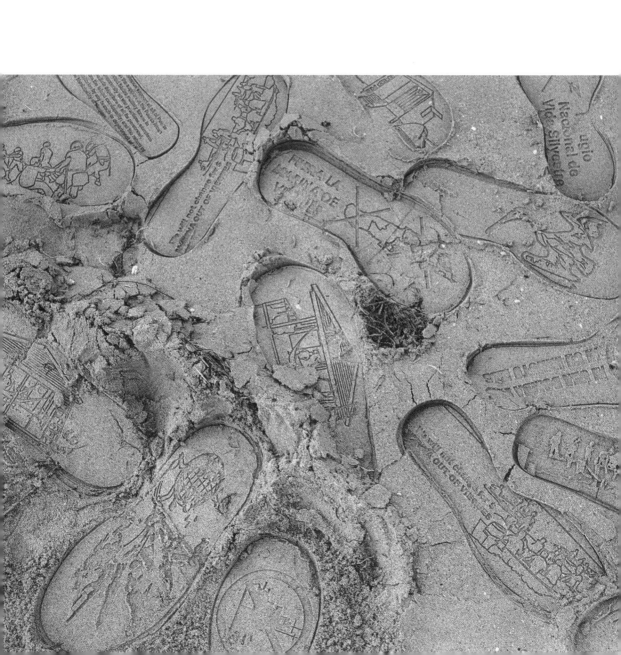

Art and the Ends of Environmentalism:
From Biosphere to the Right to Survival

Yates McKee

The pursuit of life by means other than life.
— Bernard Steigler, *Technics and Time 1: The Fault of Epimetheus*

Let us begin our investigation with a print, or rather, prints. Something appears to have happened. A photograph was taken, a freezing of time and a fragmentation of space, leaving us in the here and now with a petrified shard of a there and then. Preserved and interrupted by the camera, it is evident that this past present was never simply present to begin with. Then and there, at the actual click of the shutter, the moment and location in question were already marked by the remains of another event, traces that survived the actuality of their own genesis. These were traces, we can discern, that were destined to recession or oblivion, impressed into the precarious medium of sand. Yet there they were and here they are, almost, not quite. Monuments of absence, their origins are enigmatic. Yet the photograph was composed in such a way as to provide a modicum of legibility or recognition — the traces do not simply register a senseless physical force. They have the outline of vestiges, bearing witness to the pressure exerted by living creatures coming to pass across the surface of the earth. Animal tracks, then. But to what species do they belong? How many legs? Are these the steps of Homo sapiens, the animal that knows itself as such, and thus transcends its mere creaturehood, participating in a purposeful history, rather than a base struggle for existence? Such a desire to rise above the limitations of terrestrial existence recalls the most famous footprint of all time: that photographed by one of the Apollo astronauts when he set foot upon the moon — "One small step for man, one giant leap for mankind." One step, one man, one history…and one Earth, seen, as if always for the first time, from the deific perspective of outer space.

These steps differ and defer. Overlapping and interrupting one another, their humanity is uncertain and their direction adrift. Each is singular due to the irregularity of the surface on which it is impressed, but this singularity is not simply unique. Rather than

Jennifer Allora and Guillermo Calzadilla, from the series *Landmark*
(footprints) (2001).

register the physical pressure of human feet as such, they appear to have been created by a kind of stamp or seal that makes each mark infinitely repeatable and thus divisible — like photographs. Human figures, a bird, a map marked with an "X".... Hovering between death and survival, inscription and erasure, preservation and destruction, these signs call out for a response while withdrawing from legibility, their meaning exposed to the force of time like runes on an archaic crypt for which we lack any hermeneutic or anthropological cipher: "Read me — will you ever be able to do so?"

Satellite photograph annotated to indicate the recession of the Kangerdlugssaug Glacier, Greenland, 2005 (courtesy of Leigh Stearns, ASTER Science Team, University of Maine Climate Change Institute).

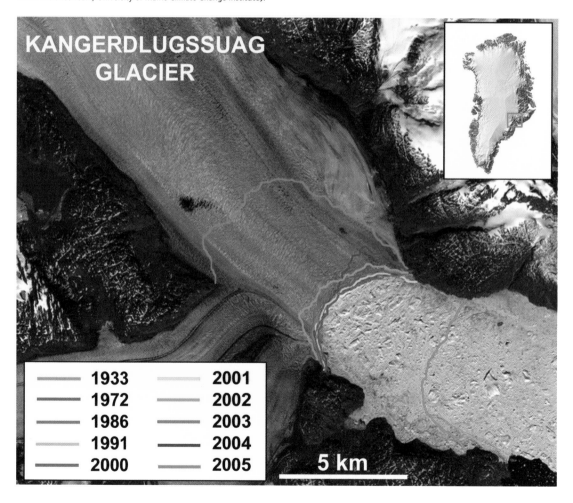

ENDS

In October 2004, a report was released at the annual meeting of the Environmental Grantmakers Association (EGA) entitled "The Death of Environmentalism: Global Warming Politics in a Post-Environmental World."[1] Based on interviews with leaders of the U.S. environmental organizations and several years' worth of public opinion surveys, the report asserts that environmentalism has ceased to be a viable social movement in the United States and that it has come to be perceived as just another "special interest" lobbying for influence in Washington, D.C. According to the report, environmentalists rely almost exclusively on a language of science and technical policy solutions. The key problem stems from what the authors refer to as a "literal-sclerosis" among environmentalists: their positing of the environment as a determinate thing to be represented, protected, and defended by experts, rather than conceiving it as a figure that mediates a network of sociopolitical, economic, and natural forces in which all citizens have a stake. The ends of environmentalism — its aims and purposes — are thus truncated by taking for granted the meaning and boundaries of its object. "If you want people to act on global warming," the authors quote one professional environmentalist as saying, "you need to convince them that action is needed on global warming and *not on some ulterior goal*."[2] Fixating on carbon emissions as the "cause" of global warming disables a politics that would target both specific policies and the larger network of concepts, values, and narratives that work to legitimize an energy economy deemed to be generally unsustainable in economic, ecological, and geopolitical terms.

Without rearticulating the politics of global warming within an expanded chain of struggles, the authors claim, such a fixation will fail to constitute a general community with the will to pressure public and private agencies into modifying their modes of governance. Echoing Antonio Gramsci, the authors assert that such a "strategic vision" would be a matter of hearts and minds as much as of scientific demonstration: "Environmentalists need to tap into the creative worlds of myth-making…not to better sell narrow and technical policy proposals but rather to figure out who we are and who we need to be."[3] As a project concerned with sustainability, the report insists, environmentalism remains unsustainable without attending to questions of seeing and framing, interpretation and meaning, desire and affect, imagination and identification, questions that all belong to the realm of the "cultural."

The increasing emphasis placed by activists on cultural production in media campaigns and policy analysis alike suggests a potentially significant role for visual culture and related artistic practices in displacing the current ends of environmentalism or in rearticulating the "environment" as a site of nongovernmental politics. Affirming the EGA report's imperatives, in this article I trace pertinent historical and contemporary instances of environmentalist visual culture, but I also ask whether the role of culture and art should be conceived simply as an instrument of "myth making" in the service of determining "who we are and who we need to be." Can artists and other cultural producers engage these ends while also attending to the *limits* of the very "we" they would help to "figure out"? Furthermore, how might cultural producers negotiate the tension between a Gramscian interest in "mobilizing the passions of the *demos*" against a general enemy, on the one hand, and a Foucauldian attention to the specificity of governing agencies' techniques and modes of modes of subjectification, on the other?[4]

These questions are all the more important in light of other contemporary invocations of a cultural-artistic imperative in environmentalist discourse, such as that made by the influential writer Bill McKibben. In an article entitled "Imagine That: What the Warming World Needs Now is Art, Sweet Art," notes that "the famous picture of earth from outer space that Apollo beamed back in the late 1960s — already that's not the world we inhabit; its poles are melting, its oceans rising. We can register what is happening with satellites and scientific instruments, but can we register it in our imaginations, the most sensitive of all our devices?"[5] McKibben appeals to the Apollo image as a kind of ruined monument for environmentalism that speaks, in principle, to a vital moment when our imaginations were able to register the crisis of the planet and thus, presumably, to animate popular desires to mitigate that crisis. Technical indices of environmental dynamics alone are inadequate for McKibben, for they fail to generate what he calls "cultural meaning" or a dramatic "plot" that would be affectively or spiritually compelling for a general public. "Cultural meaning" involves communicating

> a sense that as a species we're finally and irrevocably managing to crowd out everything else, smudge our fingerprints on every frame of the book of life. There seems to me no more telling turn in our civilization, at least since the apple in Eden (a crisis that gave rise to more great art than anything in the Western tradition). But there also needs to be hope as well — visions of what it might be like to live on a planet where we use this moment as an opportunity to confront our consumer society, use it to begin the process of rebuilding community.[6]

McKibben's positing of a "we" qua species suggests the biological and indeed geological time scale informing his sense of the environment and its anthropogenic pathologies. Set against this evolutionary horizon, the mandate of "art, sweet art" is to resolve the antinomies of geophysical system and cultural world, mechanical technology and human imagination, scientific facts and spiritual values, in the name of restoring the planetary community supposedly convoked by the Apollo image on the first Earth Day in 1970.[7]

"ENDANGERED EARTH": SYSTEM AND FIGURE

The terms invoked by McKibben have informed discussions of art and environmentalism since they were first formalized in the 1960s by figures such as Gyorgy Kepes, a student of Laszlo Moholy-Nagy and founder of the Center for Advanced Visual Studies. The center was a pioneering interdisciplinary research institute at the Massachusetts

Demonstrator at first Earth Day, United States, 1970
(Environmental Protection Agency).

Institute of Technology (MIT) whose mandate was to facilitate dialogue between the humanities and the sciences in order to "harmonize [the] inner and outer world" in the face of the "crisis of environmental scale" generated by postwar technological advances. In an article entitled "Art and Ecological Consciousness," Kepes issues an imperative for art based on a bodily analogy:

> The individual human body has an inbuilt self-defense, a physiological mechanism that protects it from extreme imbalances.... We have to begin to see that our extended body, our social and man-transformed environment, must develop its own self-regulating mechanisms to eliminate the poisons injected into it and to recycle useful matter. Environmental homeostasis on a global scale is now necessary to survival. Creative imagination, artistic sensibility, can be seen as one of our basic, collective self-regulating devices to register and reject what is toxic and find what is useful and meaningful in our lives.[8]

While he cites the Apollo astronaut's description of the earth as a "fragile ball that should be handled with considerable care," Kepes's vocabulary of self-regulation, homeostatic balance, and optimal performance, indicates his indebtedness to cybernetics, or the general theory of systems control understood in terms of the communicative feedback loops of organized bodies.[9] Indeed, Kepes's article appeared in an anthology that he edited, entitled *Arts of the Environment,* that also included an article on systems dynamics by Jay Forrester, designer of the computer-based "world model" of population, resource, and pollution flows underpinning the Club of Rome's *Limits to Growth* report. This report was the first to announce the mathematical "unsustainability" of the postwar vision of infinite industrial expansion.[10] Yet Kepes's emphasis on the moral-aesthetic dimensions of homeostasis — "the rejection of what is toxic in our lives" — also resonates with the work of another contributor to the book, René Dubos. This microbiologist-cum-philosopher developed a general environmental physiology that integrated Darwinian themes of (mal)adaptation with anthropological and theological speculations on the meaning and purpose of human history, as distinguished from, though not independent of, sheer animal existence.[11]

In books such as *Man Adapting* (1970) and *So Human an Animal* (1969), Dubos argued that the survival of humanity qua species requires an evolutionary leap in the spatio-temporal horizons of human consciousness itself that would overcome the short-term, self-interested pursuit of material gratification characteristic of "industrial civilization." These concerns framed *Only One Earth: The Maintenance and Care of a Small Planet,* the report he coauthored with Barbara Ward for the first United Nations Conference on the Human Environment in Stockholm in 1972. The report concluded with a Kantian call for

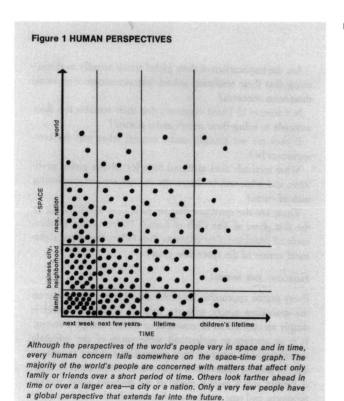

Human Perspectives graph, *The Limits to Growth* (1972).

Figure 1 HUMAN PERSPECTIVES

Although the perspectives of the world's people vary in space and in time, every human concern falls somewhere on the space-time graph. The majority of the world's people are concerned with matters that affect only family or friends over a short period of time. Others look farther ahead in time or over a larger area—a city or a nation. Only a very few people have a global perspective that extends far into the future.

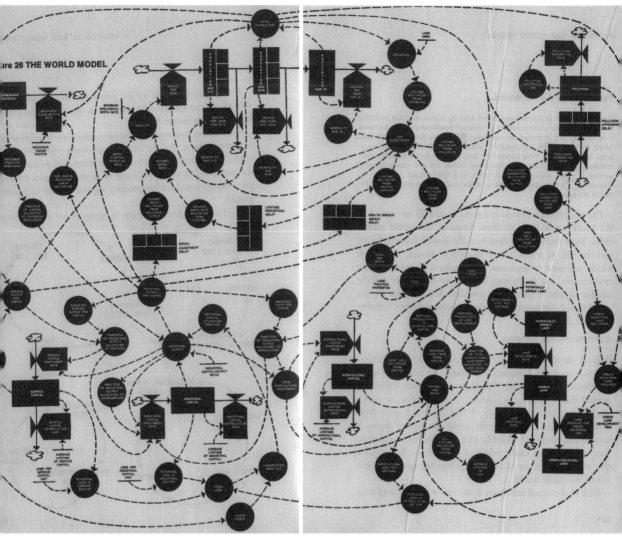

ure 26 THE WORLD MODEL

World Model diagram, *The Limits to Growth* (1972).

Figure 26 THE WORLD MODEL

The entire world model is represented here by a flow diagram in formal System Dynamics notation. Levels, or physical quantities that can be measured directly, are indicated by rectangles ▮, *rates that influence those levels by valves* ◄, *and auxiliary variables that influence the rate equations by circles* ●. *Time delays are indicated by sections within rectangles* ▮▮▮ *Real flows of people, goods, money, etc. are shown by solid arrows* ——▶ *and causal relationships by broken arrows* — — — ▶ *Clouds* ☁ *represent sources or sinks that are not important to the model behavior.*

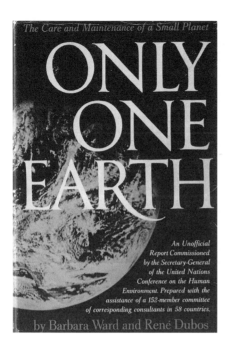

Cover from *Only One Earth: An Unofficial Report Commissioned by the Secretary General of the United Nations Conference on the Human Environment* (1970).

the recognition of "the planet as the center of rational loyalty for all mankind," based on "a profound and deepening sense of our shared and interdependent biosphere."[12]

Mediating between cybernetic systems diagrams and the categorical imperative of post-Darwinist humanism, Kepes argued that an ecologically conscious art would be concerned above all with the *future*: "Imagination is the key to pre-experiencing alternative futures; desirability in terms of human values is the decision maker that now selects the right alternatives."[13]

The other crucial originator of the discourse on art and environmentalism in the 1960s was landscape architect Ian McHarg, whose *Design and Nature* outlined a physiological and phenomenological diagnosis of the maladjustments between the human organism and its environment. These problems, he argued, have roots deeper than any particular political or economic system.[14] The extant pollution, decay, and anarchy throughout the United States were perceived by McHarg as pathological symptoms of a deep ontological misunderstanding of our relation to the world of life as a whole, symptoms of civilizational values whose "mancenteredness ensures that those processes essential to man's evolution and survival will be excluded from consideration."[15] Citing Martin Buber's proto-Heideggerian critique of anthropocentric instrumentality, McHarg claimed that humanity threatened its own existence by taking itself as the measure and master of all things, thereby forgetting its fundamental indebtedness to its planetary "inheritance": "Our phenomenal world contains our origins, our history, our milieu; it is our home. It is in this sense that ecology (derived from *oikos*) is the science of the home."[16] Informed by this sense of deep ecological memory, the architect or artist could proceed to bring the physical and visual environment into a harmonious equilibrium with the patterns and rhythms of nature, becoming both a "co-tenant" and "steward" of the biosphere, that "thin film of life covering the earth…the sum of all organisms and communities, acting as a single superorganism."[17]

The biosphere is a quasi-vitalist concept invented in 1926 by Russian geochemist Vladimir Verdansky. It refers to the "living envelope" of the planet sustained by and interacting with geological, hydrological, chemical, and atmospheric systems.[18] Understood as a "planetary superorganism," the biosphere exhibits dynamic processes and patterns that are animated above all by the sun. Life, including that of humanity, is ultimately a general, closed economy of carbonic matter and photonic energy that manifests itself in biological patterns of growth, decay, and rebirth over time.[19]

In reactivating the cosmological dimensions of Verdansky's concept, which had been underplayed by the zoologist George Evelyn Hutchinson in a groundbreaking 1968 article in *Scientific American* that unfolded its resonance with cybernetics, McHarg prefigured the so-called "Gaia hypothesis" expounded by NASA geophysicist James Lovelock. Lovelock invoked the figure of an ancient Greek "earth goddess" to emblematize humanity's moral and spiritual duty to restore a homeostatic relay with the natural systems of which it forms a part.[20] While Lovelock's mythopoetic language was greeted with skepticism by some scientists, the basic idea of the biosphere as a self-regulating organism, relative to which human activities should be made to conform in the name of species survival, has remained a cornerstone of ecological discourse since the 1960s and has until recently been imported into aesthetic discourse with unqualified enthusiasm. Indeed, as a theory of the harmonious and purposeful interdependence of parts and whole, the biosphere is a proto-aesthetic figure that resonates with various moments in the heritage of Romantic organicism, especially the antimechanistic philosophical botany of Johann Wolfgang Goethe,[21] and Alexander von Humboldt's *Cosmos* which issued a call to "generalize our ideas by concentrating them in one common focus and thus arrive at a point of view from which all the organisms and forces of nature may be seen as one living, active whole, animated by a single impulse."[22]

Exemplifying the persistence of this organicist heritage is the influential 1992 museum exhibition and the accompanying catalogue by Barbara Matilsky, *Fragile Ecologies: Contemporary Artists' Solutions and Interpretations*. The collection of works is organized according to the premise that "an understanding of ecology — the interrelationship of all forms of life in their diverse environments — is essential to the survival of the planet…. [A]n important new art movement has emerged to reestablish a vital link to nature by communicating an experience of its life-generating powers."[23] Rather than merely create images of a static, fixed nature, such artists are "in a unique position to effect environmental changes because they can synthesize new ideas and communicate connections between many disciplines. They are pioneering a holistic approach to problem solving that transcends the narrow limits of specialization…. Art changes the way people look at reality. In its most positive mode, art can offer alternative visions."[24]

The "alternative visions" catalogued in *Fragile Ecologies* revolve around various figures of decontamination, salvation, revitalization, and healing. In some cases, these visions involved converting the art gallery into a kind of displaced ecological laboratory, as in Hans Haacke's *Rhinewater Purification Plant* (1972), which diverted and repurified the water being released by a sewage plant into the Rhine river, or Helen and Newton Harrison's *Survival Piece* (1972), which salvaged orange trees from a California orchard slated to be bulldozed for suburban development, replanting them under artificial conditions in a museum. In other cases, artists performed spectacular symbolic gestures designed to register as media events, such as Joseph Beuys's planting of 7,000 trees beginning at the 1982 Documenta exhibition, or Buster Simpson's *Purge* (1983–present), in which he drops oversized antacid pills into polluted waterways. These projects oscillated between the twin pillars of what Ramachandra Guha has called the postwar Euro-American "ecology of affluence": a romantic and preservationist appeal to the "natural" environment — such as rivers, forests, and animals — on the one hand, and a moral and physiological concern with the pollution and degradation of the "human" environment, on the other.[25] While the narratives of this ecology of affluence were internally contested in important ways — epitomized by the debates between the neo-Malthusian Paul Erlich (author of *The Population Bomb*) and the liberal critic of capitalist techno-

Joseph Beuys, *7,000 Oaks*, tree-planting action, Documenta 7, Friedrichsplatz, Kassel, Germany, 1982 (Carl Ebert/AP Photo).

New Notes

ESQUIRE/NOVEMBER 1983

Contributors: Jessica Maxwell, PHOTOGRAPH · © 1983 ROGER SCHREIBER

Acid rain is polluting our waters, say environmentalists. And the government is loath to do anything about it. Above, Seattle artist Buster Simpson takes action in his own hands by placing one of his hand-carved 42.5-pound antacid pills into the Seattle water system. These river Rolaids, which are made of limestone, slowly break down in a time-released fashion, neutralize the acidity of the water and therefore bring the water back to a healthier pH. Simpson plans to treat waterways across the country with his Tums-for-mother-nature until the government comes up with a less symptomatic cure. His next stop: New York's Adirondacks.

Buster Simpson, from the *Purge* series (1983–present), Tolt Watershed, Cascade Range, Washington state (photo by Roger Schreiber).

science Barry Commoner (author of *Science and Survival*) — the basic terms of nature, environment, and humanity were left intact.[26]

Perhaps the most famous artwork of the "ecology of affluence" was the landscape artist Christo's cover for a special issue of *Time* magazine in 1989, which replaced *Time*'s annually chosen "Person of the Year" with the "Planet of the Year." Rather than featuring the face of an exemplary statesman or celebrity, Christo's cover depicted an oversized biophysical model of the planet, wrapped in plastic and precariously bound with ropes, set against a desolate landscape illuminated by the glow of an infernal, apocalyptic sunset. Suspended between suffocation or strangulation, on one hand, and protection or salvation, on the other, the image of the anthropomorphized planet, accompanied by the caption "Endangered Earth," functioned as a supplement to the narratives of planetary emergency elaborated in the magazine's articles on global warming, overpopulation, deforestation, biodiversity loss, and oceanic pollution. Synthesizing these topics, Senator Al Gore's leading article, "What Is Wrong With Us?" pleads with "humanity" for the reconciliation of economic growth, natural systems, and spiritual values. The

Christo, *Endangered Earth, Time Magazine* (January 2, 1989).

terms of Gore's article, later to be developed into his best-selling election-year book *Earth in the Balance: Ecology and the Human Spirit* (1992), were borrowed almost word for word from the United Nations Environment and Development report *Our Common Future,* published in 1987:

> In the middle of the twentieth century, we saw our planet from space for the first time.... From space, we see a small and fragile ball dominated not by human activity and edifice but by a pattern of clouds, oceans, greenery and soils. Humanity's inability to fit its doings into that pattern is changing planetary systems fundamentally.... From space we can see and study the Earth as an organism whose health depends on the health of all its parts. We have the power to reconcile human affairs with natural laws and to thrive in the process. In this our cultural and spiritual heritages can reinforce our economic interests and survival imperatives.[27]

Appearing under the heading "From Earth to World," this passage points to the relay discussed above between two senses of organization: dynamic systems and signals, on the one hand, and visual gestalts of cosmic unity and moral-physiological health, on the other. Through the totalizing gaze of the astronaut, inflected at once by scientific mastery and religious awe, the planet appears as a common possession to be preserved and managed in the name of life itself, before and beyond history. It evokes a picture of humanity qua species whose own shortsightedness threatens to destroy the planetary inheritance on which it depends for its existence.[28] Along with a technical apparatus of systems monitoring, the report insists that it is necessary to mobilize our distinctively human "cultural and spiritual heritages" to enable the species to readjust to "natural laws" and thus to ensure both "economic interests and survival imperatives." There can be no biophysical life, in other words, without a certain anthropological supplement, one that mirrors and extends the purposeful, proto-aesthetic "patterns" of the planetary organism itself.

With the mandate of restoring part and whole into a healthy and enduring dynamic, *Our Common Future* formalized for the first time the principle of "sustainable development" as "development that meets the needs of the present without compromising the ability of future generations to meet their own."[29] Sustainability was defined as an intergenerational economy extending between present and future, a matter of heritage and inheritance to be shared and handed down across time and space.

Informed by the United Nations Environmental Programme (UNEP) report, the 1992 Earth Summit in Rio posited sustainability as the guiding ideal of the post–Cold War global economy. Unlike the Conference on the Human Environment held in Stockholm in 1972, the Earth Summit could not limit its participants to national governments, intergovernmental agencies, business leaders, technical experts, and an exemplary moral spokesperson such as René Dubos.

Whatever spiritual, symbolic, or identificatory attachment the figure of the planet was meant to compel, from the beginning it has been bound up with a model of ecosystemic feedback loops between populations, territories, and resources in need of adjustment and management at both national and international levels — an expanded field of biopower, in the precise sense given to this term by Michel Foucault when he characterized it as that which "brought life and its mechanisms into the realm of explicit calculation."[30] Biopower signals a shift in the nineteenth century away from the sovereign power to take or destroy life toward a set of techniques for governing "the life of the species":

> If the question of "man" was raised — insofar as he was a specific living being and related specifically to other living beings — the reason for this was to be sought in a new mode of relation between history and life: in this dual position of life that placed it at the same time outside history in its biological environment, and inside human historicity, penetrated by the latter's techniques of knowledge and power. There is no need to lay further stress on the proliferation of political technologies that ensued, investing the body, health, modes of subsistence and habitation, living conditions, the whole space of existence.[31]

Foucault writes that this mode of government was a precondition for, but irreducible to, the capitalist system; it "had to have methods of power capable of optimizing forces, aptitudes, and life in general without at the same time making them more difficult to govern."[32] In other words, by hailing and defining subjects in their biological existence, biopower potentially opens a new field of conflict and puts itself at risk: "what we have seen has been a very real process of struggle; life as a political object was in a sense taken at face value and turned back against the system that was bent on controlling it."

This results in the proliferation of rights claims addressed to governing agencies, including "the right to life" itself.[33] Foucault is ambivalent on this point. On the one hand, he seems to imply that such rights claims participate in the "repressive hypothesis," which would imagine liberating a repressed vital potential from the obstacles imposed on it by power. On the other, the "life" in question is itself shot through with technologies of power — both biophysical life-support systems and discursive practices — that withdraw the bases of any such natural liberation. Biopolitics is thus coextensive with what Bernard Steigler called the "originary technicity of the human." Any biopolitical struggle, from this perspective, must be understood in terms of nonautogenous reinscription and reinvention, rather than the restoration of a self-determining essence — a predicament marked by Steigler's phrase "the pursuit of life by means other than life."[34]

Though Foucault does not explicitly refer to environmentalism, his understanding of biopower and the unexpected modes of agency to which it can give rise enables us to comprehend a key difference between Stockholm and Rio. Responding to the very terms put forward in Stockholm by figures such as Dubos, the two interceding decades witnessed the global proliferation of nongovernmental environmental organizations concerned with holding states and corporations accountable for either activities deemed environmentally destructive — yet lacking established, enforceable juridical norms — or the violation by these agencies of their own self-professed norms and responsibilities concerning environmental welfare, defined either at a national or an international level. Neither political representatives nor technical experts in a strict sense, these agents deployed a range of legislative, electoral, legal, and agitational strategies that aimed to disseminate an "ecological sensibility." They contributed to the creation of what Paul Wapner called a "world civic politics" that compelled governments to respond to and, if possible, to contain and manage environmental demands.[35]

While hundreds of NGOs participated with unprecedented visibility in the internal processes of the 1992 Earth Summit, an extraordinary coalition of globally Northern and Southern organizations also used the event as an occasion to overflow the pacific role of "partners" and "consultants" they were expected to play (assuming, of course, that they had been invited to participate in the first place, for many organizations in the South were not). Establishing the connections for what would come to be known as the Global Justice Movement, this coalition held a countersummit that drew attention to the failure of the Earth Summit's so-called Agenda 21 to address in any substantial way the global imbalance of power between the G7 countries and the postcolonial world. They protested the unequal terms of trade, debt, and aid, the positing of poverty and overpopulation as the root causes of environmental degradation, rather than Northern patterns of production and consumption, and the assumption that corporate-led "growth" constitutes the fundamental engine of global prosperity. Rather than function as mere spokespeople for a preexisting civil society, these NGOs recast the summit's foundational terms — "environment" and "sustainability" — as questions of governmental accountability, rather than of consensual problem solving.[36]

This unsettling of roles was dramatized in an interruptive media event addressed to the summit and the global press that assembled to cover it. From the top of Rio's famous Sugarloaf Mountain, Greenpeace activists dropped a massive banner featuring the familiar figure of the planet that had served to ground and orient the discourse of environmentalism since the early 1970s. In this case, however, the figure had been rotated so as to emphasize the Southern Hemisphere and marked it with the word "SOLD" in English and Portuguese.

This event was remarkable in the history of environmental activism. While it belonged to the tradition of mediagenic civil disobedience tactics pioneered by Greenpeace in the 1970s and 1980s — banner drops, theatrical street protests, and, most famously, "David and Goliath" maritime confrontations — it also marked an important shift in environmental groups' understanding of the agencies and modes of governance responsible for environmental abuses, as well as of the nature and scope of those abuses. Widely acknowledged as one of the first "transnational advocacy networks," for the first two decades of its existence, Greenpeace claimed as its mandate "protecting the natural world from human destruction."[37] This was most evident in its campaigns to "save the whales," but also in its campaigns against nuclear weapons in places such as French Polynesia. While targeting the practices of specific governments — such as Russia's refusal to adhere to the International Convention on Whaling or France's endangering of the health of Pacific Islanders and the militarization of its own national security policy — the organization framed what Wapner calls their "witness-bearing" activities in the public sphere as a battle between the forces of mortal destruction on the one hand and an ecologically pacified humanity on the other.[38]

Greenpeace banner drop during the UN Earth Summit, Sugarloaf Mountain, Rio de Janeiro, 1992 (© Greenpeace/Morgan).

Camera-equipped activists aboard a Zodiac raft, with the Greenpeace vessel *James Bay* between two Russian whaling ships, North Pacific Ocean, 1976 (photo by Rex Weyler).

By contrast, the Rio intervention marked the planet as the surface of a relatively novel form of antagonism; rather than an opposition between destructive or negligent national governments, on the one hand, and an endangered ecosystem or species body, on the other, the banner addresses the globalization of the market as the organizing principle of society. Yet while the banner targets a general dynamic of commodification or enclosure, it does not simply oppose "capitalism" as such; it expresses, rather, an intolerance for a certain way of governing the relation between economy, society, and nature carried out between states, corporations, and Northern-dominated multilateral institutions of development and governance. The Earth Summit was thus marked as both a site for the consolidation of these modes of governing and an occasion for their contestation, from both within and without, a contestation undertaken in the name of neither the salvation of nature nor the liberation of the proletariat, but rather in the name of democratic accountability to those affected by policies found to be simultaneously environmentally, socially, and economically intolerable.

Reiterating the universalizing figure of the Earth employed by the United Nations, but questioning its assumptions about the relationships between population, poverty, and environmental degradation, countersummit participant Vandana Shiva contended that "an Earth democracy cannot be realized so long as there is global domination by undemocratic structures.... And it cannot be realized if planetary survival is used to deny the right to survival of those who are poor and marginal today because they have borne the accumulated burden of centuries of subjugation."[39] Shiva marks the biopolitical index of survival as something other than the minimal physiological conditions of species existence or the "bare life" of the population, as Giorgio Agamben's grim teleology of biopower would have it.[40] More than a predetermined set of "needs" to be calculated by governing agencies, Shiva's "right to survival" recalls Foucault's discussion of the emergence of rights claims developed in response to the governmentalization of "life as a political object" situated at the undecidable interstices of "biological environment" and "human historicity."[41] Indeed, for Shiva, survival in the biophysical sense of sustainable access to ecological life-support systems is inextricably bound up with the survival of historical memories of deprivation of such access by the colonial and postcolonial state alike — "the accumulated burden of centuries of subjugation." The traces of these memories are effaced, she claims, by the humanist vision of planetary survival projected by the agencies assigned with the task of managing the environment and its use by states or corporations. Shiva's concept reverberates retroactively into environmental historiography, enabling certain conflicts, actors, and claims to appear that have until recently been suppressed or subsumed by the Northern "ecology of affluence." These include the Chipko movement, in which Himalayan forest dwellers resisted the Indian state's plans for ski resort development by performatively "hugging the trees"; the alliance between Brazilian rubber tappers and indigenous people against the destruction of the Amazon forest by multinational logging companies, domestic ranchers, and state-induced colonization schemes; the Movement for the Survival of the Ogoni People in the Niger Delta against inequitable, environmentally destructive resource extraction by the Shell corporation and the state-tolerated paramilitary violence associated with it; and the Greenbelt Movement, the national tree-planting and sustainable development campaign carried out by rural women, which was launched by biologist Wangari Maathai, a campaign that has gradually mitigated the patterns of rural desertification perpetrated by the Kenyan state's industrialization policies.[42]

While in the passage cited above Shiva refers primarily to the endangerment of the customary rights of rural populations, it is worth noting that her first use of the phrase "right to survival" appears in a 1985 text, coauthored with J. Bandopadhayay, entitled "Science, Environment and Democratic Rights," written in the aftermath of the Bhopal disaster. There, the authors write that "the environment movement of the affluent world has decreased the hazards of pollution and toxic chemicals in their own countries,"[43] but this success has been achieved in part by relocating hazardous industry to countries such as India with little or no environmental legislation. Positing the negligence of multinational corporations such as Union Carbide as exemplary of the destructive development model adopted by the Indian state with the support of the World Bank, Shiva calls for an alliance between human rights, environmentalism, health rights, and alternative development movements in order to "challenge the slow and dispersed processes of death along with the rapid and concentrated genocide that took place in Bhopal. Will we struggle to ensure that everyone has a right to survival?"[44]

Activists with the Movement for the Survival of the Ogoni People
demonstrate against the environmental impact of the Shell
corporation's activities in the Niger Delta, early 1990s.

Shiva's understanding of pollution as a question of governmentally determined patterns of uneven risk exposure, rather than a moral and aesthetic disequilibrium menacing a generically human environment, echoes the discourse of the environmental justice movement that was emerging in the United States in the 1970s and 1980s. The environmental justice movement was initiated by poor people of color in both rural and urban areas refusing to tolerate the disproportionate concentration of toxic industries and waste sites in their communities, and the failure of corporations and governmental agencies alike to redress their grievances.[45] While indebted to the demands for regulatory oversight and scientific transparency that animated Rachel Carson's seminal *Silent Spring* (1962), the movement was critical of the blindness of mainstream environmentalism to the specific histories of social inequality and political disenfranchisement. Significantly, delegates from the National People of Color Environmental Leadership participated in the Rio countersummit, where their "Principles of Environmental Justice" (1991) were adopted as part of the summit's platform. These principles brought together a wide range of struggles surrounding unsustainable policies — such as dumping, strip mining, weapons testing, deforestation, dam construction, climate change, gentrification, unsafe workplaces, the neglect of urban infrastructures, and inadequate emergency preparedness — aversely affecting the natural and built environments of marginalized people.

In considering the expansive rearticulation of environmentalism with claims for human rights, governmental accountability, and social justice that took place at the margins of the Earth Summit, we can read the Greenpeace banner drop as inaugurating a new biopolitical imaginary to whose imperatives any "environmental art" worthy of the name must respond. Rather than aiming to create "environmental homeostasis on a global scale," as Kepes put it in 1972, or to reestablish what Matilsky described in 1992 as "a vital link to nature by communicating an experience of its life-generating powers," or even to "confront our consumer society and…begin the process of rebuilding community," as called for by McKibben in 2005, the task of new environmental art would be to unsettle the self-evidence of "environment" itself, addressing it as a contingent assemblage of biological, technological, economic, and governmental concerns whose boundaries and agencies are perpetually exposed to conflict.[46]

While it is outside the scope of this essay to elaborate a full survey of practices responding to the imperative promulgated in Rio, it suffices to say that many aspire to take part in the expanded networks of an environmentalist counterpublic that has emerged over the past decade, especially in the aftermath of the high-profile demonstrations in Seattle against the World Trade Organization (WTO) in 1999, which saw the proliferation of new repertoires, technologies, and tactics of protest. Previous critics from Kepes to McKibben have invoked the figure of the artist as a uniquely endowed "visionary" capable of resolving the aporias of biology and anthropology, science and spirit, part and whole. The new biopolitical artist must now be understood as a contingent location within an open-ended — though not necessarily egalitarian — field of aesthetic participants, including media strategists and investigative journalists, photographers and videographers, Web and graphic designers, charismatic spokespeople and ordinary movement members, organizers and demonstrators.

I am using "aesthetic," here, as defined by Jacques Rancière in his discussion of the "partition of the sensible," as "an implicit law governing the sensible order that parcels out places and forms of participation in a common world by first establishing the modes of perception within which these are inscribed."[47] Rancière is concerned with what does or does not become sayable, audible, or visible at a particular conjuncture, whose claims can register as legitimately political "speech" as opposed to private, inconsequential "noise." Rather than simply including new elements in a common arena whose rules are shared consensually in advance, aesthetic practices have the potential to disturb the configuration of "the common" itself, or the ways in which roles are distributed and parts are arranged by governing agencies in order to constitute society as an operative superorganism — the most extreme figure of which would be that projected by *Our Common Future.*

Perhaps the most widely publicized biopolitical artistic intervention of recent years is the Yes Men's targeting of Dow Chemical Company. The group impersonated the public-relations division of the corporation by releasing to the media a simulated avowal of responsibility for the Bhopal disaster and its ongoing aftermath. Reiterated emphatically by a fake spokesperson interviewed by a BBC reporter, the statement appeared to concede to the demands of the Bhopal survivors' movement for accountability and reparations from the corporation, which inherited the assets (and historical culpability) of Union Carbide Corporation when the latter became a subsidiary of Dow Chemical in 2001. Timed to coincide with the twentieth anniversary of the disaster, the intervention was a kind of countermemorial that reactivated public scrutiny of Dow Chemical's continued impunity, thus supplementing — in a painful, but ultimately resonant manner — the concurrent media and litigious activities of the Bhopal movement itself.

Though less tactically precise in terms of its timing, mode of public address, and potential interface with actually existing biopolitical claims, another significant corporate impersonation project recently undertaken by the Yes Men targeted Halliburton, the oil and energy products and services provider firm formerly chaired by Dick Cheney and granted reconstruction contracts by the Bush administration in Iraq and New Orleans. The Yes Men designed a mirror site that parodied the official Halliburton Web site by subtly blending the corporation's own self-justifying discourse with critical analyses of its activities.[48] The centerpiece of the project, however, was an infiltration performance at the "Catastrophic Loss" conference for the risk-management industry, held at a Ritz-Carlton hotel in Florida.

Speaking on behalf of Halliburton, the Yes Men introduced a prototype of the Survivaball, an enclosed life-support capsule designed to protect and sustain corporate executives working in environments rendered unsurvivable, whether by war, industrial accidents, or climate change. As a kind of architectural prosthesis, the Survivaball recalls the microbiospheric environments created by NASA researchers in the 1960s and 1970s to determine the minimal conditions for human existence,[49] which themselves echoed the visionary science-fiction architecture of groups such as Archigram.[50] Yet whereas such experiments were undertaken with a view to restoring an equilibrium between the species body and the patterns of the planetary superorganism, the Survivaball not only hyperbolically anticipates the long-term intensification of environmental disadjustments as the condition for future profit making, but also provides the appropriate protective equipment for those contracted to manage the perpetual state of emergency generated by the energy-industrial complex.

The protective enclosure inhabited by the Haliburton executive finds its inverse counterpart in a media event staged on Earth Day 2005. There, hundreds of members of the Inuit Circumpolar Conference (ICC) used their bodies to trace the outline of an Inuit figure on the ice sheets of Baffin Island, a figure that was accompanied by the words "Arctic Warning" in both English and Inuit.[51] Photographed from the air and addressed to both the universal public supposedly convoked by Earth Day and the transnational inter-Inuit movement, the bodies marked the unevenly allocated conditions of vulnerability to which different populations and regions are exposed by the "global" phenomenon of climate change. This media event might be considered a demonstration in the ancient etymological sense of a *monstrum,* or portent, that interrupts the order of the human world with a warning of a disaster to come.[52] To affiliate this event with the inhuman or the monstrous is not to dehumanize its participants, for the human world it interrupts depends on a naturalized, unmarked polar environment to act as a mirror surface for its own precariousness qua planetary species. It is a world, in other words, that effaces the histories, economies, and cultures of polar humanity and replaces them with the melancholic pathos of the polar bear set afloat in a sea of melted ice (a ubiquitous

HALLIBURTON

SurvivaBall

TM

Model X7 Survivaball
Unit Z5-11   Version 11.7

Compatible with Halliburton power units 10x+ and 11x with PP45 adapter and TICC conversion software

1. SHF antenna with supplementary LF antennae
2. Receiver and data processor
3. Protective headgear with visor
4. Drinking straw
5. External pores (defensive)
6. Defense Enhancement Unit (1 of 3; primary)
7. Food Reprocessor (receives nutrients from Nutrition Refunction Center, 21)
8. Maniple Pods (for interaction with people, technology, and the environment)
9. Nutrition Utility Transfer (conveys nutrients from Food Reprocessor, 6)
10. Electrical Gafting (secures against power loss)
11. Dynamo
12. Motors (powered by dynamo and Maniple Pod plug interfaces)
13. Electromagnetic strips (generate electricity for dynamo and allow external linkage)
14. Maniple Pod deployed as rotor (applicable to all MPs)
15. Defense Enhancement Unit (2 of 3; non-lethal)
16. Power converter
17. Defense Enhancement Unit (3 of 3, rear)
18. Power conduits with inline power converters and dynamo
19. Medical Analysis Unit (runs constant scans on health and energy)
20. Personal Trapment Unit (conveys cast-off to Nutrition Refunction Center, 21)
21. Nutrition Refunction Center (extracts nutrients from cast-off)
22. Persistent Nutrition Unit (delivers small amounts on an ongoing basis)
23. Suspension Grid (elasticated cable system)
24. Hyperfine Elasticity Units (impart added momentum)
25. Medical Stability & Emergency Unit
26. Communications and Infrastructure Monitoring Assemblage

The Yes Men, Halliburton Survivaball diagram (2005) (www.halliburtoncontracts.com).

Arctic Warning/Naalagit media event based on a drawing by Josie
Pitseolak and directed by aerial artist John Quigley in collaboration with
the Inuit Circumpolar Conference (featuring the participation of actors
Selma Hayek and Jake Gyllenhaal) off Baffin Island, Earth Day, 2005.

figure of survival and extinction in the Northern imaginary of climate change, one that plays a starring role in Al Gore's *An Inconvenient Truth*). As a claim for "climate justice" shared with other groups in the South Pacific and elsewhere, the ICC demonstration is both a warning and a reminder to mainstream environmentalism itself about its own proclivity to neglect or to subsume historically entrenched inequalities in appeals.[53] One such example is provided by Gore in a special "Green Issue" of *Vanity Fair*: "What is at stake is the survival of our civilization and the habitability of the Earth. Or as one eminent scientist put it, the pending question is whether an opposable thumb and a neocortex are a viable combination on this planet."[54] Though we may take issue with Gore's rehetoric, it is important to attend to the ways in which his totalizing anthropological-evolutionary speculations have been inscribed, transformed, and debated within the discourses of an emergent "Neo-Green" coalition of celebrities, intellectuals, executives, technologists, architects, and NGO workers who have lent their support to the ex–vice president and his film (*An Inconvenient Truth*) over the past few years. *Wired* magazine's cover story, the "Next Green Revolution," glibly celebrates "how technology is leading environmentalism out of the anti-business, anti-consumer wilderness."[55] But its participants are a heterogeneous and agonistic group for whom the public visibility of global warming as a general planetary threat provides an important *point de capiton* for the articulation of what Ernesto Laclau calls a "chain of equivalences" linking a range of left-liberal claims in the U.S. public sphere concerning the relationship between the environment, the economy, security, and democracy.[56] Exemplary in this regard is the Apollo Alliance, which mobilizes a narrative of progressivist patriotism by calling for a program of "good jobs and clean energy."[57] In so doing, it seeks to reduce dependence on petroleum and its associated geostrategic entanglements; to reconstitute deindustrialized workforces, cities, and regions of the United States as vanguards of "green technologies" capable of competing in the markets of emerging industrial economies such as China; to encourage the internalization by developers and architects of sustainable building standards such as Leadership in Energy and Environmental Design (LEED); and finally, to reduce the overall contribution of the United States to global carbon emissions through investment in public transport infrastructure, hybrid vehicles, and alternative energy sources such as wind, solar power, and hydroelectricity.

Working in tandem with this initiative are groups known for their role in the 1999 Seattle protests such as Global Exchange and Rainforest Action Network, whose Declare Independence from Oil campaign deploys Greenpeace-style civil disobedience, legislative lobbying, and mainstream advertising in calling for Ford to invest in fuel-efficient technologies and for its consumers and shareholders to pressure it to do so.

Supplementing such targeting of large-scale corporate governance are the Green Trade Fairs staged by Global Exchange over the past five years, which showcase a range of avant-garde sustainable technologies and products, including organic consumables such as coffee, rice, and maize imported through fair-trade arrangements with peasant cooperatives in the global South. Such linkages pose an interesting question for the Neo-Green alliance: how will figures such as Gore, who obviously seeks an alternative to the world order perpetuated by the neoconservative "disaster capitalists" denounced by the Yes Men, position themselves on issues such as the liberalization requirements of the WTO in areas such as agriculture and intellectual property, requirements against which counterglobalization groups such as Global Exchange have struggled for nearly a decade?

An important aesthetic event in the emergence of such struggles was the Quit Monsanto campaign undertaken by the Karnataka State Farmers' Association in 1998. Drawing on a Gandhian repertoire of nonviolent civil disobedience, the association symbolically cremated experimental genetically engineered plants introduced to the Indian agricultural system under the auspices of the WTO. The Karnataka farmers targeted Monsanto's so-called "terminator technology," which engineers plants to kill their own embryos after each harvest, thus requiring farmers to purchase new seeds every year, rather than maintain a self-renewing "genetic commons" of seed stock to be shared freely across generations.[58]

Though the gesture of cremation expresses a certain kind of symbolic purification, it differs from the primary mode of consumer-citizenship in the United States and Europe regarding genetically modified food; whereas the consumer-citizen is often informed by moral-gastronomical anxieties about the pollution of the individual's natural body by so-called "frankenfoods," the farmers' intervention addresses instead the governmental and bioscientific technologies that enable indigenous systems of agricultural production and knowledge transmission to become the property of transnational corporations. Since the Quit Monsanto campaign, the phenomenon of "biopiracy" has become the object of a worldwide advocacy network struggling to resignify the provisions of the Earth Summit's Biodiversity Convention, in particular through initiatives such as the Porto Alegre Treaty to Share the Genetic Commons, which was announced by NGOs at the shadow convention of the 2002 World Summit of Sustainable Development in Johannesburg.[59]

Repoliticizing biotechnology and contesting its claims to the moral high ground is the point of departure for a series of public-education projects by the U.S. group Critical Art Ensemble (CAE). Displayed in art museums, on college campuses, and at activist summits, their *Gentrerra* installation recalls Harrison's *Survival Piece,* yet interrupts the older artists' rhetoric of salvation and healing. Whereas the latter displaced living botanical organisms into the gallery in order to protect their bare life from the ravages of industrial technology, CAE's project deliberately cultivates and displays plants that have been inscribed with Monsanto's terminator technology. However, the plants are presented as laboratory subjects of possible "reverse engineering," organisms capable of having their autosterilizing genetic programs undone through relatively simple biochemical interventions by scientifically informed citizens.

In a way that resonates with CAE's framing of "genetic pollution" as a biopolitical, rather than a moral and aesthetic problem, the Center for Urban Pedagogy's traveling exhibition *Garbage Problems* complicates the canonical environmentalist iconography of "waste" as the product of generic societal overconsumption by asking: "How is your

Karnataka State Farmers' Association, Cremate Monsanto campaign, 1998.

garbage political?" Designed in collaboration with low-income students from the City as School Program, the centerpiece of the exhibition is *The Garbage Machine,* a critical recasting of Jay Forrester's diagram of the interaction between population, resources, and pollution flows from *The Limits to Growth.* Forrester endeavored through cybernetic modeling to identify and eliminate the sources of "entropy" in the functioning of the planetary system with the aim of ensuring a long-term global equilibrium. Forrester's diagram epitomized a certain kind of "technocratic" project that sets up a world picture to be monitored and managed by experts. The Center for Urban Pedagogy at once deploys and displaces the graphic procedures of the ecological feedback diagram in order to chart the infrastructural circuits and governmental architecture of waste management in New York City and, tangentially, the global garbage industry.

Crucially, the diagram is annotated with visual and textual materials in such a way that the diagram transforms the totalizing gestalt of "the System" into a dynamic citizen interface with a sociotechnical network of differently positioned and empowered "garbage people" or subjects for whom waste is a field of knowledge, problematization, intervention, and conflict. Along with city agencies, planning boards, private companies, and academic experts, these "garbage people" also include — on unequal and contested terms — nongovernmental activists. These activists have targeted specific practices of sanitational governmentality, such as the disproportionate siting and inadequate

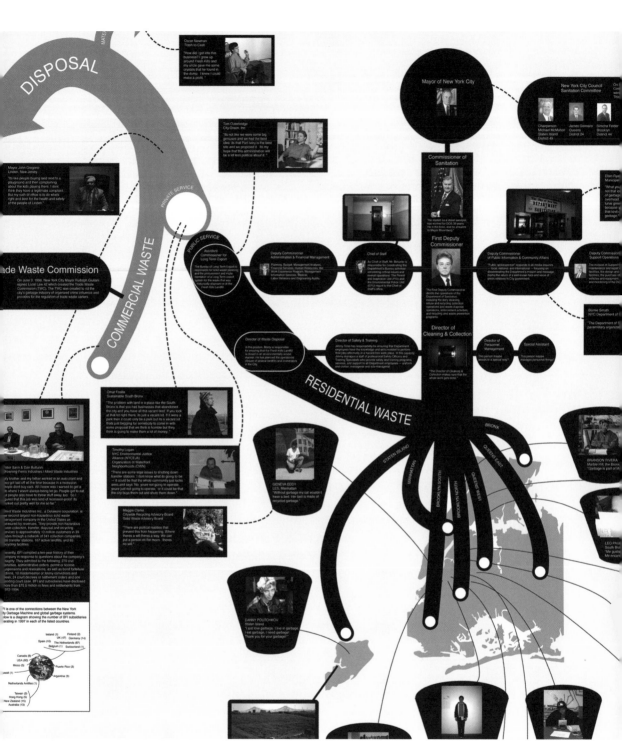

Center for Urban Pedagogy, *The Garbage Machine* (2002)
(design by Justyna Judycka and Damon Rich).

oversight of privately contracted waste-transfer stations in poor communities of color, resulting in high levels of asthma, weakened prospects for alternative economic development, and an overall degradation of the quality of life. Rather than agents of abstract oppression, scientific expertise and governmental technologies are crucial sites of debate and mobilization for groups such as Sustainable South Bronx, whose expressions of intolerance for general patterns of "environmental racism" are accompanied by partnerships with foundations and city agencies to "green the ghetto" through new forms of investment in technology, transportation, employment, and recreation (a vision that resonates with the grand design of the Apollo Alliance referred to above.).[60]

RETRACING "OUR" STEPS

Let us retrace our steps, assuming there is a "we" to whom they might belong — which we shouldn't necessarily do. Taking as our point of departure the "Death of Environmentalism," we have traced the constitutive role of aesthetico-cultural means — including, but not limited to artistic practices — in the deconstruction of the ends of environmentalism. These ends have been understood as a spatial question concerning environmentalism's conceptual boundaries and relations with other discourses, a temporal question concerning the potential obsolescence or survival of its historical task, and an ethico-political question concerning its motivations and aims and the subject or object in whose name these aims are pursued (until recently defined as nature, humanity, or as some superorganismic adjustment between the two). Having touched down in Stockholm and Rio, Baffin Island, and the Bronx, what's the next step? Where, if anywhere, are we going with this? Back to the beginning, or rather, the *arche* beginning. Not, in other words, to the dialectic of deathly, technical ossification and inspired mythic rebirth put forward at the Grantmaker's Association, but to the stamps, or stomps, that broke the ground of our investigation in the first place, the traces of traces that called out "Read me — will you ever be able to do so?"[61] Have we been or will we ever be successful in so doing?

By definition, no. And it is because of this impossibility that we have a responsibility to read the image historically: to place it in relation to other times and places that, strictly speaking, are not evident in the image as such.[62] This history neither subsumes the part into the development of a superorganismic whole (the history of "Man" and "his" evolution, for instance, or even that of capitalist globalization and its antagonists from below), nor encloses it upon itself as a part with no claim to a common world, isolated like an island. Indeed, when read historically, the image with which we began alludes to such an island whose particular kind of isolation has by no means involved simple exclusion or disconnection from global economies, governing agencies, and, more recently, transnational advocacy networks. It is an image of Vieques, a small, inhabited territory belonging to Puerto Rico, two-thirds of which was used as a weapons testing range by the U.S. Navy from 1941 to 2003.

The island gained a certain visibility in the global media in 1999, when a resident named David Sanes was killed by an errant bomb that fell in the civilian area of the island. While the military attempted to frame the death of Sanes as an unfortunate case of bad targeting, this "accidental" entry of violence into the civilian world became an occasion for the exposure of a fundamental violence haunting the island in its entirety, reactivating grievances and claims that spanned several generations of Viequenses.[63] In 1941, the military used the power of eminent domain to evict thousands of peasants, sugarcane workers, and fisherfolk from 70 percent of the island in order to build a base, a munitions storage facility, and a bombing range. These expropriations were followed by several attempts to relocate the entire population to the island of Saint Croix, a policy which was met with local resistance and ultimately a successful lobbying campaign by the governor of Puerto Rico. Though the Viequenses remain on the island, the living conditions of residents continued to decline, as evidenced by chronic unemployment, high cancer rates, the destruction of the costal ecosystem, and the endless acoustic barrage emanating from the bombing range. In the mid-1970s, these conditions aroused popular antagonism toward the military, primarily in the form of a fishermen's movement against the disruption and restriction of the island's common fisheries. The fishermen used a range of civil-disobedience tactics intended to interrupt naval operations and to draw international attention to their grievances and, by extension, to those of the entire population. Most dramatically, a flotilla of fishing boats laid a huge net of buoyed chains in the path of a warship, tangling and incapacitating its propellers. Groups of fishermen also regularly trespassed on the primary bombing range itself, activating the military's security protocol, which required a temporary cessation of

Fishermen confront the U.S. Navy off Vieques, Puerto Rico, 1976.

exercises each time it was triggered. In the early 1980s the fishermen filed a suit against the Navy in a U.S. federal court, attempting to reinscribe domestic law in terms of a universal "right to livelihood" for which the government itself could be held accountable. However, the case was immediately overshadowed when the governor of Puerto Rico incorporated the cause of Vieques into a broader campaign for statehood, which ironically involved a commitment to *allowing* the Navy to stay on the island, albeit with a small development package for its residents.

It was this history of expropriation, resistance, and failed promises that informed the response to David Sanes's death. One of the first acts of protest was to trespass onto the bombing range in order to plant a white cross in memory of Sanes. This inaugurated a larger campaign of civil disobedience, which grew as calls for solidarity began to circulate in the electronic counterpublic spheres of Puerto Rico, the United States, and Latin America. An entire "Peace and Justice Camp" was erected outside the fence of the naval installation, which hosted activists, journalists, and eventually, politicians seeking to harness the Vieques movement to a variety of electoral and legislative ends.

The photograph with which we began is, among other things, an index of these civil disobedience activities in Vieques. It forms part of a multifaceted art project by Jennifer Allora and Guillermo Calzadilla entitled *Landmark*. In 2000, the Puerto Rico–based pair began a collaboration with activists to develop protest techniques that would link the reclamation of physical territory to the symbolic remarking of historical memory. The procedure was as follows: civil disobedients were invited to design individualized protest graphics, which the artists then cast into rubber reliefs that could be attached to the soles of normal shoes. Demonstrator's bodies thus became mobile mark-making machines. With each step, or stomp, into the restricted zone of the beach, these pedestrian prosthetics would leave a mark of *pressure* — both an index of bodily weight in the receptive surface of the sand and, symbolically, a bearing down upon the navy's intolerable negligence and occupation of the island. Indeed, the logic of the technique is akin to that of the seal — a raised or incised emblem impressed on a receptive material such as wax, typically in order to authorize a document or to attest that it has not been opened or tampered with. Yet, if the seal is usually associated with the securing of secrets or the protection of spaces from unauthorized eyes and bodies, here the seal takes on the role of breaking and entering. Rather than introduce violence from the outside into an unbroken space, it decrypts or unseals a deeper extant violence, suggesting that the smooth surface of the sand already bears within it traces of destruction, loss, and conflict. To be clear, this is not to say that we are witnessing here the "instigation of strife" in the Heideggerian sense of the term.[64]

Yet, even as they are activated by a certain kind of material force, the soles are irreducible to the immediacy of "direct action." Whereas the index is classically defined as a sign that bears a uniquely physical, rather than referential or symbolic relation to the world, these marks are themselves textually inscribed in a way that gives them a certain virtuality, repeatability, and mobility that take them beyond the living moment of their genesis — like photographs. "Fuera a la Marina" — "Navy Out" — was the explicit, unconditional demand that the protesters shared and addressed to civil society. While this phrase was incorporated into many of the individual shoe soles, the latter do not express a homogenous political will. Looking down at the disturbed ground like investigators at the scene of a crime, what we witness in the photograph is a cacophony of overlapping, mutually effacing inscriptions marking everything from Puerto Rican nationalism, to the memory of the fishermen's original civil-disobedience activities, to demands for reparation from the federal government, to calls for the protection of local ecosystems. Most striking is a territorial outline of the island itself with an "X" incised across it. The physical terrain is thus marked as a target for both military bombardment and activist claims, but the negativity of the "X" also speaks, unwittingly perhaps, to the incalculable future of the island itself.

After three years of civil disobedience, massive street protests in San Juan and New York, intensifying media scrutiny, and eventual pressure from U.S. civil-rights leaders and legislators, the situation in Vieques was deemed by the Defense Department more costly than beneficial to the success of its testing operations. To great relief and celebration, the navy officially vacated the island in May 2003, and the land was returned to "public" control. With this undoubtedly spectacular victory achieved, the name "Vieques" began to disappear from both the mainstream media and counterpublic spheres. The Peace and Justice Camp was dismantled, nationalist politicians returned to their satisfied mainland constituencies, and solidarity listservs started to go cold.

For local activists and residents, however, this victory was precarious: the land had not been transferred to the municipality of Vieques, where its future might have been democratically debated, but to the U.S. Department of the Interior (DOI). The traumatized landscape had now been officially redefined as an ecological preserve under the jurisdiction of the U.S. Fish and Wildlife Service. But in claiming to restore the land to its natural balance and to preserve it for future generations, the DOI was enacting its own form of destruction and obliteration. Marking the site as purely "natural" required *marking over* the memory of those who lived and worked there before being evicted by the navy. Thus, the descendants of the evicted — in effect, the entire population of Vieques — could not be recognized as having a legitimate claim on the future of the land. With this history effaced, the DOI could position the Viequenses as an external *threat* whose lack of aesthetic and ecological appreciation for the biosphere could potentially put the natural heritage of the island at risk — an echo of hegemonic development discourses that cite unsustainable resource use by the poor as a root cause of environmental degradation. Ironically, the new status of the land as a "preserve" provided an alibi for *not* addressing the continuing contamination of the air, water, and soil of the *entire* island.

Activists were thus faced with a more insidious governmental apparatus than the U.S. Navy, which had lent itself quite well to a David and Goliath narrative during the period of civil disobedience. In place of fighting a symbolically potent war machine bent on death and destruction, the question became how to engage tactically a new regime of what Timothy W. Luke has called "environmentality," whose raison d'être is the management of the interrelation between living beings and their ecosystems.[65]

Around the time that the land was being transferred to the Department of the Interior, Allora and Calzadilla received a grant from the U.S. National Endowment for the Arts under the auspices of a landscape design project in Vieques. They combined these funds with an exhibition budget from the Tate Museum in London in order to produce another component of *Landmark* that would attend to the new dilemmas facing the island.

Along with the political and operational inconvenience caused by the protest movement, an important factor in the navy's ultimate decision to vacate the island was the fact that new Geographic Information Systems (GIS) had to some extent rendered the physical terrain of Vieques obsolete: war games could now be conducted in the open ocean using a precise spectrometric simulation of the island's topography.[66] Using the funds provided by the museum, Allora and Calzadilla were able to purchase this data from the private GIS company contracted by the military. In the hands of the navy, these spectralized traces of Vieques were used in ballistic experiments ultimately intended for material targets in Iraq and elsewhere. Refusing to accept this dominant application of GIS technology as its necessary telos, Allora and Calzadilla translated the data into what they described as a "counter-memorial" installation at the Tate.

Working from the precise measurements provided by the military contractor's infrared satellite, they reconstructed the gallery space as a full-scale topographical environment replicating the crater-marked surface of the Vieques bombing range. This procedure was an implicit challenge to the artistic principle of "site specificity," which stresses the dependence of aesthetic experience on the inviolate materiality of a given location, as opposed to the "placelessness" and "disembodiment" often attributed to digital media by art historians. Rather than violate the unity or uniqueness of a site through technological displacement, Allora and Calzadilla's intervention suggested that the singular history of Vieques is inseparable from its inscription *in* and *as* media. This lack of self-identity is what enables the island to share its wounded history with other times and places. Without claiming to speak for a unified constituency in Vieques, Allora and Calzadilla staged the sharing of this history in the museum gallery.

They also worked with planning students from the London School of Economics to organize a conference on the politics of disaster recovery — a field that had for the past three years often taken September 11 as its point of departure. Taking place in a sculptural environment bearing the indexical marks of U.S. military violence, the conference worked to decenter September 11 as the exemplary instance of world-historical trauma. Rather than simply a forum for anti-imperialism, however, the conference sought to test the quasi-utopian phrase "Another World is Possible," beloved by politicized artists, in relation to the discourses of land use and sustainable development in both the North and the South. They posed the following questions: How is land differentiated from other lands by the way it is marked? Who decides what is worth preserving and

(TOP) U.S. Geological Survey, aerial photograph of former U.S. Navy bombing range, Vieques, Puerto Rico.

(BOTTOM) Jennifer Allora and Guillermo Calzadilla, *Landmark* installation, Tate Modern Museum, London (2003).

what should be destroyed? What are the strategies for reclaiming marked land? How does one articulate an ethics and politics of land use?

With the remainder of their grant money, the artists returned to Vieques and produced a small, freely distributed research publication that sought to negotiate this tension between the affirmation of possibility and the specific political techniques required to transform the way in which the relations between economy, ecology, and society were being governed. The publication featured a variety of photographs, diagrams, archival materials, a veteran's oral history of the fishermen's movement, interviews with activists, scientists, and local officials, a set of ecological and risk-distribution maps provided by the Vieques Technical Support Group, a Web directory of relevant organizations and human-rights documents, and an artists' statement concerning the complicity of Euro-American landscape aesthetics with the effacement of marginalized cultures and economies. Finally, a section entitled "Protesting with Proposals" presented a set of project proposals for the bombing range generated by college art students in an Interrogative Design workshop held by Allora and Calzadilla.

Unlike the Hippocratic physiology of McHarg's *Design With Nature,* which claimed to resolve social and ecological problems through the readjustment of the built environment according to organic norms of self-regulation and homeostatic equilibrium, Interrogative Design, in the words of Krzysztof Wodiczko, "takes a risk in exploring, articulating, and responding to the questionable conditions of life. Interrogative design questions the very worlds of needs of which it is born. It responds interrogatively to the needs that should not, but unfortunately do, exist in the present 'civilized' world."[67]

Exemplary in this regard is *Re-Direction* by Miguel Velez, a monumental ventilation and hydraulic system whose output of effluents could be "re-routed directly to those governmental agencies which deny the continuing existence of deadly pollutants on the island."[68] Recalling the hypertrophic landscape monuments of Claes Oldenburg or Superstudio in the 1970s, Velez's "visionary" infrastructural proposal called for these agencies to take responsibility for the "negative externalities" they have deemed tolerable in calculating the costs and benefits of their policies. The residues of such governmental decisions are to be found in the trace amounts of heavy metals that mark the life-support systems of the island — soil, water, air — and thus the bloodstreams and organic tissues of island residents themselves. Like the effluents to which people are exposed in Bhopal or the Bronx, this pollution bears the traces of history and social violence and cannot be "decontaminated" through a simple readjustment of society toward an organic equilibrium, as called for by McHarg and his latter-day disciples in the field of ecological landscape design. Indeed, rather than restoration or readjustment, Velez's project insists, in the name of a trace, residue, or contamination, on *disadjustment* between past, present, and future as the condition of environmental justice.[69]

In offering a hyperbolically unrealizable response to intolerable environmental conditions, a project such as Velez's provides a "pro-testimonial" supplement to a document such as the Guide to Sustainable Development prepared by the Committee for the Rescue and Development of Vieques (CRDV), the local NGO that formed in the

Miguel Velez, *Re-Direction* (2003).

aftermath of the civil-disobedience campaign. Along with demanding that the land be properly decontaminated by the federal government and returned to the municipality, the CRDV has had to grapple with the risks and possibilities of ecotourism as an engine for the redevelopment of the island.

This is the point of departure for another project by Allora and Calzadilla entitled *Under Discussion,* which combines Surrealist collage with Constructivist equipment design in an unlikely act of reengineering: retrofitting an overturned conference table with an engine and a rudder grafted from a local fishing boat, the artists transform it into a hybrid vehicle at once practical and symbolic. In liberal planning theory, "sitting down at the table" suggests an ideal space for conflict resolution through ratio-

Jennifer Allora and Guillermo Calzadilla, *Under Discussion,* video still (2004).

nal dialogue in which different "stakeholders" assent to a common set of ground rules from which they proceed to negotiate. Yet this ideal fails to account for the inequalities that underwrite the space of the table to begin with, such as the hierarchical division between scientific expertise and local ecological knowledges.[70] *Under Discussion* is an experimental device for publicizing such counterknowledge in the form of a "guided tour" around the restricted areas of the island. Marking the inheritance of the fishermen's movement, Diego de la Cruz, the son of one of the civil disobedients from the 1970s who inaugurated popular antagonism against the navy, pilots the table boat. Indeed, the vehicle might be thought of as an homage to the fishermen's *détournement* of their own equipment during their Greenpeace-like confrontations with the navy in which a tactical assemblage of boats, buoys, and nets served to paralyze a U.S. warship temporarily. To evoke this memory at a moment when the island is undergoing a process of official environmentalization is to claim the "right to survival" theorized by Vandana Shiva, an imperative to bear witness to the traces of past injustice that unsettles the given partition of positions and functions in the present — including, for instance, the treatment of island residents as simply one set of "stakeholders" sitting around the table of a new ecoconsensus.

Encrypting a reference to the etymological link between the figure of the helmsman, the art of government, and postwar cybernetic ecology, *Under Discussion* is a subaltern *Spaceship Earth* for the twenty-first century, articulating a "lifeboat ethics" quite different from that envisioned by a still-powerful neo-Malthusian ecology.[71] Conceived as a device of both protest and testimony, the work reminds us that the departure of the navy was not primarily the result of a rational negotiation of interests within a governmental framework, but required years of heterogeneous discourses and tactics on numerous institutional and geographical scales—not least of which were the risky modes of civil disobedience practiced by the fishermen's movement and later by the hundreds who trespassed onto the bombing range in memory of David Sanes. *Under Discussion* thus warns against linear narratives that would posit a neat transition from a phase of impassioned activism to sober institutional deliberation. In so doing, it does not necessarily call for a renewed campaign of "direct action," but seeks to track the survival of certain logics of exclusion that can be addressed only by exceptional, even "absurd" nongovernmental means. It is significant that the table is not simply *destroyed* in a gesture of resistance to "compromise." It remains intact, but only insofar as it is supplemented and redirected from its intended purpose. The picturesque route traveled by the vehicle around the island is shadowed by the aporia of ecotourism, that is, the necessity of "developing" the island's primary resource: its "natural heritage." Can ecotourism be organized in such a way that it is sustainable not only for nonhuman ecosystems, but for redistributive democracy, as well? On what terms would private capital invest in the "biodiversity" of the island, widely understood as a common inheritance by Viequenses?[72] To what extent can the 2002 Quebec Declaration on Ecotourism—a joint venture between the United Nations Environment Programme and the World Tourism Organization—become an instrument for demanding accountability from capital and the state? Will fishing be recognized as a biodiverse mode of subsistence, or will fishermen once again have to struggle to reclaim access to the marine commons—this time from official environmentalism, rather than from the military? Can the landscape be strategically "conserved" as a resource without marking it as *unmarked* nature and thus obliterating the memories of dispossession encrypted in it?

Confronting this aporia, the right to survival traced by Allora and Calzadilla involves a constitutive contamination of life by forces that are outside of its control, a life that is inseparable from, but irreducible to, the condition of being governed. This is not to capitulate to a cynical reformism that would take for granted the given techniques of government, but it is to suggest that without marking and being marked by them, "environmental art" cannot survive as anything more than gestural utopianism.

The photograph with which we began our discussion—the prints in the sand—thus comes to light as something more than a mere documentation of protest. As a photograph, it allows traces of a singular event to live on, but only on the condition of a certain dislocation and loss of self-identity. It preserves and destroys evidence simultaneously, demanding to be read while withdrawing the grounds of legibility. In this survival and withdrawal, the photograph allegorizes the ends of environmentalism, namely, the loss of "environment"—or even the loss of the "loss of environment"—that would secure the identity and purpose of a movement concerned with global survival. But the ends of environmentalism do not entail any simple extinction. Survival survives as an end of environmentalism, but only insofar as it ceases simply to be itself.[73] As suggested by Shiva, survival is viable only as a matter of rights, which always involves a disruptive address to others on whom the living — the survivors — are in some sense dependent for recognition, reparation, and redistribution. The photograph bears witness to this precarious condition. Inscribed in the sand at the edge of the sea, these frozen vestiges of the right to survival impart themselves as an uncertain inheritance from the past and an incalculable promise to future generations: sustainability without guarantees.

Let us end our investigation with another footprint, another set of traces that stage the emergence and vanishing of the "environment" and the humanity it would sustain. The place of this image is at once ultraprecise and endlessly insecure. It is ultraprecise in that that the Light Detection and Ranging (LIDAR) technology that produced it registers in great aerial-perspective detail the differential elevation of a determinate sector of the

Light Detection and Ranging (LIDAR) image of New Orleans, Louisiana, annotated and distributed by the Spatial Information Design Lab, Columbia University, 2005.

earth's surface, distinguishing on a gradual chromatic scale high-lying areas (light) from low-lying areas (dark). It is insecure because, along with the sheer metric data it offers to the expert eye, the image is already characterized by a strange familiarity, a perceptual resonance marked by the memory — and oblivion — of disaster. Reiterated for a year by government agencies, scientific authorities, news organizations, and academic conferences, this crescent-shaped gestalt comes to us, or rather returns from within us, as a kind of afterimage that carries the singular place name "New Orleans" and, with it, inevitably, "Katrina." But we must ask: To whom or what do these names refer? Who or what does the referring, and how? When and where does "Katrina" start and stop? These are questions that the image cannot answer by itself, even as it poses them with the greatest urgency. As a technological artifact and aesthetic apparition, the image renders the topos of the city ghostly to itself, as if to mark the absence or disappearance of the hundreds of thousands of residents that remain dispersed throughout the country — an ongoing biopolitical emergency that crystallizes the questions of ecological risk, governmental accountability, and historically inherited inequality that have informed our discussion of the ends of environmentalism.

In so doing, this uncanny inscription of the light of land also reverberates through the genealogy of environmental art sketched above, specifically the work of McHarg, whose Design and Nature *has reemerged in the aftermath of Hurricane Katrina as a touchstone for architects calling for the readjustment of New Orleans in its proper environmental milieu. Taking for granted the self-fulfilling prophecy of the Rand Corporation that the majority of New Orleans's displaced residents will not in fact return, Aaron Betsky, coeditor of* Artforum *magazine, hails this situation as an opportunity for the "rebirth" of New Orleans as a "smaller, lovelier, more compact city," and celebrates the "visionary" impulse at work in an architectural exhibition entitled* A Newer Orleans: A Shared Space. *"These projects seek to house a sense of community, attract attention and activity, and make the landscape visible. They propose a shared space, both physical and mental, around which the city can organize itself in a meaningful manner. And in so doing, they not only suggest an architecture for a Newer Orleans but also a potential way for making all of us at home in an increasingly alien world."[74] Betsky urges the "housing" of the urban community, but only as an ecophenomenological horizon, rather than as a political demand for a "Human Right to Housing" and its corollary, the "right to return," demanded by organizations such as the ACORN Katrina Survivors Association and the United Front for Affordable Housing Coalition.[75] One form taken by these rights claims has been the setting up of a small tent city or "Survivors' Village" outside the barbed-wired premises of St. Bernard Housing Development, a housing project that, like the majority of others in New Orleans, has remained empty and boarded up since the storm, despite suffering relatively little damage. In June 2006, the Department of Housing and Urban Development announced plans to demolish five thousand such units of public housing in order to make way for "mixed-income" redevelopment, an ambiguous term that, left uninterrogated, has often served to justify programs of aggressive gentrification in the name of "deconcentrating" the urban poor.[76]*

Addressed to passing motorists, media outlets, and urban and federal authorities, the Survivors' Village is designed to "serve as a reminder…that public housing residents will continue to fight for the right to return to their homes."[77] As a performative intervention in the visual, architectural, and mnemonic landscape of the city, the Survivors' Village resonates closely with Foucault's sense of the aesthetic imperative of nongovernmental activism: "to always make an issue of people's misfortune, to keep it in the eyes and ears of governments — it is not true that they are not responsible. People's misfortune must never be a silent remainder of politics. It founds an absolute right to rise up and address those who hold power."[78] Foucault's figure of the "remainder" is crucial here — it refers to "the mute trace or leftover of politics and its calculations" and "affirms the right to memory of a future survival, a rest where it might be effaced and its effacement silenced."[79] Without allowing the visually striking force of this intervention to direct attention away from the long-term, large-scale constraints, mediations, uncertainties, and inequalities that mark the reconstruction environment in which nongovernmental activists are struggling to operate in post-Katrina New Orleans, we can read Survivors' Village as a cipher for the ends of environmentalism whose quasi-transcendental condition is the unsettling of the oikos of "Man": the desire to be properly at home with oneself and the world, untroubled by the trace of the Other.

Residents and evictees of public housing demonstrate at the fenced-off perimeters of St. Bernard Housing Development, New Orleans, as part of the Survivors' Village campaign, July 2006 (photos by Craig Morse).

1 Michael Shellenberger and Ted Nordhaus, "The Death of Environmentalism: Global Warming Politics in a Post-Environmental World," *Grist,* January 13, 2005, www.grist.org/news/maindish/2005/01/13/doe-reprint.

2 *Ibid.*

3 *Ibid.*

4 I address these issues again from a different perspective in "'Eyes and Ears': Aesthetics, Visual Culture, and the Claims of Nongovernmental Politics," pp. 327–55 in the present volume. As I hope to show in this essay, the question of culture — and more particularly, the aesthetic — has been associated by environmentalists with the realm of "human" meaning, which must supplement and guide the technical abstractions of ecosystems analysis.

5 Bill McKibben, "Imagine That: What the Warming World Needs Now is Art, Sweet Art," *Grist,* April 21, 2005, www.grist.org/comments/soapbox/2005/04/21/mckibben-imagine.

6 *Ibid.*

7 As Kirkpatrick Sale argues in *The Green Revolution: The American Environmental Movement, 1962–1992* (New York: Hill and Wang, 1993), Earth Day, which was initiated by the liberal Senator Gaylord Nelson, was met with skepticism by many on the radical left, who saw it as an ideological smoke screen obscuring issues of race, class, and militarism in favor of a pacified, depoliticized humanity. While questioning certain assumptions and figures of environmentalism, I will attempt to avoid the temptation of radicalist demystification in this paper. For a subtle, early negotiation of these problems from a Marxist perspective, see Hans Mangus Enzenbeger, "A Critical of Political Ecology," *New Left Review* 84 (March–April, 1974), pp. 3–31.

8 Gyorgy Kepes (ed.), *Arts of the Environment* (New York: George Braziller Press, 1972), p. 15.

9 On Kepes's engagement with cybernetics, especially his interest in Norbert Weiner's idea of "information patterns" that occur in natural and social systems alike, see Reinhold Martin, *The Organizational Complex: Architecture, Media, and Corporate Space* (Cambridge, MA: MIT Press, 2003), p. 38.

10 See Jay W. Forrester, "Planning under the Dynamics of Complex Social Systems," in Kepes (ed.), *Arts of the Environment*; Donnella H. Meadows (ed.), *Limits to Growth* (Cambridge, MA: MIT Press, 1972); and Dennis L. Meadows, Donnella M. Meadows, and Donnella H. Meadows (eds.), *Toward Global Equilibrium: Selected Papers* (Cambridge, MA: MIT Press, 1973).

11 See René Dubos, "The Perils of Adaptation," in Kepes, *Arts of the Environment,* pp. 35–50.

12 Barbara Ward and René Dubos, *Only One Earth: The Care and Maintenance of a Small Planet* (New York: W.W. Norton, 1972), p. 220.

13 Kepes, *Arts of the Environment,* p. 12.

14 Ian L. McHarg, *Design With Nature* (New York: Natural History Press, 1969). On the genealogy of physiology and its application to the "maladies" of social organization, see George Canguilhem, "On Organic Norms in Man," in *The Normal and the Pathological,* trans. Carolyn R. Fawcett and Robert S. Cohen (New York: Zone Books, 1989), pp. 257–73.

15 McHarg, *Design with Nature,* p. 28.

16 *Ibid.,* pp. 28–29.

17 *Ibid.,* p. 47.

18 Vladimir Verdansky, *The Biosphere,* trans. D.B. Langmuir (New York: Copernicus, 1998). This is the first translation and publication of the book in English, a fact that is celebrated by a group of earth scientists, including Lynn Margulis, in a special preface.

19 Before being translated into English and thus into Anglo-American systems ecology, Verdansky's book took a strange detour through the Parisian avant-garde. Although Georges Bataille states that he offers a "different perspective" from that of the geochemist, the philosopher nonetheless cites geochemistry as a crucial influence on Verdansky's theory of the general economy of cosmic energy. See *The Accursed Share,* trans. Robert Hurley (New York: Zone Books, 1991), p. 192. This difference undoubtedly lies in the fact that while Bataille emphasizes the irrecoverable waste and excess generated by any system (art, for instance), Verdansky posits a closed, cyclical economy of birth, death, decay, and regeneration.

20 See George E. Hutchinson, "The Biosphere," *Scientific American* 223, no. 3 (1970), pp. 45–53. On Gaia, see James Lovelock, *Gaia: A New Look at Life on Earth* (Oxford: Oxford University Press, 1979).

21 In *The Metamorphosis of Plants,* Goethe claims that "all parts of a creature have a direct effect on one another, a relationship to one another, thereby renewing the circle of life." For a discussion of Goethe on this account, see Elaine P. Miller, "Vegetable Genius: Plant Metamorphosis as a Figure for Thinking and Relating to the Natural World in Post-Kantian German Thought," in Bruce V. Foltz and Robert Froedmen (eds.), *Rethinking Nature: Essays in Environmental Philosophy* (Bloomington: University of Indiana Press, 2004), pp. 114–34.

22 Alexander von Humboldt, *Cosmos: A Sketch of the Physical Description of the Universe* (Baltimore: Johns Hopkins University Press, 1997), p. 55. On the periodical recurrence

of Humboldtian holism in the history of ecology, see John Bowler, *The Earth Encompassed: A History of the Earth Sciences* (New York: W.W. Norton, 1995).

23 Barbara C. Matilsky, *Fragile Ecologies: Contemporary Artists' Solutions and Interpretations* (New York: Rizzoli Press, 1992), p. 3.

24 *Ibid.*

25 Ramachandra Guha, *Environmentalism: A Global History* (New York: Henry Holt, 2000), p. 89.

26 See Jeffrey Ellis, "On the Search for a Root Cause: Essentialist Tendencies in American Environmentalism," in William Cronon (ed.), *Uncommon Ground: Rethinking the Human Place in Nature* (New York: W. W. Norton, 1995), pp. 198–231.

27 The World Commission on Environment and Development, *Our Common Future* (Oxford: Oxford University Press, 1987), p. 1.

28 For a concise genealogy of the figure of the planet in the history of environmentalism, a genealogy that tracks the planet's ambivalent position between ecosystems theory and religio-aesthetic holism, see Wolfgang Sachs, "Environment," in Wolfgang Sachs (ed.), *The Development Dictionary: A Guide to Knowledge as Power* (London: Zed Books, 1992), pp. 27–37. Sachs's argument resonates with Heidegger's claims in "The Age of the World Picture" insofar as he associates the bird's-eye perspective of the astronaut with a transcendental subjectivity and cybernetics with the "enframing" of the earth, understood as an enormous standing-reserve network of resources and populations to be calculated and optimized. Bernard Steigler argues that Heidegger's condemnation of cybernetics as "calculation" speaks to the latter's inheritance of a long philosophical tradition that attempts to rescue the properly human from the contamination of what Steigler calls "originary technicity." See Bernard Steigler, *Technics and Time 1: The Fault of Epimetheus,* trans. Richard Beardsworth and George Collins (Stanford, CA: Stanford University Press, 1998), p. 4.

29 *Our Common Future,* p. 10.

30 Michel Foucault, *The History of Sexuality,* vol. 1, trans. Robert Hurley (New York: Vintage, 1984), pp. 143.

31 *Ibid.,* pp. 143–44.

32 *Ibid.,* p. 141.

33 *Ibid.,* p. 145.

34 Steigler's term is useful for evaluating the humanist condemnation of technocracy as the evacuation of rational communication and meaning from public life. Without simply embracing those discourses and practices accused of being technocratic, Steigler's insistence on technicity as the condition of the human has important implications for a theory of nongovernmental activism that would go beyond 1960s thematics of alienation, spontaneity, and self-organization. See *Technics and Time 1,* p. 135.

35 See Paul Wapner, "Politics Beyond the State: Environmental Activism and World Civic Politics," in Ken Conca and Geoffrey D. Dabelko (eds.), *Green Planet Blues: Environmental Politics from Stockholm to Kyoto* (Boulder, CO: Westview Press, 1998), pp. 118–31. For a good general history that traces the internal political debates of U.S. environmentalism (including the creation of the Environmental Protection Agency itself in 1971), see Sale, *The Green Revolution*. Guha's *Environmentalism: A Global History* deprovincializes this narrative and cogently identifies the movement's origins in the tension between capitalist "scientific conservation" techniques and the moral-aesthetic claims of Romantic anti-industrialism in the nineteenth century. This tension unfolded in the colonies as much as in Europe and the United States. Guha mentions, for instance, the experiments in German forestry — pioneered by Alexander von Humboldt — that were performed by the British in India, as well as Gandhi's indebtedness to John Ruskin and the reception of Gandhi by environmentalist civil-disobedience activists in the United States. Guha challenges Sale's understanding of the "Green Revolution," contending that Sale neglects the effect of World Bank and USAID policies on the restructuring of Third World agrarian systems. For a Foucauldian analysis of the Green Revolution as a technology of subjectification that reproduces the "unproductive" image of the postcolonial peasantry, see Arturo Escobar, *Encountering Development: The Making and Unmaking of the Third World* (Princeton, NJ: Princeton University Press, 1995). Escobar combines his analysis of governmental technologies with an attention to the visual cultures of developmentalism. He opens a path for further art-historical research, much in the same way that Edward Said's *Orientalism* influenced scholars of nineteenth-century painting and photography.

36 See Ken Conca, "The Earth Summit: Reflections on an Ambiguous Event," in *Green Planet Blues,* pp. 161–69. Brian Wallis cites the Greenpeace Rio banner drop intervention in his survey of environmental art in Jeffery Kastner (ed.), *Land and Environmental Art* (New York: Phaidon Press, 1998), p. 21, but he does not unfold its unsettling implications for the Euroamerican "ecology of affluence" underpinning the majority of the practices he discusses.

37 See Margaret E. Keck and Katherine Sikkink, "Transnational Advocacy Networks in International and Regional Politics," *International Social Science Journal* 51, no. 159 (1999), pp. 89–101. The article draws heavily on Wapner's "Politics

Beyond the State." This quote illustrates the organization's description of its goal. See *Greenpeace: An Inside Look at the World's Most Dynamic Environmental Pressure Group* (New York: Harper Collins, 1990), p. iv.

38 Wapner, "Politics Beyond the State," p. 120.

39 Vandana Shiva, "The Greening of the Global Reach," in Jeremy Brecher, John Brown Childs, and Jill Cutler (eds.), *Global Visions: Beyond the New World Order* (Boston: South End Press, 1993), p. 60. Also available at www.newint.org/issue230/tread.htm.

40 Agamben understands the advent of biopower only in terms of the neutralizing management of "man's own animality": "Genome, global economy, and humanitarian ideology are the three united faces of this process in which posthistorical humanity seems to take on its own physiology as its last, impolitical mandate." See Giorgio Agamben, *The Open: Man and Animal,* trans. Kevin Attell (Stanford, CA: Stanford University Press, 2004), pp. 76–77. He implicitly affirms, through negative critique, both Dubos's post-Darwinist humanism as well as the ecocratic managerialism of systems theory put forward in *The Limits to Growth.* He ignores the existence of biopolitical rights claims proffered by Shiva. For a critique of the equation drawn by Agamben between biopower as a set of technologies for sustaining the "bare life" of the human organism, and the biopolitics of human rights, see Jacques Rancière's "Who Is the Subject of the Rights of Man?" *South Atlantic Quarterly* 103, nos. 2/3 (2004) pp. 297–310.

41 For the utilitarian genealogy of this term and its place in mainstream development discourse, see Ivan Illich, "Needs," in *The Development Dictionary,* pp. 88–101.

42 Guha mentions these four movements as examples of "the environmentalism of the poor." See "The Southern Challenge," in *Environmentalism,* pp. 98–124.

43 Vandana Shiva and J. Bandopadhayay, "Science, Environment and Democratic Rights," *People's Union for Civil Liberties Bulletin,* April 1985, www.pucl.org/from-archives/Industries-envirn-resettlement/science-environ.htm.

44 *Ibid.* We might take issue here with Shiva's use of the term "genocide" with reference to the Bhopal disaster. Historically and legally speaking, the term designates a state-sponsored practice to exterminate a particular national or ethnic group. It implies a certain international responsibility to intervene and protect the populations concerned. It is fair to say that the Union Carbide Corporation did not kill thousands of people by design, but by gross and irresponsible negligence and, in the longer term, through the evasion of legal and financial accountability. Yet Shiva's invocation of the term speaks to

the attempt by human-rights activists around the world to reactivate and rechannel the moral authority associated with the idea of "crimes against humanity" put forward by the United States, Europe, and the United Nations after the Second World War. Shiva's use of the term "genocide" appeals to the universal normative horizons within which most governments claim to participate and demands that these norms be brought to bear by governments on the conduct of corporations operating within their borders.

45 On this history and its contemporary inheritances in the United States and beyond, see Robert Bullard (ed.), *The Quest for Environmental Justice: Human Rights and the Politics of Pollution* (Berkeley, CA: Sierra Club, 2005); and Julian Agyeman, Robert D. Bullard, and Bob Evans (eds.), *Just Sustainabilities: Development in an Unequal World* (Cambridge, MA: MIT Press, 2003).

46 See Bruno Latour's discussion of "hybrid assemblages" and "socio-technical networks" in *We Have Never Been Modern,* trans. Catherine Porter (Boston: Harvard University Press, 1991), and Arturo Escobar, "Constructing Nature: Elements for a Poststructural Political Ecology" in Richard Peet and Michael Watts (eds.), *Liberation Ecologies: Environment, Development, Social Movements* (New York: Routledge, 1996), pp. 46–68.

47 Jacques Rancière, *The Politics of Aesthetics,* trans. Gabriel Rockhill (London: Continuum Press, 2004), p. 85. This is a point of departure to which I return in "'Eyes and Ears'," pp. 327–55 in this volume.

48 See www.halliburtoncontracts.com.

49 These were the predecessors to the Biosphere 2 project in Arizona, established by John Allen, who authored a report for NASA entitled *Biological Life-Support Technologies: Commercial Applications* (1973). For a discussion of his career and his engagement with the thought of Verdansky, see John L. Allen, *Biosphere 2: The Human Experiment* (London: Penguin Books, 1989).

50 Mark Wigley discusses Archigram's techno-utopian envisioning of humans as "nomadic explorers of the outer limits whose bodies are symbiotically entangled with the high-tech mechanisms of our architecture" in "The Fiction of Architecture," in *Out of Site: Fictional Architectural Spaces* (New York: New Museum, 2002).

51 The Inuit Circumpolar Conference is the transnational governing body of the Inuit people with representation at the United Nations. See the ICC Web site, www.inuit.org, for their statement on "Climate Change and Inuit Human Rights."

52 "Monster> Middle English monstre> Old French> Latin monstrare, to warn> monstrum, portent, from monere, to warn." *American Heritage Dictionary.* The most deliberate political theorization of monstrosity is to be found in Michael Hardt and Antonio Negri's *Multitude: War and Democracy in the Age of Empire* (New York: Penguin, 2004), where they invoke the Kabbalistic golem as a figure "warning" of the disaster of globalized war and for the "exceeding of the measure of sovereignty" by the anticorporate globalization movement. Jacques Derrida discusses monstrosity in a different vein in "Passages—from Traumatism to Promise," in *Points: Interviews: 1974–1994,* trans. Peggy Kamuf (Stanford, CA: Stanford University Press, 1994): "The monster is that which appears for the first time and is thus not recognized. A monster is a species for which we do not yet have a name…. Simply, it shows itself [*il se* montre]—that is what the word means—it shows itself in something that is not yet shown and that therefore looks like a hallucination, it strikes the eye precisely because no anticipation had prepared one to identify this figure" (p. 386). The relationship between aesthetics and monstrosity has been addressed in Yates Mckee, "The Monstrous Dimension of Art: An Interview with Allora and Calzadilla," *Flash Art* (Winter 2005), pp. 96–99.

53 On climate justice, see "What is Climate Justice?" Environmental Justice and Climate Change Initiative, home page, www.ejcc.org. The organization starts from the premise that "global warming is fundamentally an issue of human rights and environmental justice that connects the local to the global. With rising temperatures, human lives—particularly in people of color, low-income, and Indigenous communities—are affected by compromised health, financial burdens, and social and cultural disruptions. Moreover, those who are most affected are least responsible for the greenhouse gas emissions that cause the problem—both globally and within the United States."

54 Al Gore, "The Moment of Truth," *Vanity Fair,* May 2006, p. 187.

55 "The Rise of the Neo-Greens," special issue, *Wired,* May 2006.

56 Ernesto Laclau is concerned with how a range of particular struggles and claims come to coalesce against a common enemy such that the negation of any link in that chain is seen as negating the whole. This depends, for Laclau, on which of these particular struggles comes to be seen as the exemplary figure of resistance—that is, which part comes to metonymize the universality of the *socius* itself. In the case of contemporary environmentalism, the particular struggle

that seems poised to raise itself to this level of universality is that surrounding global warming and the geopolitics of energy. See Ernesto Laclau, "Identity and Hegemony: The Role of Universality in the Constitution of Political Logics," in Judith Butler, Ernesto Laclau, and Slavoj Žižek, *Contingency, Hegemony, Universality: Contemporary Dialogues on the Left* (New York: Verso, 2000), pp. 44–89. In considering phenomena such as the ICC intervention, my interest is in the possibility that subaltern parts of a chain of equivalence might reinscribe the scene of the universal itself in the manner described by Judith Butler when she asks, "Who occupies the line between the speakable and the unspeakable, facilitating a translation there that is not the simple augmentation of the power of the dominant? There is nowhere else to stand, but there is no 'ground' there, only a reminder to keep as one's point of reference the dispossessed and the unspeakable…. Another universality emerges from the trace that only borders on political legibility; the subject who has not been given the prerogative to be a subject, whose *modus vivendi* is an imposed catachresis. If the spectrally human is to enter the hegemonic reformulation of universality, a language between languages will have to be found." See Judith Butler, "Competing Universalities," in *Contingency, Hegemony, Universality,* p. 178.

57 On the Apollo Alliance, see Mark Hertsgaard, "Green Grows Grassroots: The Environmental Movement Today," *The Nation,* July 31, 2006, pp. 11–18. As a participant in the left-liberal public sphere, Hertsgaard is unique in ideologically mediating between the race-conscious and class-conscious discourse of environmental justice and the moral-physiological concerns of the liberal elite, as evidenced in his article on the potential implications of climate change for East Coast cities in Gore's special "Green Issue" of *Vanity Fair.* As Hertsgaard reports, the key figure in such a mediation of the practical world of NGOs and foundations is Jerome Ringo, a former labor organizer who now heads the National Wildlife Federation and sits on the steering committee between the Apollo Alliance. A fact of world historical significance: Ringo was the only African-American present at the 1998 Kyoto conference on climate change. See "The Pioneer: An Interview With Jerome Ringo," *Mother Jones,* April 25, 2005, www.motherjones.com/…/05/jerome_ringo.html.

58 See Professor Nanjundaswamy, "Cremating Monsanto: Genetically Modified Fields on Fire," in Notes from Nowhere (eds.), *We Are Everywhere: The Irresistible Rise of Global Anticapitalism* (New York: Verso Press, 2003), pp.152–159; and Vandana Shiva, *Stolen Harvest: The Highjacking of the Global*

Food Supply (Boston, MA: South End Press, 2000), p. 11.

59 Available at www.ukabc.org/genetic_commons_treaty.htm.

60 For the Sustainable South Bronx project, see their Web site at www.ssbx.org. See also Majora Carter, "Setting the Example for a 'Greener' New York," *New York Daily News,* April 12, 2005.

61 This is Jacques Derrida's ventriloquization of what he calls the "secret," which assigns to the living a responsibility both to inherit from the past and to transform that heritage in the name of those yet to come. See *Specters of Marx: The State of Debt, the Work of Mourning, and the New International,* trans. Peggy Kamuf (New York: Routledge, 1994), p. 16.

62 On this structural feature of photography, see Eduardo Cadava, "*Lapsus Imaginis:* The Image in Ruins," *October* 96 (2001), pp. 35–60. Cadava's text deeply informs my reading of Allora and Calzadilla's work, especially his opening contention that "there can be no image that is not about destruction and survival, and this is especially the case in the image of ruin" (p. 35).

63 This historical gloss is drawn from Mario Murillo, *Islands of Resistance: Puerto Rico, Vieques, and U.S. Policy* (New York: Seven Stories, 2001), and Deborah Berman Santana, "Vieques: the Land, the People, the Struggle, the Future," in *The Quest for Environmental Justice,* pp. 222–39.

64 For Heidegger, the essence of the "happening" of the work of art is to "instigate strife" between the "open region" of the historico-cultural world and the being of the Earth, which at once gives itself as sustaining ground and withdraws into concealment. Rather than mere "discord or dispute," Heidegger emphasizes, "in essential strife…the opponents raise each other into the self-assertion of their essential natures." See "The Origin of the Work of Art," in David Farrell Krell (ed.), *Basic Writings,* trans. David Farrell Krell (New York: Harper Collins, 1977), p. 172. Heidegger's terms bear comparison to the eco-aesthetic claims of other critics of anthropocentric instrumentality such as McHarg. Significantly, for our present discussion of Allora and Calzadilla, the artistic example Heidegger gives is Van Gogh's painting of peasant shoes, which he discusses in terms of "reliability" and "equipment": "By virtue of this reliability the peasant woman is made privy to the silent call of the earth; by virtue of the reliability of the equipment she is made sure of her world" ("The Origin of the Work of Art," p. 91). While these are taken for granted existential dispositions of the peasant woman's lifeworld, Van Gogh's painting *discloses* their essential being qua equipment: their status as noninstrumental agents of the opening of the Earth.

65 Timothy W. Luke, "Environmentality as Green Governmentality," in Éric Darier (ed.), *Discourses of the Environment* (Oxford: Blackwell, 1999), pp. 121–50. Following Foucault, Luke understands "environmentality" as a set of techniques not only for constituting and managing "natural" resources and ecosystems, but also for the production of environmentally self-regulating subjects, whether in voluntary recycling programs in the global North or forestry training in the global South.

66 Jane Sutton, "U.S. Navy Training Goes Virtual as War Games Move," *Reuters,* October 22, 2002.

67 Krzysztof Wodiczko, Interrogative Design Group, www.interrogative.org. Allora and Calzadilla were artists-in-residence at Wodiczko's MIT Interrogative Design lab in 2001, a kind of politicized counterpoint to Kepes's Center for Advanced Visual Studies (CAVS), with which it shares a building. Since 2003, CAVS has rethought its mandate and has worked with groups such as Critical Art Ensemble and the Center for Urban Pedagogy (both groups are discussed above).

68 Cited in Jennifer Allora and Guillermo Calzadilla, *Landmark* exhibition pamphlet, Tate Modern Gallery, London (2003).

69 Here I draw on Derrida, who writes: "Justice carries life beyond present life or its actual being-there, its empirical or ontological actuality: not toward death but toward living-on, namely, a trace of which life and death would themselves be but traces and traces of traces, a survival whose possibility in advance comes to disjoin or disadjust the identity to itself of the living present, as well as of any effectivity." See *Specters of Marx,* p. xx. Derrida's emphasis on disjunction and disadjustment challenges the traditional ecological ideal of properly adjusting part and whole, organism and environment, humanity and *oikos.*

70 For a critique of the Habermasian assumptions underlying the "Communicative Planning" paradigm, see Susan S. Fainstein, "New Directions in Planning Theory," in Scott Campbell and Susan S. Fainstein (eds.), *Readings in Planning Theory* (Oxford: Blackwell, 2003), pp. 173–95.

71 As suggested earlier, the task of figures such as Kepes and McHarg was to mediate aesthetically between a post-Romantic concern for the spontaneity and the purposiveness of the living organism and the theory of self-regulating feedback systems, otherwise known as cybernetics. Norbert Weiner derived the term "cybernetics" from the ancient Greek *kybernetike,* or the art of nautical steermanship, noting that this was also the etymological origin of the word "government" — a vestige of which remains in the French word for rudder, *gouvernail.* See "Government and

Governors," in G.T. Guilbaud (ed.), *What is Cybernetics?* (New York: Grove Press, 1960), pp. 1–7. Also see Buckminster Fuller, *Operating Manual for Spaceship Earth* (New York: Pocket Books, 1969). Fuller's techno-utopian horizon was contested on social-Darwinian terms by Garret Hardin, *Exploring New Ethics for Survival: The Voyage of the Spaceship* Beagle (New York: Pelican Books, 1972).

72 On the possibility of rearticulating "biodiversity" with democratic rights claims, see Arturo Escobar, "Cultural Politics and Biological Diversity: State, Capital, and Social Movements in the Pacific Coast of Colombia," in Lisa Lowe and David Lloyd (eds.), *The Politics of Culture in the Shadow of Capital* (Durham, NC: Duke University Press, 1997), pp. 201–26.

73 My sense of this unsettling of ends — neither apocalyptic extinction nor glowing reappropriation — is indebted to Thomas Keenan's "No Ends in Sight," in *The End(s) of the Museum/Els límits del museu* (Barcelona: Fundacio Antoni Tapies, 1995). Keenan's text is, of course, informed by Jacques Derrida's "The Ends of Man," in *Margins of Philosophy,* trans. Alan Bass (Chicago: University of Chicago Press, 1985), pp. 111–36.

74 Aaron Betsky, "Sites Unseen," *Artforum* 44, no. 7 (2006), pp. 268–71.

75 National Economic and Social Rights Initiative, *The Human Right to Housing: Access for Survivors in the Gulf,* June 29, 2006, www.nesri.org/fact_sheets_pubs/index.html.

76 See Mike Davis, "Who is Killing New Orleans?" *The Nation,* April 7, 2006.

77 A good portal for housing-rights activism in New Orleans can be found at www.survivorsvillage.com. For extensive photographic documentation of this activism, see the work of Craig Morse, www.culturesubculture.com.

78 Michel Foucault, "Confronting Governments, Human Rights," trans. Thomas Keenan, in James D. Faubion (ed.), *Essential Works of Michel Foucault, 1954–1984, Vol. 3: Power* (New York: The New Press, 1994), p. 474.

79 This is Thomas Keenan's reading of Foucault's text. See *Fables of Responsibility: Aberrations and Predicaments in Ethics and Politics* (Stanford, CA: Stanford University Press, 1997), p. 159.

DESIGNS

CIVIL SOCIETY

"Revolutions" Clothed in the Colors of Spring: Exporting Democracy to the East

Laëtitia Atlani-Duault

In 2003, thanks in part to local NGOs supported by international development agencies, the Rose Revolution broke out in Georgia.[1] The result was the resignation of President Eduard Shevardnadze, the former first secretary of the Central Committee of the Communist Party, who had been elected chair of the Georgian parliament in 1992 and president in 1995 and 2000. He was replaced by Mikhail Saakashvili, a young politician with graduate degrees from universities in the United States and France. In November 2004, in the Ukraine, the Orange Revolution occurred, in which local NGOs — with the backing of their Georgian colleagues — protested the results of the presidential election after a representative of the political old guard was declared the winner. In a second round, called after the Supreme Court annulled the election, the winner was Viktor Yushchenko, who had been prime minister from 1999 to 2001 and had become the leader of the opposition coalition. February 2005 saw the outbreak of the Tulip Revolution in Kyrgyzstan. Like the Ukrainians, the Kyrgyz citizens protested elections that appeared to have been rigged. Kyrgyz NGOs organized the demonstrations with the support of Georgian and Ukrainian colleagues, themselves "children" of international aid who had become "experts" in revolution. In a few short weeks, the power structure was overthrown. President Askar Akayev, who had held office since independence, fled to Moscow. A new government came to power under Prime Minister Feliks Kulov, the former vice president and the most popular Kyrgyz opposition leader, who had been in prison since 2000.

In May 2005 and March 2006, it was time for the citizens of Uzbekistan and Belorussia to demonstrate and express their opposition to the existing regimes, whose power they considered illegitimate. This time, those in power responded with violence, and the population was subjected to fierce repression. In Uzbekistan, the police and the military shot hundreds of civilians, including children and elderly people, and arrested even more. The repression also affected NGOs, which were accused of fomenting revolution. Many were simply declared illegal, while others were made to submit to increased surveillance of their activities. Other former Soviet republics took measures to prevent

Supporters of Viktor Yushchenko, who was then Ukraine's opposition leader, hold a mass rally as Yushchenko speaks on a stage in the main square of Kiev, November 29, 2004 (David Guttenfelder/AP Photo).

the revolutionary "epidemic" and to curb the NGOs they considered the source of the scourge. New laws — such as those passed by the Russian parliament in January 2006 — were drafted to circumscribe and control NGO activities, and efforts were made to discredit the organizations in the eyes of the general population through accusations of collusion with Western intelligence services.

These "revolutions" perhaps gave concrete expression to the democratic aspirations of the former Soviet republics, and no doubt they offered new hope. However, the conditions under which these supposedly spontaneous revolutions occurred were not put in place yesterday, nor were they a result of the policies of George W. Bush. In fact, since the disappearance of the USSR, international agencies such as the UN have given enormous assistance to the creation and support of local NGOs in the region, with the idea that such organizations could be useful opposition forces against the state and, if needed, act as levers in overthrowing certain governments.

When, in the early 1990s, United Nations agencies started large-scale development initiatives in the former USSR, there were few local NGOs, in the Western sense of the term, for the simple reason that the USSR forbade all associations independent of official structures. While there were a large number of organizations in each Soviet republic, any whose activities deviated from the party or the government line was immediately dissolved. With the demise of the USSR, however, the United Nations provided massive support for the creation of local NGOs in the region.

This international aid had two foci. The first was the promotion of a legal and social framework favoring the creation of local NGOs. To understand this, it is useful to remember that the United Nations needs the approval of the governments of the countries in which it implements assistance activities in order to put into action large-scale projects for the nongovernmental sector. One might well ask why these governments were willing to sign agreements that would benefit local NGOs, which at this point were still discouraged by the authorities. The reason was the policy of conditionality. The international assistance given to governments was conditional on their engagement in the "flowering of civil society" (to use one professional's phrase). This policy of tit for tat played out in the form of bargaining between United Nations professionals and governmental actors. For example, a typical demand was for the reform of legislation on associations: according to the UN, all organizations that applied should be able to enjoy official status, should not be harassed or pressured, and should not be subjected to political control of their activities. At the same time, the United Nations negotiated the apportioning of aid budgets to make sure a large part of their assistance budget would go to the nongovernmental sector.

The second focus of the United Nations' effort was to provide technical and financial assistance for local NGO members. The aim was to "build capacity" among existing or nascent NGOs, giving them the means to grow. The UN offered training sessions on the techniques developed by NGOs in other parts of the world for planning and designing projects, fund raising, managing programs and people, attracting volunteers, implementing all kinds of activities, networking, and so on. The training sessions were for anyone who was interested. The dates of these sessions were announced in the press to reach as wide an audience as possible. It was, therefore, a period rich in encounters and the exchange of ideas among people who otherwise had little opportunity to air and debate their different points of view.

The UN also offered financial assistance to local NGOs. Somewhat surprisingly, the UN gave less financial assistance than other agencies, which at this time had also begun to fund local NGOs in the region. Though relatively small, these budgets did cover a large number of NGOs. To help decide which projects to finance in each country, the United Nations set up a selection system that was as transparent as possible, both to avoid undue pressure from any source and to make it impossible for a limited group of well-informed actors — particularly those close to powerful political circles — to become the only candidates for financing. Again, United Nations agencies regularly published their requests for proposals in the local press to reach the greatest number of people. They also brought together local civil-society actors (professional associations of jour-nalists and doctors, human-rights groups), government specialists, and members of other international agencies involved in development work in the region to create a temporary independent authority charged with selecting projects from the propos-als received. This effectively limited the possibility of the corruption that is so wide-spread in the post-Soviet region, but it should also be emphasized that many varied proposals from local NGOs were accepted. (I discuss below why the UN focused on the strengthening of civil society, rather than on the nature and content of the proposed activities.)

Because of this strategy, the United Nations was able, in a few short years, to help groups of people or members of former Soviet institutions to create NGOs, register them with the authorities, train their staff, find funding for them, and connect them to international networks. This was the case for a wide range of aid and development ini-tiatives that sought to do everything from supporting the creation of private enterprise to aiding organizations in areas such as women's rights, education, biodiversity, and HIV prevention. As unrelated as these issues may appear, the initiatives formed part of a common approach: the construction of a "shared morality."

Why did United Nations' agencies invest so much energy in supporting the creation of an active and strong civil society? A neo-Tocquevillian vision is certainly part of the answer. But this is only a partial answer, and one informed by a specific interpretation of post-Soviet societies. This interpretation clearly directed the advisory activities of the United Nations.

It is worth remembering that the new post-Soviet states had been integral parts of the USSR, which was once the leader of the "Second World." As the head of the Com-munist bloc of countries, the USSR was on par with the "First World," composed of Western countries, and a rival model for a "Third World" said to be on the road to devel-opment. In a very short amount of time, these post-Soviet republics not only became independent states but also fell from being members of a great power to the lowly status of "developing countries."

In the UN's advisory effort, a certain vision of Communist societies became evident, one that followed the critique of totalitarianism advanced by many Westerner countries during the Cold War. According to this view, the destruction of civil society was a central element in Soviet totalitarianism, one that limited all independent action in all spheres of activity. The fundamental characteristic of Soviet-style totalitarianism was understood as the suppression of the people's capacity to form a political "space" where they could move collectively and freely. This capacity to thwart human nature in order to maintain control was seen as the most efficient and effective feature of the Soviet regime. Totalitarian terror in the Soviet Union succeeded in preventing any flowering of an independent political sphere and civil society, and imprisoned individuals in the fragmented universe of confiscated social space. The suppression of civil society thus aimed to produce individuals isolated by the lack of political space and oppressed by terror.

This vision gained even greater currency with the Polish critique of totalitarianism, which originated with the Polish philosopher Leszek Kolakowski's seminal publication *Main Currents of Marxism* in 1973.[2] According to Kolakowski, a historical parallel could be drawn between the fully realized man in Marxist terms and the real-life experience of Communism. In other words, he argued that Communism had adopted totalitarian forms, replacing civilian groups and organizations with dictatorial state structures. This critique of totalitarianism manifested itself in Poland with the conflict between the Communist party-state and the independent trade union movement called Solidarity. From that moment on, the notion of civil society permitted critics of Soviet totalitarianism to identify the dead ends and dramas of this society of "impossible citizens." Tasks were assigned both to the forces fighting for their freedom and to groups aiming to reform and eventually abolish the system by liberating civil society from the party-state or even by creating civil society in countries where it had never existed.

After 1991, for the first time in the history of East/West relations, international development aid was one of the principal vectors of massive change — change that is still under way. By slowly subverting longstanding forms of domination, development aid turned the generally accepted opposition between the "political" and the "cultural" on its head. For the United Nations staff, a "culturalist" explanation was useful because it preempted traditional criticisms of Western cultural hegemony. First, it presupposed that civil society is not a Western social construct but "natural" to all democratic organizations and therefore independent of the culture where it might be applied. Second, it assumed that the form taken by civil society depends on cultural context.

This naturalization of civil society proved crucial, giving a new type of legitimacy to democratization efforts. No imposition of a Western model was presumed; rather, a specific culture *reemerged* in opposition to the once oppressive Soviet model. In other words, the "Sovietization" of the region could be seen as an imposed monolithic model, whereas the advent of civil society was Sovietization's organic, pluralist opposite. The development-agency actors based their work on a supposedly universal idea that they could adapt to each and every context and that they could work against democratic centralism. As they saw it, local NGOs in the region were not imposed from without (that is, from the West) on minority cultures, but rather facilitated the emergence of local movements that were increasingly conscious of realities denied during the Soviet era.

This explanation legitimated the United Nations policies in the region that were, *prima facie,* undertaken without hegemonic intentions. But even more importantly, it freed them of responsibility for failures and delays, which could be ascribed entirely to persistent anachronisms inherited from the Soviet model. This was an impressive rhetorical feat, simultaneously ignoring the reality of post-Soviet conditions and sidestepping questions about the political implications of the problems that accompanied the "march of progress." The victory for democracy represented by the emergence of local NGOs — a force capable of overturning centralized power structures — could be seen as having been brought about through culture; at the same time, culture was absolved of responsibility for the slightest resistance to the movement, since such resistance could be blamed entirely on the social uniformity of predemocratic days. The trick for the development agency was to ignore cultural specifics while spreading the notion of a culture that had been obstructed and denied.

The fall of the USSR marked the victory of a point of view formulated in the United States during the Cold War. To confirm this victory over the defunct Second World, it was necessary to demonstrate this victory in the place where it had been most strongly resisted: the former USSR. It was not enough for the Soviet Union to have disappeared: its defeat needed to be crowned by its *conversion,* because its very absence left open the possibility that the universality of the long-awaited "global consensus" might be brought into question. Yet the post-Soviet reality did not seem to fit the story being demonstrated. In fact, the social consequences of introducing a market economy and party politics actually imperiled this putative victory over the Second World. There remained (and remains) the risk that state structures might veer back toward a model of government inherited from the Soviet era, although the task of the international development agencies was to thwart this possibility by building up local NGOs that would counterbalance the state and guarantee the liberal political model.

And so it has come to pass in the "revolutions" clothed in the colors of spring.

1   This article draws on my *Au bonheur des autres: Anthropologie de l'aide humanitaire* (Nanterre: Société d'ethnologie, 2005).

2   Leszek Kolakowski, *Main Currents of Marxism* (New York: W. W. Norton, 1978).

Velvet Agitators

a profile of Eastern European movements by Philippe Mangeot

Minsk, Belarus, March 23, 2006. On a snow-covered October Square, a group of about twenty tents formed a miniature image of the "Orange Revolution" that had taken place in Kiev, the Ukraine, the previous winter. Four days earlier, Aleksandr Lukashenko had been reelected president of the republic with 83 percent of the country's votes in an election that international observers deemed not to have responded to democratic norms.[1] To obtain these staggering results, the president had not skimped on any means: among other things, he had pushed up the date of the vote by three months so as to hinder the opposition's campaign; he had submitted anyone contesting his regime to a combination of administrative, fiscal, and police harassment; and he had ordered a stay against the distribution of the independent press. Determined to stave off anything resembling the Ukrainian movement, Lukashenko kept repeating that "there will not be any rose, orange or even banana revolutions in our country."[2] On television, he promised that he would "break the neck" of anyone contesting his victory, while his security chief announced that anyone taking to the streets to demonstrate against the results would be treated as a "terrorist."[3]

In the ephemeral campsite erected in a corner of the square, the remaining five hundred diehard demonstrators were already conceding that the "blue revolution" would not happen this time around. But they also noted the gains of the previous days. As the election results were announced, more than ten thousand people defied the police interdiction and descended into the streets of Minsk to form the largest demonstration the country had seen for a decade. When Lukashenko had won an anticonstitutional referendum in the fall of 2004 that allowed him to run for a third term, a demonstration that had assembled one thousand people had been immediately repressed. Mindful of this precedent, the campers on October Square were counting the days. They knew that entry to their "village" was carefully filtered by the police and that many of those who tried to join them had been taken away. They also knew that Belarusian television had been presenting them in countless stories as a gang of hooligans who enjoyed vodka

Supporters of Ukraine's Pora beat barrel drums during a protest in front of Kiev's city hall, March 23, 2006 (Ivan Chernichkin/Reuters).

and pornography. Eventually, what they had been waiting for happened: on the night of March 24, the police leveled the "freedom village," and four hundred and fifty people were arrested.

For the student movement Zubr ("Bison" in Belarusian), founded several months before the presidential elections of 2001 and one of the instigators of the 2006 demonstrations, this was certainly yet another failure. Zubr had explicitly declared its models to be Otpor ("Resistance" in Serbian), the group that contributed to the 2000 eviction of Slobodan Milosevic, and Kmara ("Enough" in Georgian), the group that had worked toward the fall of Eduard Shevardnadze. Although they could not claim the same victories as their models, Zubr's organizers were still proud of the progress they had seen. There had been many more of them than in previous demonstrations against Lukashenko's regime, and they were better organized. They could thus contend that their days in October Square would go down in history as a foundational act, and as they disbanded, they were already talking about a future date, April 26, 2006, when they would meet again, to mark the twentieth anniversary of the Chernobyl catastrophe.

Minsk, Thursday, April 27, 2006. Arrested the night before, Alexander Milinkevich, the regime's principal opponent, was condemned to fifteen days in prison for having organized an unauthorized public gathering: the April 26 demonstration had gathered several thousand Belarusians.

Ukraine, March 9, 2001. A large demonstration organized in the streets of Kiev by Ukrajina bez Kuchmy (Ukraine without Kuchma) ended with a violent clash between demonstrators and police forces. Ukrajina bez Kuchmy had been created several months earlier, when the dead body of opposition journalist Georgiy Gongadze was discovered. President Leonid Kuchma's involvement in the assassination of the journalist, as well as that of his minister of the interior, seemed quite clear. Originally launched by journalists demanding an independent investigation into Gongadze's death, the movement had grown more radical. Its promoters now demanded Kuchma's resignation.

After the violent termination of the March 9 demonstration, support for Ukrajina bez Kuchmy started to decline. However, within the movement's ranks, the idea of importing the Serbian model of Otpor into the Ukraine gradually became feasible. Adopting this model entailed the organization of a civil, nonpartisan campaign — albeit one with electoral goals — whereby people would mobilize less in favor of an opposition candidate than against the powers in place. The plan was to mount such a campaign in time for the next presidential election, which was to take place at the end of 2004. To that end, Ukrainian activists began to work closely with former Otpor activists — from March 2003 on. As a result of this collaboration, Pora (It's Time) was created by eighteen Ukrainians in April 2004 at the end of a workshop organized in Novi Sad, in northern Serbia. Part of the text presenting the group's project read: "Our inspiration, partners and advisers are Otpor in Serbia, Kmara in Georgia, Mjaft in Albania, and Zubr in Belarus."

Belgrade, October 6, 2000. The day before, a march gathering seven hundred thousand people in the Serbian capital brought to a dramatic conclusion the fall of Slobodan Milosevic's regime, the crisis inaugurated a dozen days earlier when the Serbian leader invalidated the much-anticipated presidential elections that he had lost. That day, having accomplished its mission, Otpor might have chosen to disband. Founded in 1998 by Belgrade students who sought to protest a law aiming to increase the government's control over universities, the group was formed in the wake of the 1996–1997 demonstrations against Milosevic's invalidation of the municipal elections that had been won by the opposition. Milosevic ended up ceding the elections, but nonetheless stayed in power. Thus, Otpor decided to attend to what it saw as an unfinished business, ending Milosevic's rule. For that purpose, the group used any means available to diminish the legitimacy of the regime. Lacking a precise political program, Otpor managed, partly for that reason, to draw on extremely heterogeneous feelings of dissatisfaction and to recruit supporters far beyond traditional politicized populations. Operating as a semiunderground network, the group resorted to a wide variety of protest techniques and devices, mostly aimed at ridiculing Milosevic and, by doing so, conveying that his regime was in its last throes. Using graffiti and massive collages of stickers, Otpor launched successive campaigns with simple slogans such as "It Is Time" and "He Is Finished." Its members also organized gatherings outside military tribunals whenever a deserter was tried. To establish their popularity, Otpor activists largely relied on humor. They set up farcical operations — such as mock fundraisers where the public was asked to pay for Milosevic's ticket to exile — and put on comical performances in the spirit of the dissident movements in the former Soviet bloc. For example, several hours after Milosevic declared that politicians had saucepans for heads, Otpor made sure that wearing a pan as a hat became all the rage throughout the country. As the election drew near, the group had gained notoriety and thus succeeded in multiplying and intensifying its interventions.

After the regime's collapse, Otpor decided not to disband. To justify its decision, its members stressed the need to monitor the practices of the new regime. However, in the new context, the group rapidly lost its appeal with the general public, and tensions started to mount among its founders. While some of them sought to transform the organization into a political party — rather unsuccessfully, since they merely got 1.6 percent of the vote in the 2003 parliamentary election — others refused to become professional politicians and, instead, decided to develop and sell their expertise as protest organizers. This latter group founded the Otpor Center for Nonviolent Resistance.

The postcard "It's Time to Choose" was used by Pora during Ukraine's 2004 presidential election campaign (www.pora.org.ua).

"When Milosevic was overthrown," Stanko Lazendic explains,

> Otpor was so famous that we were contacted by NGOs from all the pseudodemocracies of Eastern Europe. We had developed an analysis of the functioning of these new forms of autocracy, where elections are organized as window dressing, and we had also acquired a real expertise on how to weaken this kind of political regime. In particular, we had devised a number of tactics aimed at creating tensions and rifts among the various institutions that buttress these regimes, such as the army, the police, and the courts. And we were eager to share our expertise. So, Aleksandr Maric went first to Belarus, then on to Georgia, where he trained the people in Kmara. As for me, I worked for a year in the Ukraine. (Both Maric and I were denied access to the Ukraine territory just before the 2004 presidential elections. At this point, we are on the blacklist of many countries.) But before being persona non grata, we were a part of the creation of Pora, as well as of Znayu (I Know), another Ukrainian NGO, less well known than Pora, which sought to organize a get-out-the-vote campaign and to devise methods for preventing vote manipulation. In the workshops leading to the creation of these organizations, we didn't give precise recommendations for what Ukrainian, Georgian, and Belarus activists should do. Instead, we analyzed with them the specific mechanisms of the regimes they wanted to

"We started from nil!" (www.otpor.com).

oppose; we also explained how we got organized and passed on to them what we had learned—for instance, how to behave when you're arrested, how to write press releases, and how to collect contributions.[4]

Bringing Down a Dictator was the title of an American documentary produced in 2002 about the Otpor adventure. The film drew on two different genres, that of heroic narrative and that of pedagogical treatise. It was allegedly shown to the instigators of Kmara. "How to Make a 'Rose' Revolution?" was the name given to a workshop held in Amsterdam in November 2004 during a Dutch social forum. Members of Otpor, Kmara, and Pora were among those participating in the workshop. The idea of formalizing a method of protest that could be licensed and adapted to various regimes, with all the necessary adjustments that each situation would call for, was not merely an a posteriori usage of the techniques that were initially developed and tested on the Serbian ground: in a way, this setting up of an exportable protest "kit" could be perceived as the most important of these techniques. Moreover, Otpor's efforts toward the formalization of their own work preceded the fall of Milosevic's regime—and thus preceded their project of becoming international protest experts. Indeed, since the early days of their struggle, the founders of Otpor had been keenly aware of the risk of relying too much on leaders, who could be arrested at any moment. To limit this risk, they made sure that their movement spread throughout Serbia in the form of relatively autonomous local cells. In order to maintain a certain unity of action and method despite the decentralized structure of the group, an activist's "manual" was drafted by Otpor's founders and distributed to their local affiliates. In this manual, Gene Sharp, an American political scientist and founder of the Albert Einstein Institution in Boston, was frequently cited. Sharp is the author of many books and articles, including *From Dictatorship to Democracy* — available in Ukrainian on Pora's Web site — in which he develops a theory of civil action based on his observations of a wide variety of liberation movements, in India, South Africa, Burma, the former Soviet bloc, and the United States (the civil rights movement), among others. Sharp's book also advocated "political marketing" designed to weaken the institutional pillars of autocratic rules.[5]

In the spring of 2004, Pora's very first action elaborated on its own name: it was called "It's time to love one another." Young women went out to meet soldiers to give them flowers and condoms, inviting them to "protect their country."

Based on the records of Otpor, Kmara, and Pora, the protest kit or expanded manual that could be passed on to new affiliates probably included the following suggestions:

1 Organize a civil campaign to reappropriate national and local elections: make sure that this civil campaign precedes and duplicates the official electoral campaign and endeavor to turn the vote into a referendum against the government.

2 Support the (preferably) united opposition candidate, but only insofar as he or she is capable of defeating the representatives of the regime.

3 Discredit the people in power by any means available — stickers, tracts, newspapers, underground pamphlets (in the venerable tradition of Soviet era samizdat), and the Internet. Use, to this effect, satire, humor, caricature, and derision. Remember that slogans are even more successful when a song is made out of them.

4 Take full advantage of the spontaneous sympathy generated by students. Build your social movement as a fashion fad: make the group's T-shirts and badges a hot commodity. If possible, exploit the potential malaise experienced by soldiers and policemen when they are told to repress peaceful demonstrations and emphasize the ridiculous character of the authorities when they use words such as "terrorism" to describe your movement.

5 Try to spread your reach by leaning on preexisting networks — for the ultimate goal is to draw big crowds on the day of the vote.

6 Resort to different types of action, in terms of both register and scale: mass demonstrations are good, but so are small commando actions.

7 Dramatize the issues as the vote approaches and, in the final weeks, jump the gun by spreading the rumor that the government's defeat is a foregone conclusion.

8 Call on diasporas, if there are any, so that the movement reaches beyond the country's borders and attracts the interest of foreign media — for the vote needs witnesses and the movement needs funding.

9 Study the history of rigged elections and the scripts according to which they usually unfold: it will enable you to be prepared for the crisis that will follow the evidence of fraud. Learn, at that point, how to block roads, erect barricades, and how to exploit the divisions that the outcry about the fraud may produce among the parties and institutions that support the regime.

10 From election day on, put your movement at the service of the victorious, yet defeated opposition by taking care of its infrastructure: open dorms in the opposition's offices, put up tents in public spaces, contribute a symbol to the postelectoral demonstrations that has a chance of circulating throughout the world.

11 Be ready to be accused of collaboration with foreign powers, especially the United States — an accusation that will inevitably be leveled at your movement, both from within the country and from abroad. In that respect, rather than be defensive, admit that funding and training were provided by American foundations close to (according to each country) George Soros, the Democratic Party, or the Republican Party. Deflect this criticism by declaring that you would happily accept Russian or European — or for that matter domestic — financing, as well. (Moreover, stress that only very naive and very disingenuous people would claim that the outcry of hundreds of thousands of people could be manipulated and that the same attributes would apply to people acting surprised by the fact that this kind of mobilization requires money.)

Kyrgyzstan, July 10, 2005. The electoral sweep that brought Kurmanbek Bakiyev to the Kyrgyz presidency ended a period of uncertainty that had begun in February and March with the so-called "Tulip Revolution." The protests had started in the southern areas of the country during the weeks leading up to parliamentary elections that were largely believed to be rigged, and they kept growing as it became clear that President Askar Akayev's party would indeed be declared the winner. Organizing roadblocks, occupying local public buildings, and assembling mass gatherings, the protesters succeeded in launching a vast movement that eventually spread to the capital city, Bishkek, and enticed all the opposition parties to unite behind former prime minister Bakiyev. The protest movement had its own colors (yellow and pink scarves), and it included a student organization called KelKel ("Come Join Us" in Kyrgyz) that had been founded a few months earlier, as well as an NGO forum called the Coalition for Democracy and Civil Society, which was supported by several American foundations. Edil Baisalov, the president of the Coalition for Democracy and Civil Society, had been in contact with the Serbian representatives from the Otpor Center for Nonviolent Resistance for quite some time, and had gone to Kiev in November 2004 in order to observe Pora's activists at work on the ground.

Would Kirghizstan follow the now familiar script tested in Serbia, Georgia, and the Ukraine? Only to an extent. As had been the case with Milosevic in Serbia, Shevardnadze in Georgia, and Yanukovych in the Ukraine, Akayev eventually yielded. Despite his numerous denunciations of the "new international techniques for velvet revolutions" and his repeated proclamations that he would not cede to pressure from the streets, on March 24, 2005, he abandoned the presidential palace as it was surrounded by twenty thousand demonstrators. However, Akayev's capitulation seemed surprisingly quick to the protesters, who had conceived their mobilization as a dress rehearsal for the October presidential elections. Moreover, Bakiyev, who immediately became the interim president, and his new prime minister, Feliks Kulov, former head of the secret services, were both inside men, longtime collaborators of the deposed president and backed by Russia. Akayev himself confirmed the growing suspicions of those who had precipitated his fall when he declared to the Russian daily *Kommersant* (on July 11, just after Bakiyev's victory in the presidential election): "I have been supporting this tandem (Bakiyev and Kulov) from the beginning.... I am the one who raised Bakiyev." Thus, for the leaders of the civil protests, the presidential election of July 2005 could hardly be perceived as a full-fledged victory. Keenly aware of the fact that the Kirghisz "yellow and pink" revolution was at best an unfinished process, Baisalov did all he could to put a positive spin on the situation, claiming that Bakiyev's victory should not be read as a plebiscite, but merely as "a unanimous rejection of the past."[6]

Yet Baisalov knew full well that the past was far from repudiated. Several weeks earlier, he himself had publicly protested against the practices and lies of those now in power when it became clear that the Kyrgyz authorities were closely collaborating with Uzbekistan's president, Islam Karimov, in forcefully repatriating refugees who had fled their country after the Andijon massacre on May 13, 2005. On that day, the Uzbek army had opened machine-gun fire on demonstrators demanding reform.[7]

Baku, November 2005. Everything seemed to be in place for President Ilham Aliyev's Azerbaijani government to become the next domino in the series of velvet revolutions. First, the November 6 parliamentary elections had given the party in power an absolute majority in parliament. Second, opposition party members had been arrested just before the elections. Third, there were a number of reports from international observers that pointed to fraud and that questioned the election's legitimacy. Fourth, there was a student organization, called Magam ("It's Time" in Azerbaijani), that had been trained in the ranks of Otpor, Pora, and Kmara. Fifth, there were substantive opposition coalitions, albeit split between two separate blocs, Azadliq and YeS (Yeni Siyaset). And finally, there was the on-the-ground presence of the Freedom House, an American NGO directed by former CIA head James Woolsey and reportedly a source of funds for Otpor in Serbia several years before.

As expected, three days after the election results were announced, a well-oiled series of events, nearly identical to those in previous color-coded revolutions, were repeated: fifteen thousand people gathered at Victory Square in north Baku, wielding carnations and orange flags and demanding the government's resignation, while hundreds of police officers sent out for the event looked on. The joyful protests continued for a while, though it had no visible effect on the government, whose representatives were not showing any sign of nervousness. However, after two weeks of demonstrations, when the opposition leaders asked the ten thousands demonstrators occupying Victory Square to stay beyond the authorized cut-off time for assemblies and to camp out on the square, the police immediately brought a definitive end to the mobilization by bringing out clubs and water cannons.

What went wrong in Azerbaijan? Was it a case of a drama acted out one too many times? Was it the lack of credibility of a too heterogeneous opposition? Was it the faultless efficiency of Aliyev's regime? While the precise reasons why the Azerbaijan regime did not fall are subject to debate, for its part, the Azerbaijani opposition soon came up with an explanation. According to its representatives, the movement failed because of what they called the "treason" of the Americans. This assessment followed a statement made by the United States embassy in Baku that said that the American government was both optimistic about the possibility of working with the new members of parliament and satisfied by the constitutional court's decision to cancel electoral results in ten districts where fraud had been noted and where several of the seats had been won by opposition party members. On November 26, an orange banner read, in English: "Stop Trading Our Democracy for Oil."

Moscow, December 21, 2005. It didn't even take an hour for the Duma, the Russian parliament, to debate and pass a law (by 376 votes to 10) regulating the activity of nongovernmental organizations. A first draft of this law, sponsored by the ruling party, United Russia, had already been overwhelmingly approved a month before. Had it been promulgated in its original form, the law would have made it illegal for Russian NGOs to receive foreign funding. It would also have allowed foreign NGOs to work in Russian territory only on the condition that their statutes be changed to conform to Russian law — changes that would have made them subject to the political control of the Russian authorities — and that their leaders be Russian nationals. Some of those who supported the project made no mystery about what they expected. Over the course of the debate, the nationalist deputy and cosponsor of the legislation, Alexei Ostrovsky, had stressed the influence of "foreign NGOs financed by the CIA" in "what happened in the Ukraine, in Georgia and in Moldavia." "We want to defend our citizens against the risk of their being led into chaos," Ostrovsky added.[8]

Though overwhelmingly approved by the Duma, the first draft of the law had been strongly criticized by international institutions. This led the Kremlin to propose a series of amendments to tone down the text without completely changing it: according to the new draft, foreign NGOs could continue to operate without modifying their statutes as long as they didn't threaten "morality and national sentiment," among other things. A few days before the vote, Vladimir Putin gave his support to the new measure in the following terms: "This bill is needed to safeguard our political system against external interference and to protect our society and citizens from any terrorist or misanthropic ideology that could be spreading under this or that sign."[9]

In Russia, the next parliamentary elections are scheduled for the end of 2007. They should be followed in the spring of 2008 by presidential elections.

July 18, 2006. Has the epidemic of velvet revolutions been successfully contained? The fate of the protest movements in Azerbaijan, Belarus, and to a lesser extent, in Kyrgyzstan, as well as the tightening of Putin's rule in Russia, show that the remaining post-Soviet regimes have learned quite a bit from the experience of their deposed colleagues. To respond to the transnational spread of the kind of protest technology developed by Otpor and its offspring, the Russian government has set up a whole department entirely devoted to the task of stopping the "orange contagion" in the countries of the CIS (the Commonwealth of Independent States, which comprises most of the former republics of the Soviet Union). Among other accomplishments, this department has been responsible for the launching of Russia Today, a twenty-four-hour English-language television news station. One of the station's main leitmotifs consists of insisting on the idea that democracy comes in many different varieties and that no single model — for instance, the Western liberal model — should prevail over the others. At the same time, the Russian government has no qualms about modulating the prices of natural gas bought by the ex-USSR republics according to their political loyalty — thereby threatening the social and economic stability of countries that would be tempted to stray from Russia's fold.

Aside from Putin's pressure, the mixed results obtained by the governments that were installed in the wake of the mulitcolored revolutions have undoubtedly had the effect of chilling some of the revolutionary enthusiasm. In the Ukraine, the Orange Revolution coalition — composed of Our Ukraine, President Viktor Yushchenko's party, the Yuliya Tymoshenko bloc, the party of the charismatic former Prime Minister Yuliya Tymoshenko, and the Socialist Party — collapsed in the wake of the March 2006 legislative elections, after the Socialists' defection and amid growing animosity between the president and Tymoshenko. The split of the Orange Revolution coalition enabled Viktor

Yanukovych to become prime minister less than two years after having been defeated by the protest movement in Kiev.

Much ado about nothing? Such a pessimistic conclusion is unwarranted at least on two counts. First, it underestimates the importance of a normalized democratic process, however disappointing its workings may be. Second, it also ignores the real value of the velvet revolutions, above and beyond any skeptical or cynical judgments one might pass on them: these revolutions did not aim to bring a "good" government to power, but to make those in power aware of the fact that they are being watched. On April 29, 2006, ten thousand people, led by a large portion of the leaders of the March 2005 uprising, demonstrated in the Kyrgyz capital, Bishkek, demanding that the Bakyev-Koulov regime keep the promises of reform upon which its legitimacy rests. And in July 2006, a young man who had camped out on Independence Square in Kiev throughout most of the Orange Revolution had this to say to the French television journalist who was interviewing him: "Power may well be disappointing! But we knew we were going to be disappointed. That's not really the issue."

Translated by William Bishop and Michel Feher.

1   The Office for Democratic Institutions and Human Rights (ODHIR) of the Organization for Security and Cooperation in Europe (OSCE) reported that "the conduct of the 2006 presidential election in Belarus failed to meet OSCE Commitments for democratic elections." OSCE/ODHIR Election Observation Mission Report, Warsaw, June 7, 2006.

2   Lukashenko was speaking at an Orthodox cathedral in Minsk. The sentence was quoted by *The Independent*, London, January 10, 2006.

3   Lukashenko's statement was made on March 17, 2006, while that of his security chief dates from March 16. See *Belarus News and Analysis*, March 28 and March 17, 2006, respectively.

4   Stanko Lazendic, interviewed by the author of this article in February 2005.

5   Gene Sharp, *From Dictatorship to Democracy: A Conceptual Framework for Liberation*, 2nd printing (Boston: Albert Einstein Institution, 2003).

6   Quoted in *Deccan Herald*, July 12, 2005 (online edition).

7   On May 13, 2005 in eastern Uzbekistan, thousands of citizens descended into the streets to protest against an arbitrary court case accusing a group of Muslim entrepreneurs of being part of a movement of radical Islamists. According to observers, the slogans for this peaceful demonstration, the first of its kind under Islam Karimov's regime, had to do with living conditions and political repression. At the margins of the gathering, activists were said to have taken control of the prison and other administrative buildings to free prisoners. Police forces responded by opening fire on the crowd, killing 173 people, according to their own count, while international human-rights organizations spoke of some 745 victims. After the massacre, Karimov justified the police response and the hundreds of trials organized in its wake by describing the demonstration as an attempted coup d'état aimed at putting an Islamic state in power. At the present time, the Uzbek government has rejected all appeals for an independent international investigation.

8   Quoted by Current World Affairs (CWA), www.currentworldaffairs.com/?p=138.

9   Quoted by Radio Free Europe/Radio Liberty, online edition, www.rferl.org/featuresarticle/2005/12/515c41a8-c443-4005-a6ac-fe5bef3079f7.html.

Must We Defend Society?: Governmentality, Civil Society, and Political Activism According to Michel Foucault

Mathieu Potte-Bonneville

To appreciate fully the new perspective that Michel Foucault's notion of governmentality has brought to the analysis of civil society, it is useful to begin by examining the debates that have surrounded two contemporary events — the French referendum on the Treaty Establishing a Constitution for Europe (TCE), in May 2005, and the so-called Orange Revolution that took place in the Ukraine at the end of 2004. Foucault, after all, always constructed his concepts in close relationship to the crises and contradictions that affected the historical context of his work. Thus, understanding the relevance of Foucault's concepts today requires the same sort of immersion in the present on the part of his readers. In that respect, the paradoxes that currently accompany the reference to civil society on both the western and eastern sides of Europe provide an excellent introduction to the way in which Foucault approached the concept of civil society in the final session of his 1978–1979 lecture course, published as *Naissance de la biopolitique*.[1]

A PEOPLE OR A SOCIETY?

In the months preceding the referendum on the European Constitution, the discussion that led to the rejection of the treaty by French voters mainly focused on the treaty's so-called *libéral* dimension. In French, one must recall, the word *libéral* does not fully correspond to the English "liberal." While *libéralisme* applies to the philosophical tradition of political liberalism from John Locke to John Rawls, it also refers to the supporters of free-market economics, starting with Adam Smith and stretching all the way to contemporary neoliberal and rational-choice theorists. Thus, unlike the United Kingdom and the United States, where liberal economists include the likes of John Maynard Keynes and John Kenneth Galbraith, in France, those who qualify as *économistes libéraux* are, to a large extent, the followers of Friedrich von Hayek and Milton Friedman. Stressing that the semantic fields of *libéralisme* and liberalism do not entirely overlap is especially important in the context of the debate over the TCE. While those on both sides of the issue — at least those belonging to the left of the political spectrum — largely based

Michel Foucault at a demonstration in support of immigrant workers'
rights, Paris, France, 1973 (Gilles Peress/Magnum Photos).

their argument on the *libéral* character of the treaty, their disagreement can be traced to the meaning of *libéralisme* to which they gave precedence.

On the one hand, those who opposed the TCE saw it as an attempt to institutionalize the principles of economic *libéralisme* once and for all. They argued that the treaty defined social activity solely in terms of commercial exchange, thereby subordinating the former to the rules of free trade and to the imperative of profitability. A constitution predicated on such principles, critics of the TCE claimed, would inevitably mandate the elimination of the social protections characteristic of the European welfare state. In other words, the treaty would provide a legal basis for the destruction of the noncommercial sector of society that, until now, had been under the control and management of national governments. (According to the logic of the welfare state, this sector was meant to guarantee citizens equal access to those services that have been deemed too indispensable to be measured in terms of economic rationality alone and that thus have been maintained outside the realm of commercial competition.)

On the other hand, those in favor of the TCE, while recognizing the *libéral* character of the contested text, refused to see it merely as an instrument of market fundamentalism. In their view, what primarily made the treaty a *libéral* — and in this case, liberal — document was the fact that it enshrined as constitutional rights and protections a series of legal tools and citizens' initiatives that European constituents could use in order to challenge the policies of EU member states and European institutions. Thus, according to "liberal" and leftist advocates of the TCE, countering the hegemony of shareholder capitalism was just as much their objective as it was the objective of the treaty's leftist detractors. However, they considered that to meet such an objective, seizing on the opportunities offered by the treaty's political liberalism would prove a better strategy than taking shelter behind the walls of nation-states — which, as Marx himself had suggested, are poor ramparts against transnational economic interests.

It is worth noticing that the dispute over the interpretation of the TCE's *libéral* character extended beyond the contents of the text: supporters and opponents of the treaty also argued about what the latter meant, how to use it, and, even more importantly, about the type of collectivity that was to vote for or against it. In other words, the question was not only whether the voters should agree with what the TCE said, but also whether they could recognize themselves in the entity that produced it. In that regard, two positions confronted each other. The first, stressing the constitutional aspect of the text, pointed out that a constitution requires, as a subject, a "people" united enough to form a body politic and capable of instituting itself as an agent of its own destiny. Noting that the conditions under which the TCE had been drafted did not meet these requirements, given the technocratic and secretive procedures through which the drafting commission had established the text and balanced European interests with that of the member nations, the proponents of this first position concluded that no real citizenry could be instituted by such a treaty. Those who held the second position, on the other hand, emphasized the hybrid nature of the project. Insisting on the fact that the

A demonstrator distributes posters during a protest against the
European Constitution in Paris, January 22, 2005. The poster reads
"Vote against the European Constitution" (Charles Platiau/Reuters).

TCE was as much a treaty as it was a constitution, they contended that, as such, it
should be treated as a legal tool that jurisprudence could reinterpret and transform.
Rather than as the expression of a *people* speaking with one voice, the TCE should be
perceived as both a framework and a target for a multiplicity of strategies developed
from within a *society* whose members necessarily have conflicting interests. (Accordingly, members of such societies approach the law pragmatically, as a way of advancing their interests and arbitrating their conflicts; whereas from the point of view of a
people, the law is primarily a mode of self-representation.)

This divergence between the two positions was manifest even in the way their
respective advocates presented the act of voting in the referendum. On the one hand,
those who accused the TCE of not meeting the standards of a real constitution claimed
that voting "no" might turn out to be the founding manifestation of a European body
politic. As they saw it, the referendum vote could potentially open the way for a true

institutional process through which a "Europe of peoples" would institute itself by means of its rejection of the TCE. On the other hand, those who banked on the potential of an amendable treaty argued that strategic thinking with regard to the consequences of the vote should take precedence over concern with expressing oneself and having one's voice heard. In short, whereas some meant to express with their *voices* the *people's* will to reject a *constitution* predicated on economic *libéralisme,* others were instead casting their votes to endow their *society* with a *treaty* that seemed like a useful tool from the perspective of political *liberalism.* Hence the difficulty, for the proponents of both positions, even to hear their opponents' claims. To put it another way, the debate over the TCE revealed a profound division on the left over the opportunity — or, conversely, the risk — of bracketing the relationship between the body politic, established as a free subject through its representation in the institution of a protective national or even European state, in favor of an instrumental relationship between a transnational civil society and a set of legal tools that could be used as Trojan horses for social objectives.

IMPERIAL GEOPOLITICS OR TRANSNATIONAL PROTEST?

The 2004 presidential elections in the Ukraine should have resulted in the victory of Viktor Yanukovych, the candidate supported by the Russian government. However, the outcry over the fraud that had damaged the election's integrity and the tireless determination of the protesters who occupied Kiev's Independence Square eventually led to new elections that brought Viktor Yushchenko to power. Instrumental in this succession of events was a student activist group named Pora (It's Time), which played an essential role at every stage of what is now commonly referred to as the Orange Revolution. First, the group actively worked at discrediting the elections before they were even held. (In that respect, Pora's strategy proved remarkably subtle: while its members sought to persuade the public that the vote would be tainted by fraud, their purpose was neither to obtain the suspension of the elections because of the likely fraud nor simply to monitor the electoral process in order to report, on the night of the elections, that fraud had indeed occurred. Instead, their plan was to let the electoral campaign run its course, out of respect for democracy, while simultaneously raising the electorate's awareness of the fraud to come and thus getting people prepared to denounce the inevitable result of the vote — again, out of respect for democracy.) Second, in the wake of the fraudulent election, Pora stuck to a strictly nonviolent strategy and thus contributed to the elaboration of a pacifist approach to challenging power. Third, once the government yielded to the protesters and agreed to organize new elections, Pora did not transform itself into a political party. Instead, it chose — at least provisionally — to assume the role of a watchdog group that would scrutinize the new administration.

What is most interesting for the purpose of this essay is the disagreement between political observers about the group's activities — a disagreement leading to two quite different assessments of the Orange Revolution. As is well known, Pora was not an isolated group: its founders were part of a network of activist groups in Central and Eastern Europe (including Zubr in Belarus, Mjaft in Albania, and Kmara in Georgia, among others) that were all inspired by Otpor, the Serbian student group that had proved instrumental in the downfall of Slobodan Milosevic.[2] These various groups shared information and pursued the same goal — to exploit the trappings of democracy used by the strong-man regimes of Central and Eastern Europe in order to overthrow those regimes by nonviolent means.

During the months that followed the Orange Revolution, some commentators pointed out that the network to which Pora belonged, including Otpor and the groups directly inspired by it, was largely supported and financed by private foundations and institutes based in the United States — most notably George Soros's Open Society Institute (OSI) and the Albert Einstein Institution (AEI). (Dedicated to the development of nonviolent forms of resistance, the AEI was founded in 1983 by a researcher at Harvard, Gene Sharp, and is currently run by Robert Helvey, a retired colonel in the U.S. Army.) Accordingly, these commentators were inclined to see the American organizations funding Otpor and its network as the true instigators of the movement and thus to perceive the latter from a strictly geopolitical perspective.[3] In their view, groups such as Otpor and Pora served no purpose other than establishing U.S.-friendly governments in Central and Eastern Europe — governments that would treat liberal democracy and open markets as articles of faith and that would remove their respective country from the Russian sphere of influence. In short, this first analysis of activist groups such as Pora and Otpor associated these groups with some kind of pacifist and *Mitteleuropa* version of what Operation Gladio had been, in Italy, in the 1950s and 1960s — an imperialist maneuver orchestrated by the United States.

As for the second assessment of these same groups, its focus was less on funds than on dates. For the proponents of this less cynical view of Pora and its associates, one could not see these groups simply as the tools of an American strategy without dismissing the fact that the forced resignation of Milosevic occurred only about a year after the large demonstrations against the World Trade Organization in Seattle. A founding moment in the resurgence of a radical critique of neoliberal globalization and U.S. hegemony, these demonstrations resulted from the so-called "Teamsters and Turtles" alliance between unions and nongovernmental activists, which could be seen as the forerunner of the partnership between Otpor and the miners' union in Serbia one year later. Similarly, the Orange Revolution in the Ukraine happened at around the same time as the massive demonstrations in England and in Spain against the participation of the British and Spanish governments in the war in Iraq. (Still in the same vein, the leader of Mjaft, the Albanian exponent of the Otpor network, often claimed that his way of harassing Albanian authorities was modeled on Michael Moore's techniques.[4]) Therefore, according to commentators sympathetic to Pora and Otpor, these groups should not be perceived as the instruments of an imperial strategy, but rather as expressions of a genuine and widespread dissatisfaction with regimes that were largely deprived of popular support. This dissatisfaction, which existed in each society where these groups were based, fueled protest movements that extended past national borders and that circumvented geostrategic concerns. Consequently, insofar as Otpor, Pora, and the other members of the network remained faithful to the movements from which they stemmed, their activities should neither be reduced to the stakes of state politics nor to those of the relations between states.

WHAT IS CIVIL SOCIETY?

Both debates — on the merits of the TCE and on the nature of the Orange Revolution — revolved around the same question, the question of the political meaning that should be attributed to "society" once the latter is distinguished from the traditional tenets of the political realm: the people as sovereign, the state as institution, the government as enactment of the state, and international relations as the domain of governments. In the first debate, what was at issue was the meaning of a "European civil society" within the European Union: should it be perceived as the main vector of a massive depoliticization of Europe whereby the European space would be reduced to a vast free-trade zone or as the platform for a politics of autonomy enabling the members of such a society to avail themselves of various legal instruments? In the second debate, the contentious issue concerned the nature of an international civil society extending across the national borders of the Central and Eastern European nations: should one interpret this society as a mere tool of American policies in the region, or as an agency manifesting itself through its refusal to subordinate the defense of civil liberties to the question of whether its advocacy might benefit this or that great power?

It is noteworthy that, from one debate to the other, supporters and detractors of civil society traded priorities in at least one respect. While in the French dispute over the TCE, the advocates of civil society gave precedence to an instrumental logic (one that subordinates political action to strategic concerns in terms of means and ends) and their opponents emphasized an expressive logic (one that identifies a citizens' initiative with the voicing of a claim), the positions were reversed in the case of the controversies over the Orange and other "velvet" revolutions. This remarkable reversal of positions shows — and this will be my thesis in fine — that both the definition of civil society and the categories through which this notion is either claimed or criticized are largely a function of the historical context in which they are debated.

"MUST WE DEFEND SOCIETY?"

So far, this essay has made little mention of Michel Foucault. And yet, the preceding descriptions of the debates over the TCE and the Orange Revolution could serve as an exegesis of the title — "Society Must Be Defended" — that Foucault gave to his lecture course at the Collège de France in 1975–1976, and they could also help us appreciate the strange irony of this title.[5] The course alternated between two main themes. To begin, Foucault addressed the genealogical question of how the modern state came

Supporters of Ukraine's president Viktor Yushchenko attend a
ceremony to mark his inauguration at Independence Square, Kiev,
January 23, 2005 (Efrem Lukatsk/AP Photo).

to legitimize its own action in the name of the imperative of "defending society." He
also sought to present archival evidence of a discourse — the discourse of the "war of
the races" — that had been repressed by modern philosophical-political notions such
as sovereignty, the common good, and the general interest. What the discourse of the
"war of the races" claimed, throughout the seventeenth and eighteenth centuries, was
the impossibility for some members of society to identify with the power to which they
were subjected. Thus, the statement "Society must be defended" could be understood
in two diametrically opposite ways — in quotes or out of quotes, as it were. On the one
hand, it could be taken as the denunciation of a pretext used by the state to tighten its
control over the individuals under its administration — in other words, as the denunciation of a formula whereby the state predicates its tyranny on solicitude. On the other
hand, it could be seen as a claim truly purporting to protect society from the exercise of
a power to which it is loath to submit.

The ambivalence and irony surrounding Foucault's thematization of "society" in
this way seems to resonate in today's debates. Indeed, the disputes regarding the TCE

and the Orange Revolution both attest to the fact that (civil) society can alternatively be perceived as the instrument through which neoliberal globalization and American imperialism perpetuate their hegemony and as an entity capable of opposing a dual resistance — to the power of the state and to the rule of the market. Hence the potential heuristic benefit of rereading Foucault in the current context.

The following pages will engage the Foucauldian corpus in three successive ways. First, I will try to show how the published works, *Discipline and Punish* above all, undertake a deconstruction of the philosophical notion of civil society.[6] Second, I will describe how Foucault, having circumvented the discourse of political philosophy, proposes, in his lecture course devoted to liberal and neoliberal governmentality, a historical and critical reconstruction of civil society. Finally, I will stress that Foucault considers the notion of civil society to be inseparable from the kinds of mobilizations that are manifest in his own activist interventions, the trace of which is preserved in his collected works, *Dits et écrits*.[7]

THE PHILOSOPHICAL INCONSISTENCY OF CIVIL SOCIETY

Let us first briefly revisit what is known in philosophy as the question of civil society. There are three essential figures of this notion, corresponding to three historical moments:

The first moment is that of Aristotle's *Politics,* later revived by medieval philosophy — Thomas Aquinas, in particular. In this initial instance, civil society (*politikē koinonia*) has two major characteristics. It can be defined negatively as a community that is based on neither the natural and private relationship among kin nor the kind of cooperation existing in a village and aiming at the survival of the villagers. More positively, civil society can also be defined as a community bound by the pursuit of the "good life." As such, civil society proves irreducible to a system of contractual relations, whether established for the purpose of trading or for fending off enemies, and is thus bound to goals that transcend the individual interests of its members. That civility is primarily defined by such a *telos* implies that the political philosophy for which civil society is an object must also take up the question of the ends of social existence. To put it differently, the political philosophy to which this first figure of civil society corresponds is a discourse of ends, because its specific ends are what makes a society truly civil.

Civil society's second moment emerges with Machiavelli's *The Prince* and finds its full expression in the works of philosophers, from Hobbes to Rousseau, whom Leo Strauss has assembled under the common tradition of "modern natural law." The major transformation that the concept of civil society undergoes in this second stage pertains to the involvement of the state, which conditions every individual's membership in society and refashions it as follows: to be a member of society entails, first, the representation of the individual by the state, in a juridical, rather than elective relationship in which one is asked to recognize the state's decisions as one's own. Second, it entails submission to the state, insofar as it is representative of one's will. And third, it entails participation (in Rousseau's version, at least), through the action of the representative state, in the exercise of the general will.

The third moment in the genealogy of the concept of civil society is to be found in the empiricist tradition of John Locke, David Hume, and the eighteenth-century Scottish empiricists. Adam Ferguson's *Essay on the History of Civil Society* is the best-known expression of this third approach to civil society. Its main distinctive feature consists of separating the existence of society from the institution of sovereignty, thereby affirming the primacy of a nonpolitical relationship as the basis of social existence.[8] This nonpolitical relationship is twofold: it involves exchanges of goods and services and the division of labor, and, at the same time, relations of "sympathy" among individuals. These interactions are predicated on a bond that can neither be equated with the community of the good life nor subsumed under a sovereign authority. Instead, such a bond demonstrates that the social is irreducible to the political; better, it conveys that the nonpolitical dimension of the social is both the common ground upon which political institutions are built and the boundary that limits the field of action of these institutions. Hence the ambiguity of the expression "civil society" in this third instance: the political meaning of society resides precisely in the fact that society is neither originally nor entirely civil.

These three ways of problematizing the notion of civil society frame most of the canonical debates in political philosophy — debates that, beyond philosophy itself, affect politics, as well. In particular, they preside over the debate about whether there is such a thing as a civic form of political subjectivity that transcends individual ends. It also informs discussions about the meaning of law, as well as about the boundaries between the prerogatives of the state and those of social agents. Though heterogeneous and ostensibly exclusive of one another, these three definitions of civil society also can be perceived as three levels of the same notion. In his *Elements of the Philosophy of Right,* Hegel operates this dialectical unification of civil society in the following way: he makes the state the *telos* of the political community and sees the realization of this teleological process as the development of an order of economic exchanges that transcends itself in the state and that is in turn structured by it.[9]

In contrast, Foucault's approach neither chooses among these three models nor attempts to synthesize them. Instead, he endeavors to bracket them. Consequently, his genealogy of power relations is less about advancing a new political philosophy than about undermining political philosophy as it is traditionally understood. This corrosive perspective clearly manifests itself in what Foucault calls the "microphysics of power" in *Discipline and Punish.*

The most obvious break that Foucault's inquiry into the nature of power makes with traditional political philosophy regards the Aristotelian discourse of ends. Indeed, organizing the reflection on power around the empirical and unassuming question "How does it work?" — which is what Foucault's "microphysics" is about — does not amount to conducting a preliminary inquiry on means before addressing the main issue, that of the common good, and thus returning to the proper register of philosophy. Rather, what

Foucault's perspective emphasizes is that the ends that a political community sets for itself do not determine the mode of the operation of government; in other words, the same ends can give rise to completely different governmental technologies, and vice versa. Therefore, it becomes impossible to characterize civil society in the Aristotelian fashion, by reference to the specific ends that it assigns itself. Accordingly, any attempt to evaluate modern civil society according to whether its members continue to differentiate between life and the pursuit of the good life no longer makes sense from Foucault's point of view. (For that reason, Foucault's perspective can neither be reconciled with the kind of nostalgic critique that is typical of Hannah Arendt and Leo Strauss — the lament over a modern society that has become indifferent to the common good — nor be associated with Giorgio Agamben's Heideggerian contention that the contemporary world order is achieving a process always already enveloped in Western metaphysics, that of reducing all forms of life to "bare life.")

The project of a microphysics of power also breaks with the second figure of civil society, whereby the latter is predicated on the institution of a sovereign power that both transcends the individuals that are subjected to it and yet subjects itself to them by presenting its authority as arising from their authorization. To this legal approach to popular sovereignty, Foucault opposes several arguments. First, he points out that both the authority of the state and the rule of law presuppose that human groupings have already been ordered. The state and the law thus require an ordering of the social that they cannot manage on their own and that pertains to a mode of rationality and intervention than their own. Second, Foucault claims that, instead of operating through the representation of wills, this other mode of rationality and intervention consists of training and disciplining bodies. Accordingly, insofar as this latter mode of social ordering uses language, the discourse that it relies on is not one of expression, but of action, protocol, and watchwords. Finally, Foucault contends that this technical training of bodies not only is a necessary condition for the institution of the state and the rule of law, but also appears to be the truth of the state itself. This is why Foucault talks about the process of the "statification" (*étatisation*) of disciplines and even considers the state as an effect of this very process. Thus, from Foucault's perspective, the cult of the state, as the only structure capable of transcending social divisiveness, no longer has any place. The state's purpose is not to defend each from each, or to express the common will, but to *defend society* as a reality already constituted and pervaded by disciplinary processes.

Foucault's emphasis on training and disciplining techniques is also what makes him break with the third version of civil society, whereby society is envisioned as a system of exchanges that naturally unites its members and thereby possesses both a unity that precedes the institution of the state and a rationality that can be opposed to overbearing governments. For his part, Foucault conceives of the training and disciplining techniques that he distinguishes from the workings of sovereignty as power relations, and he defines power as an action on a possible action. Therefore, from his perspective, power and social existence are coextensive; there is no such thing as a society without — or "before" — power. One cannot even say, as Marx did in his critique of Hegel's philosophy of law, that the state and the political order are mere reflections of the truth of civil society. This thesis would presuppose that the relations of production are anterior to power relations right where Foucault attempts to show the contrary: that the political configuration conditions the organization of the dispersed multitude of workers, making labor possible in the first place. In short, Foucault rejects the notion of a prepolitical civil society, because, in his view, society is always already pervaded by a system of command and obedience that makes it impossible to lay claim to a prepolitical reality against which the value of institutions might be measured.

The first main feature of Foucault's genealogy is thus its skepticism. Accordingly, adopting his perspective amounts to straying from three familiar discourses. The first uses the reflection on civil society as a way of stressing the need to rediscover the meaning of the good life lost in the modern age — or, conversely, as a way of defending the abstraction of modern individualism against postmodern (and/or neo-archaic) identity politics. The second calls for the restoration of the state's transcendence, against — or at least as a necessary counterweight to — the centrifugal forces of individualism. Symmetrically, the third discourse calls for the liberation of market forces, unjustly constrained by governmental institutions. In short, Foucault's genealogy succeeds in eschewing pretty much all the discourses that stem from civil society as a philosophical topos.

THE HISTORICAL ADVENT OF CIVIL SOCIETY

It is not enough, however, to show how microphysical analysis makes it possible to escape the all-too-familiar topoi — in particular that of the state–civil society antinomy. Genealogy must also explain how this antinomy emerged in the first place and became so entrenched as to become one of these obligatory topoi of political philosophy for two centuries. In other words, while Foucault's perspective sidesteps the notion of civil society as essential reality, whether prepolitical or instituted by the state, it still considers civil society as a crucial historical problem: as such, its emergence must be dated and its conditions of formation analyzed.

Foucault devotes the final sessions of *Naissance de la biopolitique* to exactly this task. In one of the sudden turns typical of his lecture courses, this focus on civil society follows a sustained discussion of the neoliberal conception of the art of government according to postwar German "ordoliberal" and Chicago School neoliberal economists. In Foucault's view, civil society should be regarded as an essential tenet in the redefinition of modern governmentality that took place in the eighteenth century. His presentation proceeds in the following stages.

First, the course of 1978–1979 is largely dedicated to the formation of the different modalities of liberalism understood as an art of government. From 1977 on, Foucault had substituted the analysis of what he calls "governmentality" for that of the microphysics of power. The purpose of this shift was to stress that his perspective is not one that merely focuses on the local manifestations of power. Indeed, the notion of governmentality is meant to show that the state itself can and should be analyzed in terms of the various modes of exercising power that it integrates and combines, rather than solely by examining the legal foundations of its sovereignty. The inscription of liberal theory and practice in this framework, from their emergence in the eighteenth century to their contemporary variants, modifies the perception of liberalism as a primarily economic theory centered on Adam Smith's idea of the "invisible hand" and leading to political consequences and choices. Instead, from the point of view of governmentality, liberalism is first a practical art of governing and, as such, constitutes a matrix of economic concepts. Accordingly, Foucault does not perceive liberalism as the doctrine that calls for less government in the name of the self-organization of the market. Rather, he sees it, as we just claimed, as the art of governing that not only takes the self-organization of the social into account, but that makes it its own goal to protect and even to enhance this capacity for self-rule. Once liberalism is understood in these terms, what remains to be explained is the emergence, in the history of governmental arts and practices, of this mode of governing, a mode whereby a government seeks to limit its own involvement. In other words, what is the meaning of this paradoxical governmentality, and how does it take shape?

To answer these questions, Foucault takes us back to the crisis at the end of the seventeenth century of the regime of governmentality designated by the French notion of *État de police* and the German notion of *Polizeiwissenschaft*. This regime consisted of broad government intervention in and control of the various sectors of social activity. Its aim was to police all human endeavors at every level of society — under the aegis of a centralized authority — in order to optimize the economic and demographic potential of society. The crisis of this "police" regime during the first half of the eighteenth century — a crisis that should not be reduced to its repressive dimension — was essentially due to a series of economic transformations. In particular, national governments found it increasingly difficult to regulate the price and availability of grain. Consequently, governmental logic and doctrine were confronted by a new problem: that of the sovereign's structural inability to have full knowledge of the specific events determining the overall economic picture and thus to respond appropriately. In other words, the agents of sovereign power suddenly realized that they were blind to some of the processes that took place in what they considered to be their field of intervention. They also realized that their blindness could be traced to the discontinuity between the individual choices made by their subjects — each pursuing his or her economic interest — and the global effect of these choices. Therefore, the organization of society by the "political anatomy of detail" that characterized the "police" regime was fundamentally challenged. And the challenge it faced did not come from individual demands for rights — something for which the police regime was prepared. Rather, it came from the mere realization, on the part of governing agencies, that general prosperity was guaranteed only by the indifference of individual economic agents to the overall consequences of their pursuit of selfish interests. From this point forward, writes Foucault, governments predicated on policing technologies were left with two equally ruinous options. On the one hand, they could hold on to their conception of sovereignty as omnipotence and pervasive competence — except for what pertained to the economic sphere, which would become both a blind spot and a free zone with respect to sovereign power. On the other hand, they could claim that when it came to the field of economics, sovereign intervention should be limited to overseeing passively and monitoring both the conduct of individual agents and their global effects, thereby reducing the role the sovereign to a measurement and survey function with respect to the market.

The notion of civil society emerged at this very juncture, providing governments with a way out of two equally unacceptable alternatives — either relinquishing part of their domain of sovereignty or defining their prerogatives. The notion of civil society offered a solution by means of rearticulating the legal and political (the "civil" part of civil society) with the socioeconomic (the "society" part of civil society) in such a way as to mandate a new mode of intervention on the part of the agents of sovereign power. This new regime would not reduce either the purview or the pervasiveness of sovereignty, but it would predicate it on two imperatives: that of abiding by the rule of law and that of respecting the specificity of economic mechanisms.

"I believe," Foucault writes, "that the notion of civil society, the analysis of civil society, the ensemble of the objects or elements that have been made to appear within the frame of this notion of civil society, all of this in the end is an attempt to respond to the issue that I have just raised: how to govern, according to the rules of law, a space of sovereignty which for better or worse, as you prefer, is populated by economic subjects."[10]

Thus, according to Foucault, civil society should not be understood as a natural phenomenon preceding the institution of political sovereignty, but as a redefinition of sociality whereby sociality could be perceived simultaneously as a political (civil) and nonpolitical (social) realm. Defined in this way, civil society appears as the concept that made it possible for governments to continue to lay claim to their art of governing at a moment when they were faced with the realization that economic rationality challenged their sovereignty.

From the preceding presentation of Foucault's perspective, one could get the impression that, in his view, the invention of "civil society" was merely a "ruse of power" whereby governments ostensibly recognized a measure of autonomy in the governed — as members of civil society — only to better retain their hold on them. However, such a conclusion would prove unfaithful to Foucault's thought for several reasons. First, while the last session of *Naissance de la biopolitique* does envision the concept of civil society as a strategic construction, it also stresses that this construction was a response to a real crisis affecting the early modern art of governing that effectively challenged those who relied on this art. Second, the fact that the notion of civil society sought to circumscribe a realm that was partly ruled by law and partly submitted to economic mechanisms raised, rather than solved, the problem of how to combine the two intrinsically heterogeneous forms of subjectivities that such a realm involved — that of a subject of rights and that of a *homo oeconomicus*. Though he rejects both the assertion that liberal civil rights merely provided a convenient framework for dominant economic interests and, conversely, that these same rights formed the necessary and sufficient mode of resistance to the abusive potential of economic interests, Foucault nonetheless emphasizes that these two positions, and thus the rich history of the conflicts between them, originated in the crisis of governmentality from which the notion of civil society arose. Third, in his analysis of Ferguson's work, Foucault shows that the role of economic rationality in the liberal definition of civil society is at the same time central and ambivalent: indeed, the *Essay on the History of Civil Society* presents civil society as simultaneously predicated on and undermined by the system of economic exchange and the confrontation of interests that it entails. "The economic bond," Foucault writes, "is rooted in civil society and is not possible without it; it holds it together from one side, yet undoes it from another."[11] Finally, the fourth reason not to interpret Foucault's position as one that reduces civil society to a ruse of power is that it would contradict his claim that the meaning of a concept is not reducible to the strategy from which it stems. In other words, even if the notion of civil society was originally constructed in order to minimize the autonomy of the governed at a moment when the prevailing regime of governmentality was in crisis, the fact remains that, once constructed, the notion of civil society also became a tool that the governed made use of in order to challenge the mode of government to which they were submitted.

Consequently, the meaning of civil society should be perceived as the result of an ongoing negotiation between the way in which society governs itself and the way in which it is governed. Accordingly, the most important change that the notion of civil society has brought to the art of government regards the point of reference for what governing is about. Rather than being based on the wisdom of the sovereign, governing in the age of civil society is predicated on "the rationality of the governed...insofar as they are economic subjects and, in a more general way, subjects of private interest."[12] In short, the emergence of civil society, according to Foucault, was neither a ruse nor, conversely, the mere result of popular conquest and emancipation, but the marker of a global reconfiguration of power relations.

CIVIL SOCIETY'S OPENNESS AND ITS USES

At this point, we come to the most interesting aspect of Foucault's approach. One passage in particular should be quoted here:

> Civil society is not a pre-existing or immediate reality. Civil society is something that is a part of modern governmental technology. However, to say that civil society is a part of modern technology is not to suggest that it is just a pure and simple result of that technology, nor is it to say that civil society is bereft of any reality. Civil society is like madness, like sexuality — it is among what I will call transactional realities. These transactional, transitory figures are born out of the interplay of power relations and what continually escapes them, an interplay that takes place at the interface of governors and the governed. No less real for not being eternal, these figures include, in the present case, civil society, elsewhere, madness, and so on.[13]

The comparison with the other objects of Foucault's concerns, such as madness and sexuality, is enlightening. (Moreover, Foucault has rarely expressed so clearly the status he gives to madness and sexuality themselves.) What this comparison emphasizes is threefold. First, Foucault stresses that the historicity of these phenomena, their contingent and transient character, does not make them less real or effective. Second, he also insists on the fact that, while inherent in a specific regime of power, figures such as civil society, madness, and sexuality do not have a stable meaning, since power, in Foucault's view, is not an institution that secretly manufactures its effects, but a web of relations and confrontations. Third, that civil society, sexuality, and madness are all characterized as transactional realities implies that the "transactions" from which they arise are never resolved and closed once and for all: the meaning of these notions evolves according to how they are used, and the ways in which they are used are themselves functions of the changing relations of power between those who govern and those who are governed.

Claiming that the meaning of a reference to civil society is a function of the context where this reference takes place does not amount to disqualifying the concept of civil society as ill-conceived. On the contrary, the fact that its meaning is, if not undetermined, at least underdetermined is crucial to its political use-value. For instance, the malleability of the concept of civil society is what makes it usable — even in its original liberal sense — against a regime of governmentality that, for its part, resorts to the mechanisms of the old "police" state. This is exactly how Agnes Horváth and Arpád Szakolczai analyzed the resurgence of the notion of civil society in the discourse of Central and Eastern European dissidents in the 1980s. Adopting Foucault's perspective, these two authors stressed that the new currency of the notion of civil society among dissidents did not attest to the transhistorical reality that this notion would designate, but merely reactivated a discourse "linked, across the last two centuries, to specific and relatively brief periods."[14] At the same time, Horváth and Szakolczai also defended their perspective against a historicist objection that would point to the radical difference between the figure of the despot, who was the target of the eighteenth-century critique, and the bureaucratic state of the 1980s. In their view, despite the clear differences between the two regimes, one could still point to "a functional equivalence between Western Europe at the beginning of the nineteenth century and the contemporary political scene in Central and Eastern Europe…the common mechanism they shared was the party apparatus — the Bolshevik-style apparatus, the kind of apparatus critical for so-called absolutist states: the modern police."[15]

Thus, for Horváth and Szakolczai, what justifies the militant use of the liberal notion of civil society is less the nature of the political model that is being promoted or the institutional and ideological status of the regime that is being confronted than the presence of certain specific power mechanisms. Conversely, of course, Foucault's perspective reveals that civil society and the celebrated autonomy of its members can also become a formidable instrument of control and domination. Foucault himself endeavors to demonstrate just this point in his analysis of neoliberal governmentality, which presents the unfamiliar picture of a government tirelessly working to withdraw from the social sphere while encouraging the governed to submit all their conduct, in every sector of their existence, to the rules of economic rationality and competitiveness.

In sum, one could say that Foucault's radical pragmatism gives a new meaning to the idea of an "open society": indeed, from his perspective, society is primarily open to interpretation — open because it can be invoked in different ways and for very different purposes. While this definition implies a preference for those societies that are open to debates about how the notion of society should be interpreted — Foucault is a liberal to at least that extent — it also conveys that opening and reopening society is a perpetual task and that any invocation of civil society is bound to be reappropriated.

I will conclude by noting that Foucault's own political initiatives and involvements are paradigmatic of this process of reappropriation, insofar as they interweave two divergent logics. One may, in fact, distinguish two series of "causes" that Foucault embraced as a public intellectual. On the one hand, as demonstrated in a string of international involvements running from Spain during the last years of Franco's regime, to Iran at the time of the upheaval against the Shah, and to Poland in the wake of Jaruzelski's coup, Foucault was clearly on the side of "society against the state," addressing governments from the standpoint of the governed in confrontations that sought to demonstrate that civil society could not recognize itself in its rulers. Such activism, whereby the governed challenge the legitimacy of the sovereignty to which governments lay claim, amounts to a kind of "political strike": it seeks to manifest the autonomy of society and constitutes a social and moral experience that is indifferent to the mechanisms of political representation. But, on the other hand, Foucault's political activism also includes various instances of siding with those who face rejection from civil society — prisoners, the mentally ill, and homosexuals. The relationship between these two types of activism — activism that speaks out against the state in the name of society, and activism that questions society in the name of those it marginalizes and rejects — is hardly straightforward. It is as though Foucault's endeavor consisted of working on the time-honored pairing of society and the state, probing both the philosophical interplay and the historical solidarity between these two notions in order to extract from them an element that would enable him to examine and question the current sociopolitical configuration of power. The point of this endeavor was not to reconcile society and the state: Foucault never prophesized that the state would eventually disappear or that society would be at peace with itself. Rather, what he was looking for was the common denominator of the two types of struggles — for and against society, as it were — in which he alternatively took part. That common denominator, which each instance of political activism must recreate for its own purposes, is something that one might call an uncivil sociability.

Translated by Michel Feher and Blake Ferris.

1 Michel Foucault, *Naissance de la biopolitique: Cours au Collège de France* (1978–1979), ed. Michel Senellart (Paris: Gallimard/Seuil, 2004).

2 See Philippe Mangeot, "Velvet Agitators," included in this volume, pp. 592–603.

3 See, among others, R. Genté and R. Rouy, "Dans l'ombre des revolutions spontanées," in *Le Monde diplomatique,* January 2005.

4 See www.mjaft.org. See also Victor S., "Otpor, Zubr, Kmara, Pora, Mjaft: Eastern Europe's Children of the Revolution or Front Groups for the CIA?" in *The Apostate Windbag,* January 1994, avalable online at http://apostatewindbag.blogspot.com/2004/12/otpor-zubr-kmara-pora-mjaft-eastern.html.

5 Michel Foucault, *Society Must Be Defended: Lectures at the Collège de France, 1975–1976,* trans. David Macey (New York: Picador, 2003).

6 Michel Foucault, *Discipline and Punish: The Birth of the Prison,* trans. Alan Sheridan (New York: Pantheon, 1977).

7 Michel Foucault, *Dits et écrits: 1954–1988* (Paris: Gallimard, 1994).

8 Adam Ferguson, *An Essay on the History of Civil Society* (Edinburgh : Kincaid and Bell, 1767).

9 G. W. F. Hegel, *Elements of the Philosophy of Right,* ed. Allen W. Wood, trans. H. B. Nisbet (Cambridge: Cambridge University Press, 1991).

10 Foucault, *Naissance de la biopolitique,* p. 299.

11 *Ibid.,* p. 306.

12 *Ibid.,* p. 316.

13 *Ibid.,* p. 301.

14 Agnes Horváth and Arpád Szakolczai, "Du discours de la société civile et de l'auto-élimination du parti," in *Cultures & Conflits* 17 (1995), pp. 47–80, available online at www.conflits.org/document328.html.

15 *Ibid.*

The Closing of American Society

Gara LaMarche interviewed by Michel Feher

Gara LaMarche is vice president and director of U.S. programs for the Open Society Institute, a private foundation established by George Soros to build vibrant and tolerant democracies whose governments are accountable to their citizens. He is the author of nearly one hundred articles on civil-liberties and human-rights topics, and editor of Speech and Equality: Do We Really Have to Choose? *(1996). He serves on the board of directors of several human-rights organizations.*

Until the mid-1990s, the Open Society Institute (OSI) and the George Soros Foundations were best known for their initiatives in countries that were in the midst of a transition to democracy, especially the former Communist countries of central and eastern Europe. So my first question is about the rationale behind George Soros's and the Institute's decision to develop U.S. programs.

George Soros has been active philanthropically for twenty years or so. He made money long before he started to spend it in a significant way through his foundations. Originally, he did so in Hungary, where he is from, and then throughout Central and Eastern Europe and in what became the former Soviet Union. And so over a period of time between 1989 and the mid-1990s, he established a vast foundation network essentially by building foundations within each country, foundations that were indigenous in their governance, if not in their funding.

The money came from him, but there were local boards and staffs that spent the money along the broad themes of open society, civil society, independent media, independent academy, and so on. When he started, Soros never thought of working in the United States. Soros had, however, initiated two projects in the United States before he started working more comprehensively there. One had to do with the so-called War on Drugs and the other focused on death and dying. First, he established the Lindesmith Center, which was a policy think tank to deal with what he thought of as the failed drug policy, the failed

Homeless individual at the entrance of the White House Metro station, Washington, D.C., 2005 (photo by Kike Arnal).

War on Drugs; then he set up the Project on Death in America to examine the status of care at the end of life in the United States and to reflect on ways of improving how people die there. At the time, he didn't conceive of these as the underpinnings of a more general involvement in domestic policy issues, but it is interesting to look at what he first chose to deal with.

What the drug policy program and the Project on Death in America had in common was a concern with addressing taboos. In the wake of the 1980s hysteria about drugs — which led to people being locked up for minor drug offenses, the appointment of a drug czar, and all that kind of stuff — Soros believed that you couldn't have a legitimate and open discussion about drugs in the United States. On this issue, at least, the United States reminded him of the closed societies of the Communist world, which he had tried to combat through his foundations and the Open Society Institute. You couldn't get research funded on drug policy or speak out for a more sensible drug policy without being ostracized. So he wanted to break through that barrier. He didn't then, and doesn't even now, have a strong feeling about what drug policy should be — contrary to what is often said, he does not advocate legalization. He just believed, and still does, that the current policy is not working and that we need to have an open debate about what might work.

Where death and dying are concerned, it's somewhat different because it is not a political taboo, but it is a social taboo. Very few people in the United States are comfortable with talking about their own death and dealing with it or thinking about it, particularly doctors. Soros really wanted to open up the discussion, and his desire to do so was drawn from his very personal experiences with his parents. Both of his parents had recently died, and his father had the kind of death that Soros thought was awful. He was in a lot of pain, and the pain wasn't being dealt with well. He was in a hospital, removed from his family. It seemed like a terrible way to die. His mother's death, on the other hand, a few years later, was at home. She had pain management. She died surrounded by her family and had an opportunity for closure. She had time to say goodbye. He looked at those two deaths and he wanted to do more to promote the second kind of death. He's a billionaire, and he decided he could do something about it. We took different paths in each program, but those were the first two things that he did in the United States — both the Project on Death in America and the Lindesmith Center were created in 1994 — before focusing on the United States as a whole.

How and when did that focus come about?

The Open Society Institute's U.S. programs began in 1996, but the event responsible for their creation took place in the fall of 1994. The midterm elections that enabled Newt Gingrich to take over the House of Representatives and gave Congress a conservative Republican majority amounted to a real sea change in American politics. What Soros saw in the results of these elections was the ascendancy of an ideology exalting the marketplace as the answer to everything. (Now, of course, this same ideology dominates not just Congress but all branches of government.) While Soros clearly believes that the market has a place in society — he himself has done particularly well by it — he is also very wary of its hegemony.

In his view, you just can't apply market standards to the professions or to politics. After the 1994 elections, he was especially concerned with the Republicans' assault on government, with their desire to sap government of its capacity to serve human needs. Thus, what Soros perceived as a threat in the United States to what he calls an open society in the mid-1990s did not have to do with civil liberties, as was the case in the former Communist world, but with the growing inequalities produced by market fundamentalism — the growing gap between rich and poor. His particular focus was on the racialized dimension of this gap and on the way it gets manifested in the justice system in the United States.

So these were the issues that made for the broadening of the U.S. programs of the OSI. I was hired to build and run these programs in 1996, and I have been doing so for the last ten years. Our initial focus was the criminal-justice system; then we turned to immigrants' rights; and later we expanded our programs to a variety of democracy issues, such as campaign finance reform and media policy. We have also promoted a variety of youth empowerment initiatives, particularly for minority youth. But until 2001, the general rubric under which these programs developed was that of inequality. That is, we sought to counter the growing inequalities fostered by market fundamentalism.

Did you have a stance on welfare reform?

 Well that's an interesting example. When we started in 1996, welfare reform — along with immigrants' rights, for that matter — was not something that Soros had thought of dealing with. (This, by the way, points to the advantage of working for a living donor who makes quick decisions and is willing to be bold, which is not characteristic of many foundations.) We were in the early process of building a U.S. program, and I was just a couple of months into the job, when Clinton signed the welfare bill. Regarding the project of reforming welfare, both Soros and the rest of us at the Open Society Institute were somewhat agnostic: many progressives certainly felt that it was a terrible idea but, on the other hand, one could say that the existing welfare system wasn't working very well. However, we did object to the way welfare was actually reformed, both in terms of its devolution — the fact that the power to set the standard for welfare programs was basically thrown back to the states — and, when it came to its treatment of immigrant workers, the fact that there was a provision in the welfare bill that cut off benefits to legal immigrants as a punitive measure to save money. I am not referring to undocumented people, but to legal immigrants who work and pay their taxes.

We got involved in the welfare reform issue by addressing these two aspects of the bill. And our interventions in these two matters turned out to be important and enduring programs. First, Soros, as a former immigrant who had actually been aided by the National Health Service when he was a young man in Britain, was extremely struck by the unfairness of a measure that would deprive immigrant workers of the benefits of social safety nets (what is left of them at least) when they fell on hard times. So, within less than a month, he established a fund of a magnitude equivalent to the one he had created to provide humanitarian aid to Sarajevo a few years earlier. With that money, we ventured two kinds of initiatives. First, we financed a combination of services designed to help immigrants become citizens; there are a lot of people who want to be naturalized, but there is such a huge bureaucratic backlog that they can't actually reach this goal. Second, we supported a lot of advocacy so that the voices of immigrants could be heard in the policy debate. I guess this is a significant aspect of our philosophical approach, especially in the U.S. programs: rather than concentrating on what a policy should be — in this case, welfare reform policy — our main concern is to make sure that the people who are the most affected by the policy in question have the opportunity to be involved in the process. We thus tried to help immigrant advocates organize on their own behalf. What happened was that, within a year or so, the benefits were substantially restored, and that was a victory.

As for the devolution issue, the question was: given that the fifty states now have so much power, how do you work so that the welfare plans that emerge at the state level are not worse than what the federal standards used to ensure? How can they be better than before, more humane and responsive to human needs? This was obviously a tall order. In order to attend to it, we looked for foundations seeking to fund various state-based groups — welfare-rights groups, minority groups, associations of low-income people — whose purpose was to lobby the congress of their state in order to influence its welfare policy in a positive direction. In other words, we searched for and found other foundations, raised money for them, and gave it to them through a grants pool. On the whole, this approach resulted in many improvements at the state level. Once again, these improvements came from the fact that we enabled the people most affected by the policy to be at the table, to have their voices heard.

As you explained, Soros's decision to devote a substantial part of the money and efforts of the OSI to U.S. programs was made in the wake of and as a reaction to the midterm elections of 1994, a decision motivated by the strains put on the openness of American society by the growing inequalities produced by market fundamentalism. Would you say that the presidential election of 2000 and the reaction of the Bush administration to the terrorist attacks of September 11, 2001 modified the purview of your programs in the United States?

We can speak both of continuity and of major change. Continuity, because the problems of inequality — the gap between rich and poor, the racial dimension of this gap, and the way social inequality and racial discriminations shape the justice system — have not disappeared. There is no starker example of the gravity and endurance of these problems than what happened with Hurricane Katrina, in terms of both the social conditions that made the people in New Orleans so vulnerable and the response, or lack thereof, of the government to the disaster. We need to persist in countering those policies responsible for the perpetuation and widening of inequalities, especially because the current administration allows market fundamentalism to prevail even more than in the mid-1990s.

At the same time, especially since 9/11, something has changed quite fundamentally: the openness of American society is not only undermined by the nefarious effects of tax cuts and government-bashing, but threatened by the Bush administration's assaults on human rights and civil liberties. The United States is suffering from problems opposite to those once faced by the closed societies of the Eastern European bloc. That is, deregulation and dismantling of the government. However, increasingly, our society is confronted with the same types of problems as well: torture and secret detention, abuse of executive power, the government's alarming unchecked license to act because of the Patriot Act, assaults on academic freedom, and de facto restrictions of the freedom of the press (insofar as a few conglomerates own a large portion of the media and control its discourse). Under the aegis or the pretext of national security, American society is actually exposed to a process of closure that, as an institute devoted to promoting open society, we must try to oppose.

And this is not all: aside from the issues pertaining to the widening of inequalities, abuse of executive power, restrictions of civil liberties, and violations of human rights, we also have to deal with remarkable, and frightening, efforts on the part of the dominant party to manipulate the democratic process itself. This is not only about what happened in Florida with the presidential election of 2000. From the Gingrich days to Tom Delay's infamous tenure, the Republicans have engaged in redistricting in order to lock in their majority in the House of Representatives.

This is why Soros has been so overt about spending his personal money to defeat George W. Bush and his party. Paradoxical as it may seem, this is not a partisan move on his part. It is not about loyalty to the Democratic party, but about staving off the closing of American society. And as far as I am concerned, having worked with Human Rights Watch and the American Civil Liberties Union before joining the OSI, I can say that I am still working for a progressive, yet nonpartisan organization. Our main concern is not to make sure that particular candidates are in power, but to see to it that whoever is in power is properly checked and abides by constitutional standards.On that score, the current administration poses a real threat.

While in the former Soviet bloc the OSI purported to facilitate transitions to democracy. It seems as if your current mission in the United States is to help prevent a transition *from* democracy.

Let's return to your statement about the continuity that you perceive between your job at the OSI and your previous affiliations. Isn't there a contradiction, or at least a tension, between your claim that the OSI belongs to the same realm of watchdog groups as the ACLU and Human Rights Watch and Soros's declared ambition, shared by other progressive and liberal philanthropists, to challenge the big conservative foundations on their own turf? I am referring here to a series of articles, starting with Matt Bai's essay "Wiring the Vast Left-Wing Conspiracy," published in the *New York Times Magazine* in July 2004, about the so-called Phoenix Group and the Democracy Alliance. According to Bai and others, the progressive billionaires who formed the Phoenix Group and who now contribute to the Democracy Alliance — George Soros, Peter Lewis, Tim Gill, and Andy Rappaport, among others — are intent on countering, but also on emulating what the major conservative dynasties of donors, such as Richard Mellon Scaife and

John M. Olin, have done since the 1960s: funding the construction of the progressive counterpart to what Rob Stein, the founder of Democracy Alliance, calls the "conservative message machine." Though the OSI as such is not involved in the Democracy Alliance, it also includes programs that openly seek to revitalize liberal and progressive movements in the United States. So to rephrase my question: How can you combine the task of resisting what you see as a partisan hijacking of institutions with that of fostering openly progressive initiatives without either seeming disingenuous as an impartial monitor or tying your own hands as a political entrepreneur?

I think that you need to undertake both tasks. Regardless of how polarized public discourse has become in this country, or maybe for that reason, I believe that it is crucial to keep differentiating between the realm of fundamental rights or, to put it differently, of independent institutions, and the realm of policies and their ideological foundations. I remain convinced that, in any open society, the former ought to remain essentially beyond the reach of political majorities, while the latter can and must be contested. That the other side does not respect the boundary between the two realms should not, in my view, persuade us to do the same. Preserving the independence of institutions such as the courts, the media, the academy, and not letting them be subject to political vicissitudes, are obligations that we cannot dispense with if our mandate is to protect the foundations of an open society.

These principles are quite consequential. After all, what has saved us in the United States in the last couple of years is that the independent institutions are not yet totally gone. The media, while relatively spineless in recent years, has uncovered some scandals. For instance, it can be credited for throwing a spotlight on what is happening with the Katrina disaster. The courts have actually blocked some of the more excessive measures taken by the administration, because we are not yet at the point where all judges determine their rulings according to their political affiliation. We have seven of the nine justices on the Supreme Court appointed by Republican presidents, and yet they have opposed the executive branch in a couple of significant matters.

At the same time, I certainly agree about the need to meet the challenge of the Republican right in the field of policies and ideology, about the need for progressives to match the self-confidence, clarity, and organization of their conservative opponents. And I will also concede that there are ways in which the border between the two realms can become an object of contestation. For instance, you know that in the United States most economic justice matters have not been viewed as matters of fundamental rights. We don't tend to use the language of fundamental rights for labor or welfare-type issues because of the peculiarities of American political culture. So there certainly is a place for a debate about what a political majority is or is not entitled to undo or, conversely, to inscribe, in the realm of fundamental rights. But having such a debate is not the same thing as deliberately blurring the lines between what should and what should not be up for political grabs.

In fact, if the progressive camp, or at least the Democratic party, can be blamed for something, it is not for overemphasizing the distinction between the two realms but, on the contrary, for mixing them up. On the one hand, in the contestable domain of policies and values, Democrats tend to triangulate, look for compromises, and downplay their own beliefs, thereby making their opponents seem more clear-eyed, confident, and trustworthy. On the other hand, they have managed to let the Republicans portray them as partisans when they defend the independence of institutions. As you know, one of the greatest conservative accomplishments has been to persuade the public that progressives are guilty of judicial activism, that the mainstream media is liberal, that the academy is controlled by a leftist thought police, and so on. I maintain that we must stick to the double task of protecting the realm of fundamental rights and independent institutions from political hijacking while, at the same time, rebuilding the infrastructure of a vibrant progressive camp.

Regarding the second task, what we know about the so-called conservative message machine is that its construction dates back to the mid-1960s, in the wake of Barry Goldwater's defeat in the presidential election of 1964 and that the key to its eventual success was the combination of patience and intransigence demonstrated by its constructors. According to John Micklethwait and Adrian Wooldridge, the authors of *The Right Nation: Conservative Power in America,* the various conservative foundations and think tanks whose ideas are now dominant have consistently given precedence to their radical messages over tactical considerations. Until their agenda prevailed, they never mitigated their stance in order to help the Republican party win the next election. Is this a lesson that the people gathered in the Democracy Alliance think they should learn?

The Democrats' lack of conviction has obviously been very bad. Some are beginning to find their voice, but it is a slow process, at best. There are people on the progressive side, and I would count myself among them, who believe that we not only need to assert our basic principles more forcefully, but also think anew about what these principles mean today and how to frame them. We need to produce a vision of what our society should look like, even if realizing such a vision is not politically feasible right now. Just as the right did forty years ago, we should articulate this vision and work toward it patiently and obstinately, rather than simply trying to come up with some fine-tuning that will allow the Democratic Party to win the next election. At the same time, however, each election is quite consequential. Let's remember that we have the war in Iraq and two more right-wing Supreme Court justices because of the outcomes of the last two elections.

I would add that the reason why Democrats and their progressive supporters are so often prone to think in terms of doing whatever it takes to get across the finish line with 51 percent is that they are not sufficiently marginalized. They suffer from being too close to the possibility of power. When you're in the wilderness, like the Republicans were after Goldwater, you have the luxury of thinking boldly. But when you are that close to winning — or at least believe that you are — you don't tend to encourage boldness and innovation. And that's a bit of a problem for the progressives. This is why there is such a need for the kind of institution that the conservative side has been so good at setting up, that is, institutions that take a step back from immediate electoral concerns in order to produce ideas, articulate visions, fashion and frame messages, and train future leaders and opinion makers. Building an infrastructure on the progressive side, an infrastructure capable of competing with the various conservative institutions, is clearly the ambition of groups such as the Democracy Alliance, OSI, and of Soros himself.

Can you speak about the structure and strategy informing the OSI's American programs in that respect?

We have recently consolidated our work under three major rubrics, which means that some projects, such as Death in America, have ended. The first project is the Justice Fund, which is our main contribution to the task of keeping institutions independent and fundamental rights protected. It is a unified fund that includes all the aspects of the justice system with which we are involved. For instance, both the Constitutional and Legal Policy Program and the Justice at Stake Campaign — the former is a funding program; the latter, a coordinator of a coalition of organizations — endeavor to protect the fairness and impartiality of courts, including thorough monitoring and reform of the judicial selection process. The Gideon Project seeks to reduce inequalities in the administration of criminal justice by funding organizations that either advocate for the reform of the system that provides defense attorneys for indigent people or provides training to public defenders. The Racial Justice Initiative funds a series of organizations involved in advocacy regarding the enduring effects of racial discrimination or critical research on the relationship between race and poverty. The Program in Prison Expansion and Sentencing Reform addresses the issue of overincarceration, which is a huge problem in this country, by promoting both reforms in sentencing policies and alternative solutions to incarceration. We also have an After Prison Initiative that campaigns for more humane reentry policies and practices for the six hundred thousand people who return home from prison each year. Moreover, the OSI is also involved in the defense of immigrant rights (especially in the wake of 9/11), in lesbian, gay, bisexual, and transgender rights (including the extension of marriage benefits to same-sex couples), and in funding organizations that seek to abolish the death penalty.

Our second project is what we call the Strategic Opportunities Fund. It is in some sense a catch-all, since it covers a vast array of concerns, yet it has a specific purpose, which is to give us the flexibility we need in order to conduct a more rapid response to new open-society challenges. We have been using that fund for all our Katrina-related work. Last year, we also spent a substantial amount of money from that fund on public-education campaigns to preserve Social Security from privatization and to preserve the so-called filibuster rule in the Senate so that it would be available to stop the worst judges. And we've put a fair amount of money toward helping the public understand what is at stake with the Supreme Court.

Would you say that the purpose of this Strategic Opportunities Fund, setting up a structure capable of responding rapidly to unexpected events, echoes Soros's claim that his foundation's work in the former Soviet empire was about "seizing a revolutionary moment"?

To an extent, yes, though in many cases the moment we are trying to seize is less than revolutionary. After all, situations such as the ones created by the collapse of the Communist bloc in Central and Eastern Europe, but also those for many of the former clients of the West in Central and South America, in particular, are not so frequent. At the same time, there are some events, and among them some tragic events, that provide an opportunity for soul searching and reassessing the conditions under which these tragedies actually took place. Thus, what we hope to do with this Strategic Opportunities Fund is not only help respond to a disaster, but also encourage the kind of conversation and research that such an event should generate.

Now, to be honest, our efforts in this latter domain are not always successful. In particular, I feel a sense of failure, for both society and the foundation, because I don't think we seized the moment that Katrina provided to look at the reality of racialized poverty as a nation and say, "My God, this is the country we live in." We seemed to be on the verge of such a realization for a little while — even Bush was forced to acknowledge what had happened. However, the moment has passed and the national debate never really took place. I think Bush has paid a political price for the incompetence of his administration's efforts, but not for the underlying structure of society that was revealed by Katrina. (Not that that should be entirely laid at his door — it goes back hundreds of years.) Another missed opportunity was 9/11. Some people thought that, thanks to the firemen and the policemen, 9/11 would be the end of the antigovernment crusade, the end of conservatives' assaults on public services, and the end of tax-cut mania. But, of course, that did not happen, either. The Bush administration managed to make the post-9/11 era about national security, about justifying executive privileges, and curbing civil liberties, rather than about rehabilitating public services and institutions.

To come back to our Strategic Opportunities Fund, we resort to it for two types of situations. On the one hand, as I mentioned before, the fund is intended for unexpected emergencies, such as Hurricane Katrina. In this particular case, we awarded funds to ACORN — the Association of Community Organizations for Reform Now, which is organizing some of the evacuees — and to several other community-based agencies that are either providing legal representation to hurricane victims, immigrants, in particular, or seeking to involve low-income people and racial minorities in the policies that will shape the future of the New Orleans communities and neighborhoods affected by the hurricane. We have also created a media fellowship for writers, journalists, and photographers who are writing about either the scandalous aspects of Katrina, such as the failures of the relief operation, or the underlying structural issues, in particular, the racialized poverty, that were exposed by the hurricane.

On the other hand, we also use the Strategic Opportunities Fund to respond to issues that are more like dangerous trends or developments than actual emergencies. These include threats to academic freedom, the Bush administration's various assaults on science, including emergency contraception, "Intelligent Design," and research on global warming, and troublesome projects regarding media policy. All these issues represent looming menaces to the fabric of an open society.

Both the Justice Fund and the Strategic Opportunities Fund pertain to what you define as the realm of fundamental rights and independent institutions — the conditions

necessary for an open society. I imagine that the third tenet of your threefold structure relates to your other mission, that of building a strong infrastructure for progressive organizations and policies.

The funds for this third project are provided by the Special Chairman's Fund, and our board has identified three priorities for allocating them. First, we fund a series of multi-issue policy centers. These include organizations such as John Podesta's Center for American Progress, which seeks to be the progressive counterpart of the Heritage Foundation; Demos, which is especially involved in promoting reforms of the democratic process; the Center on Budget and Policy Priorities, which specializes in the impact of fiscal and budgetary policies on low-income people; and the Center for Economic Policy Research, which seeks to promote both debates on and the identification of the stakes involved in social and economic policies. We have also started to fund smaller university-based think tanks such as the Jamestown Project at Yale, which gathers a group of African American scholars working on race and democracy; the Longview Institute, which is a new progressive research and advocacy program based at the University of California; and the Roosevelt Institute, which is a student think tank. Finally, we are funding and looking for more community-based organizations — ideas, after all, are as likely to emerge from outside as well as from within the academy — such as the Center for Community Change, which has become as much a think tank as an advocacy group. Now, this search for policy centers, for organizations that combine research and advocacy, is very much a work in progress. I don't want to pretend that we have it all figured out, or even that all the organizations that we would like to help already exist, but we are actively searching.

Our second priority is building a progressive legal infrastructure that would be a counterpart to the conservative Federalist Society, which is both the main intellectual resource that has enabled the right to transform the courts and constitute jurisprudence as well as a career pipeline for conservative judges. So we have funded the American Constitution Society, which does not merely attempt to revitalize progressive legal scholarship, but also endeavors to inscribe it in a longer-term vision for what the Constitution should look like and how it should be interpreted. The right has been doing this for twenty-five years, while progressives have mostly been busy putting out fires. Of course, we have to keep putting out fires, and there is no shortage of them, but at the same time, it is crucial to start thinking about the day when we will have regained the power to forge a positive vision of constitutional jurisprudence. If we are to challenge the political and philosophical hegemony of the conservatives, there is hardly a more important domain than this one.

Finally, our third priority is youth organizing, campus organizing, in particular. In recent years, the right has become quite active on campuses. However, universities, whether you look at faculty or at students, are still more progressive places than the rest of the country. So we are trying to help students and younger people in general with leadership opportunities, with organizing campaigns, media access, and other such issues. Our purpose is to create opportunities for progressive activism among the emerging generation. Among the groups we fund, some are the youth wings of existing organizations. For instance,

People For the American Way has developed Young People For, which is good and aggressive. We also support the United States Student Association and United Students Against Sweatshops. There is a lot of energy in campaigns for particular issues pertaining either to discrimination against minorities or to the various social struggles around globalization. You have to meet people where they are. One issue that has become quite big on campuses and that is also an important concern for our Justice Fund is prison incarceration and privatization. The prison-industrial complex is a target of choice on campuses, but also a target of opportunity, because so many of the university cafeterias are run by Sodexho Marriott, which has ties to the prison industry. So students have something right at hand that they can boycott and embarrass.

You are clear about the fact that the U.S. programs of the OSI pursue two distinct goals: that of warding off the transition away from democracy and the closing of the American society that you impute to the Republican majority, and building a strong infrastructure, one that would in part mirror — for what is still a timid and beleaguered progressive movement — the accomplishments of conservative foundations in the last thirty years. But what should a revitalized progressive agenda look like? Can it simply be about protecting the strictures of an open society against the assaults of the conservative message machine, or does it need a vision of social change that would be as proactive and transformative as the vision evolved by the conservative movement in the post-Goldwater era?

It would be both premature and presumptuous on my part to try to answer this question. What I can say, however, is that liberals are often criticized — and the very fact that they now prefer to call themselves "progressives," rather than "liberals" attests to the soundness of this critique — for their overreliance on the law and, in particular, on the courts as arbiters. Such a tendency, critics contend, reveals that they no longer believe in the popular appeal of their ideas and values. Now, there is sometimes a rightist populist slant to this indictment of the left, such as conservative ranting against unelected and activist judges, but it is nonetheless true that, on a number of issues, progressives have eschewed public organizing and public support to rely on the courts and their rulings. The good and the bad news, of course, is that they can no longer do that: conservative judges with a clear political agenda are now in a dominant position. So, for progressives, there is no way around doing the hard work of political persuasion and ground organizing. This is why building an infrastructure for progressive advocacy is such an urgent task.

01/28/2006

(LEFT TO RIGHT) Cindy Sheehan, Jodie Evans (Code Pink), Hugo
Chávez, and Medea Benjamin (Global Exchange), Caracas, Venezuela,
January 2006.

"A Partner for Peace and Justice"

a profile of Global Exchange by Yates McKee

"We're not all just Bush supporters or imperialists.... I wish the people in the U.S. would try and understand Hugo Chávez."[1] Appearing in a March 2006 *New York Times* article entitled "Visitors Seek a Taste of Revolution in Venezuela," this appeal for cross-border understanding was issued by a U.S. graduate student participating in a "reality tour" organized by Global Exchange (GX), which describes itself as "a membership-based international human rights organization dedicated to promoting social, economic and environmental justice around the world."[2] This appeal was accompanied by testimonials to the beneficial effects of Chávez's oil-financed social programs and his determination to forge "an alternative to neoliberalism and the policies that have ravaged Latin America for twenty years."[3]

The appearance of such an antineoliberal appeal in a major national newspaper—especially one whose editorial pages have been consistently hostile to the Chávez regime—and the appearance of critiques of the U.S.-driven project of economic liberalization, more generally, constituted a relatively successful moment in a campaign aimed at what GX describes in its "Program Summary" as "increasing global awareness among the U.S. public."[4] But if the *Times* article is a register of success for GX (it is posted prominently in the Venezuela section of the group's Web site), it also speaks to an emergent aporia in the history of post–Cold War nongovernmental politics: it is a de facto apology by an NGO for a specific governmental regime, one that is widely considered by the radical left in the United States and elsewhere to embody what the organization calls "a new, progressive model of socioeconomic development that is shaping Latin America's future."[5]

Whatever one may think of Chávez per se—the coup attempt orchestrated with U.S. acquiescence by right-wing media mogul Gustavo Cisneros notwithstanding, the regime has unquestionably initiated significant redistributive measures in arenas such as land reform, health care, education, and industrial relations—such progovernmental support raises interesting paradigmatic questions about the relationship between the heritage of human-rights discourse and a neoanti-imperialism that strongly valorizes the principle of national-popular sovereignty, an ideal of political representation in which the interests of governing agencies coincide with the will of those they aim to govern in the figure of the independent "people" set off against a general capitalist-imperialist enemy.

Designed to "provide people from the U.S. with an understanding of a country's internal dynamics through socially responsible travel" and typically coordinated with small-scale sustainable tourism projects in host countries, "reality tours" are an important source of revenue, publicity, and connection building for GX.[6] They constitute the founding paradigm of the organization itself. However, they are only one element in the organization's broad array of program types, modes of operation, and levels of engagement both within the United States and abroad. This array has grown to include election monitoring, corporate accountability campaigns, legislative lobbying, street demonstrations, a speaker's bureau, and a network of fair-trade commercial enterprises. Devoted to "increasing public awareness of the root causes of injustice while building partnerships and mobilizing for change,"[7] the organization is arguably one of the most emblematic articulations of the contemporary U.S. left; a crucial node linking it historically, ideologically, and practically to the project of "globalization from below" that has begun to coalesce over the past ten years in venues such as the International Forum on Globalization and the World Social Forum.[8]

With approximately forty full-time employees at its San Francisco office, three fair-trade stores, several foreign project sites, hundreds of occasional volunteers, and an annual budget of around 7 million dollars (raised through donations, tour fees, fair-trade sales, and foundation grants), the organization offers itself as a "partner for peace and justice"[9] to think tanks, trade unions, social movements, and other NGOs in the United States and abroad. While the mechanics of these partnerships are various — they include the direct initiation of campaigns, interorganizational coordination and cooperation, and electronic news transmission for domestic and international progressive causes generally — GX consistently assumes a role of ideological hegemony, translating the effects of corporate and governmental practices deemed to be intolerable into accessible, affectively compelling stories of injustice for audiences of citizens, consumers, and in some cases investors in the United States. These audiences are addressed as potential collaborators in a broad project of social transformation encompassing both technical policies and ethical horizons: "Our campaigns seek to build alternatives to the economic status quo by linking global analysis with local action. Please help us spread the message that the current system does not have to be tolerated — we can and must change it!"[10]

The questions surrounding GX's stance on Venezuela in fact mark the historical origins of the organization itself. GX was founded in 1988 by Medea Benjamin, a former public-health specialist with the UN Food and Agriculture Organization and the World Health Organization, and Kevin Danaher, a sociologist trained in the post–new left milieu of the University of California–Santa Cruz, in the 1970s. In the 1980s, the two were senior analysts at the Institute for Food and Development Policy (IFDP, later known as Food First), an Oakland-based think tank that generated pioneering critical research on the social and environmental effects of U.S. development aid to Third World countries — especially in the realm of agriculture and food security — and helped lay the intellectual and organizational groundwork for what would become the Global Justice movement. As outlined in landmark Food First publications such as Walden Bello, David Kinley, and Elaine Elinson's *The Development Debacle: The World Bank and the Philippines* (1982) and Susan George's *A Fate Worse than Debt: The World Financial Crisis and the Poor* (1987), IFDP's analyses sought to draw systematic connections between U.S. Cold War geopolitical strategy and the evisceration of redistributive economic nationalisms in the postcolonial world (coordinated, for a time, through the United Nations Conference on Trade and Development) by the export-led development models and structural adjustment programs enforced by the World Bank and International Monetary Fund.[11] Much of the work of the IFDP in the 1980s also focused on experiments in Third World socialism and U.S. policy toward them, not least of all in Cuba and Central America — Benjamin's areas of specialty.

Of Benjamin's Food First publications, two are especially significant for the eventual program of GX. The first is *Don't Be Afraid Gringo: A Honduran Woman Speaks from the Heart* (1987), a translated *testimonio* in the style of *I, Rigoberta Menchu* (1984) that tells the exemplary life story of Elvia Alavarado, a *campesina* activist working to establish rural women's groups in Honduras during the U.S.-backed dictatorship there.[12] *Testimonio* is a genre that emphasize links between localized, embodied first-person experience and abstract geopolitical dynamics, constructing a cross-border educational encounter assumed to humanize otherwise dry policy analyses and thus to provoke U.S. citizens to pursue acts of ethical solidarity and material support.[13] The second of Benjamin's (co)publications offered a practical interface for this kind of humanizing, face-to-face encounter with others: *Alternatives to the Peace Corps* (1985–) a serially produced, multiauthored directory for "finding community-based, grassroots volunteer work — the kind of work that changes the world." With the aim of challenging paternalistic, top-down "charity" with respectful, horizontal "solidarity," this directory provided the basic terms for GX's "reality tours," which began with delegations to post-Duvalier Haiti (1986) that aimed in principle to support artisans' and musicians' cooperatives through the coordination of niche markets for their products in the United States.

With grant money acquired via contacts with Jamaican-American celebrity entertainer Harry Belafonte, a participant in the 1986 Hands Across America benefit fund, Global Exchange was incorporated as 501(c)(3) charity organization in 1988 and extended its efforts to Honduras and Nicaragua. Allied with progressive trade unions and liberation theology groups in both the U.S. and Latin America, the aim of the group's "solidarity work" was to bear witness to the effects of U.S. policy in the region and to set up support structures such as sister cities programs, speaking tours for Central American activists, and, tangentially, conduits for the resettlement of refugees.

Due to its founder's longstanding engagement with postcolonial agriculture, an important consequence of this "citizens' diplomacy" was the eventual development of relationships with Central American coffee-growers' cooperatives, which became the basis for the long-term, globally networked fair-trade program that now constitutes a significant portion of the organization's activity, public image, and revenue. The formative years of GX were thus marked by a concern with state repression perpetrated by U.S.-backed

GLOBAL ⟨A⟩ EXCHANGE

get involved
Take Action Now
Donate/Membership
Join a Chapter
Get our eNewsletter
Hear a Speaker
Interns and Volunteers
Job Opportunities

building people-to-people ties

Global Exchange is a membership-based international human rights organization dedicated to promoting social, economic and environmental justice around the world. Since our founding in 1988, we have successfully increased public awareness of root causes of injustice while building international partnerships and mobilizing for change.

fair trade store • *press room* • *search*

travel with reality tours
by Date
by Country
by Issue
Bike Aid

what's new
World News Update
Upcoming Events
GX Newsletter

regions
Africa
Americas
Asia
Middle East & Central Asia
Europe

war, peace & democracy
Iraq
Oil & Autos
Code Pink
Right To Travel: Cuba
Vote Justice

the global economy
FTAA, CAFTA
WTO
IMF/World Bank
Sweatshops
Green Festivals
Fair Trade

Global Exchange, detail of home page (www.globalexchange.org).

authoritarian governments in Latin America — a residual model of anti-imperialist Third World solidarity that would come into crisis with the defeat of Sandinista candidate Daniel Ortega in 1990 — and an interest in constructing sustainable alternative economic circuits between the United States and local groups in what would come to be known in the aftermath of the Cold War as the "global South."

It is with this transitional historical conjuncture in mind that it is necessary to understand GX's description of itself as a "human rights organization…increasing public awareness of root causes of injustice."[14] The organization aspires to overcome what it calls the "false division" of rights discourse drawn during the Cold War in which the capitalist democracies (selectively) emphasized the civil and political rights of individuals in relation to the repressive practices of totalitarian states, while the Soviet nations, repudiating such an emphasis as bourgeois mystification, claimed to secure the fundamental social rights of the proletariat.[15] While lauding the work of Amnesty International and Human Rights Watch — both of which have done important work concerning Latin American dictatorships and their aftermath — GX nevertheless perceived them as being too exclusively focused on the activities of nation-states and as limiting their definition of rights to issues such as freedom of conscience, freedom of association, electoral participation, and due legal process. Such terms were of course central to the emergent discourse of "civil society" — especially in the countries of South America — but by themselves they appeared to be inadequate in the eyes of organizations such as GX.

However crucial, the formal processes of democratization, demilitarization, and the internalization of human-rights norms were occurring against the backdrop of the massive liberalization of trade and finance known as the "Washington Consensus," a process in which multinational corporations, supranational regulatory bodies, and indigenous elites were enforcing a "race to the bottom" in the labor laws, environmental protections, and redistributive capacities of already vulnerable nations of the South. These developments required an expanded interpretation of what constitutes a human-rights violation and who or what could be held accountable for it. Such a reframing was legitimated by an appeal to historically underappreciated elements of the United Nations Universal Declaration of Human Rights (UNDHR), which declares, among other things, the right to work, the right to form independent unions, the right to public education, the right to an adequate standard of living, and the right to social services. In the words of GX spokesperson Jason Mark, "Together, the economic security articles of the declaration underscore that political rights can only be enjoyed when basic human needs have been satisfied," and vice versa.[16]

A typical scenario requiring this double analysis would be the state-tolerated use of coercion against workers struggling to form an independent union in a free-trade zone *maquiladora* subcontracted by a U.S. multinational. In such a context, the sites of accountability for the abuse are multiple, and the task of GX is to narrate the systematic relation of such sites for a public of Northern citizen-consumers — and in some cases shareholders — who are called to apply pressure in a variety of ways on the specific corporation in question, the intermediary businesses involved with the corporation — including institutional consumers such as universities and local governments — and the elected representatives responsible for the trade policy that structures the conditions for such abuses in the first place. Indeed, GX was an import actor in the emergence of the campus antisweatshop movement in the mid-1990s and continues to work on a nationwide "sweat-free" campaign that has resulted in cities such as San Francisco passing ordinances that require their urban procurement agencies to comply with the principles of the Designated Supplier Program pioneered by United Students Against Sweatshops—an important precedent for institutional investors and consumers nationwide.[17]

In a similar vein, in 1999, the organization led the Down to the Last Drop campaign that successfully pressured Starbucks to enter into an agreement with Transfair, the primary certification agency in the United States for fair-trade coffee. The introduction to a report entitled "Justice and Java" gives a sense of the mode of public address often used in the organization's campaigns, which frames an everyday act of First World consumption as the crystallization of uneven historical and geographical ties:

> Sip a steaming brew at Starbucks, and you might associate coffee with prosperity. The image of carefree consumers enjoying $3 lattes seems totally unrelated to that of coffee-bean farmers and workers, who live with grinding poverty, illiteracy and a long legacy of economic colonialism. But the two groups are part of an intricately related system that has existed for centuries, leaving coffee harvesters immiserated, and coffee drinkers mostly unaware to the suffering that goes into making their beverage.[18]

Fair-trade coffee has been an important component of GX's network of activities in southern Mexico, which has also prominently included a long-term project of human-rights monitoring in the state of Chiapas, the site of the Zapatista uprising in 1994 against the deleterious implications of the North American Free Trade Agreement for indigenous peasant farmers. In tandem with other projects concerning biopiracy in indigenous areas, these fair-trade activities have been extended since the reduction—though by no means termination—of military and paramilitary violence in Chiapas after the defeat of the Institutional Revolutionary Party (PRI) in the 2000 elections in which GX and its Mexican partners such as Enlace Civil played a significant role as monitors.

In the mid-1990s, GX—especially through the efforts of Kevin Danaher—was instrumental as a U.S. partner in coordinating and mobilizing the international NGO coalition 50 Years is Enough, which targeted the practices of the Bretton Woods institutions. These initiatives included the World Bank Boycott Campaign, which sought to apply pressure on public and private shareholders—universities, pension funds, municipalities, and churches—to demand accountability from the bank regarding issues ranging from dam construction to debt relief using the threat of disinvestment.

The cross-border organizational linkages formed by GX through its work on policies in Central America, sweatshops, coffee, Chiapas, and Third World debt, among other issues, enabled the organization to play a central role in organizing the 1999 demonstrations and civil disobedience actions against the World Trade Organization in Seattle, which sought to frame globalization as a locus of general struggle between democratic citizens and an unaccountable supranational elite. Despite the spectacular antistatism of anarchist youths (whose violent provocations were publicly repudiated by Benjamin), and despite the theoretical enthusiasts of the postnational multitude, it is important to remember that a key dimension of the democratization narrative put forward by GX and its allies in the International Forum on Globalization was to defend the protective and regulatory mechanisms of Southern economies, although not necessarily the specific political regimes nominally in charge of them. As GX sees it, such a defense is one of the preconditions for "establishing popular governance of the global economy," although in 1999 no existing national government seemed capable of becoming the vehicle for such aspirations.[19]

GX was primarily known throughout the 1990s for its work on issues pertaining to global economic justice, although specific issues of militarization and conflict were also on its agenda (exclusively, it should be said, in places where the United States could be shown to be have strategic interests, such as Columbia and Palestine). GX took an ambivalent position on the invasion of Afghanistan, dedicating itself to lobbying for compensation for civilian victims of U.S. attacks. But in the lead-up to the invasion of Iraq, GX helped launch what has become the primary antiwar organization in the United States, United For Peace and Justice (UPJ), and coordinated the historic global demonstrations of February 15, 2003.

Alongside UPJ, Medea Benjamin also colaunched Code Pink: Women for Peace, a direct-action group that has staged a number of media interventions (such as interrupting the live broadcast of Donald Rumsfeld's congressional testimonial on Abu Ghraib) and street-performance demonstrations marked by a color-coded maternalist-feminist pacifism. Along with celebrity supporters such as Susan Sarandon, Code Pink includes among its spokespeople war mother Cindy Sheehan, and has coordinated speaking tours by Iraqi women in the United States.

Global Exchange cofounder Kevin Danaher delivers a lecture at the 2004 Green Festival, San Francisco.

The Iraq war has also provided an occasion for GX to supplement its analyses of corporate globalization with a new emphasis on the relationship between security, energy, and the environment. Coordinated with the Rainforest Action Network, its newest campaign is Declare Independence from Oil, which uses a rhetoric of progressive patriotism and a range of media tactics (many involving the sports utility vehicle as an icon of arrogant over-consumption) to demand that automakers and legislators invest in green technologies for reasons of both ecological and geopolitical sustainability — an argument not entirely unfamiliar to neoliberal opinion makers such as Thomas Friedman, who has recently proclaimed that "green is the new red, white and blue."[20]

Interestingly, GX's anti-oil positions are in tension with its embrace of Hugo Chávez, for whom petroleum — and U.S. consumption of it — are economically and politically fundamental. That the organization is able to overlook this tension suggests the extent to which Global Exchange is happy to have found a formally democratic government that is both ideologically anti-imperialist and genuinely committed to securing the social rights of its citizens in the face of neoliberalism. The same could not be said for other targets of U.S. censure such as Libya, Iraq, Iran, or Serbia. (While heroic in its precarious survival, Cuba does not make for much of a long-term model; however, GX has sustained a long-term reality tour program in that country that focuses on themes such as organic agriculture and the development of the arts-and-crafts sector.) In other words, for the first time since the end of the Cold War, a demonized foe of Washington also appears as a viable friend of the left, one that shares the "Another World is Possible" narrative that organizations such as GX have labored to construct and disseminate for the past fifteen years.

Rather than an unfortunate lapse from an otherwise rigorous nongovernmental autonomy, GX's support for Chávez is consistent with its early investment in a discourse of Third World solidarity that sees the state, when properly animated by the demos rather than hijacked by the postcolonial elite, as a privileged locus of freedom and justice. As the GX statement on human rights explains, "Article 21 of the UNDHR states that 'the will of the people shall be the basis of the authority of the government.' Indeed, individuals and communities must be sovereign over their own affairs if they are to be free. In the new, globalized world, this means not just democracy in the political realm but also democracy in the economic one."[21] While the statement posits some differential, constitutive tension between "individual" and "community" — and by extension between liberty and equality, civil rights and social rights, and so on — we might conclude by asking whether it does not risk resolving this tension too hastily in the figure of the sovereign, self-governing people for whom the political would be a realm of empty form in relation to the full substance of the economy. From a certain perspective, such a resolution would spell the end of politics itself, enabling a specific mode of governing to masquerade as the universal administration of things. That said, the analyses, claims, and campaigns of GX can lead us toward a defense of policies, practices, and alliances tending toward a version of sovereignty in economic matters, but they do not relieve us of the responsibility to probe constantly the gap between governing agencies and those they govern, on whatever scale.

1 Juan Forero, "Visitors Seek a Taste of Revolution in Venezuela," *New York Times,* March 21, 2006.

2 "About Global Exchange," www.globalexchange.org/about/.

3 Forero, "Visitors Seek a Taste of Revolution in Venezuela."

4 "Program Summary," www.globalexchange.org/about/programSummary.html.

5 "Venezuela," www.globalexchange.org/countries/americas/venezuela/.

6 *"How are Reality Tours related to Global Exchange?"* www.globalexchange.org/tours/faq.html#1.

7 "Program Summary."

8 Set off against the "globalization from above" enforced by the U.S.-dominated governing agencies of the post–Cold War global economy, "globalization from below" is a phrase coined by Jeremy Brecher and Tim Costello to describe the network of development, labor, and environmental movements that coalesced in the anti–World Trade Organization demonstrations in Seattle in 1999.

9 "About Global Exchange."

10 "Democratizing the Global Economy," www.globalexchange.org/campaigns/index.html.pf.

11 Walden Bello, David Kinley, and Elaine Elinson, *Development Debacle: The World Bank in the Philippines* (San Francisco, CA : Institute for Food and Development Policy, 1982); Susan George, *A Fate Worse than Debt* (London: Penguin, 1988).

12 Elvia Alvarado, *Don't Be Afraid, Gringo: A Honduran Woman Speaks from the Heart; The Story of Elvia Alvarado,* ed. and trans. Medea Benjamin (San Francisco, CA: Institute for Food and Development Policy, 1987); cf. Rigoberta Menchú, *I, Rigoberta Menchú: An Indian Woman in Guatemala,* trans. Ann Wright (London: Verso, 1984).

13 For critical, yet sympathetic assessments of the claims of this genre, see Georg Gugelberger, ed., *The Real Thing: Testimonial Discourse and Latin America* (Durham, NC: Duke University Press, 1996).

14 "About Global Exchange" www.globalexchange.org/about/.

15 Jason Mark, "At the Millennium, a Broader Definition of Human Rights: Justice, Dignity, and Democracy" (January 2001), www.globalexchange.org/about/newhumanrights.html.

16 *Ibid.*

17 Www.globalexchange.org/campaigns/sweatshops/SanFranciscovictory.html.

18 Deborah James, "Justice and Java: Coffee in a Fair Trade Market" (2000), www.globalexchange.org/campaigns/fairtrade/coffee/nacla1000.html.

19 Mark, "At the Millennium."

20 Thomas Friedman, "Green: The New Red, White and Blue" *New York Times,* January 6, 2006.

21 Mark, "At the Millennium."

DESIGNS

GOD'S WORK

Building of the Association for the Support of the Islamic Resistance
(exhibition and donation center), Fatima Gate, south Lebanon, near
the Israeli border, August 2005 (photo by Jérôme Béllion-Jourdan).

Are Muslim Charities Purely Humanitarian?: A Real but Misleading Question

Jérôme Bellion-Jourdan

In a live interview on the satellite news channel al-Jazeera, Hany el-Bana, the director of the organization Islamic Relief Worldwide, declared: "To connect Islamic charity efforts to terrorism almost amounts to falsification and lying. The majority of the foundations closed in the last few years have been shut down without any proof of terrorist ties." Speaking on the program *Bila hudud* (Without Borders) on January 26, 2005, the international organization's charismatic leader asserted, "Since the end of the war in Afghanistan, a new international trend has emerged undermining Islamic charity work." El-Bana, an Egyptian doctor who, since the 1980s, has lived in Great Britain, where he founded Islamic Relief, is convinced that allegations of terrorist ties are being used irresponsibly against Islamic charity organizations.

Ever since I began research on Islamic charities, in the spring of 1996, journalists, United Nations officials, diplomats, and heads of NGOs have repeatedly asked me whether these organizations are truly "humanitarian." At the same time, the directors of various Muslim charities whom I have met with in London, Khartoum, Sarajevo, and even Peshawar have rejected allegations that they are political activists or involved in violence and that their organizations are anything other than humanitarian. Both accusers and defenders alike seem to recognize that a nonpartisan response to human needs is the legitimate conception of humanitarianism. Indeed, this is the very definition the International Red Cross and Red Crescent Movement advanced in its 1994 code of conduct: "The prime motivation of our response to disaster is to alleviate human suffering amongst those least able to withstand the stress caused by disaster. When we give humanitarian aid it is not a partisan or political act and should not be viewed as such."[1]

In this context, whether an NGO is truly a "humanitarian" organization or not is a real but misleading question. It is a valid question if it addresses the development of these organizations in their historical and political contexts. Islamic charities were initially devoted to activist, even military, objectives. However, pressured by the changing international situation, some of these organizations have changed their directive and sought recognition as what we now call "humanitarian" organizations. Questioning

their status is misleading or partisan when motivated by a political bias aimed at stig-
matizing specific organizations. In fact, well before the attacks of September 11, 2001
on New York City and Washington, D.C., a number of Islamic charities were already
targets of a witch hunt. The official pretext was that these organiations' missions were
not strictly speaking "humanitarian." In reality, however, the goal was to deprive these
would-be "terrorist" groups of financial support.

ACTIVISM AND STRUGGLE:
CHARITY WORK IN THE SERVICE OF "ISLAMIC CAUSES"

The creation in the 1980s of international Islamic charities largely resulted from
increased attentiveness to two major issues. This was especially the case with the
Muslim Brotherhood.[2] First, charities were created out of concern that indigent Muslim populations, especially in Africa, had been receiving aid almost exclusively from
Western organizations suspected of combining relief with cultural indoctrination. In
response, the Islamic African Relief Agency (IARA) was founded in 1981 in Khartoum as
an organ of Munazzamat al-Dawah al-Islamiyah (Organization of the Islamic Call) — a
larger organization created in 1970 to promote Islam among Muslim and non-Muslim
populations alike. In an IARA brochure published in 1985, the agency described itself as
"the first aid organization of its kind in Africa where a preponderant number of foreign
and evangelistic agencies are operating." The brochure declared that the IARA was able
"to build a solid foundation for Islamic work in this new territory of the *dawah* [the
invitation to Islam] in a short time because of its ability...to deliver aid services."[3]

With similar objectives in mind, Kuwait's International Islamic Charitable Organization was created through the initiatives of the Egyptian Shaykh Yusuf al-Qaradawi.
Exiled in Qatar and maintaining close ties with the Muslim Brotherhood, al-Qaradawi
had mobilized fundraising campaigns to counter Christian evangelical missionary projects throughout the world. A major player in stimulating investments in Islamic charities, al-Qaradawi invented the slogan "Donate a dollar and save a Muslim," and published numerous books, including *The Problem of Poverty and How Islam Can Solve It*.
According to a 2001 biography, al-Qaradawi recognized the "particular importance of
social work and benevolent action," and admonished "Islamic renewal" movements for
making words, rather than deeds, the central focus of their political activities. In al-
Qaradawi's view, if Islam was to restore the faith and identity of Muslims, it would have
to pursue these tasks "under the guise of social services" — for example, by building
schools and hospitals.[4] To summarize, the original and explicit impetus for the creation
of Islamic charities, such as those in Khartoum and Kuwait, was to preach Islam and to
serve the *dawah*.

The second central issue for Islamic charities in the 1980s was found in the struggle
to defend the Muslim community, the *ummah*, in any lands where Muslims were being
persecuted. After the 1979 Soviet invasion of Afghanistan, Islamic movements such as

those affiliated with the Muslim Brotherhood in various countries and with the Jamaat e-Islami in Pakistan began to receive funding from both public and private sources.[5] Political and religious leaders united to support the jihad in Afghanistan, including the possible necessity for armed struggle. Seeking to contain the Soviet threat, the United States tolerated and even encouraged, via Saudi Arabia, the Islamic mobilization and support of armed guerillas in Afghanistan.

Al-Qaradawi's voice resonated at the heart of this mobilization: "*Jihad* is an obligation [*fard ayn*] for military and medical experts and for all those who master a skill needed by the mujahideen. They should help the mujahideen in any domain where they are competent and capable."[6] Al-Qaradawi transmitted this message in April 1985 in the magazine *al-Jihad,* the publication of the organization al-Jihad al-Islami, founded in Peshawar in October 1984 by the Palestinian-born Jordanian, Shaykh Abdallah Yusuf Azzam. Azzam's Maktab Khadamat al-Mujahideen al-'Arab (Afghan Services Bureau) provided logistics and training for volunteers who wanted to join the armed struggle. Initially, the organization received funding from Osama bin Laden. In March 1986, however, a dispute between Azzam and bin Laden resulted in the latter withdrawing support from the Afghan Services Bureau and eventually founding his own group, al-Qaeda ("The Base").

In line with the vision of Shaykh al-Qaradawi, preaching and relief were often complements to military activities. Pakistan's North-West Frontier Province saw the arrival of different types of "Arab NGOs," some dedicated to spreading their ideological message among refugees, whom they saw as potential fighters in a war where the distinction between civilians and military personnel was fading. But the rhetoric of the call to "Islamic solidarity," with its appeal to unity, hid the dissension among the different organizations that were competing to take control of the Afghan crisis. For example, the Organization of the Islamic Call — a Kuwaiti group linked to the Muslim Brotherhood and initially run through a Canadian NGO, Human Concern International — competed with the Islamic Renewal Organization, also a Kuwaiti organization, that is, however, composed of Salafi ("following the forefathers of Islam," sometimes referred to as "Wahhabi"). One can also cite in this context the Islamic Relief Agency (the Sudan), the International Islamic Relief Organization (Saudi Arabia), and even Muslim Aid (founded in Great Britain by Yusuf Islam, the Muslim name of the pop star formerly known as Cat Stevens). All these organizations competed to exert their influence over the situation in Afghanistan.

Most of these organizations were represented at the Islamic Coordination Council, created in 1986 in Peshawar. In a 1996 Council document that summarized the activities of Islamic organizations, the necessity of helping orphans was presented as "a purely Islamic project to compensate for the absence of the *mujahid* from his household and community, and to replace him as the agent transmitting the way of God to widows and to the poor [*miskin*]."[7] Material aid and ideological work were envisioned as integral to the duty to educate this new generation living in a universe of armed struggle.

Thus there can be no doubt about whether the Muslim charities operating in Peshawar during the 1980s were partisan and militant.

All the same, it would be wrong to assume that Western organizations were themselves paragons of neutrality. Approximately two hunded and sixty-five groups came to Afghanistan after the Soviet invasion, and many of them became politicized — the Salvation Army and Catholic Relief Services, as well as Save the Children and Médecins Sans Frontières, ended up becoming de facto supporters of the opponents of the Soviet Union. This benefited the United States, the other protagonist in the proxy war between the two blocs. Particularly after 1986, the American administration used every resource at its disposal to support the Afghan "freedom fighters" — its expression for the jihadist soldiers. Humanitarian aid played a major role alongside American military support, and with the United States Agency for International Development (USAID) launching its cross-border humanitarian assistance program, the United States became the main funding source for relief projects aimed at ailing Afghan refugees in the 1980s. The two diametrically opposed poles of humanitarian action, the "Islamic" and the "Western," thus found themselves united in a war against the Soviet enemy.

MUSLIM CHARITIES MEASURED AGAINST THE "HUMANITARIAN" STANDARD

At the beginning of the 1990s, Islamic charities were directly affected by changes on the international scene. After the collapse of the Soviet Union and the accession of the mujahideen into the Afghan government, the United States no longer had any real reason to rely on Islamic movements to pursue its objectives. On the contrary, the State Department openly began to express concern about the danger such movements posed in countries such as Egypt and Algeria. Finally, Israeli officials, who had long described the operations of the Palestine Liberation Organization as "terrorist," now applied the term to all military activities associated with groups such as Hezbollah (Party of God) in Lebanon and Hamas (Palestine's Islamic Resistance Movement) in the Palestinian occupied territories, and repeatedly lobbied Washington to follow suit.

A series of events then transpired that forced certain Islamic charities to rethink their strategy. The new international climate was such that any connection to activist or violent activities now entailed the risk of repression. The February 26, 1993 attack on the World Trade Center in New York was a turning point in this regard: one of the suspects was identified as an "Arab Afghan."[8] This event had repercussions in Pakistan, where employees of "Arab NGOs" were arrested by the dozens. Many organizations, such as Muslim Aid, were also forced to shut down. Second, beginning in 1992, Egypt began pressuring the Pakistani authorities to control the activities of Egyptian mujahideen residing in the country, as well as of Egyptian employees of Islamic organizations. The very first trial of "Afghanistan veterans" opened in Cairo before Egypt's high military court, which handed down death sentences in absentia.[9] Third, following the November 19, 1995, attack on the Egyptian embassy in Pakistan, Pakistan's minister of the interior openly accused the regional director of Human Concern International, an

A Chechen man carries a box of humanitarian aid distributed by the international organization Islamic Relief in the Sputnik refugee camp near Sleptsovsk, January 28, 2000 (Vasily Fedosenko/Reuters).

Egyptian-born Canadian, of helping to fund a training camp for the armed Egyptian group al-Jihad in the Khost Valley in Afghanistan. Finally, Israeli authorities began publicly to accuse certain charities of funding the activities of the military wing of Hamas. After a February 1996 attack that killed twenty-five people in Israel, the Israeli government asserted that some of the funds that Hamas had raised in Great Britain — ostensibly destined for its social-welfare activities in Palestine, such as education and health projects — were actually being used to finance military operations.[10]

Given this environment, certain charities were prompted to publicly distance themselves from both activism and militarism. For example, in response to the Israelis' allegations, the executive director of Muslim Aid recalled that "it is a duty in our religion to provide charity." He then proceeded to assert that "we have always been careful to distance ourselves from the political situation in Palestine." For his part, Fadi Itani, the director of Islamic Relief–UK (the local branch of Islamic Relief Worldwide), observed that while the allegations were not new, they were "false and unjustified." Itani made clear that contributions to his organization were partially allocated to respond to the enormous needs of the Palestinians: "We donate money for schools and hospitals." A few months later, parallel allegations were leveled at the International Islamic Relief Organization in Jeddah, which was accused of supporting Hamas and of providing funds for its "suicide commando units." Similar accusations and matching denials from the Saudi directors ensued.[11]

The "humanitarian" transformation of some Islamic charity organizations is not fully explained by state pressure. There was also a strategic dimension to this transformation: adopting the humanitarian mantle allowed groups to diversify both their funding sources and their symbolic profiles. The IARA was a pioneer in the quest for international support, a strategy largely determined by the career of its founder, Abdallah Suleiman al-Awad. As a doctor who worked for several years at the regional office of the World Health Organization in Egypt, al-Awad had absorbed the culture of an international organization and understood how his own group could benefit from a network of international contacts. In the 1980s, preferring "dialogue on the ground" to an "intellectual dialogue between Islam and Christianity," al-Awad sought to work with Christian and Western organizations. He followed a simple principle: "As Christians, you seek to help the poor, just as we Muslims also seek to help the poor."[12] After having obtained consultative status at the United Nations Economic and Social Council, the IARA worked with agencies such as the United Nations High Commission on Refugees and UNICEF.

Another organization, Islamic Relief Worldwide, enjoyed the most international recognition. As early as 1992, when the war in Bosnia and Herzegovina had inspired a new wave of humanitarian activity, Islamic Relief Worldwide joined British Christian and secular organizations such as Oxfam and Save the Children in the fundraising campaign launched by the London daily *The Independent*.[13] This initiative allowed the NGO to dispel any suspicions about its objectives and to demonstrate that it distributed aid to populations regardless of whether they were Muslim, Serb, or Croat. Accordingly, the British newspaper recognized Islamic Relief as an organization that aided "distressed people of all races and all religions." The organization was able to emphasize the universal and nonpartisan character of its work.[14]

On this occasion and numerous others, Islamic Relief consolidated its profile as a humanitarian organization. After 9/11 and during the American military action in Afghanistan carried out by the "international coalition against terrorism," Islamic Relief once again played the humanitarian card. On October 17, 2001, a day after American bombs destroyed an International Committee of the Red Cross (ICRC) depot in the center of Kabul, Islamic Relief, Oxfam International, Christian Aid, the Catholic Agency for Overseas Development (CAFOD), Tearfund, and Action Aid signed a joint communiqué calling for the United States to halt all military strikes so that humanitarian convoys could reach populations in need of assistance.[15] Shortly thereafter, on November 1, 2001, the NGO had the "honor of receiving HRH the Prince of Wales" (who had come at his request, the group pointed out) in its London office. The prince commended the "wonderful work of Islamic Relief in alleviating the terrible suffering of refugees in Afghanistan."[16] Finally, Islamic Relief, along with other Islamic organizations, such as

Muslim Aid and Mercy International, supported the code of conduct adopted in 1994 at the initiative of the International Red Cross and the Red Crescent Movement, thereby affirming its commitment to a form of humanitarianism that was neither partisan nor political.

Either as a response to pressure or by strategic calculation, certain Islamic charities have thus incorporated contemporary "humanitarian" norms into their publicity materials. This evolution obviously presents problems because it means they officially renounce *dawah* and jihad. These organizations drew criticism from Islamic groups that saw this "humanitarian" reorientation as a betrayal of "Islamic causes," in particular the cause of Palestine. However, those charities that did convert to humanitarianism never lost sight of their need for Islamic legitimacy. Invited by al-Jazeera in October 2005 to discuss the use of *zakat* (obligatory giving) during the month of Ramadan, Yusuf al-Qaradawi asserted that disbursing *zakat* in the fight against illiteracy and poverty was a way of participating "in the struggle along the path of Allah." He explained further that if a "unified Islamic directive" existed, it would then be possible, by the end of Ramadan, to collect enough *zakat* so that some would be allocated for natural disasters — such as the earthquake in Pakistan in 2005 — and some for other causes, such as the restoration of the al-Aqsa mosque in Jerusalem.[17] Al-Qaradawi's message thus had a double dimension: on the one hand, he affirmed the Islamic legitimacy of fighting poverty; on the other, he evoked the importance of sustained support for the Palestinian cause through the potent symbol of the al-Aqsa mosque. For certain Islamic organizations, then, social-welfare assistance remained integral to their belief in partisan action.

TO SUPPORT "RESISTANCE" OR "TERRORISM"?

By August 2005, more than five years had passed since the celebration of the first "Resistance and Liberation Day," which marked the retreat of the South Lebanon Army from the Lebanese and Syrian territories it had occupied since 1982. Nonetheless, visitors to the Fatimah Gate checkpoint on the border between Lebanon and Israel still found themselves greeted by military songs celebrating the "Islamic resistance" victory over the "Zionist enemy."[18] Here, one does not speak of "Israel," but only of the "occupied territories." The loudest sounds of all emerge from a large tent that belongs to the Hay'at da'm al-muqawamah al-islamiyah (Association for the Support of the Islamic Resistance). Inside the tent, a wide range of merchandise is for sale — audiocassettes, videotapes, and DVDs recounting the battles of Hezbollah; T-shirts bearing portraits of Hezbollah's Shaykh Sayyed Hassan Nasrallah; caps and scarves emblazoned with the emblem of the movement, bearing calligraphy reading "Hizb Allah" (Party of God) in the form of an outstretched arm holding a machine gun. In the parking lot, as in the interior of the tent, small urns are set out for donations.

For the man running the association's stand, the resistance must continue as long as the Shebaa Farms area at the foot of Mount Dov remains under Israeli occupation. He answered my questions openly. In a receipt book, he records donors' orders to finance the armed resistance or to support the poor or the families of "martyrs." A little further north, at the entrance to the historic site of Baalbek, visitors can choose between two options: either a tour of the Temples of Jupiter and of Venus or a visit to Hezbollah's Museum of Islamic Resistance, a two-room building at the foot of the entrance's wall. In this other stronghold of Hezbollah, the atmosphere resembles that of the stands at the Fatimah Gate — video projections recount military operations with close-ups of enemy victims succumbing to Hezbollah attacks; exhibits of the personal belongings of "martyrs" (such as watches, glasses, and passports) and of military equipment seized from the "enemy" are on display. At the reception desk, I was told that all donations to the Association for the Support of the Islamic Resistance finance the armed resistance unless a donor has specifically indicated otherwise. In this world of "resistance," every resource serves the cause.

The gulf between local support for Hezbollah and its stigmatization internationally is striking. The shopkeeper at the Fatimah Gate does not carry arms — he sells souvenirs — yet he considers himself an activist all the same: "I am part of the resistance," he told me matter-of-factly. He is aware, however, that for years the U.S. State Department and Israel have listed Hezbollah as a "terrorist" organization.[19]

This designation is intended to be both strategic and effective. Long before 9/11 — albeit more vigorously thereafter — the United States launched a campaign aimed at cutting off financial support to organizations believed to have "terrorist" affiliations. As early as September 24, 2001, during a press conference announcing the freezing of assets belonging to some twenty-seven organizations, including charities, a combative George W. Bush declared, "Just to show you how insidious these terrorists are, they oftentimes use nice-sounding, non-governmental organizations as fronts for their activities."[20] These remarks prefigured the political line the State Department itself adopted. The tone hardly changed a few years later when, during a hearing before the U.S. Senate on July 13, 2005, E. Anthony Wayne, the assistant secretary for economic and business affairs, underlined the importance of international efforts "to prevent charities and not-for-profit organizations from being abused by those with malicious intentions."[21] During the same session, Stuart Levey, the under secretary of the Office of Terrorism and Financial Intelligence at the Department of the Treasury, observed, "With respect to the Palestinian territories, we continue to grapple with the problem of charities being abused to support terrorism." He specifically mentioned Hamas and the Palestinian Islamic Jihad, which, he said, "have infiltrated the charitable sector in the territories and have corrupted badly needed relief organizations."[22]

As early as September 2001, an expert from the Bush administration asserted that "these organizations do a little bit of legitimate humanitarian work and collect a lot of funds for military equipment and weapons."[23] Directors of organizations suspected of supporting Hamas or other groups deemed as "terrorists" were targeted by police operations and prosecutors: this was the case, for example, with an American organization, the Holy Land Foundation for Relief and Development.[24] The Bush administration also exerted pressure on Great Britain to shut down Interpal, a group providing assistance to the Palestinians. The Charity Commission for England and Wales froze Interpal's assets, but released them in September 2003 due to a lack of evidence supporting allegations that the group had channeled funds to Hamas.[25]

The underlying logic of the administration's policy is problematic on more than one level. Based on the debatable assumption that Hamas's activities are illegitimate because they are "terrorist" (an assumption that is not unanimous, as we have seen, since what is unacceptable "terrorism" for some remains legitimate "resistance" for others), any humanitarian activity linked to Hamas will be branded illegitimate. Moreover, claims by American officials regarding the abuse of Islamic charity organizations with "malicious intentions" are in large part false — the influence of Hamas, for example, resulted directly from its successful response to social-welfare needs in the West Bank and Gaza. Ultimately, this proved to be one of the reasons why Hamas won the January 2006 parliamentary elections, thereby allowing the movement to form a government.[26]

Finally, Islamic movements do not seem to have a monopoly on using charitable activities for political ends. On November 15, 2001, in a speech delivered at the beginning of Ramadan, George W. Bush referred to "the Islam that we know" as a faith that "teaches the value and importance of charity, mercy, and peace." Citing the Koran, the president expressed his enthusiasm that "Americans now have turned to acts of charity, sending relief to the Afghan people, who have suffered for so many years. America is proud to play a leading role in the humanitarian relief efforts in Afghanistan."[27] A month earlier, the United States had dispatched military forces to Afghanistan to topple the Taliban regime, which was accused of harboring Osama bin Laden and a certain number of Islamic groups, including both armed and charity organizations. Such declarations help explain the intentions of the Bush administration: to weaken the Islamic organizations supporting causes contrary to the interests of the United States or their allies, while invoking the principles of Islamic charity to mobilize "humanitarian efforts" when they support military objectives that are legitimate in the eyes of Washington.

An identical situation has now been reproduced in Iraq. In an October 2005 speech, President Bush said, "Our goal is to defeat the terrorists and their allies at the heart of their power. And so we will defeat the enemy in Iraq.... Area by area, city by city, we're conducting offensive operations to clear out enemy forces.... Within these areas, we're working for tangible improvements in the lives of Iraqi citizens." Tanks and missiles are followed by aid convoys with the aim of winning the support of the population, and a mission of persuasion is carried out in a region where "the seeds of freedom have only recently been planted."[28] The United States thus provides a perfect example of the very articulation of combat, aid, and activism that it condemns in the case of Islamic organizations. Are Islamic charities "purely humanitarian"? This is a real but misleading question — a trick question — in a world where state humanitarianism has more than ever before taken on partisan and political dimensions.

Translated by Blake Ferris.

1 International Federation of Red Cross and Red Crescent Societies, "Principles of Conduct for the International Red Cross and Red Crescent Movement and NGOs in Disaster Relief Programmes," www.ifrc.org/publicat/conduct/code.asp.

2 Founded by an Egyptian teacher, Hassan al-Banna, in 1928, the Society of the Muslim Brothers has grown as an influential movement calling for Islamic reform. Its ideology has inspired other movements in countries such as Algeria, Kuwait, Libya, and Palestine. Some of them are directly connected to the Muslim Brotherhood in Cairo.

3 Dawah Islamiya, *Dalil* (Khartoum, 1985), p. 21.

4 Shaykh Yusuf al-Qaradawi, *Shakhsiyat al-'am al-Islamiyah, 1421 H. / 2000 M.* (Cairo: Maktabat Wahbah, 2001), p. 27.

5 Founded in 1941 by Maulana Sayyid Abul A'la Maududi, the Jamaat e-Islami (Islamic Group), which has its headquarters in Lahore, remains one of the most influential Islamist movements in contemporary Pakistan.

6 Interview with Shaykh Yusuf al-Qaradawi, *al-Jihad,* April 21, 1985, pp. 20–22. *Fard ayn,* a mandatory individual duty under Islam, is different from *fard kifaya,* which is a collective obligation assumed by the community as a whole. A *mujahid* (plural *mujahideen*) is an individual who engages in jihad.

7 Islamic Coordination Council, *Al-ta'ssis w-l-injazat* (Foundations and Achievements), 1985–1995, Pakistan, July 1996, p. 47.

8 *The News,* February 10, 1995.

9 See *al-Hayat,* December 1, 1992.

10 *Daily Telegraph,* March 2, 1996.

11 Agence France Presse, June 30, 1996.

12 Interviews by author with Abdallah Suleiman al-Awad, then chairman of the IARA-ISRA, Khartoum, May 1 and 5, 1996.

13 "Relief News," *Partnership: The Newsletter of Islamic Relief Worldwide* 5 (1994).

14 Joanna Gibbon, "Bosnia Appeal: The Charities that Need Your Support," *The Independent,* December 8, 1993.

15 The president of the United States, like the British prime minister, responded to these calls in a highly paradoxical manner, asserting that the possibility of humanitarian action depended on military intervention: "We will continue our military operations," George W. Bush declared, "so that urgent aid deliveries of food and provisions will not be compromised." "Bush rejette toute pause dans les raids," Agence France Presse, October 19, 2001.

16 "HRH Prince of Wales Visits Islamic Relief," Islamic Relief Worldwide, December 15, 2001, www.islamic-relief.com/submenu/About%20Us/visits/charles.htm.

17 Interview with Shaykh Yusuf al-Qaradawi, al-Jazeera, October 16, 2005.

18 Details gathered by the author during a trip to Lebanon in August 2005.

19 See United States Department of State, Office of the Coordinator for Counterterrorism, "Foreign Terrorist Organization Designations Table," Washington, DC, 2004; available online at www.state.gov/s/ct/rls/fs/2004/40945.htm. As for Israel, on July 12, 2006, after Hezbollah captured two Israeli soldiers, Israeli retaliated with military strikes all over Lebanon, killing hundreds of civilians and destroying civilian infrastructure. A FAQ document on the Israeli Ministry of Foreign Affairs Web site describes the operation of July 12 as an "an unprovoked cross-border attack from Lebanese territory" that was "carried out by the Hizbullah, a terrorist organization which is a party to the government of Lebanon." It then states that "Israel had no alternative but to defend itself and its citizens. For this reason, Israel reacted to an act of war by a neighboring sovereign state. The purpose of the Israeli operation was two-fold — to free its abducted soldiers, and to remove the terrorist threat from its northern border." Israeli Ministry of Forein Affairs, "Why did Israel conduct military operations against Lebanon?" August 15, 2006; available online at www.mfa.gov.il/MFA/About+the+Ministry/Behind+the+Headlines/Israels+counter+terrorist+campaign+-+FAQ+18-Jul-2006.htm#why. The EU's views can be found at Council of the European Union, "Press Release: 2581st Council Meeting, General Affairs and External Relations," May 17, 2004, p. I; available online at www.consilium.europa.eu/cms3_applications/Applications/newsRoom/LoadDocument.asp?directory=en/gena/&filename=80497.pdf.

20 "President Freezes Terrorists' Assets: Remarks by the President, Secretary of the Treasury O'Neill and Secretary of State Powell on Executive Order," September 24, 2001, www.whitehouse.gov/news/releases/2001/09/20010924-4.html. See also Office of the President, "Executive Order on Terrorist Financing: Blocking Property and Prohibiting Transactions with Persons Who Commit, Threaten to Commit, or Support Terrorism," 2001, available online at www.whitehouse.gov/news/releases/2001/09/20010924-1.html.

21 E. Anthony Wayne, "Money Laundering and Terrorist Financing in the Middle East and South Asia," Testimony before the Senate Committee on Banking, Housing, and Urban Affairs, 109th Cong., July 13, 2005; available online at www.state.gov/e/eb/rls/rm/2005/49564.htm.

22 Stuart Levey, Testimony before the Senate Committee on Banking, Housing, and Urban Affairs, 109th Cong., July 13, 2005; available online at www.treasury.gov/press/releases/js2629.htm.

23 *Wall Street Journal,* September 26, 2001.

24 *BBC News,* July 28, 2004.

25 *BBC News Online,* October 15, 2003.

26 Hamas has continued to be exposed to considerable international pressure as the United States and the EU still continue to consider it a "terrorist" organization and have called for aid to the Hamas led government to be cut. Attending the American Jewish Committee's Centennial Dinner in May 2006, President Bush, for instance, stated: "Democratically leaders [*sic*] cannot have one foot in the camp of democracy and one foot in the camp of terror. (Applause.) Hamas must accept the demands of the international community to recognize Israel, disarm and reject terrorism, and stop blocking the path to peace. (Applause.)" Available online at www.whitehouse.gov/news/releases/2006/05/20060504-15.html.

27 Bush quotes Koran 2:177: "Piety does not lie in turning your face to the East or West. Piety lies in believing in God." Office of the President, "President's Message for Ramadan," November 15, 2001, available online at www.whitehouse.gov/news/releases/2001/11/20011115-14.html.

28 "Transcript: Bush Discusses War on Terrorism," *Washington Post,* October 6, 2005; available online at www.washingtonpost.com/wp-srv/politics/administration/bushtext_100605.html.

Faith, Liberty, and the Individual in Humanitarian Assistance

Erica Bornstein

Religion in America takes no direct part in the government of society, but it must nevertheless be regarded as the foremost of the political institutions of that country; for if it does not impart a taste for freedom, it facilitates the use of free institutions.... The Americans combine the notions of Christianity and of liberty so intimately in their minds, that it is impossible to make them conceive the one without the other.

— Alexis de Tocqueville, *Democracy in America*

America has a strong, thriving nonprofit sector. Recent figures indicate that the 1.4 million organizations comprising the independent sector receive over $621 billion in total annual revenue, representing 6 percent of the national economy. Charities and other nonprofits employ over 10 million individuals, comprising over 7 percent of the American workforce.

— George W. Bush, *Rallying the Armies of Compassion*

A silent revolution has taken place in the nongovernmental sector in the United States. The new focus on faith-based initiatives has transformed U.S. legislation regarding charitable organizations to the degree that a potential infringement of civil liberties — hiring on religious grounds — has become a religious freedom. The source of this metamorphosis can be found in the ideas of liberty and choice in Christian conceptions of the individual. Transformed through the alchemy of law, these ideas are swiftly becoming techniques for governing the needy through their "liberties" and "choices." The choice passed from the federal government to NGOs and from NGOs to individuals is the choice of responsibility and conversion. I argue that the trend in American politics toward faith-based humanitarianism is related to the work of NGOs more globally; behind both international aid policies and domestic legislation on charity lies the assumption that the individual is a key component in narratives of human

Texas governor George W. Bush speaks in front of a painting of Jesus Christ during a presidential campaign stop at Teen Challenge of the Midlands, a Christian-based community home, in Colfax, IA, January 21, 2000 (Eric Draper/AP Photo).

progress. The individual as such represents an entire constellation of American democratic ideals, which include individual rights and freedom, limited government involvement, and equal opportunity.

Faith-based organizations are not a new interest for me, nor are they new to the global landscape. Elsewhere, I have examined how Protestant ideas entered into the economic development work of transnational nongovernmental organizations in Zimbabwe and how this discourse was informed by neoliberal concepts of the individual.[1] My current analysis shifts the focus to the discourse of humanitarianism from the perspective of donors and U.S. government policies on aid. The work of NGOs in places like Zimbabwe is informed and even shaped by the philanthropic trends of donor nations such as the United States. What giving means in the United States will affect the types of projects supported by the United States Agency for International Development (USAID), the World Bank, the International Monetary Fund, and individuals who give directly to faith-based organizations. It will also affect the types of projects that NGOs embark on, anticipating philanthropic support.

CHARITABLE CHOICE IN THE UNITED STATES

A bit of history is in order. In 2001, the U.S. government passed legislation to support federal funding for faith-based humanitarian organizations. When President George W. Bush launched this initiative, known as "Charitable Choice," he released a report called *Rallying the Armies of Compassion*. I quote from the report:

> Government has a solemn responsibility to help meet the needs of poor Americans and distressed neighborhoods, but it does not have a monopoly on compassion. America is richly blessed by the diversity and vigor of neighborhood healers: civic, social, charitable, and religious groups. These quiet heroes lift people's lives in ways that are beyond government's know-how, usually on shoestring budgets, and they heal our nation's ills one heart and one act of kindness at a time.... Americans believe our society must find ways to provide healing and renewal. And they believe that government should help the needy achieve independence and personal responsibility, through its programs and those of other community and faith-based groups.[2]

Bush established the White House Office of Faith-Based and Community Initiatives as part of his "compassionate conservatism" campaign strategy.[3] The executive orders of January 2001 codified a movement in the Republican Party to "ease restrictions on government funding for faith based institutions."[4] This movement started in 1996, when Senator John Ashcroft, a Republican from Missouri, introduced an amendment to the 1996 welfare reform act (officially titled the Personal Responsibility and Work Opportunity Reconciliation Act). By 2004, the Office of Faith-Based and Community Initiatives had executive centers in seven cabinet departments and was embedded in the U.S. government, domestically and internationally.[5] The reach of this legislation was persistent. For example, one of the departments is USAID.

The Charitable Choice legislation allows religious NGOs to compete for federal funds for domestic humanitarian aid, and it offers individuals and corporations tax incentives for making charitable donations. When the legislation was introduced, it was contentious. Some religious groups even organized in opposition;[6] in April 2001, the *New York Times* documented 850 clergy members who opposed Charitable Choice on the grounds that government should stay out of churches, temples, synagogues, and mosques.[7] Politicians also debated whether the government should restrict funds to religious groups to ensure that no federal money supports religious activities. Liberal politicians sought restrictions, while conservatives saw these restrictions as a threat to the spiritual nature of religious organizations. It was at this juncture that the debate twisted itself into one surrounding ideas of liberty.

LIBERTIES

> I recognize that government has no business endorsing a religious creed, or directly funding religious worship or religious teaching. That is not the business of government. Yet government can and should support social services provided by religious people, as long as those services go to anyone in need, regardless of their faith. And when government gives that support, charities and faith-based programs should not be forced to change their character or compromise their mission.
> — George W. Bush[8]

At issue in the debates surrounding the Charitable Choice legislation were the hiring practices of faith-based organizations. That religious organizations stipulate in institutional missions that staff identify with the religious agenda of the institution (whether Christian, Jewish, or Muslim) is exactly what makes such organizations faith-based.[9] For example, World Vision International, an organization I studied in the United States and Zimbabwe, requires all its staff members to sign a "statement of faith" confirming their commitment to accepting Jesus Christ as their savior. Although the intensity of adherence to Christianity and denominational affiliation varies widely within the organization, World Vision requires its staff to be Christian and actively excludes those who are not. The organization, however, did not require the beneficiaries of its aid to adhere to Christian beliefs. All the better if they did *not*. That made it easier for World Vision to demonstrate by deed and not word, to provide living examples of Christian acts of charity and "love" toward one's neighbor, and therefore to show the power of Christianity. Religion, in this faith-based organization, was not promoted directly — it was modeled through a process I have called "lifestyle evangelism."[10] In practice, it is impossible to disaggregate the secular from the sacred in such institutions.

Historically, religious organizations have received federal money in the United States. However, before Charitable Choice, there was a legal requirement to separate religious from secular activities, because tax dollars were not allowed to support particular religious activities.[11] With the Charitable Choice legislation, there was neither a need to account separately for religious activities nor a question of whether faith-based organizations could hire along religious lines. Key here is that what had been a discriminatory practice was transformed into an example of individual religious freedom. As secular freedom yielded to religious freedom, a major discursive shift occurred that depended on the polysemy of the word "freedom." The state as a protector of freedom against religious authority became an instigator of freedom for religious authority.[12] This is how the language of freedom became part of the art of institutionalizing compassion, "unleashing" what Bush has called "armies of compassion." This paradoxical pairing of militarization and benevolence has accrued velocity since the legislation was first introduced in the welfare reform bill of 1996.

Religious (and community) organizations make up these armies of compassion. Bush describes their inclusion in the provision of social services as the removal of barriers. The government promotes Charitable Choice as providing "equal opportunity" for faith-based groups that have been "neglected or excluded in Federal policy" in order to create a "level playing field."[13] What was earlier considered a potentially unconstitutional support of religion has been transformed into an effort to "curb bias." By including religious organizations, Charitable Choice supposedly removes barriers, thereby eliminating government bias against religious charities that fight poverty.[14] The government argues that the new legislation is not an attack on civil rights. On the contrary, the administration claims, it promotes civil rights and religious liberties.[15]

The discourse of the individual is not unique to humanitarianism in the United States. My research in Zimbabwe in 1996–1997 focused on the work of transnational NGOs that were perpetuating the Christianity inherent in neoliberal economic discourse, for example through programs that encouraged individual economic responsibility and depended on ideas of salvation, progress, and the individual in relation to a Christian God. The discourse I found in Zimbabwe was similar to that promulgated by the United States internationally. In both contexts, there is an art of governing (in the Foucauldian sense) at work; it is an art of governing faith.[16] Here I must remind readers that the state is not a monolithic entity but a series of embodied practices, and this is crucial to its success.[17] The move in the U.S. to reassign federal funds, through states, to local grassroots community organizations — many of which are religious — is in harmony with global directives sponsored by the World Bank in places such as southern Africa to shrink the state and to support what has been called "civil society" through nongovernmental organizations. Critics of these efforts, including me, have pointed out the social costs placed on individuals and the diminishing safety net of welfare states in the face of aggressive global capitalism. Those of us who study Africa, or the "least developed" world, have explored processes of structural adjustment as instances of a larger, less-identifiable trend in neoliberal economics toward placing responsibility on individuals and diminishing the role of the state.

The liberty in question is, in a truly American sense, the liberty of individuals. In the Charitable Choice legislation, categories of persons made socially dangerous (the poor, criminals, and so on) are actively socialized through their liberty.[18] Faith-based humanitarian aid could be seen, through this lens, as a tactic of neoliberal governmentality, an effort to control the population morally and to increase the power of the state through individual bodies (and souls).[19] Although the reintroduction of the discourse of religion into legislation regarding charity at this particular time in the United States — an extremely religious nation — may seem commonplace, more remarkable are the techniques and tactics of an increasingly refined merging of the discourse of morals and markets with the instrumental rationality of neoliberal economics as it is applied to a universal compassion.[20]

The state is involved through a discursive devolution of power with religious organizations, which are now in charge of rehabilitating a dangerous social body, the poor. Categories of need in Bush's armies of compassion include prisoners, "second-chance maternity group homes," and after-school activities for low-income children.[21] That is, the initiative includes welfare mothers, children, and prisoners as categories of need. One cannot help but note that members of these groups represent those left out of modernist narratives of productivity: those who can no longer be, or are not yet capable of being, responsible. In this way, Charitable Choice extends the earlier welfare-to-work objectives of the 1996 welfare reform act and refashions individuals as productive members of society.[22]

In Charitable Choice, faith-based organizations represent the institutionalized effect of an individualizing discourse. Charity is distributed through individuals, not through the reciprocal relationships of kin or civic groups. The U.S. government relies on charitable institutions to do the work of "compassion," to mop up the wreckage of social relations left by neoliberal capitalism. In Charitable Choice, the individual chooses his or her own savior and social-service provider. It has become the responsibility, or freedom, of American citizens to carry the burden of their own welfare. In neoliberal economics, individuals are actors with choices and preferences. This contrasts with a conception of persons as identified with their roles in society.[23] The discourse of Charitable Choice reflects the Christianity inherent in neoliberal discourse, which grew out of post-Reformationist (specifically Calvinist) doctrine.[24]

The Protestant Reformation took away the church's power to mediate and navigate the communicative expanse between God and persons and gave individuals direct access to God and thus to the sacred. In an odd twist, the decentralized neoliberal state now uses the church as a mediator with its citizens. The final gesture — offered suggestively by Charitable Choice — is to give individuals responsibility for their own welfare. It is now the duty not of the state, but of faith-based organizations to assist individuals, and individuals' well-being is now the responsibility of individuals themselves.[25] The concept of the person in American foreign policy and domestic humanitarianism is also distinctly Christian. Perhaps this is why faith-based aid makes so much sense in the context of the United States, an intensely Christian nation. It reifies implicit assumptions about the category of person, as Marcel Mauss has noted, as a "metaphysical entity of 'moral person' (*personne moral*)." Mauss argues that what we "still call by the term 'moral persons' ('legal entities'): corporations, religious foundations, etc., which have become 'persons' (*personnes*)" is part of the Christian definition of person as a "rational substance, indivisible and individual."[26]

One subtext in the narrative of Charitable Choice is conversion: individuals can make a change through a choice. Christianity is a religion one can choose — one can be "born again" in it, in contrast to many other religions, into which one must be born and in which relations of blood determine relations with the sacred. Underlying the discourse of choice, responsibility, and liberty are narratives of conversion. That individuals can be transformed and reformed — converted, born again — from drug addicts, welfare mothers, and prisoners into responsible working (and tax-paying) citizens is an unspoken element of the legislation governing charity in the U.S.

At the risk of individualizing an already individualizing discourse, a recent article in the *New York Times* with the headline "Evangelicals Sway White House on Human Rights Issues Abroad" describes an account that Charles W. Colson, the born-again Christian who spent seven months in jail for his role in Watergate, had given of his interaction with the president: "After the meeting, Mr. Colson said he went up to Mr. Bush and said emphatically that faith-based policy worked. 'He said, "You don't have to tell me,"' Mr. Colson said the president replied. 'He said, "I'd still be drinking if it weren't for what Christ did in my life. I know faith-based works."'"[27] Bush's personal experience here becomes a model for his faith-based initiative, Charitable Choice. This is more than as an example of federal policy personalized by the president. Instead, we must consider this an example of "lifestyle evangelism" or "faith in action" — proselytizing by deed and not words. It is an example of the "conduct of conduct."[28]

In Zimbabwe, such efforts by transnational Christian NGOs emerged from missionary and colonial histories in the region. It is easy enough to explain relationships of power and discourses of empowerment (which actually serve to mask the real relations of power) in terms of missionary histories. But when the same discourse appears in the United States, it seems that liberty is exactly what is being used to govern the poor. Through a discourse of liberty, individuals choose their welfare with the assistance of "compassionate" faith-based institutions supported by individual donors' ability to give. Tax breaks for individuals and corporations — a significant part of the Charitable Choice legislation — facilitate the devolution of state power to individual responsibility. If individuals (discursively formed as sovereign by the state) are encouraged to give to charities, then there will be even less need for the state to mop up the damage done by economic exclusion, the free market and its failures, and the neoliberal interest in individual responsibility. This art of governing, through laws such as Charitable Choice, is not a monolithic attempt to control, but — more insidiously — represents techniques for governing a population.

CONCLUSION

In Zimbabwe, I saw how contemporary NGOs, both religious and secular, echoed the paths of missionaries who came before them; similarly contentious and collaborative relationships with the state were also evident and identifiable. However, what differentiated contemporary humanitarian efforts from those of the colonial era was a new system of control: the conduct of conduct, or governmentality, that was transnational, decentered, and focused on the individual. It was, in Foucauldian terms, akin to earlier forms of pastoral power. Yet without the empire of kings, who is to blame? As anthropologists, we are less accustomed to turning the searchlight for injustice onto our own ground. Could the same process be taking place in the United States? Is the United States the seat of a new form of empire?[29] Or is it more nebulous, more insidious, and more curious? Is it simultaneously everywhere and nowhere? In the case of Zimbabwe, what disturbed this secular academic was that Christian NGOs were good at what they did precisely because they saw their work as holistic: secular and sacred; material and spiritual. There is a danger in thinking like the natives when one's loyalties are not clear. I now find myself inside a Trojan horse, having positioned myself inside the language of "conservative compassion" in order to understand it. Yes, there are things that are right, that work. Yes, faith-based development may indeed be more effective in an instrumental, means-ends manner, because people's entire beings are taken seriously as unified "wholes."[30]

Charitable Choice does not propose to strengthen society so it will have no need for charitable institutions. The legislation does not encourage the development of social relationships to mitigate need. The underlying emphasis on individualism is a socially isolating mechanism. Linked to democracy, it severs relationships and places responsibility on the person.[31] Charitable Choice, as an artifact of contemporary democracy, constitutes the individual as autonomous and responsible for his or her own welfare. On the one hand, those in need choose their providers of compassion. On the other, individuals choose to be charitable or not. Charitable Choice embeds a deeply Christian discourse of individual choice into government. Individuals' growing responsibility to care for themselves reciprocally supplements the power of the state by means of individual actions. Individuals are charitable, work for faith-based organizations, and can be assisted. The federal government in the United States is transferring the responsibility of the welfare of its citizens to the states, which are passing it on to faith-based organizations, which have been doing this business all along. As in the international context, this is not a particularly novel constellation of relationships. It is novel, however, and alarming, that there is a radical increase in need and that this need is being discussed in a language of choice instead of relational social obligation.

1   Erica Bornstein, *The Spirit of Development: Protestant NGOs, Morality, and Economics in Zimbabwe* (Stanford, CA: Stanford University Press, 2005).

2   Office of the President, *Rallying the Armies of Compassion* (Washington, DC, 2001), pp. 2, 4–5. Available online at www.whitehouse.gov/news/reports/faithbased.pdf.

3   See Kathryn Dunn Tenpas, *Can an Office Change a Country? The White House Office of Faith-Based and Community Initiatives; A Year in Review: A Report Prepared for the Pew Forum on Religion and Public Life* (Washington, DC: Pew Forum on Religion and Public Life, 2002), for the history that follows.

4   *Ibid.*, p. 1.

5   The office had centers in the Departments of Justice, Agriculture, Labor, Health and Human Services, Housing and Urban Development, and Education, and in the United States Agency for International Development.

6   Including the Baptist Joint Committee for Religious Liberty, the American Jewish Committee, and the United Church of Christ.

7   Tenpas, *Can an Office Change a Country?*, p. 10.

8   Quoted in White House Office of Faith-Based and Community Initiatives, *Protecting the Civil Rights and Religious Liberty of Faith-Based Organizations: Why Religious Hiring Rights Must Be Preserved* (Washington, DC, 2003). Available online at www.whitehouse.gov/government/fbci/booklet.pdf.

9   Notably not Wicca, Santería, or any other alternative religious practice.

10 Bornstein, *Spirit of Development*.

11 Stephen V. Monsma, *When Sacred and Secular Mix: Religious Nonprofit Organizations and Public Money* (Lanham, MD: Rowman and Littlefield, 1996).

12 U.S. Constitution, First Amendment: "Congress shall make no law respecting an establishment of religion, or prohibiting the free exercise thereof; or abridging the freedom of speech, or of the press; or the right of the people peaceably to assemble, and to petition the Government for a redress of grievances."

13 "We will focus on expanding the role in social services of faith-based and other community-serving groups that have traditionally been distant from government. We do so not because of favoritism or because they are the only important organizations, but because they typically have been neglected or excluded in federal policy. Our aim is *equal opportunity* for such groups, a level playing field, a fair chance for them to participate when their programs are successful." Office of the President, *Rallying the Armies of Compassion*, p. 5.

14 "Charitable choice does not codify government favoritism toward religion but *curbs widespread government bias against many religious poverty-fighting charities.*" Stanley W. Carlson-Thies and John J. DiIulio Jr., "Charitable Choice: Is Progressive Social Policy Promoting the Public Trust," First Amendment Center, www.firstamendmentcenter.org/commentary.aspx?id=6375.

15 "Charitable choice also retains the well-established right of religious organizations to hire staff of similar faith. Some call this government-funded job discrimination and an attack on civil rights. In fact, this long-standing right is itself a cornerstone civil rights protection enshrined in the 1964 Civil Rights Act, not a violation of it. Under charitable choice the government funds the best providers it can find, some of whom — as protected by settled civil rights law and the courts — consider religion when staffing in order to preserve their faith-driven community-service mission." Carlson-Thies and DiIulio, "Charitable Choice Is Progressive Social Policy." For more extensive debates on the subject, see Barry W. Lynn, Marc D. Stern, and Oliver S. Thomas, *The Right to Religious Liberty: The Basic ACLU Guide to Religious Rights,* 2nd rev. ed. (Carbondale: Southern Illinois University Press, 1995); Center for Public Justice, *A Guide to Charitable Choice: The Rules of Section 104 of the 1996 Federal Welfare Law Governing State Cooperation with Faith-Based Social-Service Providers* (Washington, DC: Center for Public Justice, 1997), "Charitable Choice: Constitutional Issues" (www.cpjustice.org/charitablechoice/constitution), and "Charitable Choice: Frequently Asked Questions" (www.cpjustice.org/faq); Margy Waller, *Charity Tax Credits: Federal Policy and Three Leading States* (Washington, D.C.: Pew Forum on Religion and Public Life, 2001); Pew Forum on Religion and Public Life, "The Faith-Based Initiative Two Years Later: Examining its Potential, Progress and Problems" (Washington, D.C., 2003), event transcript available online at http://pewforum.org/events/print.php?EventID=41; and Office of the President, *Unlevel Playing Field: Barriers to Participation by Faith-Based and Community Organizations in Federal Social Service Programs* (Washington, DC, 2001), available online at www.whitehouse.gov/news/releases/2001/08/20010816-3-report.pdf.

16 While for Foucault "governmentality" or the government of populations coincides with the rise of the welfare state, the weakening of the state does not mean the reversal of governmental processes; rather, it is a delegation of authority for the government of the poor. Jacques Donzelot, "The Mobilization of Society," in Graham Burchell, Colin Gordon, and Peter Miller (eds.), *The Foucault Effect: Studies in Governmentality* (Chicago: University of Chicago Press, 1991), ch. 8.

17 James Ferguson and Akhil Gupta, "Spatializing States: Toward an Ethnography of Neoliberal Governmentality," *American Ethnologist* 29, no. 4 (2002), pp. 981–1002.

18 Michel Foucault, "Governmentality," in Burchell, Gordon, and Miller (eds.), *Foucault Effect,* ch. 4.

19 See Andrew Barry, Thomas Osborne, and Nikolas S. Rose (eds.), *Foucault and Political Reason: Liberalism, Neo-liberalism, and Rationalities of Government* (Chicago: University of Chicago Press, 1996); Burchell, Gordon, and Miller (eds.), *Foucault Effect*; Ferguson and Gupta, "Spatializing States"; Colin Gordon, "Governmental Rationality: An Introduction," in Burchell, Gordon, and Miller (eds.), *Foucault Effect,* ch. 1; and Max Weber, "Religious Rejections of the World and Their Directions," in *From Max Weber: Essays in Sociology,* ed. and trans. H.H. Gerth and C. Wright Mills (New York: Oxford University Press, 1946).

20 Public opinion of the Charitable Choice legislation is mixed. In a Pew-sponsored survey, 64 percent of respondents "favored funding for faith-based organizations"; 78 percent "oppose" the idea of "government-funded religious organizations hiring only those people who share their beliefs"; and 68 percent "worry that faith-based initiatives might lead to too much government involvement with religious organizations." Pew Research Center for the People and the Press, *Faith-Based Funding Backed, but Church-State Doubts Abound* (Washington, DC: Pew Research Center for the People and the Press, 2001). Available online at http://people-press.org/reports/display.php3?ReportID=15.

21 That is, the Charitable Choice legislation allocates government funding for rehabilitation and child support for prisoners; maternity homes (which are an alternative to abortion and speak to the moral authority of the Christian right) via individual vouchers and grants to providers; and after-school programs, again via vouchers and grants.

22 See the discussion of the reformation of prisoners in Michel Foucault, *Discipline and Punish: The Birth of the Prison,* trans. Alan Sheridan (New York: Vintage, 1977), p. 212.

23 Michael Carrithers, Steven Collins, and Steven Lukes (eds.), *The Category of the Person: Anthropology, Philosophy, History* (Cambridge: Cambridge University Press, 1985), p. 299.

24 Louis Dumont, *Homo Hierarchicus: The Caste System and Its Implications,* trans. Mark Sainsbury (Chicago: University of Chicago Press, 1974) and "Christian Beginnings: From the Outworldly Individual to the Individual-in-the-World," in *Essays on Individualism: Modern Ideology in Anthropological Perspective* (Chicago: University of Chicago Press, 1986); Max Weber, "Religious Rejections" and *The Protestant Ethic and the Spirit of Capitalism,* trans. Talcott Parsons (New York: Scribner, 1958).

25 In the conclusion to Carrithers, Collins, and Lukes (eds.), *Category of the Person,* Lukes cites Foucault's definition of the individual in relation to power as the "effects of bodies, gestures, discourses that come to be identified and constituted as individuals.... The individual which power has constituted is at the same time its vehicle" (p. 294).

26 Marcel Mauss, "A Category of the Human Mind: The Notion of the Person, the Notion of the Self," in Carrithers, Collins, and Lukes (eds.), *Category of the Person,* pp. 19–20.

27 Elisabeth Bumiller, "Evangelicals Sway White House on Human Rights Issues Abroad," *New York Times,* October 26, 2003.

28 Gordon, "Governmental Rationality: An Introduction," in Burchell, Gordon, and Miller (eds.), *Foucault Effect,* pp. 1–51.

29 See Michael Hardt and Antonio Negri, *Empire* (Cambridge, MA: Harvard University Press, 2000); that is, not the British style of empire, to which the United States is frequently compared.

30 Missionary anthropologists point to the historical link between the idea of holism and anthropology and continue to use the language of holism in their writing; see, for example, Paul G. Hiebert, *Anthropological Reflections on Missiological Issues* (Grand Rapids, MI: Baker Books, 1994).

31 De Tocqueville, cited in Dumont, *Homo Hierarchicus,* p. 18.

A World Vision International cargo plane prepares to deliver
humanitarian aid.

A Vision of the World

a profile of World Vision International by Erica Bornstein

World Vision International is the largest Christian nongovernmental organization involved in emergency humanitarian aid (also known as relief) and economic development in the world. According to a recent annual report, in 2004, the organization "served 100 million people, worked in 96 nations, directly benefited 2.4 million children through child sponsorship, raised $1.546 billion (US) in cash and goods for its work, [and] employed 22,500 staff members."[1] Its growth rate is staggering. From 1998 to 2004 alone, its income grew from $665 million to almost $1.55 billion. If asked "Where is World Vision?" one could easily answer "Almost everywhere." Where there is need, it is there.

The NGO is spatially diffuse, multiheaded, and governed as an international partnership. It is local and global. Its scope is the world; its focus is changing "one life at a time."[2] Chameleonlike, the NGO is indigenous and "acculturated" (as its missionary predecessors would say) in local settings. Staff members at project sites share national citizenship with those in need, speak local languages, and have long-term commitments to their projects. Sometimes they live at project sites. Motivated by Jesus Christ's example of service to humanity, the NGO translates acts of relief and development into Christian acts of love. World Vision promotes a view of the world with the potential to be a better place, progressing on a path toward utopia where there is no poverty and there is love for humankind—a universal love, Christian love. It promotes development from misery to progress, in local terms, but always for the better. The path to change is one of conversion: converting one spirit or one community at a time to technological improvement, to development, to economic progress, and, potentially, to Christ.

Much of World Vision's current profile emerges from its history. It was founded in the late 1940s by Bob Pierce, an American evangelist and journalist stationed in Korea.[3] Pierce's concern about the plight of a young child in an orphanage inspired him to send monthly remittances toward her support. This commenced what has become a global process of "child sponsorship," whereby individuals in donor countries send monthly payments to support children in need. Once sponsors' donations are received by World Vision support offices, they are pooled together to fund economic development projects such as school

Web promotion for World Vision's thirty-hour famine, an event aimed at youth groups in more than twenty countries. Participants collect donations, then go thirty hours without eating to experience hunger first-hand and to learn about global poverty issues and take part in a variety of charitable activities (www.30hourfamine.org).

construction and improvements in health, sanitation, and agriculture. Child sponsorship remittances are channeled through offices in donor countries toward offices in recipient countries — usually in what is considered the "developing world." The organization's extensive administrative and bureaucratic apparatus monitors and tracks both its sponsored children and the development projects in the communities where they live. Child sponsorship is the core of World Vision's fundraising success and accounts for much of its project funding. Stories of personal transformation, echoing the organization's origin narrative of support for one child at a time, are told and retold in its public documents: a donation or loan transforms a person's life. For instance, in the 2004 annual review, the chair of World Vision's International Board describes the transformation of a woman brought about by a loan:

> As World Vision regularly works on such a large scale, I often like to instead focus on that "one person" who feels the impact and genuine care of what we do. From my perspective, the difference we are making may sometimes not seem so big, but for those we are blessed to serve, the experience is often life-changing.
>
> While I was in Cambodia in 2004, I met a woman whose husband had left her a year earlier after having passed on HIV to her. This woman was left destitute, yet she had a child and

seven family members to take care of. With a World Vision loan of $37.50 (US), she was able to set up a grocery business from her home and sell produce to village locals. This woman now has a monthly income of $150 with which she provides food, medicine and shelter for her family, and pays for school fees. All from the beginnings of $37.50. Through our caring staff, World Vision continues to make this kind of personal difference in the life of "one person."[4]

In addition to emphasizing individual transformation, World Vision is a complex transnational corporation. It defines itself as an international partnership structured as a network of interdependent national offices (for example, in southern Africa, it has offices in Tanzania, Malawi, Zambia, Zimbabwe, and South Africa). World Vision International governs the World Vision partnership through an international council and board of directors and is the registered legal entity that coordinates its structure. In practice, national-level World Vision offices work with local governments and community groups to provide assistance with economic development. At some of the NGO's larger projects, World Vision staff members live and work with members of rural communities to facilitate such development. World Vision also employs community members from local project sites for this purpose.

In places such as sub-Saharan Africa, the NGO follows a long tradition of missionaries in the region, focusing on what it calls the "holistic" synthesis of material and spiritual "human development." World Vision proclaims that its organizational mission is to follow Jesus Christ in working with the poor and oppressed, "to promote human transformation, seek justice, and bear witness to the good news of the Kingdom of God."[5] Although World Vision is a Christian organization, it generates some of the same types of development and relief projects as secular NGOs. Despite World Vision's apparent similarity to nonreligious NGOs, Christianity determines its "core values." All World Vision staff members must sign statements of faith proclaiming their adherence to Christianity. While World Vision's Christian orientation serves as a solid corporate philosophy, the ways religious beliefs are interpreted in local contexts vary greatly. World Vision's work, like that of other transnational humanitarian NGOs, is in keeping with contemporary trends in international development, such as a focus on gender equity and participatory rural appraisal. While the degree to which these programs achieve World Vision's goals depends on local contexts and leadership at national and field project offices, the meaning of World Vision's work—the degree to which its presence is felt by those giving and receiving assistance—cannot be measured by project reports or fiscal assessments.

1   World Vision International, *2004 Annual Review* (n.p.: World Vision International, 2005), p. 3. Available online at www.wvi.org/wvi/pdf/2004%20Annual%20Review.pdf.

2   *Ibid.;* Robert A. Seiple, *One Life at a Time: Making a World of Difference* (Dallas: Word, 1990).

3   Richard Gehman, *Let My Heart Be Broken with the Things that Break the Heart of God* (New York: McGraw-Hill, 1960).

4   World Vision International, *2004 Annual Review,* p. 3.

5   Graeme S. Irvine, *Best Things in the Worst Times: An Insider's View of World Vision* (Wilsonville, OR: BookPartners, 1996), p. 277. See also Tetsunao Yamamori, *Serving with the Poor in Africa* (Monrovia, CA: MARC, 1996).

Posters by the Voice of the Martyrs, "a non-profit, interdenominational organization with a vision for aiding Christians around the world who are being persecuted for their faith in Christ, fulfilling the Great Commission, and educating the world about the ongoing persecution of Christians" (www.persecution.com).

Theologizing Human Rights: Christian Activism and the Limits of Religious Freedom

Elizabeth A. Castelli

The ideal of universal human rights emerged as a global political project in the wake of the devastation and horrors of the Second World War and was codified, in 1948, in the United Nations Universal Declaration of Human Rights (UDHR) and in 1950, in the European Convention for the Protection of Human Rights and Fundamental Freedoms. Subsequent conventions, declarations, and covenants have further specified and articulated this ideal on behalf of victims of genocide, refugees, women, children, the poor, victims of racism, the disabled, and so on. Apparently straightforward articulations of the rights of all human beings to dignity, civil liberty, self-determination, and sociopolitical and economic equality and well-being, these documents remain simultaneously idealized portraits of the as-yet-to-be-achieved and contested sites of struggle in the realm of the real.

The Enlightenment and its values haunt the contemporary world of human-rights discourses — their optimism, their universalism, their belief in the human capacity for solidarity, their insistence on the adequacy of the linguistic and conceptual framework of "rights" as the forum for negotiating competing claims, and their critique of the hegemony of religious authorities and institutions. Indeed, it is commonplace to trace the genealogy of contemporary human-rights arguments and stances back to a wide range of texts that have canonical or near-canonical status in the history of Western political thought: the English Bill of Rights, John Locke's *Letter Concerning Toleration,* the French Declaration of the Rights of Man of 1789, the U.S. Declaration of Independence and Bill of Rights, and other such foundational Enlightenment texts. (Less frequently do the contributions of socialist and feminist thought to the history of human-rights theory come centrally into view, despite their important role in shaping modern ideas about justice and rights.[1])

Meanwhile, scholars have long debated the proper, authoritative origins of human-rights discourses — whether secular or religious, ancient or modern, Western or global, universal or particular, and whether the answers to these sorts of binaries present obstacles to or opportunities for meaningful change on the ground.[2] Questions about origins can, of course, be illuminating both archaeologically and genealogically, but most origin stories also tend to serve particular contemporary interests or to feed into larger stories that underwrite claims to authority or legitimacy. Origins do not, or rather need not, determine the ongoing paths of a particular discourse.

Whatever the origins of human-rights discourses, what interests me in this essay is the relatively recent adoption of human-rights language, arguments, and values by specific activists: U.S. Christians (predominantly evangelical) working on particular strategic goals having to do with activism against religious persecution and advocacy for religious freedom. This adoption embraces the universalism of human rights as a framework and a domain in both practical and theological terms. It is part of a broader development within U.S. Protestant social and political engagement in recent years to put modes of argument grounded in the idioms of other social and political activist movements to work within a Christian frame. Such idioms draw on the histories of civil rights activism in the U.S., the rhetoric and strategies of identity politics, and the post-war emergence of a robust and internationally based human-rights movement.

The movements I identify here organize around a lengthy agenda of domestic and international concerns, and it is part of the political genius of these movements that they link the issues that they do. These movements first came to my attention when I began to track their collaborative work on issues of religious freedom and religious persecution.[3] And it is especially within the context of work on religious freedom that the U.S. movement finds allies in certain European Christian organizations. So although this essay will focus on the political terrain I know best (that of the U.S.), I will also make reference to cognate discourses and modes of organization in Europe, since there are important parallels between movements, including important parallel tensions over theory, strategy, and tactics.

In the American context, two different, but complementary gestures characterize the movement's appeal to human rights as a governing framework for activism: one involves the direct appeal to the moral authority of "human rights" as a category; the other involves framing "human rights" as the product of God's authorship and author-ity, rather than as the articulation of a hard-won (if also always fragile) consensus that emerges out of human negotiation and deliberation. In other words, "human rights" may have historical roots in Enlightenment and secular ground, but for evangelical human-rights activists, God is ultimately the author of and authority for such rights.[4] One can see how such logics work themselves out in the framework of one particular part of the human-rights agenda that has especially animated evangelical Christians: religious freedom.

Guarantees of religious freedom are codified in the Universal Declaration of Human Rights, Article 18: "Everyone has the right to freedom of thought, conscience and reli-gion; this right includes freedom to change his religion or belief, and freedom, either alone or in community with others and in public or private, to manifest his religion or belief in teaching, practice, worship and observance."[5] Whereas the authors of the UDHR presumed the normative ground of the document to reside in notions of human equality and solidarity, U.S. evangelical Christians who have taken up Article 18 as a prooftext for their organizing, by contrast, have made an explicitly theological originary claim for the normative ground of human rights. The founding document for evangelical activism in the mid-1990s, the "Statement of Conscience of the National Association of Evangelicals Concerning Worldwide Religious Persecution," is a case in point. It concludes with these words:

> Religious liberty is not a privilege to be granted or denied by an all-powerful state, but a God-given human right. Indeed, religious liberty is the bedrock principle that animates our republic and defines us as a people. We must share our love of religious liberty with other people who, in the eyes of God, are our neighbors. Hence, it is our responsibility, and that of the government that represents us, to do everything we can to secure the blessings of religious liberty to all those suffering religious persecution.[6]

In this framing of the matter, God and the state (presumably a synecdoche for all human political institutions, whether nation-states or international bodies) are positioned in opposition to each other. The state is figured as a capricious (if all-powerful) entity, bestowing or withholding privileges on a whim, while God emerges as a faithful and reliable gift giver who confers irrevocable rights upon humanity. (There is, it should be noted, no mention here of, for example, Job 1:21: "The Lord gives, and the Lord takes away.")

But there are other rhetorical effects of this framing of the matter. For one, if religious freedom is God-given, then it occupies a privileged position over any and all other human-rights claims. Any cursory consideration of the tensions within the human-rights framework comes to focus quickly on the potential conflicts that exist between human-rights claims of religious freedom, on the one hand, and human-rights claims by groups experiencing subordination, discrimination, or both, such as women and sexual minorities. One sees, in the American context, how claims of religious freedom by conservative Christians have been used to underwrite the legitimacy of hierarchical gender relations, the barring of women's access to certain medical services, and discrimination against lesbians and gay men.

Two brief examples illustrate the point. In recent years, a growing number of Catholic and evangelical Protestant pharmacists in the U.S. have refused to fill prescriptions for contraception, including emergency contraception, arguing that to do so would violate their religious beliefs and therefore their religious freedom. As a result, a dizzying array of pieces of legislation to address all sides of this controversy has appeared on state legislatures' dockets in recent years. Several states have passed laws allowing pharmacists to refuse to dispense these legal medications.[7] In a different vein, conservative Christian groups in the United States have framed their opposition to hate-crimes legislation as a defense of religious freedom.[8] Meanwhile, internationally, cross-religious alliances — between, for example, the Vatican and some Islamic leaders — have proven to be powerful obstacles to the realization of the United Nations Convention on the Elimination of All Forms of Discrimination Against Women (CEDAW) of 1979. This is not to say that "religion" is uniquely responsible for discrimination based on gender or sexuality, but to notice how, in these examples, religious freedom trumps other forms of human freedom, especially reproductive and sexual freedom.[9]

Organizing around the global problem of religious persecution enjoyed a resurgence in the United States and Europe during the 1990s, although many of the organizations involved in such organizing have roots in Cold War Christian anti-Communist work. These organizations—the Voice of the Martyrs (VOM), Open Doors, and Christian Solidarity International, among others—now express their self-understanding primarily as Communism's and Islam's other. The appeals and public presentations of these organizations are similar in many respects. An examination of their publications, direct-mail campaign literature, and Internet presence suggests several things in common: all focus in particular on the situation of Christians around the world, a situation dubbed "the persecuted church." (By putting this name in quotation marks, I wish to denote the heuristic function of the category, not to judge the truth claims of these organizations.)

The organizations involved in advocacy on behalf of the "persecuted church" and the promotion of religious freedom can be mapped onto a kind of continuum. On one end are organizations that are explicitly focused on Christianizing and missionizing; on the other are those that address themselves to broader structural changes and pursue activism within legislative contexts and international human-rights protocols.

Organizations on the Christianizing end of the continuum focus their activities on fundraising and direct service or action. They are explicit in their evangelizing goals, combining solidarity with missionary and evangelical outreach. This overlap between solidarity and support for the "persecuted church," on the one hand, and missionary outreach to non-Christians, on the other, is immediately evident in even the most cursory review of the mission statements of these different organizations, of which the Voice of the Martyrs and Open Doors are perhaps the best known.

The Voice of the Martyrs is the current name for an organization formerly called Jesus to the Communist World, which was founded in the 1960s by Richard Wurmbrand. The organization's Web site describes it as "a non-profit, interdenominational organization with a vision for aiding Christians around the world who are being persecuted for their faith in Christ, fulfilling the Great Commission, and educating the world about the ongoing persecution of Christians."[10] The organization's headquarters are now in Bartlesville, Oklahoma, from where it focuses on grassroots outreach and involving individuals in acts of solidarity and transnational missionizing. The activism of the Voice of the Martyrs blends two distinct projects: solidarity with persecuted Christians and evangelical missionary outreach. From the organization's many publications, both print and electronic, it is clear that it situates its mandate in opposition to Communism and Islamism. The Voice of the Martyrs makes no attempt to link the persecution of Christians with the repression of other religious traditions, nor do its publications use the language or logics of "human rights." In addition, the Voice of the Martyrs seems not to be particularly concerned with stopping religious persecution, since, like some other organizations, it figures the persecution of Christians as the defining feature of "Christianness." At least one journalistic report about the movement focuses on the tendency of some Voice of the Martyrs members to romanticize the experience of persecution by indulging in dangerous "undercover" missions into "enemy" territory.[11] Meanwhile, the organization's rhetoric is mobile, adaptable, and attentive to changes in the political terrain: a recent Voice of the Martyrs publication promoted the idea that Christianity is the most potent weapon in the war on terror.

Akin to the Voice of the Martyrs in its origins and sensibilities is Open Doors, an organization that also has Cold War roots, tracing its origins to 1955, when "Brother Andrew, founder of Open Doors, made his first trip behind the Iron Curtain to take Bibles to persecuted Christians," according to the group's Web site.[12] Like the Voice of the Martyrs' use of experiential rhetoric to build up solidarity among First World Christians and their suffering coreligionists, Open Doors—especially its youth branch, called Underground—also encourages an experiential relationship to the "persecuted church," especially for young First World Christians. Open Doors' youth ministry produces curricula that encourage church youth groups to stage a "night of persecution" or "lockdown," during which group members enact the kidnapping and torture of Christian "tribes" and the subsequent perseverance of the persecuted Christian tribespeople.[13]

Meanwhile, like the Voice of the Martyrs, Open Doors organizes its activism exclusively around Christian sources and objects. In particular, the Bible is simultaneously the source of the group's mandate and the material object of its activity. The "Vision Statement" of Open Doors makes a series of associations—between persecution and mission, between suffering and church growth—that are all grounded in citations from the Bible:

> Our purpose [is] to strengthen and equip the Body of Christ living under or facing restriction and persecution because of their faith in Jesus Christ, and to encourage their involvement in world evangelism by providing Bibles and literature, media, leadership training, socio-economic development and through intercessory prayer; preparing the Body of Christ living in threatened or unstable areas to face persecution and suffering; and educating and mobilizing the Body of Christ living in the free world to identify with threatened and persecuted Christians and be actively involved in assisting them. We do so because we believe when one member suffers, all members suffer with it (1 Corinthians 12:26), all doors are open and God enables His Body to go into all the world and preach the Gospel.[14]

The group's three arenas of activity—Bible distribution and missionizing, activism among Christians to prepare for persecution, and outreach within "the free world" (likely holdover terminology from the Cold War)—are grounded, as the vision statement makes clear, in the generative figure of "the Body of Christ" (a biblical metaphor with a complex historical, theological, liturgical, and cultural legacy) and in the Bible itself as a materially mediating force in geopolitics. Targeting various regions around the globe—"the Far East" (by which they mean China), "the Muslim world," the former Soviet Union, Latin America, and Africa (where Islam is said to be "encroaching") — Open Doors is explicitly centered on Christianity and Christians and does not concern itself more broadly with efforts to ensure "religious freedom" as a human-rights issue. The organization explains under the heading "How We Set Limits": "The determining factor for Open Doors involvement anywhere in the world is the presence of a Persecuted Church. We stand alongside when the Body of Christ has run into problems because of its own identity."[15]

The organizing principles of Open Doors, like those of the Voice of the Martyrs, emphasize biblical mandates, not international human-rights protocols. Both groups focus not on ecumenical efforts toward the promotion of human rights and religious freedom, but on stressing the creative and mutually reinforcing links between suffering and conversion. Persecution and missionary activity are unapologetically implicated in each other in the work of the Voice of the Martyrs and Open Doors. Their version of internationalism is predicated not on the formal political bodies that generate international coalitions devoted to shared values of human solidarity, as one might characterize many human-rights entities, but rather on a biblically grounded internationalism aimed toward Christian universalism. This internationalism has recently come into view in the organizing efforts of the youth branch of Open Doors, which encourages young people to wear clothing and accessories that testify to their "citizenship" in the Underground.[16]

While organizations such as the Voice of the Martyrs and Open Doors (and its subsidiaries) use the Bible as the source for their activism and focus their attention exclusively on the experiences of Christians globally, other Christian NGOs seek to build different kinds of international alliances, ones that place the Universal Declaration of Human Rights, especially Article 18, at the center of their organizing and activism, usually either downplaying their biblical or creedal mandates or placing Christian theological prooftexts alongside the UDHR. For example, the National Association of Evangelicals, which led the campaign to get Congress to pass the International Religious Freedom Act of 1998, produced just such an imbricated vision of Bible-based Christianity and human-rights language in its promotion of that piece of legislation.[17] In this framing of activist projects, a Christian imperative to promote religious freedom grows out of the mixed grounds of Christian universalism and international human-rights protocols.

A telling example in this regard is the organization Forum 18, which is based in Oslo, Norway. It describes its aims in this language: "Forum 18 is an instrument for promoting the implementation of Article 18 of the Universal Declaration of Human Rights, and concentrates on serious and obvious breaches of religious freedom, and particularly on situations where the lives and welfare of individual people or groups are being threatened and where the right to gather around one's faith is being hindered."[18] Its media outreach initiative, Forum 18 News Service, understands its mandate in clearly Christian terms, as an enactment of a Christian commitment to human solidarity:

> Forum 18 News Service (F18News) is a Christian initiative which is independent of any one church or religious group. Its independence is safeguarded by a board whose members

are Protestant, Orthodox and Catholic Christians, and who are responsible for matters of policy and fundraising. F18News is committed to Jesus Christ's command to do to others what you would have them do to you, and so reports on threats and actions against the religious freedom of all people, regardless of their religious affiliation.[19]

The commitment to covering threats to religious freedom across traditions is displayed in the organization's "Latest News" catalog of cases, where Muslims and Christians both appear as objects of repression or violence in an almost equal number of stories.[20] Moreover, a search of the news service's archives generates accounts of global conflicts over religious practices, affiliations, and identities that are by no means focused only on Christians.

If Forum 18 represents what seems to be a deeply ecumenical activism based on a subtle blend of human-rights discourses and Christian commitments—and an activism that is predicated on a studied form of objectivity[21]—other organizations that strive to combine the imperatives of the Universal Declaration of Human Rights with the demands of Christian conviction seem to struggle more with the tensions between these two registers of ethical obligation. Christian Solidarity International (CSI) is exemplary in this regard; it joins American evangelicals in claiming that the human rights articulated by the UDHR are a divine gift: "CSI's primary objective is worldwide respect for the God-given right of every human being to choose his or her faith and to practice it, as stipulated in Art. 18 of the Universal Declaration of Human Rights."[22] This general commitment to religious freedom, however, narrows in CSI's framing of its project as one that is devoted to Christian solidarity with persecuted Christians. As CSI's analysis unfolds in its literature and publications, it becomes clear that it shares the opinion of groups such as the Voice of the Martyrs and Open Doors that Islam and Communism are the main "causes" of Christian persecution. CSI also includes "authoritarian regimes" and "war" within its taxonomy of such causes. Strikingly, the CSI Web site conflates one of the categories it identifies as a cause of Christian persecution, "Militant Manifestations of Religion," with Islam as a whole. Although the site goes on to concede that "militancy" is not solely attributable to Islam—"The world is experiencing not only the rise of radical Islamic fundamentalists, but also a surge of violent tendencies in other religions and sects"—Islam serves as the exemplar for "religious militancy" *tout court.*

CSI organizes itself around a Christian mandate to help other Christians, and it draws upon an eclectic array of scriptural, theological, and human-rights prooftexts to articulate its vision of religious liberty. Genesis 1:26–27, the creation of humanity in the image of God, becomes the foundation for CSI's argument that human rights are divinely created and commanded. CSI's theological framing here links Gregory of Nyssa, whose *On Perfection* argues that human freedom has its foundations in the human likeness to God; the twentieth-century Protestant theologian Karl Barth's view that human rights came into being out of God's love; and the Second Vatican Council's assertion that religious freedom is rooted in divine revelation. In short, the Bible and its traditional

(FOLLOWING PAGES) Map from the International Day of Prayer Web site (www.idop.org). The Religious Liberty Commission of the World Evangelical Alliance organizes a day of prayer for persecuted Christians each year (© 2006 WEA Religious Liberty Commission; all rights reserved).

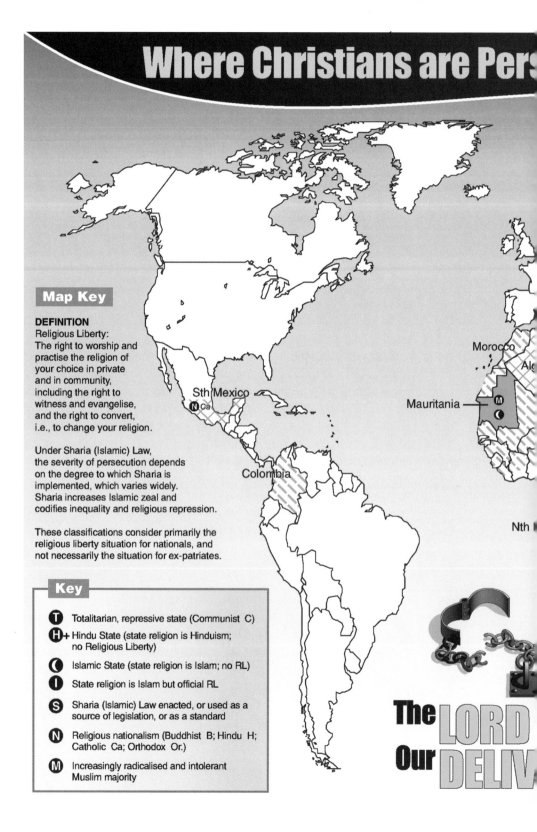

Where Christians are Pers

Map Key

DEFINITION
Religious Liberty:
The right to worship and
practise the religion of
your choice in private
and in community,
including the right to
witness and evangelise,
and the right to convert,
i.e., to change your religion.

Under Sharia (Islamic) Law,
the severity of persecution depends
on the degree to which Sharia is
implemented, which varies widely.
Sharia increases Islamic zeal and
codifies inequality and religious repression.

These classifications consider primarily the
religious liberty situation for nationals, and
not necessarily the situation for ex-patriates.

Morocco
Al
Mauritania
Sth Mexico
Ca
Colombia
Nth

Key

T Totalitarian, repressive state (Communist C)

H+ Hindu State (state religion is Hinduism;
no Religious Liberty)

☾ Islamic State (state religion is Islam; no RL)

❶ State religion is Islam but official RL

S Sharia (Islamic) Law enacted, or used as a
source of legislation, or as a standard

N Religious nationalism (Buddhist B; Hindu H;
Catholic Ca; Orthodox Or.)

M Increasingly radicalised and intolerant
Muslim majority

The LORD
Our DELIV

ated

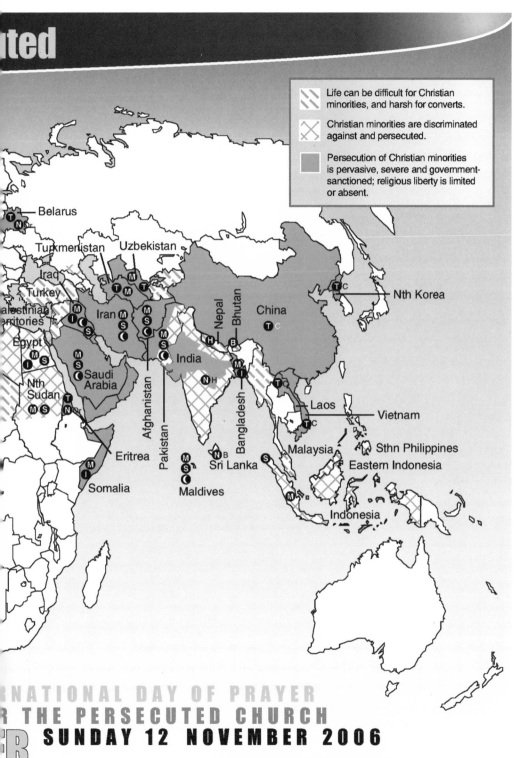

Life can be difficult for Christian minorities, and harsh for converts.

Christian minorities are discriminated against and persecuted.

Persecution of Christian minorities is pervasive, severe and government-sanctioned; religious liberty is limited or absent.

Belarus

Turkmenistan   Uzbekistan

Iraq

Turkey   Iran   Nepal   Bhutan   China   Nth Korea

Palestinian territories

Egypt

Nth Sudan   Saudi Arabia

Afghanistan   India   Bangladesh   Laos   Vietnam

Eritrea   Pakistan   Sri Lanka   Malaysia   Sthn Philippines

Somalia   Maldives   Eastern Indonesia

Indonesia

reception by Orthodox, Protestant, and Catholic interpreters produce a unified vision of the theological basis of human rights. Indeed, as CSI's framing of the matter would have it, religious freedom is rooted in natural law "and as such is both anterior and superior to state law. The state is thus under a duty to recognize the right and create conditions favorable to its exercise."[23] According to this point of view, documents such as the Universal Declaration of Human Rights simply articulate, as a second-order correlate, states' obligation to enforce the affirmation of religious freedom's fundamental character, one "both anterior and superior to" anything that a national or international system of law might assert or codify.

It is impossible to consider Christian activism against religious persecution and for religious freedom expressed in the idiom of human rights without noticing how it is interwoven with the idealistic foreign policy of the Bush administration, dominated by neoconservative principles and commitments.[24] This idealist, moralizing, evangelizing, coercive use of force in the service of spreading "democracy" and "freedom" tends to be utopian, unmoored from any knowledge of historical specificities and contingencies, and immune to critique. Just so, one sees important parallels between the uninterrogated and self-evident belief that all people want American-style democracy and the expression of the view that "religious freedom" is the sine qua non of democracy, even as only certain religious ideas and practices qualify for protection under the banner of religious freedom. In the process, "religion" itself must be defined and framed, and categories of "good religion" and "bad religion" must be produced and applied to specific examples.

The efforts of the Center for Religious Freedom, a New York City–based project of Freedom House, are exemplary of this paradoxical interweaving of advocacy for religious freedom as a human-rights absolute within U.S. foreign policy with efforts to confine and contain certain religious practices (especially the imposition of Islamic law in certain countries) with the promotion of the U.S.'s geopolitical interests.[25] The opening paragraph of the center's self-description on its Web site makes these commitments explicit:

> The Center for Religious Freedom is a self-sustaining division of Freedom House. Founded in 1941 by Eleanor Roosevelt and Wendell Willkie to oppose Nazism and Communism in Europe, Freedom House is America's oldest human rights group. Its Center for Religious freedom defends against religious persecution of all groups throughout the world. It insists that U.S. foreign policy defend Christians and Jews, Muslim dissidents and minorities, and other religious minorities in countries such as Indonesia, Pakistan, Nigeria, Iran and Sudan. It is fighting the imposition of harsh Islamic law in the new Iraq and Afghanistan and opposes blasphemy laws in Muslim countries that suppress more tolerant and pro-American Muslim thought.[26]

Statements such as these call attention to the selective convictions of some advocates for religious freedom, who promote an abstract ideal of religious freedom as an inalienable human right at the same time as they place some elements of religion—in this example, "harsh Islamic law" and blasphemy laws—outside the protections accorded under the banner of religious freedom. Under this logic, "tolerant and pro-American Muslim thought" (good religion) should enjoy shelter under international protocols and U.S. foreign policy, whereas "harsh Islamic law" (bad religion) should not. My point is not to defend Islamic law, harsh or otherwise, but to observe that it functions here as a singular and exemplary limit within the rhetorics and logics of some advocates for religious freedom.

Calling religious freedom "the most neglected human right in U.S. foreign policy," the Freedom House narrative explicitly links advocacy for religious freedom as a human right to the war on terror:

> Religious freedom faces hard new challenges. Recent decades have seen the rise of extreme interpretations of Islamic rule that are virulently intolerant of other traditions within Islam, as well as of non-Muslims. Many in our policy world still find religious freedom too "sensitive" to raise. But since 9/11, the link between our own security and freedom, between our national interests and our ideals, has never been clearer. Winning the War on Terror turns on the battles of ideas and at its heart is the principle of religious freedom.[27]

In this portrait of the current situation, the security, freedom, national interests, and ideals of the United States are collectively arrayed on one side of the battlefield in the "War on Terror"; on the other side are the "extreme interpretations of Islamic rule." Religious freedom, framed as "the most neglected human right," becomes the fragile, but crucial fulcrum on which the outcome of the war without end hinges. If victory in the war on terror requires victory on the battlefield of ideas, then religious freedom becomes a kind of gospel, spread by geopolitically savvy missionaries in the service of U.S. values and goals. At the same time, this program imagines religious freedom as an exclusive privilege of those forms of religion deemed legitimate, moderate, tolerant, tolerable, and consistent with American security and national interests.

In *The Impossibility of Religious Freedom,* the lawyer and anthropologist of religion Winnifred Fallers Sullivan demonstrates how such theoretical and practical impasses are inevitable.[28] One of the foundational ironies of legal protections for religious freedom, she notes, is that such legal protections require that governments or international bodies to define the very object of protection—religion. Ironically, in their efforts to oppose limitations on "religion," national governments and international governing bodies in fact find themselves delimiting what counts as religion. Given that religion as a category is always produced ideologically—as the other of reason, according to one reading, or as the privileged resource for ethics, according to another—defining religion, Sullivan argues, depends upon a deep-seated ambivalence toward the object of definition itself. The impossibility of religious freedom emerges from this ambivalence, as she puts it quite elegantly toward the end of her argument:

> Legally enforced religious freedom as a political goal denies and conceals the profound ambivalence toward religion revealed in this split personality [religion as irrational/savage/other versus religion as the primary source of ethical thought and behavior]. Furthermore, the denial is arguably accomplished, in part, through the use of the Delphic utopian language of human rights, whether in national constitutions or in international instruments. The denial may certainly be necessary to the political consensus underlying the promotion and protection of religious freedom. But the denial also conceals the fact that religion is not always, in fact, absolutely free, legally speaking. The right kind of religion, the approved religion, is always that which is protected, while the wrong kind, whether popular or unpopular, is always restricted or even prohibited.[29]

Sullivan's characterization of human-rights language as "Delphic" and "utopian" emphasizes the performative, prophetic, and idealizing functions of such language in the field of religious freedom. It glosses the rhetorical impact of repeated insistences that "religious freedom" is a God-given human right, insistences that render the contents of the category and the effects of its imposition closed to discussion or critique, threaded through by an unsettling impulse toward absolutism. When human rights and religious freedom come to occupy the full terrain of the thinkable vis-à-vis "freedom," nonreligious subjectivities — groups of people who organize themselves under other kinds of identities and claim rights that are contrary to some religious teachings (women and sexual minorities, most notably) — find themselves in the impossible position of seeking to make their claims on religious grounds or having no ground from which to speak.

The turn toward a theologized version of human rights needs to be historicized in several different ways. In the United States at least, it is intelligible only in relation to very specific histories and cultural realities — in particular, the rise of the religious right since the 1980s, with its grounding in a particular narrative about American history and American values (always interwoven with biblical themes and citations, invocations of God's promise, and so on), and its increasingly militant attitude with respect to both domestic politics and international affairs. It was, at one time, possible to imagine an American international human-rights project that was not explicitly theologically inflected — and, indeed, there are many U.S.-based human-rights NGOs that derive their rationales from humanistic values and self-described secular notions of human solidarity and justice.

And yet it is not the case that a realm of "the purely secular" ever actually existed, nor do I mean to advocate for it. As recent analyses of secularism have shown, the secular in U.S. contexts has often underwritten a civil religion that is broadly Protestant in its assumptions and imaginations.[30] As the anthropologist of secularism Talal

Asad has observed, the "human" in "human rights," as it is deployed in contemporary U.S. argument, is thoroughly interwoven with Christian and—in particular—Protestant ideas about private and public and confusion over "Religion" as a general category and "religion" as a uniquely Protestant conceptuality.[31] The move on the part of religiously grounded movements to lay claim to the "human rights" banner is also tied, in the United States, to other appropriations of strategies, arguments, and political themes—especially drawing on identity politics and civil rights. In other words, human rights, identity politics (often grounded in narratives of victimization, injury, and suffering),[32] and civil rights have all become highly mobile discourses in U.S. political life. Whereas they were once the privileged idioms of the progressive left, they have increasingly become the adopted languages of the religious right. To understand the theologization of human rights, it is necessary to trace the process by which this discursive change has taken place.

A final point: it is critically important to understand how the rhetoric of human rights in relation to religious freedom works in some quarters as a highly effective tool for silencing political debate and dissent. To raise questions about the effects of this rhetoric is to open oneself to the damning response "Oh, so you are *for* religious persecution?" When "human rights" is theologized, grounded in an idealized category called "religion," the unhappy result may be the evacuation of the political terrain. Grounding human rights in theological precepts, religious claims, conceptions of God, and biblical authority effectively renders any claims that proceed from that ground by definition unassailable and immune to critique, interrogation, or dissent. Since, as Asad has famously observed, the "human" in "human rights" is an autonomous Christian subject (produced through Protestant theorizing about both "humanness" and "religion") whose "rights" come to be guaranteed through the threat or practice of violence by the state, and the human-rights project thereby emerges as an evangelizing tool, one wonders what space remains in the conversation for those whose religion does not enshrine conservative or traditional values, those whose religion does not fit the reigning framework, or those who are simply nonreligious.

Moreover, the rhetorical move reinscribes a flatfooted and unhelpful dualism—religion versus secularism—that makes nuanced conversation about how to constitute and sustain social and political arrangements nearly impossible.[33] Any discussion of these pressing matters, it seems to me, must avoid any simple reduction to a facile binary—"religion" versus "secularism." And yet there are many incommensurabilities, competing sets of claims to rights and recognitions, and complex (and also concrete) effects produced by the movements outlined here. Moreover, the double-edged character of the "universal," as it asserts itself in all of these discourses—whether in UN ethical declarations or in Christian activist formulations—needs to remain both fully in view and under continued interrogation.

1   See, however, Micheline R. Ishay, *The History of Human Rights: From Ancient Times to the Globalization Era* (Berkeley: University of California Press, 2004), which seeks to reintroduce the voices of socialists and feminists into the history of human rights theorizing.

2   See, for example, the essays based on the Symposium in Celebration of the Fiftieth Anniversary of the Universal Declaration of Human Rights in the *Columbia Human Rights Law Review* 30 (1998–99): Catherine Powell, "Locating Culture, Identity, and Human Rights," pp. 201–24; Tracy E. Higgins, "Regarding Rights: An Essay in Honor of the Fiftieth Anniversary of the Universal Declaration of Human Rights," pp. 225–47; Michel Rosenfeld, "Can Human Rights Bridge the Gap between Universalism and Cultural Relativism? A Pluralist Assessment based on the Rights of Minorities," pp. 249–84; Ruti Teitel, "The Universal and the Particular in International Criminal Justice," pp. 285–303; and Jeremy Waldron, "How to Argue for a Universal Claim," pp. 305–14.

3   See Elizabeth A. Castelli, "Praying for the Persecuted Church: U.S. Christian Activism in the Global Arena," *Journal of Human Rights* 4, no. 3 (2005), pp. 321–51.

4   Whether human-rights discourses are "religious" or "secular" in origin remains a question openly and passionately debated among human-rights historians and theorists. Ishay's *History of Human Rights* offers an excellent overview of the issues at stake in this debate. For an impassioned defense of the view that human rights are historically grounded in theological or religious claims, see, for example, Michael Freeman, "The Problem of Secularism in Human Rights Theory," *Human Rights Quarterly* 26 (2004), pp. 375–400. For a sympathetic overview of the alliances involved in U.S. activism, see Allen D. Hertzke, *Freeing God's Children: The Unlikely Alliance for Global Human Rights* (Lanham, MD: Rowman and Littlefield, 2004).

5   *Universal Declaration of Human Rights,* General Assembly Resolution 217A (III), adopted on December 10, 1948. Repr. in *American Journal of International Law* 43 (1949), pp. 127ff.; available online at www.unhchr.ch/udhr/lang/eng.htm.

6   National Association of Evangelicals, "Statement of Conscience of the National Association of Evangelicals Concerning Worldwide Religious Persecution," January 23, 1996. Available online at www.pcahistory.org/pca/3-476.html. The statement was drafted by Michael Horowitz of the Hudson Institute.

7   National Conference of State Legislatures, "Pharmacist Conscience Clauses: Laws and Legislation," www.ncsl.org/programs/health/conscienceclauses.htm.

8   Robert Knight and Lindsey Douthit, "'Hate Crime' Laws Threaten Religious Freedom," Culture and Family Institute of the Concerned Women for America, November 29, 2005, www.cwfa.org/articles/9672/CFI/papers/index.htm. See also "Hate Crimes Bill: Good News and Bad News," *Rick Scarborough Report on the War on Faith* 1, no. 32 (October 27, 2005): "Adding homosexuals to US hate-crime law is a clear and present danger to religious freedom and freedom of expression" (www.visionamerica.us/site/DocServer/rsr0132.pdf?docID=204).

9   See Janet R. Jakobsen and Ann Pellegrini, "What's Wrong with Tolerance?" in *Love the Sin: Sexual Regulation and the Limits of Religious Tolerance* (Boston: Beacon Press, 2003), pp. 45–73, for a provocative critique of the imaginative and practical impasses embedded in the efforts to set "religious freedom" and "sexual freedom" in opposition.

10 The Voice of the Martyrs, "About VOM," www.persecution.com/about/index.cfm?action=vom.

11 Claudia Kolker, "The Blood of the Lambs," *Los Angeles Times Magazine*, March 28, 2004, pp. 18–21. Available online at www.latimes.com/features/printedition/magazine/la-tm-martyr13revmar28,1,7501348.story.

12 Open Doors International, "Open Doors History," http://sb.od.org/index.php?supp_page=od_history&supp_lang=en&PHPSESSID=15b5517f2d3a153b617cf0fdfe83b650.

13 See Elizabeth A. Castelli, "Shockwave! New Media Warriors Try to Shake the World," *The Revealer,* March 4, 2004, www.therevealer.org/archives/feature_000224.php. On the "night of persecution," see also www.undergroundusa.org/nop.html.

14 Open Doors International, "Vision Statement," http://sb.od.org/index.php?supp_page=statement&supp_lang=en.

15 Open Doors International, "Our Work," http://sb.od.org/index.php?supp_page=our_work&supp_lang=en.

16 On the Underground Web site, one can order "the official 'Citizen Kit.'" The kit, which costs $25, includes an olive-colored "Citizen" T-shirt, an Underground beanie, an Underground sweatband, a poster of Eritrea (the focus of the current Underground project), and a copy of a book recounting Brother Andrew's ministry "that will challenge your spiritual growth" (http://odusa.org/Store/ResourcesStep2.asp?Group=154).

17 See Castelli, "Praying for the Persecuted Church," for an analysis of the NAE's statement.

18 Forum 18, "About Forum 18," www.forum18.org/Forum18.php.

19 Forum 18, "Forum 18 News Service's Mission Statement," www.forum18.org/F18NewsMission.php.

20 Forum 18, "Latest News," www.forum18.org/index.php.

21 See Forum 18, "Forum 18 News Service's Mission Statement," which claims that "F18News is objective, presenting news in a deliberately calm and balanced fashion, and presenting all sides of a situation. The overriding editorial objective of F18News is to as accurately as possible present the truth of a situation, both implicitly and explicitly. F18News aims to ensure that threats and actions against religious freedom are truthfully reported as quickly as possible across the world." The concern for "objectivity" and "truth," expressed in emphatic and repetitious language, suggests that the authors of the statement are seeking to distinguish themselves from practices that fall outside the purview of these privileged categories.

22 Christian Solidarity International, "About CSI," www.csi-int.org/about_csi.php.

23 Christian Solidarity International, "Religious Liberty," www.csi-int.org/csi/csi-rliberty.php.

24 The canonical expression of these commitments may be found in Office of the President, *The National Security Strategy of the United States of America* (Washington, DC, 2002), available online at www.whitehouse.gov/nsc/nss.html. The theological foundations of this imbrication of neoconservatism and "theoconservatism" is compellingly analyzed by Erin Runions, "Biblical Promise and Threat in U.S. Imperialist Rhetoric, Before and After 9/11," in Elizabeth A. Castelli and Janet R. Jakobsen (eds.), *Interventions: Activists and Academics Respond to Violence* (New York: Palgrave, 2004), pp. 71–88. See also William E. Connolly, "The Evangelical-Capitalist Resonance Machine," *Political Theory* 33, no. 6 (2005), pp. 869–86.

25 Freedom House's right-wing political slant has been the object of study and critique by progressive watchdog groups and policy analysts. See, most recently, International Relations Center, "Freedom House," Right Web Profile, IRC Right Web (Silver City, NM: International Relations Center, 2005), http://rightweb.irc-online.org/profile/1476.

26 Freedom House, "About the Center for Religious Freedom," www.freedomhouse.org/religion/about/about.htm.

27 *Ibid.*

28 Winnifred Fallers Sullivan, *The Impossibility of Religious Freedom* (Princeton, NJ: Princeton University Press, 2005).

29 *Ibid.*, p. 154.

30 See Janet R. Jakobsen and Ann Pellegrini, "World Secularisms at the Millennium," *Social Text* 18, no. 3 (2000), pp. 1–27.

31 Talal Asad, "Redeeming the 'Human' through Human Rights," *Formations of the Secular: Christianity, Islam, Modernity* (Stanford, CA: Stanford University Press, 2003), pp. 127–58.

32 See Wendy Brown, *States of Injury: Power and Freedom in Late Modernity* (Princeton, NJ: Princeton University Press, 1995), especially ch. 3, "Wounded Attachments."

33 A guide to first steps toward thinking beyond such dualisms can be found in William E. Connolly, *Why I Am Not a Secularist* (Minneapolis: University of Minnesota Press, 1999).

Contributors

LAËTITIA ATLANI-DUAULT is associate professor of cultural anthropology at the Institute for Research on Development at the University of Lyon II. Since the 1990s, she has worked extensively for international agencies and development NGOs in Vietnam, the former USSR, the United States, and Canada. She is the author of *Au bonheur des autres: Anthropologie de l'aide humanitaire,* and the editor of *Les ONG à l'heure de la "bonne gouvernance"* and *Pentru fericirea celorlalti: O antropologie a ajutorului umanita,* among others.

MARK BARENBERG is professor of law at Columbia University, and has been a visiting professor at the universities of Yale, Beijing, Tokyo, and Rome. He serves on the board of directors of the Worker Rights Consortium. He is the author of many articles on global labor rights, including "Democracy and Domination in the Law of Workplace Cooperation," "Toward a Participatory Model of Labor Monitoring," "Coordinated Decentralization of Labor Rights in Supranational Regimes," and "The FTAA's Impact on Democratic Governance." His current project traces the constriction of workers' rights of association in the current era of globalization.

JÉRÔME BELLION-JOURDAN has a PhD in political science from the Institut d'Etudes Politiques de Paris and a diploma in Arabic from the Institut National des Langues et Civilisations Orientales (INALCO). He has published many articles on international Islamic relief organizations and their activities, especially in Bosnia, the Sudan, and Pakistan. He is coauthor, with Jonathan Benthall, of *The Charitable Crescent: Politics of the Aid in the Muslim World.* He has worked notably for the International Secretariat of Amnesty International in London, and most recently was posted at the Delegation of the European Commission in Cairo. His contribution to this volume was written in a private capacity.

ERICA BORNSTEIN is assistant professor in the department of anthropology at the University of Wisconsin-Milwaukee. She is the author of *The Spirit of Development: Protestant NGOs, Morality, and Economics in Zimbabwe* and is currently working on a book on humanitarianism in India.

ELIZABETH A. CASTELLI is associate professor of religion at Barnard College at Columbia University. She is the author of *Martyrdom and Memory: Early Christian Culture Making* and coeditor, with Janet R. Jakobsen, of *Interventions: Activists and Academics Respond to Violence.* Her current research concerns the political effects of accusations of religious persecution in the United States.

BRIDGET CONLEY-ZILKIC is project director for the Committee on Conscience at the United States Holocaust Memorial Museum where she has worked since 2001. She is currently curating *From Memory To Action,* the Museum's exhibition on the challenge of preventing genocide, due to open in summer 2007. She has worked on several educational films concerning contemporary genocide, acting as researcher and writer for *The Arusha Tapes* (2000), cowriter and researcher for the *A Good Man in Hell: General Romeo Dallaire and the Rwanda Genocide* (2003), producer and director for *Witnessing Darfur* (2005), and producer for *Defying Genocide* (2006). In April 2004, she was a member of the United States delegation to the official commemoration ceremonies in Rwanda marking the 1994 genocide. She supervised elections in Bosnia-Herzegovina with the Organization for Security and Cooperation in Europe in 2000. Among her published essays are "Hope Dies Last: On Women Suicide Bombers and Human Rights Abuses in Chechnya" (2004) and "What Barbed Wire Can't Enclose" (2000). She is currently working on a volume, coedited with Alex de Waal, on how genocides end.

ALEX DE WAAL is an anthropologist, a program director at the Social Science Research Council, a fellow at the Global Equity Initiative at Harvard University, and the director of Justice Africa in London. He is the author of *AIDS and Power: Why There Is No Political Crisis—Yet* (2006), *Islam and Its Enemies in the Horn of Africa* (2004), *Famine Crimes: Politics & Disaster Relief Industry in Africa* (1997), *Famine That Kills: Darfur, Sudan, 1984–1985* (1989), *Facing Genocide: The Nuba of Sudan* (1995), and coauthor of *Darfur: A Short History of a Long War* (2005).

ESTELLE D'HALLUIN is a PhD student in sociology at the Ecole des Hautes Etudes en Sciences Sociales—CRESP—Maison des sciences de l'homme Paris Nord. She is researching asylum policy, refugee status, determination process, and nongovernmental organizations.

DIDIER FASSIN is professor of sociology at the University of Paris North and directeur d'études of political anthropology at the Ecole des hautes études en sciences sociales, Paris. He recently published *When Bodies Remember: Experiences and Politics of AIDS in South Africa.* He is coeditor of *Le gouvernement des corps, Les constructions de l'intolérable: Etudes d'anthropologie et d'histoire sur les frontières de l'espace moral,* and *De la question sociale à la question raciale? Représenter la société française.*

MICHEL FEHER is a founding editor of Zone Books and the author of *Powerless by Design: The Age of the International Community.*

BRIDGET HANNA is director of the Bhopal Memory Project and coeditor of *The Bhopal Reader,* an anthology on the Bhopal disaster. She is currently a PhD candidate in anthropology at Harvard University.

ALAN KEENAN is the South Asia regional editor and senior analyst for the International Crisis Group. He is finishing a manuscript entitled *Between the Devil and the Deep Blue Sea: The Politics of Human Rights and Peacebuilding in Sri Lanka.* He is the author of *Democracy in Question: Democratic Openness in a Time of Political Closure,* as well as articles in a number of academic journals and edited volumes.

THOMAS KEENAN teaches human rights, media, and literature at Bard College. He is the author of *Fables of Responsibility: Aberrations and Predicaments in Ethics and Politics* (1997), and the coeditor, with Wendy Chun, of *New Media, Old Media* (2006). His current research, for a book entitled *Live Feed,* focuses on the role of media in post-Cold War conflicts, from Somalia to Bosnia to Iraq and the global jihad.

GAËLLE KRIKORIAN is associated researcher at the Research Center on Health, Social and Political Issues (CRESP)—Inserm—Paris 13 University—Ecole des Hautes Etudes en Sciences Sociales. She is currently conducting a research project on the impact of U.S. free trade agreements on access to medicines in developing countries. She is a member of Act Up–Paris.

LAURA KURGAN teaches architecture at Columbia University's Graduate School of Architecture, Planning, and Preservation, where she is the Director of the Spatial Information Design Lab (SIDL). She also runs an interdisciplinary design practice in New York City, blending academic research with design, information, communication, advocacy, and architecture. Most recently, Laura Kurgan Design has been working with New Visions for Public Schools on the reprogramming and master planning of twenty-one large public school buildings, and with the Committee on Conscience at the United States Holocaust Memorial Museum on an exhibition entitled *From Memory to Action.* Her research and art practice has followed the declassification of satellite imagery and GPS technology in a series of projects that address significant political events of the last decade. *Architecture and Justice,* the first major project of SIDL, was exhibited at the Architectural League of New York in 2006.

CLAUDIO LOMNITZ is the William H. Ransford Professor of Anthropology at Columbia University. He is the author, most recently, of *Death and the Idea of Mexico,* and editor of the journal *Public Culture.*

PHILIPPE MANGEOT is a founding editor of the French journal *Vacarme,* and former president (1997–1999) and long-time member of Act Up–Paris. He teaches French literature in *classes préparatoires* at the Lycée Richelieu in Rueil Malmaison.

NOORTJE MARRES works as a postdoctoral researcher in the philosophy department of the University of Amsterdam. Having been trained in science and technology studies, she draws on social perspectives on technology and nature to make sense of democratic practices. In 2005, she defended her PhD thesis, "No Issue, No Public: Democratic Deficits After the Displacement of Politics."

YATES MCKEE is a critic and PhD student in the department of art history and archaeology at Columbia University. An alumnus of the Whitney Museum Independent Study Program and a frequent participant at 16 Beaver Group, his writing has appeared in *October, Vacarme, Flash Art, Springerin,* and the *Journal of Aesthetics and Protest.* In 2004, he co-organized *Art and Everyday Life: Building a Critical Public Sphere for the Biotech Century* at the Massachusetts Institute of Technology's Center for Advanced Visual Studies. He is currently working on "The Ends of Art and the Right to Survival," a monographic study of the work of Jennifer Allora and Guillermo Calzadilla.

MEG MCLAGAN is a New York-based cultural anthropologist and documentary filmmaker. She has published essays on global social movements, human rights, and technologies of publicity. Currently, she is codirecting a feature-length documentary film about American female soldiers who have served in Iraq.

ANGELA MITROPOULOS is a writer living in Melbourne, Australia. She has written a number of essays on migration and labor, including, most recently, "Autonomy, Migration, Recognition in Constituent Imagination" and "Precari-us?" for *Mute.* She is currently revisiting the questions of human rights, borders, and citizenship.

BRETT NEILSON is senior lecturer in cultural and social analysis at the University of Western Sydney, where he is also a member of the Centre of Cultural Research. He is author of *Free Trade in the Bermuda Triangle...and Other Tales of Counterglobalization.* He is currently working with Angela Mitropoulos on a book entitled *On the Borders of Politics.*

ADI OPHIR is an associate professor at the Cohn Institute for the history and philosophy of science and ideas at Tel Aviv University and a research fellow at the Van Leer Jerusalem Institute and the Shalom Hartman Institute for Jewish Studies. Among his recent books are *The Order of Evils* and, with Ariella Azoulay, *Terrible Days.* He is currently editing, together with Michal Givoni, a volume of essays and documents on the Israeli ruling apparatus in the Occupied Palestinian Territories.

TREVOR PAGLEN is an artist, writer, and experimental geographer working out of the department of geography at the University of California, Berkeley. His most recent projects take up secret military bases, the California prison system, and the CIA's practice of "extraordinary rendition." Paglen's artwork has been shown at the Chicago Museum of Contemporary Art (2003), the California College of the Arts (2002), MASSMOCA (2006), Halle 14–Stiftung Federkiel (2006), and Diverse Works (2005), among others. He has had one-person shows at Deadtech (2001), the LAB (2005), and Bellwether Gallery (2006). Paglen is the coauthor of *Torture Taxi: On the Trail of the CIA's Rendition Flights* (2006).

MATHIEU POTTE-BONNEVILLE is a founding editor of the French journal *Vacarme* and the author of *Michel Foucault: l'inquiétude de l'histoire* (2004) and *Amorces* (2006). He is a member of the Centre Michel Foucault and teaches philosophy in *classes préparatoires* at the Lycée Jean Jaurès in Montreuil-sous-bois.

IAN ROBINSON is a Lecturer in the Residential College's social science program and the department of sociology at the University of Michigan. He is also codirector of the Institute of Labor and Industrial Relations' Labor and Global Change Program, and cochair of the Ann Arbor Campus Council of the Lecturer Employees' Association, AFT, AFL-CIO. A list of his publications on labor, globalization, and other matters can be viewed at http://www-personal.umich.edu/~eian/.

CLAIRE RODIER is a lawyer working for Groupe d'information et de soutien des immigrés (GISTI) and president of the Euro-African Migreurop network. Her fields of research are immigration issues, European policies on asylum, externalization, and detention camps for foreigners.

PHILIPPE RYFMAN is a lawyer and associate professor and researcher at the political science department of La Sorbonne (University Paris I, Panthéon-Sorbonne) and Centre de Recherches Internationales de la Sorbonne (CRIS). He is former director of MD Coopération Internationale, Action Humanitaire et Politiques de développement at the same University Paris I. His fields of research include international NGOs, international relations, and humanitarian questions. He has written several articles and books including *Les ONG* and *Non-governmental Organizations, Controversial Players in International Relations*. He currently works on NGOs' governance, NGOs' transnational and globalized networks, and the history and future of humanitarian aid.

SVATI P. SHAH is an assistant professor/faculty fellow in New York University's gender and sexuality studies program. She completed her PhD in Columbia University's joint anthropology and public health program, where her dissertation research focused on sex work and migration in Mumbai, India. Her work has been published in several scholarly journals, including *Gender and History* and *Rethinking Marxism,* and in nonacademic venues, including *SAMAR: South Asian Magazine for Action and Reflection.* She has also been a long-time activist in South Asian queer and progressive organizations in the U.S., as well as a part of the queer and autonomous feminist movements in India.

ÉLISE VALLOIS is a lawyer specializing in immigration. She is a member of Groupe d'information et de soutien des immigrés (GISTI).

SOENKE ZEHLE teaches transcultural literary and media studies at Saarland University in Germany. He holds degrees in comparative literature, philosophy, translation, and political science and has contributed to multiple online projects, most recently incommunicado.info. His research explores the intersections of Net theory, political ecology, and postcolonial/transcultural approaches. His publications include the *Incommunicado Reader* (2005) coedited with Geert Lovink.